34-

D0925466

# The Urban Condition: Space, Community, and Self in the Contemporary Metropolis

Written and Edited by the Ghent Urban Studies Team

# [GUST]

Project Directors: Dirk De Meyer and Kristiaan Versluys
Collaborators: Kristiaan Borret, Bart Eeckhout,
Steven Jacobs, and Bart Keunen

# The Urban Condition: Space, Community, and Self in the Contemporary Metropolis

010 Publishers, Rotterdam 1999

# Contents

## Chapter Three: Self

# [Part Two] Case Studies

Edited by GUST

# General Introduction

This is a book about the urban condition, as it manifests itself in the Western world at the beginning of the new millennium. As such, it is a syncretic and synthesizing work. In dealing with the urban condition *in toto*, this study draws on a great number of disciplines. The city is looked at both as a physical phenomenon in the landscape and as a cultural and even mental (arte)fact.

The scope of the investigation is wide-ranging. To give only two examples: sections on urban sprawl and architectural reactions to the thinning of urban density are found next to speculations about urban humor or consumer aestheticism; identity politics as a diversification strategy is discussed alongside the virtualization of urban space. While each aspect of the urban condition that is dealt with in these pages has been the subject of scholarly work before, our intention has been to avoid fragmentation into separate disciplines, each featuring its own separate range of favorite topics. This study positions itself firmly in the thriving (but especially in Europe still underdeveloped) field of urban studies, in which findings from several disciplines are combined and enter into a dialogue.

Traditional approaches to the city borrow from investigations in architectural criticism and theory, urban planning, geography, history, and sociology (and usually from only one of these). We have drawn on all of these fields simultaneously, while also literature and film have been included in our research. The narrative we have developed deals with morphological change, but it does in no way limit itself to the city in its materiality only. Cultural reflections and representations of the city have been considered as constituent parts of the urban condition, as well as psychological realities fostered or accentuated by urban surroundings.

To flesh out the realities of urban existence and to sketch an image as nuanced as possible, we have opted for a two-pronged approach. The first part of the book is a theoretical description of the contemporary urban condition in the developed countries of the West. The discussion in this first part is on a high level of abstraction, even though by means of concrete material and through the use of specific instances we have tried to keep the argument accessible to specialists and non-specialists alike. In a second part, case studies are offered which substantiate and deepen the findings presented in the theoretical part. Complementing abstract speculations by concrete examples, we hope to develop a dialectic whereby detail and generalization stand to each other in a relation of productive tension. On the one hand, we have been inspired by the continuing need to construct synthesizing metanarratives. To the extent that facts become more dispersed and knowledge more compartmentalized, the need for a synthesis (however tentative and provisional) increases. On the other hand, we realize that no synoptic overview can be adequate unless it is qualified by in-depth detailed investigations. In other words, in combining a theoretical part with a substantial number of case studies, we have sought to establish a balance between synthesis and analysis, universalism and particularism, between the demands of the Enlightenment tradition and the insights of postmodernism, both of which belong to our common intellectual heritage.

In the wake of the poststructuralist revolution, the problematical tension between the general and the specific has been highlighted so much that it has come to mark language use itself. In academic parlance especially, plurals are deployed to indicate nuance and difference and to suggest an aversion to homogenizing or totalizing explicatory schemes. Following this trend, we, too, could easily have entitled our book *Urban Conditions: Spaces, Communities, and Selves in Contemporary Metropolises.* Such a title, however, apart from taking pluralization to ridiculous extremes, would have belied the old-fashioned drive for synthesis characteristic of the first theoretical part of this volume, even though the case studies break up the theoretical rigor and introduce reality closer to the bone.

To fulfill their function as particularizing qualifiers, the case studies have not been conceived as point-by-point illustrations of the theoretical part. Rather they must be considered as reactions, elaborations, reflections on, and sometimes even correctives to, the generalizing speculations. The theoretical section itself, however, is governed by a tight tripartite logic. Already in 1938, in his influential essay "Urbanism as a Way of Life," Louis Wirth wrote: "Urbanism as a characteristic mode of life may be approached empirically from three interrelated perspectives: (1) as a physical structure comprising a population base, a technology, and an ecological order; (2) as a system of social organization involving a characteristic social structure, a series of social institutions, and a typical pattern of social relationships; and (3) as a set of attitudes and ideas, and a constellation of personalities engaging in typical forms of collective behavior and subject to characteristic mechanisms of social control." In aiming at a comprehensive view of the contemporary metropolis, we have followed this tripartite definition in the theoretical discussion and have dealt successively with space, community, and self in the contemporary metropolis.

The section on space describes at length how in the postwar era various urban functions and programs have dispersed over a much wider area and how this process has transformed both traditional core cities and their peripheries. In the section on community, the tension between the increasing autonomization of the individual on the one hand and the growth of new lifestyles and subcultures on the other leads to an extensive description of the contemporary social landscape and recent transformations of urban public space. The section on self, finally, starts from the classical perspectives on the urban mind to deal at length with contemporary forms of urban arousal as well as with constructions of the symbolic metropolis. Taken together, the three sections of the theoretical part constitute a round-up of the urban condition as it presents itself in North America and Western Europe, even though a great number of the topics touched upon have considerable relevance also for the fast-changing cities in Eastern Europe, South-East Asia, and for the expanding megalopolises in the Third World.

As urban space has been hybridized and become more complex and as urban lifestyles have scattered far beyond the confines of the city, it has become more difficult to give a hard and fast definition of what makes up the contemporary metropolis, certainly if also cultural phenomena are taken into consideration. Hence the title to our volume: our focus is the city, more in particular the big city or metropolis. Since, however, the phenomena we describe have spilled over (often in an attenuated form) into smaller cities and suburbia, it is fair to say that the city *per se* has been replaced by something much more encompassing that we have referred to as the urban condition. Part of that condition is shaped by morphological developments within the city itself, part is shaped by broader social and economic trends. As Melvin Webber put it somewhat hyperbolically, "urbanity is no longer the exclusive trait of the city dweller; the suburbanite and the exurbanite are among the most urbane of men." Even though the city is the originator of many new social and cultural trends and often harbors their most distinctive manifestations, sometimes it works the other way round: the city merely illustrates trends that are determined by more general developments in society at large.

In order to cover today's far-flung and widespread urban condition, this book has been undertaken as a collective enterprise and the logistics behind it has been directed by the need for a wide scope and a great diversity. The Ghent Urban Studies Team (GUST), responsible for this volume, is an interdisciplinary group of researchers at the University of Ghent (Belgium), consisting of two specialists in American and comparative literature, one philosopher and sociologist of literature, one architectural historian, one theorist of urban planning, and one philosopher-cum-art historian. The theoretical part of this study is the result of the sustained collective efforts of GUST and represents the sum total of its common ideas and research. However, the concrete working-out of the several chapters has been entrusted to individual members of the group. The chapters on space and community were developed by Bart Eeckhout and Steven Jacobs; the chapter on self by Bart Eeckhout and Bart Keunen.

The case studies were farmed out both to members of GUST and to specialists from all over the world. In choosing their topics, authors of the case studies were given total autonomy. Yet in order to ensure greater consistency within the volume, all contributors received a 40-page synopsis of the theoretical part, which served as background to their own research. Practical editing of the case studies (including translations from French and Dutch), as of the book overall, was done for the most part by Bart Eeckhout.

This volume could never have been written without the help of a great number of persons and institutions. We would like to thank Charles Vermeersch, William Sharpe, and Donatella Calabi for helping us launch our team; Andrew Beveridge, Gert Morreel, and Trui Vetters for providing essential sociological materials; and Judit Bodnár, Christophe Den Tandt, Hilde Heynen, and Jo Smets for their intellectual stimulus. Judit Bodnár joined our group too late to have a direct hand in this book, but she helped to lay the groundwork for further activities. At a crucial juncture, Peter Ruyffelaere helped us along with valuable practical advice. Chris Bulcaen, Willy De Bie, Veronique Slock, and Rik Vanmoerkerke provided much-appreciated logistical help, while Annie De Rijcke (what's in a name) continues to serve as our reliable accountant. The enthusiasm and high-quality professionalism of our publishers at 010 and our designer, Piet Gerards, allowed us to produce a handsome book. Financially, GUST was first subsidized by the Research Council of the University of Ghent. At present we are the beneficiaries of long-time sponsoring by the Fund for Scientific Research — Flanders (FWO). We received a grant from the European Science Foundation to organize an international workshop. And the publication of this book was made possible by the generous support of the Netherlands Architecture Fund.

*Ghent, July 1999*
*Dirk De Meyer*
*Kristiaan Versluys*

[PART ONE]

# THEORY

Written by GUST

# Chapter One: Space

# Introduction



In the latter half of the twentieth century, every metropolis and city in North America and Western Europe has undergone far-reaching morphological and spatial changes. The precise nature and form of these changes is often complex; sufficient allowance should be made for local variations determined by specific geographies, climates, cultures, histories, economic systems, and types of political organization. Yet for all these differentiating categories it remains possible to present a general overview of the most basic ways in which the urban landscape has been transformed. For a combination of spatial, political-ideological, and sociological reasons, those transformations have been most outspoken and most clearly delineated in North America, more particularly in the U.S. The following chapter, therefore, relies above all on American examples and materials. Yet much of the general outline that thus emerges also applies, in locally modified forms, to Western European cities. Many of the transformations under discussion have occurred widely enough to constitute a master narrative for the postwar Western metropolis. This claim will be corroborated at several points by European examples.

Central in the following narrative is the story of how traditional urban space has undergone a sea-change as the result of suburbanization. This process affects more than a residential redistribution of the urban population. Over the years, suburbia has itself been changed out of all recognition: other than residential functions, too, have spread to the former peripheries of cities, giving rise to a new sort of built environment sometimes described as posturban or postsuburban. Today's urbanized realm as a whole has complicated earlier categorizations in at least four ways: **1** by stripping the traditional hierarchical distinction between center and periphery of much of its validity and self-evident character; **2** by simultaneously accommodating antithetical tendencies of concentration and decentralization; **3** by giving rise to a discontinuous urban landscape full of voids; and **4** by radically, often chaotically mixing the functions that modernist urban planners so carefully tried to keep disentangled. The new urban landscape thus poses considerable challenges to contemporary architects and urban planners, who must seek to introduce meaningful relationships in an ostensibly chaotic environment.

Meanwhile, the success of new transportation systems and communication technologies, the globalization and increasingly flexible organization of the economy, and the growing mobility of capital and investments have collectively worked to reduce the importance of spatial limitations. Thus, the fragmented posturban landscape no longer consists principally of physical objects in relative proximity to each other, but is composed more and more of invisible networks individually established by urban residents. At a global scale, these networks increasingly link cities to each other rather than to their immediate hinterlands and national contexts. This relative virtualization of the materiality of cities, finally, is also translated into new ways of representing the contemporary city on the basis of cybernetic metaphors.

# 1 From Density to Dispersal

**The Culture of Congestion** Although the notions of congestion and density have fundamentally shaped the image of the modern metropolis, they were never really prized by the theorists of modernism in architecture and urban planning. In the early decades of the 20th century, two apparently antithetical urban models were developed that might be called, for the sake of convenience, the *modern* city and the *modernist* city. The modern city, which took shape in the course of the 19th century, corresponds to the well-known image of the kaleidoscopic metropolis with its bombardment of visual stimuli, and was impressively evoked by the historical avantgardes. This urban model figures prominently in the works of writers like James Joyce, John Dos Passos, and Arnold Döblin, artists like Ernst Ludwig Kirchner, Paul Citroën, and Umberto Boccioni, and movie directors like Walter Ruttmann and Dziga Vertov. The modernist city, by contrast, formed the subject of utopian urban planning ideas that went back to the late 19th century and inspired the discipline of urban planning as it was given concrete shape during the interbellum by above all CIAM (the *Congrès Internationaux d'Architecture Moderne*). The modernist city, in a way, is the result of an attempt to destroy the modern city. While the literary and artistic avantgardes were waxing lyrical over the metropolis as an exaltation of modernity, modernist urban planners turned their backs on the city. In their attempts at formulating solutions to the miserable conditions and suffocating atmosphere of the industrial metropolis inherited from the 19th century, the English "garden city" model of Ebenezer Howard, the German *Siedlungswesen*, the designs of Soviet "disurbanists," and Frank Lloyd Wright's *Broadacre City* tried to circumvent the existing metropolis. André Corboz has summarized these policies as "urban planning *alongside* or *outside* the city" [1992: 50; editors' translation]. Other modernist designers, like Le Corbusier (with his *Ville Radieuse*) and many proponents of the CIAM doctrine, strove to replace the existing city by a rational city based on a strict separation of functions. The traditional city of high density was swept off the table and no longer treated as a planning problem in the first place. In the case of such planners, Corboz speaks of "urban planning *against* the city" [ibid.].

Manhattan, the preeminent embodiment of the modern metropolis which has played such a huge role in the collective imagination and in the arts, is strikingly absent from the architectural theories of modernism. Although some protagonists of the so-called modern movement, such as Erich Mendelsohn or Le Corbusier, regarded New York as a fascinating machine, the city was viewed as one gigantic failure from an orthodox modernist perspective, both architecturally and in terms of urban planning. Le Corbusier talked of a *catastrophe féerique* and jokingly noted how the skyscrapers were admittedly much taller than their designers, but that from the point of view of urban planning they were nevertheless far too small and placed too close to each other [1937: 49-94; see also Cohen & Damisch 1993]. Only in 1978, after countless literary and artistic eulogies, was Manhattan finally celebrated by an architect. Not coincidentally, Rem Koolhaas, the architect in question, described his *Delirious New York*, which is a humorous and lyrical ode to the modern metropolis of skyscrapers and high density, as a *retroactive manifesto*. "How to write a manifesto," Koolhaas wondered, "on a form of urbanism for what remains of the 20th century — in an age disgusted with them? The fatal weakness of manifestos is their inherent lack of evidence. Manhattan's problem is the opposite: it is a mountain range of evidence without manifesto" [1978:9].

Koolhaas composed his ode to the modern metropolis at a time when the theory and practice of modernist urban planning had been completely discredited. The late seventies saw the construction of a number of icons of postmodernist architecture and urban planning, like Charles Moore's Piazza d'Italia in New Orleans or the housing complexes near Paris by Ricardo Bofill. At the same time, architectural debates were strongly shaped by the ideas of Aldo Rossi (laid out in his 1966 book later translated as *The Architecture of the City*) and by the brothers Krier [see the collection of Krier 1992], who sought to retain or repair the morphological and typological structure of the historical city. Increasingly also, the visionary aspirations of modernism were being exchanged for eulogies on small-scale projects or, in the case of Lucien Kroll [1987], for a process in which designs were worked out in close collaboration with local residents and inhabitants. Although these architects deployed utterly different designing strategies and operated from totally different ideological positions, they all sought to come up with alternatives to the architectural and urbanistic *tabula rasa* of modernism. Koolhaas's fascination for the modern metropolitan culture of congestion, which had been such an eyesore to modernist urban planners, testified to the attempt at revaluing the city and its urban culture. Nevertheless, his retroactive manifesto struck a dissonant chord even among those architects denouncing the radical demolitions of modernist planners. Critics of the CIAM doctrine and sceptics of any type of planning were not necessarily also great proponents of the modern metropolis as a place of high density and congestion. Jane Jacobs, for instance, whose 1961 book *The Death and Life of Great American Cities* became something of a cult book, radically rejected all types of planning and functional division and made a passionate plea for the city of diversity. She went so far even as to ridicule suburbia, which in the eyes of millions of Americans at the time was precisely becoming the highest residential ideal. Yet her plea had different accents and carried nostalgic overtones. The urban neighborhood life of Greenwich Village that she evoked and held up as a model had little to do with highrise Manhattan or with the celebrations of chaos and congestion typical of the 1920s avantgarde and of Koolhaas. As Deyan Sudjic observed, "much of the West Village around Hudson Street, with its small scale tree-lined streets, is closer to an English suburb than it is to the kind of metropolis she praises" [1992:22].

**The Story of Suburbanization** Modernist planning ideologies are one thing, reality is another. The classic modern metropolis — the city of high density and congestion — has been radically transformed in the postwar era. In large parts of the Western world, an ever growing number of people has chosen to move out of the city into a new sort of urbanized territory called suburbia. The history of suburbanization, however, is not one of quantitative increase only, but also of qualitative change. Increasingly and especially since the 1980s, new types of suburban landscape have emerged, and they have drastically complicated the traditional distinction between city and suburb. North America has been at the forefront of this evolution and it is no coincidence that the eighties also produced three American classics in urban studies, all of them zooming in on the story and metamorphosis of suburbia: Kenneth Jackson's *Crabgrass Frontier: The Suburbanization of the United States* [1985], Robert Fishman's *Bourgeois Utopias: The Rise and Fall of Suburbia* [1987], and John Stilgoe's *Borderland: Origins of the American Suburb 1820-1939* [1988].

Especially Fishman's analysis proves useful for situating contemporary and future trends against their historical backgrounds. The suburban ideal, notes Fishman, emerged in the course of the 18th century in London, which may therefore be called "the birthplace of suburbia" [1987:ch.1]. The rise of the phenomenon is not so much the result of social changes in the city itself as of certain general and momentous transformations in middle-class culture, more particularly the formation of the closed domestic nuclear family [1987:31-33]. While in the 18th century physical proximity could still go hand in hand with enormous social distances, in the 19th century the idea grew that social distinctions also required physical segregation. This idea was strengthened by the success of the Evangelical movement (which considered the city to be the preeminent locus of vice) as well as by the ongoing industrialization and construction of railroads. Unlike what happened in for instance Paris, where the working classes were exiled to the periphery and the middle classes opted for living in apartments in a huge *immeuble* along a boulevard in the city center, in the Anglo-Saxon world it was especially the middle classes that left the busy, noisy, dirty, unhealthy, and supposedly immoral metropolis. Even then, however, these middle classes did not altogether turn their backs on the city. Suburbs only served a residential function. For almost any other social and practical purpose their residents continued to be dependent on downtown facilities. In the first stage of its historic evolution, therefore, the suburb merely consolidated the importance of the city center [Fishman 1987:137]. This hierarchical relationship between center and suburb was also morphologically visible: in the age of railroads, the cityscape often displayed a concentric pattern.

It was only after World War II that the suburbanization process entered a second stage. New transportation facilities began to undermine the conditions of the classic suburb. The success of the car eroded the concentric structure of railroad systems and of the suburbs developing alongside them. Although the car is often associated with suburbia in the popular imagination, Robert Fishman argues that in fact it did not so much stimulate as destroy the classic model of suburbia: "The automobile, when it came, helped to destroy the basic conditions for classic suburbanization; the true suburban means of transportation has been the commuter rail line" [1987:135].

With the advent of the car, suburbs underwent a number of momentous transformations. Los Angeles, the city above all associated with the car, became the new metropolitan model. It should be noted, however, that the structural pattern typical of the L.A. area started to develop before the mass-marketing of the car. Already around the turn of the century, the urbanistic pattern of detached single-family houses that has come to be synonymous with suburbia had been much further advanced here than in other cities. This has to do with the fact that the spatial expansion of Los Angeles occurred relatively late and almost simultaneously with the construction of a public transportation system. As Martin Wachs notes, "the timing of the growth of Los Angeles resulted in a significantly different pattern of development than was typical in Boston, New York, or Philadelphia. Those cities had developed to considerable size before the advent of streetcars, and because walking was the primary mode of transportation, they were characterized by areas of extremely high population density" [1996:108].

By the 1920s, L.A. possessed the largest mass transportation system in the U.S. Only when this system began to obstruct the expansion of a residential pattern of low density was it exchanged for another, car-based transportation system [see Bottles 1987]. This decision was influenced to a large extent by economic interests: the urban economy in L.A. was intimately linked to real estate development [Fishman 1987:164-65]. Sacrificing the city center and the public transportation system appeared like a modest price to be paid for opening up a vast territory for real estate development. Los Angeles thus became the first large city to demonstrate that a universalization of the classic suburban ideal was impossible. Instead of a

1 Grid patterns, it should be noted, do not always and automatically imply a centrifugal and open structure: see Pope 1996.

classic concentric pattern in which a downtown is surrounded by dependent suburbs, a highway system was developed in which every place was close to a North-South or East- West boulevard. In other words, the traditional morphology of suburban expansion — the clustered settlements along railroads that John Stilgoe labeled "metropolitan corridors" [1983] — disappeared in Los Angeles. The urban infrastructure came to be dominated by a grid pattern, which allowed connections to be made without the lingering necessity of passing through a central point. Such a pattern implied a radical decentralization.[1] Not the advent of the car, therefore, but the suburban ideal and its implications on the real estate market form the deeper causes of the conspicuous spatial transformation of Los Angeles [see Fogelson 1967: 85-107].

The new grid system facilitated the spreading of formerly central elements and functions across the entire built environment. Already in the L.A. of the 1920s, industry and commerce were beginning to be decentralized — a process that gave rise to among other things the famous *Miracle Mile* along Wilshire Boulevard outside the downtown area. The classic metropolitan model with its hierarchical relationship between center and periphery was left behind: everything became suburban and thus in some sense also central. Los Angeles, in other words, turned into the first suburban metropolis, and it was soon to set the example for many other cities in North America. In his overview of the twentieth-century American city, Jon Teaford even talks of the "Los Angelesization of America" [1993: 152]. By the 1960s, suburbia became the most important residential environment for Americans. Ten years before, in 1950, 58% of the population still lived in the twenty biggest metropolitan cities, but within a decade this figure had shrunk to 49%. Since then, the ongoing increase in residents witnessed by practically every metropolitan area needs to be ascribed almost entirely to the growing share of suburbs [Teaford 1993: 109]. The success of suburbia was facilitated and embodied by a number of crucial phenomena: the enormous growth of the fleet of cars, a multi-billion-dollar endeavor to construct urban expressways and federal highways (in the U.S. especially after the passing of the 1956 Federal-Aid Highway Act), and a spectacular increase in the number of houses. The large majority of houses built after 1945 are detached suburban single-family homes inhabited by their owners. The culmination of this process in the U.S. is embodied by the famous or infamous Levittowns, which were constructed in the late 1940s near New York and in the early 1950s near Philadelphia. These new suburban towns, named after the Levitt brothers from Long Island (who were into real estate) and consisting entirely of prefabricated houses, formed the biotope of new car-oriented communities, while their spatial organization simultaneously tried to reduce the risks inevitably produced by those cars [Teaford 1993: 102]. In the course of the fifties and sixties, almost every American metropolitan area would come to include one or another version of these (almost exclusively white-middle-class-oriented) residential communities.

The postwar process of suburbanization (or disurbanization) entailed more than this quantitative shift. From the 1950s onwards, it no longer affected only the residential distribution of the urban population. Commercial activities, too, started to spread out over vaster areas. Although the phenomenon of the shopping center goes back at least to the 1920s (with the Country Club Plaza in Kansas City as a famous example), it came to full fruition only after the Second World War with the twin successes of the car (for transportation) and the refrigerator (for storage). Accordingly, the suburbanization of the fifties went hand in hand with a massive increase in the number of shopping centers or malls. Soon also these places began to transcend their merely practical function as facilities for retailing consumer goods: they became themselves a touristic attraction of sorts. Shopping no longer compelled suburbanites to visit downtown. The increasing availability of a car for every family — and in recent decades also of a second or third car — released especially housewives from regular visits to shops and department stores downtown. Parking space became a more important asset than accessibility by public transportation. "By 1984," says Kenneth Jackson, "the nation's 20,000 large shopping centers accounted for almost two-thirds of all retail trade, and even in relatively centralized cities like New York, Boston, and San Francisco downtown merchants adapted to the suburban shift. Easy facilities for parking gave such collections of stores decisive advantages over central city establishments" [1985: 259]. With some delay, European cities likewise were confronted with a sharp increase in shopping malls, and these, too, were often situated at traffic junctions in the periphery.

Gradually, the large-scale spreading of residential and commercial activities was accompanied by yet a third kind of dispersal: that of industry. The growing possibility of freight traffic by road enabled and stimulated the development of industry on the edges of cities. Morphological requirements for new industrial plants added to this trend: whereas earlier industrial architecture often consisted of multifloor buildings, the increasing organization of labor along conveyer belts necessitated the construction of monovolumes with a single stretched-out floor. The large plots of land required for such plants were only available in suburbia. "As early as 1963, industrial employment in the United States was more than half suburban based, and by 1981, about two-thirds of all manufacturing activity took place in the 'industrial parks' and new physical plants in the suburbs" [Jackson 1985: 267]. By the early sixties, the image had emerged of suburban highways surrounded by low-density industry. "A new 'Americanism' even entered the language," writes Kenneth Jackson, "beltway — to describe the broad expressways that encircled every important city by 1975 and that attracted employers of every description" [ibid.]. Especially in California and in the Boston area with its Route 128, this process took place at an unusual speed. "In the popular imagination suburbia may have connoted row after row of split-level homes and manicured lawns. By the early 1960s, however, Route 128 and its counterpart in metropolitan areas across the country were as much part of the suburban scene as Levittown or Park Forest" [Teaford 1993: 107].

The spatial dissemination of residential, commercial, and industrial activities that characterizes the history of postwar suburbia did not fail to cast a shadow on traditional downtowns. As Teaford notes,

> *the role of the downtown was narrowing. At the turn of the century, the downtown had been the center of urban transportation, business, industry, amusement, and government. It was the unchallenged focus of economic endeavor and public policymaking in the metropolitan area. By the 1960s, however, the American metropolis no longer had a single dominant nucleus. Instead, retailing was increasingly dispersed, outlying airports dominated intercity transportation, industry was spread out along the superhighways and rail lines, each home was equipped with a color television and stereo that provided a center of entertainment equal to the old vaudeville theaters, and government authority was distributed among the multitude of municipalities that made up the metropolitan area* [1993: 114-15].

The service sector, including the headquarters of large banks and law firms, often stayed downtown, yet little was left of the functional diversity of the earlier metropolis. The image of a polychrome and polyphonic metropolis was exchanged for that of identical office buildings populated by a lonely crowd of identically tailored office workers who fled to their suburban homes in the evening. The population that continued to live in inner cities underwent severe changes in composition. A racial polarization took place, with especially middle-class white people moving out to suburbia and financially less fortunate blacks immigrating (or staying) downtown. This factual segregation spawned the so-called urban crisis, which especially in the 1970s began to determine the image of just about every metropolis and which consisted of a mix of race riots, crime, and municipal bankruptcy. Ethnic and social polarization was accompanied by political and governmental fragmentation. Since well-to-do suburban towns refused to pay for the poorer inner cities, they created separate governmental units, which in turn only served to deepen the economic, ethnic, and social rifts between the central city and its surrounding suburbs. More than ever, the 19th-century suburban logic of physical segregation seemed to have established itself firmly in the cultural unconscious.

In the course of the 1980s, yet another stage in the process of dispersal was reached. After the rise of suburbia as a domestic-residential phenomenon, and after going on to assimilate commercial and industrial functions, suburbia now also assimilated the increasingly important service industries that are deemed so characteristic of postindustrial society. Especially in the area around shopping malls, clusters of office complexes began to be built. This led Deyan Sudjic to claim that "in the 1980s, when even the most conservative banks joined department stores and corporate headquarters in the exodus from the old city centres, the city changed out of all recognition" [1992: 5]. Changes in the real estate market and innovations in mass communication made rigidly centralized office organizations in downtown buildings no longer necessary. "Many companies," observed Kenneth Jackson already in the mid-eighties, "are now balkanizing their accounting departments, data-processing divisions, and billing departments. Just as insurance companies, branch banks, regional sales staffs, and doctors offices have reduced their costs and presumably increased their accessibility by moving to suburban locations, so also have back-office functions been splitting away from front offices and moving away from central business districts" [1985: 267-68]. For white-collar workers, living almost all in suburbia, the new locations tended to be more easily and more quickly accessible [Rowe 1991: 149], although the relative importance of this factor has been disputed by among others Kenneth Jackson and William Whyte. According to Jackson, "Several studies have pointed out that the most important variable in determining the direction of corporate shift was the location of the home and country club of the chief executive officer of the particular company. In fact, top officers were often the only ones to benefit from the suburban shifts" [1985: 269]. In *City: Rediscovering the Center*, William Whyte substantiated this claim by making his own tabulation: of the 38 companies that left New York at the height of the exodus, no less than 31 moved to a place close to the top man's home [1988: 287-88].

The tendency of suburbia to assimilate postindustrial activities has been everywhere in evidence in the U.S. Already in 1970, the suburbs of 9 of the 15 most important metropolitan areas formed the largest source of employment to office workers, and ten years later their share had grown to almost 67% [Rowe 1991: 149; Garreau 1991: 5]. Although in the 1970s, many companies in the U.S. relocated to the Sunbelt, the majority of relocations still took place between cities and suburbs within the same metropolitan region [Muller 1978]. Because Manhattan as the center of international corporations occupies a dominant position in the public imagination, the phenomenon became most conspicuous there. Between 1955 and 1980 giant companies like International Business Machines, Gulf Oil, Texaco, Union Carbide, General Telephone, American Cyanamid, Xerox, Pepsico, U.S. Tobacco, Cheeseborough Ponds, Nestlé, American Can, Singer, Champion International, and Olin left Manhattan's central business district [Jackson 1985: 268]. Simultaneously, in the suburban surroundings of New York, large-scale investments in the expansion of office space took place. By 1984, Fairfield County in Connecticut had already risen to the rank of third most important site for company headquarters in the United States, after New York and Chicago.

For the new generation of suburban office buildings, a new architectural typology was developed, analyzed at some length by Peter Rowe [1991: 149-81]. This typology gave expression to the widespread conviction that a calmer environment would also positively influence the productivity of employees:

*Free parking and easy access to interstate highways presumably make possible a longer work day, while stone piazzas, landscaped gardens, impressive sculpture, and splashing water fountains, as well as gymnasiums, showers, and saunas presumably make possible a more relaxed one. Company-owned cafeterias replace the downtown restaurants, shopping districts, and even noontime concerts of the city centers. To some employees the result is "close to perfect." Others find the campus environment boring and bemoan that "the main thing of interest out here is what's new in the gift shop"* [Jackson 1985:269].

Increasingly, office buildings turned into autonomous entities equipped with an *ersatz* urbanity. Suburbia had left its past definitively behind and developed into a more complex landscape, alternatively called postsuburban or posturban.

# 2 The Complexities of Posturban Space

**The Hybridization of Center and Periphery** Since World War II, the relationship between urban center and periphery has radically altered. Some of the roles even appear to have been reversed. Yet the evolution has not therefore been a simple, unilinear one. The overall process of decentralization did not, for instance, prevent other processes of downtown revitalization from simultaneously taking place. Especially since the 1980s, a boom of downtown office buildings, together with phenomena like gentrification and the construction of festival marketplaces, contributed to a revitalization of (parts of) the old downtowns. Thus, Los Angeles, the preeminently centerless city that stood as the model for much of postwar urban America, saw its own central business district bloom in the shape of an eye-catching cluster of highrise buildings. And the proverbial example of the dense modern city, Manhattan, instead of being completely drained and sapped, turned out to act as an ever greater, ever more powerful, ever more expensive magnet. The most we can say is that the oscillation between urban and suburban, centripetal and centrifugal forces, at the regional level, has drastically undermined the traditional distinction between center and periphery.

Already in 1938, Louis Wirth called our attention to the fact that "urbanization" was spreading beyond the traditional city and that the concept had begun to refer also to the "cumulative accentuation of the characteristics distinctive of the mode of life which is associated with the growth of cities, and finally to the changes in the direction of modes of life recognized as urban which are apparent among people, wherever they may be, who have come under the spell of the influences which the city exerts by virtue of the power of its institutions and personalities operating through the means of communication and transportation" [1938:146]. To this we might add today a "cumulative accentuation of the characteristics distinctive of the" *suburban mode of life* as typical of an end-of-the-century urbanization. Not only features of a suburban *way of life*, moreover, but also typical *architectural and urbanistic elements* from suburbia have invaded and changed traditional city centers. As urban functions, forms, and signs tended to sprawl, suburban phenomena like the shopping mall also began to encroach upon classic metropolitan downtowns [see Teaford 1993:154; Ellin 1996:ch.3]. Today, barely a block away from the Empire State Building, there is a "Manhattan Mall," and city-boostering politicians like the New York Mayor Rudolph W. Giuliani work hard to draw shopping malls and Disneyfied theme park entertainments into the city. To a great many suburbanites, in fact, these commercialized urban fragments have become their only points of contact with the metropolis:

*Just as the urbanite used to feel a need for "nature," the suburbanite currently feels a need for "the city" ... Yet just as the nature that promised to fulfill the urbanite's desire was rarely a "wild nature," but only a specially organized and adapted nature, the suburbanite's current desire for the city is not answered by the city so much as by the simulacra of an urban culture, some of which might still be in the city (pedestrian shopping streets), but most of which no longer are (the amusement park, the shopping center). In the competitive battle with the successful extra-urban simulacra of urban culture, the city imports typologies from outside the city and organizes itself as an amusement park* [Lesage 1997: 136; editors' translation].

The distinction between city, periphery, and countryside gradually dissolves. The result is a built environment that is particularly hard to define or identify — an environment for which Edward Soja devised the term "exopolis":

*Perched beyond the vortex of the old agglomerative nodes, the exopolis spins new whorls of its own, turning the city inside-out and outside-in at the same time. The metropolitan forms that have become so familiar to us — with dominating downtowns, concentric rings of land uses spreading out from the tightly packed inner city to sprawling dormitory suburbs, density gradients declining neatly from core to periphery — are now undergoing radical deconstruction and reconstitution, exploding and coalescing today in multitudes of experimental communities of tomorrow, in improbable cities where centrality is virtually ubiquitous and the solid familiarity of the urban melts into air* [1992: 95].

In many cases, the outskirts of metropolitan areas have adopted almost all the characteristics of the classic city and adapted them to a lower density. Thus, the new urban nodes that have emerged may be said to "lack skyscrapers, subways and other symbolic structures of the central city, but they have acquired almost all its functions" [Fishman 1990: 26]. The result is a kind of no man's land displaying features of both city, suburb, and countryside, which Peter Rowe has consequently labeled a "middle landscape" [1991]. The current success of suburbia as a place for living, working, and recreation can no longer be referred back to the suburban ideal of the 18th century: it is rather the embodiment of a new kind of city [Fishman 1987: 184]. Instead of the earlier concentric pattern, we now find an amorphous structure, an urban nebula that spreads out in all directions and that has given rise to the contradictory notion of centers within the periphery. "Metropolitan cores," says Peter Hall, "lose their significance, as not merely factories and warehouses, but also offices and shopping centers, increasingly move out from city to suburb and even to exurb" [1988: 45]. The at times strongly paradoxical nature of posturban space appears most clearly from the countless names that have been devised to denote its confusing constituents: these names range from wordplays on the etymological roots "urb" and "burb" (such as slurb, the burbs, the technoburb, exurbia, disurbia, superburbia, shock suburbs, suburban downtown, suburban activity center, nonplace urban field, dispersed urban regions, the rurban fringe) to word combinations with "city" (edge city, outer city, technocity, galactic city, elastic city, polynucleated city, spread city, perimeter city, città autostradale) and other labels (sprawl, megalopolis, exopolis, outtown, growth corridor, multinucleated metropolitan region, Nowheresville, Anywheresville, autopia...).

Increasingly, the new posturban reality is beginning to be the object also of critical analysis. One of the most mediatized instances is that of a book published in 1991 by a senior writer at *The Washington Post*, Joel Garreau. In *Edge City: Life on the New Frontier*, Garreau claimed to be able to identify already more than 200 so-called edge cities in the United States.[2] To this end, he devised a working definition with more or less precise, largely quantitative criteria. "Edge City," he proposed, "is any place that: **1** *Has five million square feet or more of leasable office space — the workplace of the Information Age....* **2** *Has 600,000 square feet or more of leasable retail space....* **3** *Has more jobs than bedrooms....* **4** *Is perceived by the population as one place....* **5** *Was nothing like 'city' as recently as thirty years ago*" [1991: 6-7]. In the same year as Garreau's book came out, Rob Kling, Spencer Olin, and Mark Poster attempted to map the process of deconcentration and to reconceptualize the new spatial organization with the help of the term "postsuburbia." In *Postsuburban California: The Transformation of Orange County since World War II*, they demonstrated how, contrary to what is the case for traditional suburbs, today's postsuburban environments evince an economic vitality and cultural diversity formerly only associated with the classic central city. Not Los Angeles, but Orange County seemed to them to be setting the example for a new urban pattern — a claim that was subsequently supported by Robert Fishman, who in a review of the book (quoted as a blurb) announced that Orange County "is as much the 'shock city' of the late twentieth century as Chicago was for the early twentieth century."

In their "Preface to the Paperback Edition," Kling, Olin, and Poster point to the limitations of Garreau's concept of edge city in terms that do much to help clarify the debate:

2 The four most typical examples provided by Garreau are the zone around Route 128 and the Massachusetts Turnpike near Boston, the Schaumburg area west of O'Hare Airport near Chicago, the Perimeter Center area at the north end of the Atlanta beltway, and Irvine in Orange County south of Los Angeles [1991: 4-5].

3 Jon Teaford, too, points out how the new urbanistic pattern is most clearly visible in zones that were formerly mere satellites of a big city, but that have come to affirm themselves in the meantime as independent metropolitan regions [1993: 162].

*Garreau's conception of edge cities is blind to the social ecologies of postsuburban regions. In defining edge cities primarily by their centers, those spaces in which commercial or retail activities occur, he completely obscures the essence of what we have called "postsuburban" because he ignores the fundamentally decentered or multicentered nature of these emerging regions. His criteria do not permit us to draw boundaries around edge cities or to conceptualize relationships among these "new downtowns." His edge cities, then, do not interact and therefore are situated in a region such as Orange County in much the same way that widely separated cities like Pittsburgh and Philadelphia are located within the state of Pennsylvania. Edge City thus misses much of the fundamentally decentralized and interactive character that makes postsuburban regions so complex, incoherent, and dynamic. Such regions are not merely multicentered in their commercial activities. As we have noted, their commerce, shopping, arts, residential life, and religious activities are all conducted in different places on a spider web of interconnected travel paths linked primarily by private automobiles. In Orange County, as in Fairfax County and other similar regions, residents drive as much between Garreau's edge cities as within them* [1995: XIII-XIV].

According to Kling, Olin, and Poster, postsuburban regions have become the most common form of metropolitan development in the U.S. Their claim is backed up by figures appearing elsewhere in their book, most notably in the contribution by M. Gottdiener and George Kephart [1995: 31-54]. These two contributors inventoried 21 very different counties where postsuburban settlements turn out to be determined by four common features. First, they are all situated in the vicinity of traditional metropolises like New York, Boston, Washington, Baltimore, Atlanta, Detroit, Chicago, Miami, Los Angeles, or San Francisco.[3] Secondly, these multinucleated metropolitan regions show growing population numbers and a rising workforce. They are also, thirdly, large and highly urbanized: almost all of them had a population of more than half a million already in 1980, and they offer employment to at least 100,000 citizens. And finally, they appear to be zones that are no longer dominated by a single urban center.

The fourth and final feature is of considerable importance. Instead of being organized around a single center, postsuburbia consists of several nuclei that form nodes within a vast extended network. Zones of relatively high density sprawl across hundreds of square miles, without a single focus. Millions of urbanites live their lives without the least inclination to set foot in classic metropolitan downtowns. "The technoburbs," notes Fishman, "which might stretch over seventy miles from the core in all directions, are often in more direct communication with one another — or with other techno-cities across the country — than they are with the core" [1987: 185]. This phenomenon makes itself felt not only in the U.S., at the so-called desert frontier of the Southwest, but even in Western European cities. In Barcelona, for example, city authorities have explicitly begun to counter this evolution by devising an urbanistic policy in which new sites of centrality are created [Busquets 1992; Meyer 1996: 147-80].

The absence of a centripetal structure in the new-fangled urban zones appears also from some of their designations. According to Joel Garreau, "We're still in the process of giving each Edge City its name ... In New Jersey, for example, there is one with only the laconic designation '287 and 78.' The reason there are no 'Welcome to' signs at Edge City is that it is a judgment call where it begins and ends" [1991:6]. Technoburbs, too, are often simply given the names of counties or of conjunctions of two or more larger municipalities: a famous example is that of Nassau-Suffolk (two counties on Long Island), which in the 1980s changed from a suburban satellite of New York to a governmentally and administratively independent metropolitan area [Teaford 1993: 163].[4]

The precise structure of post(sub)urban space is a bone of contention. Some scholars like Fishman find only an anarchic pattern in it, while others like Teaford believe the whole is kept together, be it ever so loosely, by the infrastructure of highways. "To the extent that there was a plan to the unprecedented metropolitan formations of the late twentieth century," writes Teaford, "the network of expressways defined it. Moreover, freeway interchanges were becoming the crossroads of metropolitan America, supplanting the nineteenth-century courthouse square and the early-twentieth-century downtown streetcar hub. But there was only one courthouse and a single dominant focus for streetcar traffic, whereas freeways had numerous interchanges. Thus, the superhighways spawned a series of commercial districts, in effect a string of automobile-oriented downtowns" [1993:162]. This network pattern should not be confused with the centralized structure of metropolitan corridors that emerged in the earlier stages of the suburbanization process. The morphology of postsuburbia, which should be viewed at a wider regional scale, evinces more similarities with the concept of "megalopolis" as introduced by the French geographer Jean Gottmann in his highly influential book from the early sixties, *Megalopolis*. A megalopolis, according to the *American Heritage Dictionary*, is "A region made up of several large cities and their surrounding areas in sufficient proximity to be considered a single urban

4 By 1990, Nassau-Suffolk (with a population of more than 2.6 million inhabitants) had become the 10th most populated metropolitan area in the United States. In 11th place it was followed by the no less famous Riverside-San Bernardino area in the south of California. Still in the same year, the nearby Orange County or Anaheim-Santa Ana-Garden Grove metropolitan area occupied 16th place [for all these figures, see Teaford 1993:163]. Often, these sprawling postsuburban areas eat up fertile farm land at an unusually high rate; at the same time, local residents have come to view New Yorkers or Angelenos with marked indifference or even hostility [see Goldberg 1996].

complex." Gottmann was one of the first to draw our attention to the fact that the spaces in between cities were almost entirely silting up — a process elucidated in his book on the basis of the corridor between Boston and Washington and later analyzed in other regions like the Tokyo-Hiroshima axis or the planes of the Po River in Italy [see Gottmann and Harper 1990]. Gottmann paid particular attention to socioeconomic transformations in the labor market: "Studying in the late 1950s the evolution of the American megalopolis, I saw as the most significant trend incubated in that urban region the 'white-collar revolution.' The central city was shifting its function from manufacturing to information work, from factories and warehouses to offices which were being piled up on the rising skylines" [1979:187]. A few decades later, this trend, which in Gottmann's analysis was still rooted in the central city, would be corroborated by among others Kling, Olin, and Poster [1995], who likewise related the rise of postsuburbia to the transformation of the economy into an information capitalism.

Although the built environment has been swallowed more and more by exurbia's non-places, until the late 1980s the phenomenon received very scant attention from architectural critics or, for that matter, from name architects. The only major exception was Robert Venturi, who already in 1972 teamed up with Denise Scott Brown and Steven Izenour to write *Learning from Las Vegas*, in which he tried to valorize the commercial highway strip as a form of American urban planning. After that, it took almost twenty years for the topic of the periphery to raise the widespread interest and enthusiasm of architects and urban planners. Especially a handful of important American architects has sought to devise adequate responses to disurbanization processes in their own designing practices. By the late 1980s, Steven Holl for instance proposed new urbanistic solutions for the periphery in his so-called Edge of a City projects for Cleveland, Phoenix, and New York. "In the middle zone between landscape and city," says Holl,

*there is hope for a new synthesis of urban life and urban form. Traditional planning methods are no longer adequate. Looking back at the city from the point of view of the landscape, these projects consider untested programs and new kinds of urban spaces. The exploration of strategies to counter sprawl at the peripheries of cities — the formation of spaces rather than the formation of objects — are primary aims of the Edge of a City projects. The expanded boundary of the contemporary city calls for the synthesis of new spatial compositions* [1996:51].

For more than ten years now, the phenomenon of the changed urban periphery has also occupied Rem Koolhaas and informed his influential writings. In 1987, in a journalistic piece on Atlanta (revised in 1994), Koolhaas was struck by the "basic *formlessness*" of that city in which "the center/edge opposition is no longer the point. There *is* no center, therefore no periphery. Atlanta is now a centerless city, or a city with a potentially infinite number of centers" [1987/1994: 836]. Ten years after the publication of *Delirious New York*, in which he had hailed the bustling metropolitan culture of Manhattan, Koolhaas, writing up a postscript to his own cult book, again pointed out how much urban reality had changed, how "Today there is no equivalent of that New York architecture, that — starting from mutations and rapid changes — influenced contemporary developments" [1988:152]. What must occupy us today rather is "a number of apparently spontaneous and independent processes, at work in cities as different as Paris, Atlanta, or Tokyo. These processes all seem to lead to an unavoidable fragmentation of the existing city, a displacement of the centre of gravity of urban dynamics from the city centre to the urban periphery and a remarkable ingenuity in avoiding urbanistic rules" [ibid.]. One year later, in an essay called "Toward the Contemporary City," he went on to specify the importance of the periphery to the work done by him and other architects:

*In the last ten years, the projects I have been working on have been situated in a territory that can no longer be called suburbia but must be referred to as the borders or limits of the periphery. It is here on the edge of the periphery that we should observe how things take shape. The contemporary city, the one composed of these peripheries, ought to yield a sort of manifesto, a premature homage to a form of modernity, which when compared to cities of the past might seem devoid of qualities, but in which we will one day recognize as many gains as losses. Leave Paris and Amsterdam — go look to Atlanta, quickly and without preconceptions: that's all I can say* [1989: 15-16].[5]

**Concentration and Decentralization in Europe** The transformations which the European urban landscape, too, is currently undergoing are more likely to remind us of Gottmann's notion of the megalopolis than of the concept of postsuburbia, which seems more specifically restricted to the United States [see Fishman 1990: 35-36]. A tendency towards urban sprawl is no less in evidence in Europe, but the distinction between historic city and periphery remains more firmly in place.[6] The outspoken hierarchic relationship between center and periphery, nevertheless, no longer holds in Europe either. "The periphery is not peripheral anymore," note Roger Keil and Klaus Ronneberger. "In Europe it has ceased to be merely the

5 For a critique of Koolhaas's views on the changing urban landscape and its repercussions on architectural practice and urban planning, see Lieven De Cauter (Part II).

6 An analysis of a traditional European downtown is offered in the case study by Rudi Laermans with respect to Brussels, and Transatlantic contrasts between London and Houston are at the heart of the case study by Alan Hollinghurst (Part II).

problem container of cities, [the] perverted product of social reform bred in the inner city. In North America, the periphery has left suburbia as we knew it behind. In other parts of the world where urbanization is even more rampant, the center seems to have collapsed altogether" [1994:141].

In some of the most dynamic European metropolitan regions, too, edge cities are emerging. As Klaus Kunzmann observes, several factors contribute to their success, from the mechanisms of the metropolitan real estate market constantly looking for new possibilities of investment, over the severity of planning restrictions in historic city centers, down to chronic gridlock in historic downtowns and the wish to uphold an urban image even in the periphery. European edge cities, according to Kunzmann, "consist of a conglomerate of affordable office spaces (back offices) and apartment buildings for young and educated workers, institutions of higher learning, and flanking entertainment and shopping facilities. They are zoned, planned, and executed at strategic points within regional infrastructural networks, in the twilight zone between the built-up area and the suburbanized hinterland. Paris, Frankfurt, or Munich are clear examples of metropolises with edge cities" [1997:25; editors' translation]. The tendency towards sprawl, moreover, is no longer restricted to the concentric model of expansion associated with the image of the growing oil stain. Not only did edge cities surface in the immediate surrounding of European metropolises, but the space in between metropolises has also silted up, giving rise to so-called metropolitan corridors.

According to André Corboz, it has become well-nigh impossible to talk of cities anymore: what remains in many cases are no more than "urbanized regions forming chains" and "megalopolises that cover ever greater territories. Soon all of Europe will be one urban nebula" [1992:51; editors' translation]. The French geographer Roger Brunet graphically talks of a "blue banana," an urbanized corridor that stretches from Manchester, via London, the Benelux, the Ruhr area, the Rhine and Main Rivers, over Switzerland, all the way down to the Milan-Turin agglomeration [1989]. In this European nebula city, however, decentralization has been less extreme than in the multicentered metropolitan regions discussed in *Postsuburban California*. Harm Tilman notes, for instance, how

*unlike what happens in America, the process of deconcentration in Europe is accompanied by a certain continuity in the position of the central city. Whereas in America attempts are made to instill a certain hierarchy at the regional scale in an utterly diffuse pattern dictated by mobility, what happens in Europe at the same level is precisely an attempt to attune the existing centrality to processes of increase in scale and speed. Thus, the development of the European city clearly moves in the direction of a network city* [1997:85; editors' translation].

The weight of a central hub or node is in fact decisive for the morphological development of the periphery. Studying the problem of the periphery in Europe, Hilde Heynen, André Loeckx, and Marcel Smets have drawn a useful distinction between two different varieties of the European metropolitan system: the spiderweb metropolis and the network metropolis. "Spiderweb metropolises extend concentrically around a dominant (capital) city of the first order. Examples are Paris, Rome, Athens, and Madrid.... In the spiderweb metropolis the core city is the physical centre of a radial system of links" [1989:4]. Over the past two decades, for example, a number of attempts were made in Paris (the preeminent example of the centralized capital) to redefine the relationship between central city and periphery. The plan by the 75 021 group illustrates "that it is time to stop imagining Paris as a clearly-defined city, and consider it instead as a territory that extends much further. Paris is not a municipal city, but a territorial city which also includes Versailles and the new Disneyworld.... The negative effects of the spiderweb development pattern must be countered by intensive development of new energy poles in the periphery (airports, touristic attractions, high speed rail terminals, etc.)" [ibid.:12]. Although the age-old centripetal power of Paris remains important, an active choice in favor of stronger *de*centralization was made here with an eye to making the periphery (the famous *banlieue*) more livable again. An analogous reasoning underlies the new *Schéma Directeur* worked out by the Ile-de-France region in 1994. "In general, France suffers from the insignificance and insufficient internationalization of its bigger cities and profits from the global role played by the Ile-de-France region," writes François Ascher. "To diminish this role in favor of other regions would be dangerous, but to restore some balance in the French urban system appears to be necessary. The choice has fallen on a moderation of growth ..., on the stimulation of a more selective development, and on a maximum expansion of the megapolitical zone. This zone was expanded to include the entire 'Paris Basin,' which is to say that also cities which are almost two hundred kilometers away from Paris (but can be reached within an hour thanks to the high-speed train) have been included" [1997:48].

Thus, the spiderweb metropolis of Paris has begun to borrow also from the network metropolis, for as Heynen, Loeckx, and Smets define their second category, "Network metropolises are based on a network structure of different towns. They can be found, for instance, in the UK (Greater London, Manchester, Leeds), the Netherlands (the Randstad), Belgium (the Brussels-Ghent-Antwerp triangle), and Germany (the Ruhr-Rhine area and the Upper Rhine Valley)" [1989:4]. The Randstad, which already in 1966 was described by the British urbanist Peter Hall as a polycentric metropolis [see Hall 1966], constitutes one of the most remarkable and most frequently analyzed examples in this respect. Its structure is determined by a ring of cities (Rotterdam, Den Haag, Amsterdam, Utrecht) and by the network of these cities' mutual connections. The dichotomy between center and periphery has lost much of its validity in this environment, since the interurban periphery has acquired a certain autonomy and become less dependent on the bigger, well-defined urban centers. In some smaller cities or towns, the periphery has itself even begun to function as a magnet (through its shopping malls, movie multiplexes, and so forth). "The Randstad," in Harm Tilman's words,

*no longer consists of the large, compact, and clearly delimited conurbations of Amsterdam, Rotterdam, Utrecht, and Den Haag, but of undefined, sprawling units that lie spread out across the entire territory. The Green Heart [the open space in between urbanized zones] has in the past years ... been sliced by highways, subways, railroads, and high-voltage cables. Shopping centers, sheds and hangars, wrecker's yards, business zones, allotment gardens, discotheques, and brainparks, alternating with various residential zones, have become the constituent elements of the Randstad, as have the proverbial plains of hothouses and bulb fields* [1997: 77-78; editors' translation].

Besides the Randstad, other urban regions in Europe also correspond to the model of the network metropolis proposed by Heynen, Loeckx, and Smets. Especially the Ruhr Area in Germany and parts of Italy and Belgium became both the subjects of theoretical inquiry and the action fields of designers and planners. In Thomas Sieverts's *Zwischenstadt* [1997], the Ruhr Area is described as a hybrid mix of urbanized landscape and ruralized city. Accordingly, Sieverts makes a plea for allocating this in-between city a full place in our daily lives and for investing sufficient creativity in it in terms of urban planning. He for instance argues the need to develop a regional system of public transportation and to emphasize the specific character of different suburban centers so as to throw into relief the rich diversity of the region. Cultural or sports events, according to Sieverts, may serve as symbolic indicators, enabling residents to feel better about their environments and affording them opportunities for identifying with a place. The ideas proposed by Sieverts are based on his experience as one of the directors of the *Internationale Bauausstellung (IBA)* Emscher Park, a project that was started up in 1988 and that charted out a new policy for the mining area of the Emscher region. An urbanized region full of damaged landscapes and industrial wastelands, the Emscher region was adapted to the needs of the forceful tertiary economy, while care was also taken to rebuild the urban landscape [see von Petz 1997].

In Italy, the phenomenon of the *città diffusa* — most outspoken in the Milan area, the metropolitan territory encompassing the Venice-Padua-Treviso axis, and the coasts of the Marches — has become the object not only of a considerable number of planning projects, but also of intensive theoretical analysis.[7] Stefano Boeri and Arturo Lanzani [1992; see also Boeri, Lanzani, and Marini 1993b] have been among those to note how

*the most advanced stage of reflection in our discipline today, the horizon beyond which new experiments and hypotheses for the modification of the territory can take form, no longer concerns only large cities. In growing measure, the attention of scholars, architects and planners is turning toward the territory known as the "dispersed city," that heterogeneous accumulation of edification which has sprung up in many parts of Italy around the road network of the urbanized countryside. This new focus is not only the reflection — tardy as it is — of the proliferation of professional opportunities, but is also perhaps the sign of a convergence toward a new subject of research regarding territorial disciplines. A sizeable portion of design and planning activity today is concerned with the dispersed city: with the proliferation of lifestyles linked to the single-family house, to the landscape of the "merchandising mile," to the open spaces enclosed between the edified streetfronts and the dissonant settlement rules of industrial and artisan activities* [44].

Even in well-preserved medieval towns with a clearly defined structure, like Siena, urban planners try to look at the periphery no longer as an isolated entity. In the plan for this Tuscan town by Bernardo Secchi, the periphery (where most activities of a modern society take place) is interpreted as an essential element in the functioning of a total urban system [see Taverne 1989].

In Belgium, which has one of the most densely interlaced and extended highway infrastructures in Europe, many small to medium-size businesses and shops started to settle outside the city in the early 1980s. The phenomenon of residential, industrial, and commercial "ribbon development" along the most important federal roads and freeway exits has reached an unseen level of penetration in this country [see Lagrou 1993: 273]. "The decentralization tendency is indeed so strong," writes Marcel Smets, "that Belgium is on its way to degenerating into one big periphery, in which the historic centers serve as tourist attractions and the population is endlessly underway to move from nowhere to nowhere along gridlocked highways" [1993: 287; editors' translation]. The phenomenon of the "ribbon development" in Belgium inspired the Dutch architect Willem-Jan Neutelings to write an essay on the "ring culture" [1988; see also 1989]. Starting from a study of the Antwerp ringroad, Neutelings formulated a number of ideas on the contemporary European city in general. "In European metropolises," he wrote, "we observe a spontaneous rejuvenation cure, the ring mechanism. The ring mechanism is

7 Practising architect Cino Zucchi offers his own meditations on the posturban Italian cityscape in his contribution to Part II.

able to transform a peripheral zone into a spatial-programmatic element in the city. As soon as this ring zone reaches its critical mass, it becomes the ignition coil of its own ring culture" [1988: 5; editors' translation]. Neutelings observes how the "programs" of mass culture — like jogging tracks, event halls, recreation parks, rock palaces, do-it-yourself malls, motel chains, allotment gardens, furniture stores, commodity exchanges, tire dealers, or sports complexes — are beaded like a necklace around European cities, between center and suburb, along the elongated urban freeways. This zone constitutes to Neutelings a condensation of modern culture, and he considers it incomprehensible and irresponsible that the disciplines of architecture and urban planning utterly disregard this process. While architects and urban planners have heated debates on stylistic issues and cosmetic adaptations, the largest part of building assignments relates to peripheral areas, where they are solely determined by economic and bureaucratic powers. The ring zone is a kind of architectural free zone, which shirks any planning and turns a blind eye to the supervision that is deemed so important in the historic centers. Thus, today's planners repeat the mistake made by the modern movement, which slighted the historic cities and in so doing gave free play to real estate speculation. Instead of lamenting the deurbanization process and coldshouldering it in one's designs, architects and urban planners, according to Neutelings, should realize the important task of devising designing strategies that are tailored to the new environment.

All the foregoing examples clearly indicate how the European urban landscape is subject to processes of sprawl and deconcentration as well, and that in its case, too, the dichotomy between center and periphery has weakened. A general morphological and sociocultural theory about these processes, however, is much harder to formulate than in the United States. Spatial and morphological processes in Europe are even more complex and follow more varied patterns. In some European cities, two ostensibly antagonistic processes even run side by side. Frankfurt is a conspicuous case in point: there two forms of urban growth and two different discourses on growth go hand in hand. The situation in Frankfurt is such that, in Roger Keil and Klaus Ronneberger's view, the whole idea of growth needs to be reconceptualized:

*Centralization and decentralization, and concentration and deconcentration, must not be seen as antagonistic poles but as different aspects of one complex regional growth process. The flexibilization of production and logistics make it possible for segments of economic activity to be located in so-called underdeveloped areas of the city and the region. What might look like disurbanization from the central perspective is, in fact, a dramatic increase in density anywhere else in the region. In fact, other cities and towns in the agglomeration, supported by growth policies of their municipal governments, are growing increasingly and are creating a pattern of decentralized reconcentration in formerly rural areas* [1994:146].

In this sense, Frankfurt offers an example of the double development model that is typical of many European cities: at the same time as it displays the familiar pattern of an expanding oil stain or spiderweb, the urban landscape is also characterized by an autonomous development of the periphery. The growth of the central city goes hand in hand with an increase in density within the periphery, which finally blots out the line between center and periphery. A particular zone within the periphery (around the airport, for instance) can itself become the center of important sectors in the post-Fordist economy. Ultimately, the periphery begins to interact not only with the central city, but with the entire region, which is characterized by different degrees of density. "The spatial form of the periphery is being produced by a series of often contradictory dynamics. The periphery not only has been colonized by the core but also appears as the product of exchange processes of core and periphery and of various subcenters on the fringe" [1994:151]. Keil and Ronneberger further note that almost every municipality in the region has reproduced some or other modernist urban form, for instance by building ambitious housing projects close to traditional village centers, thereby increasing the urban density. Instead of uniform urban sprawl, we thus find a multitude and multiplication of centralization effects: "post-Fordist German agglomeration, as exemplified here by the Frankfurt case, has a tradition of nodalization stemming from earlier periods of decentralized concentration" [ibid.].

**Urban Discontinuities and Urban Voids** The hybridization of center and periphery and the interaction between processes of concentration and of decentralization in the contemporary urban landscape are themselves accompanied by one further complicating factor: the radical fragmentation of the landscape. In his overview of the 20th-century American city [1993], Jon Teaford judiciously opted for framing that history in terms of an ever-increasing fragmentation process. The exemplary postmodern metropolis, Los Angeles, has been presented in similar terms at least since Robert Fogelson's 1967 classic, *The Fragmented Metropolis.* And Richard Weinstein has written about this same city that "fragmenting discontinuities operated on both the new development and the infill between existing (but already dispersed) communities that preceded the automobile, becoming the nonhierarchical, flexible, extended matrix that characterizes Los Angeles" [1996:30]. Weinstein further emphasizes "the spatial porosity of the system, its void/positive character" and points to "the blockages represented by parking structures and the emptiness of parking lots" [ibid.]. In this sense, too, L.A. has become a model for other cities: its spatial fragmentation lends a discontinuous structure to the contemporary cityscape — a discontinuity that is further stimulated by the presence of so-called urban voids. This is true both of the traditional core city and of the current posturban environment of edge cities and technoburbs.

While cities seem to be for ever expanding, their cores have in turn become subject to processes of dilution. As a result of suburbanization, many core cities have for instance seen the rise of monofunctional districts consisting of no more than isolated office towers. The suburbanization of industry, likewise, has laid waste large industrial sites in the earlier centers of cities. These literal forms of fragmentation and literal voids in the urban fabric have been accompanied by a fragmentation in the image that inhabitants as well as visitors have come to form of a particular city. At a time when most traditional urban functions have been assimilated by posturban slurbs, the central city is forced to present an image of itself as above all a cultural or historic center. The urban environment overall is being shaped more and more by the car, yet many old inner cities (especially in Europe) have been made precisely car-free to add to their profile of historic cities. The traditional inner city has thus come to serve the restricted function of an open-air museum first and foremost, and is presented as the embodiment of a collective memory. This museum character has strengthened the fragmentation process in its own way, since only isolated, contrasting fragments of static tableaux are used to suggest a shared past. In *The City of Collective Memory*, M. Christine Boyer convincingly demonstrates that political and commercial attention tends to be only directed at privileged sites, and that as a result the zones in between these sites, the residual spaces, are either ignored or stashed away. "A city of increasing spatial differentiation results," she writes, "and the gap looms larger between neglected land and revalued places, between the poor that the market ignores and the well-to-do that it privileges" [1994: 449-50].

The discontinuity of the contemporary metropolis, however, comes to the fore much more prominently in the peripheries, which have adopted so many of the functions and programs of the urban centers. Again, the phenomenon is no longer typical of American cities only, but also increasingly of European cities. The Dutch architect Willem-Jan Neutelings famously called the Randstad a "carpet metropolis" [1989]. In an urban planning study for the southern periphery of Den Haag, Neutelings even seized on the fragmentation and discontinuity of the contemporary cityscape to enhance the metropolitan character of the area. Rejecting the dichotomy between city and periphery, he aimed to kindle the metropolitan potential of the periphery, taking as his cue the example of Los Angeles, where the fulfillment of individual residential desires no longer conflicts with the immediate availability of metropolitan facilities for a mass culture [see Heynen 1990]. Neutelings sees the whole Randstad as a carpet of juxtaposed activities and in his own surprising way he underlines especially the positive characteristics of this carpet metropolis: the existing chaos yields a rich variety of intense experiences. In his designs, he does everything to retain this polychromy and to intensify it. This stands in marked contrast to the usual effect of fragmentation processes, which is one of sapping urban intensity. Posturban space, by and large, is determined by pockets of emptiness and shallowness. In between the developed sites of the urbanized landscape, we find undefined residual spaces, non-sites, or urban voids.

Indeed, characteristic of the dispersed city is precisely the predominance of large, open spaces — a characteristic already signaled in the early seventies by John Friedmann [1973]. The importance of a wider territorial scale interspersed by large, open spaces is also strikingly expressed by the growing role of landscape architects in recent discourses on architecture and urban planning. According to the French critic Sébastien Marot, the very dichotomy between city and countryside has even lost its validity altogether. As causes he cites the monoculturalization of agriculture, the appropriation of supposedly rural or picturesque sites by tourism, and the encroachment upon rural space by sprawling cities. "More striking, and indeed more usual," he adds, "is the transformation of the countryside into a transit area, its surface furrowed, with a relative indifference to the geography, or else from purely technical considerations, by the numerous vectors and infrastructures of modern systems: roads and motorways, railways, high-voltage lines, etc. A new form of territoriality has been superimposed upon the old one, substituting its transfers, its multimodal platforms, its own distribution points, for the former centres of non-specialized communication which the small town used to be" [1995: 13].

The presence of open interspaces is not only striking at a wider territorial scale and from a panoramic vantage-point. Voids are often quite tangibly real both at previously industrial sites in the inner cities and in the new landscape of technoburbs. Contrary to the chaotic and kaleidoscopic modern metropolis, which was above all associated with the notions of superimposition, congestion, density, and visual overload, the chaos of postsuburbia is associated primarily with notions of a void. Jon Teaford paints us a vivid picture of the new landscape:

*By the early 1990s so-called suburban downtowns loomed over freeway interchanges in metropolitan areas throughout the nation. These centers included shopping malls, office parks, and hotels, yet they bore little resemblance to old-fashioned downtowns. Adapted to the automobile rather than the pedestrian, they tended to sprawl, unlike the relatively compact older business districts. They had plenty of parking but few sidewalks. Their office buildings did not hug the thorough-fares or stand cheek by jowl next to one another.*

*Instead, they were in campuslike settings, removed from the highway and surrounded by well-watered lawns and well-paved parking lots. Each element of the outlying complexes tended to be self-contained and isolated from the other parts. Shopping malls stood in a sea of parking lots and faced inward. Windowless and forbidding on the outside, the malls turned their backs to the world and reserved their pleasures for those shoppers who penetrated their cores. Standing apart in individual parks, pristine glass office towers certainly did not invite casual visitors. Similarly, each hotel was a world apart and complete, with its own convention facilities, health spa, and complement of restaurants. The suburban downtowns were fractured conglomerations of commerce with an internal structure appropriate to the increasingly fragmented metropolis* [1993: 164-65].

Peter Rowe, who coined the term "middle landscape" to describe this new environment, strikes an even darker note. "The most disconcerting physical characteristic of the middle landscape," he writes,

*is the desolate and inhospitable space left between many buildings and building complexes. Commercial strips extend out into the surrounding countryside without any suggestion of a center or of termination. Bland residential subdivisions and office parks leapfrog over one another, leaving vacant land and unfinished developments in their wake. Many buildings have a temporary quality, suggesting that they might be here today and gone tomorrow. The surrounding landscape is pervaded by parking lots that offer little definition of their primary function, let alone an inviting environment. Entirely absent are characteristics of traditional city streets that graciously provide for public life* [1991: 249].

Both Teaford and Rowe point to the role of the car — and especially the dominant presence of parking lots — in the establishment of empty interspaces. According to William Whyte, more than half of the surface area of certain American cities is taken up by parking lots [1988: 6]. This means that posturban space has ironically come to assume a central feature of the most orthodox kind of modernistic urban planning. One of the most influential publications to have lambasted modernistic urban planning, Colin Rowe and Fred Koetter's *Collage City* [1979], is precisely predicated on the claim that modernism tended to invert the relationship between built and open space and how this inversion was bound to have the most deleterious effects at street level. By declaring buildings to be autonomous objects, modernist planners created desolate fields of nonurban space that made brutal cuts through neighborhoods and radically isolated people. The ensuing wastelands, wholly tailored to the car, lacked all form of human scale and any of the sense of shelter and coziness that are generally deemed to be characteristic of premodern public space in Europe. As an alternative to large-scale, megalomaniac planning practices, Rowe and Koetter proposed the small-scale collage as a method for designing public spaces. Twenty years later, the reality that has actually materialized ironically indicates how wastelands are not only the side-effects of megalomaniac modernist practices, but are just as prominent in the fragmented layout of the posturban landscape.

The isolated position of buildings in posturban space, it should be noted however, carries different connotations from those accompanying the autonomous modernist object. The reason is that the uncoupling of building and environment serves a different purpose. Whereas Le Corbusier, for instance, placed buildings on *pilotis* (piles) to create a new, utopian space that ostentatiously turned away from the decaying and ravaged urban fabric of its surroundings, the cases of the atriums of office towers or of the sunken plazas of shopping malls are different: in the latter instances "no larger protopolitical Utopian transformation ... is either expected or desired" [Jameson 1991:41-42]. Disjunction in modernism was clearly and sharply delineated and had a symbolic meaning, while characteristic postmodern buildings like the Westin Bonaventure Hotel in Los Angeles, Beaubourg in Paris, or Eaton Centre in Toronto no longer seem to care about the urban fabric. They try to sell themselves rather as "a kind of miniature city" [ibid.: 40]. The postmodern building no longer wishes to be part of the city, but rather "its equivalent and replacement or substitute" [ibid.].

The omnipresence of voids in the urban fabric renders new urbanization patterns particularly hard to identify or label. Yet it is not the presence of open spaces itself that posits a real problem. Open spaces can be used — and have always been used — to lend a certain character to a given environment. "It is probably the open spaces of pre-modern cities, rather than the buildings, that stick in the memory," writes Peter Buchanan. "But even famous open spaces would be unrecognisable if stripped of their enclosing frame of buildings. So a major problem of the sprawling and fragmented modern city is not a lack of open space, but rather an excess of it and its lack of definition. Too much openness means there is little real and memorable open space" [1993:32].

The importance of providing a definition to voids and open spaces has begun to be recognized by architects and urban planners alike. For some designers the concept of the void has thus even come to form a potentially productive concept in the construction of public spaces.[8] Rem Koolhaas is again one of the first to have explicitly thematized this potential in his writings. "In my opinion," he noted already more than ten years ago,

8 See, for a further analysis of this issue, the case study by Kristiaan Borret (Part II).

*there are two reasons that make urban voids at least one of the principal lines of combat, if not the only line, for people interested in the city. The first is quite simple: it is now easier to control empty space than to play on full volumes and agglomerate shapes that, though no one can rightly say why, have become uncontrollable. The second is something I've noticed: emptiness, landscape, space — if you want to use them as a lever, if you want to include them in a scheme — can serve as a battlefield and can draw quite general support from everyone. This is no longer the case for an architectural work, which today is always suspect and inspires prior distrust* [1989:16].

Instead of importing Manhattan's culture of congestion, today's European city, according to Koolhaas, should start to realize the metropolitan potential inherent in its forms of emptiness. "For Koolhaas," notes Paul Vermeulen, "the contemporary European metropolis [is] entirely different from Manhattan — less dense, less massive. In his view, in Europe today metropolitan potential is to be found less in the historic centres than in the peripheral areas. It is less a matter of the building volumes than of the empty gap. How to give that emptiness an urban significance? — that seems to him the most relevant town planning issue today" [1994:225]. Various of Koolhaas's designs can indeed be interpreted as attempts to bestow a surplus value on urban emptiness, without filling and thus canceling that emptiness. It is a principle that is central also to Neutelings's study of, and design for, the Antwerp ring, in which he talks of "the density of the void" [1989:42]. To Neutelings, the ring constitutes a zone in which a low density of volumes may be linked to a high density of functions and a minimum of architecture may provoke a maximum of activity.

**The Posturban Contamination of Functions** During the first half of this century, many artists, writers, and intellectuals were mesmerized by the modern metropolis as a site where different and even antagonistic objects, forms, activities, and functions influenced each other and strove to get the upper hand. It was precisely this chaotic and kaleidoscopic image of the metropolis that was swept off the table by modernist planners. The chaos of the city was to be replaced resolutely by a rational order. In the Charter of Athens, which formed the written reflection of the CIAM doctrine, the built urban environment was reduced to four functions: residence, work, recreation, and traffic. Each function, except for that of traffic, was allocated a separate urban sector. This famous principle of the separation of functions has since been subjected to much theoretical criticism. By now it should be clear, however, that the principle has also come to very little in practice. The classic suburb, whose sole function was residential, has undergone a veritable metamorphosis. One of the main reasons for the relative demise of the difference between cities and suburbs is the fact that in both zones we now find a mix of functions: both are used for living, trading, producing, and recreating. To Sharon Zukin, the dense urban landscape of production and transport should be understood to coexist in time and space with the suburban landscape of "small-scale outcroppings in the hinterland of shopping malls, ranch houses, and office parks" [1991:17]. The periphery has adopted the functional complexity of the traditional metropolis rather than the monofunctional character of the classic suburb.

Although the urban landscape has become fragmented and seems to be subject to an atomization into ever smaller units, it also displays a mix of functions. "The new suburban house of the 1950s," argues Fishman,

*like its predecessors for more than a century, existed precisely to isolate women and the family from urban economic life; it defined an exclusive zone of residence between city and country. Now a new house might adjoin a landscaped office park with more square feet of new office spaces than in a downtown building, or might be just down the highway from an enclosed shopping mall with a sales volume that exceeds those of the downtown department stores, or might overlook a high tech laboratory making products that are exported around the world. No longer a refuge, the single family detached house on the periphery is preferred as a convenient base from which both spouses can rapidly reach their jobs* [1987:195].

Functions, activities, and typologies are once again mixed. Some zoning is of course used as a planning principle, but it is no longer imposed in any dogmatic or absolute sense. At times, the built environment is being celebrated again as a chaotic surrounding. There has been almost a reversal in contemporary urban planning theories: whereas modernist planners tried to impose an order on chaos (so perceived by the individual because of the tremendous impact of capitalism on the shape of the city), their successors often seem to want to impose a sort of chaos on relative order [see Marcuse 1995]. Not everyone joins in this celebration of chaos, yet many American and European scholars are still agreed that the contemporary posturban landscape in all its hybridity offers more potentialities for urban planning than the classic suburb or any other traditional embodiment of the periphery. As Stefano Boeri, Arturo Lanzani, and Edoardo Marini are happy to note, "the landscapes of the diffused city are not 'large peripheries'; we also encounter areas and points of significant social and morphological complexity" [1993a:124].

Even the urban voids described in the previous paragraph may be subjected to a contamination of functions. After all, many of these voids take the form of traffic infrastructure, and this infrastructure invites a certain revalorization after an era of modernist urban planning in which streets were only viewed as circulation channels, not as a theater for public life. On the one hand, authors like Bernardo Secchi rightly note that the modernist principle of streets as mere circulation channels has also been adopted by the dispersed city: "The space 'in-between things,' between objects and subjects next to one another, between my house and my neighbour's, between their office and mine, is traversed by many strangers, and is not a meeting place; it has become 'empty' because it plays no recognizable role; this space is only required to be permeable, and should be traversed with as little friction as possible" [1993:116]. On the other hand, however, there has been a growing awareness since the publication of Robert Venturi's *Learning from Las Vegas* [1972] that the road today also has a billboard function — a function that has somehow come to displace the bombardment of urban signs with which people were showered in the traditional core city. Even in Europe, for instance in the "ribbon development" of Flanders, this is somehow the case [see Jacobs 1995]. The function of the landscape there constantly changes: a gas station is "converted" into a brothel, though it might just as well have been a Chinese restaurant. Signs become interchangeable: brothels, Chinese restaurants, and gas stations use similar neon lights and multi-colored signposts. The landscape itself, moreover, becomes an extrapolation of its component parts: the multi-colored, geometrical blocks built alongside the road resemble the shelves in the department stores that are linked up to the road system.

In the organization of space around the strip, the simultaneity of visual stimuli, which dominated the image of the modern metropolis, has vanished. Visual coincidence has been replaced by a gradual concatenation of images. As the posturban landscape is the realm of motorized traffic, the speed at which these seriated signs and stimuli are read depends on how hard one chooses to step on the accelerator. The chaotic spectacle of the modern metropolis and the modernist principle of zoning, which was precisely out to neutralize and counter that chaos, appear to merge again in the posturban landscape. The dogma of zoning was transformed into a politics of fragmentation and juxtaposition in which the size of various units has drastically shrunk. The increasingly long distance between different urban fragments is reduced by the car, yet that car has also turned the spectacle of the modern metropolis into a cinematic experience. In his study of the ring culture, Neutelings has linked the phenomenon of kinetic perception to the principle of productive juxtaposition [1989:43]. Precisely because of its extreme juxtapositions, the ring zone has become a laboratory of new programs and types. Neutelings does not stop to be amazed, then, by the surrealistic quality of the principle of juxtaposition which is at the heart of his concept of the carpet metropolis.

# 3 The Virtualization of the Metropolis

**The Rise of the City à la Carte** The isolated fragments of the posturban environment are not only separated from each other by urban voids, but are also linked by barely perceptible networks, which often seem to escape all spatial logic. The Italian urban planner Bernardo Secchi notes how

*together, the cities and the territory have become immense collections of objects tactically placed next to one another, mute. Similarity does not imply proximity. Each object and place takes different itineraries; the origin and the destination of each is specific and personal: here is my house, here is my school, here is my place of work, and here far away is my wife's; the cinema, the tennis, the gym I go to are all in different parts of the city, in other municipal areas; during weekends each individual moves in an even bigger territory, and during vacations this territory expands even further and turns into a continent, etc. This network of relationships between places is totally different from my neighbour's, from my colleague's, but also from my son's* [1993:116].

Every urban resident, in other words, composes his own city. The urban environment, thereby forced to sacrifice traditional notions of a public space, is reduced to little more than the sum of a series of subjective trajectories. This phenomenon reaches its apogee in the car-oriented technoburb. As Robert Fishman argues, "distance in the new cities is generally measured in terms of time rather than blocks or miles. The supermarket is 10 minutes away. The nearest shopping mall is 30 minutes in another direction, and one's job 40 minutes away by yet another route. The pattern formed by these destinations represents 'the city' for that particular family or individual. The more varied one's destinations, the richer and more diverse is one's personal 'city.' The new city is a city à la carte" [1990:38]. To Fishman, the new urban environment may be viewed as composed of three overlapping networks — the household network, the network of production, and the network of consumption — which all possess their own spatial logics. Because these networks overlap, the pattern on the ground is one of juxtaposition and interpenetration. Instead of a logical distinction between functions "one finds a post-modern, post-urban collage" [ibid.:39].

Urban space, then, has been uncoupled more and more from a materially identifiable entity and been subjected to a proper spatial logic that robs the classical notions of proximity and distance of much of their meaning. Already in the 1930s, when the future of Los Angeles was shaped, an enormous grid of freeways was superimposed on the denser network of surface roads that had developed in the decade before. "The freeways," as Fishman observes, "were truly to unite the whole region into one decentralized city, permitting rapid travel in any direction and between any two spots on the map. Once these high speed corridors were in place, even the vast distances of the Los Angeles basin could be covered in minutes" [1987: 173-74]. Not distance, but time has become the criterion that most determines the spatial organization of the various parts of the posturban landscape. According to Paul Virilio, who analyzed the fascination of modernity for speed in several of his texts [see especially Virilio 1984], the speed of modern transportation constitutes the most important factor in the current disurbanization process. Categories like time and speed undermine the geographical identity of a city. A city region like Rotterdam, Harm Tilman has argued [1997], is today much more strongly connected to other city regions in other countries than to those in the Netherlands itself. During his work on EuraLille, Rem Koolhaas even went so far as to claim that Englishmen would massively start buying houses in Lille (in the north of France) because they would be able to get to the center of London faster from there than from London's own periphery. "If you imagine not distance as a crucial given but time it takes to get somewhere then there is an irregular figure which represents the entire territory that is now less than one hour and thirty minutes from Lille. If you add up all the people in this territory, it turns out to be 60 million people. So the TGV and the tunnel could fabricate a virtual metropolis spread in an irregular manner, of which Lille, now a fairly depressing unimportant city, becomes, somehow by accident, completely artificially, the headquarters" [1996: 334].

The marriage of the newest means of transportation with other decisive transformations like the new communication technologies, the growing mobility of capital and investments, shifts in the organization of labor, and more flexible systems of production and consumption, has done a lot to diminish spatial limitations and subject the urban environment to what David Harvey has called "the annihilation of space through time" [1988 and 1989a]. In postsuburbia, spatial and sociocultural fragmentation is accompanied by the development of vast networks. Some of these networks, moreover, are almost entirely symbolic, prompting Bernardo Secchi to claim that "the physical territory is more and more the result and the recipient of contracts, laws, procedures, regulations and administrative practices, and less and less of technical operations linked to methods of production" [1985: 19]. The urban landscape, in other words, is shaped by vectors that are no longer visible, on the basis of a logic that remains impervious to outsiders and laymen. Still according to Secchi, this condition poses new challenges for architects and urban planners as well, for these are now forced

*to understand and to distinguish exactly the different features and roots of phenomena, subjects and events which appear irreducible, and to patiently try to reconstruct these into a web of connections, into a rule of associations or significant oppositions, as a reference to other things. It is not a question of conserving, preserving, limiting and preventing; nor is it a question of replacing a constructor, a promotor, an architect, a ladder, a measurement, or a language with another: it is a question of modifying and reinterpreting* [ibid.].

**Technopoles and the Global Network** Today's urban space is not only cut through by countless overlapping networks, it is in its entirety also part of a global network. Already in the early 1960s, the American urban planner Melvin Webber proposed a conceptual model for describing this changing status of urban space: the "nonplace urban realm" [see Webber 1964]. Webber demonstrated that increased mobility and global communication technologies had reduced the importance of distance for human interaction, and that as a result the principle of centrality, which until then had been at the ideological base of urban spaces, was being eroded. The city, he argued, could no longer be seen as a static arrangement of objects in a unitary space, but had to be approached as a nonplace urban realm, a giant grid consisting of near-invisible transportation and communication networks. The radically innovative developments in the fields of media and communication technology in particular have involved a rupture with an age-old process. The traditional 19th- and early-20th-century metropolis, it should be remembered, formed the culmination of a tradition reaching back all the way to the first settlements in the Old Near East — a tradition famously described in 1938 by Lewis Mumford in *The Culture of Cities*. To solve the slow, cumbersome, and expensive problem of transportation, people had consistently tended to opt for a concentration of goods and people in one and the same place. The construction of railroads in the 19th century did not fundamentally alter this pattern. Although long-standing city walls might have been torn down, the advantages of a centralized system remained in place: the system was only expanded to form a pattern of concentric circles. But in the early decades of the 20th century, at the moment when the centralized industrial metropolis was at its height, a handful of technological innovations were introduced that began to undermine the advantages of a centralized city. Communication and transportation networks that supported the center were replaced by networks spreading over entire regions. Not only the car and the growing road network, but also the general spreading of electricity, and the telephone network undermined the economic advantages of proximity and density.

To be sure, none of these transformations happened overnight. They were part of a complex and at times contradictory history that influenced the urban landscape gradually and stimulated it in various conflicting ways. The example of the telephone is but one instance of the quirky ways in which new telecommunication systems intervened with the process of urban growth. One of the early effects of the telephone was that it robbed traditional monofunctional trade zones of much of their meaning — zones like the fishmarket, the egg market, the hatters' neighborhood, the wool neighborhood, the shippers' district. It thus facilitated the formation of a modern and multifunctional downtown and contributed to the image of a vibrant, multicolored metropolis. At a later stage, however, it became one of the major factors behind the success of suburbia and thus contributed to the postwar process of disurbanization. The telephone, in other words, originally

*helped dissolve the solid knots of traditional business neighborhoods and helped create the great new downtowns; but at a later stage, it helped disperse those downtowns to new suburban business and shopping centers.... Thus we find many relationships between the development of the telephone system and the quality of urban life; strikingly, the relationships change with time and with the level of telephone penetration. The same device at one stage contributed to the growth of the great downtowns and at a later stage to suburban migration. The same device, when it was scarce, served to accentuate the structure of differentiated neighborhoods. When it became a facility available to all, however, it reduced the role of the geographic neighborhood* [de Sola Pool et al. quoted in Graham and Marvin 1996:315].

After the telephone, other communication technologies further eroded the need for proximity and residential density: radio first, then television, and in the last few decades video, fax, satellites, optic fiber cables, computers, and the Internet contributed to this evolution as well. Traditional face-to-face communication has in many cases come to be replaced by electronic forms of communication [see Graham and Marvin 1996]. As Robert Fishman reminds us, the term "technoburb" was originally devised to refer less to archetypical areas with high-tech industries like Silicon Valley, Orange County, or Route 128, than to the advanced communication technologies that enabled new urban decentralization patterns in general [1987:184].

To these new communication media should be added new means of transportation: not only cars, but also vans, motor homes, buses, motorcycles, helicopters, and airplanes. Together with high-tech industries in general, and the microelectronic industry boosted by military defense budgets in particular, these innovations played a crucial role in the economic development of especially postsuburbia. Proverbial zones like Silicon Valley, Orange County, and Route 128 are only the most eye-catching results of what might be called a new phase in capitalism, in which the new advanced technologies become responsible for important sociospatial changes in cities and suburbs. These changes, it should be noted, did not only take place in areas where high-tech products are fabricated but, given the growing overall importance of high technology in the production process, have had an impact on a far wider scale. According to M. Gottdiener and George Kephart, "the importance of high technology does not have to do as much with the product as with high technology as a means of production. Automation, robotics, and computers have revolutionized the production process, increasing the capital intensiveness of firms, expanding information processing, and even transforming financial strategies. High technology, it is argued, is emerging as a new means of production that is altering firms' decisions regarding location and organization" [1995:36].

All of these evolutions are indeed inextricably intertwined with wider economic changes in the West. Especially the fact that a free-market economy and its monetary system are fueled by expansion, and thus by processes of globalization, has been of paramount importance. Instead of being geared to local markets, whose self-evident nucleus is the commercial-industrial city, the post-Fordist economy of the past few decades is driven by a transnational financial system that lives off a dizzying mobility of capital flows. The termination of the Breton Woods agreements in 1973, which uncoupled the U.S. dollar from the value of gold, and the subsequent digitalization of the financial world, have transformed the world economy into a system of ceaselessly shuttling capital flows, devoid of any lingering materiality and only perceptible through the flickering figures on a computer screen [see Harvey 1989a&b and Castells 1989]. This "virtualization process" of the monetary economy stands in a complex relationship to the parallel transformation of urban space into a more "virtual" environment.

Especially Manuel Castells has been preoccupied with exploring the relationship between technological advances and the transformation of capitalism. The title of his classic study, *The Informational City* [1989], suggests at the least a number of repercussions on urban space. According to Castells, the most significant consequence of parallel technological and organizational changes in the realm of the "social" is the reconstruction of social meaning in a *space of flows*. The space of places is superseded by the space of flows. The new economic space is organized through an asymmetrical network of exchanges which do not depend on any specific locale for fulfilling their goals. "People live in places, power rules through flows," Castells succinctly notes [ibid.:349]. Cities, or rather, certain cities have become nodes within this space of flows, while others are losing their relevance. Castells convincingly demonstrates that, as the result of transformations in the late capitalist production process, the traditional hierarchies between cities and between center and periphery have been radically altered. To Castells, we may clearly speak of a "crisis of urban civilization. Because cities, after all, have always been communication systems that have brought together, in a spatial form, power and experience, function and meaning, knowledge and action. These systems of communication are now broken, because these forces are pulling in different directions. Experience is being contained within territorial spaces, into the space of places. And power is being propelled into electronic circuits organized in nodes and hubs, into the space of flows" [1996: 203].

Saskia Sassen also has shown how new technologies and the globalization of the economy have changed the very meaning of our notions of geography and distance. Studying the links between global economic restructuring and urban change, Sassen noted that the combination of spatial dispersal and global integration has created a new strategic role for major cities [1991: 62]. According to her, globalization is not attended by dispersal and decentralization. On the contrary, a new geography of centrality, which does not respect national or city boundaries, has sprung up. "The most powerful of these new geographies of centrality at the interurban level," writes Sassen, "binds the major international financial and business centers: New York, London, Tokyo, Paris, Frankfurt, Zurich, Amsterdam, Los Angeles, Sydney, and Hong Kong, among others. But this geography now also includes cities as Sao Paulo and Mexico City" [1996: 210].

Centrality remains a key property of the economic system, but the spatial correlates of centrality have been profoundly altered by the new technologies as well as by globalization. This poses a new challenge for architects and urban planners, among others. Thus, Sassen observes how "the 1980s brought a new architecture of centrality that represented and housed new forms of economic power — that is, the hyperspace of international business; witness the corporate towers, corporate hotels, and world-class airports that have constituted a new geography of the built environment of centrality. Though this new space of centrality is trans-territorial, it is still a type of place" [ibid.: 208-209].

The buildings occupied by the hyperspace of international business tend towards the same architectural features worldwide. The nodes in the space of flows more and more resemble each other. Cities start to look like airports, Rem Koolhaas has provocatively argued in his influential essay on "The Generic City," and the airport in this comparison stands for "a concentrate of both the hyper-local and the hyper-global — hyper-global in the sense you can get goods there that are not available even in the city, hyper-local in the sense you can get things there that you get nowhere else" [1994: 1251]. The Dutch architectural critic Hans Ibelings claims that "airports are to the nineties what museums were for the postmodern eighties" [1998: 79; editors' translation]. The airport, in his opinion, constitutes the paradigmatic building program of the 1990s. Mobility, accessibility, and infrastructure are primordial to these buildings, which have themselves become centers of growing economic significance. Ibelings has termed the formal vocabulary of these architecturally interesting airports and of other similar large-scale works "supermodernism." Instead of taking an interest in the contextual and historical factors of architecture (as in the 70s and 80s), supermodernism is characterized by a susceptibility to categories like the neutral, the indistinct, or the implicit [ibid.:62]. The buildings of, among other people, Renzo Piano, Norman Foster, OMA, Toyo Ito, Jean Nouvel, Herzog & de Meuron, Dominique Perrault, and Wiel Arets are often viewed in terms of a flexible envelope. Smooth facades are covered with solid or moving texts and images and architecture seems to have become just as footloose as all globally operating corporations [ibid.: 88-89].

One of the more striking results of this process is that global, international networks and communication technologies often serve to enhance rather than cancel processes of fragmentation. "Telecommunications and telematics play a paradoxical role" according to Stephen Graham and Simon Marvin. "They tend not to be used to link innovators together because the ongoing innovation requires intense face-to-face contact and ongoing trust-based relationships. Rather, the growth of telematics actually encourages the appearance of new specialised production activities, which themselves then cluster together in geographical space" [1996:159]. The resulting clusters are those of so-called technopoles like Silicon Valley and Route 128 in the U.S., the Toulouse area in France, certain smaller cities in Italy's Tuscany or Germany's Baden Württemberg, or the Flanders Language Valley in Western Belgium. To Manuel Castells and Peter Hall [1994], these technopoles, emerging in the periphery of almost any dynamic urban environment, possess a campus-like atmosphere and often seem to be cut off from existing cities. They appear to be especially linked to each other, rather than to their immediately surrounding urban contexts. Together they form a kind of decentralized "smart city" — a technologically linked city that has furthered the demise of the traditional metropolis. John Naisbitt and Patricia Aburdene provocatively conclude that "if cities did not exist, it now would not be necessary to invent them ... truly global cities will not be the largest, they will be the smartest" [1991:329].

The formation of global networks, finally, has also strengthened fragmentation processes in another, more cultural-political respect. David Harvey [1988] points up a paradox in this respect: the lifting of spatial frontiers has actually increased the importance of spatial differences. Precisely the development of a

9 For an analysis of these analogies with special reference to the cyberpunk of William Gibson, see the case study by Maarten Delbeke (Part II).

global socioeconomic system and of a cultural universalism has spawned an obsession with local and regional factors. Manuel Castells [1989 and esp. 1997] likewise suggests that the tribalization of local communities constitutes the flipside to the globalization of power structures. The establishment of far-flung, worldwide networks does not only stimulate new connections between the fragments of a new posturban environment, it also enhances spatial and sociocultural fragmentation. A manifest regionalism has developed in response to the rise of global networks. In *The Urban Experience* [1989b], Harvey points to the growing importance of an ideology of interregional competition in an economy of advancing globalization. This is corroborated by Roger Keil and Klaus Ronneberger in their study on the periphery of Frankfurt, an area that has developed into a cynosure of cutting-edge sectors in the post-Fordist economy. According to this study, it is possible to argue that "just as multiculturalism has become a typical unifying node in the discursive chain of inner-city consensus building, regionalism has become the buzzword for the agglomeration: it constitutes an ideological bracket linking the global with the local planes of agency" [1994:162].

**Cyburbia and Invisibility** In their introduction to *Visions of the Modern City*, William Sharpe and Leonard Wallock recall the 19th-century habit of representing cities by way of organic metaphors. "Today," they add, "the Metropolitan Statistical Areas definition relies on the atom — a nuclear city and 'orbiting' electron-suburbs — thereby combining connotations of both space and energy. The shift from the organism to the atomic particle, from biology to physics, from something familiar and instantly apprehendable to a structure that we have probably seen only in diagram and that represents lines of force — all this is indicative of our increasingly complex and insecure sense of the contemporary city" [1987:36]. Not only physics has served the purpose of reconceptualizing an increasingly elusive metropolitan ambiance: the same can be said of cybernetics.

Even as postsuburbia economically developed through the high tech of late capitalism, the computer became itself a popular symbol or metaphor for evoking the patterns of contemporary urban space. Analogies between the virtual space of computers and the spatial organization and layout of posturban landscapes have frequently been pursued, most notably by M. Christine Boyer in *Cybercities* [1996].[9] The metaphor of the city as a human body or as a machine, typical of the 19th and early 20th centuries, has given way to the image of a city as an overlapping of diagrams, matrixes, and spreadsheets. In theoretical debates, space has often ceded to the new categories of "metaspace" and "hyperspace," in which audiovisual jumps serve to disrupt our traditional sense of space and time. The electronic communication technologies that both ease and strengthen urban isolation and alienation are pictured as all-devouring entities that swallow up all of our surroundings into one giant continuum. Mapping the city, under such circumstances, seems no longer possible: the only thing we can still do is talk of non-linear visions on a multicentered, non-hierarchical, discontinuous organization — the sort of organization that bears a marked structural resemblance to that of a computer matrix. The many kinds of void that characterize the late-20th-century metropolis, for instance, are "lag-time places" (Boyer); they illustrate how a logic comparable to that of the computer now dominates the organization of urban space. Much as the electronic media have taught us endlessly to rearrange data (by cutting, copying, pasting), the urban matrix imposes itself on our perception as an aggregation of atomic particles surrounded by empty spaces. Posturban space is repeatedly represented as a virtual city, hard to fit into traditional cognitive schemes and constantly resisting all forms of mental mapping.

No matter how appealing, however, the metaphor of the computer has its limitations. Although there has been a clear uncoupling of socioeconomic and cultural structures, on one hand, and the physical condition of the built environment, on the other, the city obviously stays a material given, to which even the virtual world of computer networks is forced to adapt. According to Gabriel Dupuy [1991], also networks correspond to the logic of the existing urban structure. A cash automat, for instance, is not installed anywhere, but in spots where a high concentration of potential users can be expected, and preferably also where there is sufficient social control. These infrastructural elements, in other words, belong both to the network itself and to the space in which they are installed. Besides the system of transactions and relations, nodes are equally essential to the network. "These nodes are not in the first place pure geometric abstractions. They have a social and geographical weight that makes them the expression of an individual or collective self" [101; editors' translation].

The metaphor of the computer nevertheless raises our awareness of how today's urban networks, in their uncoupling from a relatively restricted territory, blatantly resist traditional forms of cartographic representation. Countless alternative cartographic and statistic systems have been devised to catch the new posturban reality [see Teyssot 1988, esp. the contributions by Pierre Pinon, Jacques Bertin, and Richard Saul Wurman]. According to Daniela Daniele in *Città senza mappa*, the difficulty of mapping the contemporary urban environment also plays an important role in representations of the city in for instance postwar American literature. "Also when they paint hybrid geographical palimpsests, cosmopolitan zones, and deserted cities," Daniele notes, "the stories of William S. Burroughs, Thomas Pynchon, Donald Barthelme, and later the performances of Laurie Anderson — who translates into a multimedia language the entropic climate evoked by those authors —

seem to offer a reflection of the transformations, the language, and even the furniture of an urban landscape which is still visible but which, in its enormous expansion, resists cartographic representation" [1994:6; editors' translation].

Assimilated into the continuum of global networks, cities have become in some sense invisible entities. In a classic of 1970s postmodernist fiction, *Invisible Cities*, Italian novelist Italo Calvino has ingeniously portrayed a series of fantastic cities that consist merely of scraps, memories, or representations. Thus, in the city of Eudoxia we come across a tapestry that contains a complete map of the city — or is the city merely a reflection of the tapestry? In Eusapia, the people have built catacombs replicating the city — or was it the other way round and did the dead erect the city above ground? When cities can no longer be mapped and become somehow invisible, they all start to resemble each other. Urban space loses its markers of identity and is increasingly determined by what Marc Augé has called *non-lieux* or non-places [1995]. These are places with which nobody feels a special tie and that do not function in a traditional way as meeting-places. To Augé, the world consists increasingly of these kinds of non-places, which are especially to be found in the realms of mobility and consumption (airports, hotels, shopping malls, stopping places along the highway, etc.). Such non-places consist principally of networks and junctions in a world without frontiers: they lack the peculiar features of places and sites (like centers and monuments) because they cater only to average demands. From this point of view, not only airports, freeways, parking lots, or communication networks can be called non-places, but the whole of urban space to the extent that it is leveled to meet average demands. More and more, cities generate the same kinds of experiences. In every city, the same shops and cafés pop up, rendering places ever more anonymous and exchangeable. The new urban space, in its ideal-typical format, no longer possesses a clear-cut identity, a particularity, an individuality, but has become, in the words of one of Rem Koolhaas's most famous essays, "generic" [1994].

*Developed by Bart Eeckhout and Steven Jacobs*

# Chapter Two: Community

The ongoing spatial fragmentation of the urban landscape described in the previous chapter goes hand in hand with a number of momentous social shifts. No monocausal determinism, however, will do to establish the connection between spatial and social phenomena. Both levels interact in complex ways: at times, new social patterns can be seen to underlie morphological alterations in the urban landscape; at other moments, new types of spatial organization appear to stimulate certain social evolutions. This unsteady relationship is natural insofar as evolutions in the human environment are always the outcome of a dialectic between freedom and determinism: while people freely and autonomously seek to give shape to their surroundings, they are themselves also to a certain extent limited and determined by these surroundings. And while many social evolutions may thus be aligned with changes in the physical layout of a society, some can also be at odds with these changes.

An analysis of the contemporary social fabric of cities is not only made difficult by the confusing spatial fragmentation that characterizes the end-of-the-century urban landscape, but also by processes of social fragmentation. Central to these is the overall tendency in Western societies towards what in sociology is widely called "individualization" — a tendency that defines at once the modern era and the very concept of modernity. Although this individualization process appears to have produced the most radical effects in the latter half of the 20th century, it goes back a long way to at least the 18th century. Nor is it by any means new as an analytical category in urban studies. Already in the first classics of urban sociology, the city was described as that kind of social environment that offered to the individual — or to the self, as it will be called in chapter 3 — the best opportunities for freely and autonomously composing his or her own life. This liberating aspect of city life has left its indelible mark on the ways in which urbanites have come to deal with their social needs. Since the modern industrial city is largely founded on the principle of rationalized interaction, communities (loosely defined as socially supportive networks) are increasingly composed *ad libidum*, based on particular interests and practices. Already in 1937, one of the founding fathers of urban studies, Lewis Mumford, answered the question "What Is a City?" by arguing: "The city is a related collection of primary groups and purposive associations: the first, like family and neighborhood, are common to all communities, while the second are especially characteristic of city life" [1937:184]. One year later, in an even more influential essay called "Urbanism as a Way of Life," Louis Wirth contended in analogical fashion:

*By virtue of his different interests arising out of different aspects of social life, the individual acquires membership in widely divergent groups, each of which functions only with reference to a certain segment of his personality. Nor do these groups easily permit of a concentric arrangement so that the narrower ones fall within the circumference of the more inclusive ones, as is more likely to be the case in the rural community or in primitive societies. Rather the groups with which the person typically is affiliated are tangential to each other or intersect in highly variable fashion* [1938:156].

By the early 1960s, the analyses of Mumford and Wirth could already be expanded to apply to the entire urban-suburban nexus of "nonplace urban realms," which were described by Melvin Webber as "ambiguous, shifting instantaneously as participants in the realm's many interest-communities make new contacts, trade with different customers, socialize with different friends, or read different publications" [quoted in Sharpe and Wallock 1987:29].

Just as the contemporary city in its spatial components has come to resist representation in traditional cartographic terms, social networks in Fishman's *city à la carte* have come to evince a greater complexity than before and to appear more and more resistant to synthetic analysis. What is more, the urbanization of Western society in general has robbed the city as a social entity of much of its meaning, so that a discussion of urbanized social life overall is bound to be more loosely connected to its spatial-material referent. The splintering of larger social patterns at the heart of the following analysis is a wide-ranging phenomenon that cannot always be geographically circumscribed and contained. The best terms for conceptualizing this splintering are probably those of individualization and fragmentation — two terms that will return frequently in the course of the following pages. In talking about individualization, however, we should realize how, as the German sociologist Ulrich Beck has suggested [1992:87-90], the process may refer to at least two different phenomena: the phenomenon of an increased autonomization and mobilization of individuals and that of an emerging and continuously widening range of subcultures and lifestyles. Especially the latter phenomenon poses conceptual challenges. Yet the overall trend in Western societies is clear: today's urbanized citizens identify less and less with the disciplinary and hierarchical collectivizing institutions of the past (religious institutions, moral authorities, political parties, socioeconomic class, neighborhoods...) and more and more with so-called peer groups (frequently conceptualized through the notions of subculture and lifestyle).

In what follows, we start by offering a general picture of the influence of individualization processes on the social behavior of urbanites (and more widely, of urbanized/modernized citizens overall). Our main focus is on the vexed question of community building, more specifically on the tension between emancipatory, diversifying trends toward a multicultural urban society and more antagonistic, polarizing tendencies toward social segregation. This general discussion is fleshed out more concretely in a second section, which is devoted to the changing status and place of some of the major groups that make up today's metropolitan social landscape. With respect to the question of postsuburbia and its social diversification, for instance, we will see how totally opposed ideological positions have been taken. While apologists are inclined to celebrate postsuburbia as the realization of a democratic, egalitarian, and emancipatory ideal, others have rejected much of its deurbanized space for being socially reactionary and based on doubtful selective practices. The positive view that would picture an increase of pluralism and social diversification in the contemporary metropolis is frequently offset by the negative view that would see a marked increase in forms of social segregation and separatism. This debate between social gains and losses returns in a third and final section, which focuses on the conditions of interaction for members of the urban population and centers on the much-contested transformations undergone by urban public space.

# 1 Individualization and Community Building

**The Autonomization and Mobilization of the Individual** Throughout the history of the Western world, cities and their cultures have carried two diametrically opposed connotations. While they have often been denounced as cesspools of moral turpitude and vice (with famous Biblical antecedents ranging from Sodom and Gomorrah to Babylon the Whore or sinful Nineveh), they have also frequently been hailed as the necessary condition for a democratic and emancipatory social project. "Ever since Pericles of Athens declared his city 'thrown open to the world,'" notes John Parker, "cities have fostered democratic, open societies and opposed feudal and dictatorial ones" [1995:13]. This democratic and emancipatory aspect of urban culture was catchily compressed in the popular medieval dictum *Stadtluft macht frei* ("city air liberates"). At several crucial moments in the history of the West, cities have prided themselves on offering a physically protected social space in which individuals were able to enjoy the necessary freedom to escape from feudal and other oppressions. Yet this liberation of the individual has also entailed a rise in individual responsibility. If the city is the biotope of the free, autonomous individual, it is also that of the sociopolitically participating citizen. The city depends for its success on the construction of some form of *communitas*.

Although the influence of cities on the development of communal and social life in Western societies is not quite as direct and unproblematical as it is sometimes held to be, the development of cities is at least historically closely connected with the development of that communal and social life, and the city has certainly functioned as one major catalyst in the process of Western community building. To understand the present effects of that process, we must go back at least to the emancipation of the bourgeoisie starting in the 18th century and to the egalitarian and democratic inheritances of the Enlightenment and the French and American Revolutions. Although bourgeois emancipation was not necessarily or simply urban, the bourgeoisie — based as it was on trading and commerce — did have its principal historical roots and power base in the city. According to Richard Sennett in *The Fall of Public Man* [1976], 18th-century bourgeois life, however, was still quite different from today's: it was strictly divided between a public and a private life, which kept each other in a careful balance. The former was highly theatricalized and "civilized," while the latter was taken to be "natural" (in the sense of corresponding to the nature of the human species). In the course of the 19th century and with the rise of industrial capitalism, the scales of this balance were tilted: more and more the public domain began to cede to a new private domain of intimacy, personality, and authenticity. This interiorization resulted in what Sennett pictures as a social atomization and what in recent sociology is especially known as individualization. Its driving force, in the more moralist language of everyday, is individualism. The word "individualism," significantly, was introduced into English by the French political philosopher Alexis de Toqueville precisely in the context of analyzing the American city as an exponent of a type of society that in the 19th century most embodied the political model of a bourgeois democracy [Rybczynski 1995: 109 and ch. 4 & 5 overall]. At least historically, then, individualism — or the growing dominance of the private over the public persona — can be shown to have been most prominent and conspicuous in the city, so that the overall spreading of originally *bourgeois* values and attitudes in the 20th century has come to be construed by many as the spreading of quintessentially *urban* values and attitudes, or of what is sometimes called "urbanism." In *City Life*, Witold Rybczynski demonstrates the pioneering role which the U.S. historically played in fostering this general spreading of bourgeois values over the entire population. As a result of the country's egalitarian ideal, he argues, the U.S. as a nation was not built on the Old-World dictum "city air liberates," but on the less geographically circumscribed, more homogenizing "American air liberates" [ibid.: 113-14]. Thus, the tie between political values and specific places in America has always been less strong than in Europe and the process of urbanization in the U.S. has happened less through the building of cities than through the spreading of an urbanized bourgeois culture [ibid.: ch. 5].

The leading historical role played by the U.S. in the overall individualization of people in Western societies also serves to highlight the importance of geographical and social mobility in the process. Transnational and intranational migration in the last 300 years has principally occurred in the direction of metropolitan areas, whether we are talking about New York around the turn of the century with its millions of immigrants channeled through Ellis Island or of London and Paris acting as magnets for their national and postcolonial hinterlands. It is above all migration also — more than general demographical evolutions — that led to the late-19th and early-20th-century phenomenon of the exponentially growing megacity or "metropolis." Such migration was and is the result of a complex interplay of push and pull factors, in which the positive or oneiric dimensions that motivate the desire of migrants for a better life are easily overlooked in light of the crisis character of escape motives (from political persecution and pogroms to starvation and economic exploitation) as well as of the sociopolitical problems of reception and accommodation.

Since cities have tended to support or facilitate the autonomous development of individuals, they have also become the preeminent places in which traditional social patterns are being replaced by new ones. The independence gained by individuals has found its clearest expression in the cutting of existing social ties and the establishment of alternative ones — a phenomenon that is widely summarized by the concept of social mobility. The evolution towards greater individualization and enhanced social mobility, however, is a slow and very gradual one, and concepts of this sort are highly relative. The history of ethnic immigrants is a clear case in point. During the first stage of moving into a new city, immigrants of the same ethnic (and socioeconomic) background will frequently stick together in certain neighborhoods, appropriating their own collective spaces and setting up networks of material and spiritual support. In many cases, however, these relatively homogeneous neighborhoods are only transitional phenomena that do not survive beyond one or two generations. As immigrants accommodate to their new cultural environment, they will seek to move up the social ladder and out of their poor housing. Especially in the U.S., where social mobility is strongly predicated upon geographical mobility, neighborhoods have been known to change ethnic composition from one generation to the next.[10] One telling example is that of Manhattan's Lower East Side in New York (historically the port of entrance for many immigrants to the U.S.). In *Gateway to the Promised Land: Ethnic cultures on New York's Lower East Side* [1994], Mario Maffi has surveyed the immigration history of this neighborhood from the late 19th century through the early 1990s. It is a story that starts with the settlement of especially Irish and German immigrants. It takes a first turn with the massive arrival of Eastern European Jews (on the run for pogroms in their shtetls) and of large quantities of Chinese and Italian immigrants (the birth of, respectively, Chinatown and Little Italy). The story changes again shortly after World War II, when a major influx of Puerto Ricans adds a new face to the area, that of Loisaida, and again by the late 1960s, when the area began to attract not only a whole variation of Asian peoples (Filipinos, Koreans, and Vietnamese) — thereby turning Chinatown into an increasingly Asian-American quarter — but also a variety of Middle and South Americans (Haitians, Dominicans, Salvadorans, Ecuadorans) — which in turn changed the face of Loisaida into a more mixed Latino or Hispanic area.

The example of New York's Lower East Side illustrates how the kind of group solidarity that is often a cultural-social condition and practical necessity for first-generation immigrants arriving in a big city frequently melts away in the course of one or two generations to make room for the kind of individual ambition that, for better or worse, is still mythically embodied by the American Dream. This Dream is built on the hope of financial improvement and upward social mobility — the rise from rags to riches. It is spatially expressed through the

10 That this nexus of social and geographical mobility is often considerably less strong in Western Europe is illustrated for London by Hebbert 1998: 164.

phenomenon of geographical mobility. Thus, a second, intranational kind of migration ensues, only this time it no longer occurs collectively. The tightly knit groups of first-generation immigrants give way to individualized descendants disbanding and dispersing again over a wider territory in their individual pursuits of happiness. Again it is especially Americans, as de Toqueville already noted, who have taken up the habit of voting with their feet [Rybczynski 1995:31]. By and large, they have shown themselves much more attached to their families and political institutions than to their cities.

Frequently, the only remaining mainstay in this individualization and mobilization process is the nuclear family. As Ulrich Beck has pointed out [1992], the social importance of nuclear families has grown in the course of the twentieth century in response to a waning of the disciplinary authority of external persons and institutions (political, religious, educational, or professional). Especially in suburbia, but to a considerable extent also in core cities, social life for urbanites has become principally centered on an interaction between family units. At the same time, these units have undergone something of a sea change and been typologically diversified: this is especially true of metropolitan centers, where the heterosexual married couple with kids no longer serves as a dominant template. The internal functioning of families has changed as well in response to a growing contestation of patriarchal, autocratic, and gender-stereotypical behavior, a decrease in average number of children per household, and a growing sexual independence of family members (especially women). The emphasis in the functioning of urban/suburban households has come to lie more on a mix of affection and upbringing. These and other processes have made family life more fickle: the more individualized and independent family members become, the more pressure is also put on their mutual relationships. The nuclear family has often turned into a battleground for conflicts between the individual aspirations and desires of family members. Familial ties have become more tenuous and families more subject to realignment (the rise of "serial" marriages and relationships). Several factors have also prompted or facilitated the reconfigurability of family units: the drastically increased life expectancy as the result of medical advances and improved hygienic conditions; the growing economic and financial independence of individuals (in particular through the huge postwar influx of women in the labor market); and the continuing division of labor upon which the modern city as an environment of rationalized transaction depends. Many of the functions traditionally performed by the family (protection, physical care, relaxation) have been farmed out to specialized institutions like daycare centers, schools, or social and cultural organizations that cater to the individual's interests.

**Individualization through Identity Politics** Individualization processes are by definition relative, not absolute. They indicate a tendency that can only be understood if it is set within a social and historical framework. They do not, in other words, preclude the formation of social groups. The human animal is a social animal and to picture the contemporary metropolis as a collection of absolutely individualized monads would be an egregious simplification. Even in the most metropolitan environment, all sorts of social groups continue to be formed or to exert their influence. What may be said, however, is that the number of these groups appears to have multiplied as a function of the overall emancipation and diversification of the metropolitan population. Especially youths, women, and sexual minorities have played a major role in boosting this diversification. What is more, many of today's social groups have become more mobile and flexible in adapting to changing environmental conditions or consumerist fashions. The resulting sociological pattern is one of increasing fragmentation — a fragmentation that in turn either reflects or actively affects the material permutations of today's urbanized environment.

Since any tendency towards social fragmentation must have strong political repercussions, it has been — and continues to be — the cause of hot political and intellectual debates. Depending on local political climates and historical circumstances, the social actors involved will opt for working out new models of multicultural collaboration or be up in arms against each other. This may best be illustrated with the rise of identity politics, again a larger societal phenomenon that is played out most conspicuously on the metropolitan stage, since that stage affords the most direct and daily confrontation between various segments of a country's population. When the American writer Henry James, after years of living in Europe, visited his home again in 1904, the overwhelming plenitude and intellectual uncontainability of New York threw him off balance [see Buelens 1999]. At the same time, they produced an insight that takes up a climactic place in his famous report, *The American Scene*: "No kind of person — that was the admonition — is a very good kind, and still less a very pleasing kind, when its education has not been made to some extent by contact with *other* kinds, by a sense of the existence of *other* kinds, and, to that degree, by a certain relation with them" [1907: 705; emphases added]. The category of the "other" and the question of our relation to it gain automatic prominence in a society that is built on the opposition between public and private persona, and bustling multicultural metropolises will be the sites where people are most immediately faced with the ethical and intellectual consequences of that opposition.

The development of a politics of cultural identity, more particularly as it is played out in a postwar metropolitan environment, has both an emancipatory and reactionary potential. The emancipatory potential comes to the fore in the relative autonomization, visibility, and empowerment of formerly disenfranchized groups. If it is not always easy to assess whether and how the composition of metropolitan populations has become more diverse in the postwar era, the sociopolitical sensitivity to this diversity has undoubtedly grown and become much more of a topic. Thus, the *Harvard Encyclopedia of American Ethnic Groups*, published in 1980, already distinguished between 106 different ethnic entities. This enhanced sensitivity to social difference has affected the discipline of urban studies as well. One arbitrary example among many is that of Sidney Bremer's literary-historical study, *Urban Intersections*, in which the political bias of earlier traditions is explicitly deplored:

*When minority status — whether of region or gender or race — makes group identity a dominant feature of one's experience, it does so whether one lives on a farm, in a small town, or in a big city; one is still southern, woman, black. This suggests that the rural/ urban dichotomy in our generalizations about cities since the standard Chicago novel and the sociological "urbanism" of Louis Wirth ... has been mostly the privilege of northern white, middle-class males. Like our other cultural generalizations, it must be contextualized by region, ethnicity, class, and gender* [1992: 191-92].

Bremer's perspective is clearly marked by a post-sixties academic evolution in the humanities and social sciences that has given rise to such disciplines as women's studies, cultural studies, African-American studies, queer studies, neomarxism, postcolonialism, or various strands of poststructuralist theory. Although working from highly different angles, these disciplines have collectively foregrounded theories and practices of "difference" — either in response to changing cultural environments or as active proponents of emancipatory projects. Ideologically, they have shored up a "postmodern" kind of liberalism (often walking under the banner of "multiculturalism") that differs from a more traditional liberalism or humanism in that it sets less store by universalist ideas and values and puts greater emphasis on an antihomogenizing, nonassimilationist discourse. Heterogeneity, difference, and hybridity are recurrent values among the leading theorists and spokesmen in these fields: the concept of hybridity, for instance, is to be found with many cultural authorities on the subject of ethnicity and postcolonialism, whether academics like Henry Louis Gates, Jr., Paul Gilroy, Edward Said, and Homi Bhabha, or writers and essayists like Salman Rushdie and Anil Ramdas (an important postcolonial voice in the Netherlands). In many of these cases, moreover, the metropolitan inspiration and connection, both theoretically and biographically, is unmistakable.

Neither the theory nor the practice of identity politics, however, are of necessity progressive and emancipatory. For one thing, the sophisticated theory (often insisting on some form of social constructionism) regularly clashes with the militant activism of grassroots organizations. As Steven Epstein laconically puts it, "People who base their claims to social rights on the basis of a group identity will not appreciate being told that that identity is just a social construct" [quoted in Garber 1995:86]. What is more, the insistence on group-based difference does not only liberate: it may also wind up recuperating or reencapsulating the individual. In being defined, group identities are frequently also polarized. And as David Theo Goldberg notes, "There is a long history of racialized or gendered exclusion in the name of difference. Those deemed different are not part of the social formation, are not included under values of moral treatment, respect, and love" [1994:12]. At an urban scale, this polarization is translated into a tension between the city as an intercultural meeting-place and the city as a culture-ideological battleground. "In place of the dissolution of borderlines," writes Marjorie Garber, "today's cultural politicians offer the strictures of Identity Politics. Borderlines are back: Ethnic, racial, religious, and sexual minorities assert their visibility and, thus, their power" [Garber 1995:20]. Or as David Hollinger in *Post-ethnic America* has argued [1995], ethnic consciousness and identity politics can be of a piece with more reactionary right-wing phenomena such as patriotism and an emphasis on family values in that they all erect social boundaries and seem to depend on a confrontational logic. Too much ideological self-enclosure may lead to physical separatism and segregation.

The recent political history of Western European cities further demonstrates the flipside of identity politics, for in these cities the political insistence on cultural identities comes from a radically different angle: it inspires the thinking of especially extreme-right and neofascist parties. European cities have a past that is less multicultural and less supportive of social mobility than that of North American cities. The most important recent influxes of foreign-born immigrants were attributable to non-European "guest laborers" (attracted to fill in a shortage of blue-collar workers in the economic boom years of especially the fifties and sixties) and to inhabitants from former colonies. Both types of immigrants by and large did not find the same opportunities for moving up the socioeconomic ladder as immigrants to the U.S. generally do, and in a time of economic crisis and labor shortage they became easily delineated and targeted again as scapegoats. The animosity towards these groups is voiced and fed at a transurban political level (that of the nation-state), but it is again enacted most critically on the stage of cities, where the political success of extreme-right and neofascist parties has been greatest (see the Allianza Nazionale in Rome, the Front National in Marseille, or the Vlaams Blok in Antwerp).

One important reason why the question of identity politics has become so deeply entrenched in postwar Western societies is that it is frequently moored in the fragmented morphology of the contemporary urban landscape. To an increased mobilization of the liberated and autonomized individual corresponds a fracturing of urban space into sometimes highly homogeneous neighborhoods. This leads to a remarkable paradox: whereas posturban space appears to resist all attempts at mapping (in cartographical and functional terms), it goes hand in hand with a social polarization that is at times all too easily mapped (in residential terms). This is especially true of the U.S. (in particular suburbia), but increasingly also of Europe. In some cases, then, spatial fragmentation turns out to be a natural corollary of social fragmentation.

# 2 The Contemporary Social Landscape

**Postsuburban Heterogeneity and Fragmentation** The formation of group identities and the dynamics between a diversification and a polarization of metropolitan communities have obtained new meaning in light of the morphological-functional transformations of the postwar urban landscape. In the traditional (idealized) paradigm of the modern metropolis, urban space is inhabited by autonomous and emancipated individuals relating to each other through a constant series of free interactions. The preeminent embodiment of metropolitanism proposed by Rem Koolhaas in *Delirious New York* is the bachelor who stays at a residential hotel [1978: 158]. In the modern metropolis, individuals are made to fall back on themselves, roaming like monads through the anonymous crowds. This image of the urban loner has often been enlisted by artists and writers to figure a condition of metropolitan alienation.[11] In the cultural imagination, moreover, it was frequently opposed to the domestic security and familial unity characteristic of suburbia. Robert Fishman extensively demonstrated how the historical rise of suburbia was intimately linked to the ideological constitution of the modern family unit.[12] While the metropolis was felt to be the habitat of the lonely individual and even prided itself on being hospitable towards nonconformist ways of life, the suburb presented itself as the natural biotope of what historian Lawrence Stone analyzed as the "closed domesticated nuclear family" [quoted in Fishman 1987: 33-34].

Recent tendencies towards deurbanization have inevitably affected also this distinction. With the development of posturban space, phenomena like the diversification of family types and the autonomization of individual family members have spread beyond traditional core cities [Poster 1991]. Compared to the suburb of the immediate postwar years, today's postsuburbia displays not only greater demographical variety but also greater cultural and ethnical diversity. By 1967 already, in a pathbreaking study of Pennsylvania's Levittown, Herbert Gans could be seen to modify the classic distinction between bustling metropolis and soporific bedroom community. Gans argued that suburbia was not necessarily less lively than the central city, only that social life was organized differently there: instead of revolving around the more active streetlife that comes with high-density housing, it was concentrated especially around familial activities and private institutions like clubs and associations. Moreover, partly for want of high-class

11 For an analysis of how the image of the urban loner has affected the fate of public art in the 20th-century city, see the case study by Sven Lütticken (Part II).

12 This connection between suburbia and the construction of a culture of domestic intimacy is further explored in the case study by René Boomkens (Part II).

cultural institutions like museums and opera houses, suburban cultural life displayed a more provincial than cosmopolitan character. Even so, it proved increasingly impossible, according to Gans, to hold up a strict division between city and suburb in an age that witnessed the rapid success of mass media and the concomitant spreading of a commercial culture over urban and suburban zones alike.

The evolution pointed up by Gans in the 1960s has only gained momentum in the ensuing decades, when we have seen the increasing success of various communication technologies. This technological success, as we have seen, came on top of a gradual transformation of suburbia from an exclusively residential zone to a zone that also accommodated industrial, commercial, and recreative activities. Although recent studies emphasize that postsuburbia continues to evince less visual variety than core cities and that its cultural activities are tailored first and foremost to the twin realms of domesticity and material consumption, today's postsuburbia nevertheless displays far greater diversity than its classic suburban predecessor. Postsuburban regions, according to Kling, Olin, and Poster, "are not sleepy provincial regions, although they have their quiet suburban neighborhoods. Their most important aspects ... are their origins in the suburban periphery of another urban core ... from which they have broken away, and the emergence within them of a new decentralized environment possessing the economic and cultural diversity formerly associated with the traditional central city. Through decentralization, the parochial and primarily residential suburb becomes a vital metropolitan region" [1991: 8-9].

In postsuburban areas like Orange County, the east of Long Island, or the northeastern corridor outside Atlanta, inhabitants are no longer dependent on the nearby city for work, consumption, or cultural satisfaction. More importantly, they have become ethnically and racially more diverse — in the case of Orange County, for instance, as the result of a series of massive immigration waves from Latin America and Asia. Consumption patterns have likewise also become more cosmopolitan than in the traditional WASP middle-class suburb. Such consumptive cosmopolitanism, to be sure, does not of itself guarantee the active construction of multicultural communities and does not necessarily extend beyond the acquisition of new and exotic (frequently expensive) foreign products. Yet the phenomenon points to the fact that postsuburbia has come to assume some of the diversity of the traditional metropolis as well. Socioeconomically lower classes, too, for instance, are leaving their marks on the deconcentrated urban space. Almost as in any average metropolis, ethnic groups have set up their own restaurants and shops. Local business life, in addition, which is strongly interwoven with a globalizing economy, has contributed to the formation of a more cosmopolitan cultural elite:

*Many of these highly educated employees ... developed cosmopolitan tastes in other urban areas before emigrating to Orange County. They created a ready clientele for ethnic restaurants, European and Japanese cars, a wide variety of imported goods, and cultural events such as modern theater, foreign films, and classical music. Not satisfied with mainstream goods and services that were available in their neighborhood shopping centers, these residents were willing to patronize establishments virtually anywhere in the county that catered to their tastes. They were able to support a sufficient number of business and arts organizations with world-class aspirations so that, by the 1980s, a cosmopolitan culture was well developed in the county* [Kling et al. 1991: 21].

Although real-estate agents still seek to attract potential settlers by conjuring up the utopian middle-class image of the traditional suburb, the character of Orange County is much more determined by such postsuburban social complexity than by the monotony of white-bred suburban tracts. Kling, Olin, and Poster list the examples of Hispanic and Asian concentrations, of boulevards with almost exclusively Korean and Vietnamese store signs, of the large artistic and gay communities that people Laguna Beach, only to conclude that "Orange County's vast size allows a degree of anonymity and freedom of life-style that would be much more difficult to achieve in tightly knit suburban villages" [ibid.:22]. Postsuburbia, in other words, possesses a polychromic and polyphonic quality that is more reminiscent of the modern metropolis than of 1950s suburbia. Unsurprisingly, therefore, it has been presented sometimes as the decongested continuation of an essentially urban ideology, in which the emancipation and liberty of individuals take pride of place.

Needless to say, such a positive, apologetic perspective is not shared by all scholars. William Sharpe and Leonard Wallock, for example, though willing to grant that the morphological-functional alterations suburbia has undergone in recent decades are indeed striking, have disputed the easy link with radical sociocultural changes. In their opinion, sociocultural evolutions have not really followed suit and no real metropolitanization of suburbia has taken place. "In our view," they write, "equating suburbs with cities implies that suburbs possess a diversity, cosmopolitanism, political culture, and public life that most of them still lack and that most cities still afford" [1994:3]. By focusing on questions of morphology and aesthetics, as Garreau and Fishman tend to do, "suburbanophiles" have ignored the fact that "parochialism and separatism" continue to be very strong in (post)suburbia. The diversification of Orange County, from Sharpe and Wallock's critical perspective, has given rise above all to a "culture of consumption" that, in Paul Goldberger's words, bolsters "a community as product more than a community as place" [ibid.: 11].

The supposed diversity of the contemporary postsuburban landscape is also questioned by Peter Marcuse [1995] with respect to urban planning practices. Marcuse observes a kind of inversion of the theory of modernist urban planning: whereas modernists were typically out to impose order on what they perceived to be chaos, the present-day tendency seems to be, rather, to impose chaos on order so as to obfuscate and elide the hierarchical socioeconomic relationships between people as well as the ordering principles of urban space. In hailing chaos, urban planners cover up the power imbalance with a veil of calculated arbitrariness. Diversity and heterogeneity, in this context, do not serve a progressive and liberal purpose, but are ideologically enlisted to function as instruments of a fundamentally conservative or reactionary strategy.

Terms like homogeneity and heterogeneity may themselves be part of the problem here. They tend to lose significance whenever people fail to clarify what exactly it is that postsuburban environments are being measured against. Little discussion is possible about the fact that postsuburbia evinces greater functional and social heterogeneity than the classic suburb, which served an almost exclusive residential function for a more restricted segment of the population. The fact that this diversification is indisputable, however, does not imply that postsuburbia has also assumed the active social heterogeneity invited by the compact multicultural mix of the dense metropolis. The social mix in metropolitan downtowns typically involves fine-grained patterns, while the variety of postsuburbia is much more spread out and serially linked. Thus, while heterogeneity seemed like a perfect concept for summarizing the clearly visible variety of the modern metropolis, the notion of "fragmentation" — not only spatially but also at a social level — would appear to be more apt for characterizing evolutions in the new postsuburban environment.

**The Multicultural and Subcultural Metropolis** The postsuburban evolution toward social fragmentation cannot be seen independently of a longer history, which is that of the spatial separation of social groups in the city. Already the etymologies of words like "town" (originally meaning "fence" or "enclosure"), "borough," "burgher" (the German *Bürger*, Dutch *burger*), or the French *faubourg* (all these words deriving from references to castles and fortresses) recall the walling of medieval cities, which created an important social and political opposition between inside and outside [Rybczynski 1995: 37-38]. Throughout Western history, moreover, cities have also been to some extent *internally* divided. Certain streets or zones have always been reserved for particular socioeconomic, cultural, professional, religious, or ethnic segments of the urban population — if not always reserved *de iure* then at least *de facto* [see, for instance, Fourcaut 1996 for French cities between the 18th and 20th centuries]. The entire history of a city like London has even been told as a story of basic fragmentation in which the various parts combined to form a whole more by chance than by design [Hebbert 1998]. Similarly, *The Encyclopedia of New York City* today contains articles about 416 different neighborhoods within one and the same city [Jackson 1995]. In this sense, New York may well stand as the epitome of the modern metropolis with its densely organized discontinuous pattern of distinctly recognizable neighborhoods. Whether we are talking about Greenwich Village, Soho, the East Village, the Lower East Side, the Upper East Side, the Upper West Side, Harlem, Spanish Harlem, Morningside Heights, Washington Heights, the South Bronx, Crown Heights, East Flatbush, Bensonhurst, or Flushing Meadows, the names all immediately bring to mind specific social constellations to anyone familiar with the city. This applies not only to the modern but also to the postmodern metropolis, where the phenomenon is only diluted and further stretched out over larger areas: in *Heteropolis*, Charles Jencks has drawn up a social cartography of L.A. that mixes "identity areas" (like the Barrio, Watts, Koreatown, Little Tokyo, Little Philippines, the Gay District, University Town, and Beverly Hills) with sometimes dubiously labeled "lifestyle consumption groups" (Affluentials, Metro Sophisticates, Greenbelt Families, Singles and Couples, Mid-City Mix, the Outer Fringe, Urban Melting Pot) [1993: 26-29]. The shopworn image for this social-spatial pattern is that of the mosaic. Other images recur, too, and although they have all been righly questioned, they signal an important underlying ideological battle: from the "melting pot" and its culinary counterparts, the "salad bowl" or the "buffet table," to the "garden of plants," metaphors bespeak specific views of the cohabitation of diverse peoples on a relatively compact surface area.

Political discussions about the need for an up-to-date multicultural model for Western cities are of course part of a larger political context that involves all of Western societies. At the level of nation-states, for instance, Canada has been the first to translate the multicultural diversity of its population into law. The *Canadian Multiculturalism Act* made law in 1988 states that "The Government of Canada recognizes the diversity of Canadians as regards race, national or ethnic origin, colour and religion as a fundamental characteristic of Canadian society and is committed to a policy of multiculturalism designed to preserve and enhance the multicultural heritage of Canadians while working to achieve the equality of all Canadians in the economic, social, cultural and political life of Canada" [quoted in Peters 1996: 404]. This law illustrates the long way sociopolitical discourse has come in recent decades. In a discussion of the term multiculturalism, David Theo Goldberg has analyzed the historical roots of the "imperatives of monocultural association," tracing them back to 19th-century European universities, which — combined with the then-current preference for universalistic discourses — were copied as a general sociopolitical model in the U.S. [1994: 3-4]. At the beginning of the 20th century, Goldberg argues, powerful attempts to construct a national American identity were steered by a racial immigration politics and the propagation of an ideology of the "melting pot." This metaphor frequently covered up radical power imbalances and separatist realities, especially in cities: as Sharon Zukin points out, the fiction of a shared, homogeneous culture could be kept up more easily in the early-20th-century metropolis mainly because ethnic, class, and sexual cultures inhabited separate spaces that remained largely invisible to one another [1995: 264-65]. These separatist tendencies have not waned in the course of the century, but their relative invisibility and political incontestability clearly has. Today, the various groups that make up the population of any metropolis on either side of the Atlantic tend to be much more in each other's faces in the sense that they demand their rights and confront each other directly, both in the media and in the political arena. Urbanites are thus more forced to take up ideological positions towards their multicultural surroundings. In analogy with the tension between a modern and postmodern liberalism, Goldberg today sees a tension between "liberal multiculturalism," which is based on a tolerance of cultural differences, and "managed and difference multiculturalisms," which instead seek to emphasize boundaries between groups and to celebrate differences [1994]. Goldberg's own middle-of-the-road attitude typically involves a plea for hybridity and heterogeneity as central values in this debate.

Multiculturalism literally refers to a plurality of cultures. The concept of "culture," however, is one of those contested concertina concepts whose definition may be narrowed or expanded at will, even if we restrict ourselves here to the sociological and anthropological use of the word. The advantage of opting for a wider definition in this context is that it helps us identify a number of crucial social changes in the postwar metropolis. One way in which the transformation and diversification of our understanding of cultural groups may be gauged is by the importance sociologists like Pierre Bourdieu have come to attach to a concept like "cultural capital" [1979]. Offering the best social environment for nonconformist, antiestablishmentarian, and independent individuals, big cities function as magnets to people who depend on cultural rather than financial capital: intellectuals and academics (from the *Rive gauche* in Paris to New York's Morningside Heights) as well as artists, performers, and entertainers. Especially the latter groups frequently crave the city as a soil for their creativity and socialization. In *Loft Living* [1982], Sharon Zukin provides an extended example of the influence that artists have exerted on the landscape of Manhattan: in conjunction with middle-class owners and political and social elites, artists during the 1970s and 80s put up a successful fight to claim New York's Soho for themselves, although for this they had to counter the plans of realtors, trade unions, and powerful bankers like the Rockefellers, who all wanted to build sports stadiums and skyscrapers in the area.[13]

The importance of cultural classes in analyzing the contemporary social landscape of cities is further confirmed by the striking rise of an entirely new phenomenon in the postwar city: that of the youth subculture. The autonomization of youths, spearheaded again in urban environments, must be seen against a background that is both economic (the increasing prosperity and rise of a consumerist culture since the 1950s) and social (the substitution of peer-group identification for traditional identifications with authority-based institutions). After the economic and military crises of the 1930s and of W.W. II, when any autonomization for youths was naturally out of the question, urban teenagers and twens in the more peaceful and prosperous postwar years soon developed habits of rebelling and setting up countercultures: first the mods and beatniks, then the hippies and flower-power adepts, next the punks devised lifestyles and communities of their own, until by the 1980s and 90s such movements branched out into countless different subcultural trends, some still oppositional, others largely recuperated or even actively produced by the fashion industry. London with its famous clubbing circuit, Berlin with its annual Love Parade (a ravers' festival attracting hundreds of thousands of youngsters), or Seattle as the capital of grunge are but a few of the most obvious icons of today's urban youth subcultures. The concept of "subculture," as Sarah Thornton has explained, may be usefully distinguished from that of "community":

*"Community" tends to suggest a more permanent population, often aligned to a neighbourhood, of which the family is the key constituent part. Kinship would seem to be one of the main building blocks of community. By contrast, those groups identified as "subcultures" have tended to be studied apart from their families and in states of relative transience. It is also often assumed that there is something innately oppositional in the word "subculture." While struggles over territory, place and space are core issues, subcultures would appear to bring a little disorder to the security of the neighbourhood. Subcultures are more often characterized as appropriating parts of the city for their*

13 That the power base of artists in this coalition was not necessarily all-determining or long-standing is demonstrated by the fact that Soho in the 1990s returned to its original (early-19th-century) status as a fashionable shopping district. More particularly since the opening of the luxurious and touristic Soho Grand Hotel in 1996, artists have moved out of the neighborhood again by the hundreds, due to skyrocketing rents and property values.

14 As this same study shows, the growing need for health facilities in suburbs and the increasing number of elderly people no longer able to drive is posing new infrastructural and social problems for suburbia.

*street (rather than domestic) culture.... "Subcultures" (as they have been written about over the past three-quarters of a century) have come to designate social groups which are perceived to deviate from the normative ideals of adult communities* [1997: 2].

The attraction exerted by big cities on youths has had clear demographic effects: in most big cities, the population has become younger relative to a country's general population — a trend most visibly demonstrated by post-sixties downtown Amsterdam, where streetlife is almost entirely dominated by people in their teens, twenties, and thirties. Both in Europe and the U.S., this relative influx of youths has gone hand in hand with a departure of elderly people to suburbia. Michael Hebbert notes, for instance, how "Modern London consistently draws young people from all parts of the UK and loses them after the age of 45" [1998: 164]. And a comparative study between 1950 and 1990 shows a shift in residence for people aged 65 or more in the states of New York, New Jersey, and Connecticut from almost 80% urban vs. 17% suburban in 1950 to only 37% urban vs. 56% suburban in 1990 [Fein 1994: B5].[14]

The continuing appeal exerted by the central big city on various subcultures, artists, performers, entertainers, and intellectuals testifies to the need to keep distinguishing between the social constellations of classic metropolitan downtowns and postsuburban technoburbs. The drastic spatial transformation of urban landscapes in the second half of the 20th century has not always eroded the centripetal cultural status of the earlier metropolis. Most classic metropolitan centers have consolidated their position as the locus of cultural diversity and heterogeneity by continuing to attract marginal groups and cultural elites, providing places for them that remain largely visible to the overall population. This aspect of visibility constitutes an important difference with diluted urban spaces, to the extent that they, too, have undergone a social and cultural diversification. Because of its decongested nature, posturban space may turn into a catalyst for a polarization of the various communities that make up the multicultural spectrum of the contemporary metropolitan landscape.

**The Multiethnic and Dual Metropolis** Among the first five hundred settlers that inhabited embryonic New York (then still called New Amsterdam) in 1643, already 18 different languages were spoken [Jackson 1995: 581]. Today, the New York metropolitan region houses roughly 20 million people and the number of languages spoken in the area has only multiplied accordingly. New York City remains the most eye-catching and emblematic example of the multiethnic metropolis, partly because, as Philip Kasinitz writes [1996], the density of Manhattan forces people to be constantly "in each other's faces" and the cramped housing and high subway use prompt people to spend much time in public. In addition, the visibility of ethnic groups and of their social contribution is enhanced by a strongly developed tradition of streetparades and festivals. What is true of New York, however, has also become increasingly true of other postwar metropolises. "Almost half the entire ethnic minority population of Britain lives in London," Michael Hebbert informs us. "The 1991 Census found that 22% of the population had migrated from overseas: three births in every nine were to a mother born outside the United Kingdom. The capital has immigrant communities over 10 000 strong from 37 different countries" [1998: 164-65]. Today, at least a quarter of London's population is black or Asian [ibid.: 170]. Figures for Los Angeles show an even more radical picture: between 1970 and 2000 (based on projections), the share of non-Hispanic white Angelenos dropped from 71 to 31%, while the share of Afro-Americans remained stable at around 10% and the proportion of Hispanics and Asians rose from 15 to 44% and from 3 to 15% respectively [for these and related figures, see Ong and Blumenberg 1996: 324; also Sabagh and Bozorgmehr 1996]. The number of Mexican immigrants alone for L.A. has gone up from 320,000 in 1960 to 2.5 million thirty years later. Even in absolute numbers, the immigration figures for the L.A. area in the 1980s exceeded those for the New York City area, with 2 million vs. 1.5 million new immigrants respectively.

Distinctions between categories like "multicultural" and "multiethnic" are often merely a nominal matter, especially in the U.S., where the word "culture" is almost automatically equated with "ethnicity" [Zukin 1995: 263]. The term "ethnicity" itself, as Werner Sollors has demonstrated, stands in a complex relationship to other proximate notions with which it does not fully overlap, like peoplehood, class, race, and identity [1996]. Its precise content is often elusive, but the acts of group identification to which it refers are nonetheless powerful in their social and political effects. This is illustrated, among many other ways, by disparities arising within one and the same race, as when recent African immigrants to the U.S. appear to do better on the job market than inner-city African-Americans whose ancestry reaches back to the era of slavery [see Roger Waldinger's carefully weighed 1996 study *Still the Promised City?*]. In "Race, Ethnicity and New Forms of Urban Community" [1975], Joseph Bensman and Arthur Vidich argue that the new bases for community organization in the contemporary city are increasingly connected to racial and ethnic identities. The question of the formation of these identities is a hotly disputed one, with biological essentialists pitted against social constructionists, and discussions on the subject often prove to be political-ideological

15 Sam Bass Warner, Jr., has for instance argued that in the Philadelphia of the 1930s "intense segregation based on income, race, foreign birth, and class rose to preeminence as the organizing principle of the metropolis" [quoted in Sharpe and Wallock 1987: 10].

dynamite: the inclination to use *exclusive* definitions of ethnic identity and to reduce phenomena of great social complexity to a one-dimensional issue of ethnicity easily feeds into all kinds of extremist politics (from neofascist racism to reversed racism). According to Michael Smith and Joe Feagin in their introduction to *The Bubbling Cauldron: Race, Ethnicity and the Urban Crisis,* racial and ethnic formation today functions "as a dynamic arena of domination and resistance, division and self-definition in a 'cool' world where people have lost compassion for the distant other" [1995: 4].

Ethnic polarization has been enhanced by the postwar process of suburbanization, most clearly in the U.S., but also in many European cities and suburbs. As Robert Fishman's historical analysis indicated, the whole suburbanization process is predicated on a logic of social, ethnic, and sexual segregation. The suburbia to which postwar urbanites fled in droves was first and foremost the habitat of the white middle classes, and this fact materially consolidated the tendency towards socioeconomic and ethnic segregation already apparent in the modern metropolis.[15] In the 1950s American suburb in particular, Protestants, Catholics, and Jews of similar income groups were able to live in relative harmony, telling themselves that they were "finally to realize the dream of the melting pot, creating a homogeneous amalgam of persons with diverse roots" [Teaford 1993: 104]. But in this melting pot there appeared to be no place for the color black. "Suburbia was a white haven, perpetuating the racial fragmentation of the metropolis. It was a place where one could escape from the social, economic, and racial heterogeneity of the central city" [ibid.]. With the poorer ethnic minorities staying behind in the central city, this process led to the urban crises of the 1970s and early 80s. While well-to-do suburbanites withdrew into their comfortable leafy cocoons, central cities were left to fend for themselves. With heavily reduced tax bases, this was tantamount to courting bankruptcy. For a variety of reasons, many metropolitan centers have managed to scramble to their feet since, but the lack of financial solidarity between an increasingly autonomous periphery and the center on whose presence that periphery historically depends continues to be a heavy burden on urban policy-makers.

Any discussion of the multiethnic composition of contemporary cities is thus complicated by the fact that it must factor in socioeconomic class, and that although there is a strong connection between ethnicity and class, the relationship is not simply a symmetrical one. One reason why debates on ethnicity take up such a prominent place in the North American political system is that in many senses they substitute for debates on class in European politics. This holds true especially for lower-class, working-class, or unemployed members of these groups, who have seized on ethnic identity as a political tool for claiming rights they would have more trouble claiming through a class-based identification. Yet the discussion is complicated by the fact that no ethnic group will contain only people from one socioeconomic class, and that those members who fare better economically also tend to identify less and less with their ethnic backgrounds.

In a context of ethnically and racially inspired discrimination, large-scale unemployment, and other forms of "social exclusion" — a term introduced in France to refer precisely to the diminished citizenship of blacks in the *banlieues* [Hebbert 1998:163] — it should come as no surprise that ethnic and racial frustrations in the postwar metropolis have upon occasion also erupted into bursts of violence. London saw its first race riots in 1958, when white mobs attacked the homes of blacks in Notting Hill, and it witnessed further flares in the 1980s in Brixton and Tottenham [Porter 1994:354]. Los Angeles, New York, and especially Detroit acquired notoriety for their race riots in the 1960s. The *banlieues* of French cities became restless in the 1990s. But it is above all in the L.A. riots of 1992 that the nexus of ethnicity and race was most clearly articulated as a social problem. Roger Waldinger and Mehdi Bozorgmehr's *Ethnic Los Angeles* [1996] provides the background story to these riots: the tension erupted first between blacks and white police officers (after the brutal beating of Rodney King), but the former were soon joined by recent Latino immigrants. Significantly, the direction of their anger did not remain limited to the police only: it took on a further ethnic dimension when it was extended towards local landlords and storeowners, most of whom happened to be Korean. The riots shook many proverbially laid-back Angelenos out of their dreams and confronted them with the reality of a multi-ethnic metropolis in which cohabitation, no matter how widely spread out over a vast area, was ridden with conflicts that not even the rich in their splendid isolation could hope to avoid completely.

Much of this combustibility must be seen against the background of a growing income disparity between rich and poor. Such a disparity has characterized postwar Western countries overall: it appears to be the inevitable downside of an economy of free-market liberalism. But it has produced the starkest contrasts and the greatest social inequality in cities. Every metropolis has its pockets of excessively rich and its visible share of excessively poor. London, for example, is famous for the congregations of "fabulous, luxurious, ostentatious wealth"

16 The average family income of residents living in the housing blocks bounded by Fifth Avenue, Madison Avenue, 63rd, and 67th Street was $730,000 for 1990, with a population consisting of 711 non-Hispanic whites and 34 Japanese, none of them under 21 years old. By the mid-90s, hotel suites in the area could charge as much as $2,500 per night [for these figures, see Beveridge et al. 1996:6]. Around the same time, the price of local luxury apartments (organized in the form of co-operatives or "co-ops") skyrocketed to figures between $3 and 10 million [Kleinfeld 1995:B2], to be paid cash, without taking out loans, and on the basis of a buyer's net worth that could reach up to $100 million [Rozhon 1995].

17 For more on this, see the case study by Liam Kennedy (Part II).

that may be found in parts of the city like Belgravia, Barnes, Holland Park, or Hampstead [Porter 1994:387] and the city has seen the gap between rich and poor widening faster than the rest of Britain [Hebbert 1998:162]. Similarly, Manhattan's Upper East Side is host to New York's wealthiest citizens, who pay mind-boggling prices to live in the area.[16] Except for a leper colony in Hawaii, Manhattan is the most unequal county in the U.S., with about the same level of inequality as Guatemala [Beveridge 1996:8]. And on Manhattan, too, the gap between rich and poor has been steadily widening over the past few decades [Roberts 1994].

The counterparts to these exorbitantly wealthy areas and neighborhoods are the no less proverbial urban ghettos that have sprung up most glaringly in American inner cities. Historically, the first "ghetto" was formed in 16th-century Venice, a once-prosperous city then past its prime: in that city, one formerly well-assimilated category of inhabitants, the Jews, got stigmatized as "alien" elements in a Christian society and were subsequently isolated into the first official urban ghetto. According to Richard Sennett, this move marked the beginning of the overall "divisive desire for community" in the modern metropolis [1994:228]. The term "ghetto" has remained a politically loaded one in the 20th century, covering as it does both the horror of officially installed, literally occluded spaces (like the Jewish ghetto in Warsaw under the Nazi regime) and more metaphorical instances of involuntary sequestration that are the structural results of wider socioeconomic and ideological processes. In the latter case, the discussion has been mixed up with parallel debates about the urban "underclass" — a term that was coined in the 1980s to designate those people suffering from an intense deprivation that is almost self-perpetuating.[17] The urban underclass that has surfaced since the economic and urban crises of the 1970s is built on an unusually forceful constellation of spatial, socioeconomic, and racial/ethnic disadvantages. The history and fate of this group has been explored by scholars like William Julius Wilson in his aptly named *The Truly Disadvantaged: The Inner City, the Underclass, and Public Policy* [1987] and by Douglas Massey and Nancy Denton in *American Apartheid: Segregation and the Making of the Underclass* [1993]. Wilson, who debunks several popular myths concerning social problems and the underclass in the U.S., identifies principally economic realities as responsible for the growing social isolation of a group of long-term unemployed and welfare-dependent inhabitants of inner cities. This condition, he further exemplifies, is not one that can ever hope to be truly remedied by measures that stay locked within the current mindset of American politics and economic policy-makers. Wilson downplays the immediate role of racism in this process, but he has been contradicted in this respect by Massey and Denton, who trace the effects of a long history of racism and structures of institutional segregation on the subordination of the urban poor.

References to the specifics of American society and politics are important in that they signal a difference with European cities. Although every European metropolis has its own problem areas with high ratios of socioeconomically disadvantaged citizens, this has not led to the emergence of equally outspoken ghettos. As Michael Hebbert notes, no radical ghettoization seems to have taken place in for instance London [1998: 177]. And Loïc Wacquant has demonstrated how the French *banlieues* should not be confused with American inner-city ghettos: in the former, ethnic and territorial stigmatization do not overlap completely, neighborhood and family ties remain stronger, and districts continue to be better serviced by municipal and state institutions [Wacquant 1993]. In another comparative French-American study, Sophie Body-Gendrot has also insisted, however, that despite different historical constructions, the American and French models of social integration (of diversity including class, ethnicity, religion, etc.) are converging because of economic changes. The integrative and universalizing force of French citizenship promoted earlier by official policies has diminished [Body-Gendrot 1995]. Although the racial dividedness of the French *banlieues* is still a far cry from that of U.S. cities, according to Body-Gendrot, and state interventions still hold French society better together, the increasing number of expressions of a need for cultural plurality and the inability to respond to these expressions are signs of the eroding strength and importance of the link between nationality and citizenship. The political repercussions of race and ethnicity prove to be strong factors in the growing concern over the fragmentation of society and politics everywhere.

**The Multisexual Metropolis** The growing importance of interest-based subcultures and peer groups in the self-identification of urbanites may be measured from the way in which the multicultural city has also become a multisexual city. The variation in sexual lifestyles has probably never been as great as at the end of the twentieth century, nor has the (mediatized) visibility of sexual minorities ever been as high. Since socially persecuted minorities by definition tend to gather in places that offer the highest possible anonymity, the least rigorous social control, and the greatest supply of likeminded people (both in numbers and in variety), sexual minorities, too, have gathered and developed their lifestyles principally in big cities. A result of this has been the emergence of what is sometimes

18 Since bisexuals have hardly any sexual and social circuits of their own and tend to move back and forth between gay and straight worlds, they form a particularly problematical group to situate geographically. It should be noted, in addition, that the category of the "transgendered" may itself be unwieldy in covering a wide range of different people: from drag queens and drag kings (themselves either gay, straight, or bisexual) to transsexuals (either surgically treated or not, and again with varying sexual preferences or orientations).

hyperbolically labeled the "gay ghetto." Proverbial examples in North America are San Francisco's Castro District and Polk Street, Manhattan's Greenwich Village, East Village, and Chelsea, L.A.'s Santa Monica Boulevard in West Hollywood, and Montreal's Rue Ste. Cathérine, while European counterparts are to be found in London's Earls Court and so-called Pink Village, Manchester's "Gay Village," Berlin's Schöneberg, Wittenbergplatz, and Nollendorfplatz, the Le Marais and Les Halles districts in Paris, or various parts of downtown historical Amsterdam. Like ethnic neighborhoods, these gay neighborhoods relocate relatively fast from one place to the next, though the rationale behind such movements tends to be different: it is less dependent on the drive for upward social mobility than on such factors as the availability of neglected urban zones (with their potential for collective appropriation) and the presence of external cultural-political pressures operating on the housing market and limiting or enabling the formation of sexual subcultures. Although metropolitan by definition, gay neighborhoods also have their own satellites outside the city in the form of gay and lesbian holiday resorts — from Key West, Palm Springs, Provincetown, or Cherry Grove on Fire Island, to the Spanish town of Sitges or the Greek island of Mykonos.

Studies attempting to map the geographical distribution of glbt's (gays, lesbians, bisexuals, and the transgendered) need to be handled with a considerable dose of scientific skepsis, yet a few relatively reliable American studies executed in the early 1990s gave striking results at least for gays and lesbians. According to Simon LeVay and Elisabeth Nonas, one of those surveys showed how

> *27 percent of lesbians and gay men, but only 18 percent of heterosexuals, live in metropolitan areas with populations over 3 million, and 61 percent (versus 45 percent) live in cities with populations over 1 million. As a consequence, the fraction of the population of very large cities that is gay or lesbian is much larger than in nonmetropolitan or rural areas. According to the 1992 NORC study, this urban bias is considerably more marked for gay men than for lesbians. That study reported that men identifying as gay or bisexual form 9 percent of the population of the central districts of the country's twelve largest cities, 4 percent of the population of smaller cities, 3.5 percent of the population of suburbs and only 1 percent of the rural and small-town population. The corresponding figures for women were 2.7 percent, 1.9 percent, 1.6 percent and an unmeasurable percentage* [1995: 103-104].

Whether or not such inevitably contestable figures are accurate, the indicated trend as such is extendable to other Western countries, especially with regard to gays, lesbians, and what is often the most carnivalesque and flamboyant segment of the so-called "rainbow coalition," the transgendered.[18] According to a survey conducted by the city authorities of Amsterdam, for instance, the number of gays in the male population of that city is around 10% [Hekma 1999:85]; and a 1993 study of French sexual behavior indicated that 46% of the country's gay population was living in the Paris region, which is home to only some 20% of the national population [Sibalis 1999:12]. The metropolis often exerts a double appeal on young gays and lesbians: it provides them with an escape from traditionally more conservative and narrow-minded environments outside the big city and at the same time carries the promise of enhanced sexual and relational opportunities. To many of these youngsters, the move to a big city involves "as much a psychological as a physical journey, distancing the gay person from his or her family of origin" [LeVay and Nonas 1995:104]. It also produces the remarkable social scenario of what Alan Sinfield has called "a reverse diaspora" [1996:281]: "Instead of dispersing," notes Sinfield, "we assemble" [ibid.:280]. Contrary to other components of the urban population, glbt's have no shared origin in some specific place and time — and thus, unlike for example immigrants, cannot be sent back in the rhetoric of their right-wing political opponents.

In *City of Friends: A Portrait of the Gay and Lesbian Community in America*, Simon LeVay and Elisabeth Nonas usefully distinguish between three types of gay neighborhood: **1** the type that is "residential as well as a center of social life"; **2** the type that is "mostly defined by the location of gay bars and other nightspots"; and **3** the type where "the gay and straight bars and restaurants are largely intermixed to form a single social focus to the city" [1995:120]. Until recently, the first type appeared especially in the U.S., where it takes the form of "mini-cities where one can work, play, pray, and sleep around without ever leaving the neighborhood" [ibid.]. Social networks in these cities-within-the-city are so fully developed as to provide all possible services and facilities within what is ironically and somewhat treacherously referred to as "the family": from insurances and health care, over lawyers and retail businesses, to travel agencies, churches, and political organizations, all stay within the same community. The only two places in the world where even high schools for gay and lesbian youths were founded are not coincidentally the two most populated American metropolises, New York and Los Angeles (with, respectively, the Harvey Milk High School and the EAGLES Center, an acronym for Emphasizing Adolescent Gay, Lesbian Education Services).

19 In tracing the genealogy of "queer spaces" in Western history, Aaron Betsky usefully reminds us that the building of gay neighborhoods is but one, highly visible and materialized way of queering urban spaces. Another, older, and far more invisible way, which has its roots in 17th-century Holland, is that of the appropriation of public spaces through the ephemeral practice of cruising [1997:141-77]. For further analysis of these topics, see Sanders 1996, Brent Ingram et al. 1997, and Higgs 1999.

20 Some of these problems are discussed in the case study by Anne Gotman with special reference to the question of community building among HIV-positive inhabitants of Paris (Part II).

University-based research centers like CLAGS (the Center for Lesbian and Gay Studies at the City University of New York) or universities and colleges offering full-fledged programs in queer studies are typically also to be found in larger cities. Thus, it is possible to speak of fully developed, autonomous communities in cities like New York, Los Angeles, and San Francisco — and increasingly also in European cities like London, Amsterdam, Berlin, or Paris, though for historical reasons residential concentration there tends to be less high.[19]

Today, the community of glbt's is arguably the most diverse minority in cities on either side of the Atlantic. By the same token, it offers one of the best (and most complex) illustrations of the problems attendant upon contemporary metropolitan community-building in those cases where individuals recompose a social life *à la carte* that is not principally based on traditional patterns like a person's family, ethnic group, or socioeconomic class.[20] The ethnic model in particular, which Michael Warner has called "the default model for all minority movements" [quoted in Sinfield 1996:271] and which Steven Epstein has described as "particularly suited to the American experience, with its history of civil-rights struggles and ethnic-based, interest-group competition" [1990:255], poses serious problems for non-ethnic communities that factually seek to unite a wide range of subcultures. Some distinctive elements that go to complicate the formation of a glbt community do not apply to ethnic groups: the fact, for instance, that the potential to engage in same-sex is spread over a far greater part of the population than just among members of the core movement of self-affirming and well-organized glbt's; the fact that high-profile glbt communities often fail to reach out to people who are unclear or uncertain about their sexualities or unable or unwilling to rupture the ties with their own cultures; and the fact, finally, that the identity of glbt's is not so easily established and gives rise to endless juridical and scientific disputes about the question whether sexual orientation is a matter of unchangeable genetic predisposition or of changeable preference [Sinfield 1996:271-73]. In a multisubcultural circuit that depends upon the individualized formation of sexual lifestyles and that operates without much of a shared history, cohesion is hard to achieve once the binding element of oppression is taken away: what is left then is often little more than the fluidity, natural egocentrism, and apolitical character of sexual energies. "The trouble with sexual desire," argue LeVay and Nonas, "is that it arises from a part of our mind that is singularly uninterested in co-gender issues, multiculturalism, political correctness, confronting ageism or anything of that kind. Sexual desire takes one outside one's own self like nothing else does, but it is also incomparably selfish. And falling in love means excluding the world (except for one person) from one's sphere of concern. Thus sexual desire divides as well as binds our community" [1995:395]. Or, as Marjorie Garber has formulated this tension, "the politics of identity, necessary for the attainment of equal rights," may on occasion "come into conflict with the political incorrectness of human desire" [1995: 277].

**The Gendered Metropolis** Gay neighborhoods in big cities act as magnets to gay men in the first place, and only secondarily to gay women. Lesbians, by and large, appear to lead a more dispersed life over larger metropolitan areas [LeVay and Nonas 1995:105]. At the same time, however, "Lesbian communities have tended to be stronger, longer-lasting, and less exclusive, so that they point the way toward the making of a realized social sphere that does not repeat the ghettolike isolation in which gay men have found themselves" [Betsky 1997: 176]. These differences (less spatial concentration, more inclusive and supportive socializing networks) are typical also of the theoretical complexities that arise from the attempt to isolate the category of gender in sociospatial analyses of community building in the contemporary metropolis. Unlike what is the case with many ethnic, subcultural, socioeconomic, or sexual minority groups, women tend to be much more evenly divided across the rural-suburban-urban spectrum. Their presence cuts across all these groups, often complicating the picture by posing specific gender issues that are "oblique, ex-orbitant to the general story" [Spivak 1996: 246].

Nevertheless, some metanarrative of 20th-century evolutions with respect to the place of women in urban environments remains possible, and it should start by reminding us that women's lib, like so many other emancipations spearheaded by a mix of intellectual and artistic elites, was born in metropolitan environments. The great pioneers of the women's movement, the suffragettes at the end of the nineteenth and the beginning of the twentieth centuries, made their claims for independence and equal rights in the metropolis. Dolores Hayden, whose 1981 essay "What Would a Non-sexist City Be Like?" started off widespread debates about the relationship between urban design and the needs of women, showed how in the early years of the century — more particularly in Denmark and Sweden, but as of the twenties also in the Soviet Union — the first attempts were made to design special housing facilities tailored to the needs of women. This embryonic movement in urban planning was radically set back, however, in the 1930s, when the economic depression sent many women back to their homes; in 26 American states, married women were even literally forced to return to their homes by acts of law [Marsh 1994: 43]. Two decades later, moreover, the place and role of women in the city underwent a major transformation with the onset of postwar suburbanization.

Since its earliest beginnings in the 18th and 19th centuries, the phenomenon of suburbanization had always relied on a heavily gender-inflected ideology.

The call of suburbia was predicated on a domestic ideal that sought to separate women and children from the "demoralizing sphere of work" in the early-industrial city [Fishman 1987:96-97]. Suburbanization thus consolidated the ideology of a "city of separate spheres," in which women had a place only in the home [Sandercock and Forsyth 1992:414], and enhanced the separatism by moving women out to the "bedroom communities" of suburbs, which led Susan Saegert to formulate an opposition between "masculine cities and feminine suburbs" [1981]. In the immediate postwar years, mass-scale suburbanization further contributed to these classic patterns of gender role by mooring it even more deeply in a spatial opposition. As Deborah Chambers notes:

> *It is now acknowledged that the built environment tends to institutionalize not only class relations, but also patriarchal relations. New suburbs ... were thought to nurture desirable values and lifestyles through the design of straight, regular streets and houses with space around each side, separated by fences so that their occupants could retreat into the private world of the family. The suburban lifestyle was not simply a response to the rising patterns of consumption of an expanding economy. It was also a material and cultural expression of the ideology of feminine domesticity: woman as homemaker* [1997: 87].

In this sense, too, then, the postwar suburb turned its back on the central city, in which the women's movement had been based. With suburbanization, moreover, also came the deterioration of inner cities, involving among other things an increased safety risk for women that made cities seem particularly inhospitable to them.

The suburban housewife in the fifties who listened to the radio and then started watching T.V. was bombarded with soap operas and publicity, heralding the age of consumption. By 1963, Betty Friedan could already score a bestseller with her provocative *The Feminine Mystique*, which gave a voice to the isolation and growing discontent of suburban housewives. The following years saw the symptomatic rise of tranquilizers for women that were marketed with the shamelessly sexist slogan "You can't change her environment but you can change her mood" [quoted in Hayden 1981:145]. Yet with the birth of Mrs. Consumer the need for double family incomes also grew to be able to keep up with the new consumerist lifestyle [ibid.:144]. The sixties brought not only further economic prosperity, but also the democratization of education — two factors that boosted the emancipation of women and radically altered their place in the urban landscape again.

With the gradual transformation of classic suburbia into the hybrid complexity of postsuburbia, the gender dichotomy of city and suburb began to lose much of its clear-cut neatness. The demise of old-style manufacturing industries at the expense of a fast-rising service economy played a major role in this process. According to Robert Fishman,

*women have been a not-so-hidden force behind the new city's economic success.... More than half of all women are now employed outside the home. Much of the economic life of the new city, especially with its concentration on retail trade and back-office data processing, would be impossible without these new workers. Indeed, the presence of employment opportunities so close to home — convenient, with decent pay and flexible schedules — is surely reponsible for the remarkable influx of married women into the work force.... The outcome is more than a little ironic, considering the fact that the bedroom suburb had originally been designed to separate women from the corruptions of the world of work* [1990:41].

Fishman has hailed this evolution towards female employment in the suburbs by claiming that "in contrast to the old metropolis, the economic and spatial structure of the new city tends to equalize gender roles" [1990:41], and Joel Garreau in *Edge City* has even talked of "the empowerment of women" [1991:111]. But others like William Sharpe and Leonard Wallock have contested this optimistic view by countering that "the fact of [women's] paid employment does not guarantee an end to their exploitation. Given the continuing expectation that they will do most of the housework and provide most of the child care — not to mention chauffeuring the children — their opportunity to labor outside the home carries with it an invitation to perform double duty" [1994:14] — or what sociologist Arlie Hothschild has labeled the "second shift" [quoted in Marsh 1994:43]. "Moreover, the jobs they usually fill ... offer low pay, few benefits, inadequate day care, and little security or chance of promotion to managerial positions" [Sharpe and Wallock 1994:14]. All is not necessarily well, then, for women in the new posturban environment, as Allen Scott has also demonstrated with respect to manufacturing industries in the L.A. area, where "the presence of foreign-born and female workers in any sector is strongly and negatively correlated with the average wage rate" [1996:224].

The huge influx of women in the labor market has also involved a greater diversification of jobs: national American figures spanning the period between 1970 and 1990 indicate that "women now constitute a majority of workers in a wide range of occupations long male-dominated, including psychologist, accountant, journalist, bus driver, bartender, and insurance or real estate agent" [Roberts 1995]. Many of these jobs are also urban in the widest sense. Especially for professional and managerial career women, in particular those who choose to have no children or postpone the arrival of children for a long time, the metropolis acts as a greater social magnet than suburbia. This attraction is one of the factors behind the relative preponderance of single residents in cities compared to suburbs and the countryside. Of all adults between 25 and 55 that were living in Manhattan in 1990, 61% was single, over against some 30% on average in the surrounding counties [Berger 1995: B1].

The result of women's increased opportunities and autonomizing life stories has been that the relationship between women and the city today offers a particularly complex picture. This has prompted the need among scholars and activists to diversify also among women in discussing gender issues. Leonie Sandercock and Ann Forsyth have pointed up how the analysis of specific gender-related problems has been diversified and multiculturalized since the 1980s; the voice of women from minority groups has been heard louder than before. Partly as a result of this, the awareness has grown in women's studies that "women are divided by geographical, political, religious, class, and cultural boundaries" [1992:410]. This awareness, however, is still to seep through to the agenda of, for instance, urban planners. The latter, according to Sandercock and Forsyth, are still a long way from considering questions that today are crucial to the sociospatial organization of the urban landscape: "How do different groups of women use and experience cities? Do public spaces hold the same intimidation for middle-class and poor women, for African Americans, mothers, Chicanas, Jewish women, or lesbians? How are experiences of lone parenting different for women from different communities? Taking account of the systematic differences among women, as well as the systematic differences among women and the men in their various communities, is an important task for gender-conscious planning" [ibid.: 417].

# 3 Recent Transformations of Urban Public Space

**The Virtualization of Public Space** The overall diversification of the urban population in recent decades has not simply been a story of emancipation and multiculturalization. It has been coextensive also with a certain homogenization of that same population at the local scale of particular neighborhoods or districts. One of the most striking and momentous outcomes of this process is the so-called dismantlement of "public space" — that part of the urban territory that is supposed to be accessible to everyone. To the extent that the contemporary city has begun to give up on public space (ideally and traditionally conceived), it may even be said to undermine its own historical roots. Historically, the development of urban culture is inextricably intertwined with the rise of the city as a *polis* [Weintraub 1995]. For a long time, urban space formed the representation of a political system in which the public domain played an important role. Typically, the character of historical cities is determined by buildings with public functions and by various kinds of public spaces. The political forum is historically bound to a specific place. Yet the city was also more than a public space representing political authorities: it was at the same time a place of sociability and interaction. Cities were meeting-places.

With the development of a modern, industrial society and the growing social and geographical mobility of individuals, the intimate association between *communitas* and place was largely lost. The city became a social network first and foremost. Social relationships were uncoupled from physical proximity. "During the past two decades," notes sociologist William Flanagan, "researchers have embraced the idea that 'community' is not a place but a set of social ties, that it is an extra-spatial social phenomenon not to be confused with neighborhood" [1993: 23]. The dispersal of the contemporary metropolis has only strengthened this process. In Robert Fishman's concept of the city *à la carte*, social interactions are excruciatingly hard to map in spatial terms. Posturban space has not only weakened and complicated the geographical distinction between center and periphery, it has also brought in its wake a weakening and complication of the notion of public space.

Today the public domain often no longer resides in (parts of) the city: it has been displaced to the realm of the mass media and has sprawled through the global networks of communication technologies. As Craig Calhoun remarks, "large cities are at once dissolving into a plethora of local communities and being absorbed into a larger-scale and more tightly-knit web of indirect relationships" [1986: 329]. Traditional public space, in its most immediate material sense, is not only eroded by the fragmentation and separation of diverse groups in a multicultural society, but also by the immersion of today's urban dwellers in what David Harvey has come to call a "time-space compression" [1989a: 284-307] — a compression that results from the speeding up of production, distribution, and consumption systems in the economy as well as from the overall spatial globalization of the market. The "global city" studied by Saskia Sassen [1991] — with its constant international flux of information, capital, goods, and people — has yielded a new tension between electronic spaces and urban places [see also Graham and Marvin 1996]. The material urban spaces of streets, squares, shops, cafés, salons, and clubs are no longer the primary civic *loci* of public debate. As Marc Augé notes [1995], public space has often become no more than a transitional space which is being used in a traditional sense only by outcasts. In cases like Los Angeles, critics have gone so far even as to argue that "the phone and the modem have rendered the street irrelevant; social hierarchies, once fixed, have become 'despatialized'" [Dear 1995: 31]. The virtualization of space described in the first chapter may thus be taken to have its social equivalent in the mediatization and technologization of public space. And the new communication technologies have not been responsible for a virtualization of the public domain only: they have arguably also weakened the ties between individuals and society and stimulated various forms of homeliness and cocooning. According to Nan Ellin, "new home technologies (particularly the VCR and computer) and growing privatism have conspired with a diminished public realm to make people stay home more" [1997: 31].

**The Privatization of Public Space** If in some sense public space has been dematerialized by the various media and communication technologies, it has physically and materially also been threatened by economic and social privatization processes. The distinction between public and private space, however, has never been a simple one: although it has been at the heart of Western urban planning, sociology, and political philosophy since at least the end of the 19th century, it is by no means clearly delineated and waterproof. Recent theorists like Manuel de Solà-Morales have felt the need to finetune it by pointing to the phenomenon of "collective space." The latter term may be used to refer to those meeting-places in the city which, though privately owned and hence in some respects exclusionary, continue to form the scenes for various public activities: places like the shopping mall, the sports stadium, the theme park, or the grand café. In de Solà-Morales's opinion, "Collective space is much more *and* much less than public space in a restricted sense (as public property). The civil, architectonic, urbanistic, and morphological riches of a city are those of its collective spaces, of all those spaces in which everyday life unfolds, presents itself, and remains as memory. And perhaps these are increasingly spaces that are neither public nor private but both at the same time: public spaces that are used for private activities or private spaces allowing a collective usage.... Public and private disintegrate as categories and no longer suffice" [1992:6; editors' translation]. One of the important tasks of current urban planning, according to de Solà-Morales, consists precisely of interconnecting private, enclosed spaces, so that these spaces, too, may eventually be turned into parts of the collective heritage: "To give an urban, public character to those buildings which would otherwise be merely enclosed — the urbanization of the private domain — that's the concept. Which is to say: to include the particular in the sphere of influence of the public" [ibid.: 5].

The category of collective space introduced by de Solà-Morales helps us to conceptualize today's impure relationship between public and private space in the city: it serves to highlight how, on the one hand, an increasing number of private spaces has come to serve public or semi-public purposes, while on the other, traditional public spaces are constantly undergoing processes of privatization and collectivization. Introducing a third term into the debate may thus facilitate also a discussion of those instances where the selective accessibility of public spaces has been pushed so far as to be restricted almost entirely to a very specific and homogeneous segment of the population. Today's urban public space appears increasingly subdivided into particular sections taken over by particular groups and other sections avoided by them. The most radical instances are offered by street gangs and neighborhood patrols. "Street gangs use spray paint while homeowners associations use neighborhood watch signs," notes Steven Flusty; "either way we are talking informal militias" [1997: 57]. Yet the process also works more surreptitiously. Some of the most discussed examples of the appropriation of public space by private institutions or selective groups are those of the park, the atrium, and the shopping mall.

The social history of parks in cities is not a straightforward one. Especially in Europe (the Tuileries in Paris, the Mall in London's St. James Park), many urban parks were for a long time the exclusive domain of the upper classes. The construction of entirely democratic parks open to the general public is a nineteenth-century phenomenon, with Frederick Law Olmsted as its most famous American proponent [Rybczynski 1995: 124-26]. It was only by the early twentieth century that parks in cities on both sides of the Atlantic could generally be equated with public oases accessible to every urbanite in need of quiet, relaxation, green, and some fresh air. Today, at the end of the century, however, the situation seems to have again become more complex. During the past two decades, many parks have undergone momentous transformations. This has happened mostly in response to the growing presence of "unwanted" or "undesirable" visitors — in the U.S. especially homeless people (many of them deinstitutionalized mental patients), in European cities like Zurich (Platzspitz Park) especially drug addicts (semi-officially tolerated by political authorities). Many parks have accordingly been revamped to meet the needs of the gentrified middle classes and keep unwanted visitors out. In *The Cultures of Cities*, Sharon Zukin demonstrates how the design of parks in such cases rests on an implicit code of inclusion and exclusion [1995:24-38]. Authentic and cultivated feelings of fear have led people to request a transformation of parks, which, in application of Oscar Newman's theory of "defensible spaces," have been temporarily evacuated and redesigned with an emphasis on see-through perspectives and fenced zones. The most notorious case is that of Tompkins Square Park on New York's Lower East Side. The transformation of this park gave rise to considerable commotion in the years 1988-91, when the park developed into "a national symbol of the struggle against gentrification and homelessness" [Smith 1996a:96]. Another example comes from downtown Los Angeles, where "the development agency responsible for the design of Grand Hope Park has sought to avoid security problems by not providing restrooms (regarded as magnets for transients) and by asking the park architect Lawrence Halprin to design an eight-foot-high fence, the gates of which would be closed after dark, paralleling a trend around the country toward privatizing park space" [Ellin 1996:72].

The wish for safely shielded, constantly monitored public environments likewise speaks from architectural evolutions in the construction of skyscrapers. The Atlanta-based architect and developer John Portman has been of great influence in this respect. According to Rem Koolhaas, Portman should be credited with "single-handedly perfecting a device that spread from Atlanta to the rest of America, and from America to the rest of the world (even Europe): he (re)invented the atrium" [1987/1994:841]. In his famous analysis of Portman's Westin Bonaventure Hotel in Los Angeles, the neomarxist critic Fredric Jameson pointed out how atriums not only respond to the postmodern aesthetic preference for an inversion of interior and exterior, but also simulate an urban totality. "With a certain number of other characteristic postmodern buildings," notes Jameson, "such as the Beaubourg in Paris or the Eaton Centre in Toronto, the Bonaventure aspires to being a total space, a complete world, a kind of miniature city; to this new total space, meanwhile, corresponds a new collective practice, a new mode in which individuals move and congregate, something like the practice of a new and historically original kind of hypercrowd" [1991:40]. The masses inside these atriums, however, do not automatically offer a cross-section of the metropolitan population overall. In the controlled space of atriums, visitors are silently filtered: undesirable individuals or groups are kept out. By attracting selective parts of the population, skyscrapers tend to become cities-within-cities, places that take up the function of what Koolhaas has called "an *ersatz* downtown," adding that

"The more ambitious these autonomies, the more they undermine the real downtown — its messy conditions, its complexities, its irregularities, its densities, its ethnicities" [1987/1994:843]. This effect has been strengthened by a second architectural novelty, again popularized by Portman: the construction of skywalks to connect skyscrapers. The result of both architectural evolutions — atriums and skywalks — is, in Koolhaas's polemical words, that "Once you [venture] into the system, there [is] almost no incentive to visit the rest of downtown, no way to escape.... Downtown becomes an accumulation of voided panopticons inventing their own voluntary prisoners: the center as a prison system" [ibid.:841]. "The American city," as Mike Davis also notes, "is being systematically turned inside out — or rather, outside in" [1990:226].

A third and final development symptomatic of this encroaching privatization of public space in metropolitan areas is to be found in the immense popular success of shopping malls — institutions that themselves played a prominent part in the suburbanization of cities [Teaford 1993:105-106] and that have become, in the eyes of certain critics, no less than an architectural paradigm for the late twentieth century [Ghirardo 1996; Langman 1992]. Between 1970 and 1990, no less than 25,000 new shopping malls were built in the U.S. alone — one every seven hours [Rybczynski 1995:207]. Originally an entirely suburban phenomenon, the malls have also found their way into city centers or airports. More importantly, they have increasingly started to include extraneous facilities like hotels, fitness clubs, banks, and medical centers, and have made room for entertainment industries. To Witold Rybczynski this means that the suburban mall has today become urban, a new type of (privately owned and privately run) downtown. Rybczynski has in fact defended malls for being public spaces

> *where rules of personal conduct are enforced. In other words, they are more like public streets used to be before police indifference and overzealous protectors of individual rights effectively ensured that* any *behavior, no matter how antisocial, is tolerated. This is what malls offer: a reasonable (in most eyes) level of public order; the right not to be subjected to outlandish conduct, not to be assaulted and intimidated by boorish adolescents, noisy drunks, and aggressive panhandlers. It does not seem much to ask* [ibid.:210].

From Rybczynski's perspective (which voices that of many middle-class suburbanites), malls figure as cities that have been cleaned of all traces of conflict or subversion. For that very reason, other critics have taken them to represent precisely the antithesis of metropolitan downtowns. In Kenneth Jackson's view, for instance, they "cater exclusively to middle-class tastes and contain no unsavory bars or pornography shops, no threatening-looking characters, no litter, no rain, and no excessive heat or cold" [1985:260]. To William Whyte they "reject many of the activities of a true center. They do not welcome — indeed, do not tolerate — controversy, soapboxing, passing of leaflets, impromptu entertaining, happenings, or eccentric behavior, harmless or no" [1988:208]. And Diane Ghirardo has held shopping malls responsible for destroying public space in two ways: first, by weaning shoppers and shops away from downtowns, and secondly, by reducing the notion of a public space to a zone exclusively oriented towards consumption. "The types of unorganized political and social activities associated with cities," she writes, "have often not been allowed in malls: in the United States, the Supreme Court has ruled that because they are private, they may prohibit or control such activities. This ruling cast in sharp relief the function of the carefully controlled mall, reducing the notion of civic participation to that of consumption" [1996:66]. In addition, the fact that today's malls "are usually designed in a panopticon fashion around a police substation" [Ellin 1996:73] signals a trend toward militarizing public space that is itself intimately linked to the depicted privatization processes.

Although parks, atriums, and shopping malls today present us with adapted forms of urban public space, they do not seem devised to cater to all segments of the urban population. In all three cases, accessibility is monitored and sometimes clearly restricted. Because of the subsequent loss of possibilities for interaction, they may also be said to lack the socioeconomic riches and diversity of the traditional metropolis. Not surprisingly, then, they have been called "pseudo-public spaces" by a social-activist critic like Mike Davis [1990:26], or instances of a "post-public" space by Steven Flusty [1997:51]. What these exemplary spaces offer are concrete material symptoms of wider sociopolitical trends — trends that may be further gauged from the several ways in which the contemporary metropolis has been fragmented administratively and managerially. The current tendency towards privatizing culturally and/or commercially profitable areas is further illustrated by the phenomenon of BID's (Business Improvement Districts) — first in a city like New York, but increasingly also elsewhere. By 1997, already some 1,200 of these BID's were active all over the U.S., and the phenomenon has begun to spread to Europe, the Caribbean, Australia, and South Africa [Hannigan 1998:139]. The principle of BID's, which consists in "allow[ing] business and property owners in commercial districts to tax themselves voluntarily for maintenance and improvement of public areas and take these areas under their control" [Zukin 1995: 33], may look at first sight like a form of grassroots democracy and local responsibilization. But what its implementation really achieves is often only the institutionalization and consolidation of the socioeconomic inequality of neighborhoods. Manhattan's wealthy and commercially prosperous BID's are able to organize their own neighborhoods (from private sanitation teams, security forces, and strictly enforced rules for pedestrians, down to the hiring of lobbyists and even the closing off of streets), while less prosperous and influential BID's in Queens may have to limit themselves to questions about the instalment of Christmas lights [ibid.:33-34]. BID's represent limit-cases of urban policy-making by threatening to become non-democratically controlled local governments, the administrative and managerial equivalents of the spatial fragmentation that characterizes the contemporary metropolis overall.

**Wallification and Gated Communities** The privatization of public space takes many different guises and comes in different degrees. In most of the above cases, it is indirect and surreptitious, but in other cases it may become quite blunt and unmistakable. The most extreme and most clearly visible instances are those where certain parts of a city are physically walled off from others. The trend towards a materialized separation between parts of the metropolitan population has been such that the topic of physical segregation has made a comeback in critical debates, often with a vengeance. *Provocateur* Mike Davis served as a prosecutor to the case in a chapter called "Fortress LA" in *City of Quartz*. "Welcome to post-liberal Los Angeles," Davis snidely exulted,

*where the defense of luxury lifestyles is translated into a proliferation of new repressions in space and movement, undergirded by the ubiquitous "armed response." This obsession with physical security systems, and collaterally, with the architectural policing of social boundaries, has become a zeitgeist of urban restructuring, a master narrative in the emerging built environment of the 1990s.... In cities like Los Angeles, on the bad edge of postmodernity, one observes an unprecedented tendency to merge urban design, architecture and the police apparatus into a single, comprehensive security effort* [1990:223-24].

As Davis illustrates, the fear of crime has had a major impact on the shape and outlook of the contemporary metropolis. Today's most typical collective spaces like the shopping mall or the atrium are also the preeminent domain for deploying all types of private security forces. Since the socioeconomic privatization of public space is intrinsically motivated by a desire to protect material property and physical integrity, it is unsurprisingly accompanied by an increasing militarization of public space. Heavily guarded public buildings and private residences, formerly only associated with Third World countries and an extreme polarization between haves and have-nots, have surfaced everywhere in Western cities, too.[21]

21 For a more extensive analysis with particular respect to architectural history in Los Angeles, see the case study by Dirk De Meyer (Part II).

Whether or not this evolution should be painted in terms of "building paranoia," as Steven Flusty has done [1997], the trend has undoubtedly marked urban architecture, in particular the ways in which buildings are positioned. Especially in the landscape of contemporary technoburbs, we may notice a proliferation of isolated architectural units that are turned inwards like ever so many autonomous entities. Again the architectural typology of the shopping mall — with its strong contrast between "a highly articulated interior and a relatively blank exterior" [Ghirardo 1996: 65] — proves to be a model. The fear of crime in the street, which is itself both cause and result of the ongoing privatization of public space, has given rise to a new type of urban layout, "one of closed, defended islands with blank and windowless facades surrounded by wastelands of parking lots and fast-moving traffic" [Jacobs and Appleyard 1987: 114]. Buildings are separated by prominently displayed voids, but also by conspicuous walls. In an article tellingly entitled "Walls of Fear and Walls of Support," Peter Marcuse ironically observes how the new urban layout represents a shift from earlier patterns of urban settlement: while the whole of a medieval city was surrounded by a wall, the contemporary city is internally divided by local walls. To a considerable extent, posturban space is characterized by the phenomenon of "wallification," and once again Los Angeles appears to be something of an example. In *City of Quartz*, Mike Davis paid special attention to the emergence of "stealth houses" in that city — houses hiding their luxurious interiors behind proletarian or gangster facades [1990: 221-69]. And both Charles Jencks and Steven Flusty extensively studied the phenomenon of "defensible architecture" as well as of a recent architectural style graphically called "riot realism" [Jencks 1993: 89-93; Flusty 1997].

The tendency towards walling off private property and the obsessional attention to security and control have found their most extreme expression in the much-publicized phenomenon of the "gated community." Gated communities, which started mushrooming in the U.S. in the 1980s, extend a logic that also lies behind apartment buildings with private security services and a private parking lot. They are entire neighborhoods or subdivisions, newly built or existing, that are literally walled off with a fence and a gate. In their study of the phenomenon, Edward Blakely and Mary Gail Snyder define them as "residential areas with restricted access in which normally public spaces are privatized" [1997: 2]. This privatization includes ordinary civic responsibilities, like the organization of police forces, as well as social and cultural services like education, recreation, and entertainment. According to Evan McKenzie in *Privatopia*, in 1990 already more than 11% of the American population lived in such secluded communities or "common-interest developments" [1994: 11-12]. Several years later, Blakely and Gail Snyder counted some 20,000 gated communities in the U.S. with over 3 million residential units. In their (lower) estimate (based on a narrower definition), some 8 million Americans currently seek to escape urban threats in these collective hideouts — but their potential would be much higher [1997:7-8]. Originally restricted to retirement villages and residential areas for the exorbitantly rich (the "equestrian" and "golf communities"), the phenomenon has clearly begun to catch on with other social groups as well. Today those original groups account for only one third of gated communities: another third is inhabited by the middle class, while the number of working-class gated communities, too, appears to be growing [ibid.: 6]. The greatest concentration is to be found in the periphery of big cities like New York, Chicago, Los Angeles, Houston, Phoenix, and Miami, and they are especially eye-catching in California and Florida. According to Blakely and Gail Snyder, three types may be distinguished [ibid.:38-45]: **1** *lifestyle communities* like retirement villages and golf and leisure developments, which are especially to be found in the Sunbelt; **2** *elite* or *prestige communities*, which lack the recreative facilities of the first category and offer little more than "a standard residential subdivision except for their gates"; and **3** the *security zone communities* in poor inner-city neighborhoods, which besides using private security forces to protect buildings have been given the permission by local authorities to screen the streets from public use and limit access to residents only.

Collectively, these three types of gated community use a list of defensive and exclusionary strategies that leaves nothing to the imagination: walls with gates operated by security codes or remote controls, surveillance cameras, infrared sensors, motion detectors, canine patrols, antiterrorist bollards, security-oriented gardens with particularly thorny plants, armed guards, helicopters, moats, and even drawbridges. In conjunction with other collective spaces in the city that are increasingly monitored and patrolled, gated communities seem to represent a postmodern variant of medieval feudalism. The image of guards at gates, of walls, moats, and drawbridges perfectly ties in with the metaphor of the New Middle Ages that Umberto Eco developed already in the 1970s in essays like "Travels in Hyperreality" and "The Return of the Middle Ages" [collected in Eco 1986].

Scholars have emphasized how such new forms of highly materialized segregation are mostly voluntary and should be understood in part as attempts at restoring a lost sense of community and grass-roots democracy. Yet what is voluntary segregation to certain groups of the population is less so to others. Walls protect, but they also lock out and lock up. As a voluntary form of isolation, the gated community may seem radically different from the involuntary ghetto, yet in indirect and complex ways it also adds to the process of ghettoization in the inner city. And as soon as one seeks to think both phenomena together, the aspect of community building presents a less rosy picture. As Peter Marcuse critically notes, "we have sometimes, in recent years, attempted to justify segregation and even ghettoization by saying that it can be a source of strength for those within the ghetto; it can produce solidarity, creativity, and bonds of mutual support that a less confined environment might not nourish. It is certainly true that ghettos have produced wonderful and heroic actions. But that is certainly no justification for the creation of ghettos. Those who have lost one arm or one leg can sometimes do wonders with the other; that is no reason to cut off an arm or a leg" [1997: 112]. Care should be taken, moreover, to distinguish between involuntary ghettos and voluntary enclaves. In certain nominal ghettos, Marcuse points out, residents "do cluster together, help each other, support each other's business, share tastes in food and clothing, celebrate the same holidays and festivals. I would not call such communities ghettos, precisely because their residents are not confined to them, but are there by choice" [ibid.: 113]. Freedom of choice may seem like the crucial category in debates about gated communities and ghettos, yet it also remains an essentially contested concept. Immigrants that "freely" form enclaves may do so for want of a better alternative. Freedom is limited by opportunity as well as socializing intention. "In today's cities," Marcuse offers as a complicating example,

*the poorer residents of the Lower East Side of Manhattan, of Kreuzberg in Berlin, and of the area around the University of Southern California in Los Angeles wish to keep the gentrifiers out as much as the residents of the suburbs and luxury housing of these cities want to keep the poor out; yet the two desires are not equivalent morally. One represents the desire of those poorer to insulate themselves from losses to the more powerful; the other represents the ability of the more powerful to insulate themselves from the necessity of sharing with, or having exposure to, those poorer. One wall defends survival, the other protects privilege* [ibid.: 109].

**Mallification and Disneyfication** The privatization of public space in cities has several material consequences. At the residential level, it leads to forms of balkanization. At a more economic level, however, it fosters still another development — that of the "mallification" of the contemporary city. Places that continue to be publicly accessible to large parts of the urban population are increasingly turned into sites of consumption. The pedestrian or low-traffic shopping precincts and streets in the downtowns of historical European cities offer one major example of this trend. While the mall, as we saw, assumes the status of an ersatz city, the city center presents itself more and more as a great open-air shopping mall. Contamination is again the keyword, since mallified city centers in turn tend to invert the traditional relationship between interior and exterior:

refurbished squares, for instance, frequently make use of tiles and "street furniture" intended to evoke an indoor coziness. Business leaders in Brussels have even suggested capping the entire historical *Grand Marché*, the city's touristic heart, by means of a glass dome. "The great metropolis will dwindle to what we would call a massive shopping mall," writes Robert Fishman, "while the productive life of society would take place in the decentralized city" [1987:185]. Whereas the modernist principle of the separation of functions has long been jettisoned and the periphery has assumed almost all the functions of the traditional center, contemporary downtowns are paradoxically being subjected to a process of monoculturalization. The late-capitalist downtown is almost exclusively geared to three functions: consumption, finance, and the symbolic economy. This postindustrial symbolic economy comprises tourism, entertainment, culture, sports, the media and fashion industries, and an amalgamation of services logistically underpinning these activities. New monocultures have thus sprung up: financial and office districts that bustle with life during the day and are spookily deserted at night; tourist zones that are populated at certain times of the day or in certain seasons only. With the exception of central business districts or CBD's, the identity of places in the metropolis seems to be determined to an ever greater extent by a consumerist variant of the pleasure principle: the potential for gratification prevails.

In *The Cultures of Cities*, sociologist Sharon Zukin points up how, over the past twenty years, the worlds of finance, politics, and the arts have teamed up to turn New York into a culture capital. Culture in those years has come to be seen no longer as a mere reflection, but as the principal economic motor of the city's material and social life [1995:109-13]. Here, too, the tendency has been in the direction of a privatization, in this case of the arts and their major institutions like museums, opera houses, concert halls, and theaters, all of which have increasingly turned from not-for-profit to for-profit. "During the 1980s," Zukin writes,

> *private investment in culture developed an extremely high profile. Museums basked in the celebrity of Wall Street's new multimillionaires. Patrons added luster to their image by sponsoring big art exhibits and capital projects — special facilities or new wings — in museums ... Art in general, and specifically collecting, became the focus of the media because of the astronomical prices paid at auction sales. ... A new nexus of auction houses, art galleries, art museums, art producers, and cultural and social elites — many of them international — contributed to New York's renewed reputation as a culture capital ... High art has become more like for-profit culture industries in many ways* [1995:118-19].

22 For more on this, see the case study on CityWalk by Kevin McNamara (Part II).

Culture draws tourists and so mass tourism has become a major source of income for traditional city centers, witness the success of "city trips" and "urban safaris" among especially middle-class and well-educated population groups — mostly "baby boomer" and "Generation X" adults [Hannigan 1998: 3]. This economic importance of tourism has led to the competitive self-promotion of cities. Terms like "civic boosterism" and "urban entrepreneurialism" have become stock phrases in politico-economic parlance [see Kearns and Philo 1993]. In a globalizing economic system that is increasingly indifferent to questions of locale for the production of goods, cities have paradoxically had to start emphasizing their identities and differences again in a competition for, on the one hand, tourists, and on the other, cultural and business elites. Competition of this sort increasingly pits metropolitan areas against each other and throws them into identity crises. And once again, the tendency has been one towards privatization. In the case of Atlanta's organization of the Olympic Games in 1996, for instance, observers noted a "shift of major urban decision-making from a mixed public and private sphere to an entirely private axis" [Rogin 1996: 27].

The competition of cities to position themselves in the markets of mass tourism and the culture industries has fostered a strong interest in the production of urban images. More and more, cities are being presented or sold as collections of images. In some respects, they have even become simulacra or mere reflections of themselves and their pasts.[22] An egregiously spectacular illustration of this simulational tendency is offered by the $460 million Manhattan hotel and casino which recently opened in Las Vegas. Rising up among the fantastic and escapist architecture that derives its inspiration from Egyptian pyramids, Roman palaces, or 17th-century pirate ships, a compacted and contorted ersatz skyline of Manhattan in styrofoam now graces the phantasmagoric landscape of Las Vegas. The hotel's architectural composition contains, among many other things, miniature replicas of the Statue of Liberty and the upper parts of the Empire State Building as well as of the Chrysler Building. If in the popular imagination New York is often still equated with crime and decadence, it apparently continues to possess sufficient value as a phantasmagoric spectacle to be able to figure as part of the glitter and glamor of Las Vegas.

The example of Las Vegas in fact offers a captivating illustration of a final trend, which has been intimately connected with that of mallification and is most typically embodied by the format and features of the theme park. Michael Sorkin's influential edited volume *Variations on a Theme Park* [1990] critically unpacks this trend, showing how contemporary public space, presented as a historical attraction and streamlined for consumption, is guarded against disturbing or subversive elements. In a study of the influence of privatization processes on

Atlanta, Charles Rutheiser judiciously borrowed the term "imagineering" for this strategy [1996]. The term is a pormanteau word combining "image building" and "engineering," and was symptomatically coined by Walt Disney. The Disney Company has in recent years become a flagship for urban privatization processes, and its views on the production of urban landscapes have often been held to set the model for actual urban transformations. "The Disney Company," says Edward Ball, "is America's urban laboratory" [quoted in Zukin 1995:55]. This means that the template of Disneyland, Disney World, and Disneyland Paris tends to be transposed to urban environments. It is the template of a privatized, consumption-oriented theme park intended to simulate a shared middle-class culture, aestheticize social differences, and offer a reassuring environment without arms, alcohol, drugs, or homeless bums. Transformations of urban downtowns draw inspiration from this laboratory of simulated community building. The complex example of New York's Times Square, a *locus classicus* of metropolitan urbanism, has been much discussed [see, for instance, Berman 1997]. Partly through the money and clout of the Disney Company, the place has undergone a veritable metamorphosis in the 1990s: from a seedy, crime-infected, prostitution-oriented, and economically slumping area to a glitzy, thriving, middle-class consumerist paradise that is meant to restore the old glory of the place and adapt it to a new electronic age. Diane Ghirardo has argued that the Disney model has also become a major town planning model in smaller cities across the U.S. "The approaches to public space, work space, and urbanism embodied in Disneyland and its successors [have come] to appeal both to developers and to architects as a standard against which to asses buildings and public spaces" [1996:46].

The (somewhat sloganistically called) Disneyfication of the contemporary city can be aligned also with the recent popularity of festival marketplaces. The model for these places was typologically laid out in the late 1970s by the building developer James Rouse when renovating the 18th-century Faneuil Hall Market Place in Boston and the nearby Quincy Market from 1826. Rouse transformed these historical sites into a new type of urban shopping mall combining shops, restaurants, small-cart boutiques, and performance spaces. The most famous festival marketplaces have become the Harborplace in Baltimore (1980) and South Street Seaport in downtown Manhattan (1983-85). In Europe, Les Halles in Paris and Covent Garden in London have become no less famous counterparts. On the basis of South Street Seaport, M. Christine Boyer has extensively analyzed the success of these pseudo-historical sites and how, in particular, the histories of cities have been manipulated, recycled, simulated, and artificially resuscitated in the process to meet commercial-tourist aims [1994:421-76]. The collective memory of cities — the main theme of Boyer's book — has been exchanged for a fictive image transforming the city like the print of a giant camera obscura: "Seductive images in the camera obscura always turn reality on its head. In a similar manner these visual narratives of South Street Seaport and Battery Park City mix theater play with actuality, publicize private place as public terrain, and push every neglected space of the city through the sieve of an imaginary matrix whose nodes are none other than well-designed city tableaux" [1994: 471]. The sections of cities in between the tableaux formed by festival marketplaces, Boyer points out, are often neglected and erased from collective memory. In this respect, festival marketplaces, too, contribute their share to the spatial and social fragmentation of the contemporary city. Collective memory is always grounded in images, but this time the images are only produced in the context of market strategies, which tends to make them even more ephemeral and short-lived than the material image of urban environments often already is. Because of the speed with which metropolitan centers are built and rebuilt, Richard Sennett has claimed that "in a hundred years people will have more tangible evidence about Hadrian's Rome than they will about fiber-optic New York" [1994: 360]. In light of this claim, it might be argued even that urban memories today are less and less anchored in material monuments (streets, squares, parks, churches, temples, palaces, city halls, museums, libraries, or statuary) and more and more in the individual urbanite's body, which has become the locus of continuity, slowness, and duration [Verschaffel 1991]. A reversal of traditional temporal relations has led to one more paradoxical situation: while people in general grow older, the buildings that surround them in metropolitan environments often grow younger. Memory in today's urban environment survives matter.

Theme parks and festival marketplaces belong to the most conspicuous strategies for projecting a profitable image of cities and their pasts. But there are still other ways. Two further examples of political and commercial strategies for cultivating a city's image are those of gentrification and of what is called New Urbanism. Both phenomena have again contributed their share towards the fragmentation of the contemporary city. The politics of gentrification, which consist in the residential rehabilitation of working-class neighborhoods, reached their climax during the 1970s and 80s [Smith 1986]. After the suburban boom of the previous decades, gentrification seemed to usher in a modest return to the central city. Yet the phenomenon stands in a complex relationship to the process of suburbanization. According to Neil Smith, it should be seen less as a response to, than as a surprising side-effect of, suburbanization. In his analysis, both phenomena are part of a cyclical movement: since suburbanization resulted in a devalorization of the inner-city housing stock, it created the very possibility of revalorization.

Gentrification has not reversed the trend of suburbanization; it is taking place parallel to it. Suburbanization has at most been accompanied, not countered, by the uneven redevelopment and revalorization of a handful of inner-city enclaves.

Smith links the phenomenon of gentrification also to a restructuring of the economy. Deindustrialization has not only brought about the downfall of certain city districts, but also stimulated the growth of a service sector, which generated a particular employment structure in central urban areas. This is explained by the simultaneous spatial centralization and decentralization of capital [Sassen 1991]. On the one hand, we witness the suburbanization of economic activities; on the other, high-level service functions and executive decision-making tend to be increasingly centralized in a downtown central business district (or CBD). In this context, Smith demonstrates that gentrification is not only a local phenomenon but just as much determined by international and global factors [1996b: 75-91]. Gentrification is more than the rehabilitation of the housing stock, argues Smith; "it has become the leading residential edge of a much larger endeavor: the class remake of the central urban landscape" [ibid.: 39]. It has become the hallmark of the unevenly developing "global city."

Although, statistically speaking, gentrification remained a relatively small phenomenon even during its boom years, its influence on the images of cities has often been considerable [Ellin 1996: 64-66]. The era of gentrification in the U.S. happened to coincide with that of a revalorization of the urban historical patrimony and a radical questioning of modernist urban planning. Urban typologies and their relationship to collective memory began to be systematically investigated: Aldo Rossi's ideas and the publication of his *L'architettura della città* [1966; English translation 1982] constituted an influential breakthrough in this respect. To Rossi, the city no longer offered a blank slate for the sanitized utopia of modernism, but a place which derived its meaning from its historical riches and typological patterns. It formed a giant man-made house, whose potentialities had to be optimized by architects. In the wake of Rossi, European cities saw the emergence of a movement like *Réconstruction de la ville* (with Léon Krier and Maurice Culot as most important exponents) as well as a growing appreciation of neotraditional architecture and urbanism (Prince Charles's notorious public interventions). The redevelopment of deserted industrial areas was often accompanied by gentrification campaigns. The outcome of such gentrification processes has been a bone of contention. While some would emphasize the undeniable contribution made towards the revitalization of city centers, others point to the concomitant displacement of lower-income residents and small-scale businesses. What gentrification has certainly *not* done, according to Neil Smith, is to solve any of the urban problems like crime and homelessness, since these problems were only exported to other neighborhoods. From Smith's critical perspective, indeed, the phenomenon amounts to little more than a greed-inspired attack by politicians and realtors against a mix of local minorities, lower classes, and homeless persons. The main result has been the transformation of the contemporary city into a "revanchist city" [1996b], finding its expression, once again, in those growing trends towards privatization and militarization already described.

Cities, finally, have also come to cultivate artificial and idealized images of themselves by promoting variants of the so-called New Urbanism and other types of neotraditional urbanism. Resembling the designs typical of the followers of *Réconstruction de la ville*, proposals of this type hark back to images of a preindustrial city, in which the dissonances and conflicts of a modern metropolis are papered over. The protagonists of this movement are Peter Calthorpe in Berkeley, who caused a great stir with his manifesto *The Next American Metropolis: Ecology, Community and the American Dream* [1993], and the architectural couple Andres Duany and Elizabeth Plater-Zyberk in Miami, who derive their reputation especially from the development Seaside built in 1981 in Florida. In New Urbanist designs, architectural models are inspired by a small-town philosophy, and attempts are made at rebuilding community life through urban design. According to Kelly Shannon, these recent developments have captured the popular American imagination, providing "a physical realization of the unrequited love for the aesthetics of the European past, of the poetics of small-town life, of the virtues of self-styled sustainable communities and of the common-sense emphasis of the pedestrian over the automobile" [1998:9]. For New Urbanists, monofunctional zoning should be avoided and open spaces deemed an integral part of residential areas. In practice, however, the critical potentialities of the movement are overshadowed by its neotraditional aesthetics and Traditional Neighborhood Developments (or TND's) consist especially of private residences for a privileged minority. "New urbanism," argues Shannon, "is nothing more than a shroud for enclaves of middle-class homeowners, under which everyday reality is buried in an enchanting transformation of town and landscape. It is a dangerous experiment in social engineering, creating homogeneous settlements with mindless controls and vigilante enforcement of the image of community. Most projects exclude low-income families by not including affordable housing in the mix" [ibid.:17]. In this sense, then, the movement is neither new nor urban. It merely offers to reformulate the dominant notion of suburbia: instead of focusing solely on a residential function, "masterplanned communities" offer a diversity in functions and land use. This diversity, however, is rigorously channeled through the prescriptions devised by Homeowner Associations (HOA's). As a result, Traditional Neighborhood Developments often pose the same problems as gated communities:

they only foster communities that do not seek to connect with external social groups or society at large. They tend towards a homogenization of the population, so that the community-building intentions of neotraditional urban planners may be seen as one more factor that has factually served to enhance the social and spatial fragmentation of the contemporary city.

*Developed by Bart Eeckhout and Steven Jacobs*

# Chapter Three: Self

# Introduction



If the overall sociological trend in Western metropolises and urbanized societies is a trend towards individualization, it follows that the so-called self (or "the individual" or "the I," as non-English languages often prefer to call it) automatically becomes more elementary as a unit of perception and experience. And if those metropolises and urbanized societies have in the past decades become socially more diversified, it also follows that the kinds of selves they have come to foster or accommodate will of necessity be more multiple and plural. This evolution is not a matter, however, of quantum leaps or of abrupt discontinuities, but rather of slow-grinding, non-linear, sometimes even contradictory, processes. Many of today's leading cultural sociologists have explicitly observed how the contemporary "urban self" amounts at most to a radicalization of — not a qualitative shift away from — previous "urban selves." Implicitly, this point of view also underlies a lot of the historical work on the city currently being done in the humanities. For most of this work, especially in the fields of literary historiography and art criticism, keeps harking back to the modern(ist) city — to such emblematic metropolises as Paris, Berlin, London, Vienna, Chicago, and New York, in the era of their most conspicuous expansion, transformation, and cultural influence: from roughly the middle of the nineteenth century through the interbellum. Similar literary-critical or art-historical studies with respect to the postwar metropolis of the second half of this century are notably rarer and for several specific themes even altogether absent. This paucity of studies that are up to the moment is partly explicable by the fact that historical work on the earlier modern(ist) city is often built on the premiss that a strong continuity exists between experiences of the modern and of the postmodern metropolis. Scholars like Mike Featherstone [1991: 66] and David Harvey [1989a] have in fact insisted on such continuity between theories of modern and postmodern urban experience.

Studies of the urban self developed above all in the tradition of urban sociology (Georg Simmel, Max Weber, Louis Wirth) and (German) cultural theory (Karl Lamprecht, Oswald Spengler, Walter Benjamin). It is in the works of the latter that we first find studies which, in the wake of artists like Baudelaire or romantic thinkers like Rousseau and Herder, link psychological phenomena to the "modern condition." Simmel's and Wirth's seminal essays situate these phenomena in a wider sociological context. Their essays are not only analyses of the social structure of cities, but also attempts at discovering invariants within the lifestyles of individuals. Thus, in 1938 Wirth explicitly announced:

*Urbanization no longer denotes merely the process by which persons are attracted to a place called the city and incorporated into its system of life. It refers also to that cumulative accentuation of the characteristics distinctive of the mode of life which is associated with the growth of cities, and finally to the changes in the direction of modes of life recognized as urban which are apparent among people, wherever they may be, who have come under the spell of the influences which the city exerts by virtue of the power of its institutions and personalities operating through the means of communication and transportation* [1938: 146].

The importance of this claim resides above all in the fact that urbanism is uncoupled from numerically strong and densely populated geographical units. The space in which urbanism becomes a way of life already with Wirth transcends those areas on the map that carry the name of "city," which means that his theory already foreshadows the relative dissociation between urban locale and urban way of life that has come to characterize the latter half of the century.

Artists and cultural theoreticians make frequent use of the argumentative patterns that were introduced by philosophers, historians, and sociologists with an interest in cultural theory. To this very day, the themes of hyperstimulation, phantasmagoria, alienation, and the decentered subject dominate the artistic and theoretical agenda. Often, however, these topics go on to lead a life of their own and serve to underwrite a monocausal reasoning in which the urban environment is presented as the principal determining force behind individual experience.[23] Not seldom does this result in normative culture-pessimistic claims that do not automatically square with those of the initiators of the discourses on which it rests. There is, however, also a second tradition of analysis, which is especially pursued by cultural sociologists and a number of urban theorists. In this tradition, we are dealing with a line of thought that frames the urban environment by means of a wider culture-sociological theory.

In what follows, we will start by delineating some of the major influential

23 This approach is particularly *en vogue* with authors who try to understand urban experience on the basis of (certain ideas in) Simmel, Benjamin, and the Chicago School of Sociology (Wirth et al.). In literary criticism in particular, the influence of such theorists is outspoken. Theoretical analyses of the city are used to approach literature through the history of ideas and thus to trace the urban condition in literary works. Obvious examples of this method are to be found in Sibley-Fries 1980, Jaye and Watts 1981, Freisfeld 1982, Anz 1982, Isernhagen 1983, Versluys 1987, Hauser 1990, Dethier and Guiheux 1994, and Lehan 1998.

24 This interest also extends to the arts and to popular culture: especially in the past two decades, a conspicuous interest in the human body has manifested itself, leading to spectacular forms of celebration as well as mutilation. In the iconography of advertisements and video clips the spectator-consumer is constantly being convinced of the elastic powers of the naked body, while that same body, through dietary strategies, plastic surgery, fitness, branding, tattooing, and piercing, has come to be presented as a do-it-yourself kit. At the same time, the impressive progress made in the fields of artificial intelligence and genetic technology, together with the specter of AIDS, have proclaimed the body an almost primitive and archaic substance that appears to be threatened on all sides.

ideas that have governed thinking about the self in the twentieth-century metropolis. In a second section, we will develop a number of contemporary variations on the ideas inherited from modernist students of the metropolis, taking as our central theme for this the place of the human body in metropolitan space. As contemporary sociologist David Chaney points out, the mode of deportment of the body in Western societies today, and especially in metropolitan environments, has increasingly assumed normative significance as an exemplification of particular modes of selfhood. The topics of self and body, two of the most prominent issues in contemporary social theory, have come to be highly interdependent [Chaney 1996:117]. Today's increased emphasis on hedonistic ideals is in fact the natural corollary of an urban condition whose evolution has been characterized by a growing individualism, a growing secularization, and expanding material and medical possibilities for enhancing personal physical comfort and health. In response to this evolution, postmodern theoreticians have understandably developed an interest in questions on the "construction" of the human body: the more open a society is and the weaker its communal bonds have become, "the more important it is to individual identity to guard the boundaries of the personal body" [ibid.:118].[24] The theme of the body and of physical experience thus runs like a leitmotiv through contemporary variations on classical urban theory, shaping recent views of the nature of hyperstimulation, phantasmagoria, alienation, and the decentered subject.

In a third section, finally, we gather materials that revolve around questions of symbolization. They are the kinds of questions that underlie the emergence of a semiotic matrix in urban studies and that have led to the widespread notion that life in today's metropolitan environment is steeped in codes and signs. These codes and signs, which find their most radical, in-your-face expression in the realm of advertising, have become a predominant aspect of a mediatized society overall. They are also intimately connected to the development of lifestyles, a phenomenon that in its equally widespread impact has come to offer a crucial concept for understanding postmodernity and its diversification of self-identifications. To conclude, we will also look at what has happened in postwar years to the most basic human tool for symbolizing the urban condition: language itself, more particularly the ways in which language may be seen to reflect, and respond to, evolutions in the changing morphological and sociological conditions of life in the contemporary metropolis.

**Perceiving and Consuming the City: Hyperstimulation and Phantasmagoria** In the course of the twentieth century, several theories have been developed in which changed conditions of perception are grounded in the physical characteristics of the big city. The city produces stimuli that are supposed to affect the urban population in direct and lasting ways, giving rise to attitudes considered typical of urbanites. In most culture-theoretical studies, reference is made to Georg Simmel's insights in this respect (sometimes as popularized by Louis Wirth) and at times to the empirical evidence adduced by Stanley Milgram. To their names should be added those of Karl Lamprecht (completely forgotten by now) and Walter Benjamin (quoted everywhere), who have played an equally great role in providing ideas for the study of urban experience. Although the phenomena discussed in this context often belong to the more general order of modernity and of "the modern," reference is constantly made to the modern metropolis. To theoreticians like Simmel, the metropolis indeed functioned as a sociological dynamo: already by its size, if by nothing else, it causes certain sociological and psychological phenomena. Urban experience in this intellectual tradition is thus mostly discussed in aesthetic terms (in the etymological sense of the Greek "aisthanomai": to feel, to sense, to perceive) and focuses on the emergence of a "new perception." Certain facets of the city environment are held to influence the perception of urbanites. This has consequences in the first place for the psychological condition of those urbanites. Although current theorists are no longer convinced of the validity and empirical verifiability of environmental-determinist arguments, we should note that especially in the first half of the twentieth century, life in the big city tended to be linked to a culture of stimulation, even a culture of irritability.[25] Urban culture has been called the symbol of modernity by many cultural historians and it functions as an important explanatory factor for historical caesuras in art history. In *The Social History of Art*, for instance, Arnold Hauser posits that the caesura of impressionism is intimately tied with the new urban *aisthesis*:

*Modern technology ... introduces an unprecedented dynamism in the whole attitude to life and it is above all this new feeling of speed and change that finds expression in impressionism. The most striking phenomenon connected with the progress of technology*

25 The German concept of a "Kultur der Reizbarkeit" cannot be adequately translated into English, since it ambiguously hovers between the neutral sense of "culture of susceptibility to stimuli" and the more social-pathological sense of "culture of irritability." In what follows we will opt for the usual shorthand phrase "culture of stimulation."

26 For more on Lamprecht's work, see Hübner-Funk 1976, Müller 1987, 1988, 1990, and Chickering 1993.

*is the development of cultural centres into large cities in the modern sense; these form the soil in which the new art is rooted. Impressionism is an urban art, and not only because it discovers the landscape quality of the city and brings painting back from the country into the town, but because it sees the world through the eyes of the townsman and reacts to external impressions with the overstrained nerves of modern technical man. It is an urban style, because it describes the changeability, the nervous rhythm, the sudden, sharp but always ephemeral impressions of city life. And precisely as such, it implies an enormous expansion of sensual perception, a new sharpening of sensibility, a new irritability, and, with the Gothic and romanticism, it signifies one of the most important turning points in the history of Western art* [1951: 168].

The work of the Leipzig historian Karl Lamprecht (1856-1915), which may well have been the common source of inspiration for both Georg Simmel and Walter Benjamin, can be considered one of the most obvious applications of an environmental-determinist hypothesis to modern experience. Lamprecht's successful studies of German history (more particularly of his own era) focus strongly on a new structure of perception in modernity. According to Lamprecht, a susceptibility to stimulation ("Reizbarkeit") constitutes the basic feature of the metropolitan way of life imported from America. In his series on German history from 1902, he calls the city "the sounding board of the culture of stimulation."[26] Lamprecht's work systematizes a then-current diagnosis, namely that the urban culture of stimulation is symptomatic of a new structure of perception. The central core of this perception involves a changed temporal consciousness — the consciousness of speed and uncontrollable metamorphosis. The stimuli that are foisted upon the individual urbanite in traffic or on the sidewalk, in the constant motion of shopping streets, arcades, boulevards, or warehouses, in the process of operating technical instruments and machines, in taking in the media, in the permutations of streetscapes ("prosperous" cities being characterized by a great number of construction sites) — all of these cumulatively pose a challenge that is unprecedented in Western cultural history. Serving as a symbol and the most outspoken emanation of this cultural condition is the modern metropolis.

In the course of recent cultural history, says Lamprecht, we may observe a rise in the intensity of human psychic life. This is caused by an increase in external stimuli — not the least of which are those typical of urban life. Thus Lamprecht writes: "The modern life is extraordinarily unaesthetic to the extent that it leads to continuous disturbances of mental concentration. The endless rushing, the whistle of locomotives, the jingling of streetcars, the constant flooding with mail, the aggressive information by newspapers, the rising number of personal physical contacts that comes with the increased lightness of personal interaction

— this and a lot more triggers off the wish to escape the servitude of the moment" [quoted in Hübner-Funk 1976: 48; editors' translation]. This idea can be found in a more nuanced form with Simmel and Benjamin, but it is especially in its more vulgarly reductive form that it has continued to exert considerable power, all the way from Oswald Spengler's 1923 *Der Untergang des Abendlandes* to this very day. For throughout the twentieth century, a remarkably great consensus can be said to exist, especially among the producers of art and among non-sociological students of the city, concerning the existence and influence of an urban culture of stimulation.

Probably the best-known source for such environmental-determinist perspectives is to be found, however, in Georg Simmel's "The Metropolis and Mental Life" ("Die Großstädte und das Geistesleben"; 1903). The opening thesis of this famous essay on the urban condition posits that individuals are under pressure from leveling objective forces that threaten to suffocate them. One of the arguments developed to flesh out and shore up this thesis is that the urban condition brings about a thorough transformation of individual experience. Although Simmel's concern is primarily with the objectifying as well as liberating influences which the modern "money economy" has on the social relations and personality traits of urbanites, he also, at a secondary level, situates the modern life of the senses against the excess of shocking and hyperstimulating impressions supposedly typical of urban experience. The urban way of life resulting from this intensification of nervous stimulation, according to him, is characterized by two experiential modes: distance and stress (or autonomy and threat). Simmel understands urban individuals in part on psychological grounds. "The psychological foundation," he writes, "is the intensification of emotional life due to the swift and continuous shift of external and internal stimuli" [1903:325]. The stimuli of streetlife and the manifoldness of social, economic, and professional life in the city create conditions that strongly diverge from life in a small town or in the country, "with the slower, more habitual, more smoothly flowing rhythm" of its "sensory-mental" life [ibid.]. The biological cause of increased sensory pressure for the urban dweller lies in the fact that the human mind functions through an ability to observe differences: the quality of a sensory impulse (both an "internal" and an "external" one) derives its meaning from the difference it makes with the previous impulse. When differences become less regular (i.e. swerve from steady habits) and less predictable (in terms of their outcome) and when, in addition, the several impressions within one visual field stand in marked contrast to each other, or the pace of impressions is speeded up, human consciousness feels

27 This issue of urban theatricality is further developed by Kristiaan Versluys in his case study on fictional representations of New York (Part II).

compelled to summon a higher degree of alertness. The supposed result is urban stress [ibid.].

What is remarkable about Simmel's essay is not so much the cultural diagnosis and its affinities with that of Lamprecht as the implications that are attached to that diagnosis. The urbanite, in order to ensure his psychical wellbeing, puts into effect a "Reizschutz" mechanism — a defense mechanism against stimulation. This defense mechanism is a strategy devised by human consciousness for reducing the redundancy of stimuli to a bare minimum. To this end, the powers of reason are activated, in particular the power of abstraction that is also homologous with the rationality of a monetary economy [ibid.: 325-26]. Simmel talks of the "calculating" reason that slides like a "protective organ" between impression and perception — an idea that was ostensibly taken up by Louis Wirth and the Chicago School. The individual thus acquires certain sociological schemata that Simmel calls "reserve" or the famous "blasé" attitude [ibid.: 329-31]. The jadedness of urbanites in particular is one of their most important personality traits. It involves an attitude whereby the emotional response to stimuli is continually being avoided, so that "indifference" and "a slight aversion" take the upperhand. It is on the basis of a similar observation that Erving Goffman in the 1950s and 60s conceived his equally influential theory of the theatricality of everyday life: to be able to keep up at least some relationship to the urban stranger, the individual chooses to play certain roles.[27]

A final strong influence on environmental-determinist perspectives is that of the cultural philosopher Walter Benjamin. More even than Simmel and certainly Lamprecht, Benjamin is today constantly quoted to characterize the urban experience [see Steinfeld and Suhr 1990: 176-79]. And he, too, appears to favor an analysis in terms of a "new structure of perception." In his essay on "The Work of Art in the Age of Mechanical Reproduction" ("Das Kunstwerk im Zeitalter seiner technischen Reproducierbarkeit"; 1935), he for instance claims that sense impressions are historically relative and subject to change in response to collective existential conditions. The metropolis, according to Benjamin, is a cultural constellation in which, through the confrontation with anonymous crowds and motorized traffic, the "shock experience has become the norm" [Benjamin 1939: 614; editors' translation]. As a consequence, defensive modes of individualization arise. "Content," "thought," and "experience" (in the German sense of "Erfahrung," associated with the acquisition of insight, wisdom, and memory) are being repressed from the psychic economy because the perceptual information-processing system is too busy registering merely superficial "experiences" (in the sense of "Erlebnisse," which points to more ephemeral adventures and occurrences).

But besides shocks that are experienced as threatening by the urbanite, Benjamin also talks of consumptive shock experiences. Especially his concept of "phantasmagoria," which has become inordinately influential in literary-critical and cultural studies of the past decades, is of importance in this respect. It is a concept tailored to grasping broad cultural changes as a transformation of the structure of perception triggered off by external stimuli from technology, consumption, and architecture. The link with the city, as Susan Buck-Morss points out, is all too obvious: "One could say that the dynamics of capitalist industrialism had caused a curious reversal in which 'reality' and 'art' switched places. Reality becomes artificial, a phantasmagoria of commodities and architectural construction made possible by the new industrial processes. The modern city was nothing but the proliferation of such objects, the density of which created an artificial landscape of buildings and consumer items as totally encompassing as the earlier, natural one. In fact for children (like Benjamin) born into an urban environment, they appeared to be nature itself" [Buck-Morss 1984: 213]. In "Paris, Capital of the 19th Century" ("Paris. Hauptstadt des XIX. Jahrhunderts"; 1935b), the synoptic text Walter Benjamin offered to the *Zeitschrift für Sozialforschung* to present his grandly conceived study of the "arcades," Benjamin even notes that the phenomenon of phantasmagoria demanded his exclusive attention.

The Benjaminian phantasmagoria is essentially a highly common, everyday phenomenon, not to be confused with psychoanalytic theories (about phantasms) or the traditional ideological notion of false consciousness. The term denotes rather the sentimentally connoted images that people associate with fairs, parades, crowded shopping areas, Christmas lights in the streets, strolling people in the park on a sunny summer's day, spectacular architectural constructions, and so forth. Benjamin defines phantasmagoria as affectively loaded images ("Wunschbilder") that live in the collective conscious of a society. In the 19th century, he argues, those images are above all of a material kind. The 19th-century citizen is especially fascinated by the countless economic and technological novelties springing up in the cultural environment: Benjamin discusses the rise of luxury goods, of interior design, the spectacle of panoramas, new building-

28 In Baudelaire's case, the flaneur is not simply conflatable with the idea of a "man in the crowd." Motivated by a strong drive for distinction, Baudelaire as a cultivated flaneur opposes the middle-class habitus. He replaces middle-class strolling by the image of a lonely flaneur, one who reads allegorically, who recognizes his own isolation in images of alienation which he isolates from the global image of the crowd.

29 For the relationship between flaneur and detective in the age of Baudelaire, see Benjamin 1982: 552-55. Baudelaire transforms popular stories by building on Edgar Allan Poe. In Poe's writings, we come across the stereotypical patterns of detective stories, but without these being used to sublimate unrest and threat: "Fear, repugnance, and horror seized those who were the first to look upon the metropolitan masses. With Poe those masses had something barbaric" [Benjamin 1939: 629; editors' translation]. For that reason, Benjamin argues, Poe's walker should not be called a flaneur, since the bourgeois flaneur does not suffer from the city; he is only absorbed by a consumerist aestheticism [ibid.: 627].

types like the big department store and the shopping arcade, the nightlife on Parisian boulevards, and the invention of the photograph. Such novelties are reviewed and celebrated by fashion magazines of the time and they are copiously simulated at the first world exhibitions (two phenomena about which Benjamin's study of the arcades also talks). The objects producing a phantasmagoric effect are very diverse, yet they all have one characteristic in common: the "kick" of the new — fashion being a 19th-century invention, after all, whose outsize influence a century later has only been due to a globalizing and mediatized expansion in mass marketing. The shocks of innovation, Benjamin demonstrates, are connected by the 19th-century citizen to a euphoric emotion. The bourgeoisie translates its pleasure into a "practical conviction" cultivated in the form of a historical optimism — the dream of progress, increasing prosperity, and unlimited expansion.

In the first place, Benjamin's notion of phantasmagoria informs an analysis of the *popular culture* in the age of Baudelaire; in that respect, it anticipates the "cultural studies" and so-called "Trivialliteraturforschung" (the study of trivial literature) in the second half of the 20th century. What should be noted about it, however, is that Benjamin (more particularly in his first study of Baudelaire) links the altered structure of perception to certain social carriers. His hypotheses may therefore be tied, in accordance with the more recent sociological theories of Pierre Bourdieu, to the idea of a new middle-class habitus. A habitus — a unit of durable and educationally transmitted dispositions for behaving and processing information — does not only show itself in the pronouncements of a cultural group, but also in that group's behavior and in the observations (images) the group deems relevant. A number of phantasmagorias in that sense are striking:

**1** The first phantasmagoria mentioned by Benjamin is the object of popular writings for the middle class — the only "popular" class then that was also literate. The urban observer in these popular stories is called in a general (and un-Baudelairean) sense a flaneur.[28] He is the "botanist of the asphalt" [1938: 538; editors' translation] who walks through the city while analyzing it. He turns the street into an interior. Dana Brand has elaborated upon this phenomenon and emphasized how the literature of the flaneur is governed, especially in its depiction of cities, by a "consumer's aestheticism" [Brand 1991: 187].

**2** The second phantasmagoric operation of the imagination, too, is related to popular literature, more specifically to the genre of the detective story. Probably based on his reading of Roger Caillois, Benjamin pays special attention to portraits of unrest, in particular the sort of unrest supposedly caused by crowds on the street [Benjamin 1938: 542]. In a way, these portraits also try to tranquilize that unrest by introducing a courageous detective who is able to tame the urban jungle.[29]

**3** The third phantasmagoria equally concerns the function of the masses in a capitalist metropolis. The metropolitan crowd opens up the way for a hedonistic life in anonymity, offering the bourgeoisie and the older hegemonic classes — but not the lower classes — the possibility to lead a life in which social control falls away and modern *anomie* becomes a positive characteristic. The urban middle class cherishes the illusion that nightlife entertainment and consumptive patterns in magically enchanting shopping streets are evidence of a society in which individuals are equal and free citizens.

Of special importance to *literary* studies is the rise of artistic defense strategies in response to middle-class phantasmagoria and popular *flânerie*. The veil of the masses (i.e. of the middle classes) deeply influences the observation of 19th-century literary writers. Not only because those writers surrender to the phantasmagoria of the middle classes but especially because they develop a typically aestheticist reaction pattern. A form of "artistic" *flânerie* is born. The flaneur (historically always a "he") derives his identity — not unlike Simmel's jaded personality — from perceptual defense mechanisms. In Benjamin's eyes, however, this does not turn him into a perversion of authentic individuality: the artistic flaneur is an aesthetic agent who reacts with aesthetic means to the city. The cultural drive for distinction by which a cultivated possessor of taste like Baudelaire is motivated (as in his *Le Peintre de la vie moderne* of 1863) plays a large role in this. Baudelaire argues that the average citizen looks for fortuitous pleasures during his strolls, while the painter Constantin Guys in his "noctambulism" sets himself a higher aim: to distill the permanent from the ephemeral. This higher aim is also injected in the French poet's pivotal literary texts. To Baudelaire, the "correspondences" he is out to detect are lasting values; visual impressions are only transient.[30]

Reactions by artistic observers may take either of two forms: euphoria or dysphoria. Dysphoric connotations are especially to be found in symbolistically inspired literature, more specifically in the theme of spleen. This theme continues to play a major role in views of the metropolis taken by late-twentieth-century writers. Time and again, fiction writers offer or imply arguments along pessimistic environmental-determinist lines.[31] This is not only the case for mainstream literature but also holds true for much hardboiled detective fiction, which continues to build on dysphoric schemes. Alongside dysphoric reactions to the

30 In early-20th-century avantgarde movements, we can notice how this distinction drive diminishes. The surrealistic flaneur does not have to find any correspondences; he can limit himself to the ecstatic observation of everyday reality. As a result, a *rapprochement* with popular culture and the practice of the average urban walker is effectuated.

31 For an overview of postwar urban fiction in which this traditional determinism receives ample attention, see the case study by Bart Keunen (Part II).

city, however, the euphoric connotations of artistic *flânerie* also gain visibility in the course of the 19th and especially 20th centuries. According to Lothar Müller, the urban culture of stimulation even developed into the object of a veritable urban cult: "The explanation of 'nervousness' was generally not identical with its diagnosis as a symptom of cultural decadence. Of considerable influence was the thesis that it was a phenomenon of the transition to a higher level of civilization, the inevitable accompanying effect of the rise of a new type of health, of the evolution of the physiological constitution of modern man" [1990: 50; editors' translation; also Müller 1987 and 1988]. In developing those positive connotations, moreover, the artistic flaneur has over the years come closer to the culture of popular flaneurs. The Benjaminian phantasmagoria has thus become itself an element of artistic *flânerie*.

**Feeling the City: Urban Alienation and the Decentered Subject** The experiential quality attributed to city life by Lamprecht, Simmel, and Benjamin has to do with aesthetic experiences in the widest and etymological sense of the word. Although urban experience (as in the phantasmagoria of everyday life) is sometimes called euphoric, most classical authors and their disciples tend to zoom in on the negative effects of city life. Those negative effects are also preponderant in the theories and empirical case studies of the Chicago School of Sociology, where they are viewed from a more strictly sociological perspective. In adapting many of Simmel's ideas to an American context and academic language, Louis Wirth simultaneously tilted the balance in a more negative direction. For Wirth paid less attention to the liberating character of life in the metropolis. Crime, marginal behavior, and other factors that undermine traditional community building generally took precedence with him and his colleagues. These factors were considered social symptoms that are at the basis of experiences of alienation. The urbanite wrestles with a structural "disorganization" that undermines his individuality. In Wirth's opinion, the heterogeneity of the urban social structure (the diverse specialized functions to which individuals have to submit) leads above all to an enhanced competition between individuals and to an estrangement from their proper "identities" [Wirth 1938: 152-53, 156-58]. "Whereas the individual gains, on the one hand, a certain degree of emancipation or freedom from the personal and emotional controls of intimate groups, he loses, on the other hand, the spontaneous self-expression, the morale, and the sense of participation that comes with living in an integrated society. This constitutes essentially the state of *anomie*, or the social void, to which Durkheim alludes in attempting to account for the various forms of social disorganization in technological society" [ibid.: 153].

As this quotation also illustrates, the attention to competition in the writings of the Chicago School issue more from the idea of anomie as conceived by Durkheim than from the Simmelian idea of value-indifference. To most theorists and empiricists of the Chicago School, the urban milieu is an environment in which, as a result of the many changes that are part of everyday life, anomic attitudes flourish. Building on Wirth's thesis, for example, Claude Fischer notes a relationship between anomie or alienation and the urban way of life: "the more urban (larger) a person's community of residence, ... the greater his sense of social isolation (or anomie)" [1973:312]. In his own urban investigations, Fischer has tried to corroborate Simmel's and Wirth's phenotypical analyses by means of empirical evidence.

In the tradition of Wirth, a rich tropology arose in which time and again the city is being represented as a labyrinth or jungle.[32] Such images usually hide a theory seeking to explain individual behavior on the basis of a struggle for life. The urban individual has to cope with, among many other things, high rents and the inescapable intra-urban migration resulting from these, pollution due to the proximity of traffic infrastructure and industrial areas, the threat of economic recessions and unemployment, and so on. Factors like these turn the city into a jungle not only to immediate victims but also to those privileged groups who find themselves indirectly coping with detrimental effects (like crime, sundry forms of violence, anomic behavior at a sexual level, racist slurs, etc.). Under such circumstances, communities can only be built in the form of enclaves that manage, for the time being, to escape the effects of the metropolis.

Especially in literary studies, the diagnosis of alienation often takes pride of place.[33] "The realistic city of early 19th-century novels," writes Diane Levy,

*functioned either as a backdrop or an objective test to be passed or failed by the protagonist. It was presented in highly symbolic terms of success or failure. The city gradually became more autonomous. It was viewed more as man's creator than as his creation. It controlled his life; it generated his realities and stimulated his unconscious fears and fantasies. Even in naturalistic novels, however, where the city was a formative agent, its influence was presented in terms of metaphor and contained a moral judgement* [1978:73].

32 Cities have been represented as jungles at least since the 18th century. Especially at times when social Darwinism was strong and laissez-faire capitalism high, the image of an urban jungle gained wide popularity [see, for instance, the success of Upton Sinclair's 1906 *The Jungle*, discussed in Allen 1993:36, and the discourse on "darkest London" discussed in Williams 1973]. But also in the postwar era, this image has continued to inform cultural and intellectual classics — from John Huston's 1950s movie *The Asphalt Jungle* to a classic of 1970s urban studies, Sam Bass Warner Jr.'s *The Urban Wilderness*. Contemporary fiction writers like Paul Auster, moreover (in *The New York Trilogy* or *In the Country of Last Things*), to this day like to represent the big city as a jungle and/or labyrinth.

33 For a cinematographic example, see the analysis of the late-modernist Italian film director Michelangelo Antonioni by Steven Jacobs (Part II).

34 For a theoretically inflected analysis of the complexities of street-level heterogeneity, see the case study by Trui Vetters (Part II).

In a great many studies on avantgarde literature, metaphors of chaos and the technique of montage in urban representations are interpreted psychologically, as the symbolic expressions of a sense of alienation [see, for instance, Meixner and Vietta 1982]. Such metaphors and literary techniques supposedly highlight the urbanite's isolation and would thus critique social atomization in a capitalist culture. "The city is a highly developed form of social organization on a large scale; it is inescapably a community, however defined. Yet during the nineteenth century the literary city came more and more to express the isolation or exclusion of the individual from a community, and in the twentieth century to express the fragmentation of the very concept of community" [Pike 1981:XII].

In more recent studies on the city, more particularly works dealing with "metropolitan experience" in popular culture and leisure culture [e.g. de Certeau 1984, Chambers 1986, Featherstone 1991, Laermans 1997], but also in discourses on multiculturalism, the heterogeneity of the urban population is frequently viewed as a reservoir of unexplored experiences and a possibility for combining social affiliations and lifestyles. Heterogeneity on the whole fosters multidimensionality, which contrasts with the onedimensionality (based on attributed status) of rural types of social life. Not the city itself, in other words, but the identity formation stimulated and enhanced by an urban environment forms the most crucial aspect of the social condition faced by the postmodern urbanite.[34] This identity formation only turns into a problem when it becomes a matter of "identity compulsion."

In contemporary theories, then, room is often made for a more appreciative view of urban experience. The city, it appears, also extends solutions to the problem of sensory overload and alienation — solutions that move in the direction of Simmel's starting point in "The Metropolis" about the enhancement of individual liberty. As indicated in the previous chapter on "Community," the new urban condition is more and more discusssed in terms of what the German sociologist Ulrich Beck has called an individualization process [1992:87-90]. This process points to the diminishing power of traditional norms and values and to the possibilities it offers for gaining individual freedom of choice with regard to selecting one's lifestyle (fashion, cultural tastes, consumption patterns) and one's personal ambitions and aims. It is no longer ideological organizations (like political parties and religious institutions) or social control (by neighbors and the family) that are all-important in the choice of a particular lifestyle, but rather the momentary and arbitrary preferences and predilections of the individual. Judgments on what qualifies as beautiful or ugly, good or bad, and true or false become to a certain extent a matter of personal volition [Laermans 1992:65]. This view of individualization throws a different light on some aspects of the contemporary urban self.

The urban environment, it might be argued, should not be seen as leading to symptoms of alienation alone. Anomic behavior should not be simply equated with anarchic or disruptive behavior; it may also be interpreted as an active escape route or a form of selective escapism. Likewise, personality traits that accompany a defensive isolation or a selective form of alienation do not need to be interpreted simply as irrational affects. The emblem of postmodernity is rather a contemporary variant on the 19th-century aesthete: P.R. boys and girls, advertising agents, and readers of lifestyle magazines are in some senses the flaneurs of this day and age. These are "the young 'de-centred subjects' who enjoy the experimentation and play with fashion and the stylization of life as they stroll through the 'no place' postmodern urban spaces" [Featherstone 1991:65]. And since these groups of postmodern aesthetes appear to be urban-based, we may call their perceptions somehow characteristic of a new urban experience. Not coincidentally, this new social class of contemporary metropolitan aesthetes is today often used to understand earlier environmental-determinist hypotheses about a new structure of perception [cf. Hebdige 1979, Chambers 1986]. Metropolitan subcultures such as the beat generation (an offshoot of the urban bebop culture), punk, new wave (Greil Marcus's *Lipstick Traces*), graffiti artists, and hiphop are usually linked to notions of an aesthetic urban euphoria.

Another example is that of individuals from groups that occupy a cultural or economic position of power (artists and managers, say), who frequently appear to escape the psychical disturbances and dysfunctions supposedly typical of urban life [Gebhardt 1988:295]. That identity compulsion is group-specific, furthermore, may also be inferred from the fact that Northern Europeans and members of the middle classes tend to experience the street as a transit zone (between the home on one hand and the work floor on the other), while Southern Europeans and the lower socioprofessional groups more often regard the street as an extension of their living rooms, as a "piazza" or area for play.[35]

For the dominant conception of psychical health, the ideal of heterogeneity that informs theories of the postmodern subject is synonymous with nurturing a tendentially schizoid personality, but to social psychologists of the "situationistic school," a mobile identity is the sign rather of a "new sanity." The philosophical anthropology on which scholars like Eike Gebhardt fall back is that of influential thinkers like Gilles Deleuze and Félix Guattari, or Georges Bataille.

## Displacing the City: Critical Remarks on the Urban Self and Its Social Conditions

The various hypotheses on urban experience gathered in the previous paragraphs

35 In the tendency among flaneurs to consider the street as a home, Walter Benjamin already detects the appearance of a popular "habitus": "Streets are the home of the collective" [1982:533; editors' translation].

have set the mental framework not only for literary writers, artists, and their respective critics, but often also in the fields of social geography, city planning, and even in certain architectural circles [Rapoport 1977: 2]. In several of these instances, however, they have acquired the status of *monocausal* hypotheses. Especially in theories that build on the classical pioneers of urban studies, aspects of individual experience are repeatedly conflated with the concept of "urbanism." In such cases, we might talk of a kind of environmental determinism. There is a certain legitimacy to this perspective or approach, yet more recent developments in urban theory indicate that a better understanding of the individual experiences of urbanites comes about only if we are willing to diversify explanatory factors. A strictly monocausal reasoning, moreover, threatens to get stuck in cultural diagnoses of a pessimistic sort. If we want to draw up a more nuanced image of urban experience, we need to consult more recent studies as well.

Monocausal reasonings are insofar understandable as there are indeed situations in which we may talk of forms of environmental determinism. As Winifred Gallagher in *The Power of Place* has demonstrated, human actions, emotions, and thoughts are not only shaped by genetic predisposition, neurochemistry, cultural history, and social relationships, but also by people's material surroundings. Although environmental sensitivity may differ greatly from individual to individual, the potential influence of ecological transformations on people is undeniable. The fact, for instance, that the industrial revolution massively drew people indoors — into homes and workplaces first and foremost, but also increasingly now into atriums, malls, and places of culture and leisure — has led some of today's scientists to "question the trade-offs we unwittingly make in order to live sealed up inside an artificially heated, cooled, and lighted world that is structured around economic rather than biologic concerns" [Gallagher 1993:13]. Sleep and mood problems are not simply caused by psychological conditions of stress or by the age-old influence of seasonal changes (affecting our biological need of light), but also by these daily built environments. The fact that urbanites live so strongly at odds with the natural world — "courtesy of electric light, air-conditioning, and central heating" [ibid.: 41] — is being taken by scientists to potentially affect people's thoughts, feelings, and actions. Moreover, individuals generally living under the condition of reduced competence (the elderly, the young, and the sick, for example) can also be drastically affected by their physical surroundings. Since the adaptability of humans is extraordinarily high, environments do not determine people in any strict, unilinear, and absolutely necessary sense, but they do impose limitations that may be quite restrictive.

Overarousal in a metropolitan environment may thus be partly conducive to the phenomenon of "fried urban nerves," which should be understood against (the principle that "we all seek a comfortable level of arousal from our settings, one that is neither so low as to court boredom nor so high as to invite anxiety") [ibid.: 20]. Recent scientists have emphasized, however, that "rather than being dealt a single mighty blow of global overstimulation, we're nibbled at by a gaggle of separate stressors" [ibid.: 149]. And the worst stress is that which is "simultaneously unpleasant, intense, unpredictable, and uncontrollable" [ibid.: 152] — like a subway ride during rush hour. Several of today's developmental psychologists, moreover, believe that "the real environmental problem faced by inner-city kids is a chronic sensory overload that drains energy from their proper pursuits. Study after study shows that intensive background stimulation hinders development, and that kids' adaptation to it is ephemeral at best" [ibid.: 159].

Material environments, in short, do have a certain determining power. But their power has also frequently been overrated. The reaction to environmental-determinist ideas, especially from Marxist and sociological commentators, has been proportionately vehement. The most famous criticism was vented by (the then-Althusserian) Manuel Castells, who argued that physical context exerted an immeasurably smaller influence than the social and economic constellations in which experiences occur. Theories about "urban culture" are to him mythical constructs, since they fail to relate urban phenomena to concrete social groups and relationships. Instead, they set off from an abstract discourse about Man in general, more particularly about the urban individual: "'urban culture,' as it is being presented, is neither a concept nor a theory. It is, properly speaking, a myth, since it tells, ideologically, the history of the human species. As a result, the themes about 'urban society' that are directly based on this myth constitute the masterwords of an ideology of modernity which is assimilated, in ethnocentric fashion, to the social forms of liberal capitalism" [Castells 1972: 114; editors' translation].

What Castells in his critique of environmental determinism implicitly lambasted was the Romantic antitechnologism of Western culture since the 18th century. (He would subsequently extend this interest in technological phenomena in his later studies of the "informational city.") To draw up a sociological theory of urbanization, according to Castells, we should bring together the different aspects that have made up its discursive tradition. First of all, the city can be considered (as in discourses emphasizing ethicopolitical value judgments) after the model of precapitalist cities, so that urbanized space appears as a center of political, religious, or juridical power. Next, it is possible (as in rationalistic discourses on the city) to start from the process of industrialization, so that the city is depicted as the center of the industrial revolution and of the new economic relationships. Finally, it is also possible to take late-19th-century and especially 20th-century transformations in capitalism as a point of departure. Only in so-called "consumption societies" does the "urban way of life" acquire specific meaning. With the help of a thorough study of these shifting types of capitalism and their corresponding discourses on the city, it becomes clear that the city functions as a centralizing institution in three different ways. If we relate these three aspects to a global theory on social structures, and only thus, are we ultimately left with an epistemic object.

The problem with Marxist theories of the Castellian sort, however, is that they tend to deny the problem of experience altogether to concentrate only on macrosocial phenomena. As a result, further criticisms were heard that opted, against the Marxist analysis, for a microsocial approach. Scholars adduced research materials indicating that the urban problem of anomie could also be interpreted differently, namely as a form of behavior not born of a disgust for urbanization processes, but testifying rather to an endorsement of the fragmentation which the social landscape in a modern, rationalized society has undergone. Environmental-determinist theories usually go hand in hand with a condemnation of the present city as culturally and psychologically deficient. A scholar like the former Yale sociologist Eike Gebhardt, however, attributes this to a normative (culture-specific) definition of the concept of culture, as well as to a faulty anthropological starting point. As is the case with discussions about the concept of "nature," discussions on urban "sanity" or "health" are permeated with value-laden judgments. "Even today," she writes, "the fascinating thing about polemical writings about urban pathology is the often unabashed mixture of causes and effects ..., and the umbrella term 'social problems' was and quite often still is more decree than diagnosis" [1988: 280-81; editors' translation]. The supposedly anomic condition of cities is no anomalous condition but the breeding ground for new types of behavior:

*Not only does the urban experience teach people the everyday consolidation — the cognitive administration, so to speak — of complex impulses towards a personal orientation; in the process, apparently, also a cumulative competence arises, which works itself out in other aspects of living — among other ways, in an ability for quick changes in estimations and judgments, indeed even for a change of identity in varying situations.... What has its central importance as a strategy for survival is taken by social pathologists to be exactly an index of "identity diffusion," of anomie, of loss of orientation* [ibid.: 285; editors' translation].

In the modern metropolis, more than in any other space, social situations are produced in which the subject is given the opportunity to develop new interests and new activities. Often social groups devise new cognitive strategies that may appear to entail a relativism of values at first sight, but that simultaneously put up their own forms of resistance against the negative aspects of anomic social behavior [see ibid.: 289-90]. To Gebhardt, such strategies amount at most to a strategic anomie, because they ignore existing value-systems while at the same time distilling a new group ethos from precisely this act of "protest." In this context, Gebhardt points to the importance of a "quasi-biological need for new stimuli" that is being viewed by a growing number of cognitive psychologists and neurobiologists as an essential component of a person's psychical household [ibid.: 299]. She refers, for example, to the conclusions drawn by J. P. Zubek, who claims in *Sensory Deprivation* that sensory stimuli take up an important function in the workings of the human psyche: "It is often assumed that crowding has deleterious effects on human functioning, yet the positive influences of high density must also be considered. Humans have a need for stimulation and novelty, which if unsatisfied (understimulation), may result in anxiety, hallucinations, and impaired perceptual and cognitive functioning" [quoted in Gebhardt 1988: 288].[36]

The precursor of the Chicago School and mentor of Louis Wirth, Robert Park, already signaled the following underexposed aspect of the urban way of life: "The city is ... a state of mind, a body of customs and traditions and of the organized attitudes and sentiments that inhere in these customs and are transmitted with this tradition. The city is not, in other words, merely a physical mechanism and an artificial construction. It is involved in the vital processes of the people who compose it" [quoted in Langer 1984: 98-99]. Underlying this quotation is the opinion that, although the urban environment may form an important setting for certain activities by offering facilities and imposing obstacles, it is not therefore the generator of those activities. Cities, no matter how high-profile their visual and cultural images, are usually no more than the emanation of wider social evolutions and relationships. Owing to their high profile, they may be strongly identified with certain new experiences in terms of social roles and the experiences these foster. But this identification has a lot to do with the fact that the economic and professional activities taking place in cities are often also the most advanced activities. The "tertiary sector" or "service economy" that flourishes there quickly acquires an exemplary function at a time when so-called postindustrial activities

36 This debate is a complex one. As psychologist Frank Farley explains, we should also reckon with a wide range in possible human personalities, from the "thrill-seeking" personality ("Type-T"), who is "so highly engaged with risk, change, intensity, complexity, and novelty that the pursuit of those things is almost their hallmark" to the more "uptight" personality ("Type-t"), whose habits are all in the direction of "safety, predictability, moderation, simplicity, and familiarity" [quoted in Gallagher 1993: 162]. The first type of personality occurs much more frequently in big cities [ibid.: 165], where we find a preponderance of "particularly thrill-seeking extroverts hooked on lots of stimulation" who are especially "tolerant of high social density to the point of enjoying it" [ibid.: 184].

are held to be one of the most defining characteristics of socioeconomic postmodernity.

The interactionistic perspective on the urban way of life ties in closely with what was already explained in the chapter on "Community." For this perspective, too, Simmel's early intuitive genius may serve as an important source of inspiration. To Simmel, the metropolis was not a spatial entity with sociological consequences, but a sociological entity that is formed spatially; in his view, interaction fills in space. This proto-interactionistic perspective is just as evident in an essay like "The Stranger" [1908a] as it is in one like "The Web of Group Affiliations" [1908b]. In the latter essay, for instance, Simmel takes the potential wealth of activities (social, economic, sexual, artistic, recreative, religious, and political), the cornucopia of goods and enjoyments within the urban agglomeration, to be responsible for the transcendence of limits imposed by the "primary group" (the family nucleus). A comparison with medieval (i.e. feudal and premodern) "group affiliations" is instructive here. In relatively closed, rural communities, a concentric pattern reigns that is built around a central (attributed) status, whereas in an urban social environment a weblike pattern imposes itself — what Peter Langer has called the "weblike pattern of the market metropolis" [1984: 104]. Individuals there belong to multiple circles, which sometimes, but not always, overlap and in which they may occupy positions of entirely different rank and weight. These different circles provide the individual with a high number of possible activities, thereby proliferating the opportunities for individualization [see Simmel 1908b: 43]. Sociologists have come to study this expanded freedom empirically using the method of so-called network analysis. Thus, Paul Craven and Barry Wellmann have talked of a structure connecting the urban individual to several other social units and have consequently defined the city as a Network City [1973].

Because of the gradual falling away of a closed, hierarchical, and concentric pattern of social relationships, the city has often been described on the basis of privative concepts, yet some social scientists like Lyn Lofland have argued that we should rather see this evolution as an enrichment of living conditions: "The city dweller did not lose the capacity for knowing others personally. But he gained the capacity for knowing others only categorically. [He] did not lose the capacity for deep, long-lasting, multi-faceted relationships. But he gained the capacity for the surface, fleeting, restricted relationship" [quoted in Gebhardt 1988: 297]. Lofland's view is confirmed by the theory of Charles Kadushin on the formation of social circles in urban life [1966]. Central to this theory are the activities deployed by individuals in social circles. According to Kadushin, such circles disrupt traditional tribal and neighborhood relations. Proximity disappears as the primary socializing factor to be replaced by common interests; new circles are formed on the basis of intellectual and humanistic interests. Each individual thus occupies a place at the intersection of particular social circles and in so doing becomes a unique individual — an idea that was already at the heart of Simmel's essay on "The Web of Group Affiliations." Several scholars, among whom Claude Fischer [1984], the contributors to Moos and Bromet's *Human Context: Environmental Determinants of Behavior* [1976], and authors of psychosocial studies like Hollingshead and Redlich [1964: 239] have demonstrated that the supposed social ills and diseases commonly attributed to the city are in fact not demonstrably specific to city life. In this respect, the hypothesis that such ills and diseases are more likely related to a person's position in the social stratification carries considerably more explanatory power [Gebhardt 1988: 282].

# 2 Contemporary Variations on a Theme: The Bodily Experience of Urban Space

**Postmodern Forms of Arousal and Defense Strategies** In the latter half of the twentieth century, many of the preceding diagnoses are still regularly found with cultural sociologists. Especially the theory about urban defense strategies and analyses of phantasmagoria continue to be popular. Such theories and analyses often remain geared to the experiential world of the dense metropolitan core. After all, the overload of external stimuli described by Simmel continues to be considerably more characteristic of that traditional core than it is of life in suburbia or exurbia. The nexus of reserve, indifference, and jadedness likewise continues to be a potent aspect of urban defense strategies above all in traditional downtowns. In the 1960s, Jane Jacobs, in "The Uses of Sidewalks: Safety," formulated her own melioristic ideas of "eyes upon the street" and "neighborhood surveillance" precisely in response to the threat of metropolitan indifference. "Great cities," she wrote, "are not like towns, only larger. They are not like suburbs, only denser. They differ from towns and suburbs in basic ways, and one of these is that cities are, by definition, full of strangers. To any one person, strangers are far more common in cities than acquaintances.... The bedrock attribute of a successful city district is that a person must feel personally safe and secure on the street among all these strangers... there must be eyes upon the street, eyes belonging to those we might call the natural proprietors of the street" [1961:30, 35]. During the era in which Jacobs was writing, sociologist Erving Goffman became equally famous by foregrounding the "culture of inattention" that historically developed in the metropolis — a culture that by now has taken on the status of a journalistic, popular, and literary cliché. Especially novelists, working in the Romantic tradition of urban alienation, have developed a habit of inserting evocations of the metropolitan culture of inattention in their writings. But also in the popular imagination, such evocations have become a veritable topos, witness the ease with which they may be set to use by humorists. "New Yorkers," says for example humorist Calvin Trillin, "assume they've seen everything, so if a guy gets on the IRT express carrying a pot roast and dressed as Catherine of Aragon, they're not going to stare at him. 'What? You think we've never seen that before? You think we're farmers?'" [quoted in Weber 1997a: n.p.].

In *Flesh and Stone*, Richard Sennett has traced the genealogy of the process of social distancing in cities by pointing to a "fear of touching" that emerged with the creation of a Jewish ghetto in Renaissance Venice [1994: 212-51]. In so doing, he has uncovered the roots of an evolution that Pasi Falk in *The Consuming Body* has described as a wider societal shift in Western attitudes towards the body: "The very civilizing process that shifts the sensory emphasis from the contact senses to the distant senses creates a growing band of 'spectator activities' ... from the theatre to spectator sport and the cinema" [Falk 1994: 64]. Because of this growing emphasis on the spectatorial at the expense of physical contact, the urban culture of distancing has spread or trickled down beyond its traditionally urban locale. This relative uncoupling appears itself partly fostered by changes in metropolitan spatiality. For spatial disorganization constitutes, in the eyes of theoreticians like David Harvey and Fredric Jameson, the characteristic *par excellence* of postmodern experience. Through its many transformations, postmetropolitan space has produced new forms of arousal and corresponding defense mechanisms. The relative disempowerment of the tactile body thus appears to have been enhanced by the relative dissipation of the traditional metropolis. A diluted urban landscape, with its vastness and intermittent vacant spaces, can barely be experienced any longer in physical terms.[37] In the world of the technoburb, spatial distance has been further disconnected from tactility. To move about in a posturban environment may even run counter to the traditional logic of physical movement. The shortest distance between two points is often no longer that of the straight line: in the logic of freeways we first swerve to the right to wind up to the left of the road. As Reyner Banham in the early 1970s noted about the confusions of traffic in L.A.: "No human eye at windscreen level can unravel the complexities of even a relatively simple intersection (none of those in Los Angeles is a symmetrical cloverleaf) fast enough for a normal human brain moving forward at up to sixty mph to make the right decision in time, and there is no alternative to complete surrender to the instruction on the signs" [1971: 219].

The vaster the metropolitan environment becomes, and the more the structure of metropolitan space is determined by the infrastructure of roads, the more circulation itself is subjected to a proper spatial logic that counteracts the intuitive physical experience of space. In outlying metropolitan areas, even vulnerable pedestrians are forced to follow a track that is shaped by the course of uncrossable roads and freeways, prompting them to make endless detours in order to reach their destinations. Time instead of space determines distance, and the "annihilation of space through time" described by Harvey in *The Condition of Postmodernity* is

37 In the dystopian posturban vision of *Blade Runner* (the most analyzed cinematographic classic in postmodern urban studies), a desensualization of the body goes hand in hand with the material decomposition of postnuclear Los Angeles in the year 2019. In this film, every sense of place or of spatial unity is lost; with every move in this environment the spectator is flooded by images [see Boyer 1996: 109-19 and Webb 1996].

38 See also Jude Davies (Part II) for an analysis of the ideologies that may in turn inform the representation of cars in Hollywood movies.

nowhere as materially legible as in the new posturban environment. The "time-space compression" that Harvey deemed characteristic of the postmodern socio-economic condition seems to have further disoriented the physical experience of the metropolis — the positioning of one's own body in relation to the built environment.

Although first the prototypically metropolitan means of transport, the subway, and later the prototypically intermetropolitan means of transport, the airplane, also contributed to this disorienting time-space compression, it is especially the prototypically transmetropolitan means of transport, the car, that has affected changes in perception of the physical environment during the latter half of the century. In the postwar metropolis and, more clearly still, in the sprawl of suburbs and technoburbs, car-based perception has become almost a visual default model. Contributing to the disappearance of congestion and a sense of metropolitan massiveness and density by facilitating the process of suburbanization and exurbanization, the car has also habituated individual observers with a faster-moving viewpoint, thereby robbing the surroundings of some of their tactility and subjecting them to a constant optical distortion. What is more, by being enveloped the body is literally occluded from the environment. Especially in diluted metropolitan areas, cars have almost entirely come to displace the walking pedestrian body. "If you get out of your car in this centrifugal metropolis," writes Baudrillard caricaturally and hyperbolically about L.A., "you immediately become a delinquent; as soon as you start walking, you are a threat to public order, like a dog wandering in the road. Only immigrants from the Third World are allowed to walk" [1988:58]. In a posturban environment that puts paid to traditional urban compactness, human bodies often seem out of place either for being too vulnerable or for being perceived as menacing; they need to be wrapped in the armor of cars.

In thus foreclosing all tactile and olfactory contact with the city, cars have helped reduce the urban experience to a visual spectacle. Like any frame, the car window confers on perceived objects a certain plastic or painterly quality [cf. Frey 1972 and Wachtel 1977/1978]. It also bears a resemblance to the television or movie screen.[38] Paul Virilio has on several occasions compared the driving of a car with a cinematographic experience. In one of his own captivating hyperboles, he has related the relatively new phenomenon of car-based seeing to perceptual disturbances like "picnolepsy" [Virilio 1991], a condition in which the senses function and yet seem closed to external impressions. Along the same lines, Arie Graafland proposes that

*anyone who regularly drives a car is familiar with a similar phenomenon. Even though we know the road, we often cannot remember whether we have passed a particular viaduct, building, or area. This has nothing to do with sleepiness; we are still driving faultlessly along our route. But there are huge, empty places in our memory. The speed of driving creates a cinematographic effect that many underestimate. The result is a loss of sensible referents and a decay of architectonic markers; a trend which runs counter to those postmodern architectures which seduce the eye with their recognizable shapes and messages. In the peripheral world of the highway, postmodern architecture can never win this struggle to communicate, and this is because the complexity of the building mass is imperceptible — it fades into a faint image which hardly persists in our memory* [1996:41].

"Driving," in Baudrillard's aphorism, "is a spectacular form of amnesia" [1988:9].

The increasingly widespread phenomenon of traffic-jams and of gridlock, however, serves to remind us of the inertia of matter, of the fact that movement does not merely involve a shifting of images but also the transportation of actual bodies. In an ironical return to the project of the elitist flaneur, who went for walks with a turtle on a leash to rebel against the ever-increasing speed of the circulation of goods, ideas, and various means of transport, the traffic-jam today returns us to a type of slowness *within* circulation. And in other respects, too, the car has come to remind us of our bodily existence. As a status symbol, for instance, it has been attributed physical properties and come to be presented as an extension of the body, even a well-fitting garment. The gratification of primary physical needs in the car, such as eating, has been made possible through drive-in restaurants — mostly fastfood chains that constitute the culinary embodiment of Harvey's time-space compression, erasing by their interchangeability all distinction between here and there, then and now. Finally, the destruction of tactility by the car is sometimes imaginarily compensated for by presenting the car as an erotic instrument, most clearly in advertising. Especially in the U.S. (but also elsewhere), the car has even served as *the* vehicle of sexual liberation. Canadian film director David Cronenberg, whose unorthodox conjunction of cars and sex (the two most important elements in the Hollywood iconography) caused such an outrage when his 1996 movie *Crash* was released, insisted in an interview that the car historically "enabled a boy to take out a girl for the first time — to pull her away, in other words, from parental protection. By means of that car they created their own environment. The connection between cars and sex is obvious; you need not be Freud to realize that" [Cronenberg 1996:74]. *Crash* illustrates Virilio's claim that "speed removes us as much from sensuous reality as it has the violent habit of bringing us closer to it" [1984:143; editors' translation]. The same car that most of the time numbs our bodies returns us after a crash with a vengeance to the sensitivity and vulnerability of those bodies.

**Consumer Aestheticism and the Neo-Flaneur** According to Fredric Jameson, the past decades have seen the rise of "a new 'society of the image' in which consumerism and market frenzy are not the issue so much as consumption by the eyes" [1996:14]. The postwar metropolis, too, as we have seen, is increasingly subject to the kind of spectatorial regime that is characteristic of "postindustrialism" or "postmodernity" at large. This predominance of a *concupiscio oculis* [ibid.] is of special importance to the many attempts there have been at adapting the nineteenth-century figure of the flaneur to a late-twentieth-century context. A frequent shortcoming of theories on the postmodern urban self is that of confusing Walter Benjamin's popular flaneur, who experiences his surroundings without taking any distance from them, with the artistic flaneur, to whom distancing defense strategies are of the essence. All too often theorists neglect or forget how Benjamin himself repeatedly associated the concepts of flaneur and phantasmagoria with specific social carriers, namely those middle classes that rose to prominence in the 19th-century city [see Buck-Morss 1989]. Today's spectatorial consumer should be seen as a direct heir to the popular middle-class flaneur described by Benjamin.

Postmodern images of the urban self do more than entail an increase in the distancing defense strategies depicted in the previous paragraph; they paradoxically also involve the postmodern phantasmagoria of an *absence* of distance. In the aestheticized perception of consumers, no form of distance imposes itself. In a major shift from Benjamin's analysis, moreover, the reach of this aestheticized type of perception has expanded far beyond the borders of the classical metropolis. Whereas Benjamin could still focus entirely on the traditional 19th-century urban center (*the* locus where the first phantasmagoric spectacles were staged), the realm of the spectacular has been radically extended by postwar audiovisual media to give rise to more widely mediatized phantasmagorias. The new media technologies, in addition, have expanded and sped up the flow of images that rose in the 19th century and that was originally still concentrated in urban centers. As Mike Featherstone in his influential sociological study *Consumer Culture and Postmodernism* has noted: "The aestheticization of everyday life through the figural regimes of signification, which Lash ... holds as central to postmodernism ... may have its origins in the growth of consumer culture in the big cities of nineteenth-century capitalist societies, which became the sites for the intoxicating dream-worlds, the constantly changing flow of commodities, images and bodies (the flaneur)" [1991:70]. According to Featherstone, the analyses by Simmel and Benjamin retain valid insofar as they

*can be used to direct us towards the way in which the urban landscape becomes aestheticized and enchanted through the architecture, billboards, shop displays, advertisements, packages, street signs etc., and through the embodied persons who move through these spaces: the individuals who wear, to varying degrees, fashionable clothing, hair-styles, make-up, or who move, or hold their bodies, in particular stylized ways. The aestheticization of everyday life in this second sense points to the expansion and extension of commodity production in the big cities which has thrown up new buildings, department stores, malls and so on, and which has produced an endless array of goods to fill the shops and clothe and cater for those who pass through them* [ibid.:76].

In this context, critics today often fall back on the cultural criticism of Jean Baudrillard. His "simulacra" share the same connotations as Benjamin's phantasmagoric images. What distinguishes Baudrillard's theory from his predecessor's, though, is that it links those simulacra with the codified modes of perception typical of a postmodern consumerist society overall, and that the infrastructure of simulated realities is thus no longer necessarily urban. Baudrillard's concept of hyperrealism (developed in *Simulations*) derives from an experience of surreality that is robbed of its artistic dimensions, which brings it close to Benjamin's phantasmagoria. "It is reality itself today that is hyperrealist," he writes. "Surrealism's secret already was that the most banal reality could become surreal, but only in certain privileged moments that are still nevertheless connected with art and the imaginary. Today it is quotidian reality in its entirety — political, social, historical and economic — that from now on incorporates the simulating dimension of hyperrealism. We live everywhere already in an 'aesthetic' hallucination of reality" [1983:148].

Despite Baudrillard's totalizing claim, it seems reasonable, nonetheless, to suppose that the images originating from, or pointing back to, the downtown centers of metropolises continue to take pride of place in today's more generally mediatized phantasmagoria. It could be argued that the phenomena described by Baudrillard merely radicalize the urban phantasmagoria of modernity. The modern city, notes Scott McGuire with respect to the *fin de siècle,* functioned as "a vast perceptual laboratory, a living experiment in 'special effects' whose impact on the human sensorium has shifted the parameters of human identity. New spatial and temporal experiences levied new demands upon representation" [1998:208]. This tendency seems to have been reinforced. The movie industry provides sufficient evidence for the continuing popularity of urban settings as an imaginary reservoir for staging and feeding the spectacular. Even in the densely populated streets of New York, for instance, more than 200 movies were shot in the course of 1996 alone [Weber 1997b]. Metropolitan streetscapes belong to the most conspicuous loci of a culture of simulacra and phantasmagorias. In traditional downtowns, moreover, the simulacrum plays a much more prominent role than in the rest of society. Even if we have witnessed the sprawling rise of "simulational environments which use spectacular imagery in malls, shopping centres, theme parks and hotels" [Featherstone 1991:70], it is still primarily places like Times Square in New York that, together with Las Vegas and Disney's monofunctional fun parks, most clearly embody a culture of the specular and the spectacular [see Hannigan 1998]. And this priority of traditional downtowns is not only a function of the built or architectural environment. If peepshows offer another type of simulacra, for instance, then these simulacra are again an urban phenomenon. And if today's cult of the body is based on a culture of simulacra, then the new middle classes that inhabit the centers of cities are clearly the trendsetting carriers of an ostensibly generalized and transmetropolitan phantasmagoria.

The city in more ways than one continues to refer metonymically to a postmodern world of simulacra. The power of city images is such that they have become popular even as backgrounds to news broadcasts and talkshows — whether in replicated forms or live. Setting up a curbside studio at Rockefeller Center in New York City from which to air its daily show "Today," NBC has tapped into the bustling street-theater potential of its urban foil with such success that competitors ABC and CBS have in turn been shopping to lease studios at Times Square to provide a similar backdrop to their competitive shows "Good Morning America" and "This Morning" [Bagli 1997]. An even more internationally oriented T.V. channel like MTV figures this media-dependency on cityscapes even more clearly: not only does MTV, too, have a live music studio with a window on Times Square, but the constant barrage of images it spews in its videoclips also shows a highly marked preponderance of urban cameos. The motif of the city is central to a great many pop songs and the endless fascination with city images in the audiovisual media alludes not only to the fact that the world of information-gathering has become a global village, but also cashes in on the erotic potential of phantasmagoric images. A flashing city image often suffices to metonymically call forth the erotic connotations of other phantasmagoric images.

The phantasmagoric spectacle of the metropolis, in short, has come to exert its appeal to the audiovisual media as much as to urban residents or visitors. Yet if shoppers and tourists are today's consumer-aestheticist counterparts to Benjamin's popular flaneur — so much so that in Zygmunt Bauman's opinion "Play, the *flâneur* mode of life, has become now the standard by which all reality is to be measured" [1994:152] — there continues to be a place also for a social type that might be called the neo-flaneur. This is a type that is out to take its artistic or aesthetical distance from its consumerist urban surroundings. A case in point is Jonathan Raban in his essayistic bestseller *Soft City*, where the argument is put forward that cities are "plastic by nature. We mould them in our images: they, in their turn, shape us by the resistance they offer when we try to impose our personal form on them. In this sense, it seems to me that living in a city is an art, and we need the vocabulary of art, of style, to describe the peculiar relation between man and material that exists in the continual creative play of urban living" [quoted in Harvey 1989a: 5]. The combination of "art," "style," "creative play," and "urban living" in Raban's formulation points to a shift in the composition and profile of this group of neo-flaneurs. The aesthetical dispositions of the 19th-century artistic flaneur return today in a wider group of tastemakers. As Mike Featherstone argues, the makers of today's phantasmagoric dreamworlds — not only "window dressers" but also "workers in fields such as advertising, marketing, design, fashion, commercial art, architecture and journalism" — bear a strong resemblance to artists and intellectuals in their "tastes, dispositions and classificatory schemes" [1991:77]. Not coincidentally, those same social groups are usually also singled out as the carriers of a "postmodern zeitgeist" [see Lash 1990].

Another shift in the profile of artistic neo-flaneurs is indicated by the fact that in recent analyses references to urban *defense* mechanisms are frequently dropped. The earlier strain of environmental determinism, so intellectually potent in the first half of the century, seems to have waned. Today's theorists are more inclined to identify culture-sociological factors as explicative of modern and postmodern phantasmagorias. This happens at the same time as the urban culture of stimuli has acquired much more positive connotations in the course of the century — an evolution that has brought the artistic and the popular flaneur closer together. Middle-class phantasmagorias and spectacles have themselves become an important motivating element in the activity of artistic *flânerie*, which has generally partaken of the postmodern erasure of boundaries between "high" and "low" culture. Especially since the rise of pop art, this evolution has been notable, yet the aesthetics of (neo)dadaists, new realists, and literary experimentalists, too, has come to borrow from the popular flaneur. The resulting hybridization of the artistic neo-flaneur has been further abetted by the emancipation of women. The historically all-male category of the flaneur has been modified to make room for the feminine variant of the flaneuse. And since women, for gender-historical reasons, tend to have closer ties with the commercial and consumerist phantasmagoria of urban life, they have in turn contributed towards a narrowing of the gap between the popular and the artistic flaneur.

The metropolitan flaneur, then, has undergone a number of transformations. He or she has also been relocated, for much of the time, to the inside of buildings (malls and atriums), prompting Zygmunt Bauman to claim that "the street is no more the *flâneur*'s hunting ground. The 'outside' is but a traffic-flow-support-nexus" [1994:149]. And finally, the flaneur has been displaced, for large parts of the postmetropolitan environment, by the postpedestrian type of the driver. The flaneur, in some respects, has become a chauffeur, although the distancing effects imposed by the act of driving do not automatically generate any artistic-aesthetical forms of distancing. What the car does manage, at least imaginarily, is to serve as a hiding place in which the individual finds protection from the dangers of the urban jungle. By increasing the detachment between individuals, it enables those individuals to take more distance from each other; it becomes a cocoon sheltering the vulnerable body from the new urban space to which that body is sometimes little adapted. Nowhere else is the atomization of the self or the isolation of the nuclear family as physically manifest as in the use of the car. In this sense, drivers can be said to re-enact a characteristic of the artistic flaneur in a non-artistic, popularized format. For *flânerie,* according to Rob Shields, involves "a sociability of Ones. It is an atomized form of sociation where individuals congregate in an anonymous crowd of randomly strolling people. Despite their proximity they keep their social distance from each other and preserve a discrete estrangement" [1994:77].

**Remappings and Revaluations of Physical Excitement** One form of *flânerie* in the metropolis continues to be of all ages. It is the widespread kind that is driven not so much by the audiovisual consumption of inanimate spectacles as by a fleeting ocular consumption of human bodies. It is driven, more specifically, by a longing for erotic excitement that reaches its apogee in the more-than-ocular acts of sexual cruising and sexual encounters. At the outcome of various sociological and economic trends in the past decades — most prominently the trends toward sexual emancipation, secularization, and a hedonistic commodification of bodies through advertising — the human body has itself become, more than ever, a phantasmagoric object. And the metropolis, with its dense masses of people constantly crossing, eyeing, and ogling each other, has always offered the greatest supply of erotic stimuli and the highest number of possibilities for sexual encounters. As the world-wise narrator of Toni Morrison's urban novel *Jazz* notes, the metropolis may hardly be a place for love, "but it does pump desire" [1992:34]. It is the primary locus of sexual lust, an environment with the continuous potential for eroticization, a playgarden for libidinal cathexis. As Rudi Laermans writes: "Only where others are truly Other, because they are at once physically near and psychically far, only in the metropolitan street in which every passer-by is a stranger to all other passers-by, does desire liberate itself from its traditional shackles and obtain so many potential wish objects as to constantly shift, dissipate, receive its rhythm from the laws of coincidence that bring now this woman then this man within the real or imaginary reach of someone's desire" [1997:18; editors' translation]. In the trendy Seattle of the 1990s, the sexual sparks so easily produced by random metropolitan encounters have even been institutionalized in a form that has since spread to cities all around the world: the "I Saw U" section in newspapers and magazines. "[W]hat the twenty- and thirtysomethings who dominate urban Seattle say about it is that everybody reads it, and that it is the first thing everyone turns to in the free alternative weekly, The Stranger, except maybe the sex column. They also say that to be featured in it is the ultimate status symbol — usually resulting in a scream of 'I've been seen!' to housemates and friends, who immediately become envious" [Goldberg 1997: n.p.].

The dissipation of the traditional metropolis, however, has left its marks on this aspect of social interaction, too. Thus, prostitution, in origin a quintessentially urban phenomenon, has adapted to the logic of the freeway. The "red-light districts" that historically sprang up in 19th-century Paris and quickly spread to other cities have not escaped recent processes of deurbanization either. Part of today's sex industry has relocated to the suburbs and become car-oriented. In Belgium, for example, window prostitution has developed along main transit roads and brothels have opened in motor homes along freeways, while in the U.S. huge striptease palaces have set up store in the suburbs of Sunbelt cities. In countries like Germany and the Netherlands, but recently also in cities like New York, the sex industry has increasingly been banned from central downtowns to so-called Eros-centers and to generally marginal zones or urban voids. Such phenomena signal how traditionally urban institutions for erotic or sexual interaction have in turn been decentered and diversified. The anonymity of urban life has assured the continued existence of these institutions well into the second half of the century, but morphological and sociological changes have both expanded and further fragmented the urban sex industry. Today, this industry also includes sex shops, with their plethora of videos, magazines, toys, and other accoutrements for pleasure and fantasy; prostitution by transsexuals; sex saunas; darkrooms; leather and striptease bars that cater specifically to gay men; internationally traveling (hence delocalized) Chippendales offering fantasy food exclusively for women; and the booming world of porn on the Internet.

The postwar history of sex in the metropolis has been marked by two major watersheds: the sexual liberation of the sixties and seventies, which led many to develop a hyperactive sexual lifestyle, and the subsequent restraints necessitated by the arrival of AIDS. Even if AIDS is not transmitted through sex only and knows no geographic bounds, there is at least a strong statistical link between its occurrence and metropolitan environments: New York City, for example, which houses 3 percent of the American population, in 1997 contained 16 percent of all AIDS cases reported in the U.S. [Altman 1997]. Partly in response to the potential health risks of sex, new surrogate and virtual forms of sexual encounters have arisen: from telephone sex, a topic already artistically explored by writers like Nicholson Baker (in *Vox*) and film directors like Robert Altman (in *Short Cuts*), to so-called electronic sex on the Internet (evoked by film director Atom Egoyan).

The precise relationship between the sensitive human body and the materiality of its urban surroundings, meanwhile, remains notoriously hard to identify. In his recent *Flesh and Stone*, Richard Sennett has gone so far as to reverse the classic environmental-determinist theory by studying the ways in which the human body itself — as a discursive, ideological, and practical given — has historically determined the architectural layout of urban environments, instead of the other way round. Speculations of this sort, however, always threaten to remain overidealistic; they remind us of the care that should be taken in delineating the interaction between bodies and buildings. The genealogy of queer spaces drawn by Aaron Betsky [1997] is probably better-suited for illustrating the balancing acts scholars have to engage in when reckoning with the various ways in which (sexually motivated) people shape and appropriate certain spaces. From the birth of male cruising areas in Dutch 17th-century inner cities, via the French salons and English molly houses of the 18th century and the often gender-dysfunctional, self-conscious makers of middle-class interiors in 19th-century homes, down to explicitly queer architects and interior decorators devising intentionally queer spaces in the post-Stonewall era, we are being reminded of how hard it is to disentangle physical drives, conscious cultural ideologies, and idealistic projections in assessing the dynamic relationship between bodies and buildings.

The dynamic character of this relationship has again been enhanced by the speed with which bodies often move through their environments. The experience of speed, one of the hallmarks of modernity, has been one of the major experiences contributing to a sense of urban phantasmagoria. “Today we do not so much inhabit our habitat any longer (whose terrain has practically disappeared) as our habit of speed,” says Paul Virilio, who adds that we have habituated to speed so thoroughly “that we no longer perceive the optical effect of speed and have come to view the distortions of our perception caused by such speed as normal” [1984:155; editors’ translation]. The experience of speed — whether in cars, buses, streetcars, trains, subways, planes, or helicopters — creates an effect of hyperreality that has settled very deep in the postmodern psyche. In the technologically explosive heydays of the modern metropolis, the experience was soon aestheticized in the works of futurists and experimental film directors. Already in 1909, in the first futurist manifesto, F. T. Marinetti exulted: “We affirm that the world’s magnificence has been enriched by a new beauty: the beauty of speed” [1909:21].

Less than a century later and with the help of the audiovisual media endlessly exploiting its potential, the rush of metropolitan existence has become a visual icon even in mainstream culture. Today's culture of speed forms the almost entirely naturalized, stereotypical climax to a technological revolution that started with the invention of electricity (and various electrically driven technologies) and that radically stepped up the pace of metropolitan life.

The rush culture that speed has brought is in a complex way also related to a culture of metropolitan euphoria. The introduction of electricity has allowed nightlife to expand almost indefinitely and to become an autonomous culture in its own right. Real metropolises, in contradistinction to smaller cities, pride themselves on being cities that never sleep. The nocturnal mix of music, dance, partying, drink, and drugs that is to be found in any metropolis responds in large part to a need for thrills and kicks that is the corollary of a metropolitan culture of speed and enhanced stimuli. Popular stimulants like alcohol and tobacco have a long standing in this nocturnal world, but the wide spreading of soft and hard drugs — endlessly documented by literary writers as well as the audiovisual media — is again new to the postwar era. A metropolitan vitalistic lifestyle has developed, especially among the young, which likes to experiment with experiences of physical shock and rapture and which shows a marked preference for everything that "lets the body contract in a cramp," as Walter Benjamin already observed [1938: 548]. The raw, aggressive, eclectic, and constantly shifting music of the 1980s New York downtown scene around John Zorn and The Knitting Factory probably offers the best embodiment of this vitalism. Such music is intimately linked to the subculturalization of urban life, which allows idiosyncratic individuals to lead unconventional lives not only beyond good and evil but also beyond beautiful and ugly, or beyond high and low. On a recording like John Zorn's *Naked City*, to take but one of many musical examples, the music changes genre about every four seconds in an endless sonic cataract. Fast changes in rhythm and tempo, noise effects, and violent contrasts are meant to apply current surges to the body in an attempt at communicating urban euphoria as physically as possible [see Keunen and Keunen 1996].

**Shifting Disruptions of Physical Integrity** The metropolis does not only offer the most fitting environment for *voluntarily* inflicting shocks upon oneself with the sole purpose of inducing a sense of physical euphoria, it has also long been an environment in which certain physical strains are *involuntarily* suffered. The cohabitation of a great number of individuals living to some extent at cross-purposes with one another necessarily produces conflicts in which physical integrity often comes under siege. Most of these infringements and short-circuits are not new to the postmodern metropolis, although they have again undergone a number of changes in terms of gradation and spatial distribution. Thus, one of the oldest of urban problems, antedating even the modern metropolis, is that of stench, often as a result of insufficient hygienic conditions. This is one of the problems that have drastically diminished in the course of the twentieth century (at least in Western cities), as has been the case also with the most typical environmental side-effect of the nineteenth-century metropolis, industrial pollution. An ecological sensitivity to issues of pollution has grown along with increased hygienic and health concerns, and it has led to the advancement of multiple legal restrictions on the potentially damaging effects of heavy industry. At the same time, however, new forms of pollution have been added: those by the new chemical industries (often invisible and insensible but with disputed long-term effects) and especially the one major new form of pollution to have enveloped metropolitan environments of any kind (whether dense or sprawled out): the emissions of motorized traffic. The proverbial black clouds of soot that hung over the industrial metropolis have been displaced by the no-less-proverbial smog of the postindustrial metropolis, in Los Angeles as much as in ancient European cities like Athens, Rome, or Paris. And more than fumes have threatened the urbanite's physical wellbeing since the arrival of motorized traffic: traffic accidents have in turn asked their toll to become one of the prime causes of death in today's urbanized society overall.

Like stench, noise is a traditional urban ingredient. Here again, it should be noted how noise levels have not always necessarily gone up in comparison with the Dickensian or machine-age city, but sensitivity to the problem has grown in an increasingly middle-class culture of withdrawal into the haven of domesticity. (An escape from stench, pollution, and noise is not coincidentally one of the important historical motivations behind the suburban dream.) And here, too, new forms and distributions of noise have been added: above all, the noise of motorized traffic again, which has not only spread in space but also in time, giving rise to round-the-clock disturbances. It is the temporal extension, in fact, that may be most characteristic of the postwar metropolis with its increased nightlife culture of high decibels. As Winifred Gallagher points out, "noise generated by people and their machines causes readily measurable physiological and psychological changes. ... Along with impairing concentration, memory, mood, and performance, noise undermines sociability" [1993: 151].

Still, in spite of all the potential or real damage inflicted by stench, pollution, noise, or traffic, it is the fear of crime and violence that takes pride of place in the collective perception of the physical perils attendant upon living in the metropolis. As Janny Scott has argued in *The New York Times* (figures in hand), "notions about crime and public safety have exercised an outsize influence on overall views of the city" [1997: n.p.]. Scott quotes the president of the New York Convention and Visitors Bureau saying: "'The single biggest impediment to getting people to visit New York City was and is perceptions about crime'" [ibid.]. Crime is obviously in no sense new to metropolitan existence either, but what is relatively new about people's fear for it is that the ties to real danger have considerably loosened: to some extent, today's fear has become a function of gut-ripping sensationalist exploitation by the media and, at times, by political parties. "Surveys show that Milwaukee suburbanites are just as worried about violent crimes as inner-city Washingtonians, despite a twenty-fold difference in relative levels of mayhem," observes Mike Davis [1990: 224]. In the collective imaginary, a terrifying Moloch like New York continues to rank as one of the most violent and dangerous places in the U.S., even though figures for both the city itself and the surrounding metropolitan area have for some time already begun to contradict this image.

Of the seven serious crimes that today are on the F.B.I.'s crime index — murder, rape, robbery, aggravated assault, burglary, grand larceny, and car theft — only the final category is entirely new to the postwar metropolis. Changes in the social fabric of metropolitan life have nonetheless been responsible for a number of changes in crime rates and victim profiles. In their least positive forms, secularization and individualization have brought about a decline in ethical standards and a concomitant increase in illegal, antisocial, and self-serving forms of behavior. A less strictly disciplinary, more hedonistic, and basically entrepreneurial culture of instant personal gratification and greed, informed by consumerist strategies and supplied with endless images, has generally increased the temptation of unlawful shortcuts, even if amends need to be made for severe fluctuations of crime rates in the postwar era.[39] On the side of victims, the diversification of the metropolitan population has multiplied the number of groups at risk: many acts of violence today are related to skin color or ethnicity (in a long

39 To take but one example, that of New York: although the number of murders in this city peaked in the beginning of the 1990s, with a record high of 2,245 victims per year, and the number of car thefts reached a high in roughly the same period (1988-93), figures also indicate that the highest number of burglaries occurred in the period 1975-82 and the highest number of rapes between 1975 and 1985. Indeed, the category of "major felonies" overall peaked in the early 1980s [see Kraus 1996]. Meanwhile, crime rates have been pushed back spectacularly (with the exception of rape and gay bashing) in the course of the 1990s, with for instance murders dropping to less than a thousand and the general incidence of crime returning to mid-sixties figures.

40 A 1997 opinion poll showed that about half of New York residents would not leave the city if they were given the opportunity to do so [see Nagourney 1997]. Deemed a sharp change in attitude for the better, this figure still means that about half of the population *would* grab the chance to leave the city. According to Robert Jay Lifton, a bestselling psychiatrist and born New Yorker, "people are acutely ambivalent about New York. They hold two extreme images in their head: New York as 'the most vital, fascinating, rewarding city on earth' and New York as 'the most terrorizing, deteriorated, impossible place on earth'" [quoted in Scott 1997: n.p.].

racist tradition), socioeconomic class (in the form of violence "contained" within inner cities), sexual preference/orientation (with the continuing phenomenon of "gay bashing"), biological sex (with especially women as the victims of rape), or age (with male teenagers and twens running the highest physical risks and elderly people feeling psychologically most terrorized). The preoccupation with safety has to many metropolitans become a deeply rooted, at times barely conscious, daily automatism. As Sharon Zukin notes: "Elderly men and women who live in cities commonly experience fear as a steady erosion of spaces and times available to them" [1995:38]. Worries about physical safety are a major factor behind the notoriously ambivalent attitude metropolitan residents tend to take towards their surroundings.[40]

Typically, the functional-morphological metamorphosis which the metropolis has undergone over the past few decades has left its mark on this aspect of metropolitan existence as well: crime rates no longer seem to respect the traditional opposition between center and periphery either. "New cities" and "edge cities" have also started to face a rise in crime rates. According to *The New York Times* reporting about the year 1996, "There are now seven cities in the region that are more violent than New York City, compared with only one — Newark, N.J. — that was more violent 16 years ago" [Glaberson 1997: n.p.]. Although residential suburban areas continue to show the safety advantage that historically constitutes one of their major attractions, even they now have to deal with "high-crime pockets with drug trading and violence" [ibid.]. It is the spreading of the fear of violence to suburban areas, as we have seen, that has been responsible for the rise of gated communities, especially in the U.S.

Today, the fear of crime and violence in metropolitan areas comes in different guises, often depending on the material shape of the urban landscape. Traditional European city centers, with their dense and frequently maze-like layouts, as well as traditional American downtowns like Manhattan, generate different types of fear than does a sprawling metropolis like Los Angeles or Miami. The crowded and pedestrian public character of the former cities produces threats that principally derive from face-to-face encounters and are bound up with such spaces as nocturnal subways, deserted sidestreets and alleys, dark porticos, dilapidated and boarded-up houses, and various pocked urban voids [Gallagher 1993: 189-94]. Kenneth Jackson and Fred Kameny have even suggested that New York is a particularly unfit place for deranged killers, since "the congestion discourages extremely aberrant behavior. We'll let you wear pajamas out at 3 in the morning and sing in the streets, but it would be hard to commit 50 murders or eat a lot of bodies. Somebody would see you or hear the screaming" [quoted in Tierney 1995: n.p.]. Diluted exurbias, by contrast, pose different threats. "The definitive L.A. sound," writes Peter Schjeldahl, is "a hovering police helicopter. ... Burglary is epidemic. Violent crime is widespread, often horror-movie vicious, and — in the basin's blanketing anonymity — somehow much scarier than elsewhere" [1991:81]. In cities like L.A., the threat does not come so much from subways as from carjacking, homejacking, or the necessity to stop the car on a highway to replace a flat tire.

Given the radical psychic impact of fear and the drastic physical impact of violence, it is only natural that the number of cultural products expressing this fear and reflecting this violence has mushroomed. Literature (with Bret Easton Ellis's *American Psycho* as a notorious case of one-upmanship), including the popular genre of urban thrillers and hardboiled detectives (from V.I. Warshawski's Chicago to Matthew Scudder's New York in the novels of Sara Paretsky and Lawrence Block), as well as televized police series and crime thrillers (from NYPD *Blue, Hill Street Blues,* or *Law and Order,* to *Derrick*), have largely kept to the classic metropolitan downtown paradigm in this respect.[41] But movies have arguably tended to be more responsive to the spreading of violence and fear to a wider urban field. From Stanley Kubrick's would-be prophetic and still controversial *A Clockwork Orange,* where random violence is perpetrated both in the metropolis and in the countryside, to David Lynch's scary evocations of suburban and smalltown America, the most impressive icons of cinematography have famously picked up this spreading of random violence and fear beyond the anonymous big city with which they were traditionally associated.

41 For an analysis of how the genre of the urban thriller and detective has responded to a multiculturalization of authorship and readership, see the case study by Christophe Den Tandt (Part II).

# 3 Constructions of the Symbolic Metropolis

**The Emergence of the Semiotic Matrix** Whereas hypotheses of the type pursued in the previous pages are directly concerned with the experiential relationship between metropolis and self, other theories need to be mentioned that focus rather on *interpretations* of cities. Such theories, more idealistic than materialistic or sociological in inspiration, arose especially within the framework of the semiotic paradigm that came to prominence in the 1970s. Explicitly or implicitly, these theories start from the supposition that although the physical environment offers possibilities for human behavior, individuals are still "free" to decide on which of these they activate or realize. At the basis of such decisions are cultural values, which are viewed as the most important filters between the environment and individual experience — a view that to this day recurs with semiotically inspired cultural theorists. Arguments along these lines are mostly developed by theories in which the interpretation and restyling of physical surroundings is believed to be of the utmost importance. For those critics, says political philosopher François Fourquet, "Every stone is a sign, every form is a symbol; the cultural person implied by this conception lives in a symbolic city, a city entirely animated by phantasms and representations" [1973:28; editors' translation].

The study of phantasmagorias developed in the wake of Walter Benjamin also has a variant at the level of cultural-semiotic theory. This variant tends to move in the direction of a phenomenology of postmodern signs. Jean Baudrillard is the most conspicuous case in point with his argument for viewing the postmodern city as no longer a locus of industrialization but a "zone of signs, the media, and the code." This argument ties in closely with the analysis of a rising consumer aestheticism, witness the following synopsis by Mike Featherstone of theories that to him depict "shifts in cultural experiences and modes of signification":

*Here we find an emphasis upon the aestheticization of everyday life and the transformation of reality into images in the work of Jean Baudrillard. Jameson too emphasizes the loss of a sense of history and the fragmentation of time into a series of perpetual presents in which there is the experience of multiphrenic intensities. A similar aestheticization of experience and breaking down of the ordered chain of signifiers can be detected in the writings of their followers where one finds an emphasis upon "the liquefaction of signs and commodities," "the effacement of the boundary between the real and the image," "floating signifiers," "hyperreality," "depthless culture," "bewildering immersion," "sensory overload," and "affect-charge intensities." While many of these examples draw this inspiration from the intensification of image production in the media and consumer culture in general, one also finds it in descriptions of the contemporary city. Here the emphasis is not only on the type of new architecture specifically designated postmodern, but also on the more general eclectic stylistic hotchpotch which one finds in the urban fabric of the built environment* [1991: 65].

In Roland Barthes's characterization of Tokyo, today's city has to several critics become an "empire of signs." Reading the city has thus become one of the most central themes in recent cultural criticism. In architectural theory, for instance, analyses of different ways of building and living have been worked out on the basis of the structuralist narratologist A. J. Greimas, and theories on the semiotics of buildings were devised as of the 1970s. Such theories ran parallel also with contemporaneous literary-critical analyses of the readings of cities produced by flaneurs. They may be connected, moreover, to longer-standing discussions about the problem of cognitive mapping, which have been framed historically by David Chaney in the following terms:

*as urban life has become the determining precondition of everyday life for national culture in modernity, so visualisation has become the central resource for communicating and appropriating meaning ... The reason why visualisation has come to dominate the hermeneutics of everyday life in metropolitan culture is that the landscape scale of the rapidly expanding cities of the nineteenth century meant that a communal cognitive order became largely unsustainable. Devising and utilising new ways of searching for visual intelligibility became necessary ways of coping with cognitive alienation* [1996:101-102].

Most consistent in this pursuit of the question of subjective cognitive maps has been Kevin Lynch in *The Image of the City* [1960], where an empirical study is undertaken, based on questionnaires, into the way a city is being read by its inhabitants and users. To this end, Lynch concentrated on a certain visual quality, "the apparent clarity or 'legibility' of the cityscape." By this he meant "the ease with which its parts can be recognized and can be organized into a coherent pattern" [1960:2-3]. This kind of inquiry was further pursued by scholars like Gerald Suttles, who, in *The Social Construction of Communities* [1972], tested the cognitive maps discovered by Lynch on their social consequences: "Cognitive maps provide a set of social categories for differentiating between those people with whom one can or cannot safely associate and for defining the concrete groupings within which certain levels of social contact and cohesion obtain" [Langer 1984: 115-16].

The need for cognitive maps derives in part from a basic characteristic of metropolitan society. "It is in the world of strangers that characterises modern urban social life," notes David Chaney, "that symbolic meaning is infinitely negotiable and continually being re-invented.... Not only has the number of things made vastly increased, but also how they are made available and how they are presented and how they are discussed have all become in themselves further services which are forms of goods and thus purchased in markets" [1996:44]. Symbolic relationships in a postindustrial society have become increasingly arbitrary and unstable. Reformulating the ideas of Michel de Certeau in this respect, Chaney has observed how "Meaning is not something 'there' in what we say or do or in the world around us to be appreciated correctly or not, but is something made in the politics of social practice" [ibid.:73]. In his *The Practice of Everyday Life*, de Certeau has demonstrated the possibilities for applying this sort of speech act theory to a sociological realm. Stressing the significance of spatial practices, he has called these practices pedestrian speech acts; "as they move through established spatial and social order, actors are telling stories through their reinforcement and confirmation of local knowledges" [ibid.:74].

**The Smorgasbord of Lifestyles** Since the socioeconomic system underlying the modern and postmodern Western metropolis sets great store by competition and individualism, these aspects have also found a sociocultural expression in the form of multiplying lifestyles. A variety of metropolitan activities and behaviors derives from the fact that competition obtains not only in economic matters but also between owners and non-owners of what Pierre Bourdieu has called cultural or symbolic capital [1979]. Already in the explosive industrial metropolis of the 19th century, a strong drive for distinction among the middle and upper classes could be discerned. It went hand in hand with the emergence of a new class of professionals and intellectuals who established their power in part by manipulating criteria of discrimination. The phenomenon of aesthetic indifference foregrounded by Simmel and Benjamin may even be referred back to behavioral characteristics typical of the *Bildungsbürgertum*. Sibylle Hübner-Funk has analyzed this early evolution whereby "the aesthetic ideal does not mirror man's existential struggle for physical survival so much as it reflects the social struggle for appreciation and self-esteem ... Despite their dependency on money as a medium for maintaining themselves, [urban middle-class citizens] cherish a self-image in which cultural individuality forms the sole measure for determining one's social value" [1984:188; editors' translation]. The human need for difference in a metropolitan environment, already in Simmel's opinion, led to "the strangest eccentricities" whose significance merely lay in "making oneself noticeable" [1903:336]. Simmel talked of the fact that "the metropolis is characterised by its essential independence even of the most significant individual personalities" [ibid.:335] and of the resulting urban plight that "extremities and peculiarities and individualizations must be produced and they must be over-exaggerated merely to be brought into the awareness even of the individual himself" [ibid.: 338].

Cities have thus become veritable hotbeds of practices that are aimed at codifying the self. These self-codifications are in the first place written upon the body: the urban body has itself, in certain respects, become a sign [Baudrillard 1983: 148; Chambers 1986: 11; Falk 1994]. But this semiotic externalization operates within the larger sociological framework of lifestyles — a concept that has been of central importance to the postwar era. As David Chaney in his book on the topic argues, lifestyles are essentially features of modernity that derive from the reflexive character of modernity's concern with social identity, distinction, and difference, and they may be defined as "patterns of action that differentiate people" [1996: 4]. They are narrower than the concept of culture in that they refer only to "sets of practices and attitudes that make sense in particular contexts" [ibid.: 5]. The concept of lifestyles is thus better attuned to the more flexible and changeable social realities characteristic of the (post)modern urban way of life. As Joseph Bensman and Arthur Vidich point up, "life-styles are artificial creations or adoptions. The bearer himself is aware of the fact that the style can be donned and discarded at will and, therefore, it can be acted out with some degree of self-irony and self-satire" [quoted in Chaney 1996: 12].

The codification of outward apparel was already a crucial and widespread feature of urban life in the 18th century, as Richard Sennett has reminded us: it is even closely tied up with the very rise of the public-private antithesis explored by him. The historical rise of a private sphere is reflected in the emergence of a concept like "sensibility" — a concept that, as Chaney argues, was imbued from the start with ethical and aesthetic significance and associated with ways of living that are fundamental to a sense of a person's identity [see also Williams 1976: 235-38]. It is in such a context of the (strongly gendered) rise of a private sphere and of an ideology of domesticity that the sensibility of later lifestyles was able to emerge. Mass marketing, with its advertising and other spectacular marketing techniques, was of the essence in this process, as was a growing emphasis by the middle classes on the luxury of leisure time and how to fill it. Already by the end of the 19th century, the culture of sensibility had spread all over an urban world of exploding popular consumption. "Lifestyle shopping" became a widely available possibility. It gave rise to a new secular form of religion — that of taste, which, in Stephen Bayley's definition, "is a new religion whose rites are celebrated in department stores and museums, two institutions whose origins lie in exactly that historical period which witnessed the explosion of popular consumption" [1991: 209].

Contrary to the concept of class, which was still crucial to the 19th- and early-20th- century metropolis, the concept of lifestyle is not based on occupation or common privileges but on the *use* made of privileges and resources. It is based, in Chaney's antithesis, on the social organization of consumption rather than on the social organization of production. Characteristic of lifestyles is that they encompass more social groups than a typology based on production traditionally does: it is, for instance, better able to accommodate groups like the elderly, the young, the unemployed, and women. In addition, it is better able to account for the diversification and fragmentation of traditional social groups: lifestyles based on consumptive patterns do not necessarily constitute inclusive groups and their emergence runs parallel with what Chaney has dubbed "a shift from communal forms of play and celebration to commercial forms of entertainment supplied by entrepreneurs" [1996: 22]. They are "a product of the privatisation of communal life" [ibid.: 95], which involves a process towards more private, personal modes of participation in cultural occasions. This shift has again a number of spatial components: whereas earlier communal forms of play and celebration, especially among the working classes, tended to be spatially more circumscribed and more territorialized, today's supply of commercial and privatized forms of entertainment happens in a more dispersed and decentered form (through the technology of audiovisual media at home, through the arcades of electronic games, through malls and fun parks).

In some respects, it has become "virtually impossible to distinguish between lifestyles and subcultures, particularly when fashion in dress and entertainment, etc. becomes a constitutive symbolic vocabulary," [ibid.: 35] although, as Chaney also points out, sometimes the former label is preferred for not implying a deviant relationship to a notional dominant culture. The concept of subcultures arose in a historical context of law-breaking, nonconformist forms of social behavior and was originally predicated upon the street life of especially male youths. Its intellectual father figures like Dick Hebdige have moved away from its categorial rigidity to develop more flexible accounts of the meaning of style, taste, and fashion. Inevitably, however, the concepts of lifestyle, fashion, and subculture continue to meet and intersect, since lifestyles and fashions, too, involve mechanisms for inclusion and exclusion and may be inflected in ways that are subversive of the hegemonic power structures in society. About the 1960s British phenomenon of the "mods," for instance, Iain Chambers writes that "the mods translated the anonymous flux of consumerism into a specific shape ... Consumerism was turned into the secret language of style" [1986: 7].

The possible manifestations of urban lifestyles are far too many to tally here; they have given rise to a multiplication of specialized market niches. Yet a few major realms of activity and expression should be listed. Apart from a marked interest in clothing and music, today's metropolitans have come to develop a strong interest in culinary matters (especially in the form of dining out and a diversification of exotic foods and cuisines), in the domestic realm of design (originally a mass marketing strategy that has since been successfully diversified and artistically aestheticized), or in no less self-defining tourist activities (with city-hopping as one particularly trendy example). To a certain extent, the autonomization of sexual lifestyles that break with the traditional norm of heterosexuality also belong in this category. All of these lifestyle interests have found their conspicuous journalistic expression in a plethora of urban-based, image-shaping magazines and an expanding supply of lifestyle television (from Martha Stewart to glbt television). The accompanying codes have been so multiplied beyond encyclopedic control that in many instances they have become legible only to subcultural insiders, from the wearing of ski glasses in the partying circuit to protest the use of drugs ("snow") to the sporting of a red handkerchief dangling from one's left pocket in the cruising circuit (signaling a taste for active fistfucking).

Among academic culture-watchers, the formation of lifestyle-based identities has frequently come to be seen as, in Diana Fuss's words, "less a function of knowledge than performance, or, in Foucauldian terms, less a matter of final discovery than perpetual reinvention" [1991:6-7]. Performance and performativity have unsurprisingly become key words, in academia as well as in literature and the fine arts. The social power base of such ideas, however, should not be overrated. At the same time as notions of a perpetually reinvented and pluralized self have started circulating, a defensive trend towards the solidification and homogenization of the self as a member of a particular sociopolitical group has been equally clear. As we have seen, the compulsion to self-identify (in ethnical, sexual, political, cultural, subcultural, lifestyle terms) has sometimes locked urbanites in oppressive stock roles and regressive stereotypes.

**The Bifurcation of Metropolitan Languages** The major evolutions delineated throughout our theoretical part — the process of economic globalization, the sprawling out of metropolises, the relative dissociation of urban locales and urban ways of life through the media, the subculturalization and diversification of metropolitan populations — have finally also found a sociolinguistic manifestation in their shaping of the language that metropolitans speak. This language has notably bifurcated. From one perspective, it has been subject to pressures which have rendered it less circumscribable *per se*, rendering any discussion of the topic necessarily more problematical. The pressure of economic forces in the direction of a global free-market economy has been conducive to the growth of delocalized languages for global use. Whereas the modern metropolis still played a centralizing role in the process of constructing nation-states — a process which largely depended on the construction of standardized, homogenized national languages through dictionaries, national academies, and a nationally organized educational system — the postmodern metropolis is increasingly caught in an international web whose communication tools transcend the traditional borders of the nation-state. This economic evolution has been paralleled by a stepped-up international interaction among intellectual and cultural elites and entertainers. As a result of these economic, intellectual, and cultural processes of globalization, the need for a new lingua franca has made itself felt — somewhat on the analogy of the role played by Latin in the Middle Ages and the Renaissance (though this time in a more democratic and mediatized form). For historical reasons, English has surfaced as this transnational (hence transmetropolitan) lingua franca now widely used by elites in the worlds of international corporations, finance, academia, entertainment, and the media. Widespread use of the Internet, moreover, has been extending the sociological reach of this lingua franca to include a younger, less class-based, and spatially even more dissipated body of users.

At the same time, however, this trend towards an international standardization and homogenization of language (primarily for functional-pragmatic purposes) has been accompanied by a disruptive trend towards diversification and subculturalization. This second trend, too, is no longer moored necessarily in the metropolis and has indeed become more a matter of sociolects than of earlier geographically circumscribed dialects. Yet it often still reaches its most extreme embodiment in the metropolis. The history of slang is instructive in this respect. In *The City in Slang*, Irving Lewis Allen has studied the history of slang and popular speech in New York City between 1850 and 1950, arguing that "At a very broad level, most historical slang can be associated with urbanization — the settlement and development of cities — and more directly with urbanism — the distinctive culture that emerges from this social form" [1993: ii]. The acme of popular lexical innovation in New York, according to Allen, was reached during the time of the greatest immigration waves (roughly between 1880 and 1920). Substandard language was popularized by newspapers (in particular their syndicated comic strips) and further disseminated by the fact that "The relaxing of certain ethnic and class barriers in the large cities, especially after the First World War, brought conventional, middle-class people into contact with a variety of formerly isolated urban subcultures, such as bohemians, theater people, socialists, ethnic minorities, gangsters, and drug users" [ibid.: 25]. Once again, however, as time progressed, such metropolitan slang got delocalized and its usage spread over the entire population: radio first, then movies, and finally T.V. familiarized everyone with cityspeak and in so doing played a prominent role in the urbanization of society overall. A word like "dude," which originally referred to a sartorially extravagant urban dandy, typically managed to become, under the influence of late-twentieth-century icons like Beavis and Butt-head, a largely placeless and neutralized apostrophe in a globalized youth culture. Suburbanization in its turn came to extend the range of slangmaking. "New slang today," notes Allen, "is as likely to come from suburban malls as from the cities. The young people who frequent the suburban shopping malls in search of social life are themselves the object of slang, in the late 1980s called *mall rats* or *mallies*, collectively a *malling* of young people in a debased quest for urban excitement" [ibid.:26]. "A few ridiculing place names of probable suburban origin have appeared, such as *New Yecch* and *New York Shitty*, but there is *Filthydelphia*, too" [ibid.:259]. Today, we might add, a major locus of lexical innovation appears to be the non-locus of cyberspace, where an improvisational culture of "smilies," codes, and rushed abbreviations has surfaced.

Characteristically metropolitan or urban language, in other words, has been subject to a sociolinguistic sprawl and fragmentation, too, as urban lifestyles and values have multiplied and spread beyond the compass of the classic metropolis. Nevertheless, books like *New Yawk Tawk: A Dictionary of New York City Expressions* [Hendrickson 1998] or *Buzzwords:* L.A. *Freshspeak* [Scotti and Young 1997] still get written, and it remains possible to identify the following evolutions in the language of postwar metropolitans — shifts that are all the more important for having shaped the tools of postwar urban fiction writers and movie directors:

**1** An evolution towards hybridization, closely linked to phenomena of immigration and the concomitant multiculturalization of the metropolitan population. The best examples in the U.S. today are offered by such hybrids as Black English (politically foregrounded at one point by the debate over the existence of a separate, inner-city Ebonics) and Spanglish, which has been called "an effortless dance between English and Spanish, with the two languages clutched so closely together that at times they actually converge" [Alvarez 1997: n.p.]. In non-English-speaking European metropolises, such hybrids are produced mainly by mixing vernacular slang with English. A recent dictionary of the language spoken by youngsters in the *banlieue* of Paris, compiled by the Sorbonne linguist Jean-Pierre Goudaillier, contains a mix of French *argot*, English slang, and words from Arabic and various North and West African languages, leading to sentences of the type

42 Thus, every self-respecting *yup* today will go to the *gym* to do *reps* until his *abs* and *pecs* look like those in the *mags*, after which he will take care of the *rez* in a restaurant with excellent *recs* and frequented by *celebs*, where he just might have a *decaf*, unless he prefers to drop by at the *deli* to grab a BLT (bacon, lettuce, and tomato sandwich) with an OJ (orange juice) and replies to your suggestion of an evening out at the opera by a curt "Been there, done that." In Paris, likewise, every self-respecting *intello* will read *Le Nouvel Obs* or one or other *hebdo* at the *resto* and worry about what is BCBG (bon chique, bon genre).

"Cette meuf (girl), elle est tellement maigre, elle a pas d'airbags [breasts] qu'on peut la faxer." In a mixed French-Dutch-speaking city like Brussels, it is even possible to hear rap groups use Spanglish and produce lines like "la vida nuestra, the street experience, soy un real wrider with en mi mana some spraycans." And a young urban writer like Pier Vittorio Tondelli became a cult figure in Italian literature in part because of his use of the typical Italian-English mix spoken by young urbanites.

**2** An evolution towards greater semantic explicitness, most notable from the spreading of intensifiers and expletives in everyday language, at least at street level and in literary and cinematic fiction (though not, for moralistic and commercial reasons, on American network television). Graphic language, which has always been part of an intrinsically competitive and conflicting metropolitan environment but was originally more restricted to the working classes, has become both more widespread and (arguably) more violent and sexually explicit. This is the logical result of an urban society that has itself become more violent and allowed for more sexual freedom, but it has also been influenced by the media tapping into the colorful reservoir of this language with a stepped-up craze for sensationalism.

**3** A fundamentally subcultural or lifestyle-oriented evolution towards what may be called "trendification," signaled above all by the usage of an urban turbo lingo that responds to a culture of speed and energy and is geared to peer-group prestige and the demarcation of social boundaries. The most striking formal attributes of this lingo are its many abbreviations, letter words, and grammatically truncated sentences — linguistic features that are not restricted to English alone, but occur just as readily in other Western languages like French, German, Italian, or Dutch.[42] As with other consumption products in the mainstream economy, the turnover time of this language has considerably shortened and the wish to be a fashion trendsetter prevails. A quintessential urban-void movie like Gregg Araki's *The Doom Generation* derives one of its major *raisons d'être* precisely from the hip California nineties slang that it continually employs and that remains almost impenetrable to outsiders.

These three evolutions, we should note, are more a matter of quantitative increase than of qualitative difference. This is even more true of one final characteristic of metropolitan language that remains a crucial psychosocial defense mechanism and outlet for urban dwellers in a secularized and competitive world: humor. Cabarets, vaudevilles, and burlesques have a long metropolitan tradition and Dorothy Parker and her friends of the Algonquin Round Table may serve as famous mid-century examples of metropolitan humor. Today, a spate of stand-up comedians, literary and non-literary writers (from Tama Janowitz, Jay McInerney, and David Feinberg to the authors of L.A. *Bizarro! The Insider's Guide to the Obscure, the Absurd, and the Perverse in Los Angeles*), actors and film directors (with Woody Allen as conspicuous godfather of Jewish New York humor), and the endlessly popular television sitcoms that seek to domesticate metropolitan life by humorizing it (*Mad about You, Seinfeld, Spin City*), all collectively bear witness to the metropolitan impulse to counter and relax daily tensions by way of humor. According to cultural theorist Andrew Ross, a certain type of New York humor has even been institutionalized. "What humor does in general is normalize situations," says Ross. "It is since the city's fiscal crisis, 1975, that the survivalist component of humor has been not only normalized but glamorized, so that in the last 20 years or so, the physical danger of residency here has become the preferred cliché of New York City boosterism" [quoted in Weber 1997a: n.p.]. A postmodern writer like Donald Barthelme, who described his work in the most carnivalesque Bakhtinian tradition as a "laboratory of discourse" [quoted in Daniele 1994:80], has tapped this humoristic potential of New York language to remarkable effects. In so doing, he has also enhanced our awareness of the postmodern city as no longer a place of capitalistic fetishes only, but also of linguistic fetishes. Writers of Barthelme's kind have continued, in a more fragmented form and with a greater mix of "high" and "low," that aspect of the modernist literary project which consisted of displaying, through alienating shock effects, the negotiating function of language in the daily construction of selves and their environments. To the extent that literature has continued to play a role in the perception of the late-twentieth-century metropolis, then, it has done so in large part by raising the linguistic and discursive awareness of both urbanites and city-watchers.

*Developed by Bart Eeckhout and Bart Keunen*

# Case Studies

# [PART TWO]

Alan Hollinghurst
Dirk De Meyer
Kevin R. McNamara
Jude Davies
René Boomkens
Cino Zucchi
Kristiaan Borret
Lieven De Cauter
Liam Kennedy
Anne Gotman
Rudi Laermans
Sven Lütticken
Steven Jacobs
Trui Vetters
Bart Keunen
Kristiaan Versluys
Christophe Den Tandt
Maarten Delbeke

Edited by GUST

# Introduction



If the preceding 150 pages of theory present an exercise in multidisciplinary compilation, synthesis, and metanarrative, the ensuing 250 pages of case studies offer to extend and complicate the insights arrived at in the theory by narrowing, deepening, elaborating, and questioning them. What the preceding narrative must lack in nuance and detail can thus be set straight in the following pages. And what that same narrative has chosen to omit or quickly sidestep can now be given special attention. Issues that have received short shrift — whether in the form of concrete architectural debates, discussions of cultural artefacts (from books and audiovisual material to the fine arts), analyses of specific cities or characteristic urban sites, or confrontations with metatheoretical writings on space and postmodernity — all receive a place in the eighteen essays gathered here.

Since each of the essays has its own rationale and style, and since several of them combine and move across disciplines and topics, they cannot be squeezed into the same format established for the theory. To insist on keeping up the neat division of Space, Community, and Self would be Procrustean, the more so since many of the following contributions precisely seek to reunite those three aspects of our urban condition and are attuned to their intricate interweavings. The order in which the case studies are presented, however, does recall the bare outlines of Part One. Thus, the series opens with analyses that zoom in above all on *spatial and architectural* issues. Since these revolve principally around the phenomenon of sprawl, most famously embodied by Los Angeles, the essays that follow continue to address questions about the representation as well as the sociological and architectural repercussions of car-based posturban environments. Gradually, however, discussions concern themselves more and more with the issue of *community building* — an issue that comes into its own with analyses of particular urban groups at risk, such as ethnic minorities in inner cities and people with HIV. Community-oriented contributions in turn give way to a series of essays that are more clearly concerned with the place and function of *cultural-artistic representations* of city life. These essays draw on concepts raised above all in our chapter on self, but they do so while often remaining sensitive to broader questions about social cohesion and spatiality as well.

*Cruising into downtown Houston.*

**Alan Hollinghurst**

# From Hampstead to Houston

*Keywords:* ■ *Architecture* ■ *Posturban Space* ■ *Redevelopment*

When I tell people that I'm working in Houston for four months, those who've been there say: "My God! The drive from the airport!" They mean the drive from George Bush Intercontinental Airport, down Interstate 45 or 59. It's a ten or 12-lane highway, flanked by teeming feeder roads, and you career along it to the gathering rhythm of power pylons, used car lots, motels, the cacophony of billboards selling burgers, judges, vasectomy reversal, everything exposed and unashamed, the great aesthetic shock of America in all its barbarity and convenience. After twenty minutes or so, the famous downtown towers of Houston appear in a distant silhouette across the utterly flat and uncharming landscape. The freeway traffic hurtles towards them with daunting confidence, and before long you are right up beside those thousand-foot-high buildings, looking among them from the circling elevation of the road as the chasms of the streets flicker past. They have an extraordinary presence, the glamorous giants of the seventies and eighties half-obliterating surviving brick-clad structures that were giants in their day, and spelling out the fiercely Darwinian message of this boom city. Then they are behind you, and you get a confused hint of the rest of the place, which looks to a British eye like an endlessly extended suburb. Houston is now the fourth largest city in the United States, but it is hard to imagine when you arrive that you could ever come to like it, much less, as I think I did, to love it.

Houston is full of space — partly because there is a Texan endlessness of space for it to use, partly because so much of it has been knocked down. Any journey across town runs through zones of emptiness, intermittent blocks of ruin and decay, garish disjunctions, seams of poverty. It is a car city, second in that only to Los Angeles, and the parking lots are themselves a part of the pattern of emptiness. They give an odd rhythm to much of Downtown, like a half-cleared game of cyclopean solitaire. Newer buildings there aim at concentration by being raised on plinths of parking-garage eight or 12 stories high. In between them are numerous other vast parking-garages, sometimes half disguised, but distinguishable by the oblique lines of their inner ramps. The buildings themselves are often linked by passages below ground, to avoid the astounding heat and humidity of the summer, so the sense of empty space is subtly intensified. There is no Manhattanish bustle between office and subway (there is no subway); just the coming and going of the cars.

In my early days there it was perhaps some unacknowledged form of homesickness that kept me perversely reading the wonderful fat new edition of Pevsner's *City of London*, revised and expanded by Simon Bradley (Penguin, 1997). I found myself repeatedly escaping from the shallow architectural culture of Houston (founded 1836, the year of Texan independence) into imaginary rambles through my own city (founded 50 BC); and indulging a slightly self-conscious relish for the lanes and livery-halls and melancholy churches of London, alongside a faintly supercilious dismay at the trashiness and sprawl of my temporary home. Bradley has written an enthralling introduction, giving a historical overview of the growth of the City and bringing out to the full its oddity and insularity as well as its almost ungraspably layered density. To marvel at it was a kind of defense mechanism while I struggled to absorb the initial disconcertment of Houston, so torrid and extreme, so faceless or recklessly ugly, its inner life so hidden. I am still haunted by the number of windowless buildings there.

Houston's Pevsner, and my main means of imaginative entry to the city, is Stephen Fox, a professor at both the large and unlovely University of Houston, where I am teaching, and the élite Rice University, which has a beautiful campus laid out by the Boston architect Ralph Adams Cram just before the Great War; Cram's original Byzantine-eclectic halls and quadrangles are still being gracefully augmented by sympathetic architects such as Cesar Pelli. Fox is the author of the covetable AIA guide to Houston, published in 1990 and so covering the immense expansion of the boom years between the Arab oil embargo of 1973 and the mid-eighties slump, but none the less ready for further revision. His knowledge of the place is inexhaustible, scholarly, loving but not uncritical, and all the more remarkable in that he does not drive. There is something touching about this last fact, as a testament to his own devotion to his adopted city (he comes from the far south-west of Texas), and to the constant readiness of others to take him round. Houston needs its defenders and exegetes. It is not a tourist city, and it strikes me early on that Houstonians don't expect their environment to be admired, and are wonderfully generous to anyone who shows an interest. Fox flatteringly offers me a Houston tour, on the obvious condition that I take the wheel.

The Sunday afternoon agreed on is one of heavy rain, and everything we see is craned at through the splosh of the windscreen-wipers. Yet, oddly, I can't remember the impediment, and recall only the communicated pleasure of looking, and the new sense of logic as the growth of the city is explicated: the competitiveness, the accelerated flux of fashion and money, the westward migrations of the rich, the impact of one or two key developers. The contrasts are certainly astounding. Houston has no zoning laws, and the mood of planning laissez-faire is both exhilarating and melancholy. Something, like nothing, happens anywhere.

The downtown area once contained the mansions of the rich, but they have all gone; some of those baking, dusty parking-lots were once their gardens. Elsewhere "little" 12-story office buildings of the boom years were mere teasers for vaster projects which never had time to be built. Or as a commercial development ran into the slump it turned into a residential one, to slightly eerie effect. Just occasionally an owner held out, and an older house huddles stubbornly in the shadow of the surrounding highrises.

Stephen directs me to go through the former Fourth Ward. It is an old African-American quarter, much of it demolished to make way for new middle-income housing in the horribly bastard sub-postmodern style common in Houston — fanlights, balustrades, other bits of tat. Beside these, the late 19th-century rows of tiny wooden "shotgun" cottages along potholed or unpaved roads exhibit an architectural dignity that is only a part of their eloquence. The type takes its name from the unhappy certainty that the discharge of a shotgun through the front door would pass through the back door without encountering any (architectural) obstacle. Most of the ones here are well kept up. One or two have slumped into the engulfing vegetation of this swampy place. Then you lift your eyes and just beyond the trees, startlingly close, the downtown towers loom and glitter. Stephen says how moving the Fourth Ward is, and I feel deeply touched by it myself — as a late symbol of close-knit urban life in a city that is all suburban dispersal and avoidance of focus; and a poignant architectural survival in a city of such rapid erasures. But apparently the black mayor does not support the preservation of these archetypal Southern working-class dwellings. And one can see

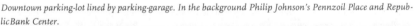

*Downtown parking-lot lined by parking-garage. In the background Philip Johnson's Pennzoil Place and RepublicBank Center.*

that they perpetuate (if that is the word) the original distinction between the white Downtown and the adjacent black area which serviced it. Later, I find myself questioning my surge of emotion. Later still, an African-American friend speaks of the place as a kind of disgrace. When I suggest showing it to a friend visiting from England, he says: "My God! Don't take him there!"

The flatness of Houston. An early arrival on the bayou sailed straight past it without noticing, so utterly did it lack elevation; certainly the later mania for elevation is part of the city's crudely defiant dynamic. When landscape is reduced to invisibility the buildings take on a new supremacy. Living on one of the steepest roads in London I find the flatness after a while emotionally oppressive, and book a flight to San Francisco, really just so as to see a hill. True, there is a northern area called the Heights, which sounds as if it ought to be the Hampstead of Houston, but the altitude in question turns out to be a mere 23 feet — not enough to notice, at least until a tropical storm comes in and the rest of the city is under water. Otherwise it is only from the raised racetrack of the freeway that you get any kind of view over things. Or of course from a high building itself. I. M. Pei's 1002-foot-tall Texas Commerce Tower has an observation deck on the 60th floor, a good way short of the summit. From it you look down into the Deco crown of a nearby twenties block, and across other rooftop areas not quite meant to be seen. The rest of Downtown clusters around, but its glamour is reduced and exposed. What strikes you more is the leafiness of the rest of the city, much of which is almost invisible among trees, browning now in the late quasi-autumn. It is like a poetic resolution of the vacancy and transience of Houston, as if nature had

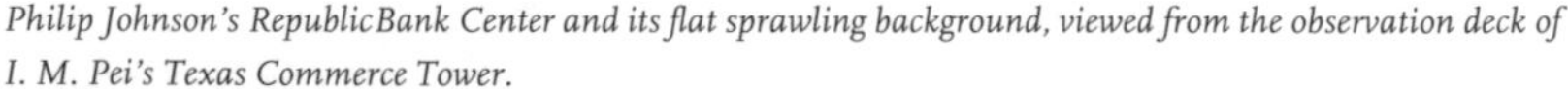

*Philip Johnson's RepublicBank Center and its flat sprawling background, viewed from the observation deck of I. M. Pei's Texas Commerce Tower.*

reclaimed the place. It looks at least like a garden city; until you see, far off, the secondary Downtown of the Galleria area, and the glinting monolith of Philip Johnson's Transco Tower.

Johnson is perhaps the most conspicuous architect in the Houston cityscape. He was brought in by the Menils, the city's great artistic benefactors, and his later career is interestingly represented here. First there is the economical Miesian minicampus of the Catholic University of St. Thomas, built in the late fifties, a place and moment at which, as Stephen Fox says, "the spirit of the new entered Houston." Nearly twenty years later he designed with John Burgee the first of his giant commercial buildings, Pennzoil Place. It stands towards the edge of the Downtown cluster of corporate towers, and makes a subversive play on them by actually being two towers, only ten feet apart. Their surface is refinedly Miesian, articulated by close-set vertical black I-beams, but in the dynamic play of forms and angles Johnson is his own man. Pennzoil Place becomes one of my favorite Houston sights, constantly changing as one circles round it or walks through the narrow ravine between its two parts — which mass and merge and separate again with a lightness and tension never quite achieved, for example, by the twin towers of the World Trade Center.

It is a repeated dull shock to glimpse, between these finely honed forms, the sterile and bombastic RepublicBank Center, which Johnson built seven years later on the other side of the street. This is one of his buildings which blows up a traditional but alien form to a colossal scale — like the broken-pedimented tallboy of his famous AT&T building in New York. Here it is the pinnacled, stepped gable

*Philip Johnson and John Burgee's Pennzoil Place.*

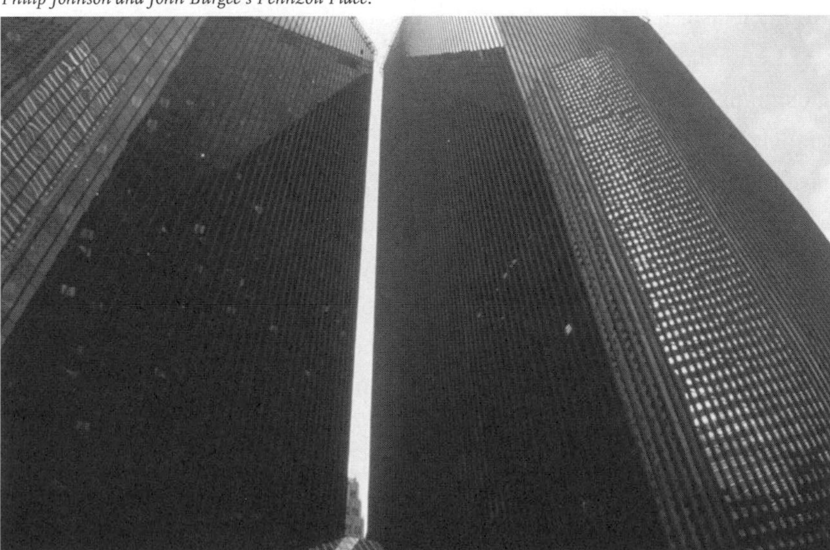

of a Flemish cloth-hall raised in overtopping triplicate eight or nine hundred feet high. It must be said that it's a popular building with Houstonians, and in a sense a trademark one among the relative anonymity of its neighbors. If the Transco Tower is more successful it is because the language it adapts is that of the visionary skyscrapers of the twenties and thirties; like much new design of the eighties and nineties it has a slightly camp quality, as if it were imitating a long-ago imagining of the future. Also it stands alone, like Cesar Pelli's more blockish but very American Canary Wharf tower in London, and its soaring glass surfaces, like Canary Wharf's stainless steel ones, help make it a theater of sublime effects when seen from a distance in storm, haze, or sunset.

I watch a documentary about the Loisaux family — three generations of demolitionists. Their technique is described, not quite accurately, as implosion: they hollow buildings out and then collapse them inwards; and there seems something efficiently nihilistic about this, unlike the dogged poking and swinging of bulldozers and iron balls, which dramatize the doomed resistance of the structures. We see them at work removing the inner walls of great sad interwar apartment and office buildings, thirty-story hotels with ballrooms at the top and huge neon "HOTEL" signs stilted up on the roof. One building has gone from being a hotel to a masonic temple to a private home: an odd recension. The Loisaux are perfectionists, bringing down their prey with the minimum of charge in the exactest area. We see them demolish the Douglas Building in downtown Omaha: rough brick sidewalls and grandiose corniced and pilastered street façades. One set of charges weakens the building, a second set brings it down. Each victim looks indescribably obsolete in its last erect moments; yet the technique is devised to assault what is essentially modern about them all: their immensely strong metal or reinforced concrete frames.

Demolitions of a slower kind are depicted in an exhibition of Paul Hester's photographs of Houston, "The Elusive City," shown at the Menil Collection, the serenely long and luminous museum by Renzo Piano which is one of Houston's most treasured resources. Hester's vision is rather at odds with it: he has a clever eye for what is actually seen but rarely isolated and framed: his subject is less architecture than the spaces between architecture, that interstitial emptiness which is so potent a part of Houston but not of New York or New Orleans or San Francisco. He observes the obviously ephemeral — shacks, strip-joints, neighborhood tarot parlors — alongside the monumental sheen of bank lobbies and Downtown towers too tall to fit the frame. Like any close observer of a place he loves, he produces anecdotes and memorabilia, but he also has pictures with no discernible subject at all: a bit of freeway, an empty parking-lot, figures waiting at a bus-stop in a featureless street. And then he has pictures in which the monuments themselves become nothing: the demolition of the Shamrock Hotel (1949-87), or of the colossal blank cylinders of the Rice Elevators. He shows the Memorial Baptist Hospital ripped and trashed against a beautiful but pitiless background of night-lit office towers.

Boomtown thoughts. I remember how in 1982 the TLS, which I had recently joined, moved to Clerkenwell, an area of obsolescent trades, little printers, and watchmenders. I liked it, despite its shabbiness and apartness and oppressive closeness, for a vegetarian, to the bloody squalor of Smithfield meatmarket. But then, as that convulsive and destructive decade continued, Clerkenwell changed. It was discovered, clustered around a deep railway cutting halfway between the City and the West End. People moved in and out. And it wasn't all bad. The stinking little cafés and third-rate trattorias were suddenly supplemented by bracingly pricey restaurants. Galleries, wine merchants, even nightclubs opened. There was refurbishment; but there was also massive destruction. A sombrely impressive Piranesian warehouse along the railway line was demolished, and replaced by a meretricious street-long office block in the ubiquitous grey and maroon of low-class eighties development. Bits of postmodern nonsense were quickly run up. Whole blocks of small-scale Victorian commercial building were reduced to rubble and anonymous new projects begun. And then the boom was over, and the building stopped, and for years and years there were just the concrete stumps, sprouting their reinforcement rods, and empty half-built frames encroached on by weeds and small bushes. They were premature ruins, and very symptomatic ones. They seemed to have a curious formal kinship with the real ruins, the Blitz bombsites which were still numerous when I first came to London in the early sixties, and the last of which, deployed as rough carparks between shattered walls, survived into the late eighties. This was the devastated City that Pevsner had had to describe in his original volume of 1957, and I realize that I was lucky to have seen it on the threshold of its delayed (and sometimes disastrous) redevelopment. The presence of the different types of ruin keeps coming back to me as I drive each day through the gappy urban fabric of Houston; though Houston, of course, has never been bombed by anything but money.

I am invited to Galveston by some friends, and taken on a windshield tour by Ellen Beasley, co-author with Stephen Fox of an excellent architectural guide to the town, and author of a book on the alleys which run behind the houses, like long, straight, slightly countrified mews. Galveston is a boomtown of the later 19th century, a port, founded, like Houston, on cotton, and a major point of immigration. It covers a long narrow island, and the journey to it, past the oil refineries and petrochemical plants of Texas City, is one of the most hideous I can remember making. Galveston suffered from a terrible hurricane in 1900, and a decade later from the opening of a ship canal to Houston, forty miles to the northwest, which effectively took its business away. In its decline it became famous as a gambling town. Nowadays it has a long, delightless front but behind it an amazing amount of the old town survives and has been beautifully conserved. We drive round block after block of raised white wooden houses, distinguishing the different formats, the variety of gables, the follies of the rich, and again the little backhouses in the alleys, where the mainly black servants once lived. The town has its own architectural hero, an Irishman called Nicholas Clayton, who designed a number of vigorous polychrome brick buildings in a medley of late Victorian styles. Ellen is deeply attuned to her subject, and has a particular appreciation of the simple geometry of the more modest houses, which have their own subtleties of vocabulary and proportion. About ten times she says: "This one is my favorite." We drive on and on, through derelict black neighborhoods, boarded-up social housing, past the last surviving bordello, gaping behind a chainlink fence, and out to the desolation of the town's edge: the vast ruined Falstaff brewery, zones of salt marsh, distant lines of grey concrete silos. The car humps over half-buried railway tracks and, caught up in Ellen's emotion, I find myself nodding and murmuring in melancholy appreciation of a scene that is undeniably frightening and sad.

The writer Phillip Lopate described Houston as a "covert, lyrical city," and as the months go past these unexpected adjectives slowly reveal their rightness. The lyric has the lightly thudding rhythm of the car's tires over the concrete blocks of the long straight avenues, and the sedated pace of American town traffic, so different from the communal frenzy of the freeway or the clogged aggression of London driving; as well as the generalized sense of aptness which comes from falling in love with a place. And as the open-sesames of Texan hospitality follow each other, new districts unfold. One evening it's a party in North Boulevard, the street at the humblest end of which I live, but which, as one drives eastward, grows grander and grander by the block, until it is a triple avenue of live oaks flanked by twenties mansions — now Spanish, now French, now severely Georgian, now picturesque Lutyens Tudor. The juxtapositions are as surreal as you could hope for from a new plutocracy, but the houses themselves have space to breathe, unlike comparable avenues of the same period in North London, with soulless and pretentious neo-William and Mary manor houses packed side by side. Next it is a party in the Heights, in a different kind of twenties house, a corner bungalow with candles on the porch and a profound suburban calm in the roads which seem to stretch away for ever under the trees.

And then, one of the best surprises of Houston, a visit to the architect Cameron Armstrong, who lives in one of a number of "tin houses" he has built in the West End (so named from its being the end of the long-vanished Blossom Street trolley line). These houses are sided in Galvalume, an alloy produced in flexible sheets which can then be crimped into rigid folds. They pick up on the forms and scale of various metal-sided sheds in the area, but their language is sophisticatedly modern. Armstrong speaks of the influence of the great Viennese architect Rudolph Schindler, who worked so inventively in the climatic conditions of his adopted California; and certainly the interiors of Armstrong's own house and of others he shows me round display a refined modernist apprehension of the ever-changing subtleties of light, the multiplicity of whites, and the ambiguous margins between inside and outside. There is grandeur and intimacy, and surprising relations between the two. Unlike most new Houston domestic architecture, the houses are both practical and beautiful. Where brick can reach 140 degrees and turn a house into a kiln, and stucco absorbs the damp, and wood rots and drops off, the tin is resistant and cools quickly and should prove to have a long life. The architectural press seems to have passed Armstrong's work by, but its new synthesis of modernism with its industrial roots is highly original and satisfying.

In general it is artists and collectors who have commissioned the best — though not by a long way the biggest — new houses. It takes time, a good guide, or good luck to come upon these quiet, unannounced enclaves, leafy, almost rural-feeling little quartiers in the West End or along the inner curves of the bayou, where you sense a sudden change of terms, and the vulgar suburban conformism of latter-day Houston is shot through with originality and beauty.

This text was written at the outcome of a term spent teaching in the Creative Writing Program at the University of Houston, Texas (Fall 1998). It was earlier published as a guest column in the *London Review of Books* 21, 6 (18 March 1999): 32-33, and is reprinted here with kind permission of the author and the publishers.

*Julius Shulman, night-time view of Case Study House #22 by Pierre Koenig, Hollywood Hills, 1959-60.*

Dirk De Meyer

# Agonizing Arcadia: Notes on Postwar Architecture in Los Angeles

*Keywords:* ■ *Architecture* ■ *Photography* ■ *Suburbanization* ■ *Wallification*

*"Whenever I happen to be in a city of any size, I marvel that riots do not break out every day: massacres, unspeakable carnage, a doomsday chaos. How can so many human beings coexist in a space so confined without destroying each other, without hating each other to death? As a matter of fact, they do hate each other, but they are not equal to their hatred. And it is this mediocrity, this impotence, that saves society, that assures its continuance, its stability. Occasionally some shock occurs by which our instincts profit; but afterward we go on looking each other in the face as if nothing had happened, cohabiting without too obviously tearing each other to shreds. Order is restored, a ferocious calm as dreadful, ultimately, as the frenzy that had interrupted it."*[1] — E.M. Cioran, *History and Utopia*, 1960

Immaculate, transparent, lighthearted, and self-confident: of all the Case Study Houses built in the 1940s through 1960s, the Case Study House #22 that Pierre Koenig built in 1959 on lot 1635 of Woods Drive in the Hollywood Hills most caught the public imagination. The photos by Julius Shulman turned it into a manifesto for this program of well-designed single-family housing affordable for the typical post-World War II American family. The Case Study Houses were intended to perfect domestic life along "contemporary" lines, to design an architectural ideal for the average American family, which by the end of the 1950s lived in greater prosperity than ever before and was not yet traumatized by the impending Vietnam mobilization. The houses were developed from 1945 onwards under the missionary impulse of John Entenza and his Los Angeles-based magazine *Arts and Architecture*. With his magazine and a handful of architects, Entenza "really made it appear that Los Angeles was about to contribute to the world not merely odd works of architectural genius but a whole consistent style."[2] Entenza reported on the construction of the Case Study Houses with dramatic pictures of building sites; he organized public showings and presented the results with lavish documentary photographs and product descriptions meant to rouse and inspire emulation. In his view, Koenig's designs evinced "some of the cleanest and most immaculate thinking in the development of the small contemporary house."[3] With the publication of the Koenig house on the cover of Esther McCoy's pioneering *Modern California Houses* in 1962, canonization was finally achieved.[4]

**Arcadian Angels** The meticulously composed nocturnal shot Julius Shulman made of C.S.H. #22 for *Arts and Architecture* shows two emphatically easy-going and chatting young ladies in cocktail dresses who, thanks to the gravitation-defeating architecture, float like angels over L.A. The photo is to Los Angeles what Robert Doisneau's *Baiser de l'hôtel de ville*, only a few years older, is to Paris. Doisneau's lovers kiss themselves a path through density, navigating between strolling and rushing pedestrians, between passing cars and sidewalk cafés. From high up on their Californian Peloponnesus, in an Arcadia where Puritan chastity reigns over French passion, Shulman's young ladies seem to slight so much sensual urbanity.[5] Not *Stadtluft* but ocean-breeze-cum-air-conditioning *macht frei*. Set at a distance from each other that is dictated by etiquette and composition, they are literally elevated above the city and congestion. They hardly even contemplate that city: they are not gaping at the endless flat plain of stars dropped from the sky. The only one to remain impressed by the abstract grid of this nocturnal Mesopotamia of pop culture is the (excluded) spectator, who still has to get used to the idea that walls may be decorated with other grid patterns than those of wallpaper. For the two silent angels with demurely crossed legs no environment would seem more natural. "Los Angeles," wrote *The Los Angeles Examiner* in 1960 about the inhabitants of this house, "is their great, big front yard."[6]

So much is clear: Hollywood and life here coincide. Here the prophecy of the Apocalypse has been realized: "And I saw a new heaven and a new earth ...

1 E.M. Cioran, *History and Utopia*, trans. Richard Howard (New York: Seaver Books, 1987), 80. Original version, see E.M. Cioran, *Œuvres* (Paris: Gallimard, 1995), 1035.

2 Reyner Banham, *Los Angeles: The Architecture of Four Ecologies* (Harmondsworth: Penguin, 1971), 225.

3 *Arts and Architecture* (February 1959): 19.

4 Esther McCoy, *Modern California Houses* (New York: Reinhold, 1962). The same photograph is also shown, as a "symbol for Los Angeles," in Leonard Pitt and Dale Pitt, *Los Angeles A to Z: An Encyclopedia of the City and the County* (Berkeley and Los Angeles: University of California Press, 1997).

5 In kind and composition, too, the photos are each other's antipodes: Shulman's renaissance staging vs. Doisneau's apparently coincidental snapshot. As to the image of Arcadia: L.A. was viewed by several of its founders and immigrants as an Eden, and twice literally even as an Arcadia. In 1888, E. J. "Lucky" Baldwin developed Arcadia, one of L.A. County's cities, at the foot of the San Gabriel Mountains. And Abel Stearns in 1858 called the first modern commercial structure of L.A. Arcadia Block.

6 "Milestone on a Hilltop/A Milestone in Steel," in *Los Angeles Examiner: Pictorial Living*, 17 July 1960.

7 See M.A. Ovnick, "Film-Making, House-Building, and the Mark of Zorro," paper delivered at the Fifty-First Annual Meeting of the Society of Architectural Historians (Los Angeles, April 1998).

8 Kurt Forster, "Improvisations on locations: on Frank Gehry's architecture," *Architectural Review*, 182, 1090 (1987): 65.

and I saw the holy city ... And the city had no need of the sun, neither of the moon to shine in it" [Rev. 21:1-2, 23]. Los Angeles has not only rendered celestial bodies superfluous, it has simply switched heaven and earth: the "real" star-spangled sky is dazzled by its artificial counterpart. In the city in which you stumble over film crews, in the Movie Capital of the World, film making and home building have been tightly interwoven ever since the end of the First World War.[7] Hollywood brought to L.A. not only money, talent, genius, neurosis, and charlatanry, but also architecture. In the 1920s, the production of *Zorro* led to a boom of Spanish haciendas. These were inspired not by Mediterranean or Mexican models but by filmsets. The houses, like the sets, combined all allusions, all clichés so that they became recognizable at a single glance. In a similar way, other buildings arose in the interstices of the grid between Sunset and Firestone Boulevards: Aztec temples, Bavarian castles, Tudor manors, and Chinese pagodas. The notion that history is absent from L.A. is one of the few clichés about the city that are *not* true: history is there alright, but it is *condensed history*, homogenized, timeless in the most literal sense, and collected without much geographical inhibition.

Entenza and Shulman had both worked for the movie industry, and neither had failed to notice the one peculiar characteristic of the city which an inspired Swiss observer, from a geographically similar position as that of the young ladies, would summarize as "a city of locations rather than sites."[8] But in the *Arts and Architecture* experiments, the influence of Hollywood reaches even further: it *precedes* the materialized architecture. Even the building-site pictures of the Case Study Houses look like film stills. When Julius Shulman in 1950 recorded the construction of the unnumbered Case Study House in Pacific Palisades, the architect Raphael Soriano — with visionary glance, fashionably cut suit,

*Julius Shulman, building site of the unnumbered Case Study House by Raphael Soriano, Pacific Palisades, Los Angeles, 1950.*

drawings under his arm — is a perfect match for Howard Roark, alias Gary Cooper, the lone champion of Modernism in King Vidor's *The Fountainhead* of one year earlier. Shulman's photograph catches the essence of Soriano's self-declared agenda for this project: "it has the virility of realness."[9]

Pierre Koenig's Case Study House #22 distinguishes itself from Soriano's quest for realness, and from other transpositions of film studios to the reality of L.A. (let us suppose for a moment that such a "reality" exists). The difference resides in the awareness that angels, liberated as they are from necessity, do not dwell in a fixed abode. Their most characteristic attribute turns them into nomads *par excellence*. Typical of the pictures from *Arts and Architecture* is the limited spectrum of discernible activities, which seems to favor only the art of flower arrangement and the nonchalant touching of a book or magazine (no signs of reading). When a man and a woman are both in the same picture, they appear as a quiet emblem of the family. They converse with each other, but keep a remarkable distance. The "contemporary minded family" is childless and (hence?), like angels, sexless.[10] In kitchens, no cooking is done, in swimming pools no swimming. The only trace of human subordination to necessity is the pouring of a drink — a task which is invariably performed by the woman, apparently lady of the house.

**Domestic Nomads** By reducing his entire architectural program to its Californian essence of "a free floating roof shelter,"[11] Koenig succeeds in realizing an architectural oxymoron that combines chaste family domesticity with unbound nomadism. What else is this Case Study House but the materialization of a site that is limited only by a roof? It suffices to consider the difference between the ostensible absence of a supporting structure *here* and the essential role of such a structure in that Olympian glass house designed by Ludwig Mies van der Rohe for Edith Farnsworth. Compared to the extreme vulnerability of Koenig's and Ellwood's houses, Mies's comes across as built by God himself.

Koenig's structure does not enclose; it knows itself free from the task of protecting, of lodging. Cheerfully it adds to the nomadic status of its residents.

9 Raphael Soriano, "Note on Case Study House 1950," in *Arts and Architecture* (January 1950): 26.

10 The childless family was described by the magazine as the "contemporary minded family" in *Arts and Architecture* (May 1958): 15.

11 *Arts and Architecture* (February 1960): 26.

12 Reyner Banham, "Klarheit, Ehrlichkeit, Einfachkeit... and *Wit* Too!: The Case Study Houses in the World's Eyes," in *Blueprints for Modern Living: History and Legacy of the Case Study Houses*, exhibition organized by Elizabeth A.T. Smith (Los Angeles: Museum of Contemporary Art; Cambridge, MA.: MIT Press, 1989), 185.

13 Kevin Starr, "The Case Study House Program and the Impending Future," in *Blueprints for Modern Living*, 143. In 1962, Entenza would in fact sell *Arts and Architecture* and move to Chicago, where he became president of the Graham Foundation and went to live in an apartment designed by Mies.

Koenig translates into all-American family values what had been the ambition of those Austrian bohemians — Neutra, Schindler, and others — who settled in Los Angeles around 1920: the Schindlers slept on the roof of their house, without any further protection, until one of those rare winter showers compelled them to build a cover. Their work was characterized by an outmaneuvering of the outdoors: in Schindler's house or Neutra's 1946 Bailey House, the garden is incorporated as an indispensable part of the spatial organization of the interior.

From the 1940s onwards, the delightfully naïve dream of Schindlerian *bricolage* was challenged by the sophisticated technologies of the war industry. Charles and Ray Eames and countless others worked for this industry and applied the results in the fields of architecture and furniture design. The ideal of a quasi-nomadic existence between inside and outside — still characteristic of the Eames House: two large trailers between eucalyptus trees — is adapted to the demands of the market and of mass production as well as to the growing demand for luxury and status affirmation. Architectural experiments get stuck in imitations of filmsets and futuristic (would-be) upper-class ambitions. To be sure, in L.A. *form* had never really followed *function* — Arcadia is not subject to necessity — and a sense of decorum had always been fundamental to American Modernism. But while Lautner's 1960 Chemosphere House, built on a supposedly unusable plot of land, is still the product of straightforward ingeniousness and evinces a liberating mix of pile dwelling and S.F. fantasy, the Case Study Houses #23 and 25 by Killingsworth, Brady & Smith (in La Jolla and Long Beach, 1961 and 1962) are status-producing *settings* — including scenic water parts and five-meter-high entrance doors.

**Cozy Consumers** The all-American family, meanwhile, feels ill at ease with the crystalline challenges set by Koenig and Ellwood. And while to some Europeans Neutra's houses are even too much old hat, "too heavily compromised by the historicism of *Heimatstil* and folksy vernacular revivalism,"[12] by the early 1960s the Case Study Houses are revealed to the American public "in [their] true nature, a prophetic experiment, not the achieved prototype of a new kind of mass housing."[13] Office workers and upscale blue collars are not buying into the *Arts and Architecture* dream. In the postwar America of McCarthy, they prefer to identify with Mr. Blanding's Cape Cod coziness in *Mr. Blanding Builds His Dream House* (1948), rather than with Howard Roark's architecture of steel, concrete, and glass in *The Fountainhead* (1949). A modern utopian architecture like Laszlo Moholy-Nagy's design for the filmsets in *Things to Come* (William Cameron Menzies, 1936) is being received with less and less enthusiasm. Moholy-Nagy's designs seem like prefigurations of Koenig's C.S.H. experiments: "Houses were no longer obstacles to, but receptacles of, man's natural life force, light. There were no walls, but skeletons of steel, screened with glass and plastic sheets. The accent was on perforation and contour, an indication of a new reality rather than reality itself."[14] But much as the Hungarian's designs were barred by movie producers in favor of Vincent Corda's Boullée-like futurism, the general public (at which both Hollywood and the Case Study Houses were directed) turned away from the utopias of Modernism. Another Utopia was waiting for the all-American family, stretched out over hundreds of square miles full of new developments in Van Nuys Town, Lakewood, Pomona, and the entire Citrus Belt. There, middle-class ambitions were combined with traditional typologies — somewhere between neocolonial and Pennsylvania Dutch, the styles most cherished by the fifties Hollywood movie.

The realm of experimentation is narrowed to mere technological experiments in production, in the scale and seriality of building. Fordism takes the place of the dream of domesticated nomadism. The ideal of an existence between naturescape and artscape is transformed into a massive, hopeful subjection to the grid and to the assured regularity of concrete and lawn. "The critics of suburbs say that you and I live narrow lives. I agree. My life is narrow. From one perspective or another, all our lives are narrow. Only when lives are placed side by side do they seem larger."[15]

The harsh laws of the market economy merely allow for experiments that are able to increase profits instantly. Suburbia-in-the-making becomes a chronometrically organized assembly line.

*In 1949, three developers bought 3,500 acres of Southern California farmland. They planned to build something that was not exactly a city.... The houses in this suburb were built in the same way. As many as a hundred a day were begun between 1950 and 1952, more than five hundred a week.... Construction crews in thirty-man teams built the rows of houses. Each team of workmen was subdivided by specialty. One man with a pneumatic hammer nailed subfloors on five houses a day. The framers finished lengths of precut lumber with new, electric saws. Another crew operated a power door hanger. Rough plaster laid by one crew was smoothed a few minutes later by another. Subcontractors delivered construction materials in exact amounts directly to each*

14 Sibyl Moholy-Nagy, *Experiment in Totality* (Cambridge, MA.: MIT Press, 1969), 129.

15 D. J. Waldie, *Holy Land: A Suburban Memoir* (New York: Norton, 1996), 94.

16 Waldie, *Holy Land*, 4, 7-8, 10.

17 In reality, the picture was staged by the publicist for the developers. He offered the opportunity to local movers to have their trucks, with respective names and telephone numbers, pictured in *Life*: see Waldie, *Holy Land*, 89-90.

18 Waldie, *Holy Land*, 34-35.

*building site. Expediters coordinated the work from radio-equipped cars. The foreman used a loudspeaker to direct the movement of his men.... If the workmen looked up from laying rafters, they saw a row of houses with bundles of shingles being lifted by conveyor belts to shinglers on the roof. Beyond them was a row of house frames being sheathed in tar paper and chicken wire. Beyond them was another row of houses gray with new stucco. Beyond that row would be another row of houses, only a few days older, being painted. Behind them, nearly out of sight, would be a street of finished houses, forty-six to a block.*[16]

Much as the experiments in "contemporary" architecture found their promotional channel in *Arts and Architecture*, the large-scale development of suburbia enjoyed the attention of a less specialized, but more widespread American press. The suburban development of Lakewood in Los Angeles County described above made it into *Time* magazine in 1950 as the "biggest housing development in the world." *Life* documented it with encomiums and an entirely staged photograph showing the arrival of families, which were then moving into their new homes at the rate of 35 families a day.[17]

The houses sold like hot cakes: "When the sales office opened on a cloudless Palm Sunday in April 1950, twenty-five thousand people were waiting.... Couples waited in line to be led in and out of a row of seven model houses, the first time that a street of model houses was used to sell a subdivision.... The models were furnished by the Aaron Schultz furniture store in Long Beach. Each model was decorated in one of four styles — Maple, Traditional, Modern, and Provincial."[18] The model houses, affordable by almost every blue-collar purse, are the pictures

*J. R. Eyerman, "Moving Day," Lakewood, Los Angeles.* Life Magazine, *July 13, 1953.*

of *Arts and Architecture* turned reality. Only, the Arcadia of hills and nature has become a rather flat Promised Land, which, because of the titanic attempt to democratize the ideal of a detached house with garden, winds up being densely occupied. And, not least importantly, "modern" has become an option. The "contemporary" experiments by Entenza and Co. were not spared. In a 1950 issue of *House Beautiful*, a magazine for interior decoration, they were called no less than un-American — a term with a then-familiar ring in circles around Joseph McCarthy. Gradually, Hollywood began to opt for more cozy-eclectic interiors, "especially if the film was a comedy or was concerned with one or another variation of mid-American goodness.... Only villains, it seems, or Europeans (frequently they are the same) were permitted to write on glass-topped tables or sit in Eames chairs."[19]

The immediate surroundings of houses reflect the same shift in values. The (apart from a swimming pool) undomesticated nature of C.S.H. #22 is transformed here into the emblem of the American cultural landscape: the lawn.[20] In a local newspaper, a reporter hears from one of the new residents in Lakewood that they "wanted to get involved in the community ... but they wanted to get the grass growing in their front yard first."[21]

**Moving Targets** Already in 1965, the latently disconcerting aspect of these environments is recorded in Edward Ruscha's photo series *Some Los Angeles Apartments*.[22] But it is a film using the presentational techniques from *Arts and Architecture* that offers the most merciless dissection of the hopes and ambitions expressed in *Time, Life, House Beautiful*, and other family magazines. With the precision for documenting materials, fabrics, furniture, and appliances usually found in *Arts and Architecture*, a camera in 1968 registers the texture of new materials in the fully equipped homes of the Promised Land: wall-to-wall carpeting, vinyl wallpaper, cigarette-proof kitchen cupboards, and so on. The same attention is paid to the claustrophobic interior of the limousine in which one of the protagonists is driven through Los Angeles. In his film *Targets*, Peter Bogdanovich records the new domesticity in these suburbs, where "Daily life ... has an inertia that people believe in."[23] It is an everyday domesticity-cum-lawn, in between highways and drive-in cinemas, those paragons of the Angeleno's nomadic disposition.

19 Starr, "Case Study," 142.

20 See Georges Teyssot, ed., *The American Lawn* (New York: Princeton Architectural Press; Montreal: Canadian Centre for Architecture, 1999).

21 Waldie, *Holy Land*, 38.

22 Edward Ruscha, *Some Los Angeles Apartments* (Los Angeles: Edward Ruscha, 1965, limited first ed.; 2nd ed. 1970).

23 Waldie, *Holy Land*, 11.

24 Banham, *Los Angeles*, 23.

It is these and similar *topoi* that, in 1971, are hailed by a cyclist and architectural critic from London, Reyner Banham. For his study on *Los Angeles: The Architecture of Four Ecologies*, Banham "like earlier generations of English intellectuals who taught themselves Italian in order to read Dante in the original ... learned to drive in order to read Los Angeles in the original."[24] In Bogdanovich's case, by contrast, the highway is not so much a refuge as the lugubrious blow-up of a shooting range: in *Targets*, the moving anthropomorphical metal plates of shooting ranges are replaced by tinplates and their passengers gliding over the highway. The highway becomes the hunting ground for the psychopath. Bogdanovich hits L.A. in the arteries.

Until the end of the 1950s, the most frequently heard demand for control in the suburbs of Los Angeles County had to do with curbing dogs and their dirty habits. In *Targets*, by contrast, the neon letters "GUNS" are more omnipresent than McDonald's famous "M." And it is surely no coincidence that the movie watched by the protagonists in the drive-in cinema should be Roger Corman's *The Terror*, starring Boris Karloff. Bogdanovich's cynicism has come to be more visionary than Banham's optimism. The claim made by the non-conformist

*Edward Ruscha,* Some Los Angeles Apartments, *1965.*

*Three stills from Peter Bogdanovich,* Targets, *1968.*

techno-prophet Banham — "Miraculously the city's extremes include an excessive tolerance ... a heritage from the extraordinary cultural mixture with which the city began"[25] — can only be read, after the Rodney King riots, with a pitying smile, as a likable but naïve apology for a lost ideal.

**Voluntary Prisoners** If, a few issues of *Arts and Architecture* under your arm and with the expectation of seeing floating roofs in nature, you look for the Case Study Houses today, you will find yourself bumping into man-high walls and signs saying "No Trespassing: Armed Response" — the most common signboards in L.A. today. The new preconditions within which Banham's four ecologies — Surfurbia, Foothills, The Plains of Id, and Autopia — are to be enjoyed, are stringent:

*Twenty years ago, I was given a premonition of what Los Angeles would be like in the 1990s. My grandparents visited our house, in what was then the far western suburbs of Los Angeles, after returning from a cruise to Rio De Janeiro, Brazil. The stories they told me would have seemed unbelievably dystopian were it not for the fact I then believed that grandparents do not lie. They spoke of how the houses of the rich Brazilians were surrounded by high walls topped with broken glass. The concierges of apartment buildings carried automatic weapons. The city's outskirts were packed with cardboard and corrugated metal shanties. Children in ragged clothes slept on the sidewalks and ate out of garbage cans in alleys.*

*My parents still live in that same suburban house, purchased twenty-eight years ago. For eighteen of those years, the house remained much the same. I would pass through a front yard open to the street, unlock and rotate the doorknob, and walk in. Over the past decade, however, the simple act of entering the residence has grown dauntingly complex. Next to the door is a small metal plate with an illuminated red L.E.D., warning for the presence of an activated alarm. Upon disengaging the dead bolt and opening the front door, I have thirty seconds in which to deactivate the alarm by entering a sequence of digits into a small keypad in the entry hall.... Next, the dead bolt must be reengaged and a separate switch, located elsewhere in the house, must be tripped to deactivate pressure pads strewn beneath the floor and contacts embedded into the interior doorways. At that point the house's interior becomes safe for passage and the alarm may be safely reactivated as a perimeter defense. At any time, the alarm may be intentionally activated by hitting "panic buttons" sprinkled throughout the house at strategic locations. The exterior of the house, once illuminated only by a porch light, now basks in the glare*

25 Banham, *Los Angeles*, 25.

26 Steven Flusty, "Building Paranoia," in *Architecture of Fear*, ed. Nan Ellin (New York: Princeton Architectural Press, 1997), 47.

*of multiple 150-watt security lights in the back and side yards, switched on from dusk to dawn by photoelectric sensors.*
*My parents' house is one of the neighborhood's less obtrusively secured.*[26]

Today's Angeleno survives by moving from homes equipped with alarm systems to privately policed office buildings, from schools with metal detectors to golf, fitness, and other clubs sequestered by sizable membership fees. In the same year as *Targets* (and hence only a few years after Koenig's C.S.H.), Frank Gehry, as alert to changing social conditions as Bogdanovich, gave the Danziger Studio in South Hollywood, on the corner of La Brea and Melrose Avenues, the shape of a bunker. It will never become entirely clear whether these interiorized sites con-

*Gated community, 1998.*

*Frank Gehry, Danziger House and Studio, South Hollywood, 1968.*

tribute to social and cultural diversity or remain solely a matter of enclaves for elites. In contrast with the light-hearted and transparent techno-bucolic existence of Eames, Koenig, Banham, and friends, the new middle class hides behind walls where technology serves protective purposes first and foremost. The American ideal of the lawn holds its ground, but the houses themselves become as accessible as *palazzo Farnese* and are similarly surrounded by a private *soldateska*. *Form follows fear*: walls, barriers, steel gates rising up from the ground are the paraphernalia of contemporary architecture. "Even as the walls have come down in Eastern Europe, they are being erected all over Los Angeles."[27] A sharper contrast with the sliding rice-paper doors in Schindler's house is hardly thinkable. Withdrawn into gated communities or streets that are only nominally part of the public domain, well-to-do Angelenos live in their small-scale, private theme parks of the American Dream.

"Los Angeles cradles and embodies the most potent current version of the great bourgeois vision of the good life in a tamed countryside."[28] The idea of Los Angeles as a Poggio a Caiano for the masses, as Banham saw the city, is more accurate than the author himself probably anticipated: we know how the villa of the Medici dynasty near Prato is encircled by a defensive wall and how the Tuscany of the sixteenth century was a hypercontrolled police state in which armed and ruthless street urchins were deployed for extortion and murder. "L.A. the Magnificent," in the lucid epithet that Bob Winter, author of the best architectural guide to the city, devised in his opening lecture at the 1998 conference of the Society of Architectural Historians: L.A. as the Florentine archduke, who produced one of the most striking urban environments of his day and age, with a sampling of the best modern architecture; a fascinating man, but merciless to large parts of the population, and with a notoriously bad character.

It would be unfair to blame Gehry, in Benjaminian terms, for aestheticizing politics. He is the architect to be most explicit in showing us the new conditions

27 Mike Davis, *City of Quartz: Excavating the Future of Los Angeles* (London: Verso, 1990), esp. 221ff.

28 Banham, *Los Angeles*, 238.

29 In this respect, Gehry was not only noted by architects: see Fredric Jameson in *Postmodernism, or, The Cultural Logic of Late Capitalism* (Durham: Duke University Press, 1991), 107-29; and Davis, *City*, passim.

30 Davis, *City*, 239.

31 Ibid.

32 Manfredo Tafuri and Francesco Dal Co, *Architettura contemporanea* (Milano: Electa, 1979), 307. In his design for the Seagram Building along Park Avenue in New York (1954-58), Mies van der Rohe pulled the building back from the alignment, thereby creating a semi-public open space in front of it.

33 Diane Ghirardo, introduction to *Out of Site: A Social Criticism of Architecture*, ed. Diane Ghirardo (Seattle: Bay Press, 1991), 9-16.

34 In this respect, the West Palm Beach condominiums go much further than L.A.'s Bonaventure Hotel, which Davis used, in a fulminating response to Jameson's analysis in "Postmodernism, or, The Cultural Logic of Late Capitalism," as an example of "systematic segregation from the great Hispanic-Asian city outside": see Davis in *New Left Review* 146 (July-August 1984): 59-92.

of production for architecture.[29] His Frances Howard Goldwyn Library in Spanish Hollywood, "the most menacing library ever built,"[30] makes no attempt at covering up the first concern of Gehry's customers — a "vandalproof" building — nor the crucial presence of a new partner in the designing process: next to an officer of the Fire Department now sits the Chief of Police. "With its fifteen-foot security walls of stucco-covered concrete block, its anti-graffiti barricades covered in ceramic tile, its sunken entrance protected by ten-foot steel stacks, ... the Goldwyn Library ... projects the same kind of macho exaggeration as Dirty Harry's .44 Magnum."[31] On the endless plains of postmodernity, the space to move for a critical architectural production has really become quite small, and Gehry's buildings reveal this condition. They also show the impossibility, in the postmodern urban sprawl, of an aristocratic critique like the one implied by the Seagram Building in New York, where "Mies takes a step backward and keeps silent."[32] A gesture that means to L.A. what Mies van der Rohe's classic *Entsagung* meant to the hustle and density of Manhattan — the parading of a void as a sign of disdain for the fundamental condition of the metropolis, scarcity of land, and this on the most expensive spot in the world — is still missing and is probably excluded in advance. Architecture in the new American metropolis, more candidly than in Europe, displays its role of "silent witness to all of the weaknesses, indulgences, and self-absorption characteristic of modern culture."[33] In certain cases, it even shamelessly contributes to the exclusion of social and urban problems: exclusive apartment buildings in West Palm Beach, Florida, turn their totally blank twenty-floor-high backs on the less fortunate (ex-)middle-class part of the city.[34]

**Alzheimer Arcadians** Is what remains of the twentieth-century Arcadia of Shulman, Koenig, and Entenza no more than "a junkyard of dreams" (Mike Davis) or even "God's own junkyard" (Peter Blake)? The physical condition of Los Ange-

*West Palm Beach, Florida, 1998.*

les in the 1980s and 90s is comparable to the Rome of Piranesian engravings: the relics of L.A.'s Antiquity — the 20s through 50s — survive, tattered and overgrown, alongside a few sublime fragments of L.A.'s Bernini, but mostly surrounded by urban and social debris. Banham's ecological-Arcadian dream clashes with Le Corbusier's "a dream × 1,000,000 = chaos." To the four ecologies a fifth has been added: the ecology of fear.[35]

The first sketches for this contribution were made in the Park Plaza Hotel, the former Elks Building by Curlett and Beelman from 1927, which dominates MacArthur Park by its American Art Deco exterior, its multi-story sculptures, and its own indoor Olympic bath.[36] MacArthur Park and the hotel were showpieces in 30s and 40s Los Angeles and a pet subject for Kodak-color postcards. In the lobby that has the size and outlook of a solid Central Station, scenes for *Wild at Heart* were shot. I stayed there paying the rate of a dubious Inglewood motel. MacArthur Park, "once a jewel in the crown of the city's park system, is now a free-fire zone where crack dealers and street gangs settle their scores with shotguns and uzis."[37] This zone, Mid Wilshire, was one of the most "active" areas during the Rodney King riots.[38]

Except for some ancient, down-and-out female country singer — Dolly Parton is said to have stayed here — the enormous hotel was empty. But not only tourists avoid the parts of L.A. that fail to meet the Beverly Hills or Santa Monica norms. The middle classes, for and by whom Los Angeles was originally built, respond to the ecology of fear by producing an *architecture of fear* — or else turn their backs on the city. Families whose budgets are ravaged by the bills of security companies, citizens who fall short of being able to afford a "Beirutized" villa (in Davis's typical language), are leaving the City of Angels, driven out by its racial and social problems.

35 Not coincidentally also the title of Mike Davis's new book: *Ecology of Fear: Los Angeles and the Imagination of Disaster* (New York: Metropolitan Books; Henry Holt and Co., 1998).

36 Kurt W. Forster opens his contribution "Along the Boardwalk of Imagination: Frank Gehry's Buildings in Los Angeles" (in *Frank O. Gehry: America come contesto/America as Context*, ed. Mirko Zardini [Milano: Electa, 1994], 8) precisely with a reprint of a postcard of MacArthur Park and the Elks Building.

37 Davis, *Ecology*, 378.

38 Contrary to the black-and-white image of the Rodney King riots projected by the media, black violence was not predominant. Police reports indicate that only 36% of riot arrestees were African-American, against 52% Hispanics. The greatest density of "incidents" did not occur in South Central but to the north of Santa Monica Boulevard, around MacArthur Park: "nearly as many suspects were booked by the LAPD's Ramparts station [which polices MacArthur Park] as by all four stations which make up the department's South Bureau in South Central Los Angeles." Davis, *Ecology*, 371. Davis forgets to mention that recently the park has become more livable again, mainly as a result of near-permanent policing.

39 S. H. Kaplan, *L.A. Lost and Found: An Architectural History of Los Angeles* (New York: Crown, 1987), 80-81.

40 This was the slogan developers used to make publicity: see Richard Longstreth, *City Center to Regional Mall: Architecture, the Automobile, and Retailing in Los Angeles, 1920-1950* (Cambridge, MA.: MIT Press, 1997), 160ff.

41 Diane Ghirardo, "Two Institutions for the Arts," in *Out of Site*, ed. Ghirardo, 120.

42 Mike Davis, "Ozzie and Harriet in Hell," *Harvard Design Magazine* (Winter/Spring 1997): 7.

For a long time the city responded to urban and moral forms of decline by urban nomadism. In an evolution encouraged by real-estate speculation, sectors that were considered degraded were promptly displaced by new ones next to them. Thus, for example, Hollywood was founded, the product of two devout Methodists, Horace and Daeida Wilcox, who hoped to realize "a genteel, bible-quoting suburb for those wanting to escape the hard-drinking, decadent life-style of downtown L.A.."[39] Westwood, the product of the Janns Investment Company, in turn became, in the 1920s and after the suburban Hollywood dream was strangled by too much density, a "Second Hollywood."[40] In the same period, Wilshire Boulevard became a success as the alternative "linear downtown" alongside the original center plagued by traffic congestion. Inglewood, a mere couple of meters below continuously landing and departing 747s at L.A.X., was once founded by Daniel Freeman because of its healthy ocean breeze. The Arcadian locations of the Case Study Houses were themselves the product of the middle-class wish to rise above the blue-collar plains. And after the Watts rebellion in 1965, white downtown L.A. fled to the former sites of the old Twentieth Century Fox Studios, since called "Century City," where "the fiction of an all-white society is fashioned by investment companies, brokerage houses, law firms, insurance companies, and mortgage bankers, an ironic variation on the old Hollywood fictions once cranked out in celluloid on the same site."[41]

L.A. as a field of class and race tensions has expanded far beyond the traditional problem areas, South Central, East L.A., Inglewood, and Watts. In the wake of the ongoing decline of the manufacturing industry, Los Angeles County's modally middle-class cities like Lakewood have suffered the effects, too. Pomona, the fourth largest city of the county, was once a veritable family-value town, known as the Queen of the Citrus Belt. Since 1970, one percent of its population has been murdered. These places, described by Mike Davis as a kind of "senile suburbia" that "in addition to the dramatic hemorrhage of jobs and capital over the last decade ... also suffers from premature physical obsolescence — the architectural equivalent of Alzheimer's disease,"[42] are being left behind by all those population groups who can economically afford it. The most important job providers, too, are decentralizing to the newer and ever more distant suburbs. The complex of office centers around John Wayne Airport in Orange County, built on land that was, until a generation ago, cultivated for lima beans, recently surpassed downtown San Francisco as the second-largest employment center in California. The new housing tracts there are encroaching further and further on agricultural and environmentally sensitive areas. The deserted zones in Los Angeles County are doubly hit: first by the drain of industries, then by the virtual inaccessibility of new jobs for those unemployed who are left behind and cannot afford daily commutes of several hundred miles.

These are not the conclusions of America's New Left or of Marxist-noir L.A. haters; they can be read in a 1996 report by the Bank of America:

*This acceleration of sprawl has surfaced enormous social, environmental, and economic costs, which until now have been hidden, ignored, or quietly borne by society. The burden of these costs is becoming very clear [and has] adverse impacts on the state's business climate. By reducing the quality of life, sprawl has made California a less desirable location for business owners and potential employees. By increasing suburban resistance to further growth, sprawl has made it difficult for businesses to relocate and expand in California. Both these trends increase the attractiveness of neighboring states such as Arizona, Nevada, and Utah. For example, a major film studio recently decided to relocate its animation facility to Arizona, principally because of lower housing prices and less traffic congestion.*[43]

Urban nomadism all over again, in other words, but this time no longer on an intracity or intercounty, but on an interstate scale.

The hunger for new locations, in quest of a new Eden, leaves in large parts of Los Angeles County a moribund Arcadia behind: "the great unbroken plains of aging bungalows,"[44] populated by political and social outcasts. L.A. is old and tired, even if it does not stop to fascinate. It is like an elderly eccentric aunt with a little too much *fond de teint* and slightly garish dresses. It lives, at times sumptuously, on the credit of its golden years.[45] And where it allows itself facelifts and prostheses — as at Two Rodeo Drive in Beverly Hills, the display window of Bulgari jewelry and New Urbanism — it appears more than a little Old Continental. The stale smell that breathes from this English-French-Italian mishmash of urban styles leaves little hope for the city but that of a sweet death.

*Translation Bart Eeckhout*

Materials for this contribution were gathered in Los Angeles thanks to the support of the Flemish Fund for Scientific Research (Brussels). Further research and writing were done in the scholarly "luxe, calme et volupté" of the Canadian Centre for Architecture in Montreal, in the margins of a Visiting Scholarship 1998-1999. I wish to thank Phyllis Lambert, Réjean Legault, and the staff of the Study Centre, the Library, and the Photographs Collection for their precious help.

43 Bank of America Report, *Beyond Sprawl: New Patterns of Growth to Fit the New California* (San Francisco: Bank of America, 1996).

44 Davis, *Ecology*, 361.

45 One might consider the autobiographical mother figure in Joshua Miller's recent novel *The Mao Game* (New York: Regan Books, 1997), a drinking Beverly Hills ex-film diva, as the personification of the city that produced her.

*Dan Graham, Jersey City, New Jersey, 1969.*

Kevin R. McNamara

# CityWalk: Los(t) Angeles in the Shape of a Mall

*Keywords:* ■ *Architecture* ■ *Public Space* ■ *Simulation* ■ *Mallification*

CityWalk is the name of a recent mutation in shopping-mall design. Opened in 1993, its 250,000-square-feet of sales space for over forty specialty shops, eating places, and entertainment venues is one of several attractions that comprise an "Entertainment Destination" in Universal City, which also includes the 6,200-seat Universal Amphitheatre, the Universal Studios Tour, and the 6,000-seat, 18-screen Universal City Cineplex, reputedly the highest-grossing in the nation.[1] The entire "City," a 415-acre unincorporated tract within Los Angeles, is owned by Universal Studios, whose corporate offices and studios also occupy the site. Designed by the prolific Californian designer of malls, John Jerde, CityWalk reverses the program of San Diego's Horton Plaza (1985), which brought him to prominence. Whereas Horton Plaza turned six-blocks of downtown into a multilevel shopping center in the style of an Italian hill town, the $100-million CityWalk's 6.25-acre site in the Hollywood Hills, five miles from downtown Los Angeles via the Hollywood Freeway (U.S. Route 101), simulates two "typical" Los Angeles streets joined at a central plaza.

My analysis of "'idealized reality,' L.A. style"[2] begins by locating CityWalk at the confluence of several trends in the design of quasi-public space that have brought ever closer in form and function historic and commercial sites. It then analyzes CityWalk's semiotic regime, drawing on Louis Marin's exploration of how Disneyland spatially represents "the imaginary relationship the dominant

1 Universal owned 50 percent of Cineplex Odeon, which it merged with Sony's Loew's unit to form Loew's Cineplex, of which Universal owns 27 percent. In 1995, an 84 percent share of MCA-Universal (now simply Universal) was sold by Matsushita Electronics to the Seagram Company. See Universal Studios, Inc., *Hoover's Company Profile Database — American Private Companies* [online] (Austin, Tex.: Reference Press, 1998) (cited 23 May 1998).

2 Amy Wallace, "Like It's So L.A.! Not Really," *Los Angeles Times*, 29 February 1992, Home Edition, A1, quoting MCA President Lawrence Spungin.

3 Louis Marin, "Disneyland: A Degenerate Utopia," Glyph 1 (1977): 54.

4 Ibid.

5 Reyner Banham, *Los Angeles: The Architecture of Four Ecologies* (Harmondsworth: Penguin, 1971), 129.

6 Fredric Jameson, "Nostalgia for the Present," in *Postmodernism, or, The Cultural Logic of Late Capitalism* (Durham: Duke University Press, 1992), 292.

7 Verne Chatelaine, quoted in John Bodnar, *Remaking America: Public Memory, Commemoration, and Patriotism in the Twentieth Century* (Princeton: Princeton University Press, 1982), 177.

8 Witold Rybczynski, *City Life: Urban Expectations in a New World* (New York: Scribner, 1995), 210.

groups of American society maintain ... with the real history of the United States."[3] Finally, an account of CityWalk's popular reception registers both its appeal to many Angelenos and the emergence with regard to CityWalk of the same race and class discord that the site was created to repress. I will suggest, however, that CityWalk departs from the narrative form that Marin uncovers at Disneyland and that one may also find at CityWalk's other precursors. Urban festival marketplaces attempt to connect a city's present to "a fantasmatic projection" of its past, and Disneyland invites the visitor to "'perform' ... the mythical story by which he imagines his social community has been constructed."[4] In contrast, at a time when the city was overwhelmed by racial and economic conflict, CityWalk was built to reaffirm the myth of exemption from history that Reyner Banham, who was seduced by his own projection of the surfer as "noble savage," declared the Angeleno's "special brand of 'innocence.'"[5] The designers' program was to distill the atmosphere of certain iconic Los Angeles neighborhoods into a space that, from its facades to its merchandise, would be a material expression of that wished-for innocence, but the result may also be read as symptomatic of what Fredric Jameson calls "nostalgia for the present." In CityWalk, one surveys "a collective unconscious in the process of trying to identify its own present," yet, perhaps, only "illuminat[ing] the failure of that attempt, which seems to reduce itself to the recombination of various stereotypes of the past."[6]

**A Brief History of Present Design** The last few decades have witnessed the accelerated convergence of two types of development that were once more or less separate: the historic district and the shopping mall. Many historic sites always had their commercial dimension, but as at Colonial Williamsburg (Virginia), Mystic Seaport (Connecticut), or Old Smithville (New Jersey), they attempt to integrate retailing into the historical ambiance. At most U.S. national historic parks, merchandise is selected for its relevance to the site's significance. To "breathe the breath of life into American history," and to convey "something of the color, the pageantry, and the dignity of the country's past" to visitors, is how the parks' mission was conceived by Verne Chatelaine, the National Park Service's first professional historian.[7]

In contrast, shopping malls were for decades as generic as the chain-stores they housed. Minor variations on the basic anchor-store plan maintained a neutral yet reassuring backdrop for the consumption of everyday goods. In this predictable environment, Witold Rybczynski contends, a trip to the mall is also time-travel; it recreates the experience of what "public streets used to be before police indifference and overzealous protectors of individual rights effectively ensured that *any* behavior, no matter how antisocial, is tolerated."[8] Rybczynski's claim that "liberals," not shopping malls on the urban periphery, are responsible for the decline of downtown shopping districts is as dubious as it will be important to understanding the motivation behind CityWalk. An emphasis on conformity of class and culture is apparent in the language of Lawrence Spungin, President of Universal's then-parent, MCA, who characterized his new development as L.A.'s Venice Beach without "somebody on every corner with a 'Work for Food' sign," and Leasing Director Tom Gilmore, who foresaw something like the trendiness of Melrose Avenue absent the feeling of having stepped into "a Third World country."[9] While praising the mall's evolution as a social space, Rybczynski fails to consider how the mall contributes to the decline of civil society by rendering poverty, homelessness, and minority cultures invisible.[10] If malls offer their automobile-dependent population one of its few pedestrian experiences, it is in a *polis* without politics as a consequence of the Supreme Court ruling in *Lloyd Corp., Ltd. v. Tanner et al.*[11] The refuge from difference and conflict that suburbs promised has been provided by the malls, which eject "drunks" and "panhandlers"; the only "boorish adolescents" in sight are one's own or the

9 Spungin and Gilmore, quoted in Wallace, "Like It's So L.A.!" 1, 23.

10 The data on the suburban shift simply refutes Rybczynski's account of the decline of downtown retail districts. Between 1945 and 1960, the urban population grew by 0.1 percent while the suburban population grew 45 percent. Of the twelve largest American cities, only Los Angeles gained in population between 1950 and 1960. By 1956, 1,600 shopping centers had been built and another 2,500 were under construction. By 1963, 80 percent of Americans owned a car. Public transportation use declined by nearly two-thirds between 1945 and 1965. (See Jon C. Teaford, *The Twentieth-Century American City: Problem, Promise, and Reality* [Baltimore: Johns Hopkins University Press, 1986], 98-110.) The reason for downtown shopping's decline was obvious to urban scholar George Sternleib: "We are asking the customer to pay a penalty ... — either to use the mass transit system ... or an automobile in an environment that cannot comfortably accommodate it" (quoted in Teaford, *Twentieth-Century American City*, 112).

11 *Lloyd Corp. v. Tanner, et al.*, 407 US 551 (1972), held that the First Amendment right to free political expression does not outweigh the interests of private property-holders. *Pruneyard Shopping Center v. Robins*, 447 US 74 (1980), upheld a California Supreme Court ruling that the state constitution's more stringent protection of free expression prevails over the shopping-center owner's property rights, but the ruling has no bearing on other states.

12 I quote Rybczynski's inventory of undesirable types found in urban downtowns (*City Life*, 210).

13 On the West Edmonton Mall, see Rob Shields, "Social Spatialization and the Built Environment: The West Edmonton Mall," in *Geography and Identity: Living and Exploring Geopolitics of Identity*, ed. Dennis Crow (Washington, D.C.: Maisonneuve Press, 1996), 337-65; and the Mall's website, http://www.westedmall.com. On the Mall of America, see Michael J. Crosbie's critique of the themed avenues' failure architecturally to evoke their models, "The Vatican of Consumption?" *Progressive Architecture* (March 1994): 70-73; and that Mall's website, http://www.mallofamerica.com.

14 Through the '40s, only the New York Yankees and Washington Senators played in a "Stadium." (Griffith Stadium was called Griffith Park in 1922 and National Park before then; the New York team moved to Yankee Stadium in 1923 after nine years at the Polo Grounds and another nine at Hilltop Park.) From the late '40s through 1990, new facilities were named "Stadium," "Colosseum," or "Dome," with the exception of Candlestick Park (in San Francisco), and some older facilities (as in Detroit) were renamed "Stadium." By 1985, twenty-two of twenty-six teams played in facilities so named. Quite recently, two Stadiums (in Cincinnati and Anaheim, California) and one Dome (in St. Petersburg) were renamed "Field." Baseball's six newest facilities include three "Fields" (in Atlanta, Cleveland, and Denver) and three "Parks" (in Arlington, Texas, Baltimore, and Phoenix). Other "Parks" and "Fields" are under construction in Houston, Milwaukee, Montreal, and Seattle.

neighbor's.[12] Without any visual evidence of poverty and injustice, shoppers need not calculate the degree to which forms of oppression underwrite their own contentment.

Even if one credits Rybczynski's portrayal of the mall-goer's sentiment, the generic mall proved too antiseptic to please many and please long. Competition for the stimulus-starved shopper's patronage has led designers on a pursuit of entertainment and novelty. The West Edmonton Mall offers nightclubs, miniature golf, a full-size ice rink, a submarine ride, "Dolphin Lagoon," and "Sea Life Cavern"; in Bloomington, Minnesota, one chooses among golf, the seven-acre Camp Snoopy amusement park, an underwater voyage through four ecosystems, and the Rainforest Cafe, all in the Mall of America (for which the Jerde Partnership was design architect).[13] Urban America has become another fantasy destination for mall-goers. Nostalgia for the trappings of city life has led developers to invoke the urban milieu from which the malls are a retreat by designs that resemble (or, at least, are named for) older shopping districts.

Nostalgia is no less marketable within U.S. cities, as the popular success of Baltimore's Orioles' Park at Camden Yards and Cleveland's Jacobs Field attest. These baseball facilities conjure an age of athletic innocence, purged of the inconveniences of authentic old stadia. Their historicist designs mix "intimacy" (as a product identifier if not in fact) and old-fashioned asymmetry with "family friendly" play areas and picnic grounds. Even their names, the pastoral "Field" and "Park" not the monumental "Stadium," contribute to the effect.[14] The Baltimore venue, whose unwieldy name is the product of a compromise between the team and the city, verbally *and physically* incorporates the ghost of the city's industrial past into the project. The former Baltimore & Ohio Railroad warehouse at the Camden Rail Yards, located behind the right-field bleachers, now houses team offices, a sports bar, a gift shop, and the team's VIP lounge.

These site-engaging alternatives to the "cookie-cutter" regularity of multiuse stadia and the dome's controlled environment follow a design strategy that originates in the "festival marketplace," so named by its pioneer, James W. Rouse. Festival marketplaces reclaim disused spaces that hold, or may be assigned, some historic significance; examples range from waterfront areas (Baltimore's Harborplace, Chicago's North Pier, New York's South Street/Fulton Fish Market area, San Antonio's Riverwalk, San Francisco's Fisherman's Wharf) to converted factories, mills, warehouses, and other significant buildings too numerous to mention. Each site is *prima facie* evidence of the shift in the U.S. to a service and information economy, but it disguises that transition by celebrating an older, seemingly more coherent world in which tangible goods were produced by intelligible processes. In a parallel gesture, the new "old" stadia hearken to that mythical time when athletes who played "for the love of the game" were loyal to their teams and teams to their players, fans, and home cities.[15]

M. Christine Boyer defines festival marketplaces as "premixed design packages that reproduce pre-existing urban forms," recreating connections "to the city's historical past."[16] Boyer further proposes that the informing ideology of these markets is at least on one level a bid to "regain a centered world, to reestablish a mythical base on which American moral, political, and social traditions might stand," an objective that certainly may be attributed to the new "old" ballparks. Festival marketplaces are nevertheless wanton in their use of the signifiers of historicity, for as Boyer also notes, "Within the space of the South Street Seaport's historic tableau and through its museum's interpretative programming, the consumer is drawn into a special network of associated meanings, enabling a transference to take place between the context and the commodities for sale."[17] The recovery of a centered world is, then, a power implicitly ascribed to commodities that become associated with a certain lifestyle-image.

Having ably described the visually acquisitive experience of consumer society, which dissolves the distinction between the object of use and symbolic attributes as well as between the commodity and its setting, Boyer continues to the more questionable claim that consumers' desire and yearning are the same emotions that in earlier times "propelled men and ships to voyage around the world."[18] This reading of how the romance of empire is encoded into the festival marketplace is compelling; yet in pursuit of her thesis Boyer herself falsifies history. She fails to distinguish between the desire for adventure and riches that propelled some men to sail and the economic or legal exigencies that compelled many others. The oversight is significant because the appeal of the festival mar-

15 Repressed in the baseball idyll are the color line, the ill repute of many players recalled today as merely "colorful," imperious owners, limited access to the major league game before television and expansion, and the irony that the owner who broke the color line also moved a successful franchise across the country from Brooklyn to Los Angeles.

16 M. Christine Boyer, "Cities for Sale: Merchandising History at South Street Seaport," in *Variations on a Theme Park: The New American City and the End of Public Space*, ed. Michael Sorkin (New York: Hill & Wang, 1992), 184, 190-91.

17 M. Christine Boyer, *The City of Collective Memory: Its Historical Imagery and Architectural Entertainments* (Cambridge, MA: MIT Press, 1994), 439.

18 Boyer, "Cities for Sale," 201.

19 Mark Gottdiener, *The Theming of America: Dreams, Visions, and Commercial Spaces* (Boulder, CO: Westview Press, 1997), 5, 85. In the Czech Republic it is (or was in 1994-95) possible, under a scenic billboard of Marlboro country, to use one's Liberty Lighter (sold under a cutout of the Statue of Liberty) to light up and "Taste the West" — a very popular brand of cigarettes is called, simply, "West." Italian-made jackets displaying the emblems of the Indiana Hawks, Utah Pistols, and New Orleans Giants, sold briskly despite the teams' non-existence. A Czech friend who spent part of a Saturday asking people why they bought clothing with the particular messages they had chosen said the common response was, "Do you think I'd buy it if I know what it said?" These people were consuming the aura of the words, but not just passively; they project an America of their own invention onto those symbols.

20 Quoted in Wallace, "Like It's So L.A.!" 23.

ketplace rests on such soft-focus history and generalization of desire. The present globalization of consumer markets often mis-referred to as "Americanization" has little if anything to do with U.S. moral, political, and social traditions, but everything to do with the use of "highly popular commercial images associated with television, advertising, films, and popular music" in the creation of themed environments conducive to consumer behavior. (The Mall of America's developers are, after all, Iranian-born Canadians.) Actual patriotic sentiment is of limited utility in these conditions, although as a receptacle of personal associations, and thus as an infinitely consumable signifier void of any clear message, *America* may function as "a consummate marketing device."[19]

Then again, commodity marketing may be all that remains of patriotism. The neo-conservative attack on the social contract, despite its cynical use of moral and patriotic nostrums, continually identifies the U.S. with its macro-economic data, which suggests that consumption is the last patriotic act.

**The Present as History** *"When Nietzsche made a big deal out of the eternal recurrence, I wonder if he was talking about popular culture.... Do you know kids today are still listening to the Rolling Stones and the Beach Boys, and those phoney old dudes are like in their* fifties? *By insisting on being always new, popular culture constantly ends up by being nothing but eternally the same. Freedom is no longer a state of being. It's now a high marketing concept."* — Charlie the Crow, in Scott Bradfield, *Animal Planet*

As only an "urban" development located in a well-off entertainment-industry enclave and accessible only by car can, CityWalk captures the multiple contradictions that inform the design of post-urban semi-public spaces. It represents a stage beyond the other kinds of space that I have discussed, in part because its site is no disused space reclaimed for consumer uses or (like Memphis's Beale Street, for example) a "revitalized" entertainment district, and in part because of how it is promoted. In place of Midwestern sincerity (either Disney's nostalgia or baseball's evocations of an Iowan *Field of Dreams* as America's mythical heart), CityWalk's sign system offers a counter-myth of local origins that celebrates self-expression and disregard for convention. These values are presented as the ethos — or, at least, the mythos — of the affluent, mobile, predominantly white Angelenos who grew up in the shadow of Disneyland but were immersed in the surf and car culture that provide two principal sources for the region's distinctive vernacular architecture. Described by Richard Orne, the chief project designer, as "A kind of 'screw you, I'll do whatever I want' [attitude] that is exactly how Los Angeles was formed,"[20] CityWalk reminds us how institutionalized what Banham called "the Angeleno's special brand of innocence" has become. The city's newspaper of record, the *Los Angeles Times*, promotes this image of Angeleno subjectivity. It is in this light that one must read the *Times*'s praise for L.A.'s "young and irreverent" designers, whose "architecture as art, attitude and lifestyle" draws its inspiration from "movies, sports cars, Nintendo games" and "flirt[s] with the ultimate taboo, bad taste," in search of "bankable" designs.[21]

The atmosphere CityWalk aspires to create has its *locus classicus* in Sebastiano Serlio's "Comic Scene," a 1545 engraving of an illusionistic stage that represents "an urban square with a corridor street receding behind it." Richard Sennett writes that the scene's "genius ... is that the corridor moves the eye forward" into the square in which the "intensely human action that is comedy will happen."[22] This world of random happening comes down to the present by way of townscape planning and its theatricalization in Disneyland and the festival marketplace, which are literally *stages* amid whose properties the everyday occurs. CityWalk itself is all foreground: a single "street" lined with three-dimensional facades, the promenade is crowded with signs and activities whose function is to maintain a constant level of visual stimulation. Indeed, the lack of "any ideal referent for the always engaging 'accidents' which it sought to promote," noted by Fred Koetter and Colin Rowe as a failure of townscape planning, is especially true of CityWalk, which also was conceived "to provide sensation without plan, to appeal to the eye and not to the mind, and, while usefully sponsoring a perceptual world, to devalue a world of concepts."[23]

Inverting Disneyland's five-eighths-scale program for Main Street, U.S.A., CityWalk offers auto-scaled signs fronting buildings that are one-and-a-half-times normal size. Among the outsized and outlandish features of CityWalk's facades are a 27-foot, neon-outlined King Kong suspended from the simulated art-deco marquee of Sam Goody's Superstore, an upside-down '57 Chevrolet convertible (pink, of course) protruding from a freeway sign for L.A. FreeZway's frozen-yogurt shop, a "spacecraft" similarly impaled at Things from Another World (science-fiction toys), a surfboard-shaped roof, fin-side up, at Malibu Ranch surf and western clothes (left over from when it was Current Wave), a lighthouse and tables in the sand at Lighthouse Beach Cafe, a retro-'60s mural and fiberglass Marilyn Monroe at celebrity-chef Wolfgang Puck's California Pizza Kitchen. Twenty-one vintage neon signs on loan from the Museum of Neon Art decorate

21 Joseph Giovanni, "L.A. Architects: They Did It Their Way," *Los Angeles Times Magazine*, 15 May 1994, 30, 34, 30, 34, 32.

22 Richard Sennett, *The Conscience of the Eye: The Design and Social Life of Cities* (New York: Knopf, 1990), 159.

23 Colin Rowe and Fred Koetter, *Collage City* (Cambridge, MA: MIT Press, 1978), 15, 36.

24 Richard Orne, quoted in Eric La Brecque, "CityWalk Remembers," *Visual Merchandising and Store Design* (August 1993): 70.

25 Boyer, "Cities for Sale," 201.

the structures' upper facades. Several signs remain outside one's normal line of sight, an excess cultivated to evoke spatially the way in which, on an actual Los Angeles Boulevard, "in time, layer is added to layer. Storefronts become aggregates. Add to this another kind of commercial layer: the billboards, and ultimately what you get is a set of layers piled up on each other that blur the original intention."[24] At CityWalk, the accretion of history is simulated in pastiche. Blurring *is* the original intention and, as in the planned communities and subdivisions from which the attraction draws so many of its local patrons, CityWalk has its own Architectural Control Board. The signs of "transgression" — the graffiti on the walls of Lucille's blues café and the gum wrappers on the pavement — were in place on opening day.

CityWalk may be the first of these quasi-public commercial spaces to make the present an object of longing. If nostalgia is "a sweet sadness generated by a feeling that something is lacking in the present ... [and] a desire to ... reexperience something untouched by the ravages of time,"[25] the objects of nostalgia at CityWalk are stations of the Angeleno imaginary: Venice Beach, Melrose Boulevard, the Sunset Strip, and, in Crabtree & Evelyn's more staid evocation of the structural rhythms of Parkinson and Parkinson's Bullock's-Wilshire department store (1928), the Golden Age of Hollywood. Unquestionably, the architectural facades of CityWalk are historicist, but so are the contemporary forms to which CityWalk alludes: Streamline Diner, Beachfront Market Stall, even Frank-Gehry-meets-*Blade-Runner* postindustrial neon and metal sculpture. Yet many of the city's surviving structures in these vernaculars maintain the presence of the past functionally

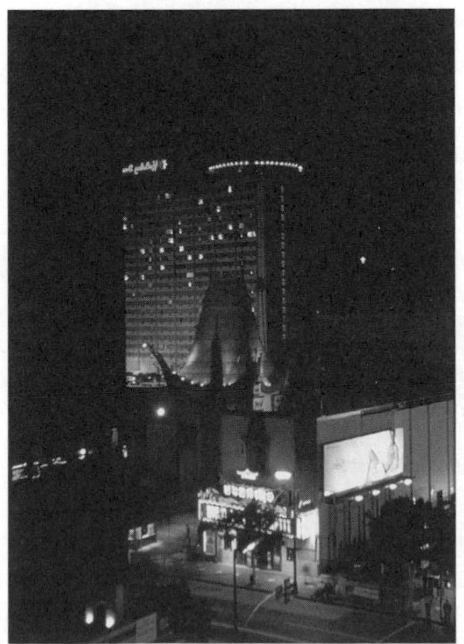

*Mann's Chinese Theater.*

as well as visually; they have not been put to new uses. More importantly, for the people who shape or maintain their identities in the terms of a no-longer-dominant cultural moment (e.g. the surf-culture of the '50s and '60s) the forms, symbols, and sounds of that cultural moment are experienced as contemporary, not as historical. Like the city's many immigrant communities, temporally displaced Angelenos live at the juncture (or the thrust-fault) of two or more cultures.

What separates CityWalk from its sources is that in the city these styles are as separate as are the subcultures they represent. Developed as a site of the city's new-wave, art, and urban-professional scene in the '80s, Melrose Boulevard mixes an avantgarde industrial vernacular and retro-kitsch. A trip through its second-hand shops distinguishes the nostalgia-'50s from the retro-'50s, which has more the feel of something imagined by David Lynch. The bric-à-brac is tacky and recalled with an ironic edge that cuts against the mood cultivated by CityWalk's '50s; the clothing might be left over from a John Waters film. You cannot wash off tattoos gotten on Melrose or in Venice Beach, where the architecture recycles a decades-old surf vernacular that remains relatively unchanged. Mural-painted buildings and stalls still house T-shirt and bikini vendors, head-shops, and pizza parlors. The beach, the grass, and the paved Ocean Front Walk are the setting for a vibrant performance culture that includes Muscle Beach bodybuilders, musicians, roller disco-ers, proselytizers, and panhandlers, with cyclists and rollerbladers weaving among the pedestrians. Here is not only a racial and ethnic mix, but a mix of classes and attitudes that CityWalkers like MCA-head Spungin find intimidating.

At CityWalk, whose true muse is the movies, any clash of styles is orchestrated to drive "a machine for the production of euphoria"[26]; it expresses no underlying collision of ideas, cultures, or codes, but suggests the jumble of studio backlots. Two attractions particularly foreground the dissolution of boundaries between the on-screen world and "real life." At Showscan Cinemania, "you don't just watch movies — you experience them"[27] in a $3-million quartet of 55-seat theaters whose "hydraulically-operated motion-base seating"[28] brings the film

26 As Disney World is described by Rowe and Koetter, *Collage City*, 45.

27 "CityWalk on the Web," http://www.mca.com/citywalk/blocks/block1.html (cited 15 May 1998).

28 "Showscan Cinemania Theater," *A+U* (June 1997): 121.

29 "CityWalk on the Web," http://www.mca.com/citywalk/blocks/block5.html (cited 15 May 1998). In 1996, an 8"×10" print cost $35.

30 "CityWalk on the Web," http://www.mca.com/citywalk/blocks/block4.html (cited 15 May 1998).

31 Ibid.

32 "CityWalk on the Web," http://www.mca.com/citywalk/blocks/block8.html (cited 15 May 1998).

33 The guides cover board games, Barbie Dolls, G. I. Joe and other backyard heroes, Pez Collectibles (two titles), Hot Wheels, Hopalong Cassidy, Matchbox Toys, Marx Toys, Tinker Toys, Howdy Doody, Snoopy, Flexible Flyer sleds, teddy bears, marbles, metal lunchboxes, piggy banks, snowdomes, old televisions, space race toys, radio premium and cereal box collectibles (two titles), and tie-ins to television shows. Other volumes track trademarks of the '20s and '30s, trademarks of the '40s and '50s, character trademarks, and 20th-century American advertising icons.

into the seats. Out-Takes photography studio takes one into the screen. Through "the magic of computer-generated composite photographs," one can follow the yellow brick road with Dorothy and friends, help Marty McFly get *Back to the Future*, or be "placed in one of a hundred [other] movie or television scenes."[29] Further reminders that Universal City is a company town include the Sunset Boulevard-sized billboard that advertises a Universal picture and posters for other films lining the garage stairway, the Universal Studios Store with its full line of clothing and gear sporting the company's logo, and other shops that feature stuffed animals, action figures, novelizations, and comic books tied to Universal's television programs and movies. Media celebrity is also for sale at All Star Collectibles, where a Ken Griffey-autographed baseball fetches $109.

If CityWalk is a simulacrum of a stage set, the "movie" it produces is one's own experience of the site, in which the scenery and soundtrack are the ever-present images and sounds of our commercial and entertainment culture and the props are merchandise on display. Capitalizing on the alienated character of consumer culture, in which one is never what one is but what one imagines one will become if properly accessorized, or what one would have been had one been raised in the happily mainstream, middle-class world of movies and television rather than the incapacious place one was, CityWalk offers nostalgia for anyone who accepts its version of who "we" are and the way "we" were. Sparky's, Dapy, and Glow, three shops owned by Universal's Entertainment group or its Spencer Gifts subsidiary, are the principal sites of retailed nostalgia. In Sparky's "modern day re-creation of a 1940s 5 and Dime store ... guaranteed to make you feel nostalgic for the 'good old days'!"[30] CityWalkers browse and buy wind-up toys, tops, yo-yos, water-pistols, dolls, lunchboxes, boardgames, and other items too numerous to list, both costly originals and reproductions. Glow "celebrates the idea of 'glow-in-the-dark.'"[31] Its version of the '60s is defined by blacklight posters, fluorescent T-shirts and peace signs, as well as new-age and Christian symbols; for the knowing, there is a Jenny Holzer L.E.D. artwork. What Glow omits is any allusion to drug culture. While Dapy is said to "place an emphasis on humor and current social expression," a particular attraction is "the '50s retro section, unique to the CityWalk locale."[32] Shelves overflow with an eclectic mix of items from several decades: slinkys, lava lamps, bead and bamboo curtains, to television and movie icons — Elvis, Lucy, James Dean, Marilyn, Three Stooges, Betty Boop, and *Wizard of Oz* busts, plates, cookie jars — to famous art throw pillows and inflatable artwork such as the angst-ridden figure from Munch's *The Scream*, in a nineteen-inch or fifty-inch model. (I bought the smaller size.) That nostalgia is lucrative is evidenced on the bookshelf at Sparky's, which features more than thirty-five titles devoted to appraising toys, games, and other trappings of childhood.[33]

The dating at Sparky's is off; too many of these items are familiar from my childhood in the early '60s, while the ambient "music" is television themes and commercials from the '50s and '60s. Of course, as Charlie crows in the epigraph to this section, all time is eternally present in postmodern pop culture; in the '90s the '50s is an effect produced by '70s and '80s television and film. Further, to insist on accurate dating is to violate the spirit of nostalgia, which runs on private time. The time that an object recalls is whenever one first encountered it, and that recollection creates the attraction for the great majority of browsers. Most everyone will find something that, like Proust's madeleine, will restore oneself to oneself. Time and again, I watched groups form around some once-popular object and recall its particular charms. The dynamic startlingly exemplifies the extent to which "commodities (have) become the unacknowledged reference points for the accounts we give of ourselves."[34] It also stresses the importance of material possession because only through ownership was play possible. Thus, in the recall that CityWalk solicits, one's primary relation is with the commodities that mediate the memories of friends and events in ways that music does not: One never asks, "Whose album?" or "Whose radio?"

**Et in Arcade-ia** The range of attractions and relative safety have assured CityWalk's popularity with tourists and the San Fernando Valley residents who are said to make up 75 percent of its visitors. While attendance at the Universal Studio Tour rose 15 percent, attendance at the Cineplex increased 60 percent, no doubt in part because the parking fee may be credited toward the purchase of two tickets.[35] A more unusual draw is the University of California, Los Angeles, which offers evening and weekend classes in Entertainment Studies and Performing Arts, Business and Management, and Writing, particularly screenwriting, in a 14-classroom building whose brick facade alludes to the older structures on the main campus. (A few doors down, UCLA Spirit offers "a slice of student life with unique logo merchandise" in a shop so popular it became the model for the new student union.[36]) Additionally, special events like holiday celebrations, auditions

34 Jean-Christophe Agnew, "The Consuming Vision of Henry James," in *The Culture of Consumption: Critical Essays in American History, 1880-1980*, ed. Richard Wrightman Fox and T. J. Jackson Lears (New York: Pantheon, 1983), 68.

35 Percentage of Valley residents, see Suzan Ayscough and Judy Brennan, "Will Movie Meccas Do the Right Thing?" *Variety* (12 July 1993): 69; increase at the Cineplex and the Tour, see Steven Fader, "Universal CityWalk," *Urban Land* (1 August 1995): supp., 23.

36 "CityWalk on the Web," http://www.mca.com/citywalk/blocks/block7.html (cited 15 May 1998). This storefront is one of the most involved; its neon sign is sequenced to the rhythm of the school's cheer. See La Brecque, "CityWalk Remembers," 71-72.

37 William H. Whyte, *The City: Rediscovering the Center* (New York: Anchor-Doubleday, 1988). L.A. FreeZway and Cafe Puccino are also operated by Universal's Recreation Group; management of Gladstone's and Hollywood Sports Grill are sourced out.

for jobs as "street" performers, and the summer "KidsWalk" program that runs children's movies in the Cineplex appeal to return visitors.

Several of CityWalk's constituencies use the venue differently. On weekend days, perhaps half or more of all visitors are families, many with children in strollers. The crowd is ethnically diverse but economically relatively homogeneous because parking costs six dollars, a sandwich and soda close to ten dollars, and because almost everyone will buy something, at least as a souvenir. A decade ago, many of these people would have gone to the mall, but on my visit in June 1996, the famous Sherman Oaks Galleria (approximately seven miles west of CityWalk) was almost empty. Reasons are not hard to find. CityWalk offers novelty beyond the capacity of the more functionally oriented mall. It is not sheltered from the delightful climate. The promenade is designed to create pleasing interruptions — musicians, magicians, mimes, patio dining, palm trees, merchandise carts (leased out by Universal) — that draw crowds and create eddies in the pedestrian flow, simulating the currents of street life. Children old enough to walk splash in the fountain at Center Court, which sprays geysers of water from scores of pipes beneath the ground while music flows from live performers or the speakers of KWGB (the radio-themed *W*orld's *G*reatest *B*urger restaurant that is one of five food venues owned by Universal). Observing CityWalk from Center Court's second level, one suspects that the planners studied William H. Whyte's brilliant analysis of what makes urban space work. Yet they omitted precisely the people to whom Whyte is most attracted — the handbill-passers, bag ladies, street-corner salesmen, and three-card-monte dealers — because part of CityWalk's attraction rests on the certainty that distractions will remain pleasing, never truly surprising, let alone shocking.[37]

The evening crowd is more racially diverse. Under full-size streetlights that burn smaller, dimmer bulbs couples stroll who come for the movies, the Hard Rock Cafe, the concert at B. B. King's. Groups of teenagers and twentysomethings, who may also go to the Hard Rock or a movie, seem more interested in checking out the opposite sex. At nine o'clock on a Saturday evening in January, the fountain at Center Court is full of teenage boys performing for girls, while others lip-sync to KWGB's music. At the far end of the promenade, people dance to live Latin music while young couples kiss in the shadows. A line of thirty people — mostly teens, but a range in age from perhaps six to sixty — wait their turn at Glow, where one kid complained, "It's so packed you can hardly breathe." The wait for a table at Wolfgang Puck's is forty minutes. This crowd reminds me of nothing so much as the boardwalks of beach towns, or at least that is the "film" I produced from my own memories of East-coast summers. Yet there is one crucial difference between CityWalk and a boardwalk: within CityWalk are no games of chance or skill, nothing that requires action. This omission is quite likely deliberate. In the popular imagination, the denizens of arcades are, like Rybczynski's "boorish adolescents," given to incivility, substance abuse, and other forms of delinquency. Gaming would also detract from the spectatorial quality of CityWalk sociality, which is based on visually consuming and being visually consumed by others, performing the rites of anonymous recognition, losing oneself in crowds.

Jerde boasted early on that CityWalk would become "its own 'real-life place,' not a mock Los Angeles, but a genuine new neighborhood."[38] Clearly, many Angelenos, particularly Valley residents, have brought their lives to CityWalk. However, the limits to CityWalk's incorporation into their lives is clear in any number of ways that relate to what Fred I. Kent III and Kathleen A. Madden describe as a sense of collective ownership of public places. "Even if they are not shopping, people feel they 'belong' on a good [public] street," the authors write; they also feel that they have a say over the street's future and "would rally to its defense if it were threatened."[39] CityWalk fails on both measures. As at a mall, loitering is prohibited, and precisely because it is not a public space purchasing becomes almost an imperative. At the very least, one pays to park.

38 Quoted in Wallace, "Like It's So L.A.!" 22.

39 Fred I. Kent III and Kathleen Madden, "Streets vs. Malls: The Modern Dilemma of Urban Public Spaces," *Los Angeles Times*, 4 December 1994, Home Edition, M2.

40 Mike Davis, *City of Quartz: Excavating the Future in Los Angeles* (London: Verso, 1990), 170. The chapter on "Homegrown Revolution" (153-219) chronicles the political activity of San Fernando Valley homeowners associations in the '70s and '80s.

41 See John D. Markman, "Coalition Formed to Fight MCA Expansion," *Los Angeles Times* [online] 22 May 1995, Valley Edition, B4 (cited 18 May 1998); Patrice Apodaca, "Homeowners Girding for Fight over MCA Project," *Los Angeles Times* [online] 5 November 1996, Valley Edition, B1 (cited 18 May 1998); Hugo Martin and Barry Stavro, "40% Reduction in Universal Studios Expansion Sought," *Los Angeles Times* [online] 7 June 1997, Valley Edition, A1 (cited 18 May 1998); and Barry Stavro, "New Theme Park Cut As Universal Scales Back Plan," *Los Angeles Times* [online] 3 July 1997, Valley Edition, A1 (cited 18 May 1998). When Universal reversed itself and requested a subway stop at the complex's entrance, the rerouting was denied because the expense was not considered in the public interest. Eventually, the MTA agreed to build two entrances on the CityWalk side of Lankershim Boulevard, widen Lankershim, and construct more freeway ramps, at a cost of $6 million. It also agreed not to collect Universal's $6 million property assessment. See Nick Patsaouras, "Valley Commentary: MTA Deal with MCA Sells Out the Public," *Los Angeles Times* [online] 20 March 1994, Valley Edition, B19 (cited 18 May 1998). Also see Hugo Martin, "Rail Station Move Called Too Costly," *Los Angeles Times* [online] 9 January 1994, Valley Edition, B1 (cited 18 May 1998); and Henry Chu, "MTA Approves Plan to Link Subway, Universal," *Los Angeles Times* [online] 24 February 1994, Valley Edition, B1 (cited 18 May 1998).

42 Gerald Silver, quoted in Barry Stavro and Martha Willman, "Studio Expansion Plan Receives Mixed Reviews," *Los Angeles Times* [online] 22 January 1997, Valley Edition, A1 (cited 18 May 1998).

43 Gerald Silver, quoted in Ed Bond, "Is Universal's Growth Plan Neighborly?" *Los Angeles Times* [online] 28 January 1997, Valley Edition, B3 (cited 18 May 1998).

44 See Jeff Schnaufer and Jeannette Regalado, "8 Arrested in Brawl at Universal Citywalk," *Los Angeles Times* [online] 7 August 1994, Valley Edition, B1 (cited 18 May 1998); "CityWalk Returns to Normal After Melee," *Los Angeles Times* [online] 8 August 1994, Valley Edition, B3 (cited 18 May 1998); Jeanette DeSantis, "Woman Arrested in Brawl at CityWalk," *Los Angeles Times* [online] 11 September 1995, Valley Edition, B2 (cited 18 May 1998); Aaron Curtiss, "Reality Intrudes upon a Polite Urban Escape," *Los Angeles Times* [online] 13 August 1994, Valley Edition, B1 (cited 18 May 1998).

Area residents have also contested who belongs at CityWalk. Consistent with their political focus over the last three decades "on the *defense* of [the] suburban dream against unwanted development (industry, apartments, and offices) as well as against unwanted persons,"[40] homeowners associations focused resistance to Universal's expansion plans to more than double the size of the entire entertainment destination.[41] The president of the homeowner's association in nearby Encino "triggered an ovation when he declared expansion certain to increase traffic and noise," and to draw "a large workforce of hot dog and hamburger salesmen attracted by a worldwide tourist attraction."[42] What his group would welcome, he told a reporter, is "An expansion of MCA film-making, taping and production facilities, [which] brings to the Valley high-quality jobs that provide a stable income for families."[43] On its face, this position advocates economic exclusivity. In fact, the racial stratification of employment in Los Angeles is such that a possible onslaught of Third-World immigrants to staff the food-stands was likely in the audience's mind, while the implicit modifier of the keyword "families" in this discourse is "like ours."

Racial exclusion is more clearly at issue in allegations of gang problems at CityWalk, which was promoted as a safer Venice or Westwood when first announced (a scant two months before the 1992 riots). The Los Angeles County Sheriff's Department maintains that the gang presence is overblown by local residents who cannot distinguish African American and Hispanic youth in urban attire from actual gang-members; their paranoia is fed by the news and entertainment media including the *Los Angeles Times*, which carried five reports of fighting at CityWalk in 1994 and 1995, all listed as possibly gang-related.[44] Nevertheless,

*CityWalk at night.*

the level of policing at CityWalk was increased after those incidents in order to quell fears of violence and to send a message that CityWalk is "neutral turf." On the Saturday evening of my mid-January 1998 visit, the 1,500-foot promenade was patrolled by twenty security guards, eight sheriff's deputies, and four probation officers. To this typical complement we must add a number of off-duty policemen employed as "greeters."[45]

Despite the manifestly low incidence of violence at CityWalk, a director of the Studio City Homeowners Association accused the *Times* of falsely portraying it as safe. "The area seems to be a magnet for gang members. ... They can be seen in groups and at times with no security around," he declared with urgency; "I have spoken with many parents who will not allow their children to go to Universal CityWalk because they are afraid of the gangs."[46] The association's president had a year earlier expressed concern "about what seems to be an increasing number of incidents."[47] The parties involved in a Mother's Day double murder in CityWalk's parking structure (in which a 30-year-old man and his girlfriend fatally stabbed his mother and former girlfriend) may have been "middle-class people from the Valley who had jobs and some success in their jobs,"[48] but that same homeowner was moved to "wonder about overall security at CityWalk."[49]

45 Sheriff's Lieutenant Brad Welker, telephone interview, 26 May 1998. Because probationers must answer any questions from probation officers, the officers have "a lien on their freedom" (Welker). Welker maintains that gang members are treated no differently from other visitors as long as they display no gang colors, insignias, or gestures. Total crime for all of Universal City in the past four years includes:

| | *1994* | *1995* | *1996* | *1997* |
|---|---|---|---|---|
| Theft (including shoplifting) | 534 | 380 | 567 | 555 |
| Aggravated Assault (including fist-fights) | 49 | 27 | 65 | 10 |
| Burglary (including automobile break-ins) | 43 | 15 | 39 | 93 |

Welker estimates that less than 10 percent of this crime occurs on CityWalk and attributes increases in theft (1996) and burglary (1997) to changes in reporting and policing strategies.

46 Jack Gold, Letter to the Editor, *Los Angeles Times* [online] 11 June, 1995, Valley Edition, B16 (cited 18 May 1998).

47 Tony Lucente, quoted in Eric Slater, "Neighbors Tell Concerns over CityWalk Safety," *Los Angeles Times* [online] 7 September 1994, Valley Edition, B3 (cited 18 May 1998).

48 Deputy District Attorney John Gilligan, quoted in Evelyn Larrubia, "Jury Votes Death For Mother's Day Killer," *Los Angeles Times* [online] 14 April 1998, Valley Edition, A1 (cited 18 May 1998).

49 Tony Lucente, quoted in Julie Tamaki and Nicholas Riccardi, "2 Slayings at CityWalk under Investigation," *Los Angeles Times* [online] 16 May 1995, Valley Edition, A1 (cited 18 May 1998). On trial's outcome, see Evelyn Larrubia, "Carrassi Given Death Penalty in CityWalk Double Slaying," *Los Angeles Times* [online] 27 May 1998, Valley Edition, B1 (cited 28 May 1998).

50 Boyer, *City of Collective Memory*, 372.

51 Michael Sorkin, Introduction, *Variations*, xv.

52 Boyer, *City of Collective Memory*, 65; see Boyer, *Dreaming the Rational City: The Myth of American City Planning* (Cambridge, MA: MIT Press, 1983).

53 In *The Uses of Disorder: Personal Identity and City Life* (New York: Knopf, 1970), Richard Sennett rejects the ideal of community as harmony and order as rooted in fear of otherness that forecloses mature self-development. In less psychologized terms, see his *The Fall of Public Man* (New York: Knopf, 1976), 294-312; and *The Conscience of the Eye*, 121-49.

These conflicts over belonging suggest that CityWalk is an allegory for the social and economic fissures that rive American cities, as well as for the functional disaggregation of urban space and the development of fortified residential enclaves that produce an urban landscape in which, Boyer writes, "Homogenized historic zones protected for their architectural value are juxtaposed and played off against areas of superdevelopment, while monumental architectural containers are designed intentionally to turn the urban street inward and internalize their own set of public spaces and services within the privatized layers of shops, restaurants, offices, and condominiums."[50] The response to such spaces must avoid substituting a nostalgia of its own for the nostalgia in which imagined cityscapes traffic. Michael Sorkin, for one, indulges in nostalgia when he invokes "The familiar spaces of traditional cities, the streets and squares, courtyards and parks" as "our binding agents," and pleads for "a return to a more authentic urbanity, a city based on physical proximity and free movement."[51] Similarly, Boyer recalls with longing "the social programs and utopian ideals embedded within the modernist view" that she once scathingly critiqued as a disciplinary apparatus.[52] Sorkin's traditional, centered city based on free movement is a noble fiction. Slavery, poverty and poor laws, race, ethnicity, and gender have all limited freedom throughout history. More likely, freedom of movement has increased as the urban spatial and social orders disintegrated.

In that respect, CityWalk represents a step backward, as if parks, which became public spaces in the nineteenth century against great resistance from the better-off classes, were suddenly re-surrounded with *de facto* barriers. Controlled, tranquilized environments of the sort I have discussed bespeak the confusion of a legitimate demand for safety with the wish for a shared space in which one is never made uncomfortable. They testify to a fear of conflict that marks a failure of urbanity, the ability to value the diversity and unpredictability that has characterized the life of cities.[53] However much the practice of architecture and planning needs to be reformed, the greater challenge, at least in the United States, is to reassert the value of the public sphere and a democratic culture in which people are responsible to others whom they do not know and may not like or even understand. If it can be done, CityWalk's version of the city as theme park may in later years be recast as a stage in the return not to an older form of the city but to a never-realized ideal of collective life.

Travel, research, and the writing of this essay were supported by a grant from the University of Houston, Clear Lake, Faculty Research Support Fund. I also want to thank Bart Eeckhout for inviting me to test some of this material as part of his panel, "The Spectacle of Identities and the Identity of Spectacles in the American Metropolis," at the biennial conference of the European Association for American Studies, Lisbon 1998.

Jude Davies

# Race, Cars, Film, and Los Angeles as (Post)Modern City

*Keywords:* ■ *Ethnic Studies* ■ *Gender Studies* ■ *Film Studies* ■ *Car Culture*

The starting point for this essay is the overdetermination of the automobile as a symbolic object in two kinds of discourse: on the one hand popular culture, to be exemplified by visual representations of Los Angeles, and on the other hand, theoretical and critical accounts of modernity and postmodernity. The significance of the automobile in American culture is self-evident to the point of cliché. From the dirtiest working pick-up to the most glamorous sports model, cars mean geographical mobility, social mobility, and power. Cars, therefore, are the objects most symbolic of the American dream. And hence as Car City, Los Angeles is the city most emblematic of "America." In addition, as indicated in the theoretical introduction to the current volume, the automobile is often used as a symbolic object to concretize more abstract discourses of modernity and postmodernity. Perhaps the best known example of this is Jean Baudrillard's *America.* In this work Baudrillard asks that we recognize a pair of metonymic chains connecting on the one hand, the metropolis, the car, the movie, and the hyperreal, and on the other hand, the car, the freeway, the suburb, Los Angeles, America. In both strands it is the car as symbolic object that exemplifies and concretizes Baudrillard's account, serving respectively to ground his theorization of the hyperreal and to underwrite the claims of the book to present "America." Appearing in both chains, the automobile links them together and thereby inspires Baudrillard's understanding of America as hyperreal.

In this case study, I want to consider some rather complex developments in the popular discourse of the automobile that are discernible in figurations of cars in Los Angeles in 1990s American culture. A context for this analysis will first be produced by investigating the limits of theoretical discourses in which the car is affiliated with notions of (post)modernity. Both these projects are informed by the necessity of rethinking the apparent universality of the modern/postmodern subject in terms of difference along the lines of race, gender, sexuality, and other frames of identity.

1 Arie Graafland, *Architectural Bodies* (Rotterdam: 010 Publishers, 1996), 41.

2 T. W. Adorno and M. Horkheimer, *Dialectic of Enlightenment* (trans. London: Verso, 1986), XIV-XV.

Foregoing theoretical sections of the present work, entitled "Postmodern Forms of Arousal and Defense Strategies" and "Consumer Aestheticism and the Neo-Flaneur," have introduced the notion that the driver is to the decentered contemporary "postmodern" metropolis what the flâneur was to the modern industrial city. In placing this section under the heading "The Bodily Experience of Urban Space," the notion of driving as a development of the activity of the flâneur is offered primarily as a means of conceptualizing direct experience of metropolitan existence. But this is not all. In keeping with the interdisciplinary nature of this book, the importance of the automobile for metropolitan culture has been investigated in its widest sense, and for ideological and experiential frameworks more generally. Hence the claims that "in the sprawl of technoburbs, car-based perception has become almost a visual default model," and, via Paul Virilio and Arie Graafland, that such car-based perception is connected to the activity of watching television or a movie.

As Graafland puts it, "The speed of driving creates a cinematographic effect that many underestimate. The result is a loss of sensible referents and a decay of architectonic markers."[1] The perceptual framework demanded by a car window, then, strongly resembles that necessary to watch a film. In most Hollywood films set in Los Angeles, the reverse is also true. No doubt due to the decentered suburbanization of Los Angeles, in films such as *Colors, Pretty Woman,* L.A. *Story, Grand Canyon, Falling Down, Devil in a Blue Dress,* a dominant point-of-view offered cinematographically strongly resembles, and is frequently identified as, that from a car window. However, due to the film grammar of shot and countershot these movies cannot help but also offer at least a doubled point of view, whereby the driver is normalized twice over, in the positions of the viewer and the viewed. What these filmic representations of Los Angeles as car city enable us to see are the limits of Baudrillard's discourse of the automobile, and in particular the workings of fantasy and power in *America,* whereby the gaze of the driver is never returned, and the freeway is never jammed.

Therefore, this essay aims to focus on exactly that which is excluded when the description of driving in terms of the conditioning of individual metropolitan social existence is used metonymically to define a cultural condition. The ideal metropolitan driver as conceptualized above via Graafland, Virilio, Harvey, and Baudrillard, replicates the characteristics of the flâneur "in an intensified form." In terms of its interiority this ideal driver may be considered to be subject to an intensified version of the modernist double-bind, as defined for example by Adorno and Horkheimer in terms of enlightenment and reification, or perhaps more directly in terms of empowerment and alienation.[2] However, if it is not to remain within the unreflectively white, male, and heterosexual subjectivities of dominant modernisms, this (post)modernist sense of the dialectical nature of the interiority of the ideal driver must be supplemented by a concern with the structural and contingent exclusions generated by cars as both material and symbolic objects.

Among others, Marshall Berman and Mike Davis have drawn attention to such material exclusions in the contexts of New York and Los Angeles respectively. For both, the costs of the apparent freedoms conferred by automobile travel are to be seen not only in terms of the individual alienation of the driver, but also in the destruction of city neighborhoods for highway construction, the decay of public transportation systems, the geographical concentration of wealth and poverty associated with suburbanization and disinvestment in downtown areas, and a host of further environmental problems.[3] What is suggested by this work is a very different modernist sense of the car as a symbolic object. Via Marx, the car appears as a dialectical combination of civilization and barbarism.

The more modernist (in its Marxist articulation) positions taken up by theorists such as Berman and Davis are clearly and often strategically mobilized against Baudrillardian "postmodernist" perspectives. From these positions, Baudrillard's observations appear complicit with the most extreme fantasies of car culture, playing a part in objectifying social relations at the level of culture as well as that of economics. As John Rundell has pointed out, Baudrillard's notion of hyperreality, heavily dependent as it is on a notion of the car and the freeway as paradigmatic social forms, is itself a "totalizing meta-narrative" in which a certain modernism "goes unnoticed."[4] Nevertheless, despite the ostentatious provocation and the flimsily concealed modernist nostalgia evident in phrases such as "Only immigrants from the Third World are allowed to walk. It is, in a sense, their privilege,"[5] Baudrillard is clearly correct in one way — it is difficult to return the gaze of a driver. Non car users do become regarded as cinematographic objects. Yet at the same time, these formulations also call attention to the function of the excluded (the third-world, the immigrant, the pedestrian), as a kind of constitutive outside of the ideal driver. I have already suggested that the exigencies of film grammar prevent the full idealization of driving. In what follows I will briefly trace the visual figuration of the automobile and Los Angeles in U.S. film

3 Marshall Berman, *All That Is Solid Melts Into Air: The Experience of Modernity* (London: Verso, 1982); Mike Davis, *City of Quartz: Excavating the Future in Los Angeles* (London: Verso, 1990).

4 John Rundell, "Beyond crisis, beyond novelty: The tensions of modernity," *New Formations* 31 (Spring/Summer 1997): 158-74, 165. For a more general discussion of filmic representations of automobiles in the context of modernity, see John Orr, *Cinema and Modernity* (Cambridge: Polity, 1993).

5 Jean Baudrillard, *America* (London: Verso, 1988), 58.

6 See Elizabeth Traube, *Dreaming Identities: Class, Gender and Generation in 1980s Film* (Boulder: Westview Press, 1992); Susan Jeffords, *Hard Bodies: Hollywood Masculinity in the Reagan Era* (New Brunswick: Rutgers University Press, 1994).

and in some significant television examples. As will be seen, these presentations make explicit the limits and the exclusions of car culture in varying degrees.

In Hollywood representations of Los Angeles, the car remains a potent symbol and emblem of the positive pole of modernity. In general, recent Hollywood films have reiterated the conventional associations of the car with mobility both geographical and social, with personal security and self-fulfillment; with the clichés I announced at the beginning. Like "America" itself, the car in Hollywood movies embodies a fantasy of democratic freedom, self-presence, and control.

In movies set in Los Angeles from *Pretty Woman* (Garry Marshall, 1990) to *Get Shorty* (Barry Sonnenfeld, 1996), from the *Beverley Hills Cop* series (Martin Brest, 1984; Tony Scott, 1987; John Landis, 1994) to *Grand Canyon* (Lawrence Kasdan, 1991), automobiles are framed by dominant and longstanding U.S. discourses of cross-country travel strongly linked with notions of social mobility, escape, and leisure. Such representations of the automobile connect it self-evidently to security, glamor, freedom, power, etc., in ways that are so naturalized as to be taken for granted by most audiences. These semiotic links have become so conventional in Hollywood representations of private autos, police cars, and limousines that they are used as the basis for the production of further meanings.

For example, in the opening minutes of *Pretty Woman*, the power and status of the Richard Gere character Edward are confirmed by his use of his lawyer's expensive sports car. Yet his inability to control the car's manual transmission emblematizes his lack of fitness for his responsibilities as corporate capitalist. He is, the audience learns later, a corporate raider who profits from closing down companies rather than producing commodities. The ease with which prostitute Vivian (Julia Roberts) operates the stick shift is a token of her good sense, which the film asks audiences to read both in terms of practicality and morality. By the end of the film this doubly good sense has enabled the regeneration not only of Edward, but also symbolically, of American business in general. Vivian, meanwhile, is rewarded by being able to marry both for love and for money, a happy ending achieved in the film's closing scene by again invoking the automobile as symbolic object. Edward depends upon his chauffeur to find Vivian's flat, but leaves his limousine waiting as he climbs the fire escape to propose.

The most direct filmic celebrations of the car as symbolic object, as distinct from utilitarian, metaphorical, and fetishistic representations, are associated with Reagan-era movies such as *Pretty Woman* and in the Chicago-set *Ferris Bueller's Day Off* (John Hughes, 1986).[6] In both these films the sports car stands unproblematically for material desire, and in turn material desire is presented unproblematically as a means of self-realization. The secret of the popularity of *Pretty Woman* lies in the way it relates romance to materialism. Rather than placing them in opposition to one another, the film presents them as ultimately complementary. This is why it is important that the first car Edward is seen to be driving is borrowed, and also not entirely under his control. *Pretty Woman* is as frank as John Hughes's film about the pleasures of consumption, but associates consumption primarily with femininity, as for example in a famous scene when Vivian goes shopping on Rodeo Drive. The trajectory of the film as a whole, in which as Hilary Radner has pointed out, Vivian negotiates her way from prostitute to wife, is anticipated in this first scene.[7] Vivian talks her way from streetwalker to driver.

As streetwalker, Vivian/Roberts had been the object of the looks both of the camera and of Edward as he drove up Sunset Boulevard. However, it is far from clear that the film grants to her the privileges of the look associated with the driver's position. The sense of Vivian's empowerment, as several critics have suggested, derives instead from the covert workings of codes of racial identity.[8] Vivian's whiteness links her to the female stars of screwball comedy, and distinguishes her from the largely Black and Latina prostitutes of the real Sunset Boulevard. A key figure here is "Skinny Marie," a streetgirl who at the beginning of the film is said to have been murdered and left in a dumpster. While the film does not assign racial or ethnic identity to this character, she occupies the position of the racialized and ethnicized underclass in contrast to which Vivian is defined. Vivian's whiteness is thus highly symbolic while it remains unspecified and in a sense invisible.

Elsewhere in Hollywood, and far less frequently, car culture is associated with modernity in its negative sense. Probably the best example is *American Gigolo* (Paul Schrader, 1980), in which Richard Gere also starred, where automobile transport, along with designer clothes and interiors, signifies Los Angeles in terms of a moral and ethical vacuum. In *American Gigolo* the car which Gere drives around a bleak L.A. is an instrument of self-alienation. It is here, as also in road movies such as *Vanishing Point*, that the car becomes most visible in terms of the interior dialectic of modernist selfhood, signaling both empowerment and alienation.

As has been suggested, this dialectic of modernity in car culture is itself ideological, and can serve to displace a sense of its exclusionary practices. Yet these exclusions have occasionally been made visible in a series of films and television

7 Hilary Radner, "'Pretty is as pretty does': Free enterprise and the marriage plot," in *Film Theory Goes to the Movies*, ed. Jim Collins, Hilary Radner, and Ava Preacher Collins (New York: Routledge, 1993), 56-76.

8 D. Soyini Madison, "*Pretty Woman* through the triple lens of black female spectatorship," in *From Mouse to Mermaid: The Politics of Film, Gender, and Culture*, ed. Elizabeth Bell, Lynda Haas, and Laura Sells (Bloomington: Indiana University Press, 1995), 224-35; Jude Davies and Carol Smith, *Gender, Ethnicity and Sexuality in Contemporary American Film* (Edinburgh: Keele University Press, 1998), 10-13.

9 John Fiske, *Media Matters: Everyday Culture and Political Change* (2nd edition; Minneapolis: Minnesota University Press, 1996), 255.

spectacles from the late 1980s on. In the 1990s, dysfunctional or limit-cases of idealist discourses of driving were broadcast nationwide via the video footage taken by George Holliday of the beating of Rodney King (widely shown in 1991-92), the L.A. riots/uprising (April/May 1992) and the pursuit and arrest of O. J. Simpson (June 1994). Each of these raised the question of the racial and economic limits of the dominant ideology of car freedoms, or what I have termed the ideal driver. The protection offered by the automobile was revealed symbolically as being over-ridden by race and class. Rodney King was of course allegedly stopped for motoring offences; while often-replayed footage from the uprising of the attack on white truck driver Reginald Denny provided a graphic illustration of the breakdown of order when not even a high cab can protect its occupant.

Although in many ways apparently the least historically important, the live television coverage, often replayed, of O. J. Simpson's flight in his friend Al Cowling's white Ford Bronco, and its low-speed pursuit by numerous police cars is perhaps the most complex of these representations. It also garnered the highest viewing figures, of some 100 million.[9] At one level, this presented the limits of the protection that can be afforded by the automobile. Here on national television was played out the tension between juridical and police power and the freedom of the individual as emblematized by auto-mobility. And for many miles and many minutes of screen time this tension was in fine balance. The forces of law and order, here emblematized by at least twelve police cruisers, pursued Simpson, but for whatever reason were unable or unwilling to penetrate the interior of the Bronco, until he gave himself up. At the same time, as part of the Simpson episode more generally, the incident raised the questions of race and wealth in connection with access to privileged ideological positions. When these power relations were played out for real, would Simpson's wealth protect him from the racially skewed power of the LAPD? In this sense, the television coverage served as a precursor to popular and racially inflected readings of the subsequent murder trial. As such, the Ford Bronco occupies the metaphorical position of Simpson's legal defence team. At yet another level, for purely technical reasons the incident enacted some elements of the hyperreal. The slow speed of the pursuit made it appear an inferior copy of car chases familiar from film representations. On its action alone, the footage would not be dynamic enough for one of the "true-life" shows such as *Cops*, and *The World's Most Dangerous Car Chases*, that it helped to spawn.

But there is something more going on here than simply a demonstration of the ideological limits of car culture. These examples are not just limit cases of a dominant ideology, but can also be read in terms of an alternative or counterdiscourse whereby cars are represented as emblems of power and tools for patrolling limits of exclusion and inclusion. This counterdiscourse is articulated in African American film, as for example in the representations of police cars in the films of Spike Lee, Matty Rich, Melvin Van Peebles, and Mario Van Peebles. Lee used the video footage of the Rodney King beating in the opening titles of *Malcolm X* (1992), to signal the historical continuities of African American experience. Both dominant and counterdiscourses are articulated with racial inflections in gangsta films such as *Menace II Society* (Albert Hughes and Allen Hughes, 1993), where private cars are presented as embodying financial success, and police cars as the mobile panopticons of the state.

Bearing in mind this sense of multiple and overlapping, though still power-inflected ideological discourses of the car in American film, I will now consider in a little more detail three films which make visible the racialized limits of car culture in significant ways: *Colors* (Dennis Hopper, 1988), *Falling Down* (Joel Schumacher, 1993), and *Devil in a Blue Dress* (Carl Franklin, 1996). Each of these offers a direct representation of the historical Los Angeles (of the 1980s, 1990s, and 1940s respectively), and each articulates the experiential and cultural space of Los Angeles to automobile culture, and other codes of identity and history. A longer study would be necessary in order to fully understand the inflection of filmic discourses of the automobile by the various important codes of identity such as race, gender, sexuality, and class. The concentration here on masculinity and race reflects the focus of the majority of Los Angeles movies, but remains theoretically exemplary rather than exhaustive.

Against the background of gang conflict in downtown Los Angeles, *Colors* focuses on the relationship of two white cops, macho authoritarian rookie McGavin (played by Sean Penn), and the more avuncular Hodges (Robert Duvall) who is one year from retirement when the two are partnered at the opening of the film. That this is a buddy-buddy cop movie raises the possibility of homosocial relations, especially since these two are the pre-eminent pairing in the film who fully return one another's gaze. The homosocial is in fact buried beneath their generational difference and the involvement of both men in heterosexual relationships, most overtly displayed when McGavin brings his girlfriend to eat at Hodges's family home. Much more explicitly, the film directly invokes associations of the car with power and the privileged position of the subject of the gaze. For much of the film, the pair patrol Watts in a succession of unmarked police cars, and go on to take part in a series of raids, during one of which Hodges is eventually killed. The opening title sequence normalizes both the association of the car with the gaze of power and white racial identity, and the driver's perspective on Los Angeles. It begins with a cut from the interior of the LAPD Headquarters, the scene of a pre-credit sequence I will discuss shortly, to an exterior shot of the building from a car. Cinematic point-of-view maintains the perspective of driver and/or front-seat passenger as the car exits what was the Central Business District and tours the deprived areas of downtown, where African Americans and Latino/as are visible as individuals and in groups on the sidewalk. These images are interspersed very occasionally with views of McGavin and Hodges through the car windscreen. Significantly, this is not a reverse shot but stands in for one. Viewers are positioned with the (white) policemen as they gaze at the (non-white) pedestrians on the sidewalk, but instead of returning this look, cinematic point-of-view switches to the front rather than the side of the car. The title sequence is concluded by a cut to a wide focus view of the skyscrapers downtown at night, which must be either from a tall building or a helicopter. Although seamless for viewers (and this seamlessness illustrates the mutually sustaining normative power of car-based perception and Hollywood conventions of point-of-view), this shift of perspective is the first of a series of ways in which the film demonstrates the limits of the power attributed to car-based subjectivity.

Throughout the film, their car is a haven of security for McGavin and Hodges, yet clearly they must frequently leave it and become vulnerable. The space they traverse is always difficult; primarily is it the bumpy, dusty alleys of Watts. The pair are never shown driving the freeways, but on these alleys and city streets. Like their contrastive styles of masculinity, linked in the film to notions of community policing (Hodges) and overt aggression (McGavin), the power of the car is presented in terms of performativity. And it is exactly the testing of these masculinities and the power conferred by the car that forms the narrative interest of the film, displacing to a large extent the dynamics of gang conflict and overt racial difference which, though privileged in terms of the film's title and soundtrack, function largely as a backdrop.

The pre-opening title sequence of *Colors* opens with a washroom discussion of masculinity, in which Hodges compares contemporary gangbangers invidiously with John Wayne, before McGavin introduces himself jokingly as "Rocky Six." When the older Hodges sarcastically asks his job, McGavin claims, "I'm a guardian of masculinity, man." This statement is quickly ironized when the effectiveness of Hodges's brand of masculinity becomes apparent, while McGavin's aggression only alienates the public. McGavin's aggressive driving occupies a pivotal point in the narrative, linking his own rite of passage into mature and caring masculinity with the gang strife that is reduced to the film's context and subplot. His determined pursuit of gang members in a car driven by a Latina results not only in the death of the occupants but also in the destruction of their own unmarked police car. The replacement car, a shabby yellow motor, draws ridicule from their colleagues and results in a temporary loss of prestige.

By the end of *Colors*, car use is repositioned in terms of stasis rather than mobility, in contradistinction to the helicopter. After a raid in the middle section of the film, a police chopper is shown occupying exactly the position of the powerful subject of the gaze that the opening title sequence had identified with car-based point-of-view. Later, as Hodges lies fatally shot, a helicopter sound vies to drown out his last words. And most strikingly of all, at the instant Hodges dies, McGavin raises his face to the sky and cries out in anger, sorrow, and frustration, and the cinematic point-of-view moves back sharply to give an aerial view of the death scene, as from a helicopter. The death of Hodges is followed by a brief coda, where McGavin is shown imparting Hodges's wisdom to his new partner, a rookie African American, and which ends with a wordless twenty-five second shot of McGavin at the wheel. The effect is a somewhat contradictory mixture of glamor and dull professionalism, of submission to the disciplines of police work while invoking also the Western motif of the cowboy's fundamental marginality and exteriority to "civilization." Having looked down on McGavin and the dead Hodges from the position of the helicopter, viewers are encouraged by these cinematic conventions to read driving from outside, differentiating themselves from it as driving is fixed as a blue-collar activity which places the cops in proximity to the gangs on which they seek to impose their authority.

A second coda of sorts follows during the end titles. These are interspersed with very brief shots or stills of downtown street scenes as seen from a car, as in the opening titles, but this time alternating with images of an arrest of several African American and Latino gang members. In the last of these, it is revealed that the arresting officer is Black. As with the final scene of the film proper, the effect is ambiguous. Following from that scene, in one sense this sequence suggests a trajectory whereby African Americans are now inhabiting the position of the ideal driver, a position whose whiteness was taken for granted in the opening title sequence. Yet there has been no countershot to establish the presence of the African American driver, and audiences are enabled to read the driving position in terms of Blackness only retrospectively, and with a little effort. Moreover, as I have argued, the panoptic power associated with the car-based perspective in the opening title sequence has been undermined by comparison with the helicopter.

1993's *Falling Down* in part employs a similar grammar of car and heli-

10 Jude Davies, "Gender, ethnicity and cultural crisis in *Falling Down* and *Groundhog Day*," *Screen* 36, 3 (1995): 214-32; Jude Davies, "'I'm the bad guy?': *Falling Down* and white masculinity in 1990s Hollywood," *Journal of Gender Studies* 4, 2 (1995): 145-52; Fred Pfeil, *White Guys: Studies in Post-modern Domination and Difference* (London: Verso, 1995); Liam Kennedy, "Alien nation: white male paranoia and Imperial culture in the United States," *Journal of American Studies* 30, 1 (1996): 87-100; Davies and Smith, *Gender, Ethnicity and Sexuality*, 31-38; Richard Dyer, *White* (London: Routledge, 1997), 217-22.

11 Kennedy, "Alien nation"; for further discussion of the complex negotiations going on here and in the film in general, see especially Davies and Smith, *Gender, Ethnicity and Sexuality*.

copter. The opening and initializing scene is set in a traffic jam. The gridlocked highway is just the first of a series of emblematic images and discourses in the film representing Los Angeles in terms of a highly territorialized and socially fragmented space (territory is policed by Latino gang members, a golf club, helicopters, and white police, among others). These territories are traversed by the film's central protagonist D-Fens, a sacked defence worker (Michael Douglas), whose decision to abandon his car in the gridlock not only initiates the action but also symbolizes the failure of the automobile as modernist ideal. *Falling Down* has been widely seen as relating specifically to the development of a new cultural visibility of white masculinity.[10] Here the abandonment of the car by D-Fens emblematizes what the film portrays as his exclusion from the economic and social status traditionally associated with whiteness. Its significance is underlined by the helicopter sounds that re-occur throughout the film, most noticeably at the close of the scene when he abandons his car, and at later moments of crisis.

*Falling Down* also makes a symbolic accommodation between white and African American males. As in *Colors,* Robert Duvall again plays an avuncular, caring cop due for retirement, only this time the film's action takes place on what is intended to be his last day on the job. Unlike *Colors,* which hardly breathes the possibility of police racism, *Falling Down,* which was made in the wake of the Rodney King video, presents the association of African American and white males as being generated against police power. In an early scene D-Fens catches the eye of an African American protesting against the alleged racism of a bank. The bank, as the protester alleges, has used the phrase "not economically viable" as a code for Blackness in refusing him a loan. As the African American is arrested and driven away in a LAPD squad car, he exchanges glances with D-Fens and his words, "Don't forget me," are heard on the soundtrack. At the conclusion of the film, when D-Fens is involved in a face-off with cop Prendergast (Duvall), he repeats the words on the protester's placard, "I'm not economically viable."

The territorialized city of *Falling Down,* and its symbolic representation of car and helicopter, is heavily overdetermined by debates over race and gender issues integrated into its action and extratextually framing its consumption as a "state of the nation" film. The episode just discussed has been read, as for example by Liam Kennedy, as appropriating Black history imperialistically, using the protester figure to give extra credibility to white suffering. However, its representation of the LAPD car links it to the counterdiscourses described above.[11] The complexity of *Falling Down* in this respect is thrown into relief by comparison with *Grand Canyon* (Lawrence Kasdan, 1991), which is initiated with a similar representation of the potential dysfunctionality of the car as modernist symbol. Kasdan's film begins when the Lexus of Mack (Kevin Kline) breaks down in Inglewood and he is threatened by Black gang members. Mack is "saved" by an African American tow-truck driver played by Danny Glover. In contrast to *Falling Down*, this film keeps faith with modernity, the automobile, and American exceptionalism, all of which are employed to realize a heavily symbolic racial accommodation via a family road trip to the Grand Canyon at its climax. Yet for all their comparable gestures of racial negotiation and their different constructions of whiteness itself, both remain white-centered films.

In comparison with both, *Devil in a Blue Dress* makes few claims for topicality (it is set with meticulous detail in the Los Angeles of 1948), but its evocation of the racialized and class-based power of automobile ownership amounts to a revisionist take on Hollywood traditions of car ownership. Carl Franklin's film does feature a scene in which a police car functions to maintain white power, as two policemen cruise by abusing the African American protagonist Easy Rawlins (Denzel Washington). But, as a suburban-living and aspirational blue-collar African American, Easy's own car is very important to him. The film opens with Rawlins driving home through his neighborhood, and the car remains visible in much of the film, largely as a safe haven. These representations place Rawlins firmly in the driving seat, occupying the normative space of the driver as exemplified in *Colors*. Also, as in the 1988 film, the mobility conferred by the car is potentially dangerous as soon as one steps outside it. Thus at one point Rawlins is attacked by two white police officers just as he gets out of the car in his drive. This danger is also articulated in specifically racialized terms when the car allows Rawlins to travel to parts of town where his presence attracts the attention of white racists. During the course of the film, as Easy is drawn somewhat unwillingly into the role of private eye, the conventions of classical Hollywood are reworked somewhat around racial difference. At one point, while essentially being used as a chauffeur, Easy wonders to himself at the danger of being found by the police with a white woman in his car.

Another scene calls attention to the ways in which this ideology of the car is imbricated within power relations structured by economic power and racial and ethnic identity. Here, while walking home at night from a police station, Rawlins is persuaded to get into an expensive car. The passenger compartment is dark, gloomy, and threatening. A middle-aged and rather overweight white man kisses a Latino boy whom he introduces as "Jésus, my adopted son," and begins to address Rawlins. Through imagery which is at least partially homophobic, Franklin effectively reverses the logic set up in the opening scenes. Here the interior space of the automobile is white-dominated and threatening, part of an overarching field of power which Rawlins has already experienced at the hands of the L.A. cops and which meant he had no real option of refusing the chauffeur's original invitation to get in the car. At the same time, the identification of the young boy as Latino implies that to be outside the dominant ideology of car culture, is to be positioned not as "Black," but as "non-white." In this scene, with both the boy and Rawlins incarcerated against their own interests, the automobile is for them more akin to a mobile jail than a liberatory mode of transport.

In conclusion, then, I have identified in films such as *Pretty Woman* and *Grand Canyon* what might be termed a mainstream discourse of the automobile which, while explicitly undifferentiated in terms of race and ethnicity, operates within the default position of whiteness. In this discourse, the car generally, but not always, emblematizes modernity in its most positive sense. Occasionally, as in *American Gigolo,* it is made clear that there is a dialectical payback for these emancipations. In addition, I have also identified the limits of this discourse by calling attention to three main topics: its silent exclusions; its failure always to compel belief; and also the existence of an alternative discourse of the automobile developed initially outside mainstream films but visible in readings of the 1990s T.V. events and in certain readings of mainstream films. This counterdiscourse makes visible the exclusions produced by notions of the ideal driver, in which the automobile functions as emblem of status and instrument of power. The epitome of the automobile in this sense is the police car as the mobile panopticon of the state. In keeping with their rather confused politics, *Colors* and *Falling Down* actually gesture towards this counterdiscourse. Such representations are sustained more fully in several films by non-white directors, especially in Franklin's *Devil in a Blue Dress.*

What is clear is the importance of race, gender, and class in understanding that when cars operate as symbolic objects, they are as much indices of power as fantastic instruments of self-fulfillment. Finally, it is worth noting that the increased visibility of non-whites in the position of the ideal driver in mainstream representations of Los Angeles has been accompanied by a curtailing of the power of that position. In the proliferating representations of Los Angeles as dysfunctional city, from daily traffic reports on local television and radio news, to the coverage of the attack on Denny and Simpson's flight, and in films such as *Colors, Falling Down,* and Robert Altman's *Short Cuts,* car-based perception no longer occupies the position of greatest power. The most powerful panoptic gaze is offered instead from the helicopter.

**René Boomkens**

# The "Middle Landscape" and the Myth of Mobility: Coming Home in Commuter Country

*Keywords:* ■ *Architecture* ■ *Sociology* ■ *Suburbanization* ■ *Car Culture*

**Modernity between Uprootedness and Homecoming** Modernity, and in particular modern urban life, is easily identified with uprootedness, nomadism, and homelessness. In recent architectural debates, this identification even functions as a somewhat intractable and undefinable stimulus for a discourse on the practice of modern architecture as a discipline that would get rid of its positive role as a supplier of housing and thus of any lingering sense of a home. This discourse, itself strongly rooted in a neo-Heideggerian and deconstructionist body of ideas, redefines the task of architecture as one that is grounded in a refusal to contribute to the destructive conditions of modern society, in which homelessness and uprootedness are supposed to have become the dominant ways of life. This idea of the *impossibility* of architecture under social conditions dominated by uprootedness is born of an originally critical research program, which drew from various sources: early-twentieth-century avantgardism in architecture and urban planning, with its longing for the "New Realism" ("Neue Sachlichkeit") and its wish to build for the proletarian masses; Marxist and neo-Marxist critiques of the capitalist system of production; and neo-avantgardist programs and movements from the sixties and seventies.

The Heideggerian hypothesis of a general uprootedness in many senses squares well with this context of criticizing capitalism and technology, but it is at the same time the expression of a growing disappointment about possible alternatives and has resulted in ever more radical strategies of rejection. The idea of the impossibility of architecture is but one of these. It is echoed in many texts by Peter Eisenman, Rem Koolhaas, Sanford Kwinter, Manfredo Tafuri, Massimo Cacciari, Francesco Dal Co, and several other renowned and trendsetting architects and architectural critics. The question is whether this increased disappointment derives principally from deteriorated social circumstances or from a significant crisis in the practice of architecture itself. The latter sounds the more plausible explanation: although the hypothesis of the impossibility of architecture under the conditions of a general uprootedness was and is especially heard in the treatises of architectural critics and historians of academic extraction, as well as in the manifestoes of non-building "paper architects," as soon as the latter nevertheless manage to obtain assignments and commissions, the impossibility thesis is soon dropped for that of a nomadic and revelatory architecture — in other words, of an architecture that renders the uprootedness visible and tangible in and through evasive, de(con)structive, and nomadic gestures. Here we only witness the return of an ancient debate, or better, of the classic conflict, between the aesthetics of a Beaux Arts architecture and the technological rationality and pragmatism of engineers, but the conflict now returns as a farce *and* within one and the same person, that of the master architect with the vision of a universal intellectual, who upon closer inspection turns out to be no more than a humble technician doing little more than executing the assignments of frequently quirky parties in the market.

What is more, these nomadic master builders and critics of uprootedness are inclined once again to appeal to the program of the historical avantgardes, and this so many decades after the death of avantgardism: Le Corbusier's self-inflation ("architecture or revolution") is once again adopted, this time as an empty gesture that in one fell swoop rejects both society and architecture. This rejection *seems* like the result of a thorough analysis of social relations and of a consistent ethical-aesthetical stand from the specific angle of a technical-artistic professional group that plays a major role in questions of urbanization and housing policy. Yet this appearance must cover up the miserable condition in which the professional ego of the late-modern architect finds itself — a condition that is again partly due to more recent technological innovations, which have robbed the profession of its last semblance of artisticity and intellectualism. Ironically, the latest avantgarde of nomadic architects is itself principally hired for projects with a high "semblance" and "design" factor (monuments, for example), in ways that are more than a little question-begging. What is the difference, say, between the monumental *kitsch* in which a historicizing postmodernist like Bofill dressed the popular housing of suburban quarters in Paris and the obtrusive monumentality with which Eisenman shaped his Holocaust monument — a monumentality not only reminiscent of tombs, but just as much of the scale on which the proverbial Nazi architect Albert Speer used to work? In terms of nomadism and uprootedness, it is probably Rem Koolhaas who continues to be the most consistent and sober-headed of the company: he appears to shun any attempts whatsoever at designing or at devising so much as an architectural style and appears to grant honestly that he can do no more than "surf on the waves" of international economic dynamics (surfing being already tough enough as it is). In practice, however, this appears to imply little more than that this Dutch master architect always turns out to be where development is fastest and scales are largest, at the crossroads and junctions in other words, those places of which Walter Benjamin argued, already in the 1930s, that they are favored by "the destructive character" (his portrait of a reckless, cynical, pragmatic, and illusionless Maker, the other face of the avantgardist).

Benjamin's short and virulent portrait of the destructive character, modeled upon both the avantgardist Bertolt Brecht and an old friend turned banker, was written under very special circumstances. This was 1931: an economic crisis had spread all over the world, the national-socialists in Germany were rising fast, and the traumas of the First World War had not in the least been healed. The position of the Jewish intellectual Benjamin in Germany seemed hopeless, and in this historical constellation Benjamin "gambled" (the phrase is Irving Wohlfarth's) on the destructive character as an ultimate opportunity for undoing the ongoing destruction through a final destructive gesture. Two years later, with Hitler already in power, Benjamin filled in the political and cultural program of the destructive character as the absolute tabula rasa. He did so on the basis of an awareness that the historical experience of European culture had become as worthless as German paper currency. There was hardly any other option left for people but to make a final attempt at surviving the culture as "new barbarians," and this promised to be most successful in the naked and functionalist building blocks of New Realism, where the past had been erased and where it would be difficult to leave behind new historical traces.

Clearly, the special historical constellation in which Benjamin wrote stood under the sign of a growing uprootedness — but neither he himself nor the avantgardes with which he associated himself (no matter how illusionlessly) derived from this a (cultural) politics which itself displayed signs of uprootedness: they were rather concerned with devising *hiding-places,* in which it was possible to survive the culture. No nomadic policy for them, in other words, but forms of hiding, and that was a sensible policy in the thirties. The New Realism and so-called functionalism survived the war and were only able to mark society fully after 1945, especially as an instrument of reconstruction. And although the loftier ideals of some avantgardes, like the dream of a New Man or a New City, turned out to be pipe dreams, many of the avantgardes' more pragmatic thoughts were realized in that reconstruction process. This became clearest in the realm of town and country planning, or better, in the ongoing urbanization process. The idea of a separation of functions was materialized in the design and construction of monofunctional residential quarters and industrial zones, and in the upscaling of traffic infrastructures. Gropius's box of blocks was translated into the large-scale standardization of popular housing projects, and urban development was engineered on the basis of new planning principles and extensive urban "surveys." Rationalization and a scientific approach were expected to deflect the proliferation of cities into more ordered tracks. Highrise construction in a green environment: that seemed to be the panacea for all urban ills; so, make room for new forms of mobility. Thus, a new, dynamical form of urbanism would acquire shape, without the chaos and the dirt of the typically modern, nineteenth-century city.

It was not to be. Things took a different turn. Especially the success of the automobile thwarted the functionalist scenario. No matter how much a rise in mobility was being anticipated, functionalism kept relying strongly on collectivist notions of urbanization. A growing individualization, however, contributed to a type of urbanization, or rather of suburbanization, in which notions like community, neigborhood, and vicinity were gradually surpassed by the autonomous status of the private home as the molecule of a new suburban, possibly posturban, way of life. Not criteria of social cohesion, but ideas of a free and unhampered private life in a secluded intimate sphere were to determine the ongoing process of suburbanization. The vocabulary of New Realism and of functionalist planning lacked the terms for attesting to this evolution. The heaviness, bareness, and undeludedness of the prewar jargon of radical avantgardes, born of the cultural uprootedness of the Interbellum, evaporated in the cloudless sky of a new homecoming in "commuter country," the new "middle landscape" of a successful middle class. Thus, without interference of the avantgardes, a "new man," or at least a new urbanite, seemed to be born. But what did he or she look like? We still don't seem to know. Let's leave the avantgardes and their nomadic descendants for what they are, so that we may focus our attention on the still underexplored social culture of suburbia, a culture that exists somewhere between uprootedness and homecoming. Afterwards, we will be able to observe how that culture relates to a typically urban culture, or what is assumed to be such.

**"Nattering in Paradise"** Suburbia, as becomes clear from Part One of this book, has been in existence since at least the late 18th, early 19th century. It was once the privilege of the wealthy, the private Arcadia for those able to escape from the smog and dirt of the early industrial city. The first commuters in the Netherlands were distinguished gentlemen who preferred to travel back and forth in first-class compartments between Bloemendaal or het Gooi and Amsterdam. At the end of the twentieth century, suburbia has become something totally different: no longer a refuge, it is rather the self-evident residential destination of a large and still growing part of the population. Suburbia has become ordinary and average.

Even so, it has persistently resisted attempts at getting a scholarly purchase on it. Knowledge about suburbia other than statistical data and morphological-functional analyses is still arriving only piecemeal. Somehow, then, suburbia has not profited much from the growing academic interest since at least the eighties in mass-culture phenomena like television, tourism, fashion, pop music, pulp fiction, and so forth. The suburbs have remained a form of sunken heritage, or worse: they are deemed cultureless *à outrance*. Already since D. H. Lawrence and Virginia Woolf, suburbanites are represented in literature as a kind of secondary creatures, who derive their knowledge from the local library and their food from cans.[1] This condescending attitude has changed little since. The two most renowned urban planners and landscape architects in the Netherlands, Rem Koolhaas and Adriaan Geuze, have never made a secret of their dislike for "the suburbs." Koolhaas once called suburbia the greatest ecological disaster ever to have struck the Netherlands; Geuze once believed he was born to design houses for people who had sooner live in water towers than in row houses. Both designers consider themselves utterly "modern" and prefer to design spaces that have to do with traffic, transportation, and communication: transfer hubs, airports, bridges, highways, railway stations, and so forth. That the suburbia they so strongly despise forms the inevitable flipside of these spaces is a fact they choose to ignore. Koolhaas and Geuze are both heirs of early-twentieth-century modernism in architecture, with its strong preference for transparency, rationality, and large scale. The coziness and comfiness of gable-roofed suburbia are a long way from their interests. Nevertheless, they remain powerless against the hard facts of the real estate market: for decades now, the row-house-cum-garden-and-garage in quiet surroundings without fast traffic, offices, shops, and nightlife has been the outspoken favorite of average Dutchmen. Safety and accessibility by car are two of the primary motives underlying this widespread preference.

What "everyone" seems to wish is nowhere on the agenda of the intellectual elite, which continues to view suburbanization as a flight from the city and not as a part or aspect of the urbanization process itself. Yet what is the "city" that is at stake here? Nostalgia is of course pointless, with its false celebration of the nineteenth-century city, which brought us endless jerry-building and social and medical misery and was thus precisely responsible for the radical plans for renewal devised by the modern avantgardes. At the same time, we cannot be unaware of the extent to which our own conceptions of urban life remain filled with images,

1 For the disdain felt by the British literary avantgarde towards suburbanites, see John Carey, *The Intellectuals and the Masses: Pride and Prejudice among the Literary Intelligentsia, 1880-1939* (London: Faber and Faber, 1992), 46-70 ("The Suburbs and the Clerks").

certainly also idealizations, that — thanks to writers, historians, painters, or photographers, and a little bit also to oral tradition — we derive precisely from that same 19th century. These images should not be seen as all-pervasive, yet they cannot be dispensed with either. For the sad thing about more than a century of history of the modern city and of modern urbanization is that none of the recent outcomes of that history any longer meet with approval. The classic modern ideals of metropolitanism or cosmopolitanism have lost their glitter and the urbanite as a world-citizen has been superseded by the *commuter,* the type of urban dweller who does not want to be an urbanite. To realize the condition that the modern city finds itself in, we will need to map the commuter's biotope.

The commuter is who we are, who we do not want to be, and who we can only be, even if we think we are not, or to some extent try not to be.

*Nattering in Paradise* is the title of a wonderful book of photographs on British Suburbia, and it is a title that quite accurately expresses our problem or dilemma. Suburbia, the suburbs, the garden city or garden village: those were the bourgeois and socialist utopias of the past one hundred and fifty years, offering a way out from the chaos and misery of the modern industrial city, a way out that, certainly in the rotund treatises of the day, took on paradisaic features. Now, a century of suburbanization later, we appear to be acting like Adam and Eve after the Fall: we are not adequately equipped to inhabit paradise. The only thing we are doing is "nattering" or chattering, and that may well be the greatest sin of all: we misuse the language of God, who gave things their names, by letting it circulate in an endless and meaningless prattle across the hedges and fences of our suburban paradise. Yet one might ask: *what* paradise? Surely that was only the inflated presumption of the earlier citizen or socialist? Indeed. But what about the prattle? In terms of statistical data, of socioeconomic or demographic facts, even in culture-sociological terms, we are not at a loss to conceptualize it. In many senses, we are talking here of the most described, most charted, and most analyzed group of all times. It was formerly known as the "middle class" and is today referred to as average consumers, a group that in turn divides into a whole series of taste communities that mutually overlap yet may be kept apart analytically on the basis of categories like income, social status, origin, or age. And even then, we again wind up in the middle group: to an important extent, the elderly and adolescents fall outside available statistics. Membership of the social "middle group," in terms of age, education, and income, coincides to a large extent with living in suburbia. The suburban way of life has become a crucial part of the identity of late-modern citizens. It marks their views of the good life, determines their self-esteem and individuality, exerts a major influence on their roles in public life, their political beliefs, their cultural sensibilities, and their attitudes towards others.[2] Yet it is and remains hard to determine precisely what this suburban culture consists of. The farmer or the urbanite might be called social types, who derive their respective identities to an important degree from their spatial positions. Something comparable, however, does not as automatically apply to residents of suburbia. Their locational status developed at a point in history when the notion of "place" had lost much of its meaning. Suburbia is part of the ongoing process of "despatialization" or "decontextualization": fast traffic and telematics have drastically reduced the distances between outlying places on this globe; city and country are merging more and more and losing their distinctive features — and suburbia is probably the most telling embodiment of these evolutions.

In sum, we are talking here of a *paradoxical spatial identity*. Most postmodern theorizations do little else than observe this fact and play an at times highly entertaining and ironical game with this paradox, without however making any true intellectual progress.[3] The problem seems to be that theorists get stuck in spatial metaphors, or in other words: they take for granted that suburbanism or suburbanity is an exclusively spatial condition, along the lines of comparable spatial conditions like centrality and periphery, city and country, inner city and suburb, and so on. The paradox disappears, however, when we no longer understand the concept to be a strictly spatial category, but try to grasp it from other angles. This requires the temporary suspension of demographical, geographical, or urbanistic notions in favor of a phenomenology of the suburbanite, or as I have just called him or her: the *commuter*.

**A Mobile Intimate Realm** The history of the suburban way of life is roughly the product of two mutually enhancing processes: first, the growing intimization of the private realm, or what the philosopher Walter Benjamin called the emer-

2 The consequences on so-called "active citizenship" that follow from living in more or less homogeneous suburbs was pointed out by among others Richard Sennett in a chapter called "Community Becomes Uncivilized" in *The Fall of Public Man* (London: Faber and Faber, 1977), 294-312.

3 See for instance the international debate among architects and critics organized annually by the so-called ANY conferences, where architects and theoreticians like Rosi Braidotti, Peter Eisenman, Sanford Kwinter, Bernard Tschumi, Rem Koolhaas, Christine Boyer, and many others discuss the future of architecture and urban life in terms of a universal nomadic subject, peppering their contributions randomly with ineptly interpreted texts by Gilles Deleuze, Jacques Derrida, and others

4 Walter Benjamin, "Der destruktive Charakter," in *Gesammelte Schriften* IV.1 (Frankfurt am Main: Suhrkamp, 1980), 396-7.

5 See for instance George Duby and Philippe Ariès, eds., *Histoire de la vie privée* (Paris: Éditions du Seuil, 1985); Richard Sennett, *The Fall of Public Man* (London: Faber and Faber, 1977); Christopher Lasch, *The Culture of Narcissism* (New York: Norton, 1978); Michel Foucault, *Histoire de la sexualité 1-3* (Paris: Gallimard, 1978-1984); Jürgen Habermas, *Strukturwandel der Öffentlichkeit* (Frankfurt am Main: Suhrkamp, 1990).

6 Joel Schwartz, "The Evolution of the Suburbs," in *Suburbia, the American Dream and Dilemma*, ed. Philip C. Dolce (New York: Anchor Books, 1976), 1-36.

gence of the "envelope man,"[4] followed by a non-gradual increase in mobility determined by technological jumps, or in other words, the acceleration, intensification, and upscaling of traffic flows and networks.

First, the process of intimization, or better: the transformation or reduction of the private realm to an intimate realm. Relatively speaking, the history of private life, of intimacy and sexuality, and of upbringing and education belongs to those historical topics that have been underexplored. This may in fact be considered one of the reasons why suburbia has long remained an academic orphan. In the past few decades, however, thanks to the work of historians like Philippe Ariès and George Duby, sociologists like Richard Sennett and Christopher Lasch, philosophers like Michel Foucault and Jürgen Habermas, and the increasing influence of feminist theory, women's studies, and queer studies, some theoretical and historical consensus has formed about the crucial and autonomous meaning of the private realm for understanding wider social processes.[5] This is not the place to argue this consensus, but it is helpful to sketch out a few of its major aspects. The most important characteristic of the modern private realm as an intimate realm is the idea of the freedom or autonomy of the bourgeois self as something rooted in the warmth and security of the intimate realm. This notion of freedom is at odds with more common notions of freedom grounded in the political or public domain. It is rooted, among other things, in an attitude towards the "world outside the family," the city culture, the world of labor and of public life, that has been radically altered since industrialization.

In his descriptions of, and comments upon, the nineteenth-century bourgeois interior, Benjamin anticipated current interests in the intimate realm. With considerable lucidity, he saw how the bourgeois family patriarch radically isolated the intimate realm from the everyday realities of work, trade, and politics, and how a pastoral ideology was extracted from this, which saddled the intimate realm with the task of looking after authenticity and unhampered identity-building, while the realms of work, trade, and politics were labeled the threatening domain of necessity, with the male patriarch as intermediary between both spheres. This description runs ahead of what we now know as the reality of suburbia or of the commuter, who, as Joel Schwartz put it, "dreamed of a private garden spot, but one never far removed from the easy camaraderie enjoyed back in the city."[6] In this formulation, we do not only hear the echoes of a crucial sexual divide in the organization of the "private spot" of suburbia, but especially the ambiguous relationship between suburbia and city, between intimate and public — a relationship that reveals the ambiguous appeal of modern urban life. Economically, suburbia is one hundred percent dependent on the city; culturally, it turns its back on that city. This fact, as I already indicated, at the same time also sealed the fate of the Modern Movement in urban planning and architecture, which equally turned against the chaos of the big city, yet explicitly looked forward in its alternatives to new, open, and transparent forms of communal life in garden cities, satellite towns, or green suburbs. The antiurban subtext of modernists was retained and even intensified in the actual realization of suburbia, but the ideal of the City of Tomorrow or of the New Man was dumped. What remained is the commuter, the theoretically dynamic, mobile, and autonomous urbanite.

The history of mobility, as demonstrated in Part One of this book, is the history of the use of cast iron and steel in architecture, of the invention of the elevator, of the electrification of the railway system, of the introduction of the automobile as a private means of transportation, of the spreading of air traffic, of the invention of the container, and finally of the so-called revolution of informatics and telematics. It is more than striking that of all these revolutionary jumps in technological development, only one is being contested, or generally deemed to pose a great problem: the introduction of the (private) car. With the car, the two processes of intimization and of expanded mobility are united with a vengeance. The commuter is the most catching embodiment of these twin processes. The overwhelming success of the private car, in other words, is more the result of an increased significance of the intimate realm than of the sheer technological possibility of getting the machine moving. Maybe the spectacular downfall of the superior public transportation system in Los Angeles can serve as evidence here: in merely technological terms, this network was better able to solve the city's transportation problem than whatever private alternative. And yet public transportation in L.A. succumbed under the pressure of the private car. Today, Union Station in L.A. has become little more than a tourist attraction.

More important, however, is the observation that the revolution effected by the private car should not in the least be considered the triumph of a free market ideology, of thinking in terms of efficiency or functionality. The private car, as the dreamed acme of mobility, is in no sense part of the world of "the market" or of economic liberalism. The car simply represents an expansion of the fortress of the autonomous individual's intimate realm, which seeks to protect itself as long as possible from the many perils inherent in the public life of work, trade, government, and politics. The car is the final line of defense against this threatening outside world. At its best, it is an intermediary world: a haven in the traffic jam on the way to countless obligations. The car is the ultimate attempt of the intimate realm to render its laws applicable everywhere. The commuter is thus an extreme character: s/he strives for the highest degree of immobility in a culture that stands under the aegis of a continual intensification of mobility. We need only wait before this paradox will start hurting.

In the U.S., the "commuter's paradox" is in fact already hurting. In the urban landscape of Southern California, daily traveling times between home and work of more than three hours (round-trip) are no longer an exception. Distances of hundreds of miles per day are not felt to be extreme. From a social-cultural perspective, hundreds of thousands of people traveling back and forth between their homes and jobs find themselves doubly isolated. As indicated, the private car functions first and foremost as an expansion of the "fortress" of the intimate realm: the stress and chaos of public life are locked out as long as possible, or regulated and contained by means of cellular phones and car radios. But also with respect to the intimate realm itself, commuter traffic by car represents a form of isolation. Commuters may well be "by themselves" while traveling, yet they lack the sheltering security and other advantages, as well as obligations and worries, that are part of the intimate realm: the relationship with a partner, with children, or other family members. More in particular, the strenuous work ethic typical of the American economy, combined with the double work load for both sexes and the longer traveling times, leads to an erosion of the private or intimate realm itself. It is no coincidence that American pedagogues introduced the term "quality time" (or even "cuddling time") in an attempt to counter this erosion. The term points to the daily necessity of spending some short extra time with the children, by way of compensation for the many hours these children have to make do with no (or only little) attention from their parents. Such emergency scenarios reveal ever so clearly the paradox of an increased mobility that has resulted in a diminished mutual reachability. They also point to the ongoing functional segmentation of everyday life into divergent time schedules — a segmentation that leaves little intact of the more or less opaque social-cultural reality of modern urban public space, where, besides much that is useful and planned, all kinds of useless, disrupting, and unplanned events, meetings, and confrontations also take place. That this evolution also disrupts the spontaneous and self-evident domestic ecology of nuclear and extended families means that we are faced here with a tendential undermining of the very breeding ground of the autonomous individual. And this situation will certainly lead to concerned or alarmed reactions more easily than the fact that our public life would be threatened.

During much of his or her working day, the commuter occupies a kind of "middle landscape," a nondescript twilight zone, which he or she obstinately tries to describe in terms of a time schedule — the number of traveling hours, the lost time in traffic jams and in waiting — but which ultimately is still determined by the limits set to one's daily timetable by physical space. The commuter differs favorably from the spatially deprived, from those who for economic or other reasons possess little or no freedom of movement: the unemployed, the disabled, the elderly, children, underprivileged minorities in slums, etcetera. Compared to the world of the supermobile, by contrast, the commuter's freedom of movement means absolutely nothing. The private car is above all the carrier of a myth, the myth of an individual freedom of movement that, in spite of everything, still associates the move to suburbia with the notion of social ascent. The truly mobile, however, the successful businessmen, artists, politicians, or scientists, who travel mostly by plane, have precisely left suburbia. This is something commuters may only dream of — an activity for which the long daily hours on freeways offer ample opportunity. It would appear as if the individual command over the method of transportation offered them all possible freedom to go anywhere they liked, to leave behind even their works and their families, in other words, to escape. In reality, however, the car binds the commuter ever so strongly to the daily routine of traveling between home and work. The private car might well be one of the most refined instruments of what Michel Foucault called the *pastoral power*, the late-modern type of power that has come to displace the era of *disciplinary power* (that of industrialization, of massification, and of standardization). In this new era, massification is not stopped, but it takes on a different guise. Authoritarian management styles make room for management based on negotiation. Moral values like submission and obedience are exchanged for values like independence and personal initiative. According to Foucault, the pastoral power exists as a sort of permanent conversation with the subject over whom power is exerted. In this conversation, a double result is achieved: the subject is continuously confirmed in his/her freedom and power to decide, as well as in his/her personal integrity, *and* is simultaneously normalized, which is to say that he or she is prompted, via the invisible (uncoercive) coercion of joining the conversation, into freely accepting the existing situation as normal.[7]

The private car is an ideal instrument for this new type of antiauthoritarian exercise of power or of social normalization. The car provides the commuter

7 See Michel Foucault, "The Subject and Power," afterword in *Michel Foucault between Structuralism and Hermeneutics* by Hubert L. Dreyfus and Paul Rabinow (Brighton: Harvester Press, 1982), 210-11; and René Boomkens, "Het subject na de dood van de mens," in *Foucault Herdenken. Over werk en werking van Michel Foucault*, ed. Machiel Karskens and Jozef Keulartz (Best: Damon, 1995), 16-19.

8 To the instruments of pastoral power since the car, a new item has been added: that of "airmiles." Airmiles can be saved when buying at large supermarkets or oil companies (the gas station!) and at other large companies, all with an eye to traveling cheaply in the end. The term "airmiles" suggests that one is saving miles for traveling by airplane. This is one possibility, but it is more than revelatory that most savers use their miles quite differently: they exchange them for days at Center Parks, a chain of family holiday parks. The new promise of mobility, too, in other words, is transformed into the motionless and sheltered world of suburbia.

9 See Edward W. Soja, *Postmodern Geographies: The Reassertion of Space in Critical Social Theory* (London: Verso, 1989).

10 Rem Koolhaas, "The Generic City," in Office for Metropolitan Architecture, Rem Koolhaas, and Bruce Mau, *Small, Medium, Large, Extra-Large*, ed. Jennifer Sigler (Rotterdam: 010, 1995), 1239-64.

with an expansion of his or her personal power realm and a form of individual distinction vis-à-vis other road users. At the same time, the car forces commuters ever so clearly into their socially desirable roles of suburban workforce and languid participants in, or victims of, the daily rush-hour traffic jams.

The social-cultural reality of the commuter and the social significance of the private car are important evidence for a critique of the influential myth of a widely increased mobility (both geographical and social).[8] This myth was and is still kept alive by international bankers like Onno Ruding, who as the Dutch Minister of Finance loved to chafe at employees (or rather: the unemployed) for staying home too long, instead of getting their butts moving (and thus finding work). But it also hangs like a mist over the debates in contemporary architecture and urban planning. These debates consistently and almost irritatingly bypass the dominant condition of our late-modern cities. That condition is called suburbia, and it is a condition that, in spite of all dreams of mobility, is marked by the immobility, the comfort, the security, and homogeneity of the everyday life-world. It is, in short, not marked by uprootedness, but by homecoming.

The problem is that this homecoming has inevitable consequences for what suburbia, despite its growing autonomization, still stands in a relationship to: the city and its culture. Has the city stopped to exist? And what would that mean? Questions of this sort are too general to be given a sensible answer. But it still remains to be seen how processes of suburbanization will mark the agenda of the debates in urban planning and in architecture. One such debate, crucial to the Netherlands, is that on the so-called "Randstad," the ring of cities in Western Holland which somehow or other refuses to grow into a new, large-scale type of city. This debate takes us from the recent history of Dutch town planning to the murky and labyrinthine world of globalization. Somewhere in the middle of this we must situate the near future of what we still refer to with a concept reminiscent of flat bicycle tires and stage-coaches: *the city*. Or not? Does what we call the city have a predictable future?

**The "Randstad" as Los Angeles?** The city *as* suburbia: that is Los Angeles, which has not for nothing been proclaimed the capital of postmodernity — which seems to imply that big cities everywhere in the world will eventually develop into the kind of urban landscape typical of L.A. and of Southern California at large. As social geographer Edward Soja so catchily quips, "L.A. is everywhere and everywhere is in L.A."[9] The motto anticipates Rem Koolhaas's Generic City,[10] but while Soja tends to see postmodern urbanism especially as the outcome of a steadily growing automobility and therefore as an almost endless horizontal suburban landscape, Koolhaas precisely detects isolated urban clusters of verticality as the nodes in a global network of powerbases, in particular airports and centers of financial-economic power. To Soja's "global village" Koolhaas opposes a "global city" — two possible outcomes of the urbanization process in the age of globalization. Both models or hypotheses presuppose that the globalization of the capitalist economy will have similar effects all over the world: either the earth will be covered by a seemingly endless grid of similar suburban lowrise housing (the triumph of individualism and of the commuter's automobility) or else the built environment will be limited to, and concentrated in, a number of spatially isolated megacities in the vicinity of international nodes of global transportation and communication located in the middle of an almost endless natural hinterland. Upon closer inspection, however, these models appear to be overeager extrapolations on the basis of rather onesided presuppositions. Soja's model of L.A. is founded on a kind of postmodern methodological individualism: the city develops simply on the basis of the preferences of atomic, individual residential consumers, who, given the present supply, will automatically opt for accessible living in an environment that is as green as possible. On the basis of such a logic, the Dutch urban historian Vincent van Rossem also concluded that the Western part of the Netherlands (the so-called "Randstad") would automatically develop into a second Los Angeles.[11] Another logic than this strictly individualistic market logic is not to be found in this model.

Just as onesided is the essentially structuralistic, even system-theoretical train of thought developed by Koolhaas, in which a global urban system simply unfolds or develops without any counterforce, in which nodes emerge without a hinterland or centers without a periphery. An obvious thing to do, then, is to juxtapose both models and rob them of their onesidedness. Quickly, it appears that urban concentration and suburban deconcentration are in many cases simultaneous processes, which are in different ways linked to the globalization of the economy and of communication, but which also, at a more local scale, depend upon specific spatial, national, interregional, as well as historic differences. Only on the basis of such differences and specific circumstances does it become possible to draw an acceptable and justified sketch of possible future developments within a certain region. Randstad Holland has been "suburbanizing" for a number of decades now, not only owing to the breakthrough of private cars, but also because of a national spreading policy founded on notions of spatial balance. This policy has been officially under review for more than ten years already, but in reality is simply continued. At the same time, huge efforts are made, especially

11 Vincent van Rossem, *Randstad Holland, Variaties op het thema stad* [Rotterdam: NAi Publishers, 1994].

by multinational corporations, to develop the Randstad further into a concentrated "mainport" (a pseudo-English term favored by powerbrokers) around the airport of Schiphol and the harbor of Rotterdam. In short: concentration and spreading seem to be able to go together. More accurately: concentration of economic power and of industries goes together with an ongoing residential sprawl. While urban centers gain an ever greater independence from every local or national dynamic or influence, the residential function spreads out to an ever growing periphery that refuses to become a city. This is also where the two crucial tasks for the coming decades lie: on the one hand, the task of reestablishing a collective purchase on the development and organization of the international nodes in our landscape, and on the other, the task of reurbanizing our ever more homogeneous and emptier suburban landscapes of residence. This requires the setting of explicit restraints on the ongoing spiral of intimization and mobilization and thus a repoliticization of space. Without this repoliticization, debates like those on Randstad Holland remain a futile tit-for-tat between the L.A. of Soja and the Generic City of Koolhaas.

*Translation Bart Eeckhout*

Cino Zucchi

# Enclaves: Cruising through the City of Minorities

*Keywords:* ■ *Architecture* ■ *Suburbanization* ■ *Spatial Fragmentation*

*"Many ancient towns derive exceptional beauty from their enclosure by ramparts or walls.... We have no occasion, and it would therefore be a pure affectation, to seek to fortify our towns with walls, nor is it desirable that we should cause undue congestion; but it is most necessary in some way to define our town areas, and in the case of large towns to define and separate new areas and suburbs.... Though we shall not copy the fortified wall of the old city, we may take from it a most pregnant suggestion of the value of defining and limiting towns, suburbs, and new areas generally. This may be done in many ways."* — Raymond Unwin, *Town Planning in Practice* (1909)

**Interiors** The sixties opened with a strong image: a polyethylene bubble, an amniotic sack sustained by a series of sophisticated technologies of micro-environmental control. This image generated a revolutionary hybrid between two deep mental associations, two archetypes of well-being: one of protection, of shelter, and one of the contemplation of nature, of nomadism.

Reyner Banham's "bubble," the ageless ideal of domestic comfort made panoptical and ubiquitous by a progressively "softer" technique, can be bought today from any car dealer. The car evolved in these years from a mechanical device to the cozy ideal of an interior moving through the landscape.

What is the present relationship between the offer of mobility and the demand for domestic roots?

Recent attempts at describing the contemporary city have explored radical changes in the use and design of collective spaces, and have directed our view to a number of new spatial situations and building types connected with the phenomenon of increased mobility: interchange hubs and stations, shopping malls, specialized entertainment centers, theme parks. To new social behaviors correspond new, often spectacular forms of buildings and spaces. What Wim Wenders calls "entertainment architecture" stages ever stronger effects, generating unusual spatial and figurative emotions.

But, as Adolf Loos was already aware of, the *chez soi* refuses architecture as art. A man in slippers does not look for emotions, merely for comfort.

Bruno Zevi's axiom of modern architecture — the correspondence between interior and exterior — staggers and stumbles every day under the blows of a "complementation of furniture." Gimmicks and gadgets are the caryatids and telamones of teenager rooms. Higher up, the revenge of interior designers, an *International Style* of oversized cushions, of golden elephants, an aesthetic surgeon's *Renaissance*, a Bécassine's *country elegance*.

Inside, the sentimental house.

Outside, the functional city.

**Layout** If the "citizen's needs" of classical urban planning are hard to translate into the forms and building types of the city, the real estate market seems to respond more quickly to the desires of its potential customers.

The desire for privacy, the desire for mobility, the desire for identity, the desire for nature, or better still, their crossed requests, generate new places in the European version of the "extended city."

The model of the single-family home, of the little villa, is the individual response to these conditions. Although efficient, this model is nevertheless unable to control what exists beyond its borders, beyond its fence.

What is there between *highway* and *home*?

Scarce are the requests made to a public space that is no longer a place for communication and social interaction. Only a few desirable attributes remain: transi-

*Cino Zucchi and Federico Tranfa (with Margherita Cugini, Carolina Prestini, and Sandro Saccuti), project design for the "tangenziale" (highway bypass) south of Pisa, Italy, 1995.*

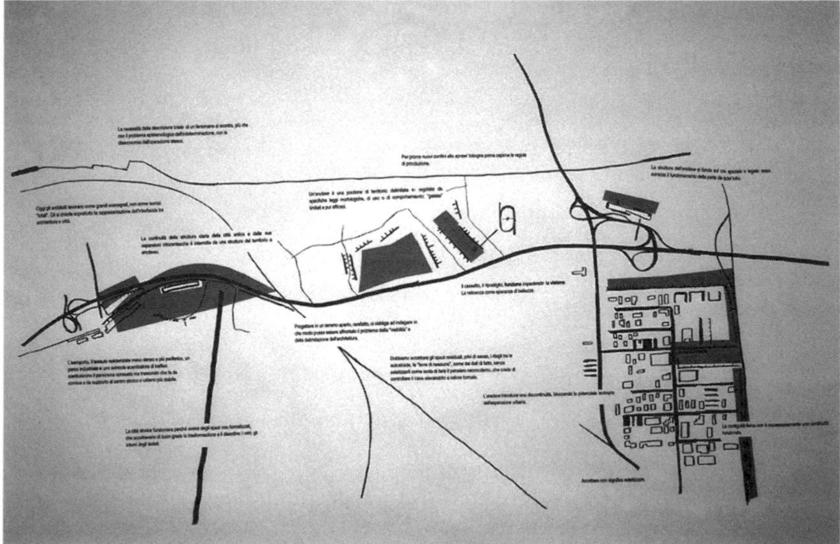

tivity (the street and the parking lot), visual pleasantness (greenery), relaxation (a children's playground).

A hedge hides the fence of a large residential complex east of Milan. You can get there fast from the "tangenziale" (the freeway ring), from the airport: "ten minutes from the center of Milan" boasts the advertisement.

An entrance booth designed by a famous architect, an open bar overlooking the border like a friendly neighborhood policeman. The names of the private roads are redolent with a thousand perfumes: Birch Alley, Elm Alley, Maple Alley.

Trees on crutches like children with polio. A path in the form of a snake (William Hogarth's "line of beauty") in prefab concrete paving blocks, evoking, in conjunction with little green mounds, the icons of a tamed nature.

The model of postwar satellite settlements is here employed in its leaf-like, or glomerule-like, structure. The roads lead you nowhere: they end up in a garage or else return you in gentle circles to the entrance booth, and from there to the hydraulics of the highway system.

The separation between pedestrians and cars, vividly figured by little bridges overpassing the streets, represents a miniature version of the paradigms of urban utopias, while they also manifest the distance between this urban scheme and the models of the historical city.

The landscape yielded by this layout is simultaneously unexpected and predictable. A plan similar to that of the English "garden city" is extruded in a vertical direction to generate buildings whose density is clearly urban: a reassuring hybrid, which tries to embody the best of both models.

**Values** The image projected by these places is not founded on parameters of a spatial nature. Their perimeter is not visible, nor explicitly represented. They consist rather of interiors without an exterior. The possibility for recognition is founded on *attributes*.

A balcony.

Identity: an offset in the plan.

The human dimension: a roof's eaves.

Neighborhood status: prestige detailing; video-interphone.

The beautiful life: the swan lake; water as a symbol of superfluity, of the departure from the condition of need.

Once identity has been affirmed, differences may arise. As with cars, where a colored strip on the side and an appealing name (Fiat Uno *Ranch*, Fiat Uno *Elegant*, Fiat Uno *Young*) are sufficient to satisfy different lifestyles, here the permutations of vernacular and modern architectural detailing cater to different market niches.

The formal value of movement.
A view, a painter's glance.
International picturesque. Atopical regionalism.
A Lombardy farm. A *piazzetta.* A portico.
Holidays all year through. The aesthetic paradigm of the holiday resort.
*Green submarine.* Submerged in the greenery.
Beauty only if it's practical, functional, easy to clean.

**Outside** Outside, whatever you like. The continuity of the city without figures, or rather: other subdivisions.

**Rewind** To be able to set new borders to the urban sprawl, we first have to understand the rules of its production. Designing in an open, rarefied terrain forces us to search for ways in which we can deal with the problem of the "visibility" and delimitation of architecture.
Physical contiguity does not necessarily imply functional continuity. An old farmhouse glimpsed from the highway, an illuminated interior appearing for a second from a train window, are only subliminal images perceived by a system that ignores them: a fishbowl city behind noise barriers.
To exist from the highway, cities, villages, places must be denoted, translated into the iconic language of the exit sign: the city center as a *bull's eye,* the rivers as a *wave,* the monuments and tourist spots simplified in white pixels on a brown background.

*Project design for the "tangenziale" south of Pisa, Italy, 1995. Experimental alterations intended to add complexity and interaction with other parts of the city.*

The relationship between dwelling as "interior art" and the city as a "flowing landscape" is today fragile, problematic. The inside and the outside of a building appear ever more as two separate identities, perceived under different circumstances.
The icons of building are no longer able to control the landscape, nor to make interiors comfortable. We keep on losing control of the intermediate scale, of "urban design."
We often envy the correspondence between physical space and social behavior that founded the condition of the historical city as that of a "common place." In its nostalgia for this lost state, modern urban planning pretended to implement a social engineering through the physical form of the environment; it pretended to transform connections into hierarchy, proximity into interdependence, cohabitation into "neighborhood unity."
But it is not easy to translate the diagram of social interaction into a spatial morphology, and vice versa.

**Codes** The contemporary city is a place where contradictory powers confront one another.
People's behaviors are understood and justified only on the basis of "minority codes." A message is clear only within the context of a subculture (whether a group of teenagers, an art historians' seminar, or a religious sect); it becomes hermetic in the absence of the semantic context in which it was produced.
It is not true that the modern city lacks order. It may be better described as a fairly casual sequence of very well-defined subsystems. These subsystems "run" well. The codes of these environments are univocal: the imperative language of highway signs, the sentimental "recollection" of an historical center, the forced neighborhood peace of residential quarters, the "freedom of choice" in shopping malls, the technical laws that regulate the functioning of infrastructural subdivisions.

**Fenced** We can label *enclave* the physical expression of this segmented structure. The extended city seems to grow as a random juxtaposition of *enclaves.*
An *enclave* is a portion of territory ruled by specific laws regarding form, use, and behavior — codes that are limited but efficient.
An *enclave* hopes to reestablish rules of behavior which are lost in the metropolis overall, such codes being shared no longer by the totality of the urban population.
The structure of the *enclave* is founded on spatial control: it disengages the functioning of the part from that of the whole. In an urban environment marked by a babel of languages, it sets a number of limited narrative conventions.
If nineteenth-century urban planning entrusted to the layout and to the continu-

ity of the street grid the "book of manners" of the city, the *enclave* introduces a discontinuity, blocking the potential isotropy of urban expansion.

An *enclave* can be both democratic and reactionary; it is identified by the act of separation. The *enclave* is the architecture of (numerical) minority groups, be they hegemonic or subaltern. It contains at the same time the positive idea of *community* and the negative idea of *segregation*.

The Fontfroide abbey, the Tuscolano quarter in Rome, an "edge city" like Milano 2, but also the closed highway system, are in this sense *enclaves*. To enter them means to accept more or less implicit rules.

An *enclave* produces discontinuity and therefore intelligibility. It sets partial codes, with strong internal congruences; it raises a number of circumscribed formal expectations which are reasonable because governed by controlled forms of consensus. In this sense, an *enclave* dispels the anguish of a "total structure" and prevents catastrophic events from happening. Butterflies can flap their wings in Japan while we rest in golden slumbers.

**Cruising** We enter and leave these semantic contexts several times a day, in accordance with the same quick rules of T.V. zapping: an instant amnesia of the previous code allows us to avoid surreal chains of meanings.

Unlike what some modern critics suppose, the violent juxtaposition of contiguous codes in the city does not create disorder, but rather indifference. Much as our brain suppresses the irrelevant information imprinted on the retina — so that while looking into a shop window we don't "see" the reflection on the glass, only the goods exposed —, in any semantic structure we easily suppress the

*Project design for the "tangenziale" south of Pisa, Italy, 1995. Places chosen to represent the spatial condition of self-enclosed realities in the contemporary periphery.*

inessential information, the "background noise." Every *enclave* suppresses deformities, interferences; triviality, the price for clarity.
Only the *flaneur* cruises the city to find chaos, surreal experiences, unexpected encounters. His ideal of urban beauty implies a temporary interruption of pragmatic, utilitarian behavior. He has, literally, *time to lose.*
Not so with the *commuter*. For him, the city is a useful object. His perception of the city is a praxis oriented towards a goal.
But as in a novel by Oliver Sachs, where a jazz drummer suffering from the La Tourette syndrome deliberately changes personality during weekends simply by interrupting the intake of medicines inhibiting his illness, the *commuter* likewise returns to the city during the weekend to become a *flaneur*. The city becomes for him a theme park, a ludic space that rouses strong emotions. He wants an entertaining city, he wants to be astonished. As the recent history of European capitals shows, the separate codes of art and urban design blend again in strange cocktails, in which the everyday humdrum and exceptionality are juxtaposed in unusual combinations.
But this happens only in the *ville lumière*. The periphery is still caught between infrastructure and privacy, in a neotechnical, or neoregionalistic, mediocrity.

**Hidden** The historical city functioned thanks to a number of informal spaces which accepted transformation and disorder very well: backyards, city block interiors. In this city, not everything was considered "architecture."
The modern ideal of transparency, of a panoptical world, is as frightening as it is impossible to realize. In its "towering infernos," nobody can change the brand of lightbulbs without spoiling the architecture, hence the entire city.
The glass house, the free-standing pavilion, in visual and spatial continuity with nature, is in need of god-like inhabitants. The *sublime*, the only aesthetic permitted to modernity, is incompatible with the *domestic*.
To the modern idea of the glass house we can today oppose "faceless" interiors. The patio houses by Mies van der Rohe deny every concept of facade and therefore every representative will. They employ total transparency and the total opacity of screens as a binary lexicon that interrupts architectural semiotics. Likewise, the studies of Chermayoff and Alexander on patio houses attempt to reform the American suburb by pushing the concept of privacy as the basis of new social forms to its very limits.
The drawer, the closet, work to *interrupt* the act of looking.
Against the modern priority of the "visual" — a totalitarian view according to which everything in the human environment has to be "pretty" or meaningful — we have to be able to devise figures only where they are necessary.

The modern "method" pretended to extend from the spoon to the city, and did not distinguish among the disciplines of architecture, engineering, restoration, industrial design, or the landscape. But these fields are today presenting themselves as counterposed ideological models, generating aesthetical subcultures at war with one another. To design in the extended city also means to move among these limited expectations, exploring their reciprocal interferences.

Thus, figures will surface as passages of condition, arising from the encounter of two systems ruled by different laws, hence in need of *communication.*

We have to start thinking again about the interfaces between *dwelling* and *landscape.*

Raymond Unwin looked for new means of controlling the form of the territory. If he saw in the housing *cluster* the icon of coziness, infrastructure and greenery made up the morphology of the large scale.

Then, *Learning from Las Vegas.*

But the analysis of Bob Venturi, cornerstone of reflections on the contemporary city, threatens to be made obsolete by the media.

"Talking architecture," no longer burdened by the need for communication, can sometimes return to being dumb.

From Venturi to H&deM, from *text* to *texture.*

Or, perhaps, two architectures, two aesthetics, as in Milton Keynes.

To the public *pop,* supergraphics.

To the private individual the *informal,* the poison ivy wall.

Control for open spaces; freedom for buildings.

Reticence, a hope for beauty.

An earlier Italian version of this text was published in Mirko Zardini, ed., *Paesaggi ibridi: Un viaggio nella città contemporanea* (Milano: Skira, 1996): 25-34.

**Kristiaan Borret**

# The "Void" as a Productive Concept for Urban Public Space

*Keywords:* ■ *Urban Planning* ■ *Architecture* ■ *Political Philosophy*

**Prologue: Agora and Asphalt** In the late summer of 1996, it became obvious that, through the incompetency of the Belgian judicial authorities and the police, the psychopath Marc Dutroux and his companions had been allowed to kidnap, abuse, and kill a series of young girls. When this unspeakable truth was revealed, a spontaneous upsurge of indignation swept over Belgium. The exceptional public outcry resulted in, among other things, an immense protest march through the central boulevards of the Belgian capital. Whatever the political content of the march may have been, the event at least rekindled one of the most cherished images of urban public space: that of an activist gathering of citizens in streets and squares with an eye to occupying these so as to request attention for certain political demands.

Countless other protest actions preceded the enormous manifestation: two of them were announced side by side in the newspaper of September 14, 1996.[1] The first journalistic piece talked of a commemorative caravan with "thousands of motorcyclists, truck drivers, and car drivers" along the homes of the four murdered girls in Hasselt and near Liège — a drive of some 40 kilometers across the Belgian language boundary. "At the point of departure for the caravan in Mechelen-Bovelingen, a 20-hectare parking lot will be made available. The destination is the shopping mall Biggs, with one of the largest parking lots in the whole of Limburg," concludes the piece. The second article deals with an expression of sympathy for the family of the disappeared girl Loubna, who used to live in Brussels. The march, which in this case departs from the Flagey Square in Brussels, is a "silent march" on foot through the city center. The "destination of the march is, symbolically, the Brussels Palace of Justice."

In this anecdotal confrontation of two newspaper articles, the contrast between two urban models is striking. In the description of the march for the Brussels girl Loubna, we immediately recognize the traditional morphology of

1 "Herdenkingsrit stevent af op overrompeling" and "Stille mars voor Loubna," *De Standaard*, 14 September 1996. The following translations are by the editors.

the European city: a compact urban fabric articulated through monumental squares and buildings. Public space still serves as an agora for the gathering of citizens, and public authorities are still represented unequivocally in the cityscape. According to this paradigm, urban space is a full and coherent whole that testifies to a glorious tradition of public life. In the other article, a new kind of diluted city emerges, which has been spreading in Belgium for some time now, but whose paradigm has not yet been calibrated. The short newspaper item depicts the urbanization pattern between Hasselt and Liège as an auto-scaled environment in which the most important feature of the assembly points for the protest drive is their size. In this diluted city, the familiar models of square, park, and boulevard lose much of their meaning, while no up-to-date alternatives seem to have been formed yet.

At the end of the pedestrian march through Brussels, demonstrators come face to face with the institution to which their reproaches are addressed. In this sense, the journalistic addition of the word "symbolic" for the almost overdeterminedly symbolic Palace of Justice is clearly redundant. By contrast, the addition of a phrase like "without symbolic meaning" to the megamall Biggs would have been very much to the point, for instance with regard to the question whether the spontaneous civic protest also involved an accusation against a moral degradation that should be seen as the result of an excessive consumerist culture. The final destination of the protest drive by car is the vast asphalt space of an unused parking lot on a Sunday afternoon. The building that dominates this site is a manifest sign of unbridled mass consumption, but does not apparently come under attack. The real target of this *posturban* manifestation is the waiting T.V. camera, not the place. The place itself is triply empty: spatially, functionally, symbolically.

**The Appeal of the Urban Void on European Architects** Places like the parking lot of a shopping mall in the periphery are widely held to be "urban voids." The urban void — such a far cry from the cherished ideal of the European city — today nevertheless enjoys the special attention of progressive European architects and urban planners. The concept of the void that circulates among these people, however, takes many different guises. A first group of architects and urban planners, which includes Italians Bernardo Secchi and Stefano Boeri, uses the concept above all within a descriptive framework. Their aim is to develop new ways of reading that are specifically tailored to the diffuse urban landscape sprawling over a vast territory and to the share of unbuilt space in this landscape. A second group, with Dutch designers like Rem Koolhaas (and his office, OMA) and Adriaan Geuze (with his West 8), is especially sensitive to the poetry of the vernacular in the dispersed city. The void is to them a productive concept first and foremost, which they use as a design instrument to develop a contemporary idiom for urban space — an idiom Liane Lefaivre has labeled "dirty realism."[2]

Already in 1984, the Italian urban planner Bernardo Secchi signaled how in both bigger and smaller European cities "large voids are opening up," which he took to be "mostly zones waiting for a morphological definition."[3] From his point of view, two kinds of urban void may be distinguished. In the first instance, we are dealing with sites and buildings that derive from the vast arsenal of nineteenth-century infrastructure, such as slaughterhouses, barracks, railyards, docks, and industrial complexes, and that are now falling into definitive disuse and disrepair. This ruined infrastructure tears huge holes — functionally as well as spatially — in the middle of the urban fabric or in the immediate periphery of city centers. The Bicocca factory site of Pirelli near Milan or the Lingotto building of Fiat in Turin are two renowned examples. In addition, Secchi identifies a second kind of void, which he detects in the sprawled settlement pattern typical of the postwar era, in which "the cities and the territory have become immense collections of objects tactically placed next to one another, mute."[4] The missing links and inept definition in these areas are the reflection, according to Secchi, of a "decomposed contemporary society" in which "the space 'in-between things,' between objects and subjects, between my house and my neighbor's, between their office and mine, is traversed by many strangers, and is not a meeting place; it has become 'empty' because it plays no recognizable role."[5]

The discourse on urban voids developed by Bernardo Secchi is for the most part detached and neutrally formulated. What Secchi does resolutely denounce are acritical urban design projects that ignore the void by trying to fill it in accordance with an anachronistic view of the city, and he goes on to argue that

2 A succinct version of Lefaivre's article in which she proposed the idea of "dirty realism" in architecture appeared as Liane Lefaivre, "Dirty Realism in European Architecture Today," *Design Book Review* 17 (Winter 1989): 17-20.

3 Bernardo Secchi, "Il vuoto," in *Un progetto per l'urbanistica* (Torino: Einaudi, 1989), 61-64. The article first appeared in *Casabella* 503 (1984). Editors' translation.

4 Bernardo Secchi, "Un' urbanistica di spazi aperti/For a town-planning of open spaces," *Casabella* 597-598 (1993): 116.

5 Ibid.

6 Secchi, "Il vuoto," 64. Editors' translation.

7 Ibid., 62. Editors' translation.

8 Maaike Dicke and Ed Taverne, "Als ik mijn gang kon gaan, zou ik alle bestuurders van de Italiaanse steden bij hun kraag vatten en ze overal met hun neus bovenop drukken. Een vraaggesprek met Bernardo Secchi," *Archis* 12 (1989): 24-27.

9 Marcel Smets, "Hoog-Kortrijk: het structureren van de hedendaagse stadsontwikkeling," *Archis* 12 (1990): 50. This article includes a discussion of Bernardo Secchi's competition design for Hoog-Kortrijk, the urban sprawl at the south end of the Flemish town of Kortrijk. In this design, Secchi's *progetto del suolo* finds a clear expression.

10 Stefano Boeri, Arturo Lanzani, and Edoardo Marini, "Nuovi spazi senza nome/New nameless spaces," *Casabella* 597-598 (1993): 124.

"designing for the void begins with its thematization and this requires a widening of the scope of one's observations."[6] On the other hand, the usual negative assessment of urban residual spaces gets its full due as well: "At a lower level, from the vantage point of the passer-by, the void appears as interrupted design, a space that is hard to cross, the settlement for weak, marginal, and barely institutionalized functions: merry-go-rounds, gypsies, parking lots for trucks, residences for marginal groups, for newly arrived immigrants, popular allotment gardens, activities on the edge of unlawfulness."[7] The urban void as represented by Secchi seems an eyesore, a vague transitional phenomenon that sooner or later will receive its destination and is best served eventually by the achievement of a decent morphological definition. In Secchi's *progetto del suolo* — the organization and shaping of the city at "ground level" or the level of open space[8] — the activity of designing the urban public realm retains "its ordering force even in today's fractured city."[9] Although Secchi's designs for the dispersed city testify to the use of refined new typologies and updated programs, they nevertheless correspond in principle to the harmonic ideal of the historical city, in which open space is the structuring carrier that articulates the city by providing it with a recognizable coherence.

Taking Secchi's "descriptive city planning" as a point of departure, Stefano Boeri develops a meticulous inquiry into the morphology of the "città diffusa." In so doing, he hopes to lend weight to his renunciation of the generalizing rhetoric that prefers to paint recent urban sprawl as tantamount to meaningless chaos: "the landscapes of the diffused city are not 'large peripheries'; we also encounter areas and points of significant social and morphological complexity."[10] Aided by what he calls "eclectic atlases" — multidimensional methods of analysis exceeding the synoptic aerial view and containing among other things taxonomies,

*From Stefano Boeri and Gabriele Basilico,* Italy — Cross Sections of a Country, *1998.*

design-like investigations, photographic campaigns, and geographic-literary essays[11] — Boeri maps recurrent patterns of use and spatial developments in the diluted city. From his innovative analysis of the "dust-cloud" urban landscape around Milan, the architect distills settlement principles and implantation typologies like "linear attractors," "hybrid machines," "islands," "repetition areas," "inserts," or "metamorphosis" — categories that cannot be ordered by means of familiar parameters like scale and proximity, yet that emerge everywhere and at different levels throughout the diluted city.[12] Thus, Boeri's pioneering work succeeds in gradually rendering the Milanese "città diffusa" legible and comprehensible as a system composed of multiply heterogeneous elements that have somehow become a unity.

In the supposedly chaotic periphery, in other words, enduring structures have been detected, and what Boeri in 1993 still indicated as "new nameless spaces" have since required at least a handful of names. Indeed, insofar as different kinds of void in the dispersed city acquire a name, they can be distinguished from each other, and they automatically start to lose a major part of their meaningless indeterminacy. Even so, Boeri feels compelled to grant the existence of a peculiar type of empty space, called *terrain vague*, which does not possess a clear or univocal identity and seems to lack any code whatsoever. The "hypocodification" (the term is by Ignasi de Solà-Morales) in such spaces often invites an ideology that is "libertarian, marginal, deviant, and certainly disrespectful of the traditional codes of the city."[13] Zones that are traversed by highly different population groups, or that bring together two clashing types of spatial development, are in Boeri's mind examples of residual or interstitial spaces in which semantic emptiness reigns supreme. Contrary to other unclear sites in the dispersed city, the *terrain vague* continues to resist all straightforward definition, because its semantic emptiness turns out to have less to do with an absence of codes than with a multiple presence of codes that are superimposed, that clash, or even destroy each other. "They are not weak in themselves," observes Boeri,

11 Stefano Boeri, "The Italian landscape: Towards an 'eclectic atlas,'" in *Italy — Cross Sections of a Country* by Stefano Boeri and Gabriele Basilico (Zurich: Scalo, 1998), 24. The collaboration between Boeri and the photographer Basilico in this book illustrates how an "eclectic atlas" may acquire shape.

12 Stefano Boeri, Arturo Lanzani, and Edoardo Marini, *Il territorio che cambia. Ambiente, paesaggi e immagini della regione milanese* (Milano: Abitare Segesta, 1993). Editors' translation.

13 Stefano Boeri, "Les paroles des habitants: où les codes entrent en conflit," in *A moving city*, ed. Studio Open City (Brussels: Studio Open City, 1998), 105. Editors' translation.

14 Ibid., 106. Editors' translation.

15 Gerrie Andela, "Challenging landscapes for explorers: Estrangement and reconciliation in the work of West 8," *Archis* 2 (1994): 38.

16 Adriaan Geuze, "Accelerating Darwin," in *Nederlandse landschapsarchitectuur. Tussen traditie en experiment*, ed. Gerrit Smienk (Amsterdam: Academie van Bouwkunst, 1993), 17. Editors' translation.

17 Ibid.

*but because they express an excessive number of interpretative codes.... It is impossible to understand these spaces without participating in the multitude of codes they manifest, without thinking of them by means of pluridirect and complex thoughts that literally jump between several points of view, using the logic of literary abstraction, like Peter Handke, or cinematographic forms of the intrigue of lives people live around a geographical space, like Robert Altman. Exactly because they are physically "hypocodified," these vague places reflect better than any other urban landscape the multiplicity of identities that each of us harbors and deploys in the course of a single day.*[14]

Boeri's concept of polysemous urban voids ties in with a characteristically postmodern insistence that personal identity is not stable and singular, and it possesses — along the same lines — a liberating potential, a possibility of moving beyond established social values. In this sense, the attribution of a clear morphological definition to these seemingly meaningless spaces, whether in Bernardo Secchi's intelligent manner or in more traditional urbanistic terms, would constitute a reductive intervention that can bring clarity only at the expense of papering over the real complexity of a fragmented society. The appreciation that Boeri and others show for the semantic void of the *terrain vague* expresses a conviction that urban life must rest on a model of conflict, in which the necessity of total determination, cohesion, and harmony does not take precedence.

**Adriaan Geuze Colonizing the Void** No urban planner flaunts the "void" more than the Dutch landscape architect Adriaan Geuze. The design method of his office, West 8, bears a close resemblance to that of Rem Koolhaas and his OMA, "for instance with respect to the scenario approach, the use of emptiness as a design instrument and the fascination with the periphery."[15] Like Koolhaas, West 8 tends to view a design as a scenario that merely sketches out a future development without entirely fixing it. The elementary framing conditions of the design thus create open potentialities for still unknown usages. Not coincidentally, Geuze propagates an up-to-date kind of urbanite who brooks no patronizing about his or her use of urban public space, but is to the contrary "intelligent, well equipped, and ever curious."[16] In his essay "Accelerating Darwin," Geuze sings the praises of local urbanites who spontaneously appropriated the Maas Plane in Rotterdam — an offshore harbor area at the estuary of the Maas River — for purposes of imaginative mass recreation: "the sand flats are used as training runs for sledge dogs or motocross, the dredging dump as a slope for hang-gliding, the dam as a fossil-supplying rock, the sand extraction pit as a site for deep-sea diving."[17] The public that successfully colonizes the void of the Maas Plane illustrates how "its norm is no longer based on preprogrammed recreative facilities, but on principles of anarchy, exploration, self-expression. It is able to search out and occupy its own sites and provides its own meanings."[18] According to Geuze, the new urbanites impose their own imaginations on their surroundings and are thus more quickly adaptive than ever.

From this point of view, the nondescript residual and interstitial spaces to be found in the urban periphery exert a strong appeal because of the open possibilities they entail. It is their programmatic emptiness that inspires many so-called "anarchitectural" designs spawned by both West 8 and OMA. "The void points to the absence of intentions. The void is the absence of architecture. The void is the domain of unfulfilled promise and unlimited opportunity. It is the projection screen of our desire," notes Hans van Dijk about their approach.[19] As the descendant of the natural open landscape, moreover, emptiness enjoys greater popularity both with the general public and with administrators, while architectural or urban planning designs are by definition suspect and mistrusted. Rem Koolhaas masterfully exploits this innocence of the void in his visionary plan for the *ville nouvelle* Melun-Sénart: "At a moment when the complexity of each three-dimensional undertaking is infernal, the preservation of the void is comparatively easy."[20] Instead of designing and fixing a built environment, the plan restricts itself to the delimitation of a structuring network of corridors within which nothing may be built. "We arrived at an almost Chinese figure of void spaces that we could protect from contamination by the city — a new controlling element that would give the city, which was obviously not a classical city, but maybe a contemporary city, a form of coherence and conviction. And then we said, 'the rest we will surrender to chaos.'"[21] Koolhaas's euphoric resignation with respect to the chaos of the dispersed city is not a little polemical, and his use of the void in a programmatic and scenic sense as a design instrument restricts itself to a considerable extent to an aesthetic level, witness his predilection for "a potentially sublime contrast between the empty areas of the site — those we had protected from building — and the uncontrollable, almost cancerous chaotic growth of the city as a whole."[22]

In the case of Adriaan Geuze, the programmatic concept of the void also dovetails with a purely spatial landscape notion. As a landscape architect Geuze is

18 Ibid.

19 Hans van Dijk, "Colonizing the void: Urbanization: The landscape as ally," in *Colonizing the void: Adriaan Geuze, West 8 Landscape Architects, Rotterdam*, ed. Adriaan Geuze et al. (Rotterdam: NAi, 1996), n.p.

20 Rem Koolhaas, "Surrender," in *S,M,L,XL* by OMA, Rem Koolhaas, and Bruce Mau (Rotterdam: 010, 1995), 974.

21 Ibid., 977.

22 Ibid.

23 Adriaan Geuze, "Het vermeende succes," *de Architect* 2 (1996): 46. Editors' translation.

almost irresistibly enthusiastic about the grandiosity of the Dutch landscape, which forms a cross between, on the one hand, the wide views and cloud masses in the polders familiar to us from the paintings of Ruysdael, and on the other, the large-scale human manipulation of nature into a cultural landscape. Each one of those, he writes, is "a perfect landscape composed of plain, horizon, and Ruysdaelian skies under which commuters, cows, and greenhouses make their appearance."[23] The semantic emptiness thematized in Boeri's analysis is not as strong in the designs of Koolhaas and Geuze. With them, the void has less to do with aspects often perceived as negative, like fragmentation, marginality, and polysemy. What they prefer to highlight, rather, are the programmatic and landscape dimensions of the void; certainly with Geuze, these are enlisted unproblematically to shore up urban planning designs.



Two fitting examples of this practice are offered by two squares in downtown Rotterdam which have been redesigned by West 8: Binnenrotte (1987-95)

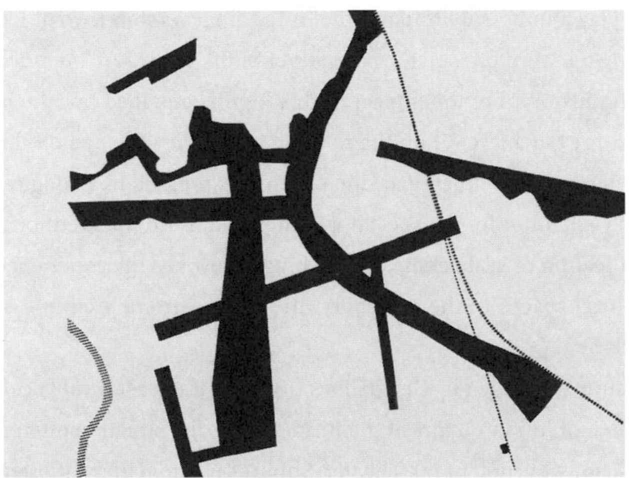

*Chinese sign formed by open spaces in OMA's project for Melun-Sénart, France, 1987.*

*Adriaan Geuze and West 8, scale model for Binnenrotte, Rotterdam.*

*Binnenrotte, Rotterdam.*

and Schouwburgplein (1990-95). Both sites display the results of a cheerful design mentality that treats the void as a positive and productive concept, set to work with as much bravura as pragmatism. In the Binnenrotte area, a sizeable strip of land almost half a kilometer long in the middle of the city became available by the demolition of a disused railroad viaduct. West 8 froze the large scale and open expanse of the exceptional site by designing an empty square, which in a flexible way also offers the logistics for the market that regularly takes place there. With the design of a bare plain, uniformly paved with concrete slabs and equipped with the paraphernalia of markets like electricity outlets, anchoring points, and parking spots, West 8 injects the vernacular of parking and trading grounds from the city's periphery into the heart of the Rotterdam downtown. At the very spot of West 8's project, in fact, the river Rotte used to flow, and it was here that after the construction of a first dam the city of Rotterdam was founded. Whereas in the original design (1987-89) several historical references to this origin as well as to other meanings attached to the site were explicitly integrated, these have come to play a quite subordinate role in the final version (1993). Extended letters forming the word DAM on the paved floor of the square are intended to recall the founding history, but the impact of this sign is equalled by a huge mention of the word FIETS ("bicycle") on the fencing of the bicycle shed on the square. Historical reference and functional sign are thus expressed in analogical fashion and vie with each other for the spectator's attention. Both interventions, moreover, provide a feeling of scalelessness, which again evokes the experience of empty infrastructural spaces in the periphery, the most extreme example of which is the Maas Plane.

If the new urbanite envisaged by Geuze does not have the least trouble colonizing the crude patch of infrastructure at the Binnenrotte, the situation offered by the redesigned Schouwburgplein (or Theater Square) is altogether different and poses more serious challenges. "The square belongs to another planet, measures itself only against the skyline, and has to be conquered and interpreted by the user. It provokes agoraphobia," notes Geuze.[24] The void as a design principle is at stake here in two ways. First of all, West 8 tries to maintain as much as possible of the spatial experience of emptiness that dominated the place already before. Admittedly, the original ambition of the plan has been curbed considerably in the meantime by the construction of a new movie multiplex, roughly taking up one side of the square. Yet the square, which is worked out as a slightly elevated stage with unusual materials like steel, rubber, and epoxy, still appears to with-

24 Geuze, "Accelerating Darwin," 21. Editors' translation.

25 Adriaan Geuze and Edzo Bindels, "Colo.voi," in *Colonizing the void*, ed. Geuze et al., n.p.

26 Geuze, "Accelerating Darwin," 21, 20. Editors' translation.

draw from its immediate surroundings. The autonomous Schouwburgplein is an "excavated urban void" amid the urban congestion of the Rotterdam downtown.[25] It relates more to the abstract urban skyline in the background than to the public-oriented theater, concert, and shopping facilities that surround it, and it evokes, partly through its industrial use of materials, the atmosphere of Rotterdam's expansive world harbor. The second scenario for the void has to do with the absence of a preprogrammed use, which stimulates both the instability of the program and the creativity drive of the urbanites. "Every step on the square is a conscious step, a choice. The square needs to be more than a stage and to be used flexibly: the square taunts urbanites and demands that they take an active stance. It returns to them their imaginations and identities," says Geuze in his motivation for the design, adding that "new urban space will manipulate the user to such an extent that he will become aware of his behavior on the spot, and that he can no longer fall back on machine-like preprogrammed acts."[26] The programmatically free zone figured by the Schouwburgplein is enhanced by the four big light towers on the square. These are equipped with a moving mechanism like those of cranes, and the public is able, through the mere insertion of a coin, to steer their positions, thus becoming itself responsible for part of the square's character in the evening. The gimmick of the light towers, the emphatic stage function, and the special surface textures of the Schouwburgplein collectively give rise to an explicitly aesthetic kind of staging that stands in marked contrast to the low-profile layout for the Binnenrotte.

Both OMA and West 8 start out by accepting the sociopolitical conditions within which they are expected to work — such as the policies of urban authorities or the late capitalism that is typical of realtors — only to comment upon these conditions, or even subvert them, in a second stage, through the design itself. But the "anarchic" freedom supposedly explored by Geuze's urbanite

*Adriaan Geuze and West 8, scale model for Schouwburgplein, Rotterdam.*

*Schouwburgplein, Rotterdam.*

appears to be limited to the recreative realm, as part of a pluralistic mass culture without sharp edges. "The euphoria of mass culture," argues Geuze, "derives from the accessibility and exchangeability of various cultures, which lend to urban life the proverbial combinatorial freedom of the videoclip."[27] The designs for Binnenrotte and Schouwburgplein square nicely with the general revitalization of downtown Rotterdam as a magnet for shopping and entertainment, and thus threaten to contribute to a further festivalization of the urban public domain. The forced construction of the multiplex *on* the Schouwburgplein (not foreseen by Geuze's design) and the similar entertainment-oriented design of the square further erase the distinction between public and private space in the Rotterdam downtown. In this context, it is worth noting how Rotterdam has recently also seen the construction of a successful pedestrian passage underneath a busy road that cuts through two shopping areas. This so-called Shopping Gutter (Dutch: Koopgoot) is entirely encapsulated by commercial facilities and playfully and imaginatively designed. The Schouwburgplein and the Koopgoot seem to belong to one and the same spectrum, so that it becomes quite unclear whether the un-preprogrammed fun on the square is also meant to accommodate the possibility of political demonstrators or of homeless people.

In a final project that serves to illustrate how West 8 treats the void as a productive concept in designing contemporary urban spaces, the familiar scale of the urban square has been left almost completely behind. In recent years, the old harbor piers along the river Ij in the Eastern Harbor Area of Amsterdam have begun to be redesigned as a new residential zone. The urban planning design of West 8 (1993- ) for two of those harbor piers, Borneo and Sporenburg, seeks to organize a very high residential density by means of two architectural types: on the one hand, three colossal housing blocks at exceptional locations — called "motherfuckers" by Geuze — and on the other, a strip subdivision of lowrise houses, spread out over the entire surface area. The dense buildings on Borneo/Sporenburg remain livable, according to the motivation of the design, because of the compensating omnipresence of the vast landscape voids of the Ij. This compensational element has prompted West 8 to keep the public space as small as possible, and to reserve the resulting gain in surface area for the patios and terraces of individual homes. What is missing from this dichotomy between the

27 Ibid., 20. Editors' translation.

28 Ibid., 15. Editors' translation.

29 Martin Knuijt, Hans Ophuis, Peter van Saane, and David Louwerse, eds., *Modern park design: Recent trends* (Bussum: Thoth, 1993), 45.

30 Geuze, "Accelerating Darwin," 16. Editors' translation.

31 See Hans Ibelings, "Variation in Housing in the 1990s," in *Housing in the Netherlands: Exemplary Architecture of the Nineties*, ed. Arjen Oosterman (Rotterdam: NAi, 1996), 9-29.

large-scale landscape texture, on the one hand, and enclosed private outside spaces, on the other, is the kind of semi-public space of neighborhood squares, inner courtyards, and green buffers that is so commonly found in Dutch housing projects. The publicly accessible space on Borneo/Sporenburg consists almost entirely of functionally indispensable streets, which also happen to be worked out quite neutrally and ordinarily.

The new city that Geuze has in mind also for Borneo/Sporenburg is the resplendent posturban metropolis, "a vital and majestic rain forest that holds the immense potential of mass culture."[28] The matching urbanite is "happy, has self-respect and has appropriated democracy," as one comment on a Geuze lecture would have it[29]; or as Geuze himself says, "within the mass culture he finds his freedom and chooses his subcultures, annexes his surroundings."[30] Geuze's optimistic view of the city bears some resemblance to the fragmented model of the post-Fordist metropolis, in which consumption culture and multiculturalism are unproblematically welded in the articulation of new social groups based on lifestyles. In the Netherlands, this type of reasoning in terms of distinct target groups based on new sociocultural parameters like lifestyle has been of exceptional influence on the housing market.[31] The Fordist model of a minimal number of residential standards has been dumped in favor of a varied gamut of housing types all tailored to their specific target groups. Such housing differentiation also leads to a wide variety of highly specific houses in the design for Borneo/Sporenburg. There is, then, a glaring paradox in the diametrically opposed ways in which Geuze fleshes out his vision of a fragmented metropolis full of individualistic

*Adriaan Geuze and West 8, scale model for Borneo/Sporenburg, Amsterdam.*

urbanites, depending on whether he operates in the public or the private realm. In streets and on squares, all forms of preprogramming are anathema, and an abstract void reigns supreme, while in the private environment of dwellings an advanced segmentation according to preestablished market niches *is* accepted. Housing differentiation, it should be noted also, often issues in a concentration of like-minded people — of residents with the same lifestyle living in homogeneous housing enclaves. The plan proposed by West 8 for Borneo/Sporenburg wants to preempt such social segregation by alternating even more frequently between diverse housing types, so as to obtain a finegrained mix of residents. The categorical line of demarcation between public and private, in the absence of negotiating semi-public spaces, coincides with the streetside. It enhances the urban character of the former harbor piers: anybody who closes the door behind him is in the street — an urban space because it is always and everywhere accessible, because it is in the open air, and is anonymously shared with differently minded people or complete strangers.

**Agoraphobia** In his introduction to the high-profile volume of essays, *Variations on a Theme Park: The New American City and the End of Public Space*, Michael Sorkin frames the collected discussions on contemporary urban public space by setting up an almost Manichean opposition between the new city and the traditional city.[32] The new city, according to Sorkin, may be recognized by "the ageographia, the surveillance and control, the simulations without end" — by the very three characteristics, that is, that in a heightened form also dominate the theme park. "In the 'public' spaces of the theme park or the shopping mall, speech itself is restricted: there are no demonstrations in Disneyland. The effort to reclaim the city is the struggle of democracy itself," writes Sorkin in his final line, which sets the agenda of the book.

Sorkin's description of the new city involves a plea for a return to a more authentic city. In his introduction, however, several suggestions are made that render the model of the good city problematical. Sorkin's text, for one thing, is steeped in the conviction that the so-called urban public realm is something we all once shared, but have now lost, and that we should somehow regain it. By viewing public space as a locus of political activity, Sorkin successfully chal-

32 Michael Sorkin, "Introduction: Variations on a Theme Park," in *Variations on a Theme Park: The New American City and the End of Public Space*, ed. Michael Sorkin (New York: Noonday Press, 1992), xi-xv.

33 Bruce Robbins, "The Public as Phantom," in *The Phantom Public Sphere*, ed. Bruce Robbins (Minneapolis: University of Minnesota Press, 1993), viii.

34 Quoted in Rosalyn Deutsche, "Agoraphobia," in *Evictions: Art and Spatial Politics* (Cambridge, MA.: MIT Press, 1996), 272.

35 Ibid., 273.

36 Ibid., 274.

lenges the mainstream discourse that would prefer to screen public space from political aspects so as to facilitate discussions of the city's shape in terms of pleasant entertainment and safe sociability. But by holding up the dazzling historical ideals of "agora, castle, piazza, or downtown," he only causes every germ of public space in the banal reality of the dispersed city to pale in comparison, which in turn serves to perpetuate the lament of the demise of public space. What is more, Sorkin totally bypasses the different levels of exclusion on which these supposedly ideal models relied for their functioning. "*For whom* was the city once more public than now? Was it ever open to the scrutiny and participation, let alone under the control, of the majority? Was there ever a time when intellectuals were really authorized to speak to the people as a whole about the interests of the people as a whole? If so, where were the workers, the women, the lesbians, the gay men, the African Americans?" asks Bruce Robbins with the present political participation of social minorities and new subcultural groups in mind.[33]

Rosalyn Deutsche shares Robbins's argumentation and concomitant critique of commentators like Sorkin who mourn "a lost state of plenitude" and chase a phantom of public space that has never really had the right to claim that title. Deutsche constructs an alternative model for a contemporary public realm, making extended use for this of Claude Lefort's ideas on radical democracy as well as of more recent contributions by Chantal Mouffe and Ernesto Laclau. According to Lefort, the hallmark of a democratic system is the "disappearance of certainty about the foundations of social life."[34] In Deutsche's paraphrase: "Democracy abolishes the external referent of power and refers power to society. But democratic power cannot appeal for its authority to a meaning immanent in the social. Instead, the democratic invention invents something else: the public space. The public space, in Lefort's account, is the social space where, in the absence of a foundation, the meaning and the unity of the social is negotiated — at once constituted and put at risk."[35] Without an external origin, in other words, the identity of a society is always relationally structured. Laclau and Mouffe emphasize that, because of this relational structure, society can never be fully defined. There is an inherent "antagonism" which renders it impossible for society's identity ever to be absolute or complete; in other words, "society is 'impossible' — which is to say, that the conception of society as a closed entity is impossible."[36] A universalizing discourse on "the" urbanite and "his" needs for a higher quality of life, for instance, commits the mistake of making absolute claims that bypass the fundamental "unknowability of the social."

The unity and significance of society are forever precarious, and public space is the site where they are constantly being negotiated. A radically democratic public space thus lives off conflict and can never be a harmonious haven of consensus. Deutsche depicts public space as a highly open site of political action, which should be careful to keep all consolidating appropriations for the sake of security, unity, universality, coherence, and so forth, at a distance for fear of losing its most fundamental characteristic. "Conflict, division, and instability, then, do not ruin the democratic public sphere; they are the conditions of its existence. The threat arises with efforts to supersede conflict, for the public sphere remains democratic only insofar as its exclusions are taken into account and open to contestation. When the exclusions governing the constitution of political public space are naturalized and contests erased by declaring particular forms of space inherently, eternally, or self-evidently public, public space is appropriated."[37] The unknowability of society and the instability of public space are to Deutsche no reason for political despair, but the starting points for a contemporary democratic politics. "True" democracy exists by the grace of a loss, a negativity, a void. Anybody who ignores these principles suffers from a kind of agoraphobia with regard to the emptiness with which democratic openness begins.

Deutsche's definition of a democratic public space cannot of course be transposed simply to the empirical field of public spaces in the city. We should beware of all forms of architectural determinism that posit a causal or immediate link between the shape of a public space and supposed sociopolitical effects. Yet it is possible to detect in the practice of urban planners who pay attention to the urban void an ideological position that has some affinities with the ideas of Deutsche. Stefano Boeri, as we saw, interprets the semantic emptiness of the *terrain vague* as a surfeit of codes that are simultaneously operative and conflicting, and that cannot be known without one's being involved as a participant. This interpretation by Boeri grants not only the polysemy of a fragmented society and the absence of a unitary code in it, but also the impossibility of taking a Sirius perspective on this pluralistic environment. Standpoints of this sort clearly square with Deutsche's political beliefs on the conflictual instability and the unknowability of a society without an absolute foundation. Stefano Boeri understands semantic voids in the dispersed city to be valuable and does not seem to suffer from the agoraphobia set up by Deutsche for critiquing among others Michael Sorkin. The designs of Adriaan Geuze, too, display an ideological background that tends toward Deutsche's theory, especially when they show an interest in the unprogrammability of the use of urban public space. The new urbanites pictured by Geuze are active participants, who are capable — if perhaps only in their recreative activities — of autonomously questioning and redefining existing or supposedly self-evident codes of urban space. In this sense, the continuous

37 Ibid., 289.

38 Adriaan Geuze, "Moving beyond Darwin," in *Modern park design*, ed. Knuijt et al., 39.

negotiation and constitution of meanings in a radical democracy is mirrored by their transgressive behavior. Apparently, the designs of West 8 are not meant to prevent subversive takes on the public realm. "We need to create surrealistic environments," writes Geuze, "we should provide anarchic environments and even subversive cities and green areas."[38]

The meticulous "eclectic atlas" of Stefano Boeri celebrates a city we are already living without knowing it yet. Today's real public space may well be relegated to the cracks and margins that appear among namable, homogeneously composed fragments. Public space in the posturban city is no longer the expression of a harmonious consensus, but the enabling site of subcultures, of friction, of the simultaneity of heterogeneous opinions. The "dirty realism" of Adriaan Geuze supplies us with virtuosic and experimental spaces that hope to offer an adequate translation of this redefined public space in the posturban city. The excitement attributed by Geuze to the new urbanite in the process of colonizing the Maas Plane is great, and the independence with which the new urbanite recalibrates values seems nothing short of heroic, but are these excitements and independence also more emblematic of the contemporary city than the utterly uneventful invasion by an anti-Dutroux demonstration, on a blue Sunday afternoon, of the parking lot of a shopping mall somewhere in the banal urban sprawl between Hasselt and Liège?

*Translation Bart Eeckhout*

Lieven De Cauter

# The Flight Forward of Rem Koolhaas

*Keywords:* ■ *Urban Planning* ■ *Architecture* ■ *Political Philosophy*

**The Trance of the Generic City** Rem Koolhaas opens his essay "The Generic City," the final and capping piece of his spectacularly successful *S, M, L, XL* (1995), by asking "Is the contemporary city like the contemporary airport — 'all the same'?"[1] Compared to the identity and character of traditional cities, the new city has no identity: it is a city without a past, without individuality or particularity, hence a "generic" city. Identity, Koolhaas writes, is linked to a center, but the center has become too small. The center is destructive. It is caught in a double bind: it has to be at once preserved and renewed. The only way out, in traditional cities, is underground (he refers to Zurich). The Generic City, by contrast, breaks with the vicious circle of center and periphery. It is homogeneous: every neighborhood looks the same; every part is an incarnation of the whole, a configuration of roads, housing blocks, and greenery. It is, he proposes elsewhere, "a *city without qualities*" [1077]. The airport is paradigmatic because "The in-transit condition is becoming universal" [1252]. The Generic City is a settlement for people who migrate, hence its instability. With his usual slyness, Koolhaas notes how Paris, in its urge to remain identical with itself, is quickly turning into a caricature, while London, which has been transforming itself dynamically, is precisely losing its identity. In other words: there is no alternative. All cities necessarily tend toward the generic.

Needless to say, the "generic" as such is nothing new: fast-food and hotel chains have been spreading the paradigm for decades now — from generic aesthetics to the generic organization chart. They testify to the irresistible attractions

1 Office for Metropolitan Architecture, Rem Koolhaas, and Bruce Mau, *Small, Medium, Large, Extra-Large*, ed. Jennifer Sigler (Rotterdam: 010 Publishers, 1995), 1248. (Further page references will be given in the text.) The book, whatever else one may want to say about it, is certainly an event. No critic, as a result, can escape the double bind that comes with talking about events. As Goethe said, "Anything that has been of great influence cannot be judged any longer." Criticism, too, becomes part of the success (the way antipublicity is also publicity) and the author remains forever beyond it. As OMA, Koolhaas abolishes the author (the book is co-authored by at least the photographer, the designer, and the editor), yet he thereby also manages to be gloriously resurrected as a star. He offers us an image of the artist in the age of late capitalism: a well-run "factory," with a lot of attention for corporate communication and P.R. At the same time, he has remained a scriptwriter, staging his own work like a movie director. And like it or not, it is clearly becoming a masterpiece. All the more reason for taking him ever so seriously. To identify his train of thought, I will start with a reading of "The Generic City." And since thinking and writing style are so intimately linked in this case, I will start by staying close to the text.

and unstoppable progress of the generic. But while the fast-food culture and the "Hilton system" have been studied extensively, Koolhaas now claims that such generic constituents have also become paradigmatic for the city as a whole. His discovery of this "new" kind of city can be dated to about 1987. His description of Atlanta then (also included in *S, M, L, XL*) already displays all characteristics of the Generic City. Later he would find back the same model in Singapore (see another included essay, "Singapore Songlines"). This physiognomy was then generalized in his essay on "The Generic City."

Drawing on concrete observations and experiences as an internationally active architect, Koolhaas offers a kind of phenomenology of the Generic City. This ideal-typical city has around 15 million inhabitants, and is more likely to be located in Asia or not too far from the equator. It is immersed in a trance, an unreal calm, and is characterized by an "*evacuation* of the public realm" [1251]. Its foremost attraction is its anomie. Koolhaas laconically sums up the "great originality of the Generic City": "to abandon what doesn't work" [1252]. But at the same time he extends a certain heroic quality to this no-nonsense attitude, since it tries "to break up the blacktop of idealism with the jackhammers of realism" [ibid.]. Koolhaas acts rough. He dispenses completely with the "idealism" of modernists, evidently without qualms.

The Generic City is "the post-city being prepared on the site of the ex-city" [ibid.]. It is not bound together by the public domain or agora, but by the residue. The street is dead. The skyscraper has become the definitive typology; it has swallowed up all the rest and can stand anywhere, aloof and untouchable. The Generic City is built on the tabula rasa, either arising from nothing or replacing whatever preceded it. It has, in Koolhaas's view, become irrevocably "unshapable": "planning makes no difference whatsoever" [1255]. The satellite towns that cluster around the Generic City rise and fall unpredictably. The population explodes and suddenly tumbles, the economy booms or collapses. In this apotheosis of multiple choice, says Koolhaas, it will never be possible to reconstruct cause and effect. "They work — that is all" [ibid.].

The housing issue is handled with similar panache: "Housing is not a problem" [1253]. People either live legally in apartment towers and slabs or illegally in a crust of improvized hovels. In the first case, Koolhaas observes with mock surprise, they consume air, and in the second, land. "It is strange that those with the least money inhabit the most expensive commodity — earth; those who pay, what is free — air" [ibid.]. An instance of Rem Koolhaas's jokes: as robust as Le Corbusier's, but without any of the latter's utopianism, humanism, or seriousness. One cannot help wonder: Does sarcasm without an agenda — in perfect impartiality, devoid of ethical choices — ultimately not turn into cynicism?

On the issue of politics in the Generic City, Koolhaas is conspicuously brief. The regime, he notes, tends toward the authoritarian, but remains surprisingly invisible in the urban landscape. The remark is typical of Koolhaas's view on the city: politics is only tangentially relevant. The same applies to capitalism, which is hardly ever called by name. Instead, Koolhaas raises a sociological smoke-screen. All sociological hypotheses, he argues, may be proven and refuted in the Generic City. The only hypothesis that may be kept is that the constant contradiction of hypotheses constitutes the riches of the Generic City.

In his attempt at viewing the Generic City simultaneously as it is *and* from an optimistic perspective — both as ineluctable fate *and* as opportunity — Koolhaas does away with all nostalgia. He points up how history, despite its absence, has become the biggest industry of the Generic City, and how tourism expands in direct proportion to the destruction of the past. But again he reverses the roles: it is not this destruction, but the false nostalgia for the past that draws scathing remarks from him. In a city without qualities and history, people seem doomed to regress to a Disneyfied, simulated version of a collective memory. Koolhaas coolly notes that in the Generic City no real individual memories exist, only memories of memories, faint *déjà vus*, a "generic memory" [1257]. History, he notes in a reference to Marx, does not return as a farce but as a service.

In the Generic City, everyone is a tourist or a shopper. Office buildings are redundant because work is being done at home and the infrastructure of hotels has become so complete as to displace almost all other buildings. The architecture of the Generic City, Koolhaas flippantly observes, is by definition beautiful, i.e. *recherché*. The angle is the yardstick of originality. The style is (and will always remain) postmodern, for postmodernism is "the only movement that has succeeded in connecting the practice of architecture with the practice of panic" [1262]:

2 Dr. Faustroll is the inventor of pataphysics (the science of phantasmagoric solutions to real problems and of real solutions to phantasmagoric problems). This character from Alfred Jarry formulates the hypothesis that the most fundamental physical law is not that of gravity — a law according to which everything is attracted by mass and hence by a center, that everything evolves concentrically with respect to the massiveness of the middle — but conversely, that everything wants to disappear and go up into smoke, that all molecules strive to disperse in the open air. This law of pataphysics is used by Baudrillard as the point of departure for the umpteenth installment in his series on hyperreality, his *essai fleuve* on simulation (see Jean Baudrillard, L'illusion de la fin [Paris: Galilée, 1992]: occurrences tend toward their own unreality. Baudrillard talks of the unreality of political events: the Gulf War, the fall of the Berlin Wall, the democratization of the Eastern bloc. To him, these are no longer real historical events, but events that immediately go on strike and refuse to participate in world history any longer.)

3 See Marc Holthof, *De digitale badplaats* (Leuven: Van Halewijck; Amsterdam: De Balie, 1995), 78-79. Bart Verschaffel reaches an analogous conclusion about the evaporation of the public domain in his already classical text on the network, "De kring en het netwerk," in *Figuren/Essays* (Leuven: Van Halewijck; Amsterdam: De Balie, 1996), 105-20. He was the first also to point me to the seminal essay on "The Generic City" and to Koolhaas's book in general (as well as to its riskiness). For an inspiring discussion of the book, see Pieter 't Jonck, "Bij S/M/L/XL: het interieur zonder eigenschappen als ruimte van de verbeelding," *Dietsche Warande & Belfort* 1 (February 1997): 76-91.

its only aim is to keep up with evolutions. Every form of resistance to postmodernism is antidemocratic.

With sardonic humor, Koolhaas steams ahead. He wonders whether the omnipresent mirror is meant to celebrate the void or to offer a final glimpse of evaporating essences. Cultural production is reduced to the superfluous and copied from place to place: "In each time zone, there are at least three performances of *Cats*. The world is surrounded by a Saturn's ring of meowing" [1264]. Finally, Koolhaas arrives at a new definition of the city: "A city is a plane inhabited in the most efficient way by people and processes" [1263]. Surely this must be the most un-urban, vapid definition of a city ever given. Koolhaas accepts posturbanity as a *fait accompli*. He concludes his essay with what are already famous words: "The city is no longer. We can leave the theater now..." [1264].

So much for our visit to the "post-city" of the future. The vision is an uncanny one, and Koolhaas's detached, lucid, occasionally witty description conveys the alienation well. But it is and remains: the end. The disconcerting thing about the essay, and by extension about the whole book, is that Koolhaas depicts this hereafter of the city, of urbanity, perhaps even of the very idea of sociability, this post-mortem society, with an ironic, sometimes sarcastic, but ultimately cheerful view, and that he even defends it as a treasure-trove of possibilities, as the right way to go, as a new paradigm. In the Generic City, reverse gravity reigns supreme: evaporation is the rule, the centrifugal attraction of the void and the periphery, eventually resulting in centerless agglomerations. First there was the delirium of New York, but now the "culture of congestion," once so strongly promoted by Koolhaas, has been superseded by what we might term a "culture of evacuation." Like a prophet, but without any of the prophet's pessimism, Koolhaas has an eye for the latest developments. He has accepted Dr. Faustroll's Law — the law of antigravity, of universal evaporation, of growing unreality.[2]

**The Virtualization of the Public Domain** If we compare the generic urban condition with its traditional counterpart, one thing stands out. Whereas the classic metropolis used to be a scene entered by the masses, the Generic City is the place where these same masses have disappeared from the scene again. This absorption of the masses and virtualization of the public domain is summarized by Koolhaas in the final sequence of his essay in a dramatic, almost touching image: that of a spectacular Hollywood movie which shows a mass of people appearing in a market, but with the sound switched off and played in reverse. This links the Generic City to a media society: much as the Generic City entails an "evacuation" of the public realm, the "place" of the audiovisual media is that of a simulated public realm.[3] The so-called disappearance of the masses looks like an unavoidable side-effect of the end of the industrial age: the masses are a product of the modern metropolis which disappears again in the postindustrial era. Gone is the dream of dissolving the materiality of buildings through the creation of transparency, gone is the dream of a new collectivity: in its stead we witness a renaissance of the interior. The dream which enthralled both the political utopians and the artistic avantgardes — a dream detected by Walter Benjamin from the nineteenth-century arcades down to Le Corbusier and that exerted its hypnotic spell a final time in '68 — has been shattered. As with nineteenth-century interiors, which were inspired by a defense against the industrial city, against the real world of production and exploitation, people return to the paradisaic island of the new interior. Instead of the languorous shimmer of palm-trees and carpets, of upholstery and *chinoiseries*, we now have *cyber-cocooning in the blue lagoon*. Design provides the streamlined and polished if ultimately vapid synthesis between the bric-à-brac of a bourgeois culture of plush and the transparency, rationality, and functionality, the cheerfulness and light-heartedness of the historical avantgarde. The modern antithesis has been, in Hegelian terms, *sublated*. The designer house of weekly sections in newspapers is Utopia realized, according to the formula: the uninhabited island + the network = paradise. Hell, by contrast, is "paradise unplugged." *Hypothesis*: the growing success of ideal home exhibitions, of ditto television programs and glossy magazines, is directly proportional to the growing number of homeless people.

The place where the new, "evacuated" urban condition becomes most visible is, in Koolhaas's descriptions, the atrium. This emerges from his discussion of the building complexes designed by John Portman for Atlanta. Portman is to him the undisputed inventor of the atrium in its postmodern version. As usual, Koolhaas's definition of the atrium is razor-sharp. Whereas for the Romans it was a hole in a house or other building which injected light and air from outside into the center, today it has become the very opposite: "a container of artificiality that allows its occupants to avoid daylight forever — a hermetic interior, sealed against the real" [841]. Koolhaas proves eminently conscious of how the atrium produces a surrogate urbanity: "The new atrium became a replica as inclusive as downtown itself, an *ersatz* downtown.... The more ambitious these autonomies, the more they undermine the real downtown — its messy conditions, its complexities, its irregularities, its densities, its ethnicities" [843]. The atrium is the new matrix of an urban condition that should indeed be called virtual. This new, virtual urban condition is one of enclosed, artificial inner spaces. The resemblance to airports

4 "Apprenez que l'on veut faire couvrir toutes les rues de Paris avec des vitres, ça va faire de jolies serres chaudes; nous vivrons là-dedans comme des melons." Quoted in Walter Benjamin, *Das Passagen-Werk*, vol. 1, ed. Rolf Tiedemann (Frankfurt am Main: Suhrkamp, 1983), 104. English translation by the editors.

is again striking: security is the key concept. Anything that falls outside the enclosed space tends to turn into a *no-go area*. This situation cannot help but remind us of the "dark city" of Dickens, Stevenson, and Sherlock Holmes: a frightening territory of crime and fog. Outside is only darkness and night. (Not coincidentally, part of the new science fiction is set in such cities: from *Blade Runner* to *Strange Days*.)

The nineteenth-century arcade to which Walter Benjamin ascribed the dream of a new public sphere that would cancel the distinction between public and private has been transformed into the "air-conditioned nightmare" of hotel atriums, of closed, artificial spaces and esplanades that are only accessible via car parks (as in *La Défense*, Las Vegas, or L.A.). There is a topicality to Benjamin's *Passagen-Werk* that its author could not have anticipated, for the mixture of interior and exterior which so characterized the arcade — an ambiguity that sparked Benjamin's project — now takes its postmodern form in new spaces that produce a new kind of sequestered public realm. The withdrawal from a threatening outside world, which to Benjamin's mind was typical of the bourgeois interior, has definitively vanquished what he called "the *plein-airism* of the revolution." Postmodern *flânerie* has been domesticated: it takes place in new, large inner spaces, in shopping centers or malls, piazzas, atriums of office buildings or hotels, dramatized transit zones like those of new airports, and so on — empty spaces or voids that do no more than facilitate the individual delectation of a grand architectural decor. The postmodern versions of the arcade — the shopping center, the mall, the artificial piazza, the transit zone, the atrium — are increasingly generating a new urban paradigm, that of a virtual urban condition. These are all spaces that have definitively come down on the side of the interior. People seem to have given up on the street, on the world outside.

The fantasy of a covered city that Benjamin quotes from an early-nineteenth-century *Vaudeville* has acquired a new, slightly sour taste: "You know, they are thinking of covering all the streets of Paris with glass. Imagine the lovely hot greenhouses this will produce: we will be living like melons."[4] In light of this quotation, history today appears as a remake of a science fiction classic, *The Body Snatchers*, in which an invasion of plants devitalizes mankind. And this, too, Koolhaas knows. By the end of his long essay on Singapore, he announces point-blank that "the third millennium will be an experiment in this form of soullessness" [1077]. Dr. Faustroll's Law all over again: the soul, that most ephemeral element of cities, is the first element to be surrendered to the attraction of the void and to the forces of inverse gravity.

The city without qualities, nevertheless, is and remains a scenario of doom. Or at least, it would be absurd to raise these new, generic cities with their virtual-ity to a norm for older, "specific" cities. The third millennium must not become an experiment in soullessness; mankind must do all it can to avert this encroaching catastrophe. Even Koolhaas's own *EuraLille* is an exercise in soullessness. He himself describes it as "a Freudian flight forward" [1164]. But can an architect afford this kind of cheerfulness and lucidity as theorist without turning into a cynic as practitioner? Or is the cynicism of Koolhaas the author a mere mask, the cool look of an architect in shades, behind which a pragmatical moralist hides?

**Faster than Revulsion** About the Boompjes TowerSlab project in Rotterdam, Koolhaas writes in *S, M, L, XL*: "It was OMA's first *retroactive* concept, the beginning of an exhausting bombardment of idealization with which we tried to maintain a marginal advantage vis-à-vis our own increasing revulsion" [543]. This phrase, found by chance when first leafing through the book, seems to me to offer the key to Koolhaas's *magnum opus*, and maybe to his entire mental strategy. The slogan is far from unequivocal. If read in the context of "The Generic City" and particularly in light of the rallying cry "to break up the blacktop of idealism with the jackhammers of realism," it looks like an attack on (or renunciation of) all idealism by thrashing it with an illusion-free realism. But read from the viewpoint of other texts in *S, M, L, XL* (and from that of *Delirious New York*, which does not purport to be "a retroactive manifesto" for nothing), it implies rather the opposite: a re-idealization of whatever is, and thus a manner of devising a survival strategy. Let us briefly analyze the significance of this opposition between realism and idealization in Koolhaas's texts.

In "The Terrifying Beauty of the 20th Century," under the heading of "Method," Koolhaas writes that "If there is a method in this work, it is a method of systematic *idealization* — a systematic overestimation of what exists, a bombardment of speculation that invests even the most mediocre aspects with retroactive conceptual and ideological charge" [208]. In other words, this method amounts to a systematic overestimation of the status quo, a legitimation of that status quo through a battery of speculations, even an investment of meaning into a proliferation of projects that in retrospect prove to be total or partial failures: "To each bastard, a genealogical tree" [ibid.]. Prestige is imputed to even the most brainless products. Thus, the skyscrapers of Portman's Northpark, a new satellite town for Atlanta, remind Koolhaas of Malevich's "Architectons" [856]. What is behind this "overestimation"? In his essay on Atlanta, Koolhaas discusses Portman with a mixture of contempt and admiration. Indeed, no other contemporary architect in his entire 1,300-page book is discussed over several

5 Gershom Scholem, *Über einige Grundbegriffe des Judentums* (Frankfurt am Main: Suhrkamp, 1970), 135.

pages. This may seem surprising, but becomes less so when one realizes how Portman embodies Koolhaas's own ideal: he notes with some envy that the man is at once an architect and a developer, but adds that he still has to discover an extra identity, that of the theorist. It is a trinity Koolhaas himself apparently dreams of.

Koolhaas hopes to "realize" idealism (that of the modern movement) by immersing it in a bath of *no nonsense* — the bath of his own explicit antihumanism. But in reality he is only idealizing realism. Thus, he regresses to the opposite of what at first sight he appears to be arguing for. An "exhausting bombardment of idealization with which we [try] to maintain a marginal advantage vis-à-vis our own increasing revulsion" is not only tantamount to a (retroactive) idealization of the existing, but also to a denunciation of all idealism, to a strategy that elevates "realism" to a holy doctrine. And all of this to stay one step ahead of his own revulsion.

Koolhaas's method logically follows from his view on modernity. "Modernity is a radical principle. It is destructive. It has destroyed the city as we know it. We now inhabit 'what used to be the city.' In a bizarre way, Portman's Northpark — in fact, Atlanta as a whole — comes close to fulfilling that kind of modernity, a post-cataclysmic new beginning that celebrates revolutionary forms in liberated relationships, justified, finally, by no other reason than their appeal to our senses" [856]. He clearly wishes to see the utmost degradation, the debasement, the fury of destruction, as an opportunity. Destruction is accompanied by a kind of liberation, if only in the form of relief, the ditching of ballast. This desperate hope is reflected in both his reasoning and style — in his parentheses, for example, the dialectical kink in many of his sentences, in which statements are inverted. Two examples from "Singapore Songlines" must suffice. After the already quoted dictum that "the third millennium will be an experiment in this form of soullessness," he adds the parenthesis "(unless we wake up from our 30-year sleep of self-hatred)" [1077]. And a few lines down: "Singapore is a *city without qualities* (maybe that is an ultimate form of deconstruction, and even of freedom)" [ibid.]. His ambivalence towards a runaway modernization becomes readable in these and similar moments of "dialectical" reversal. Is Koolhaas perhaps a crypto-Messiah who secretly operates according to the most daring cabbalistic topoi: "Israel asks of God: When will you redeem us? He replies: When you have sunk to the lowest step, in that hour I will redeem you."[5] In more modern, neo-Marxist terms: in the extremest reification, salvation is under way. Or does nothing else remain of this mental operation today but a gamble? OMA as Russian roulette?

Koolhaas sees through the process of destruction, but his lucidity offers only two outcomes: *Realpolitik* and hedonism. On the subject of urbanism, he writes in "What Ever Happened to Urbanism?": "Redefined, urbanism will not only, or mostly, be a profession, but a way of thinking, an ideology: to accept what exists" [969-71]. What else does this mean than the freedom to swim along with the current of disastrous developments? On hedonism, he writes: "Contrary to modern architecture and its desperate afterbirths, this new architecture is neither authoritarian nor hysterical: it is the hedonistic science of designing collective facilities that fully accommodate individual desires" [7]. This quotation comes from his 1972 graduation project, "Exodus, or the Voluntary Prisoners of Architecture," a polemical design for a hedonistic concentration camp that cuts through downtown London.

But behind his method, there is also his Credo: "maybe all these arguments are in the end mere rationalizations for the primitive fact of simply liking asphalt, traffic, neon, crowds, tension, the architecture of others, even" [208]. Koolhaas the confirmed urbanite, the Baudelairean flaneur who enjoys the density, the clash, the confusion of the metropolis: a likable image in view of his other statements, but not convincing.[6] This Baudelairean Credo is at odds with his method. He appears all too willing to join others in abolishing this city, whose end he ordains, for instance by assimilating and defending the developer's logic (à la Portman). That is where an idealization of architectural *Realpolitik* takes you: the importation of this American logic into Europe. Richard Plunz has rightly deplored this import, especially when it also involves the exportation of the "model" to the second and third worlds. To him, the flight forward into deurbanization is being exported from "developed" countries to "developing countries." But the disastrous sprawl is precisely what should *not* be repeated in Asia. "The problems facing Western urbanism, particularly in the period of Post-War deurbanization of the United States, can ill afford to be repeated on an ever larger scale elsewhere." Nor is Plunz enthusiastic about the Generic City. "In Asia for example, we begin to see cities which replicate the sprawl of Los Angeles or Phoenix on a scale far more vast: de-urbanization without automobiles, enfored by the ersatz socialism of centralized power in a region of labor commodification."[7] Perhaps this statement catches the sad socioeconomic and geopolitical reality of the new generic cities better than Koolhaas's entire "bombardment of idealization."

6 The Baudelairean flaneur is explicitly invoked at the end of Koolhaas's book: see 1322-23.

7 Richard Plunz, "Größe als falsche Fährte/The Scale Canard," *Daidalos*, 61 (1996): 130-31.

8 The scene appears twice in the book, once as a photographically reproduced quotation from *Delirious New York* [36], once as an entry in the "dictionary" of quotations and fragments that runs through the book like a litany [76]. We may suppose, therefore, that it amounts to a sort of Koolhaasian *ur-scene*. We should note also how in Koolhaas's project for Welfare Island the gigantic plastic version of Géricault's Medusa serves as an entertainment for rich tourists staying at the Welfare Palace Hotel, who can go visit the larger-than-life sculpture by boat at night, after a visit to the theater formed by the inverted bow of a sunken Titanic. An instance of Koolhaas's rowdy, sardonic humor.

**Terror as Delight** The wreck of the Medusa: "After the shipwreck in the Mediterranean of the *Medusa* — a military vessel — the soldiers/castaways were left on their raft with only barrels of wine, guns and ammunition. In a premature and drunken panic they began to cannibalize each other on the second day of their journey. Saved on the 7th day of the shipwreck, they could easily have survived without eating anything at all" [36].[8] This anecdote becomes to Koolhaas an allegory: "This monumental expression of 'loss of nerve' corresponds to the premature panic and loss of nerve about the Metropolis in the present moment of the 20th century" [ibid.]. A revulsion of doom-mongering and of what he calls "the practice of panic" typifies Koolhaas's texts. Under no condition does he want to collude with the convergence of architecture and such a practice of panic. But does this not result precisely in a panicky (which is to say, also, a frightening) architecture? Is this not what causes him to worship *Bigness*?

Beyond a certain scale, Koolhaas argues, architecture takes on the properties of Bigness. Bigness is an ideological program in its own right, independently of the architect's wishes. He sums up the attributes of Bigness as follows: big buildings are characterized by an autonomy of their parts that does not necessarily amount to fragmentation; inventions like the elevator subordinate architectural compositions to mechanical possibilities; the rupture of form and function, of program and manifestation, of core and envelope, deprive buildings of their logic, their (modernist) ethos. Because of their expansiveness, big buildings acquire an amoral quality: impact. All of this means that big buildings break with scale, with architectural composition, with tradition, with transparency, with ethics, finally resulting in the most radical break: "Bigness is no longer part of any urban tissue.... Its subtext is *fuck* context" [502].

But this constellation (is it autarchy or autism?) of the mega-skyscraper still offers us, in Koolhaas's view, a final opportunity: "in spite of its dumb name, Bigness is a theoretical domain at this *fin de siècle*: in a landscape of disarray, disassembly, dissociation, disclamation, the attraction of Bigness is its potential to reconstruct the Whole, resurrect the Real, reinvent the collective, reclaim maximum possibility" [510]. But was not the lesson of Manhattan exactly that skyscrapers are only effective as a city, when they are combined at high density? That is what makes New York *delirious.* Now, however, Koolhaas detaches them to form distinct entities that may be erected anywhere. This implies no less than an elevation of the logic of deurbanization into doctrine. Urbanism as ideology: "to accept what exists." What else does this mean for the urbanist than *to celebrate* what exists?

"Only through Bigness can architecture dissociate itself from the exhausted artistic/ideological movements of modernism and formalism to regain its instrumentality as vehicle of modernization" [510]. Here the idealization of *Realpolitik* (that of developers) truly turns into a doctrine of salvation. Can architecture still be an instrument of modernization? What modernization? Techno-economic development run riot? "So what!" Koolhaas seems to be saying. His method only comes down to an aestheticization of the megalomania of capitalist building practice.

What is the aesthetic secret of this big/grandiloquent architecture? The sublime, of course. Edmund Burke defined the sublime as that which somehow produces terror. He summed up his reasoning as follows: "The passions which belong to self-preservation, turn on pain and danger; they are simply painful when their causes immediately affect us; they are delightful when we have an idea of pain and danger, without being actually in those circumstances; this delight I have not called pleasure, because it turns on pain ... Whatever excites this delight, I call *sublime*."[9] Therefore, Burke wrote, "Whatever ... is terrible, with regard to sight, is sublime too."[10] For buildings to be sublime, according to Burke, the one and only condition is "greatness of dimension."[11] But "Designs that are vast only by their dimensions, are always the sign of a common and low imagination."[12] Applied to our present day and age, this is equal to saying that, when all meanings have evaporated, all styles become untenable, all solutions unreachable, there is only one answer: size. Extra-large sizes always work. They are overwhelming and produce the elation of the sublime. The new architectural complexes are machines that exist just for the kick and — wholly in accordance with Burke's description — exclude any real danger, the outside, the real city. At least as an author, Koolhaas appears to opt for a spectacular architecture, for architecture as spectacle. Not an architecture of panic for him, but an architecture of terror as delight.

Big buildings and big interior spaces produce a *modern* sensation at a time

9 Edmund Burke, *A Philosophical Enquiry into the Origin of Our Ideas of the Sublime and Beautiful*, ed. James T. Boulton (London: Routledge and Kegan Paul; New York: Columbia University Press, 1958), 51.

10 Ibid., 57.

11 Ibid., 76.

12 Ibid.

13 See D. G. Shane, "Rem Koolhaas and the Post-Modern City," *The Los Angeles Forum for Architecture + Urban Design: Newsletter* (1995): 1-7.

14 Postmodernism is defined by Koolhaas as follows: "Post-inspirational, past erudition, intimately connected with speed, a futurism, postmodernism is a mutation that will be from now on part of architectural practice — an architecture of the flight forward" [848]. Is not Koolhaas according to his own definition also postmodern, then? Take his ode on Bigness. It might legitimately be objected that sublime monumentality, at least in Koolhaas's own designs, is shot through with irony and the temporary. His Congrexpo at EuraLille refers explicitly to the temporary pavilions of Expo '58. The Kunsthal in Rotterdam (which also alludes to '58) is again a temporary pavilion — in fact, a nomads' tent (the trees as pillars). But this temporary character, this ironical "neometabolism," ultimately contributes to the new sublime: in spite of everything, an absolute absence of illusions is the lasting impression left by Congrexpo. The irony (the imitation of rusticated stone in concrete, the plastic or galvanized corrugated plates typical of slums, the slanted posts, the incongruities) turns into a grimace as soon as it is built and thus still characterized by stability and durability.

15 Paul Virilio, "Van Plaats van Uitverkiezing naar Plaats van Uitstoot," in *Het Horizon-negatief* (Amsterdam: Duizend en één, 1989), 109-30. (Orig. *L'horizon négatif: essai de dromoscopie* [Paris: Galilée, 1984].)

when *modernity* itself becomes posthumous. Koolhaas already inhabits the hereafter of modernity: he is metamodern. Faced with the developer's architecture of Portman's Northpark, he asks the (ironical) question: "Is this the reappearance of the sublime?" [856]. The answer should be: *yes.* It is the totalizing aspect of capitalism, the language of power, which is expressed in spectacular buildings (albeit of a *postmonumental* variety, since they no longer convey meaning). Within this framework, there is room for phantasmagoria, for spectacle, for amusement. The Rockefeller Center continues to be the ur-model.[13] Which is to say, *no*: this is not sublime, in the sense of "awesomely elevated," but only the final architectural manifestation of banality, of a society of the spectacle in its transcendental, overpowering phase. It is capitalism squared. The Luxor Palace Hotel in Las Vegas is built in the shape of an enormous pyramid which encloses the biggest atrium in the world: a gigantic gambling hall and theme park in one. What can we learn from Las Vegas? That in the long run even irony or parody, even transgression, excess, subversion, the carnivalesque, etc., may be perfectly recuperated and contained. Writing of "The Voluntary Prisoners," Koolhaas argued: "From the outside this architecture is a sequence of serene monuments; the life inside produces a continuous state of ornamental frenzy and decorative delirium, an overdose of symbols" [7]. Irony, too, is ultimately no more than outward show for a postmodern "architecture of the flight forward" [848].[14]

**The City as a Transit Camp** In Koolhaas's book, the absence of violence is striking. The Generic City is quiet, "*sedated*" [1250] and of "an eerie calm" [1251]. The Bronx and the *banlieue* do not enter into the picture. (Why not? Hypothesis: The absence of violence in the book is related to the latent violence of the book itself.) What is the connection between the latent or manifest violence of the decaying inner cities and slums, and the trance and tranquility of the Generic City? Perhaps Paul Virilio can help us here. Of course, Virilio's geopolitical fantasies on the Cold War and on how cities were being sacrificed to the two remaining strategic centers, Washington and Moscow, have turned him into something of a laughingstock. Nevertheless, on the topic of cities he did have momentous things to say, even if they were steeped in the double *forte* of his heroic and prophetic tone. After all, he is the first to have pointed out the transformation of the city into an airport. In his view, however, violence is exactly ubiquitous. He sees the city as a transit zone, a place of speed and hence of violence, of migration.[15] It is impossible to get a correct picture of the Generic City without putting Virilio's vision alongside, or better even under, that of Koolhaas.

For Virilio, the politics of space (territory, defense, urbanism) is being replaced by a politics of time (transport, communication, speed, networks). The cocoon-like interior and the atrium are capsules in a politics of time that rules a world with a minimum of bodily space. So what happens when the city begins to look like an airport? In abstract terms, the answer should be: we have then, by definition, reached the age of the politics of time. In other words, farewell to the politics of space. Space does not much matter anymore, which is why the city everywhere is becoming the same. The Generic City is the product of the network and thus of the politics of time.

Perhaps in a premature extrapolation of his own lifestyle, Koolhaas observes that the in-transit situation is increasingly becoming a generalized way of life. He omits to mention that this mobility (driven by Virilio's "vectors of speed," i.e. cars, trains, airplanes) also generates violence. There is a huge difference between legal and illegal migration, between arriving in Business Class on a Concorde and as a stowaway on a tanker. The airport lounge and the nearby transit camp for illegal immigrants are worlds apart. But there is a convergence: the world's population is ever more subject to delocalization, as are today's industries. This delocalization is a source of violence, both because of the speed with which it is associated and because of attendant phenomena like exclusion, incarceration, collision, ghettoization, alienation, lack of rights, xenophobia.

In light of the Generic City, a C.I.A.M. pronouncement in "A Short Outline of the Core" (1951) acquires a prophetic overtone: "If new towns are built without a core they will never become more than camps."[16] Is the Generic City a camp? It is, says the Italian philosopher Giorgio Agamben. In his opinion, more and more people fall outside the status of communal life (*bios*) and into the status of unmediated life (*zoé*). This unmediated life is outlawed; it is governed by the logic of the camp. A camp is not a prison, not a legal institution, but a territory outside the law, an enclave within but especially outside society. And it is a place where anything can happen, even the most inconceivable horrors (not so much because of human cruelty or the barbarity of ideological indoctrination, but simply because of the legal structure of the camp itself). Transit zones, too, are extraterritorial (hence duty-free). They are potential camps (like the camps for illegal immigrants). Perhaps Agamben, despite the appearance of gross exaggeration, is not far from the truth when he proposes that the concentration camp, rather than the city, provides the paradigm of contemporary biopolitics.[17]

16 "A Short Outline of the Core: Extracts from Statements Prepared during the 8th Congress of CIAM," in *The Heart of the City: Towards the Humanisation of Urban Life*, ed. Jacqueline Tyrwhitt, José Luis Sert, and Ernesto N. Roger (Nendeln: Kraus Reprint, 1979), 165.

17 See Giorgio Agamben, "Qu'est-ce qu'un camp?" in *Moyens sans fins: Notes sur la politique* (Paris: Christian Bourgois, 1995), 47-55. See also his book *Homo sacer: Le pouvoir souverain et la vie nue* (Paris: Seuil, 1997), 195 & passim.

18 "Atlanta, Parigi, Singapore. Atlanta, Paris, Singapore," interview with Rem Koolhaas, *Lotus*, 84 (1995): 120.

On a geopolitical scale, the ever-growing refugee problem is the only evidence to support the hypothesis that an "in-transit condition" is becoming universal. We must take Koolhaas's question seriously: "Is the contemporary city like the contemporary airport?" But we should be willing to consider the airport in its totality, i.e. not only its lobbies and lounges, its catering services, cargo companies, and tour operators, but also the nearby transit camps. Only then do we obtain a true picture of the Generic City.

**Postscript: The Tragedy of the Architect** My entire analysis of Koolhaas's thinking may be based on a misunderstanding. What Koolhaas is out to offer is not a critical theory, one might argue, but a provocative framework for practice. My stubborn mistake would then be based on the fact that I read him as a theorist rather than as an architect. Maybe so. Yet I believe such a reading strategy to be necessary, since Koolhaas is almost as influential as a theorist than as an architect. And the architect interferes with the impartiality of the theorist. In a recent interview, Koolhaas has put his cards on the table in a rare moment of candor. To the question "You do not imagine a return to the traditional city?" he replied:

*I think that it is necessary to be very modest. Nothing is ever sure, and it may be that in twenty years the need to recreate the city as it was before will be rediscovered. As an architect, the difficulty I have with the existing city is precisely that this city exists. It is still part of the mythology of our profession that we have to change things, because one cannot make a contribution to a work of architecture without changing the situation, the contexts, or the city. There is, deep down in my activity as an architect, the ambition to change things and an awareness of the inevitability of this. From this perspective, it is impossible for me to stick to the conventional city — at least as an architect.*[18]

The candor is disarming. The answer explains the entire strategy of retroactive idealization, as a rationalization of the position of the architect, who will and must build. There is even an element of tragedy in it: the architect is irrevocably on the side of modernization and "postmodernization" (and thus also of transcendental capitalism). He must move ahead and help organize the destruction of the traditional city. As an architect he is, by the very definition of his profession, forced to engage in a flight forward, even if eventually he can see no other solution but to think faster than his own revulsion.

*Translation Bart Eeckhout*

An earlier version of this text was published in Dutch with an accompanying English translation in *Archis* 4 (1998): 28-34.

**Liam Kennedy**

# Representations of the Underclass: Race, Poverty, and the Postindustrial Ghetto

*Keywords:* ■ *Ethnic Studies* ■ *Journalism* ■ *Film Studies* ■ *Ghettoization*

As the cores of American cities have been radically transformed in the last twenty years, the postindustrial ghetto has emerged as a highly visible signifier of urban decline, a scene of social and economic devastation peopled by an ominous "urban underclass." The concept of the underclass has been widely disseminated, though never clearly defined. On the one hand, it is a metaphor for the sociospatial restructuring of American cities: it refers to the deindustrialization and decentralization of economic enterprise, the intense concentration of poverty in increasingly isolated inner-city areas, the deproletarianization of the urban poor, and the privatization and militarization of public space. On the other hand, the underclass is a compelling and powerful myth of behavioral deficiencies which combines common assumptions about poverty and race. It generates images of criminals, delinquents, crack addicts, and unwed mothers, and of an urban scene in which crime, drugs, unemployment, welfare dependency, indiscriminate violence, and educational failure are norms of existence. More insidiously it signifies "blackness," it is a term of racial categorization which connotes and normalizes what Daniel Moynihan once egregiously termed "a tangle of pathology" in urban black poverty.[1] In this essay I will comment on some general features of the myth of the underclass and examine how it has been treated as an issue of representation in selected texts.

The myth of the underclass is a cultural and political construct which has a

1 See Lee Rainwater and William L. Yancey, *The Moynihan Report and the Politics of Controversy* (Cambridge: MIT Press, 1967), 39-125.

2 U.S. National Advisory Commission on Civil Disorders, *The Kerner Report* (New York: Pantheon Books, 1988), 1-2.

3 "The American Underclass," *Time* (29 August, 1977): 14.

4 See William Julius Wilson, *The Truly Disadvantaged: The Inner City, the Underclass, and Public Policy* (Chicago: University of Chicago Press, 1987); Charles Murray, *Losing Ground: American Social Policy, 1950-1980* (New York: Basic Books, 1984); and Lawrence Mead, *Beyond Entitlement: The Social Obligations of Citizenship* (New York: Free Press, 1985).

distinct historical emergence and development in public discourse. It began to take distinctive shape in the wake of late-1960s representations of "urban crisis" which focused on riots, disorder, and decay in African-American urban centers. In March 1968 the Kerner Commission, reporting on the cause of urban riots, famously warned that the United States was "moving toward two societies, one black, one white — separate and unequal." While the Commission's recommendations for "ghetto enrichment" and racial integration were largely ignored, its image of "the racial ghetto [as] a destructive environment totally unknown to most white Americans" is one that emerged in more detailed and negative profile in 1970s and 1980s discourses on the underclass.[2] These discourses developed in social analysis and then more publicly in the national media toward the end of the 1970s. One notable instance of the latter is a *Time* cover story of August 1977 which stated: "Behind [the ghetto's] crumbling walls lives a large group of people who are more intractable, more socially alien and more hostile than almost anyone had imagined. They are the unreachables: the American underclass."[3] This statement represents the underclass as a distinctly separate group, all but invisible to white America, and implicitly responsible for its members' separation and immizeration — they are not only alien, but intractably so, rendering themselves unreachable. There is in this language an intimation of what have become common assumptions about the underclass: that it is outside normative (white American) considerations of what constitutes citizenship and that its members have little prospect of overcoming this isolation.

Such assumptions became hardened within a political ideology of the underclass in the 1980s, an ideology in tune with the national government's withdrawal of social expenditure programs and the Reaganite engineering of a more hierarchical society. While liberal analysts such as William Julius Wilson sought to identify class differentiation and economic restructuring as causes of the underclass condition, conservative America found more polemical and compelling evidence in the work of Charles Murray, Lawrence Mead, and others who criticized liberal welfare policies and advanced behavioral models to explain the existence of a separate poor black population in American cities.[4] The behavioral explanation (echoing the "culture of poverty" argument of the 1960s) both focuses and rejects the black poor as a social "problem" by arguing that the individual, not social conditions, is responsible for membership of the underclass.

In the mid-1980s "underclass" came to be used primarily as a behavioral term, widely used to describe what was perceived as aberrant or antisocial lifestyles and outlooks. This discourse (echoing nineteenth-century perspectives of the "undeserving poor") rearticulated the crude dualism of "two societies," but now with a powerful moralizing emphasis. It worked to transform the social problem of poverty into the moral problem of behavior. Moralizing commentary on the urban black poor has tended to accentuate the pathological difference of the underclass as a form of social degeneration signifying an essential loss or lack of social wholeness — individual, familial, and communal. The underclass is said to lack moral values and incentives; it is said to have lost role models due to the absence of a black middle class in the ghetto. This formulation of fundamental behavioral deficiencies valorizes a "middle-class morality" which is absent from ghetto cultures and focuses attention on the dysfunctional nature of family structures, gender relations, and reproduction among ghetto inhabitants. As images of teenage mothers and one-parent families became commonplace images of underclass life, "behavior" was readily taken to connote attitudes, motivations, and values which are only rarely studied in detail.[5]

If the underclass myth was originally propelled into public consciousness by the writings of sociologists and journalists, it took on a fresh impetus and even greater resonance through visualization in television and cinema. By the late 1980s images of unmarried ghetto mothers, crack users, and homeless people were common on American television, and it was television news and documentary programs which began to feed alarmist images to the public of "babies having babies." These forms of programming encoded black urban poverty as distinctively separate from the worlds of the viewing audience and contributed to the pathologization of the poor inherent in the underclass myth.[6] Issues of visuality and visibility are crucial to understanding representations of black urban poverty, especially as these take on recognizable spatial components. The framing of the postindustrial ghetto as the space of the black underclass has given rise to stock images of people positioned in a mise-en-scène of urban wasteland streets, concrete playgrounds, project housing, and derelict buildings. The ghetto appears as a carceral space, confining its inhabitants as both visible and exotic, subjected to the distanced gaze of the viewer.[7]

The emergence and dissemination of the myth of the underclass is inextri-

5 For an incisive critique of the focus of behavior in discussions of the underclass, see Adolph Reed, Jr., "The Underclass as Myth and Symbol: The Poverty of Discourse About Poverty," *Radical America* 24 (January 1992): 21-40.

6 In American television news and documentary representations of the urban black poor there is recurrence of staple images and visual frames which signify social deviancy and dangers. See Herman Gray, *Watching Race: Television and the Struggle for "Blackness"* (Minneapolis: University of Minnesota Press, 1995).

7 For an analysis of representations of the underclass in American cinema, see Liam Kennedy, "Urban Others: The Black Underclass in American Film," in *Social and Secure?: Politics and Culture of the Welfare State*, ed. Hans Bak, Frits Van Holthoon, and Hans Krabbendam (Amsterdam: VU University Press, 1996), 289-300.

8 Stuart Hall, "The Whites of Their Eyes: Racist Ideologies and the Media," in *Gender, Race and Class in Media: A Text-Reader*, ed. Gail Dines and Jean M. Humez (Thousand Oaks, CA: Sage, 1995), 20.

9 An early, seminal text is Jacob Riis's *How the Other Half Lives*, first published in 1890.

cably linked to ideological issues of race and representation. Journalism, television, and cinema are important sites for the (re)production, elaboration, and transformation of racial representations. As Stuart Hall observes, "the media construct for us a definition of what *race* is, what meaning the imagery of race carries, and what the 'problem of race' is understood to be. They help to classify out the world in terms of the category of race."[8] The myth of the underclass has become a potent interpretative framework for focusing the "problem of race" in American cities, and more specifically within the postindustrial ghetto. The "problem" is reconfigured in the proliferating narratives about the underclass that cross many modes and mediums of representation: journalism, television, documentary film, narrative film, photography, mural art, autobiography, fiction, and popular music. In this essay, I will focus on selected texts of journalism and documentary film which have proved to be influential representations of black ghetto life in the 1990s. The texts offer well-intentioned, meliorist efforts to inform and demystify, to produce fresh understandings of urban black poverty, yet, as we shall see, they also reproduce as well as challenge common assumptions about the underclass.

**How the Other Half Survives** American journalists have been venturing into the inner city to record "how the other half lives" for over one hundred years, and sociologists have followed a similar path for almost as long.[9] Their representations of the urban poor have evolved over time, both responding to contemporary social conditions and drawing on established codes and conventions of documentation and reportage. The result has been a distinctive if varied literature of ghetto ethnography which has played an important role in defining urban poverty for a readership outside that world. The underclass writings of the 1990s have significant methodological and stylistic roots in 1960s journalism and sociology. They build on the traditions of "new journalism" which melded fictional techniques with traditional forms of reporting in analysis of American subcultures and countercultures, and mimic the fieldwork aspect of progressive sociologists who immersed themselves in the cultures of the urban poor. The underclass ethnography of the 1990s is in certain ways more sophisticated and self-conscious regarding the positionality of authorship, yet continues to valorize the role of the writer as participant observer, a first-hand witness to the experiences of the urban poor.

The text which most influentially opened the way for in-depth reporting on the black underclass is Alex Kotlowitz's *There Are No Children Here: The Story of Two Boys Growing Up in the Other America*, published in 1991. Kotlowitz's book had its origins in a series of articles he wrote for the *Wall Street Journal* in 1987 on

African-American children living in a public housing project in Chicago. The articles were well received (one of them won the Robert F. Kennedy Journalism Award) and Kotlowitz returned to Chicago to closely chronicle the lives of two brothers in the Henry Horner Homes over a period of three years. The resulting book quickly became a best-seller and established its author as an expert on ghetto poverty and education. Throughout the 1990s many writers have followed Kotlowitz into the lives of black people in public housing. A large number have shared his focus on children, and notably popular have been texts which analyze the expressive culture of young black males through sport. Others have focused on drug culture and related aspects of predatory street life.[10] A common element in these works is a concern to represent the psychological and cultural damage caused by inner-city poverty. They offer personalized accounts which engage readers very immediately with the experiences of the black urban poor and offer to understand the collective "condition" of the underclass through close attention to the daily routines and thoughts of selected individuals.

*There Are No Children Here* tells the story of Lafayette and Pharoah Rivers across a period of three years, producing a very intimate chronicle of their home lives, their schooling, their relationships with their extended family (with particular emphasis on the role of their mother LaJoe), and their responses to the poverty and violence which surrounds them. In "A Note on Reporting Methods" which follows the main narrative text, Kotlowitz emphasizes the diligence of his approach to his subject:

*In reporting this book, I spent a good deal of time just hanging out with Pharoah and Lafayette, sometimes as much as four to five days a week.... LaJoe was like a second pair of eyes and ears for me. She relayed incidents involving her children that I would talk about with them at a later date.... I interviewed over a hundred other people, including the boys' friends and neighbors, police, schoolteachers, judges, attorneys, Chicago Housing Authority officials, and local politicians.... Of the numerous scenes in the book, I witnessed nearly half.... Those events at which I wasn't present I recreated from interviews with people who were.... In those instances where dialogue was re-created, it was*

10 Acclaimed examples include: Daniel Coyle, *Hardball: A Season in the Projects* (New York: Harper, 1995), which tells of the author's experiences coaching a Little League team in the Cabrini Green projects in Chicago; Darcy Frey, *The Last Shot: City Streets, Basketball Dreams* (New York: Houghton Mifflin, 1994), observes the lives of young basketball players in projects in Coney Island; Leon Dash, *Rosa Lee* (New York: Basic Books, 1996) records his intimate observances of the addictions of a black mother of eight children in Washington; and Philippe Bourgeois, *In Search of Respect: Selling Crack in El Barrio* (New York: Cambridge University Press, 1996) is based on the five years the author spent closely observing drug dealers in East Harlem.

11 Alex Kotlowitz, *There Are No Children Here: The Story of Two Boys Growing Up in the Other America* (New York: Doubleday, 1991), 307. All further references to this book will be in parentheses in the text.

*based on the memory of at least one of the participants, and often on the memory of two or three.*[11]

This explication of reporting methods underlines the veracity and authenticity of Kotlowitz's chronicle. We cannot doubt that he has been a dedicated and conscientious observer of the boys' lives. However, this commentary on his methods, as much as the narrative it follows, begs many questions about his participation in and mediation of their lives.

While Kotlowitz appears to have been omnipresent, ever-documenting the lives of Lafayette and Pharoah, he renders himself invisible in the main narrative, which is told in the third person by an omniscient voice which blends the perspectives of the key participants with social and historical information. In this manner Kotlowitz seeks to draw us into the lives of the boys (and of their mother) by opening up their interior worlds, the subjective spheres of hopes, dreams, anxieties, and fears. The effect is dramatic, as common feelings unfold in uncommon contexts and we are taken into a world of everyday poverty and violence through the perspective of those who cannot be responsible for this environment. As a narrative strategy this is an effective means of appealing to a readership which might have little direct interest in issues of urban poverty and education. However, it is also a strategy which sets the boys' lives within particular ideological and narrative frameworks the author has selected. While Kotlowitz seeks through interiorization to provide points of empathy for his readers, it is never clear to what degree the children and their mother have expressed their emotional lives to him and to what degree he imaginatively constructs subjectivity. Although this is impossible to clarify we can recognize that he uses particular modes of emplotment, focalization, and metaphorization to dramatize his chronicle.

The narrative begins with a coming-of-age episode (a stock device of countless fictional and autobiographical treatments of childhood) in which the boys and their friends visit railroad tracks near their home to hunt for garter snakes in the undergrowth alongside the tracks. Their "urban safari" [6] fails to uncover any snakes, but just as boredom sets in the boys are startled by "a commuter train approaching from downtown" [ibid.]. As the boys frantically hide themselves their fear is explained by the narrator:

*The youngsters had heard that the suburb-bound commuters, from behind the tinted train windows, would shoot at them for trespassing on the tracks.... Some of the commuters had heard similar rumors about the neighborhood children and worried that ... they might be the targets of talented snipers. Indeed, some sat away from the windows as the train passed through Chicago's blighted core. For both the boys and the commuters, the unknown was the enemy* [7].

The incongruity of unconventional setting (ghetto pastoral) and conventional motif (the machine in the garden) establishes key thematics of the narrative and signals its implied reader. The thematics — the relations between space and knowledge, innocence and experience, and self and other — are archetypal but will take on the particulars of the boys' environment and experiences as the narrative unfolds. The implied reader is correlated with the commuter in the suburban bound train who recoils in fear from the denizens of the city's "blighted core." Playing the points of view of the boys and the commuters against each other, Kotlowitz reassures his reader that "the unknown was the enemy" and implicitly asks his reader to open their minds to what lies beyond rumors about the ghetto poor.

This introductory chapter also begins the characterization of Lafayette and Pharoah. The older Lafayette is portrayed as impulsive and impatient; "almost twelve," he is on the edge of adulthood and tugs at the responsibilities of looking after his younger brother. As he grows older he becomes apprehensive about close relationships as friends die at a horrific rate; and he struggles with the role of his mother's confidant in place of his father, who has left the family. By the end of the narrative he has become a morose young man whose "face seemed incapable of expression" [280] and whose expressions of tiredness to his mother worry her that "he was just tired of being" [260]. It is Pharoah, though, whose interior world is more fully dramatized by the author and strikes the most empathic chords with the reader. Nine years old at the opening of the narrative, he is portrayed as a sensitive child given to private reveries and seems "in awe of the world" [4]. In the opening chapter he marvels at the downtown skyline: "With the late afternoon sun reflecting off the glass and steel skyscrapers, downtown Chicago glowed in the distance. As he looked south a few blocks, he glimpsed the top floors of his home, a red brick, seven story building. It appeared dull and dirty even in the brilliant sun" [ibid.]. The sense of socioeconomic disjunction is for the readers' eyes only, though, for Pharoah finds the view "pretty great" [ibid.]. This sense of wonder at the surfaces of life is used by the author to transmit the perspective of childhood, further enhanced by Pharoah's attachment to the natural world. As the other boys play around him he is distracted by butterflies and wildflowers, "lost in his thoughts, thoughts so private and fanciful that he would have had trouble articulating them to others" [7]. As his narrative develops he is depicted as yearning for a "sanctuary" to protect his childhood: "Pharoah clutched his childhood with the vigor of a tiger gripping his meat. He wouldn't let go. Nobody, nothing would take it away from him" [15].

The struggle to protect childhood lends the book its moral core. Kotlowitz shows us that the innocence associated with childhood is under extreme pressures in the projects environment and as he details the decay and danger that surrounds the boys we are led to feel concern for their very mortality as much as for their emotional and intellectual development. The author frequently draws our attention to the social and historical contexts of their imperiled childhoods. For much of the narrative he does this almost seamlessly, impelling the reader to look over the shoulder of the children at issues beyond their articulation (as in his depiction of Pharoah's view of the city above). As the children experience random shootings in their neighborhood he moves to present information on gang activities and policing; at another point the children's presence at a basketball stadium, where they seek to park cars safely for a fee, allows him to provide an insightful historical sketch of the politics of policing surrounding the stadium which is on the edge of the projects. At times, though, the narrative moves awkwardly between the children's perspectives and the broader social issues of project life Kotlowitz wants to comment upon. His commentary on the criminal activities of a gang leader and his eventual conviction stretches across several chapters and reads like a journalistic aside to the main narrative. The sometimes awkward transitions in narrative focalization and tempo render apparent the tensions between the moral thrust of his chronicle and his nascent efforts to identify causes and responsibilities for the boys' immizerated childhoods.

In the figure of LaJoe, the boys' mother, Kotlowitz means to broaden his purview of family relationships and pose questions about adult values and responsibilities. LaJoe is described as the key "guidepost" [9] in the lives of the boys at the beginning of the narrative, though it is a position she struggles to maintain. Via her memories the author documents the development of Henry Horner Homes from a place of utopian hopes in the mid-1950s, when LaJoe arrived there with her parents, to a place where she "and her neighbors felt abandoned" [12] by the late 1980s. Kotlowitz accentuates this sense of abandonment through his descriptions of the physical decay of her immediate environment — her apartment and her building which lack maintenance — and of the neighborhood which lacks public spaces for safe recreation or communal activities. This physical decay is linked time and again in the narrative to forms of individual, familial, and communal decline. From La Joe's perspective, "It wasn't just her home that was crumbling; the neighborhood was too. It was all the perfect metaphor, LaJoe thought, for what was happening to her spirit" [241]. The metaphor is too perfect, though, to hold together the manifold issues of poverty and parenting the larger narrative places before us. Earlier we are told that LaJoe "could not separate" her family and the physical ruin of the neighbourhood: "Sometimes she blamed her children's problems on the neighborhood; at other times, she attributed the neighborhood's decline to the change in people, to the influx of drugs and violence" [13]. This seesawing perspective works fine to dramatize LaJoe's insecurities and sense of despair, but it also reflects the author's own elisions of critical inquiry (as he works to sustain the illusion of the invisible, omniscient chronicler who simply reports what he hears and sees) and mystifies social and economic relations.

Whereas Kotlowitz emphasizes LaJoe's embattled but essential humanity, he depicts her largely absent husband Paul in pathological terms, as a junkie who has failed the family. Having promised Lafayette "he would move the family out of Horner to a quieter neighborhood" [167], his failure to keep this promise appears central to the family's "decay": "[Paul] had not only welshed on his promises, but he was too dejected to be of much support for the kids" [168]. The reader is not told what changed Paul from an employed father to a depressed junkie, simply that his "habit overtook him" [167]. He remains a shadowy figure in the narrative — we do not share his point of view as we do that of the children and their mother. This may be due in some part to the author's limited access to Paul, but the result is a skewing of the narrative to suggest that the absent, delinquent father is largely responsible for the family's plight. This reflects Kotlowitz's broader treatment of male role models in the book. He draws attention to the paucity of employed black men in the boys' lives, pointing out that "only a handful" of their schoolteachers are men and noting the allure of gang leaders as surrogate fathers. However, issues of male parenting roles remain largely pathological in presentation, summarized as the common occurrence of absence in "a neighborhood where men fathered children and then disappeared into the gangs and the street corners and death" [82]. The focus on behavioral deficiencies stands in for analysis of motivations and values and we learn little about the impact of the urban political economy on the role of male parenting.

The "disappearance" of the fathers is a common stereotype in mass-media portraits of black poverty and Kotlowitz does nothing to further readers' understanding of the trajectories or emotional complexities of adult black male life in the ghetto. One of the most troubling aspects of his narrative in this respect is his dissociated treatment of his own presence in the lives of the children. For all his references to conscientious "reporting methods," he retains complete, omniscient authorial control of the narrative. His stress on his closeness to the boys might lead readers to wonder just what effect he had as a role model while "hanging out" with them (especially as the epilogue hints that he has acted as both bene-

12 See Bill Nichols, *Representing Reality: Issues and Concepts in Documentary* (Bloomington: Indiana University Press, 1991).

factor and mentor). Narratologically, at least, he is another absent father, lending their lives shape and meaning at a distance. Kotlowitz's omniscience is troubling also in its effort to provide a corrective vision of the underclass condition through empathy and recognition of a common humanity based on "our" responses to children. The immediacy and strong emotional tones of the narrative convey a sense of urgency and foster both horror and pity in the reader. However, this liberal effort to evoke compassion relies on assumptions about the universality of childhood — its immanence and innocence — which deflect understanding of the very differences — of race and poverty — which make them fitting subjects for liberal empathy. In his preface Kotlowitz stresses that "despite all they have seen and done, [Lafayette and Pharoah] are — and we must constantly remind ourselves of this — still children" [xi]. *There Are No Children Here* is a reminder of this, but it also allows "us" to forget the material conditions of difference and segregation in favor of the imaginary citizenship of empathy.

**How the Other Half Strives** Documentary filmmaking has long been established as a medium of representation that offers to reveal and interpret hidden or obscured cultures, promising the viewer knowledge of the "real" based on the illusion of direct, unmediated engagement with the world of others. This illusion can be powerfully affective, feeding on the viewer's desire to know and using staple techniques and devices — talking-head interviews, fly-on-the-wall footage, *vérité* camerawork, and voice-over narration — to render transparent what appears to be the inherent drama of the filmed subject.[12] In its treatment of its subject it is akin to literary journalism due to their shared epistemological basis, but documentary film must be distinguished as a visual ethnography — it relies on the hegemony of vision to certify the real and uses the camera to insistently place the viewer as witness to or voyeur in the world of others. When applied to worlds of urban poverty, documentary film has taken many forms, including populist voyeurism (True Crime television programming), liberal investigation (ethnographic treatments of ghetto life), and the radically vernacular (residents' filming of their own conditions of poverty). It is liberal ethnography I am concerned with here, specifically as it is represented by the film *Hoop Dreams*, which is by far the most highly acclaimed documentary film treating black poverty in recent years.

*Hoop Dreams* earned astonishing box-office success and wide critical praise on its release in 1994. It is an independently funded film made principally by three young white filmmakers — Steve James, Peter Gilbert, and Fred Marx — who began in 1987 to put together a half-hour documentary about high-school basketball in Chicago. In 1994 it was released as a three-hour "epic" that won the

Audience Award at the Sundance Festival, made the Top Ten of just about every film critic's list in the United States, and caused a media frenzy when it was snubbed for an Oscar. Within a year it had grossed more than eight million dollars and the filmmakers and their filmed subjects, two young black basketball players from the Cabrini Green projects, Arthur Agee and William Gates, had become celebrities. The filmmakers were signed up by Spike Lee to assist in a fictional version of the film, while Agee and Gates were widely interviewed in the mass media and feted for photocalls by President Clinton. As several critics have noted, the success of the film has a reflexive connection to its content premised on the dream of upward mobility, the movement from margin to mainstream.[13] However, such success for a documentary film could not have been foreseen and we must look more closely at the film to consider the appeal of a three-hour documentary on inner-city black basketball players, and more particularly to analyze its representation of ghetto life.

From the point of view of the filmmakers, *Hoop Dreams* was originally intended to be an exposé of the manipulation and exploitation of young black athletes from the ghetto by agents, coaches, high schools, and universities; it was meant to feed the audience's desire to know through its illumination and critique of the making of sports celebrity. In many ways it achieves this aim, showing us how a white suburban high school poaches black basketball talent from the ghetto with little regard for educative potential, or how Nike manages a basketball summer school for such talent which is known as a "meat market." However, the critique is subsumed by a more potent narrative force: the story of two poor boys chasing the American Dream. Between intended critique and resulting narrative reside ambiguities and contradictions which the narrative momentum of the film barely allows us to reflect upon as we watch.

The powerful narrative momentum does not come from traditional docu-

13 See, for example, Paul Arthur and Janet Cutler, "On the Rebound: *Hoop Dreams* and Its Discontents," *Cineaste* 21, 3 (1995): 22-24.

14 Jack Ketch, "Beyond the Camera: The Untold Story Behind the Making of *Hoop Dreams*," *The World & I* (October 1995): 139.

15 Heralded by *Newsweek* as a "spellbinding American epic," reviewers treated it as a national story; see "Battered Dreams of Glory," *Newsweek* (7 October, 1994): 80. By the time of the film's appearance on video this had become common wisdom, eagerly reflected in the description accompanying the video: "They have nothing — except talent and a dream — and in this tough Chicago neighborhood, dreams are all they can count on. *Hoop Dreams* is the critically acclaimed true-life story of Arthur Agee and William Gates and the unforgettable five year experience that turns them into men. You will come to know them and root for them as if they were your friends, your family, as against all odds, these boys prove that with faith, talent and a little luck, anyone can achieve the American Dream." The description retains traces of documentary's epistemological allure — "true-life story," "You will come to know them" — but foregrounds the drama and pleasurable identification of narrative which will be afforded the audience through vicarious pursuit of the Dream. The description is notably short on specifics, such as the racial identity and ghetto location of the protagonists.

mentary resources, though the filmmakers imply otherwise. Over five years, as they followed the lives of Agee and Gates, they accumulated over 250 hours of film. In interviews the director Steve James accentuates both the slow pace of their enterprise and the rawness of their practice (they had only one camera, shot directly onto Beta video, and used natural lighting when possible) to emphasize that they were three years into the project before they understood what the film was about and realized "You write the screenplay in the editing."[14] This is disingenuous as an explanation of the narrative form, as it replays the stock documentarist view that the subject assumes its own dramatic form — the drama of the real. In fact, the momentum of the film draws heavily on narrative film tropes and devices, particularly those of the sports movie, which has traditionally featured narratives of impoverished athletes triumphing over great odds in pursuit of an American Dream. It is this genre of narrative film which *Hoop Dreams* appropriates to provide the dramatic force of the film, even using formulaic themes and iconography of the genre, such as the big-game finale and the slow-motion treatment of a ball play which carries the drama of success/failure in its arc. In the shaping of its material for dramatic effect *Hoop Dreams* ultimately invests in the pleasures of success. It is the narrative of upward mobility — eerily iconicized in the image of William slowly rising skyward with a ball in film advertising — that reviewers fixated on.[15]

While the dramatic focus on the Dream ultimately overwhelms the filmmakers' overt critical intentions, they do succeed in offering a fascinating portrait of ghetto life for at least half of the film's running time, before the drama of success/failure becomes almost exclusively tied to court play. The first half of the film is densely textured, cross-cutting between diverse individuals and environments, and building a complex web of social and personal relations. Family dynamics receive a good deal of attention, although they mostly revolve around the dreams of the boys. The roles of the mothers, particularly Sheila Agee, are positively presented to show them as caring and supportive of their families in general and the boys in particular. At one point Sheila asks the filmmakers: "Do you ever ask yourself how I get by on 268 dollars a month and keep this house and feed these children? Do you ever ask yourself that question?" Articulate and intelligent, Sheila also pursues her own dream of becoming a nurse and the film finds one of its few emotional highlights outside of the boys' lives when she passes her exam. Although a secondary character in the narrative, the portrait of Sheila effectively challenges common stereotypes of "welfare mothers" which were prevalent at the time of the film's making and release. Unfortunately, there is no similar challenge to stereotypes in the portraits of adult black males in the film. Indeed, there is a clear echo of Kotlowitz's narrative in the film's representation of Arthur Agee's father Bo as an unemployed drug addict who deserts his family. Once again, pathology and dysfunction characterize the role of the black male adult without any interrogation of the conditions or circumstances of individual failings. Although we learn that both Bo and William's brother Curtis have previously held employed work but now have difficulty finding jobs, there is no suggestion that they may be victims of deindustrialization. Rather they are portrayed as victims of their own failings, defeated men now living out what is left of their aspirations through son and brother respectively.

Sheila's direct address to the filmmakers is the only direct reference to poverty in the film, which, unlike *There Are No Children Here*, eschews critical examination of the socioeconomic conditions it portrays. As a result we have only very limited understanding of why (as the film would have us believe) a longing to play basketball consumes all desire in the lives of young black men in the ghetto. "Basketball is my ticket from the ghetto," William asserts, articulating the transcendent promise of the Hoop Dream. Some commentators have sought to explore why this belief is held by many young black males in ghetto poverty, and produced varied explanations: the street credibility of this route to success; the relative access to this sport within ghetto environments; the celebration of black athletes as role models; an alternative to unfulfilling wage labor.[16] *Hoop Dreams* does not explore such issues, it simply relies on the assumption that a desire to escape the ghetto is a natural aspiration. A telling scene in this respect is one in which the young Arthur comes face to face with his hero Isiah Thomas, who has visited his high-school alma mater where Arthur and William are now enrolled. For Arthur, whom we observe watching Thomas on television at the beginning of the film, the man before him is the Dream incarnate, holding the ticket from the ghetto. We watch Arthur and Thomas play a quick one-on-one in which the latter feints and leaps past the awe-struck boy, and as the camera focuses on Arthur's expression of wonder we sense how potent is his identification with this heroic figure who leaps past him, out of the film, and back into the world of mythical sports celebrity. It is, as with many moments in this film, poignant and self-sufficient. At no point with this scene do the filmmakers attempt to provide the more critical forms of interrogation they bring to the workings of the white high-school coach or the Nike training camp. There is no consideration, for example,

16 See Darcy Frey, *The Last Shot*, for a journalistic treatment of these issues. For a penetrating academic analysis of transformed meanings of "play" and "leisure" in the postindustrial ghetto, see Robin D.G. Kelley, "Playing For Keeps: Pleasure and Profit on the Postindustrial Playground," in *The House That Race Built*, ed. Wahneema Lubiano (New York: Random House, 1997), 195-231.

17 On the efforts of the National Basketball Association to display black players as model citizens and surrogate parents, see Gitanjali Maharaj, "Talking Trash: Late Capitalism, Black (Re)Productivity, and Professional Basketball," *Social Text* 50 (Spring 1997): 163.

18 Ibid., 159.

of how and why many black basketball stars have come to act as symbolic surrogates for the absent fathers of the ghetto.[17]

*Hoop Dreams* celebrates the dream of ascension even as it is selectively critical of machinations attendant on this. It simultaneously exploits and elides viewer fascination with the urban environment that constrains and motivates the Dream. The film begins with a panoramic view of downtown Chicago as seen from the projects (echoing the opening of *There Are No Children Here*) and briefly follows the movement of an elevated train before cutting to Arthur and William in their respective homes watching an NBA All-Star game on television. Surrounded by their families the boys whoop with delight as they watch their heroes at play. William is then shown going outside to play ball on a neighborhood court and the camera catches him in slow motion going for an impressive slam dunk. While this establishing sequence has some obvious meanings — the boy's fixation on the world of celebrity basketball and relative distance from the rest of Chicago — it also announces an important element of basketball's media appeal and perhaps that of the film as well: the juxtaposition of the dichotomous worlds of the professional basketball arena and the "street" space of ghetto players. The link between these worlds is widely romanticized in professional basketball and related advertizing, with images of ghetto courts and rusting, netless hoops becoming common symbols of the game's "authenticity." This is to say that the link is also commodified, as professional basketball exploits the "street" image of the game. However, this linkage is rarely treated critically in mass-media representations. This may be due, as Gitanjali Maharaj contends, to a reluctance to engage a central paradox of representations of race in the United States:

*the same late-capitalist economic practices that led to deindustrialization and the decline of black urban communities in the post-World War* II *United States also produced the black basketball star as a commodity and an object of desire for mass consumption; ... both the "nightmare" of the urban ghetto and the "dream" of being a celebrity, professional athlete are manifestations of the economic and cultural workings of late capitalism.*[18]

*Hoop Dreams* allows us to only barely glimpse this paradox and steers clear of engaging its complexities. It reads the difference between street and arena as that between failure and success, suppressing the more ideologically charged connotations of pathology and redemption.

The socioeconomic underpinnings of the Hoop Dream point us back to the effects of postindustrial decline on American inner cities, particularly to the transformations in the roles and meanings of labor and recreation among the urban poor. The romance of the ghetto as a space of play (not only in *Hoop Dreams* but in much corporate advertising) effaces the impact of the urban political economy on recreational space. As Robin Kelley points out: "Economic restructuring leading to permanent unemployment, the shrinking of city services ... the decline of parks, youth programs, and public schools, all have altered the terrain of play and creative expression for black youth."[19] One result of these processes is that "the pursuit of leisure, pleasure, and creative expression is *labor*" for many young black people in the postindustrial ghetto.[20] *Hoop Dreams* ignores the role of the urban economy in creating new conditions for play-as-labor and encouraging self-commodification among young black males. It only allows one of its protagonists a flickering recognition of how play is turned into labor late in the film when William expresses his disillusionment with the pressures on him to succeed and observes that playing basketball has become a "job." At best, this functions as an aspect of the film's fragmented critique of exploitation, but even this is defused as William's increasingly dejected characterization symbolically associates him with the failed men of the film (Bo and Curtis) and the narrative moves on to focus on the drama of Arthur's more fulsome pursuit of success.

**The "Problem" of the Underclass** As liberal ethnographies of underclass life, *There Are No Children Here* and *Hoop Dreams* effectively evoke compassion for their subjects. However, they also frame their subjects within ideological and narrative structures that reproduce one of the most common assumptions about the underclass, that it is always already outside normative citizenship. Though they encourage different modes of identification — with narratives of innocence and aspiration — these texts distance the reader/viewer from the material realities of the worlds they represent. While Kotlowitz has a coming-of-age story deflect the differences of race and poverty, the filmmakers allow the driving narrative of the Dream and the spectacle of play — the recurrent imagery of black bodies performing on court, invested with aspirations — to subsume their critical intentions. Moreover, both texts exhibit the ethnographic fallacy of sharply delineating "the behavior at close range but obscure the less proximate and less visible structures and processes that engender and sustain that behavior."[21] By ultimately reinforcing a sense of intractable difference and distance surrounding the ghetto poor, they reproduce mystifications about race, class, and poverty

19 Kelley, "Playing for Keeps," 198.

20 Ibid., 197.

21 Stephen Steinberg, quoted in Micaela di Leonardo, *Exotics at Home: Anthropologies, Others, American Modernity* (Chicago: University of Chicago Press, 1998), 121.

common to mass-media representations of the underclass. The underclass remains a "problem of race" in these texts (even as they suggest this problem may be overcome, through the struggle to survive or escape), contained within the other America of the postindustrial ghetto.

Anne Gotman

# Hospitality as a Condition of Urbanity: Ethnography of a "Stopping Place"

*Keywords:* ■ *Empirical Sociology* ■ *Welfare System* ■ AIDS

**Hospitality as an Experience of Limits** The following experience related by a woman occurred in Paris in 1989:

*"In the hospital B., I met a young man who must have been about 20 to 25 years old. My husband had to pass a load of exams, which took very long. The weather was nice and I was waiting for him outside in the garden. A young man came and sat down next to me while I was reading a magazine about fantastic cinema. We started talking about movies and I told him, 'If you like, you may keep it.' He replied, 'I'd love to, since I'm hospitalized here.' I proposed to bring him more copies of the magazine as I visited the place every day. He said, 'Alright, I'd love that' and gave me the number of his building and room number, and two or three days later I went back to see him. But when I entered the building, people were amazed I was asking to see someone. I had no idea I was in a building strictly reserved for patients with* AIDS. *I asked the nurse, 'Could you go ask this young man whether he wants to see me? I will leave you the parcel. Really, I don't want to impose myself.' She returned and told me, '*O.K.*, come along... Mind you, you will have to put on this, this, and this.' I was transformed into a sort of helmeted diver: in those days, you were still dressed all in white, even your shoes were covered with some sort of gloves. And I said, 'But what's all this?' She told me, 'These people have* HIV.*' In those days, I didn't even know what that meant. And there I discovered people totally separated and treated like pariahs; a disease that was considered dirty; insupportable discrimination; the morbid side of these services. This was really the corridor of death, completely empty, no noise, no colors, and with an utter absence of humanity. You had the impression people were dropped there and that was it. It was there I told myself something really had to be done... I joined Aides after my meeting with this young man."*

Places set up for taking in, looking after, and protecting vulnerable people in turn produce their own barriers. They bring about an impasse for individuals

1 See Donatella Calabi and Jacques Bottin, eds., *Les Etrangers et l'espace physique urbain* (Paris: Editions de la Maison des Sciences de l'Homme, 1999).

and create urbanites "outside the city." They bring to light the paradox of hospitality, which integrates and separates, includes and excludes. Hospitality issues directly from the existence of boundaries between territories and populations, yet, in order to be effective, draws new surrounding lines of demarcation, which may go so far as to integrate no longer and only to lock up. Having crossed those invisible barriers, the visiting woman was determined to reopen the city to the diseased, to push back the frontiers that had closed down on those whom society, with an eye to looking after them, had relegated to the status of non-member.

**Urban Sites of Hospitality** The passer-by and the poor, the stranger and the invalid, the pilgrim and the beggar: to those categories hospitality in the Judeo-Christian tradition is due. It was for them that the hospices, hospitals, and hostels bequeathed by that same tradition were built. The list of places and buildings reserved to people who are either temporarily or permanently deprived of a home is long. The existence of such a list itself already indicates the simultaneous processes of integration and discrimination among beneficiaries. The history of hospices, hospitals, hostels, and hostelries in the Middle Ages, the more recent history of almshouses, night-shelters, or insane asylums, the contemporary history of the medicalized hospital, of the shelters and homes with which we are familiar today — all these histories testify to the place of hospitality in the urban landscape. But they also testify to the oscillations to which hospitality has been subject — at one time included within the physical urban space, at another expelled beyond its perimeter — and to processes of a growing discrimination and specialization. The hospitality that is due to people deprived of a home, moreover, represents only one aspect of hospitality: that of being free of charge — a gratuitous character first insured by religious institutions, then largely taken over by the welfare state (at least in Western Europe). The hospitality that is due to one's equals, to friends, parents, business relations, partners, colleagues, and so forth, entails not only this gratuitous character, but also the aspect of reciprocity, which is unavailable to beneficiaries of public hospitality. The second type of hospitality, which is extended in hotels and individual homes as well as in community centers, although less visible, constitutes a dimension of urban hospitality that is no less important, witness the history of the *fondaci*, of the *scuole*, and of *guild halls* — veritable cities within the city where residing strangers were able to sojourn, conduct trade, meet up, relax, and, on certain occasions, invite inhabitants from the city.[1] Parallel to such family- or community-based forms of lodging and accommodation, there are also the commercial modes of hospitality — guest houses, boarding houses, inns, public houses, and hotels of all sorts — which constitute a resource for travelers of all types that is at once ancient and growing.

**Strangers to the Organization and the Needs of Reintegration** If hospitality has thus bequeathed an important urban patrimony to the contemporary city, its situation today touches on three major questions: that of the migration movements which continue to feed the growth of cities and which, owing to the principle of free circulation, bring society in contradiction with itself; that of the limits of institutional mechanisms of solidarity which eject a growing number of citizens from the "system" and demand new protocols of access to fundamental resources and protection; and finally, that of the multiplication of urban services which increasingly draw citizens out of their homes and give rise to new needs of reception. As an extension of migration movements and an embodiment of the heterogeneity of coexistent cultures, as a reinforcer of social inequalities and an index of the insufficiency of systems of solidarity, and as the locale of a growing public service and of an increasing institutionalization of everyday life, the contemporary city produces three categories of strangers and three levels of strangeness, depending on its growth and diversification: strangers to a country, strangers to a city, strangers to an organization. To the strangers and the poor who constituted the classic beneficiaries of a public, free, non-reciprocal hospitality, we should today add the beneficiaries of public services who, for different reasons, cannot be reintegrated into the city: those unemployed who stay locked up in their homes, unable to regain their footing in the economic city; or those hospitalized incapable of asserting their autonomy, removed from public life, even though included in specific systems of protection. The reasons for their deadlocks are numerous.

Specifically with reference to persons affected by HIV (our concern here), people will point to the disease itself and its social dimension, which in more than one respect is "exceptional." To be sure, the double stigmatization (social *and* physical) of those who are called "high-risk groups" has ceded, in the case of AIDS, to a more "liberal management" of the epidemic. This has been translated in the abandonment of discriminatory terminologies and the renunciation of coercive measures of removal. The appeal to an individual mastery of risks and to solidarity with infected people, moreover, has opened an unusual space for associative and cooperative action that, by being aimed at supporting infected people, turns its back resolutely on the epidemic model of isolation. Still, "the norm of tolerance remains fragile" and infected people continue to be confronted with multiple forms of rejection.[2] In addition to social representations of the disease, we should also invoke the evolution in urban life overall, which makes that

2 See Claudine Herzlich and Philippe Adam, "Urgence sanitaire et liens sociaux: l'exceptionnalité du sida?" *Cahiers Internationaux de Sociologie* 102 (1997): 5-28.

3 Jane Jacobs, *The Death and Life of Great American Cities* (New York: Random House, 1961), 30.

today, as Jane Jacobs says, "To any one person, strangers are far more common in big cities than acquaintances."[3] As cities are more and more populated by strangers, the urban way of life calls for an ever greater number of go-betweens and translators. The shortage of the latter explains the growing number of misunderstandings, incomprehensions, and rebuffs. The fragmentation of specialized interventions, the distancing techniques employed by the occupants of "front offices" faced with the demands of the public, the anonymity and impersonal character of bureaucratic relationships — all of these contribute to the structuring of everyday relationships in terms of "members" and "non-members." The latter become "strangers to the organization" to which they have managed to gain access without therefore succeeding to make themselves heard, and without truly entering in a relationship with the members of the service. The AIDS epidemic has functioned as an eye-opener in this respect, and the initiatives taken by the associative sector at the heart of institutions (most notably in hospitals) or in their periphery emphasize the multiple occasions for urban hospitality engendered by the contemporary city.

**Definition of a "Stopping Place"** In 1996, seven years after the episode related above, the Ile-de-France committee of *Aides* opens a "place of reception" in the center of Paris under the name of "Arc en Ciel" ("Rainbow"). The place, to which you gain access through a small staircase, occupies three floors of a local-style apartment block (a so-called *immeuble*) that also comprises other occupants. The lateral and streetside blocks contain both apartments and professional and commercial premises. This "big warm house with its colors, light, and comfortable furniture, where it is good to spend a moment," inspired by foreign reception centers like The Lighthouse in London, has been conceived for maintaining the "well-being" and the "quality of life of persons afflicted by HIV." It is at the disposal of women, men, and children who are confronted with the virus on a daily basis. Without extending medical care, it offers a collection of resources aimed at helping to fight the disease, directly or indirectly. Breaking the isolation of afflicted persons — including the isolation which attends contact with medical personnel — and reconstituting social links around the disease are, in conjunction with the recovery of physical and individual well-being, the objectives of a place that seeks to inscribe itself in individual geographies which have been rudely shaken by the disease and, frequently, by the loss of the near and dear. The ground floor comprises two salons, a library, a dining room for sixty people opening onto a garden, a commemoration room, several activity rooms for various workshops, and more general service rooms. The second floor comprises offices and a meeting room reserved in principle to administrative staff and volunteers. Finally, the basement contains still more activity rooms for other workshops. Admission, free of charge, is subject to an introductory interview. In the first two years since its opening, the active body of "participants" (in the designation chosen by users) has been around 700 people.

**Newcomers** Although the place is only a few years old, it already contains different generations of afflicted people. "Seniority" in being HIV positive divides the population into "old" and "new" — into those who have begun their "careers" before the arrival of tri-therapies and seen their circles of friends melt away, and those who, having lived with those therapies from the start, are nevertheless less numerous to follow treatment than their fellows of longer standing. We find, in other words, both people who are undergoing treatment — the large majority, some 85%, in the form of bi-, tri-, and quadri-therapy, and as part of research experiments — and people who do not, or are no longer doing so, either because they have no need for it, or else because they refuse to. There are those who have known periods of hospitalization and those who have not; those who support treatment well — the majority: some 70% — and those who do not, and live alone most of the time. It should be noted also that the treatment is itself an entire way of life. It involves a relationship with your body, a relationship with yourself, and a relationship with others. It also structures everyday life. The majority of participants live alone; others live in couples or families, and many live "with" a television set. A majority again does not have a professional occupation, and less than half of these are officially invalid. The income level is less than 6,000 French francs (some 1,000 U.S. dollars) per month for more than 50% of participants. Ties with the family (preserved, tightened, or broken) as well as with friends (still numerous or drastically dwindled) in turn make up for strongly contrasting situations. Participants are on average between 30 and 50 years old, with a very strong preponderance of men (80%). The dominance of homosexual participants is obvious and even more outspoken because it is almost all male. A majority of participants are tenants living in central Paris: only 35% come from departments in the peripheral *banlieue*. Whether the population of Arc en Ciel is representative of the epidemic? Not entirely. Still, in the course of the years, it has put on the face of the epidemic's diversity, with the arrival of women (who are among the younger participants) and sometimes of their children; of persons contaminated through toxicomania; and of foreigners (with or without papers, some at the end of immigrational procedures, others juridically in a tight spot) — a new type of sick who have never looked after themselves and often arrive in very bad shape, the descendants to a first wave of arrivals who, in the meantime, have already had to learn how to "grieve about grief."

**In Transition** Receiving while yet letting go: that is the philosophy of the center, which is precisely that of hospitality itself. As a "stopping place," Arc en Ciel in no sense wishes to bind its clientele. Rather, it aims to restore a kind of autonomy, no matter how restricted, that has been compromised by the disease. To organize the transition for people who are traversing the stages of a disease or who, suffering from a chronic illness, are being abandoned whenever they leave the hospital, is a means of preventing and acting timely: at the point when difficulties threaten to appear and not when problems are at their worst. "There are still gaps we haven't managed to close," says the initiator of the project. "We have to move from a stage where we conceive of the 'social' in terms of financial or technical aid and assistance to the next stage. Our society has shown itself able to pay for the first level of help in extending services, in building hospitals. Today, we have to move beyond that. Arc en Ciel is this new type of social aid which is something else than merely talking money."

What is this new type of social facility made of, and in which respects does it differ from traditional social instruments? There is, first of all, the composition of the body of hosting "staff," which relies on some one hundred volunteers, who belong themselves to different "generations" of volunteering: some of them are uniquely active in the field of AIDS, while others also volunteer elsewhere. To support the work of volunteers, seventeen permanent staff are employed full-time, only part of whom are paid by the organization. As far as modes of access to the center are concerned, they are comparable to those of a club, even if we are talking of an open club. Admission is preceded by an interview in the course of which the newcomer explains his needs. This rite of passage also allows the person to establish a first relationship and join the new community. The future member then receives a number, which he has to announce whenever he passes by the reception and in exchange for which he has access to messages left in place: this system insures the protection both of the place and of the identity of people. The newcomer will find at Arc en Ciel all the ingredients of aid: information on the disease and possible therapies, activities for well-being, thematic conversation groups, some assistance even; social, juridical, and therapeutic consultations; re-dynamizing workshops and workshops for physical or artistic expression; a nutrition workshop, the only one with a therapeutical import insofar as nutritional practices, for people confronted with HIV, involve a dimension of care; diverse services like a library, tickets for spectacles, and announcements. All these activities are free of charge.

Owing to the diversity in types of aid, participants can profit from different types of follow-up, and thus they can start weighing again on their own destinies. In response to the evolution of its clientele, however, the method of reception has already had to be adapted. Participation in workshop activities can no longer be the single admission ticket to Arc en Ciel, even if refocusing efforts in this direction have been undertaken. "People who have been living in the street cannot be dropped in a yoga workshop" — a comment that sums up the turning point taken by a house that is no longer dealing with a demand for physical resources only, but now also finds on its doorstep young and not-so-young people looking for a place to live, to take care of themselves, and to eat at reduced prices... Temporary shelter, springboard, switch-platform, distributor of help: only by diversifying its palette of services is Arc en Ciel able to extend a helping hand to persons in distress, who "on top of everything else" have been afflicted by HIV. One of those helping hands is the "Lift Off" program, set up for helping people who would like to go back to work, enabling them to immerse themselves in work without changing their status. The idea of a missing link between hospital and home on which Arc en Ciel is founded is equally valid with respect to employment: without gangway or transition between unemployment and work, the step can only be illusory, if not fatal.

**A Place of Confidence and Integration** Besides aid in a strict sense, the newcomer may find all the ingredients of hospitality in place, which prompt people not only to turn but to return to Arc en Ciel. First of all, during their formation hosts are given corrective instructions for courtesy on the topics of homosexuality, of AIDS, and of the relationship with others in general. "To speak a clear language" on a certain number of questions means to shatter all those prejudices susceptible of hurting the newcomer, to be able to show him interest, attention, and consideration. This courteous neutrality in its own way is a codification of rules of hospitality aimed at insuring the security of the guest when he appears at your doorstep. Such a codification of rules is all the more necessary since the guest arrives not only with a disease but often with a death wish, with grief, anxiety, distress, stories of misfortune.

A place of hospitality also treasures the memory and traces of its visitors. It is a place where you are recognized, and where you do not come incognito, without being greeted or addressed. Anybody demanding the right to tranquility must avoid these places. To anyone who looks for contact, on the other hand, they are valuable, and for those who want to remain socially visible even more so. People return to Arc en Ciel because they can deposit their misfortunes there, question them, recall the dead, but also because they exist for others there. Even when they are away for a while, their absence is noted.

4 See Anne Gotman, "La question de l'hospitalité aujourd'hui," *Communications* 65 (1997): 5-21.

The nexus of social life is the dining room, used by more than 70% of participants: "It's there that everything happens, everyone stops, exchanges take place, meals are taken; it's the heart of the place." Nutritional function, pleasure principle, and conviviality are inseparable here. Alone, you do not bother to cook, and the act of coming over to eat (or even be waited upon) for someone who is adrift is as much a gesture of survival as it is a way of reengaging with a feeding other. On the other hand, the reduction of the usage of the center to the satisfaction of needs is a threat that constantly weighs on the group. The fear of seeing Arc en Ciel turn into a canteen or club, a place to which people frequently only turn for eating in the company of others, is perceptible. It is the hospitality dimension of the place that is at stake — whether people only come to receive (in the sense of enjoying the advantage of something) or even merely to pay for receiving. An office for social aid or a service, state or market: those are the two negative poles between which Arc en Ciel tries to maintain itself in trying to balance gift and countergift.

Arc en Ciel cannot be equated with an office for social aid. This is also clear from the importance of "meetings." The attempts at restoring a rapport with others, at escaping the social torpor in which the disease winds up locking the weak, turns this place into something of a goal to achieve. The fact of having another place to go to and of once again making a move, of willingly exiling yourself for two hours every day and taking up transport — 83% of participants come by bus or metro — is a first step towards resocialization. Is it not hospitality, after all, which permits individuals or families from different places to *form a community*, to offer each other lodgings, to render each other mutual services — an *expenditure* that allows the group to expand, to circulate, and to multiply mutual relationships?[4] Having somewhere to go to is important, but having a time schedule is just as much so. Social normality is displayed in the use of time and the use of a pocket calendar, and anybody who is no longer linked to the social pendulum threatens to feel lost. Some participants come every day, others several times a week, and still others several times a month; some more during the week, others on Saturday...

**A Something Extra...** If time is a structuring element of social integration, so is space. What symbolizes the hospitality dimension of Arc en Ciel perhaps most is the fact that the place is at once perceived and intended as beautiful. This quality, noted by different audiences, is almost unanimously remarked upon. The aesthetic choices use the vocabulary of modernism without imposing that of modernity; they propose a palette of colors and of materials that combine clarity and warmth, thereby avoiding the double snag of minimalism and of condescendence.

Qualifiers like "warm," "bright," "vast," and "agreeable" used by participants testify to the non-conflictual appropriation of an aesthetic that is nevertheless devoid of complacency. Yet the aesthetic of the place is not only appreciated for its qualities of comfort but also for its moral connotation: the beautiful here refers to the better. It is something extra that does not correspond to a need but to an aspiration. The beautiful here is opposed to the "social" as well as to the functional and to the strictly necessary in which social aid ensconces itself on purpose. The beautiful, as common good, accessible to all, serves as an antithesis to the "shit" reserved to the poor. It serves as an index of universality and furthers integration. Yet again, beauty also has its "flipside" — you acquire a taste for it, you install yourself in it — and from a place of passage Arc en Ciel fears to become a place of sojourn. This raises the specter of a chronicization that bedevils the whole issue of hospitality, a movement by which the (temporal and spatial) limits supposed to warrant the protection and security of guests are inverted into barriers and become instruments of a loss of autonomy. This sedentarization, nevertheless, may signify something else: that you have found security, that you have reached the finish.

**Receiving** "Hostess," "Master of the House": this terminology reappears today in many residences and specialized centers seeking to dissociate themselves from the image of impersonal reception that obtains in institutions. Thus, the project of Arc en Ciel calls its director "master of the house" and chooses the designation "dining room" instead of "restaurant." The people in charge of reception are permanent staff. Some work in reception only, others are also engaged in the management and administration of the center. It is the volunteers, of course, who take it upon them to entertain, welcome, help, and so forth. However, participants, too, contribute their share towards a task that is non-specialized but taken care of simultaneously or successively by everyone. This modus operandi is not dissimilar with that governing domestic space, where nobody is host or guest by name and everybody may perform the roles in turn. But contrary to what is the case in domestic space, there is no "numerus clausus" or fixed number for the hosts and guests of Arc en Ciel, who are invited to take care of reception in great numbers, if for no other reason than to replace those who leave.

The idea of reception at Arc en Ciel is based on several principles. Here, first, we do not find an office window or counter, but proximity, that master word of the modes of approach between receivers and received, translated in this case into an absence of spatial barriers, so that the entire territory is accessible to all. The second principle is the proximity between volunteers and permanent staff, which means that a volunteer at the reception performs the same job as a salaried worker, and that in the dining room, salaried staff and volunteers serve indiscriminately. The third and final guiding principle for the reception at Arc en Ciel is that everyone should participate actively in the maintenance of relationships with the general public. If those in charge of reception only "do fieldwork," those in charge of administration should join them just as much, starting with the director, who is expected to be also around in his function of master of the house. Neither client nor beneficiary of a service, the participant of Arc en Ciel is treated as, properly speaking, the guest, inasfar as he has in front of him a person who is there in his name, an alter ego who is neither the representative of an institution nor the occupant of a function.

**"You Are at Home Here"** This motto of Arc en Ciel, this injunction to create your own place, expects participants to be active rather than passive; it expects them to take part in the work of hospitality and to become themselves hosts or masters of the place. In providing a first handle for integration to newcomers by placing them in a situation where they may themselves also give, the strategy of Arc en Ciel revolves around the organization of reciprocity. This demand for participation, moreover, is consistent with the option to constitute a "place of second-level reception" that excludes "extreme visitors" — this in opposition to a first-level reception that is open to anyone. This partiality in selecting people with the capacity for integration, socialization, and exchange, so as to insure the work of consolidation and prevention, rests on a concept of hospitality that operates in stages. Against an "open-door" approach, it assumes a discrimination of visitors and their inequality with respect to the capacity to engage in exchanges. Participants contribute towards the task of reception through a house committee, but also in more informal ways by helping a hand, by jointly preparing the table, by turning a particular experience into good account, or else by committing themselves to a pseudo-permanent availability for answering questions, discussing, and meeting newcomers. The installation of an S.E.L. (Système d'Echange Local), an exchange system that permits people who have been ejected from the labor system to recover a social role by putting their professional qualifications at the disposal of everyone, derives from the same wish to stimulate exchange among participants.

**Intersecting Hospitalities** Whereas participants of Arc en Ciel are not only the guests but also the hosts of the place, volunteers say they, too, find a place of hospitality there. Sometimes they have already been welcomed as former participants. As infected volunteers who have escaped a fate that has not spared close friends, they come here to look for a refuge from the assaults of culpability and of the survivor syndrome. Uninfected volunteers, wishing to escape a life of protection, in turn, feel the dire need to rejoin a more naked existence, often after having reached the truth of being that is experienced as a kind of revelation. For those exiled from the disease, the act of coming to Arc en Ciel means traveling again, exposing themselves, taking leave of a truncated self and an incomplete existence, enriching themselves. Anybody who receives the sick (and extends hospitality to them) receives from them in profusion: gift and countergift occur simultaneously here. Sometimes, Arc en Ciel functions as "an open door" for volunteers, a place of integration where it is possible to better accept their homosexuality and make friends. Finally, as a working environment, Arc en Ciel offers to permanent staff who are HIV positive a relatively protected (although fragile) environment. And for volunteers and salaried workers who are HIV negative, it offers an almost experimental environment.

Another index of the appropriation of the place by participants and their hosts is the fact that all of them invite their close relatives and friends. Likewise, life in Arc en Ciel is exported outside and participants also meet beyond its premises. Circles of sociability may thus cut across one another, to a greater or a lesser extent, and Arc en Ciel may form a locus of privileged crossings. Still, there is a certain desire to keep such circles at a distance. To the boundaries set up from within by those who have been inflicted should be added the boundaries imposed from outside by those who have not, and who are not inclined to enter what to them remains a different world.

**Primary and Secondary Hosts: "Masters" and "Servants"** That participants are "at home" in Arc en Ciel is, however, only true up to a point and derives from the same fiction that would reduce the practice of hospitality to the moment of welcome and to the space of the salon, while forgetting that this practice is performed in a house kept by hosts, or sometimes their aides, who are being mobilized beyond the act of reception in a strict sense. The fact that hosts are united in a single designation is no more than a linguistic convenience destined to momentarily erase the duality of the population — volunteers and permanent staff — that shares the responsibility of the framework within which participants support, meet, and welcome each other.

Who, one might well ask, are the masters of the house and who their aides? Who are the principal hosts and who the secondary ones? The definition itself of Arc en Ciel and of *Aides* in general, as an association of *volunteers*, in principle turns the latter group into the principal hosts. Contrary to what is the case with

5 See Felicity Heal, *Hospitality in Early Modern England* (Oxford: Clarendon Press, 1990).

benevolence, volunteer work relies on an obligatory and not a discretionary commitment. Its commitment is social and not merely moral. And indeed, the role of volunteers is primary in how the institution functions. They are hierarchically higher than permanent staff, who are in some sense at their service. It is volunteers, through the administrative council, who define the strategy, the objectives, the methodology, and the politics of the association. They are the "anima," the driving force of an action which in no case wants to be caught in the trap of social institutions, and which, for that reason, appeals to individuals and not just to qualifications. The latter, demanded of permanent staff, are only there for optimizing and giving durability to their actions. Yet again, if the instrument for promoting this durability, instead of taking the painstaking route via higher echelons normally called for, consists rather of insuring everyday business, the relationship between permanent staff and volunteers may be inverted. Permanence, an apparently secondary criterion, may in certain circumstances become principal, and the person insuring it may become the veritable master of the house. In a structure of continuous reception, without office window, back office, or front office, the permanent person actually finds himself in the front row. Compared to volunteers who drop by intermittently and perceive only fragments of reality, he performs what he calls "supervolunteer work," since he is there "24 hours a day." If permanent staff thus leave volunteers behind them, it is not hard to imagine how these "masters of the house" may begin to run the house by delegation, and how, after the image of what happened in the grand English mansions of the 17th century, visitors are received in the absence of the real masters, the latter having left for London, where aristocrats were jostling each other while still remaining attached to their reputation for hospitality. Often, the visitors' stay was all the more pleasant, since instructions had been given to servants to make sure that visitors were received generously, and that the obligations of hospitality were honored exactly as should be. Some visitors even preferred to come when hosts were absent in order to spare themselves the burden of reciprocity and to feel freer. In due course, however, when generosity started to subside, these houses became only accessible at a charge and gradually changed into museums of hospitality.[5]

**The Limits of Hospitality: Violated Boundaries...** As a place without boundaries, Arc en Ciel is a theater of proximity, but also a scene of conflicts engendered by the cohabitation of different factions of the population who either ignore the barriers and the prohibitions necessitated by the demands of cohabitation or else raise invisible protective barriers around them against whatever erupts within their common space. As an open yet structured place, the space of

Arc en Ciel is subject to all the infringements that characterize domestic spaces everyday, and to all the border wars that oppose occupants at different times of the day. Here as there, it is the ambiguity of the status of the place that causes problems — the overlapping between rights of ownership and rights of use. Common spaces are of course most frequently exposed to conflicts of territoriality and to confusions between "chez soi" and "chez nous," between "being at home" and "being among us." The outbursts when people violate the psychical limits of another person's receptivity are in turn hard to contain.

We should also reckon with the confusion between Arc en Ciel and external places not conforming to the habits of the "house." Arc en Ciel is a place for keeping up health, a place of certain sexual prohibitions. It is no sales outlet for alcoholic beverages, nor does it allow the exchange of drugs or smoking. It is no place for sexual scoring, and calls to order are just as badly taken here as in families, where the exclusiveness of power to lay down rules is increasingly being contested. In response to such outbursts, two attitudes can be found: first, a reaffirmation of the necessity of rules and, as a result, of enforcing respect for them — of surveillance, policing, explaining, remaining vigilant. Parallel to this legalistic attitude, a second attitude consists of reaffirming and preserving the particular qualities of Arc en Ciel that turn it into a protected zone where the laws of society need not be enforced when they are held to be unjust, and where humanity has to take the upperhand of legality. "Arc en Ciel has to be a place of nuance in comparison with society." The proposal by the council of the house to make sure that every expulsion is followed up, so that expelled persons "are not completely locked out," thus aims to preserve a place of belonging, a sort of sanctuary of social links that guards against all the vicissitudes of communal life, after the image of religious or familial sanctuaries...

**... and Erected Boundaries** To be able to realize itself under the best of conditions, hospitality presupposes equipments, rooms, resources, and an organization set up to this end. But hospitality also resides — to some even in the first

6 As Jean-Michel Belorgey writes, "You do not offer hospitality because you are available or prosperous. Hospitality means sharing, even of penury, even of a limited time and space. In other words, it remains an issue, and may indeed be an issue more than ever, when you have not organized yourself to practise it, when there is no pavilion or apartment for the guests, no *spare room*, and you have to give your own bed; when there is no margin or reserve, and you have to deprive yourself." ["On n'accorde pas l'hospitalité parce qu'on est disponible ou prospère; l'hospitalité est partage, même de la pénurie, même d'un temps et d'un espace compté; autrement dit elle demeure d'actualité, à moins qu'elle ne soit surtout d'actualité, quand on ne s'est pas organisé pour la pratiquer, qu'il n'y a pas de pavillon ou d'appartement des hôtes, de *chambre à donner*, et qu'il faut donner son propre lit, quand il n'y a pas de marge, et de réserve, et qu'il faut se priver."] "Etrange-étrangers," in *Ville et Hospitalité: Textes de synthèse, Table ronde du 24 avril 1997, Bilan et perspectives* (Paris: Fondation Maison des Sciences de l'Homme - Plan Construction et Architecture, November 1997), 77-81. English translation by the editors.

place — in the acceptance of the unforeseen, the capacity to make room for the newcomer, for the extra person.[6] Today, it is precisely such originally unforeseen, if not unforeseeable, newcomers that Arc en Ciel has to welcome, and it is notably between settled participants and those who seek to become so that physical and especially verbal barriers are erected. If the creational myth of Arc en Ciel should be believed, a first reigning dynasty, that of "fancy queens," was placed under the sign of homosexuality and of social prestige. These myths have as their function to proclaim and hide at the same time: proclaim the original "folly" of a place supposedly conceived of as a "holiday resort for people with HIV"; hide under the denunciation of an outrageously unsocial project the nostalgia for a golden age that was not yet troubled by precariousness and toxicomania. The all-too-real arrival of the latter, corresponding to the sociodemographical evolution of the epidemic, is both greeted and apprehended, and the uncoupling of homosexual identity proves hard to achieve.

Although open on the outside to all those affected by the disease and to all links in the chain — homosexuality, heterosexuality, toxicomania (and blood transfusion) —, the house has in reality compartmentalized on the inside. As often, the lowering of external barriers brings along the apparition of internal barriers. The first of these runs between toxicomaniacs and non-toxicomaniacs. The new precariousness hardly brings participants and hosts any closer together, since the latter tend to lose spirit in view of the complexity of social problems which push problems related to the disease into the background. Toxicomania, hepatitis C, distress, misery: coping with all these ills threatens to transform Arc en Ciel into an institution for general aid. What to do — fling the doors wide open to a mix of miseries by adding a new room for the not-yet-lost, or stop up the openings of a house that in order to welcome has to offer a protected space? This is the double snag. Besides the barriers between hosts and guests, there are the dividing lines among guests that render the geography of the place more complex than at first sight. Superimposed upon the boundary between toxicomaniacs and non-toxicomaniacs is a fault line between homosexuals and heterosexuals, which is made visible by the boundaries of sex and age superimposed upon them. Women (both European and African), mothers, young heterosexuals, and homosexuals thus exchange glances more readily than words. While participants remain deaf to one another, relationships in return become charged with images and start to fix the contours of the "other." Otherness is constructed and polarized on the basis of sex, sexual orientation, age, visibility, and so forth — to which today should be added the quality of being a foreigner. Faced with many hostile remarks (homophobic, xenophobic, or misogynistic), volunteers have to keep putting up resistance. If the spoken word may knock over barriers, it is above all by overturning fantasms, by casting a gangway, as one of the go-betweens says, between the alien, unknown, imagined stranger and the real stranger who comes to Arc en Ciel. And this involves playing the role of the host to the full.

**Hospitality, Neighborliness, and the City** Arc en Ciel is no island. As a place of hospitality, it exists only thanks to the hospitality of the outer world, the world of citizens and of neighbors. The host of a place like it, as the fable of La Fontaine put it, is the "natural" occupant and, transposed to human society, the legitimate occupant. He is entitled to the place. If hospitality consists of making room for somebody else, there are indeed a thousand reasons to refuse it. This is especially the case with institutions proposing to welcome those for whom the city does not make (enough) room. Thus, before being able to cast anchor, Arc en Ciel had to stomach countless rebuffs, "disguised" or "deflected" refusals that surfaced as soon as property owners discovered the association's goal. The phenomenon known by the acronym of NIMBY ("not in my backyard") is reproduced almost everywhere in the same fashion, and arguments are organized around a few typical schemes: threats to public order (the potential attractiveness of these centers), assaults on personal security (violence, aggression, theft), effects on property values (the risk of real-estate devaluation). The relationships with co-proprietors have been hardly more favorable. Not a single question for modifications implying the agreement of co-proprietors was granted, in particular questions related to accessibility. The relationships with neighboring occupants of the *immeubles* sharing the entrance and the courtyard, by contrast, have evolved more favorably. The early hostility has been followed by a period of acceptance and of cooperation, which persists thanks to the vigilance of all parties involved. Insults, hate mail, threats of legal action, departures: the first signs sent to newcomers, accusing them of being rowdy, irrespectful of rules and regulations, and dangerous to children, have gradually subsided. Several factors have contributed to this: the renewal of the population, which has replaced hostile tenants by occupants who are *a priori* better disposed; the sending of a delegate by Arc en Ciel charged with negotiating peace pacts; the multiplication of contacts; and finally an ostentatious surveillance. Today, young tenants come over to have coffee and eat, superintendents are used to do the cleaning, and exchanges of services are slowly beginning to happen.

With respect to shopkeepers in the neighborhood, a similar strategy has been followed. Those with whom it has proved possible to develop privileged relationships are admitted to have lunch or dinner. They are also selected for spreading a favorable image of the house. "A whole education has happened," thanks to a go-between familiar with both cultures, someone who is both a host at

Arc en Ciel *and* responsible for provisioning. Fund-raising, too, constitutes an invisible part of the work of hospitality, which implies attempts at demonstrating the value of the enterprise in terms of the public interest and of returns for society that might justify making a social contribution — subsidies, but especially gifts, the latter representing 85% of the financing of Arc en Ciel. What might the public interest gain from this type of hospitality, however? For government agencies, the advantage resides above all in actions related to "health care" — a recognized aspect of public benefit. Conviviality and sociability do not fall within their authority or jurisdiction, at least not in this field, and taking care of those aspects (if that is how the two fields may be distinguished) reverts in the main to private benefactors, ostensibly far better informed about the social benefit of hospitality than government agencies. At this stage, however, the question arises whether the situation is really balanced, whether Arc en Ciel "does not yield more to the state than the state gives," and whether hospitality should not form the object of a politics on the part of the general public. We are still a long cry from this, and although all politicians who have come to visit the center have sung its praises, Arc en Ciel at this time remains quite solidly "a commercial place." To become a "social place" is not the aim either, as we have seen. "Fifty-fifty" would be, in the eyes of those responsible, the desired formula: it would allow them not to transform the place into sheer "administration" and to retain a foot in the outside world. Fifty for durability, a necessary condition for the life of a collective that is faced with the same precariousness as its "clients," even though it is meant to fight this precariousness; fifty for remaining open to the world, since the search for private funding forces one "to take position with respect to the outer world." The latter demand in fact remains crucial for a collective institution whose *raison d'être* is openness to the outside.

At the time of writing, the medical section of the London Lighthouse has just closed down and the proceeds of *Sidaction*, the national French fund-raising for AIDS, has been particularly bad, which has allowed feelings of unrest and insecurity to spread among participants. The inscription of Arc en Ciel in the city, therefore, is not assured, insofar as this inscription relies too exclusively on the economy of gifts. Habituation and demoralization: these are the words that often return to explain the volatility of gifts and the departure of volunteers. Gifts, which are in principle the establishers of links and are kept up by these, have no stability for the very reason that they are subordinated to the quality of those links. Whenever links become complex or fall away, gifts rapidly run out. This economy is especially exhausting in that it necessitates a permanent weighing of gifts and countergifts. Many volunteers wind up telling themselves that they are not being paid back, that they have given enough, that they need to refuel themselves and tap new sources. In a culture where the obligation to give is quite relative, the sentiment of debt is easily reversed, and people pass quickly from the obligation to give to the right to receive (also). The quick turnover of benefactors has no other explanation either. In it we notice the limit of gifts consented without real expectations, distributed somewhat like alms, in passing... Such contributions are by definition fluctuating. As far as links with the state and the third sector are concerned, they, too, highlight a growing imbalance. While the cause of AIDS sets the pace and Arc en Ciel finds itself at one of its famous turning points, the organization, which has opened several branches in the city and the *banlieue*, sees its line of active collaborators expand less and less. The branches in the *banlieue* run at full blast, the lines in the structures of reception with which Arc en Ciel forms a network are overloaded, and the social services with which the collective has developed relations consider the organization as a practical refuge for hopeless situations. Threatened by financial drought, the collective allows itself to be simultaneously recuperated by institutions. Last but not least, the links between Arc en Ciel and the city pass through the volunteers, who are often engaged elsewhere as well, whether in the associative sector, in political organizations, or in specific actions. The cross-pollination of experiences is considered fruitful in itself, and a commitment outside Arc en Ciel is perceived as necessary to advance the interests of the house. However this may be, "to let a place like this live, political action is required." Hospitality invents itself and organizes itself, but it also needs to be given public recognition.

**Conclusion: Hospitality as a Narrow Gate** In calling itself "house" and proclaiming "you are at home here," Arc en Ciel has adopted the language of hospitality. By offering to newcomers well-being and conviviality, it meets the obligations of hospitality. By favoring a passage through Arc en Ciel, it partakes of the temporary dimension of hospitality. And by offering participatory rather than hierarchical modes, it follows the newest code of a contemporary, more egalitarian hospitality. Yet this gamble — for that is what it is — is not without its danger. Like any system of interaction, hospitality knows many possibilities for deviation: chronicization, instrumentalization, institutionalization. Moreover, the model itself is not without its defects. It is by nature unstable. It tolerates professionalization more or less. It creates obligations, and that is a position today that does not go without saying. The system of hospitality, finally, also has limited capacities. It creates, like social aid, its own waiting lines. It is necessarily selective and cannot reconcile the imperatives of equality and pluralism. Above all, hospitality continues to hold a weak status in a society that leaves little room between the commercial sphere and the governmental sphere for a collective action of a different kind. Still, the usefulness of such places can hardly be doubted. As spaces that are not so much indeterminate as composite and complex, they respond better than others to the limits of the provisions of solidarity. Multitudes of receptive places are today needed to reopen a society that ceaselessly shuts itself off and produces “nearby strangers.” Economic powers, those great organizers of today’s society, are unquestionably the first great imposers of barriers. But does not health, today’s most prominent resource, more than ever divide society, despite all countervailing measures, into the sound and the sick? Faced with this challenge, could not Arc en Ciel figure as a concrete utopia, the avantgarde of a long tradition?

*Translation Bart Eeckhout*

**Rudi Laermans**

# Downtown Brussels: A Portrait

*Keywords:* ■ *Sociology* ■ *Politics* ■ *Urbanism*

**1** No search for fanciful words, no elevated expressions bursting with good intentions, no resounding programmatic statements: whoever speaks about downtown Brussels, that little piece of urban reality within and just beyond "The Pentagon" formed by the inner ringroad, has to use a language tailored to the subject. Building companies and real estate developers in Brussels are always quick to come to the point; *flânerie* in this city is synonymous with carefully avoiding potholes in the sidewalk and gazing with admiration at a forest of building cranes; the local cuisine is rough but hearty. Whatever else Brussels may be, it is not a city that asks for polished expressions or glossy metaphors. The powerful, rough-hewn language of manifestoes or the sharp, urgent tone of emergency plans are better attuned to the reality of Brussels. □ Needless to say, there is no such thing as The Real Brussels: the city, its inhabitants, and its varied groups of users are too multiple-sided, too heterogeneous, too opaque to be gathered in a single panoptical glance. Moreover, the long-standing lack of governmental and political clout has resulted in a city full of black holes (urban voids) and festering scars (vacant housing lots). Brussels is an almost indescribable, at times even surreal dreamscape characterized by radical fragmentation, multilingualism, hybridity. *Les extrêmes se touchent*, but literally then: relatively well-preserved buildings are adjacent to slums; behind a historical monument may arise an exceedingly ugly specimen of 1950s functionalism; expensive or trendy restaurants are in out-of-the-way places; from the benches of the *Place des Martyrs*, drunken bums study the to-and-fro of Flemish government ministers; and in and around the *Rue Ribeaucourt*, the metropolitan walk of life (drug pushing, shady dealings in cars or clothes) seems only an inch away from that of the villager (strolling women with baby carriages, gossip on the sidewalks, typically male-bonding cafés, ...). For that reason, Brussels has little tolerance for absolute claims or univocal definitions. Yes, it is the only Belgian metropolis — but it is also a place where, because of the many immigrant communities, you continuously run into gestures, clothes, rituals, and other lively expressions that point to a disappearing localism. Yes, it is a multicultural city — but without many cross-fertilizations, exchanges, or "acculturations." A civilized indifference, which in Flemish eyes always appears a little sophisticated and mundane, predominates in social contacts. Even the local beggars address you in two words: "*Bonjour Monsieur*, you wouldn't happen to have five francs?" (And even if you fail to give, they will still often wish you "a pleasant day.") Life here is lived without many illusions, alone or in families, and you simply try to make the best of it. The typically Belgian device — *on s'en-fout-pas-mal* — is brought to a head in this city: we don't give a damn, we manage to get by, we live and let live. ☐ Question: How did it ever come to this? A rudimentary diagnosis is quickly made: urban flight, urbanicide, and the destruction of the historical patrimony since the end of the fifties; wild, governmentally uncontained immigration flows in the sixties and seventies; deindustrialization and impoverishment during the eighties and nineties. No less obvious are the remedies: reinforcement of the residential function; job creation for semi- and unskilled workers; more Belgian families with children; suitable schooling for young immigrants; decent social housing, ... And above all, the right to vote for anyone who has been living here for at least five years, and more financial solidarity between the rich and poor municipalities which the Capital Region is constituted by. (This so-called Capital Region or "Greater Brussels" is the politico-administrative compromise that makes up larger Brussels, the third of three regions in Belgium, along with Flanders and Wallonia.) With culture, let alone the arts, this has nothing to do, which is why cultural institutions and initiatives in the context of Brussels could do with a little more modesty. Neither prosperity nor well-being depend on an exhibition more or less, even if it shows Moroccan tapestries. Whoever pictures culture or the arts as an essential lever for the desired rejuvenation of Brussels seems bound to lapse into an obfuscating, *ideological* discourse.

**2** A Benjaminian thought: Brussels is modernity in a state of ruin, beyond the point where one might still believe in something like complete salvation. Optimism, therefore, is out of place, and certainly the utopian belief in wonders or miracles. A dying city has no need for quacks: it needs painkillers and nurses. In accordance with this image, in fact, Brussels continuously calls forth a single basic mood: nostalgia, the indefinable desire for a different present, or for a past which retrospectively appears always larger, more interesting, or simply more civilized than it probably ever was. Nostalgia for the long-lost grandeur of shortly after the turn of the century: Horta! *Art Nouveau*! The area around the Josaphat Park! and so forth. Nostalgia for the fifties, and for an undivided Belgium: The Atomium! Expo 58! The *Innovation* department store! and so forth. Nostalgia for home: evident from the furrowed, ever-pensive faces of elderly Spaniards, aged Moroccans or Turks, and other immigrants. In quite a different way, an analogous longing also speaks from the uniformed haste with which thousands of office workers in the evening rush to the Central Station, and from the frightening nervousness of the countless car-driving commuters who, every day from four o'clock in the afternoon, are gridlocked on the inner ringroad. These people feel at home somewhere, but certainly not in Brussels. Sometimes it would appear as though everyone in Brussels is permanently ready to leave. □ Except for a handful of intellectuals, artists, and members of subcultures, hardly anyone consciously *chooses* Brussels in its *present* state. *That* Brussels is "faded glory" and/or city to be remade, which results, incidentally, in often justified pleas for urban renewal, monument preservation, and a more democratically oriented policy. However this may be, for the majority of people living here, Brussels is probably not the always-longed-for city of their dreams. Either for financial reasons you did not get away from it in time and got stuck in the place: the fate of the many indigenous elderly, of the hangers-on from sheer necessity; or else you wound up in Brussels unintentionally, found work there, moved family members over, and eventually stayed where you had been involuntarily stranded: the life history of countless immigrants and political or economic refugees, of the permanent alien residents. During the week, however, Brussels is above all one gigantic transit center, one big passage of white-collar and other tertiary workers, in whose footsteps during weekends the tourists follow. Thus, the city is constantly being occupied by non-residents, non-locals. Or do those tens of thousands of daily commuters also belong to the city? Who is and who is not able to claim something like "membership of Brussels"? □ Brussels is currently a mere place, a rather nondescript city with hardly any outlines and associated with principally negative images: Brussels as a dirty, windy, ugly, expensive, unsafe city. It is in fact not or hardly *experienced* as a city. You live or work here, but this "here" as a rule stays limited to your proper neighborhood or the direct surroundings of your office building. The city as a whole does not come into view. Even the tourists restrict their outings as a rule to the immediate vicinity of the *Grand Marché*, where as a result everything is provided for: cafés with or without sidewalk tables, even a picturesque street with nothing but restaurants and a magnificent shopping arcade as a shelter against the world-famous Belgian rain. No wonder, then, that Brussels no longer produces a collective memory. Day after working day, as a permanent resident or eternal commuter, you can pass a statue, the *Palais des Beaux-Arts*, or the Fish Market, without even the faintest awareness of the historical meaning(s) of what you are glimpsing. Neither at the macrolevel of the overall city nor at the microlevel of streets, neighborhoods, or buildings can we talk of commemorative work, of emotional links, of imaginary identifications. Is there any passer-by who sometimes thinks "this is *our* capital," "this is *my* city"? Brussels literally belongs to nobody, which is why cultural institutions can claim it so easily.

**3** Brussels does in fact have an identity, but it is a paradoxical one: at once hypermodern and hyperruinous, forever in motion and therefore always dying. Probably this city is the preeminent place to recall modernity, in the double sense given to this expression by for instance Jean-François Lyotard: both process of mourning and rethinking. The city acquired its current shape through a policy of forced modernization. In 1958, Brussels was allowed to organize its own World's Fair, *Expo 58*, an opportunity seized by the local political-economic elite to "modernize" the city. The inner ringroad and its countless tunnels, the Martini Tower and Parking 58, the Monnaie Building, the North Quarter: ever so many expressions of a rampant modernism, of a desire, perverted by nepotism, corruption, and shortsightedness, to turn Brussels into a paragon of modernity. An image, indeed a phantasm, has dominated the postwar history of this city, but in an imperfect way. Becoming modern in Brussels became a permanent situation: an endless repetition of demolition, of building fever, of tearing down and pouring concrete. And an endless repetition of urban decay here, renovation there: the city is continuously dying, but always in different places, so that it may also be continuously reembellished, renewed, restored. Brussels, in short, is a verb. Only, there is hardly anyone left who knows why the *Grands Travaux* ever got started in the first place, and why they are continuing to this very day. And what is most surprising of all: the arguably most actively building city in postwar Western Europe has produced hardly any buildings of significance. Brussels does not suffer from an excess of architectural plans, but from drawing-board stupidity, from a lack of architectural grandeur and ingenuity in the many scale-models that *have* been realized. □ The dream of Brussels as a hypermodern economic and administrative center has long since been shattered. What is there most resembles an urban Sphinx: half residential, half working city; half *vieux Bruxelles*, half *New Brussels*. Old and new are in a jumble, form improbable combinations and frequently perplexing juxtapositions. The city has thus acquired a characteristic aesthetic after all, beyond the difference between beautiful and ugly. It is urban in a radically new sense of the word — that of a failed Modernism. Time and again one runs into a totally fragmented space, without much cohesion: Brussels is a torn-up body, a barely legible corpus or corpse that can no longer be symbolized, leave alone narrated. The city has fallen apart into dozens of neighborhoods that are hardly in touch with each other: the *Grand Sablon* vs. "Little Chicago," the North Quarter vs. the area around Brussels South, the *Grand Marché* vs. *le Vismet* (the former Fish Market), the *Place de Brouckère* vs. the *Place Anneessens*, and so on and so forth. The list of possible contrasts is impressively long, especially for a relatively small city like Brussels. And the oppositions always concern both the buildings and the residents, both the architecture and the people. Nor do contrasts allow themselves to be reduced to the famous tension between uptown and downtown, rich and poor. The fragmentation is even more complete than suggested: the oppositions characterize almost every neighborhood, albeit in different measures. In Brussels, oppositions between rich and poor, indigenous and immigrant, etc., do not beautifully fall into step, nor do they simply coincide with certain neighborhoods. Many of the indigenous residents, too, are poor; the uptown uphill areas also have their slums; the downhill area, too, has its trendy places and residential oases, even its arts centers. Precisely the non-coincidence of social, cultural, ethnic, economic, and other dividing lines has prevented the city from imploding, indeed constitutes the individuality — more than once even the phantasmagoric charm — of Brussels. In this patchwork city, the Other is often enough only a neighbor like everybody else. To take Brussels seriously is synonymous with a thorough reflection upon this fragmentation of lifestyles, cultures, ethnicities, economic patterns, housing types, etc., down to the microlevel of every street. Even the proverbially poverty-ridden *Marolles* quarter does not form a homogeneous neighborhood, but just like the rest of the city is characterized by heterogeneity. Everyone and everything (past and present) are a minority in Brussels: even the majority of immigrant residents has to be called a minority in the political and economic sense. □ Brussels has a lot of "strong spots," places that aesthetically, architecturally, or otherwise catch the imagination. As a non-homogeneous city, Brussels is in fact one big collection of separate sites, of "spatial singularities" (Gilles Deleuze), of sometimes weak, but mostly strong territorial dissonants. Examples: the North Quarter, the Ravenstein Arcade, the Fish Market, the hall of the Central Station, the *Place Royal*, the subway station *Kruidtuin/Botanique*,... The city also houses a number of barely exploited yet proverbial "grand" buildings: the South Palace, the *Petit Château*, the rooms of the Conservatory,... At the wider level of "the nineteen municipalities" (the Capital Region), examples may be multiplied *ad libitum*: the *Parvis* of Saint Gilles and of Old-Molenbeek, the Basilica, the *Concert Noble*,... Most of these places are places of transit, passages, *non-spaces* in the sense Marc Augé gives to the word: without (much) symbolic weight, without a well-articulated role in community life, without semantic charge. They are not inscribed in a symbolic network of references, they are no part of a mythic Brussels. For these places tend to be used in a mostly functional manner, either by widely different groups of passers-by or by local residents. They form in reality or potentially strong public spaces, but they usually fail to coalesce into collective spaces where the act of exchanging glances, gestures, even words with strangers, obtains a surplus value. They are not "spaces for nothing" (Olivier Mongin), not spaces where you like to spend your time and hang around. These places do testify to "the poetry of the city" (Pierre Sansot), but in unseen ways, almost in spite of their surroundings and users. The same applies to the few downtown spaces that do channel public life, like the *Rue Neuve* (the main shopping street), the *Place de la Monnaie* (at the end of that same street and lined with the National Opera and a branch of the municipal library), or the streets around the *Bourse* (the Stock Exchange). These perform their public task in a minimal manner, almost in spite of everything — in spite of the forever omnipresent litter, the dogshit, the literally misplaced neon ads, the ill-kept greenery, the concrete trash that passes for flower boxes, the windswept places,...



**4** Brussels is the cultural-artistic waterhead of Belgium. In this respect, it is no different from other capitals like Paris, Amsterdam, or London. Bilingualism, the preeminent sociocultural fact in a mixed French-Dutch-speaking country, and especially the process of federalization, the juridicopolitical response to that fact, have resulted in literally divergent, side-by-side networks of institutions. The more prominent the role of words in artistic production, the stronger the segregation: pop and classical music concerts and exhibitions are relatively multilingual events, but theater audiences are almost always monolingual. Even so: a rock concert in the *Ancienne Belgique* or the *Vaartkapoen* stand better chances of being announced and/or covered in a Flemish newspaper than a performance at the *Botanique*; and a nonverbal artform like contemporary dance has its "Flemish" and "Walloon" choreographers, with matching audiences. Exchanges across the language-divide remain limited, even after a joint and much publicized initiative like *Kunstenfestivaldesarts* (the name itself a concatenation of Dutch and French) or the change of course which a Flemish-based arts center like the *Beursschouwburg* effected in the early 1990s. Within the context of Brussels, it appears unthinkable, apart from some incidental collaboration, that a Dutch-speaking and a French-speaking institution would jointly develop a complementary program on the basis of an overall diagnosis of, say, the local situation in the performing arts. Community-based hedgehog positions and, connected to them, political patronizing preclude a durable policy of cultural development within the context of the Brussels Region. French-speaking and Dutch-speaking organizations work independently of, sometimes consciously against each other. As a rule, they also address "their" audiences in only one language, thus rendering the composition of those audiences at least partly a matter of self-fulfilling prophecy: either French- or Dutch-speaking. Cultural politics as tribal warfare, artistic policy as linguistic protectionism — and in the meantime, every institution still tries its very best, often via exorbitantly expensive advertisements (again often monolingual), to sell as many tickets as possible. Ticket sales, even the reception you receive, happen in the language of the subsidizing political authorities: in Brussels, the artistic or cultural consumer is usually expected to adapt to the language of the hosting institution, instead of the other way around. □ Brussels would not be the capital of Belgium if countless local cultural institutions were not manned or "womaned" by (semi-)bureaucrats with political connections. Sometimes this does not stand in the way of dynamic policy-making, but just as often it issues in the infamous Belgian disease: fossilization, inertia, immobilism. You acquire a cultural stronghold and then fortify it, meanwhile making sure that "friendly" politicians or administrators are not given offence. Positive or negative reviews or criticisms on the programming, as a result, more than once do not matter, as long as you do not commit any political errors. This state of affairs seems especially nefarious for the local museums (in the widest sense of the word): hardly talked about, they are merely bent on preserving, not on publicizing their collections, no matter how promising these may often look on paper.

**5** Brussels has long stopped being claimed "from within," by a proper bourgeoisie or metropolitan elite. Various economic and political actors make claims on Brussels from without. They talk *about* Brussels; their strategic words float above the lived city, even if they often produce the most real effects within the city. Their "Brussels," as a rule, is little more than a symbolical name, or an eight-letter-word in a contract, a placename without much content: "Brussels" as an empty signifier. City and region are thus alternatively plaything and stake in decisions taken externally. Both form the constant object of speculations — on the part of real estate developers and construction companies, on the one hand, and on the part of politicians, on the other. Corporations and political parties thus have their frequently secret plans for the city and the region, and as befits colonizers, they do not bother to ask the opinions of the natives, nor of the numerous temporary residents. They invest their money or their power, and in light of these investments new buildings are erected or not, obstacles are put in the way or not. Brussels as a colony to be exploited, Brussels as the breaking point in discussions about the future of Belgium... □ The fight for Brussels among the elites looks all the more surreal for being waged against a background of a massive lack of interest, if not a downright revulsion for the capital on the part of the majority of the Flemish and Walloon populations of Belgium. In Flanders, the animosity against Brussels has strong historical ties with the traditional image of Brussels as a Francophone, anti-Flemish city: Brussels = *la Belgique à papa*. A younger generation of Flemings has looked beyond this still widespread stereotype. It moved to Brussels in the 1980s to do artistic or cultural work, and gave especially the West of downtown Brussels, the area from the *Bourse* to the Canal Zone, new impulses. Thus, a new dividing line ensued, which, incidentally, is again crossed by countless other lines: in cafés like *Le Coq* or *La Cygogne*, and in shops along the *Rue Dansaert*, a lot of typically suburban

Flemish Dutch may be heard, yet at the *Petit Sablon* or in the *Marolles* hardly a Fleming will be spotted. The center of Brussels turned a little Flemish, but this little oil stain is not spreading. And above all, Brussels remains to most Flemings, and probably also to most Walloons, one huge *Terra Incognita*. One does not feel at ease in the capital, especially since the social relationships that obtain in villages, small towns, and recently also suburbia, set the dominant model for "living well" in Belgium. Brussels is the only metropolis in Belgium, and this unique position is being paid for with indifference, defense mechanisms, if not sheer animosity. As the metropolitan exception to the Belgian rule, Brussels is to a majority of Belgians by definition *other*: alien, tough, cheerless, uncomfortable... All in all, Brussels is like a foreign country to the rest of Belgium. □ The existing deidentification with the capital is shored up by a much wider dislike for all things metropolitan. This dislike is in turn rooted, at least in Flanders, in a highly ambiguous attitude towards modernity (partly determined by the Catholic tradition and a rural way of life). "The big city" — Brussels, that is — fascinates *and* repels because it is viewed as the abscess of the modern, as the blow-up of the shortcomings of that modern life which one has nevertheless begun to lead oneself, albeit in an attenuated form. Squandering and spending sprees (the consumerist ritual), adultery and prostitution, self-aggrandizement and the hunt for status, or — in a different register — social decline and impoverishment, youth subcultures and adult immigrants: just about the whole of Flanders has become acquainted with these phenomena, but in a diluted form, so that the image of the sinful city, of Brussels as a cesspool of vice, still stands. Brussels was and remains a projection screen to be used *ad libitum*, a white cloth — an unknown face — on which the average Fleming externalizes unconscious anxieties and revulsions, on the one hand, and illegitimate desires and dreams, on the other. And all too often, this image is affirmed by the media. In those media, Brussels usually is not just a problematic city — that much should be granted — but simply *the* problematic city, the city as a problem.

**6** Brussels is in many respects a fragmented, postmodern city. But nothing could harm it more than new urban planning projections of the type "Washington at the Zenne" or "the Belgian Los Angeles." So numerous have been the attempts to put the city internationally on the map, or in another stylistic register, to "save" it, that it presently craves only a single thing: to be allowed to die with dignity.

*Translation Bart Eeckhout*

An earlier Dutch version of this text was published in *A moving city*, ed. Studio Open City (Brussels: Studio Open City, 1998): 42-49.

**Sven Lütticken**

# The Invisible Work of Art

*Keywords:* ■ *Visual Arts* ■ *Public Space*

Traditionally, works of art in an urban environment are monuments. Monuments symbolize the values of a community or serve to commemorate a person or an event. A monument creates a site that is of greater importance than the surrounding space. It would appear, however, that the signifying power of monuments steadily decreased as their number in the nineteenth century ceaselessly grew. With respect to nineteenth-century France, the term "statuomania" has often been used: such was the exorbitant number of memorials that were erected in Paris, and to a lesser extent also in the larger provincial towns. Other European countries, too, experienced this kind of inflation, and by the 1920s Robert Musil was able to observe:

*Memorials, apart from having the property that we do not know how to form their plural in German ("Denkmale" or "Denkmäler"), have many more properties. The most important of these is a little contradictory. For the most conspicuous thing about memorials is that one does not notice them. Nothing in the world is as invisible as memorials. Yet they are undoubtedly erected with the purpose of being seen — more than that even, with the purpose of stimulating the attention. But at the same time*

1 "Denkmale haben außer der Eigenschaft, daß man nicht weiß, ob man Denkmale oder Denkmäler sagen soll, noch allerhand Eigenheiten. Die wichtigste davon ist ein wenig widerspruchsvoll; das Auffallendste an Denkmälern ist nämlich, daß man sie nicht bemerkt. Es gibt nichts auf der Welt, was so unsichtbar wäre wie Denkmäler. Sie werden doch zweiffellos aufgestellt, um gesehen zu werden, ja geradezu, um die Aufmerksamkeit zu erregen; aber gleichzeitig sind sie durch irgend etwas gegen Aufmerksamkeit imprägniert, und diese rinnt Wassertropfen-auf-Ölbezug-artig an ihnen ab, ohne auch nur einen Augenblick stehenzubleiben." Robert Musil, "Denkmale," in *Gesammelte Werke 7. Kleine Prosa, Aphorismen, Autobiographisches* (Reinbek: Rowohlt, 1978), 506. English translation by the editors.

2 "Es wäre falsch, sich durch einige Ausnahmen täuschen zu lassen. Etwa durch jene paar Standbilder, die der Mensch mit dem Baedeker in der hand suchen geht, wie den Gattamelata oder den Colleone, was eben ein ganz besonderes Verhalten ist; oder durch Gedenktürme, die eine ganze Landschaft versperren; oder durch Denkmäler, die einen Verein bilden, wie die über ganz Deutschland verbreiteten Bismarckdenkmäler." Ibid., 507. English translation by the editors.

3 "... der Beruf der meisten gewöhnlichen Denkmale ist es wohl, ein Gedenken erst zu erzeugen, oder die Aufmerksamkeit zu fesseln und den Gefühlen eine fromme Richtung zu geben, weil man annimmt, daß es dessen einigermaßen bedarf; und diesen ihren Hauptberuf verfehlen Denkmäler immer. Sie verscheuchen geradezu das, was sie anziehen sollten. Man kann nicht sagen, wir bemerkten sie nicht; man müßte sagen, sie entmerken uns, sie entziehen sich unseren Sinnen: es ist eine durchaus positive, zur Tätlichkeit neigende Eigenschaft von ihnen!" Ibid. English translation by the editors.

4 "Das mindeste, was man verlangen müßte, um die Aufmerksamkeit zu erregen, wären bewährte Aufschriften wie 'Goethes Faust ist der beste!' oder 'Die dramatischen Ideen des bekannten Dichters X sind die billigsten!'" Ibid., 508. English translation by the editors.

*they are somehow inocculated against attentiveness, which glides over them like water-drops over oil cloth, without lingering even the faintest moment.*[1]

Thus, monuments have paradoxically become almost invisible in the twentieth century. There are of course exceptions, as Musil admits: "It would be wrong to let oneself be misguided by a couple of exceptions. Say by those few statues that people go look for, Baedeker guides in their hands, like the Gattamelata or the Colleone, which amounts to a special *form* of conduct. Or by commemorative towers that block an entire landscape. Or by memorials that form a club, like those Bismarck memorials spread all over Germany."[2] But although there are in Musil's opinion still memorials that attract people's attention or even give expression to an idea or sentiment shared by the whole of society, "the profession of most ordinary memorials is rather to create the act of remembering in the first place, or to seize the attention and steer the feelings in a pious direction, since it is understood that this is what is somehow needed. And this chief occupation is never performed by memorials. They dispel precisely what they should attract. We cannot say we fail to notice them; we should rather say they unnotice us, they hide from our senses: it is a wholly positive, almost physically aggressive quality of theirs!"[3]

Musil assumes that the task of a monument, in a way, is unnatural: a monument should attract attention, yet permanent things are hardly consciously noticed by people and figure more like a soft background noise. If this principle were entirely correct, however, it would have to apply to all solid components of any environment, and in that case Musil would not have had to attach his observations specifically to monuments. After all, he does explicitly state that "Nothing in the world is as invisible as memorials." He comes far closer to formulating a convincing answer when he notes how traditional statues, in terms of visual appeal, are simply no match for the temptations of a modern consumer society: in the display windows of shops, we can watch mechanical figures moving in circles while opening and closing their eyes. Such attractions are altogether absent from bronze statues on their pedestals. "The least one should expect in order to catch the attention would be time-tested inscriptions like 'Goethe's *Faust* is the best!' or 'The dramatic ideas of the famous poet X are cheapest!'"[4]

Another reason for the invisibility of monuments is the said "statuomania" which at the end of the nineteenth century seized European metropolises and above all Paris: the number of persons who were honored with statues underwent a severe inflation. In a predominantly bourgeois society, statues of a few royals and saints could not possibly suffice. Instead, a whole series of heroes, poets, thinkers, and explorers had to be commemorated. The urban expansions of the late-nineteenth century, moreover, produced a lot of public gardens and squares that craved some form of decoration.[5] Because of this, statues, once a focus in the city but now omnipresent, increasingly turned into background noise. That the honored people in many cases did not catch the imagination, or were only admired by small groups within the overall population, reinforced this situation. When social cohesion diminishes, monuments can no longer offer a binding factor either. The line between visibility and invisibility in public space, however, is no fixed matter: the Surrealists, contemporaries of Musil, were fascinated by the old-fashioned monuments they saw everywhere in Paris. In *Le Paysan de Paris* (1926), Louis Aragon portrayed statues as mysterious idols surrounded by bizarre, ephemeral sects and Surrealist cults.[6] However, the statues did apparently need a little help from their friends to become truly visible again: in 1933, a group of Surrealists made proposals for "modifying" Parisian statues, thus providing them with new magic and meaning.[7] By modifying the monuments, they believed, the magical qualities of these archaic objects could be exposed, much as Max Ernst in his collages converted old reproductions into Surrealist tableaux.

In what follows, I will inquire into a number of ways in which early- and late-twentieth-century artists have dealt with the invisibility that threatens art in an urban space. Clearly, this discussion can no longer revolve around monuments in a traditional sense: because of the evolution just outlined, the foundations of monumentality have been totally undermined. Art cannot pine for a lost stability and visibility, but must find ways of dealing with the new developments.

**The Man of the Crowd** A striking analogy may be found between the increasing invisibility of the statue in the twentieth-century metropolis and the way in which, in the experience of metropolitan observers, the self is swallowed up by, and disappears in, the urban crowd. Already in the first half of the nineteenth century, Edgar Allan Poe incorporated this experience in his story "The Man of the Crowd," which opens with the narrator looking out through a pub window at the passing crowds in a busy street in London, then the biggest metropolis in the world.[8] The narrator insists on his skillfulness at categorizing the pedestrians as members of a particular social class or professional group — a highly useful skill in an anonymous metropolis, as becomes clear from the fact that the narrator is

5 Dario Gamboni, *The Destruction of Art* (London: Reaktion Books, 1997), 224-26.
6 Louis Aragon, *Le Paysan de Paris* (1926; reprint Paris: Gallimard, 1972), 186-89.
7 Gamboni, *Destruction*, 76.
8 Edgar Allan Poe, "The Man of the Crowd," in *The Complete Tales and Poems of Edgar Allan Poe* (Harmondsworth: Penguin Books, 1982), 475-81.
9 Richard Sennett, *The Fall of Public Man* (London: Faber and Faber, 1986), 213.
10 Ibid., 20.

also able to single out various pickpockets and con men who merely pretend to be decent citizens.

One apparently agitated man fascinates the narrator so much that he decides to follow him on his rambles through twilit and nocturnal London. By daybreak, both narrator and reader have come to understand that this man suffers so much from a traumatic memory or from pangs of conscience that he constantly longs to be absorbed by the masses: at any one moment of the day or night, he wants to be in a place where a great many people are gathered, and he allows his route to be determined by this drive. He is "the man of the crowd" who wants to be submerged by the masses, for only the urban crowd can assure him that he does not have to be alone with himself, while at the same time there is no need to establish contact with anybody else. Unlike what was the case in the eighteenth century, in the nineteenth century it became *bon ton* not to address strangers in the city, as Richard Sennett has argued in his study on the fall of "public man."[9] The nineteenth-century (and by extension also the twentieth-century) city stopped being a stage for social interaction and instead became a tableau for and of silent onlookers. Compared to what was the case before, people who populated the modern metropolis were hard to place:

*For instance, the mass production of clothes, and the use of mass production patterns by individual tailors or seamstresses, meant that many diverse segments of the cosmopolitan public began in gross to take on a similar appearance, that public markings were losing distinctive forms. Yet virtually no one believed that society was becoming thereby homogenized; the machine meant that social differences — important differences, necessary to know if one were to survive in a rapidly expanding milieu of strangers — were becoming hidden, and the stranger more intractably a mystery.*[10]

Significantly, it was precisely in the metropolis of London, at the time inhabited by nearly four million people, that by the late 1880s the detective Sherlock Holmes appeared on the scene in the stories of Arthur Conan Doyle. As the real-life Jack the Ripper sufficiently demonstrated, the anonymous masses of the British capital offered the ideal protection to criminals and monsters. One of the most captivating Sherlock Holmes stories explicitly thematizes the invisibility in which the modern metropolis is able to cloak people. In "The Man with the Twisted Lip," Holmes goes after a disappeared gentleman, Neville St. Clair, who turns out not to earn his living through financial transactions in the City, but as a beggar in that same City. Every workday the man disguises himself unrecognizably as the shabby beggar Hugh Boone and takes up his position at a busy spot, where he manages to make large sums of money from begging. Although Holmes, too, is at first misled by this act, he eventually finds out that the gentleman disappeared because he had been arrested in his begging outfit and stuck to his role so as to avoid being forced to reveal his "true" identity.[11] Among the uniform people in the center of London, Hugh Boone stood out as a striking figure: with him you did not have to spy for details in order to "place" him, since his whole appearance pointed to his being an outcast. On second thoughts, however, even less about him seemed certain than about the businessmen in neat suits to whom Neville St. Clair seemed to belong.

The multiplication of statues in the late-nineteenth-century European city led to a situation in which observers like Musil could treat monumental works of art, in a rhetorically exaggerated form, as though they had become invisible. They were no longer the center of attention like Michelangelo's David in fifteenth-century Florence or the equestrian statue of Louis XIV in Paris around 1700. Conversely, when modern works of art began to appear in the city, it could happen that these new works became exceedingly visible to some people and even aroused aggression. The modernist statue *Kneeling Woman* by Wilhelm Lehmbruck (1911) was quickly damaged when in 1927 a bronze version was erected in the German city of Duisburg.[12] Later, too, modern works of art in public space were frequently subject to vandalism, as we know from Dario Gamboni's *The Destruction of Art*. Especially abstract works were often taken to be a visual form of provocation: these works were all too noticeable.

Nevertheless, the fact that the opposition between visibility and invisibility in public space is never stable is also true for modern-looking works. Thus, the German artist Tobias Rehberger in 1992 made a series of miniature replicas of the kinds of modern sculptures to be found in the public or semi-public spaces of business premises. Of the nine figures, seven were small replicas of extant sculptures, in a stylistical variation that ranged from geometrical abstraction to biomorphism, while two were really new creations. The fact that it proves impossible at first sight to decide whether you are looking at a "real" or a "fictional" sculpture goes to show that these forms have become so hackneyed that their visibility is not much higher than that of traditional sculptures in Musil's day. Yet it cannot be excluded either that to haters of modern art they are highly visible: a work of art that in one person's eyes anonymously merges with the

11 Arthur Conan Doyle, "The Man with the Twisted Lip," in *The Original Illustrated "Strand" Sherlock Holmes* (Ware: Wordsworth Editions, 1989), 186-200.

12 Gamboni, *Destruction*, 130.

13 Douglas Crimp, "Redefining Site Specificity," in *On the Museum's Ruins* (Cambridge, MA: MIT Press, 1993), 150-86.

14 Marcel Duchamp, "A l'Infinitif," in *Salt Seller: The Writings of Marcel Duchamp*, ed. Michel Sanouillet and Elmer Peterson (New York: Oxford University Press, 1973), 74.

crowd is in another's view an eye-catching and irritable beggar forming a blot on the streetscape.

However, some works clearly swing in one direction or the other. In 1989, Richard Serra's *Tilted Arc* on Federal Plaza in New York was destroyed by the authorities after many public protestations.[13] Serra's warped wall of steel was an aggressive spatial intervention, no near-invisible piece of decoration: it was so extreme that one could not possibly overlook it. That it had to be removed suggests that visibility is probably not wanted by most people, since artistic visibility in this day and age is associated with extremism, with resistance against mediocrity. The fate of two sculptures at the 1987 exhibition *Skulptur* in Münster, West Germany, bears witness to this. Jeff Koons's sculpture *Kiepenkerl*, so popular with the public, was a stainless steel replica of a popular local statue that had been used by the Nazis at some point to illustrate propaganda slogans (so-called "Durchhalteparolen"). Koons cunningly used an overfamiliar image, subverted it by the use of a banal contemporary material, and yet profited from its public appeal. The contribution by Katharina Fritsch, by contrast, was equally familiar in form, but her statue of the Virgin Mary took a bright yellow color, which was deemed such a provocation that the statue did not survive the exhibition.

**The Woolworth Building as a Ready-made** The most fundamental reflection on the (in)visibility of works of art is to be found in the work of Marcel Duchamp. The term "ready-made" was borrowed by Duchamp precisely from the sort of off-the-peg garments that made the inhabitants of the modern city look so much like each other: "ready-made clothing" was a term the artist came across after his arrival in the U.S. in 1915. In Duchamp's *magnum opus, The Large Glass* (a.k.a. *The Bride Stripped Bare by Her Bachelors, Even*), on which he worked during most of the 1910s, clothes play a prominent role, more particularly in the "cemetery of uniforms and liveries" — the visual form adopted by the wretched bachelors. Duchamp took a great interest in clothing specifically tailored to a profession, like that of the gravedigger, the postman, the police officer, etc. The bachelors, in this case, have been totally reduced to their professional clothes.

"Ready-made clothing," however, pointed up a more general uniform to Duchamp: that of the citizen as such. The term was thus ideal for naming an activity with which Duchamp had been occupied since 1913: the selection of ordinary appliances and utensils as works of art — or rather, as "works which are not works of 'art.'"[14] While the popular notion holds that Duchamp took a bottle-rack and "placed it in the museum" so as to "elevate the ordinary object into art," the issue is in fact more complex. Usually Duchamp kept the ready-mades in his studio and only a few friends were aware that the objects were actually "ready-mades." A journalist who interviewed Duchamp and his friend Crotti in their studio was admittedly amazed at the snow shovel dangling from the ceiling, but did not receive an explanation.[15] The ready-mades were invisible to the general public.

Not counting the 1917 *Fountain* affair — an affair in which Duchamp, by pseudonymously submitting a urinal to the exhibition of the Society of Independent Artists, wanted to test the liberalism of the organizers, and was successful insofar as the submission was turned down — we can find only a single instance in the 1910s of Duchamp being willing to display ready-mades. That was in 1916 in the Bourgeois Gallery: *Pharmacy* (a treated picture of a landscape, an odd-one-out in the corpus of ready-mades) hung in the exhibition, while two unidentified objects hung on a coat rack near the entrance to the gallery. The latter objects, in fact, were not noticed at all, or not as works of art: at most they were considered junk somebody had tried to dispose of.[16] The ready-made did not hide its identity any less efficiently than the begging gentleman in Conan Doyle's story. Only in a context of art was it being identified as a work of art, but Duchamp took this step really only in the 1930s, for example at an exhibition of Surrealist objects. Until that date, ready-mades lived in hiding, as part of the mass of identical appliances and utensils. Quite characteristically, most of them were lost and later replaced by replicas: thus, Duchamp's sister Suzanne, although informed of the existence of ready-mades, put the bottle-rack with the garbage when she was forced to evacuate Duchamp's Parisian studio during the First World War.

The image of the discarded bottle-rack says something of the radicalness of Duchamp's approach. As I have argued elsewhere, Duchamp used his ready-mades as a point of departure for all sorts of puns and hermetic speculations on, for instance, sexuality and n-dimensional geometry; the general public was to him a potentially disturbing factor to be kept at a distance.[17] The work of art (or simply "work") existed above all inside Duchamp's head. He associated certain ideas with a preformed object and saw certain features reflected in it. In the case of the bottle-rack, one of the things that appealed to him was the phallic character of the object, although Craig Adcock has also convincingly related the work to Duchamp's interest in the fourth dimension.[18] It cannot be sufficiently emphasized, however, that such things are impossible to observe in the object itself

15 Serge Stauffer, ed., *Marcel Duchamp. Interviews und Statements* (Ostfildern: Edition Cantz, 1992), 18-20.

16 Dieter Daniels, *Duchamp und die Anderen* (Köln: DuMont, 1992), 172-76.

17 Sven Lütticken, "'Het publiek verpest alles.' Kunst en kunstgeschiedenis volgens Marcel Duchamp," *Jong Holland* 12, 2 (1996): 24-36.

18 Craig E. Adcock, *Marcel Duchamp's Notes from the Large Glass: An N-Dimensional Analysis* (Ann Arbor: UMI Research Press, 1981), 159.

19 Marcel Duchamp, "Apropos of 'readymades,'" in *Salt Seller*, ed. Sanouillet and Peterson, 141.

20 Duchamp, "A l'Infinitif," 75.

21 Adcock, *Duchamp's Notes*, 204.

without a prior knowledge of Duchamp's mindset. The object in itself, utterly commonplace in the France of its time, was as unspectacular as any inconspicuous member of a restless crowd. "A point which I want very much to establish is that the choice of these 'readymades' was never dictated by aesthetic delectation. This choice was based on a reaction of visual indifference with at the same time a total absence of good or bad taste..."[19]

In the case of the urinal which Duchamp saw in the window of a New York plumber and which led to his famous *Fountain* of 1917, Duchamp probably did feel aesthetically attracted to the object. *Fountain*, however, is above all a parody of the category of the aesthetic, and of art *tout court*, intended to demonstrate that beauty may manifest itself even in the lowest regions. The polemical character of *Fountain* distinguishes this work from other ready-mades, which, although they have started to look more aesthetic with the passing of time, are still characterized by a merely cool, stubborn beauty. Instead of refined design objects, Duchamp chose objects that are functional first and foremost, only to subsequently rob them of their function: a snow shovel, a bottle-rack, a dog's comb. Earlier in Neuilly he had been mesmerized by a simple chocolate mill in a shop window, which he later included in a schematized form in his *Large Glass*. The appeal of these objects was more cerebral and determined by Duchamp's personal preoccupations than by the primary, plain-to-see characteristics of those objects themselves.

The "invisibility" of ready-mades also applies to what would have been Duchamp's largest work, had it ever been executed. "Find inscription for Woolworth Bldg. as readymade," says a note of January 1916.[20] The Woolworth Building was a new skyscraper (finished in 1913) which was considered spectacular for various reasons: the highest building in New York at the time, it was also executed in a neo-Gothic style, procuring it the nickname of "Cathedral of Commerce." The fact that in the proudly modern United States of America a skyscraper had been dressed in a pseudo-medieval garb no doubt must have amused Duchamp. In addition, Craig Adcock has been able to link the structure of the building to Duchamp's pseudo-mathematical, n-dimensional speculations.[21] The Woolworth Building is in its external form of course anything but inconspicuous or commonplace. Yet what matters here is that this monumental ready-made — had Duchamp indeed "executed" it by providing an inscription on the building — would not have been recognizable in the least as a work by Duchamp. It would have been the ultimate invisible work of art, impossible to get into a museum (where everything becomes recognizable as art), towering high above the crowds in the street, and even hoodwinking Sherlock Holmes. Of this work, we would indeed have been able to say, with Musil, that its escape from attention constituted a "positive, almost physically aggressive quality" of the object. Thus, the problematical character of public works of art in a modern society was brought to a head by Duchamp.

**Shop Windows** In a note from Neuilly in 1913, Duchamp also expressed himself in a suggestive manner on "The exigency of the shop window." The appeal exerted by an object in a shop window is described by him in sexual terms: "When one undergoes the examination of the shop window, one also pronounces one's own sentence. In fact, one's choice is 'round trip.' From the demands of the shop windows, from the inevitable response to shop windows, my choice is determined. No obstinacy, ad absurdum, of hiding the coition through the glass pane with one or many objects of the shop window. The penalty consists in cutting the pane and in feeling regret as soon as possession is consummated. Q.E.D."[22] This fragment is clearly related to the interest in mass products that in the following two years would lead Duchamp to the discovery of the ready-made. But whereas Duchamp always emphasized the aesthetic "indifference" of objects in the case of ready-mades, the seductive power of objects in this instance clearly prevails.

The shop window in the modern city is a source of visual stimulation that in terms of visibility puts traditional forms of "high art" in the shade. As we already saw, Musil, too, related the shortcoming he observed in statues to the attractions that are offered by shop windows and that are absent from monuments: "Why do the figures of a marble group fail to turn around each other the way their better selves in shop windows do, or why at least do they not bat their eyelids?"[23] In the spring of 1945, Duchamp made use of the shop window as a stage for pointing people's attention to a new book by his friend André Breton. In collaboration with Matta he designed a window at Brentano's Bookstore that displayed, among other things, a scantily dressed, headless female dummy with a water faucet to its side. The window attracted much notice, and the Society for the Suppression of Vice and the League of Women protested so strenuously that Brentano's removed the display, after which it remained visible for no more than a week at the Gotham Book Mart.

Duchamp, then, knew how people's attention may be drawn in a metropolis with all its distractions: through an eye-catching shop window. A few years earli-

22 Duchamp, "A l'Infinitif," 74.

23 "Weshalb drehen sich die Figuren einer Marmorgruppe nicht umeinander, wie es bessere Figuren in den Geschäftsauslagen tun, oder klappen wenigstens die Augen auf und zu?" Musil, "Denkmale," 508. English translation by the editors.

24 Judith Goldman, "Windows," in *The Warhol Look*, ed. Mark Francis and Margery King (Pittsburgh: The Andy Warhol Museum; Boston: Little, Brown and Company, 1997), 113-14.

25 Sennett, *Fall*, 144.

26 Jean Baudrillard, *Pour une critique de l'économie politique du signe* (Paris: Gallimard, 1972).

er, in 1939, Salvador Dalí had been one of the first to seize upon this medium. Unsurprisingly, Dalí — who was anagrammatically branded "Avida Dollars" by Breton after their rift — proceeded rather more commercially. He received a substantial fee to decorate two windows of the Bonwit Teller store in New York. Shocked by the results, the management wanted to censor his outré compositions, and in the ensuing row Dalí emptied a bath tub which formed part of one of the displays. The tub crashed through the window pane and the resulting scandal made Dalí a celebrity in the United States.[24] While Duchamp and Matta still made their avantgarde assault on the public from within the world of culture (a bookstore), Dalí used avantgarde strategies to launch himself into the world of conspicuous consumption.

The modern display window came into existence in the second half of the nineteenth century, when in the big cities — first of all Paris — the first big department stores were constructed. These stores staged the display of products in such a way that objects acquired a surplus value. The combination of ordinary and extraordinary goods in ways that lend a certain aura to the former became a veritable skill. Richard Sennett quotes a contemporary observer noting how in the stagings of department stores, utterly disparate products enhance one another as soon as they are being juxtaposed.[25] In the twentieth century, this kind of commodity aestheticism has been refined much further and become far more dominant: Jean Baudrillard has become its principal theorist and critic. The objects themselves have also been designed increasingly with an eye to their relationship with other commodities; they have been ever more codified. Accordingly, Baudrillard has come to define the commodity as an object-sign that derives its value not from its functionality, but from the meaning it borrows from the code formed by the mutual relationship between commodities.[26]

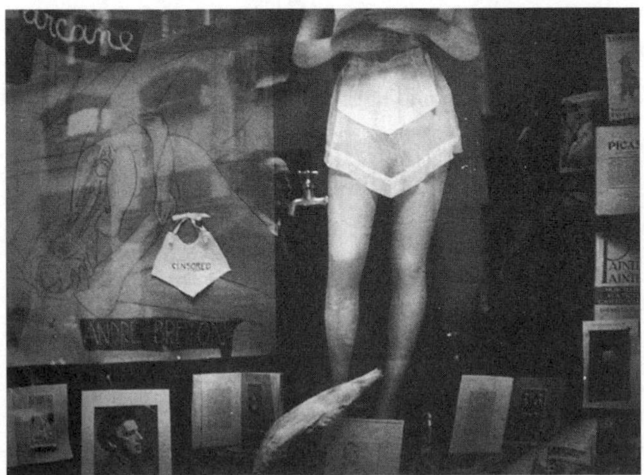


*Marcel Duchamp, window display for Breton's* Arcane 17*, Gotham Book Mart, New York City, 1945.*

In the fine arts, the Pop Art of the 1960s ostentatiously drew a link between commerce and art, between commodity and work of art. Andy Warhol had already worked as a window dresser in the 1950s, when he was still a commercial artist. Even young artists who did not want to be associated with commercialism because it might hinder their careers in "serious" art earned some money designing shop windows: Jasper Johns and Robert Rauschenberg used the joint pseudonym Matson Jones for their displays for stores such as Tiffany's.[27] In 1961, when he was struggling to become accepted as a "real" artist instead of a commercial one, Andy Warhol designed a shop window at Bonwitt Teller's in which his own early pop paintings served as the background to dummies displaying the latest sartorial fashion. While Duchamp and Matta used bizarre elements to point the attention to Breton's Surrealist poetry, it is unclear whether Warhol sought to create a "modern" ambiance for the clothes on display, or else used the display dummies as a sort of extras so as to provide his paintings with an imaginary, fashionable audience, thus making them seem even more interesting. The desirable new dress codes entered into an ambiguous relationship with Warhol's exciting new art: a fine instance of the said principle of the mutual enhancement of unlike objects.

Thus, Warhol did not want to dissociate himself completely from his commercial background in trying to launch his "serious" career. Here as elsewhere in his work, he allowed art and commerce to be married to each other. Even though in 1961 he was desperately trying to get a show with a serious art gallery, Warhol was not above using the shop window and his window-dressing skills to make his art visible in the streets. He was showing an awareness that in the booming consumer culture of the sixties, art could not be isolated from the world of commodities and shop windows. It was precisely the emerging mass culture with its pervasive production of "kitsch" that according to Clement Greenberg (in his famous essay on "Avant-Garde and Kitsch") provided the impulse for modern art to "purify" itself more and more, to cut itself increasingly loose from popular culture.[28] Pop Art, following Duchamp and the Dadaists, consciously broke with this tendency.

More recently, Jeff Koons has also experimented with the shop window as a

27 Goldman, "Windows," 115.

28 Clement Greenberg, "Avant-Garde and Kitsch," in *The Collected Essays and Criticism I: Perceptions and Judgments, 1939-1944* (Chicago: University of Chicago Press, 1986), 5-38.

29 "Interview: Jeff Koons — Anthony Haden-Guest," in *Jeff Koons* (Köln: Benedikt Taschen, 1992), 26.

30 "Das Neue ist eine vom Gebrauchswert der Ware unabhängige Qualität. Es ist der Ursprung des Scheins, der den Bildern unveräußerlich ist, die das kollektive Unbewußte hervorbringt. Es ist die Quintessenz des falschen Bewußtseins, dessen nimmermüde Agentin die Mode ist." Walter Benjamin, *Das Passagen-Werk*, in *Gesammelte Schriften V.I* (Frankfurt am Main: Suhrkamp, 1982), 55. English translation by the editors.

form of presentation. In his case, however, things were brought full circle again, for the result was precisely that the work of art, through the use of ready-mades, became invisible again. In 1980, Koons used the window of the New Museum of Contemporary Art in New York to display three vacuum-cleaners and a light box mounted on neon striplights. "The guards got very upset because all day long people were coming in, wanting to buy a new vacuum-cleaner," says Koons.[29] Whether this is true or merely a case of myth-making is irrelevant: a quick glance at the window could indeed lead to the misguided conclusion that vacuum-cleaners were being promoted at this place for commercial reasons. The vertical striplights on which they were mounted, and the spotlights pointing to them, created an almost sacred sea of light around the Hoover products, which were emphatically presented as "new." The way in which Koons used commodities differs sharply from that of Duchamp. Over against Duchamp's relative indifference and his choice of basic objects stands Koons's passion for the seductive power of industrial design. Duchamp's bottle-rack or snow shovel are above all everyday and traditional instruments, while Koons's *New Hoover Deluxe rug shampooer* and his *New Hoover Celebrity* QS are clear instances of design.

It is not for nothing that Koons called his series *The New*. As Walter Benjamin reminded us about the consumerist culture and art of nineteenth-century Paris: "The new is a quality that is independent of the utility value of commodities. It is the origin of the kind of appearance that is inalienable from the images produced by the collective unconscious. It is the quintessence of false consciousness, whose never-tired agent is fashion."[30] In the new, the dynamics of the code are manifested — a dynamics that requires continual alternation to remain interesting. The remarkable thing about Koons's installation at the New Museum is that he did not combine disparate objects in accordance with the aforementioned law of mutual enhancement, as his colleague Haim Steinbach for instance did, but only placed three related vacuum-cleaners next to each other.

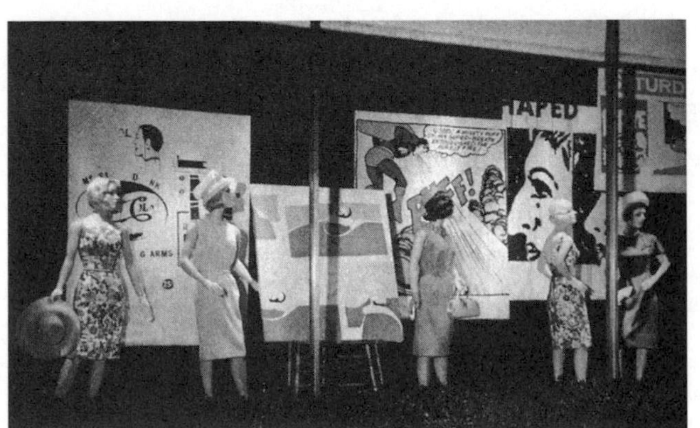

*Andy Warhol, window display for Bonwitt Teller, New York City, 1961.*

Their specific colors, forms, and materials nevertheless derived their appeal from the context offered by the code of the object-signs of their time — a context that has in the meantime come to produce a nostalgia for the days when the design of *The New* was still really new. By presenting the vacuum-cleaners in isolation, Koons emphasized the magical, almost sexual fascination that emanates from their forms and that drew passers-by into the museum-deemed-shop.

Shop windows offer a fundamentally different situation from monuments or other works in public space. Richard Sennett has described the rise of modern department stores and display windows as an indication of the emergence of "an experience of publicness more intense and less sociable."[31] Whoever looks into a shop window is cut off by the window pane from the displayed goods, which exist in another world, a world that does not belong to public space, but to that of desirable objects, of "coition through the glass pane." This world is a matter of sign-objects trying to rouse the individual into purchasing.

**"We now inhabit what used to be the city"** Another indication of the demise of sociability starting in the nineteenth-century city is the type of the flaneur. In the eighteenth century, it was not unusual for strangers in the street to strike up a conversation; the Baudelairean flaneur, by contrast, is a passive, albeit attentive observer, a kind of voyeur.[32] Walter Benjamin saw in him a prefiguration of the private investigator.[33] Baudelaire himself linked the flaneur to the "man of the crowd" found in his much-admired Poe, but it would be more logical to identify the flaneur with the narrator of Poe's story, who does nothing but observe the "man of the crowd" — although it is true that the flaneur, too, enjoys being submerged by the crowd. Today, however, the modern city has become itself the object of nostalgic sentiments, as the architectural and urban planning avant-gardes are mesmerized by Los Angeles and Asian megalopolises, where yet another step has been taken in the destruction of public space.

"Modernity is a radical principle. It is destructive. It has destroyed the city as we know it. We now inhabit what used to be the city," says Rem Koolhaas.[34] The flaneur has become an archaism in this world: "The street is dead. That discovery has coincided with frantic attempts at resuscitation. Public art is everywhere — as if two deaths make a life. Pedestrinization — intended to preserve — merely

31 Sennett, *Fall*, 141.

32 Ibid., 213.

33 Benjamin, *Passagen-Werk*, 554.

34 Rem Koolhaas, "Atlanta," in *S, M, L, XL* by OMA, Rem Koolhaas, and Bruce Mau (Rotterdam: 010, 1995), 856.

35 Koolhaas, "The Generic City," in *S, M, L, XL*, 1253.

36 Michael Fried, "Art and Objecthood," in *Art and Objecthood: Essays and Reviews* (Chicago: University of Chicago Press, 1998), 157-58.

channels the flow of those doomed to destroy the object of their intended reverence with their feet."[35] So far, the confrontation with this new situation has only happened piecemeal in the arts. An example of such a confrontation is the exhibition entitled *Framed Area*, which took place in the summer of 1997 between the Dutch airport of Schiphol and the center of nearby Hoofddorp. In this area, completely dominated by the influence of the airport, office buildings and other businesses alternate with island-like residential areas and shopping centers, connected (but also divided) by freeways and straight roads. Hotels and fastfood restaurants complement the image. The area is in fact totally geared to the car, and so many of the works in the exhibition took the form of giant billboards along the roads and freeways. Just like the shop window, the billboard may serve as a possible format for presenting art.

Here again, though, visibility may turn into invisibility. The perception of a work of art by car drivers will of necessity be restricted to a flash, a mere moment. In the case of advertisements already perceived countless times, this would not really matter: the advertising message would have been identified. In the case of (unknown) works of art, the situation is much more difficult. Does the car driver catch something of a work by Hiroshi Sugimoto, or does he merely register a billboard advertising something unfamiliar, which he is consequently unable to place? In the act of driving, the cinematographic passing-by of landscapes may have become such a dominant experience that individual images and objects are drowned in it. In the 1960s, the sculptor Tony Smith described a nocturnal drive along the unfinished New Jersey Turnpike as a revelation: this was such an overwhelming experience that surely it had to mark the end of art.[36] Maybe the German photographer Wolfgang Tillmans was simply being consistent with himself when he renounced his opportunity to contribute to *Framed Area* and instead invited Amnesty International to use his billboard for one of

*Photograph of* Giving, *the performance directed by Jeff Wall in Hoofddorp, 1997.*

their posters. He made himself invisible and allowed the billboard to merge effortlessly with the landscape: calls for support by Amnesty, after all, are familiar and do not raise further questions.

Jeff Wall chose another format than that of the billboard for his contribution to *Framed Area*. Wall gave meticulous instructions to two actors, who at regular hours and several times a day performed his piece *Giving* in the shopping center of Hoofddorp. Exactly at the hour, a shabby homeless man with Asian traits would slouch into the square; he would sit down in front of the branch store of the clothing chain C&A with his cap turned up on the ground before him. Soon afterwards, a young man in "casual" clothes would emerge from the crowd of shoppers, walk past the tramp, stop a few yards off in front of a shop window, and start to take a sneak look in his purse. The actor at that point had two options: to resume walking without giving anything, or to step back quickly and throw something in the tramp's cap. Whichever choice he made, shortly after he had left, the tramp would get up and slouch off again. The whole performance took four minutes and twenty seconds.

Although *Framed Area* was devoted to the "generic city" and to the demise of public space, Wall opted for a shopping center in which the open space is still public property, which means that tramps or other unwanted individuals cannot be kept out by a private security force. Nonetheless, the erosion of public space makes itself felt no less strongly in such a shopping center, which as a pedestrian area should be the place *par excellence* for encounters and interaction. The visitors who have just gotten out of their cars are shoppers with little eye for either their surroundings or other passers-by. They are not flaneurs but people of the crowd. *Giving*, as a result, was barely perceived. Only people who knew about Wall's work watched it consciously, and after a while some shopkeepers also started noticing that something was going on; to the shoppers, the performance was invisible. Much as the businessman/tramp managed to fool even Sherlock Holmes at first, passers-by on the Polder Square failed to notice anything suspicious. In an age when security cameras are mushrooming in urban areas, Wall's work can be interpreted as a subtle form of guerilla against the technocratic dream of total transparency. Soon perhaps we will be craving again for the kind of anonymity the modern city offered, when the man of the crowd could not be tracked down by people in control rooms staring at monitors, screening the crowds roaming through shopping centers, entertainment districts, and busy streets.

Wall's ephemeral performance does not mourn for some lost era when

37 Vito Acconci, "Public Space in a Private Time," in *Art and the Public Sphere*, ed. W.J.T. Mitchell (Chicago: University of Chicago Press, 1992), 173.

"public art" still seemed to function. Rather, it investigates how a tiny, barely noticeable addition can influence a given situation. In the words of Vito Acconci: "The city has all the design it needs. For another category — 'public art' — to have a function in the design of city spaces, 'art' has to be brought back to one of its root meanings: 'cunning.' Public art has to squeeze in and fall over and fit under what already exists in the city."[37] This cunning art, searching for whatever kinds of public space still exist, or whatever new kinds may develop, cannot take anything for granted, least of all itself. It exists always on the threshold of complete invisibility.

*Translation Bart Eeckhout*

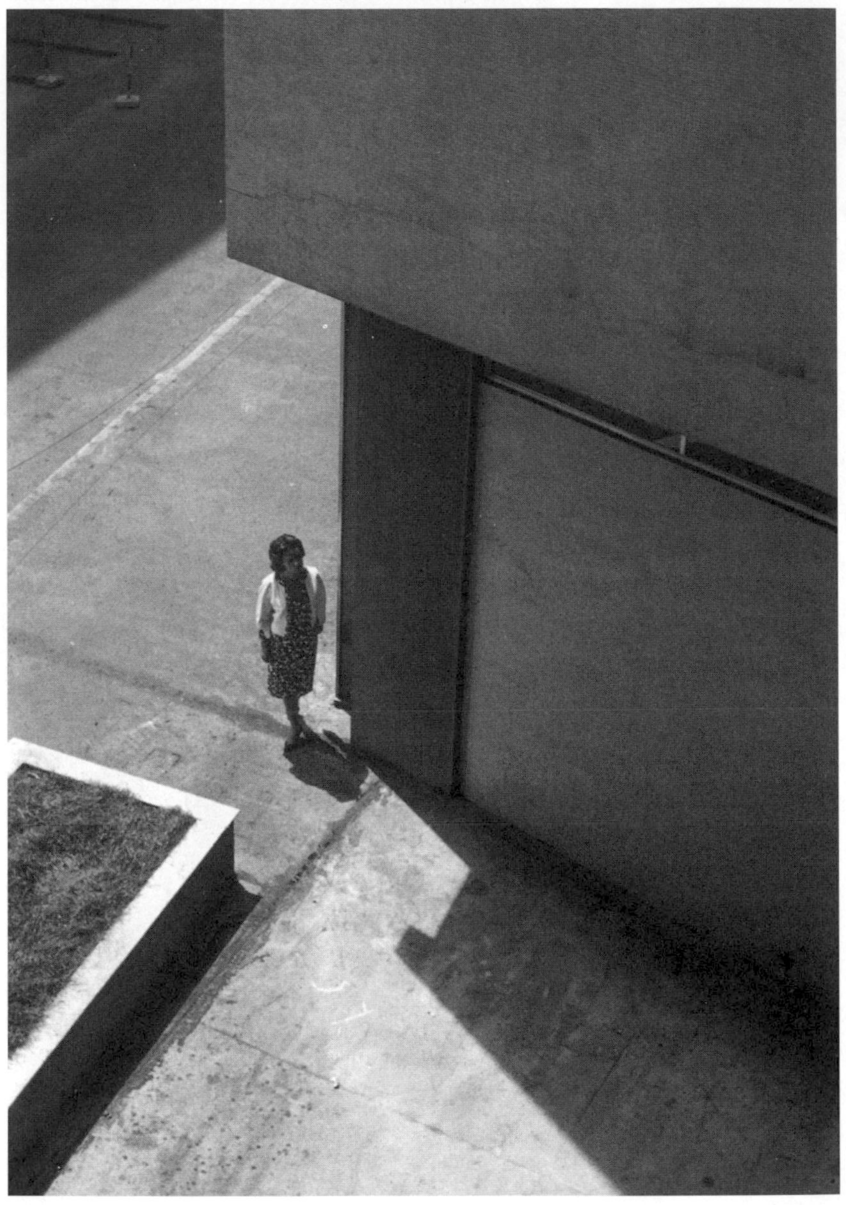

La notte *(1960)*.

**Steven Jacobs**

# Between E.U.R. and L.A.: Townscapes in the Work of Michelangelo Antonioni

*Keywords:* ■ *Film Studies* ■ *Urban Landscape* ■ *Voids* ■ *Periphery*

*"Only film commands optical approaches to the essence of the city, such as conducting the motorist into the new center."* — Walter Benjamin

*"The cinematic* derive *has itself become a form of nostalgia, a melancholic appeal to an old city. A new form of security is found in old ways of being lost."* — Mark Wigley

The subject of this case study is the townscapes of the Italian director Michelangelo Antonioni. First I will analyze in what ways Antonioni has been influenced by neorealist evocations of the city and how he distances himself from these. Next I will look at how Antonioni has transposed the romantic notion of the sublime, which was revitalized by the avantgarde of the fifties and sixties, onto the phenomenon of urban emptiness. His fascination with empty cities and urban wastelands also stimulated his interest in the periphery as the ideal setting for the treatment of his favorite subjects. The disappearance of the traditional city eventually directed his attention to Los Angeles, where *Zabriskie Point* was partly filmed. This singular road movie leads us to a discussion of the motif of "being-on-the-road" in Antonioni's productions.

**The film cartolina versus the Neorealist City** Besides the use of certain generic conventions of news reels, the participation of non-professional actors, a preference for authentic language, the attention to ordinary people in everyday situations, and the collapsing of film time and real time, filming on location is one of the most important characteristics of Italian neorealism. The explicit attention devoted to these locations immediately makes clear that the cinematographic space is more than just scenery. Already in Luchino Visconti's *Ossessione* (1942), the relation between the tragic characters and their surroundings is emphasized. Their desolate dwellings, the remote inn, the streets of Ancona and Ferrara, the sand flats along the Po are all emphatically present in this movie. Extremely lengthy medium shots, a typical feature of Visconti's mature style according to Peter Bondanella, allow the director to follow the main characters "as their destinies unfold and become shaped by their surroundings."[1] This explicit attention to the relation between characters and their daily surroundings is not only an essential feature of neorealism, but to a certain extent also determined other typical stylistic characteristics, such as the preference for medium and long shots, the use of long takes, and the dedramatization of the plot.

About half of the neorealist movies take place in a rural environment and concern the problems of agricultural laborers or fishermen. "These pictures of typically Italian situations," notes Pierre Sorlin, "had no counterpart in other European countries, whereas ... 'urban' films were comparable to other foreign productions while offering, at the same time, an original, unprecedented vison of cities."[2] Unmistakably, the city and urban life form the context in which the favorite themes of neorealism manifest themselves most clearly: the war and its effects on Italian society, poverty, political conflicts, and the tension between the individual and the masses. Particularly in the works of Roberto Rossellini and Vittorio De Sica, the city is prominently present. It often expresses the state of mind of the characters and determines to a large extent the narrative structure of the movie. In Rossellini's so-called war trilogy, the story of the characters is interwoven with the events and circumstances in a specific city: the fighting between partisans and nazis in the Italian capital in *Roma città aperta* (1945), the poverty and psychic desperation among the ruins of bombed Berlin in *Germania anno zero* (1947).[3] In the Florentine episode of *Paisà*, the city as a narrative and cinematographic element appears in its most essential form. In his monograph on Rossellini, Peter Brunette talks of "the visual 'thereness' of the built environment" in the Florence episode.[4] This part of the movie shows us nothing more than the attempts undertaken by two persons to reach the other part of town at a time when Florence is still occupied by lingering Germans and small groups of

1 Peter Bondanella, *Italian Cinema from Neorealism to the Present* (New York: Continuum, 1991), 28.

2 Pierre Sorlin, *European Cinemas: European Societies, 1939-1990* (London: Routledge, 1994), 117.

3 Since the camera has been panning the ruins of Berlin from the very beginning, even before the appearance of the credits, as well as afterwards, an obvious cause-and-effect relationship between the characters and the city is visually implied. The credits are immediately followed by a voice-over saying: "This film was shot in Berlin in the summer of 1947. It is intended to be simply an objective, true-to-life picture of this enormous, half-destroyed city." See Peter Brunette, *Roberto Rossellini* (New York: Oxford University Press, 1986), 81.

4 Ibid., 62.

5 André Bazin, "An Aesthetic of Reality: Cinematic Realism and the Italian School of the Liberation," in *What is Cinema?* (Vol. 2, Berkeley and Los Angeles: University of California Press, 1971), 16-40.

6 David Bass, "Insiders and Outsiders: Latent Urban Thinking in Movies of Modern Rome," in *Cinema and Architecture: Méliès, Mallet-Stevens, Multimedia*, ed. François Penz and Maureen Thomas (London: British Film Institute, 1997), 85.

7 Ibid., 86-87.

fascists, while the Allies prepare to march into the city. The city thus becomes the leading actor in the movie. As the French critic and advocate of neorealism André Bazin observes, "everything that is happening in Florence in the throes of the Liberation is of a like importance. The personal adventures of the two individuals blend into the mass of other adventures, just as one attempts to elbow one's way into a crowd to recover something one has lost."[5] In Vittorio De Sica's *Sciuscià* (1946), *Ladri di biciclette* (1948), and *Umberto D* (1951), the characters are likewise associated with their urban surroundings through an ingenious *mise-en-scène*, an extreme depth of field shots, and a deep-focus photography.

In their city evocations, Rossellini and De Sica characteristically brush aside the usual touristic establishing shots. In "Insiders and Outsiders," David Bass compared the representation of Rome in Hollywood productions like *Roman Holiday* (William Wyler, 1952), *20 Million Miles to Earth* (Nathan Juran, 1957), and *Three Coins in the Fountain* (Jean Negulesco, 1955) with the way in which this city plays a role in *Ladri di biciclette* and *Umberto D*. He describes the American representations of Rome as typically being made from the perspective of the outsider who tries to tame the city. "Outsiders' films of Rome violently warp the city's topography and present stereotypes of its culture and physical constitution. Such films are intimately tied to the phenomenon of tourism: filming on location is a form of visit, the plot concerns the exploits of outsiders visiting the city, and viewing represents a form of 'armchair tourism.'"[6] All important views of the city are sampled in a glorious but topographically nonsensical sequence. Hollywood-Rome is nothing more than what is known in Italian as *film cartolina*: a sort of moving postcard collection. The city is transformed and reduced to a series of wonderful attractions, in which dull or dangerous non-places get stashed away. "The *film cartolina*," writes Bass,

> *tames the city by manipulating its scale as well as by massaging its contents. While, typically, panoramic establishing shots state Rome to be a grand but distant object, the protagonists experience the city as relatively small. The film-city's collectable sights neighbour each other, and frequent chance meetings and other narrative conveniences reduce the city's potential vastness. Each of the cinematically joined-up sights in this distilled "city," on the other hand, is made to appear larger than life: shot frontally and full-frame (to eliminate its context), looking up (to stimulate its effect on the overawed pedestrian), and with a lingering gaze (after all, such monuments are the reason the producers paid out to come to Rome)."*[7]

In contrast to the *film cartolina* in which every context is erased, neorealist evocations of Rome highlight the urban context. According to André Bazin, "it would not be an exaggeration to say that *Ladri di biciclette* is the story of a walk through Rome by a father and his son."[8] Millicent Marcus adds that this accurate description does not just concern the topography, but that the movie "is also a walk through Rome's social institutions."[9] The itinerary followed by De Sica's characters appears to be a rather coincidental trip, which charts completely and in great detail certain parts of the city in their everyday contexts. "In 'urban context' movies," David Bass observes, "the insider sees the city as a strict itinerary of repulsions. If the *film cartolina* remakes the city in the service of the film, folding it to maximise the intake of touristic sights, then insider's films of resistant urban context are made in the service of the existing city, their actions guided and squeezed by its intransigent topography and the character of its areas."[10] For the down-and-out protagonist of *Umberto D*, the monuments of the eternal city are completely irrelevant. In *Ladri di biciclette*, the protagonists undertake a journey through a strange and somehow also hostile Rome. The city, consisting of anonymous residential blocks and dark spots in tunnels and under bridges, seems like a labyrinth in which figures suddenly emerge and disappear. "De Sica's Rome," writes Millicent Marcus, "is a fragmented, decentered space with few familiar landmarks and no sense of cohesion."[11] This labyrinthine townscape frequently emerges in neorealist evocations of the city. It is without a doubt partly a consequence of neorealists' agile camera work. André Bazin notes how "Traveling and panning shots do not have the same god-like character that the Hollywood camera crane has bestowed on them. Everything is shot from eye-level or from a concrete point of view, such as a roof top or window."[12]

**Nettezza urbana: Antonioni and Neorealism** In his early works, Michelangelo Antonioni shared with his neorealist colleagues an unusual interest in the city and in urban life. N.U. *(Nettezza urbana)* (1948), an eleven-minute documentary about *spazzini* or street sweepers in Rome, radically departs from the *film cartolina*. In Seymour Chatman's words, "The film reverses ordinary travelogue interests: however variegated the brilliant Eternal City may be, the street cleaner is everywhere, invisible to the populace and indifferent to the landmarks yet ironically essential to them, to Rome's *nettezza*, its propriety."[13] In N.U., the traditional

8 Bazin, *What is Cinema?*, 55.

9 Millicent Marcus, *Italian Film in the Light of Neorealism* (Princeton: Princeton University Press, 1986), 64.

10 Bass, "Insiders and Outsiders," 88.

11 Marcus, *Italian Film*, 73.

12 Bazin, "An Aesthetic of Reality," 33.

13 Seymour Chatman, *Antonioni; or the Surface of the World* (Berkeley and Los Angeles: University of California Press, 1985), 6.

14 See Sam Rohdie, *Antonioni* (London: British Film Institute Publishing, 1990), 111-12.

15 Ibid., 61.

hierarchical relation between role and context, between figure and background is turned upside down: the city itself has become the true main character and receives more attention than the pitiful fate of the street sweepers. However, this inversion is a consequence of the fact that the *spazzini* have become invisible to the city's inhabitants and visitors.[14] The movie begins with the figure of a street sweeper looming up at the break of dawn and ends with a character disappearing into the twilight. A scene where a street sweeper looks at his reflection in a display window is cut through with other movements and other people, as if the street sweeper and his reflection did not exist. The characters seem unreal or ephemeral — a motif that will frequently reappear in Antonioni's mature work. While neorealist directors or screenwriters like Vittorio De Sica or Cesare Zavattini would undoubtedly have explored the dramatic and even tragic possibilities of such a subject, Antonioni dedramatizes the lives of the *spazzini* through the abstract quality of his photography. The surroundings are shown by way of emphatically arbitrary camera movements that draw the viewer's attention to themselves. The result is a series of hard-to-define, nondescript fragments that generate a sense of disorientation.

Antonioni borrows from neorealism the meticulous selection of locations and the great care for settings, but the urban landscape no longer functions as an illustration of the social context of the characters, as is the case in "orthodox" neorealism. Instead, Antonioni develops another form of objectivity, which transcends realism and relies on an outspoken detachment. In his films, the environment is just there and leads its own life. This is even discernible in other early works that bear the mark of neorealism, such as *Tentato suicidio*, his contribution to Cesare Zavattini's "film journal" *Amore in Città* (1953), or in *I Vinti* (1952). In *Tentato suicidio*, the camera relishes in gliding over the water surface and stones instead of concentrating on the drama. In *I Vinti*, an episodic movie about urban juvenile delinquency in Paris, Rome, and London, a causal relation between environment and characters is nowhere explicitly suggested. As Sam Rohdie notes, "What stands out is not only the reticence and distance of the narration, but the presence of the backgrounds and the landscapes as central to the actions, somehow working their way into the souls and psyche of the characters, but in no way that is direct or obvious."[15] Antonioni retains from the documentary genre and the aesthetics of neorealism an interest in the environment, but leaves out any didactic dimension. As a result, his own later documentaries evolve into meta-documentaries in which perception and the cinematographic registration itself are examined — witness the much-maligned documentary on China, *Chung Kuo Cina* (1972), in which the texture of a wall gets more attention than the achievements of the revolution. Antonioni's "formalism" is in that sense not an exclusive feature of his masterpieces from the sixties, but was already apparent from the beginning of his artistic career and even determined his attitude as a film critic in the early forties. In his contributions to the journal *Cinemà*, in which the aesthetics of neorealism was laid out, his attention was not directed at the social or political dimensions of the movie, but at the narrative structure, the function of silences, the rhythm of events, the creation of a certain atmosphere, the camera movements, and the effects of light and montage.[16]

**Deserts, Voids, and the Modernist Sublime** Antonioni's distinct interest in the specific conventions of the medium film resulted in the development of a singular cinematographic language, which turned him into one of the most important masters of European modernism. The unconventional long take, the ostentatious camera movement, the "open" plot, the dedramatizations by way of *temps mort*, the use of the wide-angle lens to increase distances and the long-focus lens to flatten out the image, the idiosyncratic montage, the calculated framing: Antonioni's stylistic features appear to relate to a Brechtian dramaturgy of alienation as well as to refer to a systematic self-examination. This tendency towards self-reflection is closely related to the way in which Clement Greenberg analyzed postwar American abstract painting as the result of a search for the essence of the medium. The work of Antonioni even displays similarities with the work of painters like Jackson Pollock, Mark Rothko, and Barnett Newman. Unsurprisingly, Antonioni is also active as a painter, although he once qualified this claim by saying "I am not a painter, more a filmmaker who paints."[17] In the Antonioni museum at Ferrara, works can be seen apparently made up of photographic enlargements of abstract images — a procedure that inevitably evokes *Blow-Up* (1966). His so-called *Enchanted Mountains* resemble the vague landscapes or the ethereal mountain tops of the Romantic or Symbolist nineteenth-century paintings of Caspar David Friedrich or Ferdinand Hodler.

The cinematographic work of Antonioni has been associated with developments in modern painting before. Angela Dalle Vache, for example, pointed to similarities between Antonioni's movies in general (and *Il deserto rosso* in partic-

16 See ibid., 12-22.

17 Michelangelo Antonioni, *The Architecture of Vision: Writings and Interviews on Cinema* (New York: Marsilio Publishers, 1996), 231. The interview originally appeared in *Positif* 292 (June 1985).

18 Angela Dalle Vache, *Cinema and Painting: How Art Is Used in Film* (London: Athlone, 1996), 43-80.

19 Robert Benayoun, "Un cri dans le désert," *Positif* 66 (1965): 43-59; Roger Tailleur, "Le désert jusqu'à plus soif," *Positif* 67-68 (1965): 81-92.

20 See, for instance, Antonioni, *Architecture of Vision*, 204, 248.

21 See Richard Gilman, "About Nothing — With Precision," *Theater Arts* 46, 7 (1962): 10-12; Lee Seldes, *The Legacy of Mark Rothko* (New York: Holt, Rinehart & Winston, 1978), 64; also Chatman, *Antonioni*, 248.

22 See Richard Roud, "The Red Desert," *Sight and Sound* 34 (Spring 1965): 76-80.

ular) and the oeuvre of Italian painters such as Giorgio De Chirico, Piero Manzoni, Mario Sironi, Alberto Burri, and Mimmo Rotella.[18] French critics like Benayoun and Tailleur noted an affinity to the informal art of Jean Dubuffet, Wols, Nicolas de Staël, Pierre Soulages, and Jean Fautrier.[19] Strangely enough, the Antonioni-*Forschung* hardly devotes any attention to the abstract expressionism of Pollock, Rothko, and Newman, even though Pollock is explicitly mentioned by Antonioni in interviews.[20] The director was even friends with Rothko. In 1966, he visited the painter's atelier in New York.[21] Both Antonioni and Rothko had been struck by their common interest in representing elusive things. Ephemeral phenomena such as water, mist, haze, or smoke form important motifs in the former's oeuvre and are already prominently present in his debut, *Gente del Po* (1943-47). As in the canvases of Rothko or Pollock, forms appear and disappear in Antonioni's movies: figures fade like shadows, fore- and background melt together, shots and sequences are disconnected from perspectival space or a central point of view.

The so-called abstraction in Antonioni's movies is further realized by the two-dimensionality of many of his images, which is equivalent to the flatness in the paintings of Rothko and Pollock. Antonioni's interest in surfaces is clearly connected to his preference for ephemeral substances. Mist, for instance, transforms any depth into a surface and minimalizes the difference between fore- and background — as can be seen in *Il grido* (1957), *Il deserto rosso* (1964), or *Identificazione di una donna* (1982). In *Il deserto rosso,* the flatness is also achieved through the use of a telephoto lens. The lens is never used to bring upfront and to focus distant objects, but to reduce depth and diminish the optical distance between figures and background. The depth of focus, typical of realism, is replaced by a distinct pictorial effect that strongly resembles the way in which modernist painting explores the limits of pictorial illusion.[22] In *Il deserto rosso,* Antonioni's first color movie in which he did not hesitate to "paint up" locations, every sense of depth is undermined by the use of subdued colors, which completely breaks with the saturated color palette of the Hollywood technicolor movie. Giuliana, the female protagonist, is also flattened by pressing her literally against a wall — a motif that regularly pops up in many other works of the director. The most extreme example is undoubtedly the nymphomaniac patient in *La notte,* in which the flatness is coupled to the immensity of a formal as well as an existential emptiness. In the words of William Arrowsmith, "what the nymphomaniac wants to shut out is any knowledge of the blank immensity — it is hard to give it a name, call it the infinite, immensity, the unlimited, the object of transcendence — that we see exteriorized as she stands against the absolutely clinical white blankness of the wall, her own emptiness projected as the emptiness around her, threatening her."[23] In other movies of Antonioni, men or women are placed against big flat surfaces that are criss-crossed by two or more vertical lines in a way that is reminiscent of Barnett Newman's colorfield paintings.

Antonioni's coupling of flatness to big surfaces constitutes another likeness to American abstract expressionism; it was no coincidence that *wall-sized painting* emerged at the same time as the cinemascope format. Moreover, Arrowsmith's analysis of the scene from *La notte* evokes the notion of the sublime that played an important role in this form of art. Like Rothko and Newman, Antonioni is an artist who explores the sublimity of emptiness. Emptiness and infinity are indeed sources of the sublime, as Edmund Burke argued in his *Philosophical Enquiry into the Origin of Our Ideas on the Sublime and Beautiful* (1757). Shortly after the Second World War, the concept of the sublime was reintroduced into contemporary art precisely by artists like Newman, who attempted to find the sublime in what Jean-François Lyotard described as the here and now of paint.[24] Newman translated the Kantian dynamic sublime from nature to culture by reinscribing the force of formlessness in the sensation of paint as such.[25] In Newman's art, *The Sublime is Now* — as the title of a text by the artist from 1948 has it.[26]

Newman's confrontation of the spectator with a vast surface finds its equivalent in Antonioni's exaltation of emptiness. Characters are, for instance, often expelled to the edges of the screen. The isolated suicides in *Tentato suicidio* and the scene from *Il deserto rosso* in which figures fade into the mist, clearly refer to the sublimity of the void. In other shots or sequences, a wide angle lens enforces the distance between characters. Even in a relatively small chamber, as with the hospital scene in *La notte*, the distance between the figures appears unbridgeable. Another Antonioni feature that capitalizes on this dimension is the way in which characters tend to leave the frame so that the viewer is confronted with a long or short deserted emptiness. The director not only suggests that there is a world or image not captured by the figures, he also makes clear that the relation between the figures and their surroundings is an important factor.

Another American artist who revitalized the notion of the sublime was Robert Smithson. With his often spectacular *earth works* from the late sixties and

23 William Arrowsmith, *Antonioni: The Poet of Images* (New York: Oxford University Press, 1995), 57.

24 Jean-François Lyotard, "The Sublime and the Avant-Garde," in *The Lyotard Reader*, ed. Andrew Benjamin (Cambridge: Blackwell, 1989), 199.

25 See Mark C. Taylor, *Disfiguring: Art, Architecture, Religion* (Chicago: University of Chicago Press, 1992), 88-95.

26 Barnett Newman, "The Sublime is Now" (1948), reprinted in *Barnett Newman: Selected Writings and Interviews*, ed. John P. O'Neill (Berkeley and Los Angeles: University of California Press, 1990), 170-73.

27 See Nancy Holt, ed., *The Writings of Robert Smithson* (New York: New York University Press, 1979), 52-57 and 186-96.

28 Reyner Banham, *Scenes in America Deserta* (Cambridge, MA: MIT Press, 1982), 61-62.

early seventies, Smithson returned Newman's interpretation of the sublime back to the landscape. That same landscape, however, was no longer seen as idyllic, untouched nature. For Smithson "New York itself [is] natural like the Grand Canyon."[27] The dullness of New Jersey had a particular effect upon him. The locations for his interventions were preferably "entropic" landscapes — industrial residual spaces, dumping grounds, exhausted stone quarries, deserted mines where natural forces and human interventions coalesce — in short, the sort of landscape that is brilliantly evoked in *Il deserto rosso*, which was filmed in the industrial periphery of Ravenna with its bizarre silos, chimneys emitting multicolored smoke, radar installations, turbines, and generators. Antonioni also clearly shares Smithson's fascination with deserts. In *Zabriskie Point* (1970) and *Professione: Reporter* (1974), hot sand flats acquire almost mystical connotations, as do the Liparic island in *L'avventura* or the swampy plains of the Po in *Gente del Po* or *Il grido*.

Architectural historian Reyner Banham has foregrounded the desert as a space in which modern man feels at home:

*The desert measurably offers immeasurable space. It is therefore an environment in which "Modern Man" ought to feel at home — his modern painting, as in the works of Mondrian, implies a space that extends beyond the confines of the canvas; his modern architecture, as in the works of Mies van der Rohe, is a rectangular partition of a regular but infinite space; its ideal inhabitants, the sculptures of Giacometti stalking metaphysically through that space as far as it infinitely extends. And modern man's last frontier of exploration, in case you'd forgotten, is space itself — which is how we came to be stumbling about lunar landscapes that are uncomfortably like the desert of the earth.*[28]

Il deserto rosso *(1964)*.

Jane Tompkins likewise observes a similarity between the desert and modern architecture: "Its clean, spare lines, lucid spaces, and absence of ornament bring it closer to the abstract austerities of modern architectural design than any other kind of landscape would."[29]

**Antonioni and Urban Voids** The work of Antonioni is a perfect illustration of Banham's and Tompkins's metaphors. Not only does the desert acquire a strictly geometrical or architectural character in his movies, the effect of a sublime void is also evoked by his unusual representations of the geometrical simplicity of (modern) architecture and the estranging character of the modern city. The hostility of nature finds its peer in alien townscapes. The Romantic yearning for Arcadia and the utopian city of modernism are both rejected. Architecture and the city take up a prominent place in Antonioni's so-called tetralogy from the period 1960-64 (*L'avventura, La notte, L'eclisse,* and *Il deserto rosso*). With Antonioni architecture no longer serves realist purposes or is used to convince the spectator of the "real-ness" of the location. But neither is the built-up environment just a background. "It is hard to imagine a movie in which buildings do not appear," writes Seymour Chatman. "We tend to ignore them in most films as mere background. But in the tetralogy we come to read buildings as architects, urban planners, and designers do."[30] Characters seem to become no more than mannequins in architectural designs or spatial environments recalling the paintings of Giorgio De Chirico — something that was already striking in scenes from earlier movies, like the meeting between Clara and Nardo amidst film sets in *La signora senza camelie* (1953), or Clelia's trip through Turin in *Le amiche* (1955). De Chirico would also seem to be the source of inspiration for the presentation of the streets of Ravenna in *Il deserto rosso,* and especially for the impressive scene in the sunflooded and deserted Sicilian town from the fascist era in *L'avventura*. The city's emptiness not only refers to the barrenness of the islands in a previous scene, but also conjures up a feeling of alienation. For Antony Easthope, the void in Antonioni's dystopian evocations of the city points to the psychic and existential hollowness of the characters: "Here the city is a site of alienation — less social alienation than a full-blown transcendental alienation to be understood as the view that formerly human life in cities was real, a natural inheritance, but now is made up, a merely arbitrary construction from which

29 Jane Tompkins, *West of Everything: The Inner Life of Westerns* (Oxford: Oxford University Press, 1992), 76.

30 Chatman, *Antonioni*, 102.

31 Antony Easthope, "Cinécities in the Sixties," in *The Cinematic City*, ed. David B. Clarke (London: Routledge, 1997), 133.

32 Ibid., 134.

33 Ibid.

something transcendental is felt to be missing."[31] Whereas in the traditional aesthetics of the sublime voids suggested the presence of the invisible or the ineffable, and in Romantic painting nature is a symbol of the supernatural, Antonioni's urban emptiness precisely expresses the absence of the transcendental. Protagonists react to the same situation in totally different ways: to Sandra — an architect, by the way — the situation presents nothing abnormal; for Claudia, however, the white hollowness of the city is a cause of anxiety and fear. Like Lidia in *La notte*, Vittoria in *L'eclisse*, and Giuliana in *Il deserto rosso*, it is again a woman who feels uprooted and threatened in the city. A shot at the end of the sequence quite effectively strengthens the feeling of disorientation: as Sandro and Claudia prepare to drive off, the camera tracks towards them, viewed from a sidestreet. According to cinematic conventions, a camera movement to a character points to a point-of-view shot and thus to a present third party. Antonioni's inexplicable tracking shot can be interpreted as a modernist inclination to foreground a specific cinematographic procedure, but in Easthope's opinion it can also express the fact that "some sinister presence of the deserted city is watching the couple."[32] However that may be, "we are invited to link alienation in the city with a certain erosion of classical cinematic space."[33]

In *La notte* and *L'eclisse*, the architecture of the city is even more center-stage than in *L'avventura*, so much so that it appears to play the main role. In the former film, Antonioni's sensibility for architecture and the city shows from the very opening scene, in which the camera glides over the glass surfaces of the Pirelli tower, recently built by Gio Ponti, and pictures Milan as a busy construction site. The camera tracks down along this European skyscraper until the city seems to rise up from the ground and absorb the camera. As Geoffrey Nowell-Smith notes,

*From this moment on the city, with all that it throws up by way of human and material flotsam, allows the characters no respite. More than a background, or (as in*

*L'avventura* (1959).

*Bresson) a subjective emanation of the characters' spiritual condition, the landscape becomes a protagonist in the action and co-actor in the human tragedy. Traffic piles up in the streets in a chaotic symphony of claxons: in a slum quarter a child cries and won't be comforted. Out in the periferia, on a wasteland, two men fight each other for no given reason: rockets are let off in a cornfield and sizzle up into a featureless sky. In an almost empty night-club a coloured woman does a striptease that is mechanical to the point of obscenity. All these are accidents of the city, but they act upon the characters, or are simply observed by them, and acquire in the process an explicit role in the development of the story.*[34]

Vis-à-vis modern architecture and urban planning Antonioni often adopts an ambivalent stance. On the one hand, he cannot hide his aesthetic fascination with the power of geometrical volumes and the perfection of modern, industrial materials. On the other hand, the new architecture and its clinical hollowness contribute to an atmosphere of alienation and loneliness that hangs over the tetralogy. The new, modern architecture symbolizing the reconstruction and rapid industrialization of Italy is often confronted by Antonioni with the solidity of old churches and palazzi, just as the old urban structures dissolve into the wastelands of modern planning. This is brilliantly visualized in Lidia's walk through the periphery of Milan, in *La notte,* and in the famous coda of *L'eclisse,* which lasts some seven minutes and is a sort of mini-documentary about the E.U.R. suburb of Rome. The coda consists solely of a montage of shots of various views and details of buildings, constructions, infrastructure, vehicles, and objects.

**Learning from la periferia** *La notte* and *L'eclisse* illustrate Antonioni's increasing interest in the periphery as an environment in which the themes and motifs of his films can best be developed. William Arrowsmith notes how *La notte* displays

*Antonioni's familiar polar geography — the comparison and contrast — of center and countryside, as well as their interim world at the periphery, what the Italians call* la periferia, *that is, the neither-nor space where the city gives out, where the paving abruptly stops and the high-rise palazzi of the quartieri nuovi yield to shacks and open fields;* la periferia *is the point where city and country intersect in a momentary, fragile equilibrium. Every image is composed to declare the intersection of these two worlds, at the periphery, but also the looming imbalance that threatens them both.*[35]

34 Geoffrey Nowell-Smith, "La Notte," *Sight and Sound* 31 (Winter 1961-62): 28-31.
35 Arrowsmith, *Antonioni*, 52.
36 See Nowell-Smith, "La Notte."
37 Arrowsmith, *Antonioni*, 80.

The shift from core city to periphery in *La notte* is accompanied by a change in film technique. At the moment when Lidia slips away from a cocktail party and starts to wander aimlessly through the streets of the Milan periphery, the camera movements are replaced by a montage of images that have no inner meaning: a child, fighting men, a firework that is being launched, etc. The montage not only gives meaning to these images — they can, for instance, be interpreted as alluding to Lidia's unfulfilled desires[36] — but also enhances the spatial disorientation induced by the centerless and fragmented landscape of the periphery.

Hardly definable urban or peripheral voids are often counterpointed by Antonioni with short sequences in which the inner city is presented as similarly uninhabitable because of the suffocating bustle: for instance, the emptiness of Noto and of the fascist satellite city vs. the mad crowd in Messina in *L'avventura*, the periphery of Milan vs. the traffic congestion after the visit to the hospital in *La notte*, the strange emptiness of the Roman E.U.R. neighborhood vs. the swarming masses in and around the stock exchange on the Piazza di Pietra in *L'eclisse*. According to Arrowsmith, this last movie is

*even fuller in its architectural inflection: we move with glancing incisiveness to the planned suburb of* EUR, *with its Nervi Palazzo dello Sport; then to the stock exchange; then to a glimpse of Saint Peter's seen from Vittoria's mother's apartment; on to mixed classical and Renaissance in the shots of Piazza di Pietra, the site of the café where Vittoria meets Piero; to the middle-class ambience of Piero's parent's apartment in Roma vecchia; and then finally to the half-finished building, its skeletal ferroconcrete still masked by the drying mats of woven reed, on the corner where Piero and Vittoria meet.*[37]

L'eclisse *(1962).*

In *L'eclisse,* the montage technique is even more explicitly used to evoke hardly definable voids in the periphery. The film ends with the already mentioned sequence of images of traffic, buildings, and all kinds of objects at the place where the two protagonists have arranged to meet. Instead of choosing a romantic café or a piazza in the center, the two lovers meet on a pedestrian crossing at an anonymous street corner in the E.U.R. neighborhood. Seymour Chatman calls it "a void, not an intended place" and states that "the intersection evokes what is most transitory, casual, and ephemeral in our society: mere encounters, not genuine meetings."[38]

Antonioni's cinematographic interest in the periphery in general and E.U.R. in particular is also found in other Italian movies of the same period. One of three episodes in *Ieri, oggi, domani* (1964) by Vittorio De Sica consists of an impressive car trip through the center of Milan and the periphery into a sort of no man's land. Directors like Pier Paolo Pasolini with *Accatone* (1959) and *Mamma Roma* (1962) and Bernardo Bertolucci with *La commare secca* (1962) try to uncover the poetry of the periphery. Their principal characters — beggars, thieves, homosexuals, and whores — make up a community of social and geographical marginals, who are presented as allegorical and even mythical figures.[39] In Federico Fellini's *Le tentazioni del Dottor Antonio* (1962), in which a gigantic billboard-Anita Ekberg comes to life, the banal and terrifying unreality of E.U.R. is evoked and reduced to its true proportions: as a part of Mussolini's third Rome, E.U.R. was in fact designed as a scenographic spectacle, a sort of enormous film setting.

A cinematographic interest in the Roman periphery already surfaces in neorealism and is doubtlessly linked to the specific urban morphology of Rome. In a chapter devoted to the "blurred image" of the city in European cinema, Pierre Sorlin observes that "the Italian capital has for a long time been a city, plus suburbs, plus a no man's land."[40] The two boys in *Sciuscià* often sleep in a stable and at a certain moment are seen to ride through the city center on horseback. Val Melaina, where *Ladri di biclette* begins, is situated five miles away from the city walls. Later on, the whole roadside was filled with buildings, but in 1947 this area was still an urban desert. Distance is an important feature in this movie.

In films like *L'eclisse,* the periphery is no longer presented as a wilderness where only the proletarian part of the population lives. For Antonioni the urban void proves the decline of urban culture in general. As Pierre Sorlin remarks, "The film tells us about an eclipse, the eclipse of Rome. In 1980 or 1990 it was

38 Chatman, *Antonioni*, 108-13.

39 See Bass, "Insiders and Outsiders," 84-99.

40 Sorlin, *European Cinemas*, 118-19.

41 Ibid., 126.

42 Ibid., 132-33.

easy to say that the centre of most European towns lost inhabitants to the suburbs. In 1960 that was not clear at all, especially in capital cities where well-off people hoped they would get rid of the lower classes (sent to the outskirts) and stay in the historic districts. In contrast to their wishes, *L'eclisse* pictures a radical change which seemed overstated at the time but which squares with what was to happen during the following decades."[41]

**Voids and Vegas** In contrast with the cinematographic evocations of the city in the 1920s by Dziga Vertov, Walter Ruttmann, Paul Fejos, King Vidor, or Joe May — which suggested the glittering enchantment of the kaleidoscopic metropolis —, Antonioni's evocations seem to be built on a dichotomy in which claustrophobic masses alternate with empty streets, squares, and buildings. Although the image of empty streets regularly pops up in Antonioni's oeuvre, such emptiness is usually associated with the decline of the city. His distinct interest in the periphery underscores how his fascination with the urban void does not simply reproduce an older motif stretching back to the aesthetics of Symbolism, in which empty streets betray a feeling of fear, anxiety, or alienation. Antonioni clearly evokes another sort of emptiness that is itself a consequence of the transformations of the contemporary city. It is an emptiness that denies the city any identity at all. In his later work, the city acquires a negative presence. Although *Blow-Up* (1967) has been read by some critics as a fanciful vision of Swinging London, the British capital is hardly discernible in that movie. Every action seems to take place in anonymous neighborhoods. "We are offered glimpses of an unidentified English town," writes Pierre Sorlin, "and buses and lorries cross our field of vision, preventing us from pinpointing any recognizable site. Long rows of brick houses, coloured buildings, waste grounds and now an antique shop in a small, decayed structure: a town, for sure, but more a skeleton, an idea of a town rather than any defined place."[42]

The loss of a *genius loci* and the shift from center to periphery as the prime location for an Antonioni plot reach their predictable end in the registration of an American cityscape. In *Zabriskie Point* (1971), Antonioni links his fascination with deserts to specific features of the postwar cityscape in which the hierarchical relations between center and periphery are no longer apparent. It is no coincidence that, besides Death Valley and Arizona, Antonioni chose Los Angeles as a location for his movie, for L.A. is the paradigmatic urban space of the late twentieth century, in which core and periphery fuse into an endless, extended amalgam and the car determines life to a great extent. Although several critics have emphasized that Antonioni viewed American society as a die-hard European, we should note how he nevertheless decided to visualize America in the American way — that is, from the perspective of the car. In *Zabriskie Point*, Antonioni pictured Los Angeles in the same way as the British architectural historian Reyner Banham would do a year later in his seminal book about the city: "So, like earlier generations of English intellectuals who taught themselves Italian in order to read Dante in the original I learned to drive in order to read Los Angeles in the original."[43] Although the vastness of Los Angeles and the gradual transition between city and desert is visualized in the scenes with the airplane, Antonioni, like Banham, learned to drive and *Zabriskie Point* can easily be interpreted as a *road movie*. While the periphery of European cities in *La notte*, *L'eclisse*, and *Il deserto rosso* is defined by an almost geometrically designed emptiness, Los Angeles is foregrounded as an avalanche of interchangeable signs of corporate power and injunctions to consume. This is impressively conveyed at the beginning of the movie by a series of billboards that are blurred by a telephoto lens and evoke a feeling of disorientation. To Seymour Chatman this approach would precisely betray the European perspective of Antonioni: "The interesting shots of the dizzying array of billboards along the Los Angeles streets are taken from Mark's point of view. But what native would ever actually look at them? (Mark, unlike Lidia, is no critic of architecture)."[44] Yet Antonioni could also be claimed to have developed a cinematic equivalent to an experience that was described in the same period by the American architect and critic Robert Venturi in *Learning From Las Vegas*. One paragraph of that book in particular seems to apply almost literally to the filmmaker who exchanged the streets of Milan and Rome for the streets and highways of Los Angeles:

*Visiting Las Vegas in the mid-1960s was like visiting Rome in the late 1940s. For young Americans in the 40s, familiar only with the auto-scaled, gridiron city and the antiurban theories of the previous architectural generation, the traditional urban spaces, the pedestrian scale, and the mixtures, yet continuities, of styles of the Italian piazzas were a significant revelation. They rediscovered the piazza. Two decades later architects are perhaps ready for similar lessons about large open space, big scale, and high speed. Las Vegas is to the Strip what Rome is to the Piazza.*[45]

Antonioni's images perfectly correspond to Venturi's observation that "this architecture of styles and signs is antispatial; it is an architecture of communica-

43 Reyner Banham, *Los Angeles: The Architecture of Four Ecologies* (1971; reprint, London: Penguin Books, 1990), 23.

44 Chatman, *Antonioni*, 161.

45 Robert Venturi, Denise Scott Brown, and Steven Izenour, *Learning From Las Vegas* (1972; reprint, Cambridge, MA: MIT Press, 1991), 18.

46 Ibid., 8.

tion over space; communication dominates space as an element in the architecture and in the landscape. But it is for a new scale of landscape ... a new landscape of big spaces, high speeds, and complex programs."[46]

**On the Road** Mark and Daria, the protagonists of *Zabriskie Point*, also befit the image of the typical Antonioni hero who is continually traveling and looking for something. This hero is a nomad. Only rarely do the buildings or cities so carefully filmed by the director offer shelter to the characters. The characters are drifters who do not succeed in settling down or finding comfort at home. They are always on the road, living in hotel rooms or in the houses of others. Already in Antonioni's early documentaries, people can be seen to live in movable houses (e.g. boat cabins in *Gente del Po*) or makeshift ones: in N.U. a drifter locks himself up in a flower booth on Piazza di Spagna. In *La signora senza camelie* (1953), Clara clearly does not feel at home in the house where she has been living since her marriage with Gianni. The interior has not yet been finished. She lives, as it were, on a construction site, and leaves every decision about the decoration to her husband. Later she confesses to a friend and former colleague that everything in the house seemed "unreal." Clara prefigures Niccolo in *Identificazione di una donna* (1982), who also lives in a house decorated by another, his ex-wife. When he enters the house, the alarm goes off. He is an invader in his own house. Clara's trysts with her lover Nardi happen in typical places: a hotel room, the labyrinthine alleyways of Venice, the Potemkin city between the decors of Cinecittà, or the barren landscape near the E.U.R. district, where Libera's Palazzo dei Congressi and the Palazzo della Civiltà Italiana eerily rise up from the ground.

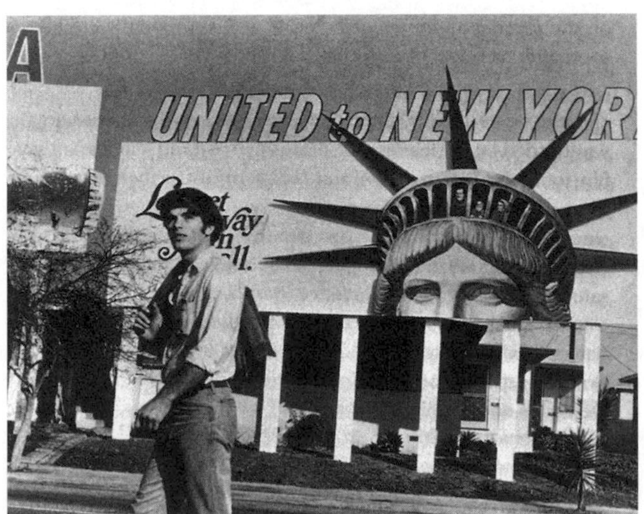


Zabriskie Point *(1969)*.

Aldo in *Il grido* (1957) is literally a drifter. When the woman with whom he has lived for seven years tells him she loves someone else, he leaves together with his little daughter and wanders downstream through the barren winter landscape of the Po. First he visits an old lover, Elvira, but finds that he cannot feel at home with her. Next he goes to see Virginia. She runs a gas station — a perfect symbol of being-on-the-road. Eventually, in the sandy plains of the Po estuary, the symbolic end of his journey, he looks in vain for shelter in the primitive hut of the prostitute Andreina. As with Mark and Daria in *Zabriskie Point*, or Claudia and Sandro in *L'avventura* and David in *Professione: Reporter* (1974), Aldo personifies the typical Antonioni hero as the drifter. Vittoria, too, wanders aimlessly through Rome in *L'eclisse*, just as Lidia does through the periphery of Milan in *La notte*, or Giuliana in the industrial wastelands nearby Ravenna in *Il deserto rosso*. Giuliana's lover, Corrado, twice explicitly tells her that he feels at home nowhere. At other times, he alludes to a feeling of restlessness, always in typical places: in the shop that Giuliana decorates, where the walls are painted with test color squares, in a hut, and in a room in a clinical hotel. Strikingly enough, in *L'eclisse*, the film in which Antonioni focuses most on the urban landscape and on interiors, we hardly get a view of Vittoria's flat. Her antagonist Piero does not live in his own house, but in that of his family — a house packed with paintings and portraits that have always been there. It is an environment where Vittoria feels even more threatened than in the empty streets of the E.U.R. neighborhood. Their lovegame clearly works better in Piero's office than in his home. Piero only feels at home when he is at work: the stock exchange, a tumultuous non-place, the exemplary site of flux and circulation. Since Fritz Lang's *Dr. Mabuse. Der Spieler* (1922), the stock exchange as a teeming mass of hooting and gesticulating individuals was never pictured this convincingly.

The queen in *Il mistero di Oberwald* (1980) calls her castles a grave in which she has locked herself since the death of the king. Her delay in Oberwald, moreover, is only of a short duration. In order to escape from terrorists and court intrigues, she continually changes residence. Even so, it is probably David, the principal character of *Professione: Reporter*, who embodies the ultimate Antonioni hero. He does not have a home at all — the film was brought out in America under the title *The Passenger*. David always stays in hotel rooms, in cars that continually break down (machines do not provide any comfort either), and indeed even lives in the body of another, the arms dealer Robertson, whose identity he has taken over.

*Translation Chris Bulcaen*

**Trui Vetters**

# "Night on Earth": Urban Practices and the Blindness of Metatheory

*Keywords:* ■ *Photography* ■ *Film Studies* ■ *Gender Studies* ■ *Theory of Space*

*"When you're finally up at the moon looking back at earth, all those differences and nationalistic traits are pretty well going to blend and you're going to get a concept that maybe this is really one world and why the hell can't we learn to live together like decent people."* — American astronaut Frank Borman, *Newsweek* (23 December 1968)

*"To grasp its secret, you should not, then, begin with the city and move inwards towards the screen; you should begin with the screen and move outwards towards the city."* — Jean Baudrillard, *America*

The view from the moon described by Frank Borman became accessible to everyone after an astronaut took a series of photographs of the earth, during the Apollo 17 mission in 1972. In the years that followed, one of these photographs, known as AS17-148-22727, became one of the most popular pictures of the earth ever produced. It was not the first time that the earth had been represented in its entirety, but what was so significant about this representation was that the image had been captured by a human eye-witness.[1] The importance of this event can hardly be overstated. As Richard Muir explains in *Political Geographies*, not only did "this photographic image of the planet ... [supplant] the Mercator map and the cartographer's globe as an icon of the Earth," it also became a symbol of the earth's "oneness": "The images obtained on the Apollo missions provided the global public with striking and timely reminders of the unitary nature of its fragile home."[2]

The desire to know what the Earth looks like "from the outside" has played a fundamental role in Western conceptualizations and representations of space, as David Harvey has shown. In *The Condition of Postmodernity*, he presents a historical overview of how fundamental changes in spatial and temporal practices have affected social life over the last 500 years. One of the most radical shifts took place during the Renaissance, with the introduction of a new way of seeing known as "perspectivism." The new rules of perspective, which were to dominate our way of looking at the world until the beginning of the twentieth century, introduced the notion of the fixed viewpoint, which, contrary to the more "sensuous" viewpoint of medieval mapping, was "elevated and distant, completely out of plastic or sensory reach." This entailed not only a heightened sense of objectivity and rationality (laying a foundation for the Cartesian principles that would dominate the Enlightenment project), but also a conception of the world *as a whole* from the standpoint of an all-seeing eye. In fact, it was precisely this belief in the "ability to see the globe as a knowable totality" that, according to Harvey, provided the necessary tools for a total systematization of space. The Ptolemaic map, which made its way from Alexandria to Florence around 1400, showed how geographical information could be arranged according to mathematical principles. It also solved the problem of representing the globe on a flat surface and as a result, Harvey explains, "it seemed as if space, though infinite, was conquerable and containable for purposes of human occupance and action."[3]

The conquest of space was as much a cause as an effect of these geographical innovations. One of the most effective and straightforward ways to both systematize and control space is to turn it into an immutable and monolithic whole.[4] In fact, one could say that to command the techniques and science of mapmaking is to command space itself. As Harvey puts it, "If a picture or map is worth a thousand words, then power in the realms of representation may end up being as important as power over the materiality of spatial organization itself."[5] Although considered a matter of fact for ages, maps are by their very nature ideological constructs and therefore never objective or impartial. The Mercator map, for

1 Denis Cosgrove, "Contested Global Visions: *One* World, Whole Earth and the Apollo Space Photographs," *Annals of the Association of American Geographers* (1994): 270.

2 Mark Monmonier, *Drawing the Line: Tales of Maps and Cartocontroversy* (New York: Henry Holt and Co., 1995), 213.

3 David Harvey, *The Condition of Postmodernity: An Enquiry into the Origins of Cultural Change* (Cambridge, MA: Blackwell, 1992), 242-46.

4 In *Writing Women and Space: Colonial and Postcolonial Geographies*, Alison Blunt and Gillian Rose formulate a critique of "imperial mapping" as the erasure of difference (New York: Guilford Press, 1994). See also Gillian Rose's *Feminism and Geography: The Limits of Geographical Knowledge* (Cambridge: Polity, 1993).

5 Harvey, *Condition*, 233.

6 Ibid., 251. As Monmonier argues in *Drawing the Line*, maps are never capable of containing all possible information at once. In fact, if a map is to be useful or readable at all, a cartographer *has* to make choices about what information to include or leave out of spatial representation: "no map is a thoroughly objective, value-neutral device for describing distances and locations. While a map might appear accurate and relevant, there usually is more to the story than one map can conveniently communicate" (7-8).

7 Monmonier, *Drawing the Line*, 16. According to Monmonier, "Mercator's worldview makes Europe's 3.8 million square miles look larger than South America's 6.9 million square miles ... Greenland looks larger than China (a country more than four times as large), and the relatively industrialized 'North' appears larger than the less economically advanced 'South'" (16-17).

8 Michel de Certeau, *The Practice of Everyday Life*, trans. Steven Rendall (Berkeley and Los Angeles: University of California Press, 1988), 120-21.

9 Ibid., 117.

instance, which "completed the Ptolemaic ambition" by presenting "ever more accurately ... the physical spatial relationships of all places on the globe's surface," illustrates very well how, even though a map may seem accurate and value-neutral, it can never be completely objective in its descriptions of distances and locations.[6] The Mercator map is one of the most popular and most widely distributed representations of the world ever produced and yet it is also essentially flawed, because it clearly favors a Eurocentric worldview. The map quite literally magnifies the size, and thus emphasizes the importance, of Europe and North America at the expense of Africa, Latin America, and certain parts of Asia.[7] Produced during the heyday of colonialism as a predominantly navigational tool, the seemingly cold rationality of the Mercator map not only represents space but also manipulates it.

In *The Practice of Everyday Life*, Michel de Certeau criticizes maps as "totalizing" devices that "colonize" space in two ways: they homogenize the rich diversity of spatial practices that constitute them, by collating heterogeneous places on the same plane, and they eliminate from their presentation the practices that produce them. "In particular, if one takes the 'map' in its current geographical form, we can see that in the course of the period marked by the birth of modern scientific discourse (i.e., from the fifteenth to the seventeenth century) the map has slowly disengaged itself from the itineraries that were the condition of its possibility."[8] These "itineraries," which de Certeau traces back to Medieval times, represent an older, more subjective, and especially more fluid sense of space, which not only includes its modes of production but also allows for the combination of different elements. In other words, whereas the map fixes and reifies, the itinerary *spatializes* and acknowledges the changing relationships between places and spaces. Itineraries are a vital part of what de Certeau refers to as *espace*, which is a fluid phenomenon "composed of intersections and mobile elements" and "actuated by the ensemble of movements deployed within it."[9] Maps, on the contrary, require stability and distance; they preclude the possibility of two things being in the same place at once, and, most importantly, they presuppose the existence of an all-seeing eye.

De Certeau begins his social critique of the spatial practices associated with the map and the itinerary with the paradigmatic experience of "Seeing Manhattan from the 110th floor of the World Trade Center." Undoubtedly one of the most monumental skyscrapers in the history of Western urban architecture, the WTC presents de Certeau with an excellent vantage point from which to criticize what he calls the "panorama-city." The "panorama-city" is an illusion, a "visual simulacrum" produced by a voyeuristic perspective, a total and therefore superior view of the city. Once he is lifted to the summit of the World Trade Center, the spectator changes into a "voyeur-god" whose "solar Eye" transforms the labyrinthine city into an "optical artifact," "mak[ing] the complexity of the city readable, and immobiliz[ing] its opaque mobility in a transparent text." In other words, the view from above converts the city into an image that can be both mastered and contained. Above all, it suggests that the city can be *known* in its totality as well as its social reality. As de Certeau points out, however, the only way to maintain this optical illusion of "seeing the whole" (produced by the urban planner and cartographer alike) is to disembody and desocialize the viewing process. This disembodiment, this "lust to be a viewpoint and nothing more," relies on the "oblivion and ... misunderstanding of practices." Practices are, by their very nature, situated, particular, and often invisible, which is why they must be erased, leveled, and overlooked in order to produce a "successful" total representation. In other words, the voyeur's city can never be anything but a fiction, both because of its unwillingness to recognize particularities and because of its inability to see those who live "below the thresholds at which visibility begins." There are always spaces that cannot be seen, movements that resist rationalization. There is always a "migrational city," de Certeau concludes, that "slips into the clear text of the planned and readable city."[10]

A recent article in *The New York Times* presents a striking example of de Certeau's argument. "A Mayor's Empire and a Cabby's Turf" describes how two photographers, Mayor Rudolph W. Giuliani and a taxi-driver called David Bradford, both fascinated by their territory and subject, adopt very different approaches to their representations of New York. Giuliani obviously favors the aerial perspective, focusing mainly on skyscrapers and bridges seen from a high vantage point. Bradford, on the other hand, is primarily interested in what happens on the streets, portraying everyday life as it unfolds in those parts of the city that often remain invisible. Visibility is very much a factor in the Mayor's version of New York. As the colonial metaphor in the article's title suggests, Giuliani likes to be in control of his representations (a fact which should come as no surprise to New Yorkers). The writer of the article notes Giuliani's desire to "look down on the city, taking sentimental stock of his vast empire," which in many of his pictures shows a "surprising lack of people."[11] Appropriately entitled "View from the Capital of the World," Giuliani's series of photographs focuses primarily on New York's monumentalism. The skies are usually clear, the buildings look magnificent, and the city as a whole, while vast, tends to look orderly and controllable. One particular picture, "City of Bridges," shows downtown Manhattan as seen

10 Ibid., 92-93.

11 Sarah Boxer, "A Mayor's Empire and a Cabby's Turf," *The New York Times*, 7 May, 1998.

12 Ibid.

from high up over Brooklyn (probably from within a helicopter or plane). The twin towers of the WTC are left of center, while the Brooklyn Bridge and the Manhattan Bridge thrust into the heart of the city, geometrically balancing the composition as a whole. This sense of structure and control over his subject matter can be found in almost all of the Mayor's pictures. Even at ground level, the writer explains, the Mayor likes to include "something long thrusting up from the bottom edge of the picture — a water main, a fire hose, a bridge, a skyscraper."[12] In short, the Mayor's city is, at all times, a rationalized space, the kind of space



*Rudolph W. Giuliani, "City of Bridges," from* View from the Capital of the World.

*David Bradford, photograph of Times Square, New York City.*

that is always already mapped and governed by what de Certeau calls the law of the "proper": "the elements taken into consideration are *beside* one another, each situated in its own 'proper' and distinct location, a location it defines." Motion in such a space is limited to movement from one specific location to the next.[13] The Mayor himself is the distant, fixed and, above all, elevated point of reference from and against which the city is measured.

Motion, however, is precisely what defines the cabby's experience of the city. Contrary to Giuliani's pictures, which are usually daytime shots that create a sense of a controlled vastness devoid of people, Bradford's photographs reflect a world where streets have cracks and potholes, encounters are fleeting, and people can be found even in the darkest of places. Often taken during a stormy night and thriving on movement, the taxi driver's images show what de Certeau calls a *practiced* place, a space "composed of intersections of mobile elements" and shaped by "vectors of direction, velocities, and time variables."[14] Bradford's New York is neither vast nor organized. A picture of Times Square on a rainy night from his rear view mirror, for example, shows cars barely visible behind their own hazy headlights, whose reflections on the wet streets blur the distinction between the city's Bright Lights and the mundane reality of life on the streets. At a quick glance, the rest of the picture seems to frame the undefined brightness of Times Square, but in fact shows another part of the same place, mostly veiled in darkness. The whole has the effect of disorienting the viewer, who cannot seem to take up any one particular perspective in this space, crossed at different angles and in different directions, "composed of intersections of mobile elements," of which the photographer himself is one. The overall result is confusion, as the viewer tries to make sense of different surfaces reflecting different versions of reality. In short, Bradford's city is anything but transparent. Its multiple layers, heterogeneity, and juxtaposition of realities make it what Brian McHale has called a "zone" in which "fragments of disparate discursive orders ... are merely juxtaposed, without any attempt to reduce them to a common order."[15]

The biggest difference between the Mayor's and the cabby's representations may be the lack of perspectival distance in Bradford's pictures. While the Mayor's photographs call for a fixed and distant viewpoint — "if he could fit the

13 de Certeau, *Practice*, 117.

14 Ibid.

15 Brian McHale, *Constructing Postmodernism* (London: Routledge, 1992), 250-51.

16 Boxer, "Mayor's Empire."

17 Maurice Merleau-Ponty, as quoted in de Certeau, *Practice*, 117.

18 de Certeau, *Practice*, 92-93.

19 See, for example, Anne Friedberg, *Window Shopping: Cinema and Postmodernism* (Berkeley and Los Angeles: University of California Press, 1994) and David B. Clarke, *The Cinematic City* (London: Routledge, 1997).

whole city in every picture, he would,"[16] as the article suggests — Bradford's snapshots establish a space of contact rather than a visual space, an "anthropological" space rather than a "geometrical" one.[17] They suggest that there is no such thing as a perfect representation of the "real" city, that it is impossible to produce an overview that allows the spectator to read all underlying spatial realities from a distance. Instead, Bradford's pictures establish a space in which we are always *immersed*, a space that cannot be observed from the outside and that, according to de Certeau, can only be explored by legwork. Urban practices such as walking are de Certeau's antidote to the "cancerous growth of vision." The tactics of everyday life, involved and yet "indefinitely other," not only escape panoptic constructs, but also expose them for what they are: a "fiction of knowledge."[18]

The possibilities for the creation of an "anthropological" space of contact are perhaps even greater in film, a medium that thrives on its audience's temporary immersion in a fictional space.[19] The title of Jim Jarmush's 1992 film *Night on Earth* seems to promise its viewers a total visual perspective. Heightening that promise, the opening shot is an image of the globe from outer space, a version of NASA's AS17-148-22727. No sooner have we been tempted with a view from above, however, than the camera zooms in on a specific location, closer and closer, until we are immersed in the urban space of, one by one, Los Angeles, New York, Paris, Rome, and finally Helsinki at the break of dawn. In a series of five simultaneous cab rides, Jarmush takes the audience on a journey that is both spatial and temporal, exploring the creative possibilities of a single night's wandering through five different metropolises. Geography and time zones are at the director's mercy, as he invites the audience to take a cosmopolitan trip around the Western world, making contact across temporal, spatial, linguistic, and cultural boundaries.

The common urban practice of taking a cab creates encounters between a casting agent and a young female cabby/mechanic, an African-American from Washington Heights and an exiled East German clown turned New York cabby, a taxi driver from Ivory Coast and a blind Parisienne, a crazy Italian cabby and a priest, and finally Mika and his three drunken fares in Helsinki. The taxi is the only constant in the film, its paradoxically mobile point of stability. The random encounters that take place in this confined space between places, which is usually invisible to all but its occupants, are fleeting and transitory, yet meaningful and in some cases life-changing. What is usually overlooked or considered unimportant is foregrounded in the taxi, where life seems temporarily suspended in a transit zone that is an integral part of many urban itineraries. As Jarmush puts it, "If you think about taking a taxi, it's something insignificant in your daily life; in a film when someone takes a taxi, you see them get in, then there's a cut, then you see them get out. So in a way the content of this film is made up of things that would usually be taken out. It's similar to what I like about *Stranger than Paradise* or *Down by Law*: the moments between what we think of as insignificant."[20] This betweenness is not the same as rootlessness. A cabby's turf is in fact quite local, even territorial: it is limited to one particular city or just a part of it. His/her car is an enclosed, often personalized, space that is both public and private. David Bradford calls his taxi "a pretty nice office" and uses it as a studio and gallery, showing his work whenever "his passengers have anywhere from eight to 30 minutes to peruse his seat-back display."[21] In this sense, the taxi driver is rooted, even though his/her existence is defined by mobility. This combination of localization and mobility, as well as its accommodation of chance encounters, makes the taxi a perfect example of what James Clifford has defined as a "chronotope."

In "Traveling Cultures," Clifford suggests the use of alternative localizing strategies in the construction and representation of cultures. He argues that, since even the most remote sites on the globe are "always already enmeshed" in "the wider global world of intercultural import-export," we need to rethink such binaries as local/global, center/periphery, inside/outside, by analyzing culture in terms of travel relationships. As he explains, his goal is "not to *replace* the cultural figure 'native' with the intercultural figure 'traveler'" but rather to focus on "concrete mediations of the two in specific cases of historical tension and relationship." Such mediations are what constitute Clifford's notion of the "chronotope," a "setting or scene organizing time and space in representable whole form" that resembles "as much a site of travel as of residence." The chronotope establishes a stationary process — "traveling-in-dwelling," "dwelling-in-traveling" — and focuses on the in-between as a cultural site. Transit zones such as hotels, motels, buses, airplanes, are not simply suspended in space; they constitute a *somewhere* that frames encounters between people who are traveling for a number of different reasons. Moreover, places that are traveled through are always localized, while also part of a wider network of intercultural "crisscrossing." Quoting from Luis Rafael Sanchez's short story "The Airbus," which tells the story of a cross-cultural encounter during a routine night flight from San Juan to New York, Clifford explains that the question is "not so much 'where are you from?' but 'where are you between?'"[22]

20 Peter Keogh, "Home and Away," interview with Jim Jarmush, *Sight and Sound* 2, 4 (1991): 9.

21 Boxer, "Mayor's Empire."

22 James Clifford, "Traveling Cultures," in *Cultural Studies*, ed. Lawrence Grossberg, Cary Nelson, and Paula Treichler (New York: Routledge, 1992), 101.

23 Ibid., 103.

24 Bruce Robbins, *Secular Vocations: Intellectuals, Professionalism, Culture* (London: Verso, 1993), 184-85. Emphasis added.

The itineraries in *Night on Earth*, then, do not constitute a free-floating exercise in displacement. They create a zone of what Clifford calls "differently centered worlds, interconnected cosmopolitanisms."[23] As Bruce Robbins points out in *Secular Vocations*, "there is always a tension between cosmopolitanism in its strictly negative sense of absolute freedom or total disconnectedness," on the one hand, and its positive or "more general sense of 'belonging' to parts of the world other than one's nation," on the other. The point is "to try and sustain this tension, valuing the negative relation to nationality without giving up an insistence on belonging — an insistence that includes the possibility of presence in other places, *dispersed but real forms of membership*, a density of overlapping allegiances rather than the abstract emptiness of non-allegiance." The personal encounters in *Night on Earth* reveal precisely such "dispersed but real forms of membership." Jarmush's characters clearly belong somewhere, situated as they are in a specific place and time, but their specificity does not prevent them from moving around freely and engaging in meaningful relationships, however fleeting and arbitrary (most emphatically *not* a contradiction in *Night on Earth*), which cut across class, gender, race, and national identity. Moreover, the urban centers themselves are not so much fixed localities but powerful sites of travel interaction. "If our supposed distances are really localities," Robbins argues, "it is also true that there are distances *within* what we thought were *merely* localities." The term he introduces to refer to these "distances within" (although he uses it specifically in relation to an analysis of universities) is "situatedness-in-displacement."[24]

"Situatedness-in-displacement," like Clifford's concept of "dwelling-in-travel," suggests the dynamic connection that always exists between the notion of residence/specificity and that of mobility/universality. It is precisely at the crossroads, the intersection of these two elements, that Jarmush situates his cosmopolitan encounters. By recontextualizing the travel motif in every new specific locale, he particularizes the idea of the journey and creates specific transit zones where different worlds meet and interact with each other. The locus he uses to represent this "situatedness-in-displacement" is the taxi, a place of transience, which, while belonging to the streets of a particular metropolis, is nevertheless in constant motion. Always *between* (between the airport and the hotel, between the city and its suburbs, between center and periphery) the taxi escapes, neutralizes, and subverts binarisms. The monumental landmarks of the Colosseum and the Eiffel tower disappear into the background, as Rome and Paris reshape and remap themselves during a nocturnal journey through a labyrinthine network of streets.

The cab ride, weaving places together, creates a new space where different people and their respective worlds engage with each other. What is usually considered an instance of lost time and space becomes the premise for a cosmopolitan experience. The New York sequence, which brings together Yoyo, an African-American, and Helmut, an East European who knows absolutely nothing about the city and even less about driving a cab with automatic transmission, is one of the most powerful and moving in the film. As two worlds that could not be more apart from each other struggle across American slang and broken English in search of common ground,[25] a short but shared journey gradually creates a communal space, in which both men are able to share a valuable if momentary experience, an opportunity to exchange stories. Their storytelling creates what Doreen Massey calls a *meeting* place, an articulated moment in a network of social relations and understanding, most of which are "constructed on a far larger scale than what we happen to define for that moment as the place itself, whether that be a street, or a region or even a continent."[26] The stories in *Night on Earth*, without any real beginnings or endings, remain forever *in medias res* and refer to other places, times, and encounters, further expanding the complex space of relationships to the larger scale that Massey describes.

In a nutshell, *Night on Earth* penetrates its emblematic opening image of the globe as a perfectly contained whole, explodes it into the complex network of experiences and interactions that characterize urban practices, and reveals the kinds of territorial complexities that belie the smooth rationalizations of the view from above. These are the kinds of practices that escape the observer on top of the World Trade Center, the kinds that must be accounted for in any meaningful theory of space. They cannot be mapped, if mapping presupposes homogenization and the totalizing gaze from a distant perspective. James Clifford, who agrees with de Certeau that the panoramic view is a potentially damaging illusion, does not propose to abandon the idea of mapping altogether, however: "The metaphor of travel, for me, has been a serious dream of mapping without going 'off earth.'"[27]

As Rosalyn Deutsche has shown, however, it has been difficult for theorists to stay on the ground. In *Evictions: Art and Spatial Politics*, she explains that de

25 The ice is broken in a hilarious scene when the two men tell each other their names. Hearing Helmut's name, Yoyo bursts out in laughter, explaining that a "helmet" is something you put on your head. But Helmut finds "Yoyo" equally funny. "Aber das ist ein Spielzeug," he chuckles.

26 Doreen Massey, *Space, Place, and Gender* (Minneapolis: University of Minnesota Press, 1994), 154.

27 Clifford, "Traveling Cultures," 105.

28 Rosalyn Deutsche, *Evictions: Art and Spatial Politics* (Cambridge, MA: MIT Press, 1996), 213-14.

29 David Harvey cited in Deutsche, *Evictions*, 215.

30 Deutsche, *Evictions*, 213-14.

31 Ibid., 201.

32 Ibid., 213.

33 Ibid., 220.

34 Ibid., 216.

Certeau's critique is aimed at "a specifically modernist model of vision," a "social visuality" that relies on the separation between a transcendent subject and an inert object and that promotes "an entire regime of knowledge as mastery." Such a model favors aerial perspectives because they promise unity and totality. As a result, the view from the top becomes a metaphor for *metatheory*, which promises to "uncover the absolute foundation of a social totality" and establishes "the illusory basis of the subject's coherence, authority, and uniqueness."[28] The theorist "sees" and claims to understand in its entirety an objective reality that lies in front of him. David Harvey thinks of metatheory as a set of infinitely expandable Chinese boxes, "a theoretical framework that has the potential to put all ... partial views together not simply as a composite vision but as a cognitive map that shows how each view can itself be explained by and integrated into some grander conception of what the city as a whole, what the urban process in general is all about."[29] In short, the all-seeing subject believes his knowledge to be both truthful and all-encompassing.

What such an epistemology lacks is precisely a critique of *vision*. De Certeau's project amounts to more than comparing and contrasting two views of the city; he socializes vision itself. According to Deutsche, this is what a number of influential theories of so-called "postmodern landscapes," which use voyeuristic models of knowledge, sorely fail to do.[30] With its promise of control and wholeness, the modernist model still dominates a number of urban discourses, especially those that deplore the fragmentation, contestation, and eclecticism of postmodern space. Most of these analyses "adopt a classic realist approach," which consists of evaluating the city's purported chaos and otherness from a critical distance. If such evaluations remain unreceptive to the sexual politics of representation, Deutsche warns, urban discourse will continue "to construct space as a feminized object surveyed by mastering subjects." As a result, the discipline will continue to "reproduce oppressive forms of knowledge,"[31] such as Harvey's blatant "misreading of de Certeau's visual metaphor for totalizing knowledge as positive or at the very least neutral."[32]

Harvey feels that the fragmentation perpetuated by postmodern art and culture is a condition we need to escape from, especially because it obscures reality. As Harvey understands it, this reality is both absolute and knowable: the "underlying unity of capitalism," concealed by postmodernism's obsession with images, must be uncovered by Marxist metatheory, "the only body of knowledge ... capable of perceiving that unity."[33] Harvey resents postmodern critics who think of unity (*any* kind of unity) "not as an impartial totality but as a fiction" and who are receptive to the potential of fragmentation to facilitate an awareness and understanding of difference.[34] Metatheory cannot function with such an awareness, which is why, Deutsche insists, "the high ground of total knowledge can only be gained by an oppressive encounter with difference — the relegation of other subjectivities to positions of subordination or invisibility."[35]

Fredric Jameson also refuses to acknowledge the mediated nature of vision and its implications for power and sexuality: other subjectivities are either relegated to a nonpolitical arena or denounced as too political. In his seminal essay "Postmodernism, or, The Cultural Logic of Late Capitalism," Jameson claims that "categories of time have been replaced by categories of space."[36] In more specifically architectural terms, there has been "a mutation in the lived experience of built space itself," as a result of which the individual human body has lost its capacity "to locate itself, to organize its immediate surroundings perceptually, and cognitively to map its position in a mappable external world." Jameson's primary example of this new labyrinthine, chaotic and, above all, "bewildering new world space of late or multinational capitalism"[37] is the Westin Bonaventure Hotel, built in 1977 by the developer-architect John Portman in downtown Los Angeles. One of the more prominent mutations that seem to mark the Bonaventure is its disruption of such traditional notions as outside and inside. Because its mirror glass surfaces reflect, distort, and fragment its surroundings, the building does not have a real exterior; it does not even have a discernible entrance. From the outside, one does not see the hotel itself but an endless reproduction of surfaces. The same glossy surfaces also distort the building's interior, which is equally confusing, as hanging streamers "suffuse this empty space in such a way as to disrupt systematically and deliberately from whatever form it might be supposed to have." In other words, the contours of this new space remain unclear and the only possible spatial experience is one of complete "immersion," as the body is unable to separate itself from the space it inhabits. "You are in this hyperspace up to your eyes and your body," Jameson explains, so it becomes impossible to maintain "any of that distance that formerly enabled the perception or perspective of volume."[38]

35 Ibid., 198.

36 Fredric Jameson, *Postmodernism, or, The Cultural Logic of Late Capitalism* (Durham: Duke University Press, 1992), 6.

37 Ibid.

38 Ibid., 43.

39 Mark Wigley, "Lost in Space," in *The Critical Landscape*, ed. Michael Speaks (Rotterdam: 010 Publishers, 1996), 34.

40 Ibid.

41 Jameson, *Postmodernism*, 54.

42 Wigley, "Lost in Space," 38.

43 Ibid., 37.

44 Jameson, *Postmodernism*, x.

45 Massey, *Space, Place, and Gender*, 224. For a more historical overview see Friedberg, *Window Shopping*.

For Jameson this distance between oneself and one's surroundings is absolutely essential if one is to negotiate this indeterminate space. What seems to be especially troubling is that postmodern space has not only lost its coherence but also its *legibility*. Since "we do not yet possess the perceptual equipment to match this new hyperspace," there is no meta-structure, no meta-narrative in which to situate the Bonaventure; it is a space all unto itself, a labyrinth that is the city's equivalent or substitute. To help overcome this condition of fragmentation and disorientation, Jameson proposes an "aesthetic of cognitive mapping," a concept that was introduced by Kevin Lynch in his work on the city during the late fifties and early sixties. It calls for mental maps that operate as symbolic systems, enabling "purposeful movement" through a space.[39] The orientation techniques proposed by Lynch rely on the successive production of spatial images that serve to locate the individual within his/her habitat.[40] In short, cognitive maps help people to make sense of their urban surroundings and, as Jameson understands them, "endow the individual subject with some new heightened sense of its place in the global system."

However, Jameson's claim that this is "not a call for a return to some older kind of machinery, some older and more transparent national space, or some more traditional and reassuring perspectival or mimetic enclave,"[41] is problematic for a number of reasons, the first of which is the fact that Lynch's project is explicitly modernist. As Mark Wigley points out in "Lost in Space," "it sustains an ideal of transparency whereby every functioning element of the city is supposedly open to inspection, the structure revealing itself to the inquisitive eye."[42] Cognitive mapping does not just assume that there is an underlying totality waiting to be discovered but also actively imposes one, making the complexity of the city readable by immobilizing it in a transparent spatial construct. Moreover, Lynch's orientation techniques are decidedly aesthetic in nature, a matter of "delight," "pleasure," "order," and "beauty," defined by terms such as "smooth," "coherent," "vivid," "continuous." In other words, aesthetic order is not only aligned with psychological order (*mental* maps), but it is also "understood as the basis of social order."[43] This in itself would not be problematic were it not for the fact that one of Jameson's major critiques of postmodernism is precisely its "'aestheticization' of reality."[44]

Finally, there is the question of the "inquisitive eye" to which the city's underlying totality reveals itself. Modernism systematically prioritizes vision over other senses, mainly because vision allows the greatest mastery over its subject matter, since it requires distance and detachment from its object.[45] Cognitive mapping, as defined by Lynch, calls for just such an eye "to locate oneself within a dislocating world." Lynch got his ideas for a visual approach from Gyorgy Kepes (painter, filmmaker, and photographer), when he was doing research for his most important book, *The Image of the City*. According to Kepes, "Vision is primarily a device of orientation; a means to measure and organize spatial events. The mastery of nature is intimately connected with the mastery of space; this is visual orientation. Each new visual environment demands a reorientation, a new way of measuring."[46] But how "new" can a reorientation be when it keeps relying on the same visual principle? It is no coincidence that Jameson feels most at ease *at the top* of the Westin Bonaventure, where he is "offered a contemplative spectacle of the city itself." Although still "alarming," it is definitely less "confusing" or "bewildering" than the space of the lobby. Like de Certeau's voyeur enjoying the sight of Manhattan from the 110th floor of the World Trade Center, Jameson relishes the fact that, once he reaches the top floor, his body is "lifted out of the city's grasp" and temporarily liberated from fragmentation and disorientation.[47] No longer immersed in the labyrinthine space below, Jameson finally acquires the necessary distance to "see the whole." In short, this elevated perspective represents Jameson's epistemological ideal, the cartographer's view from above, where the *male* gaze of metatheory can roam over the bewildering expanse of postmodern space.

That this is above all a *male* ideal, is emphasized by both Doreen Massey and Rosalyn Deutsche in their critiques of Jameson, Harvey, and Edward Soja.[48] As Deutsche points out, the "phallic pretensions" of Harvey's epistemology are quite obvious, as he mourns "the abandonment of metatheories as a retreat into 'emasculated and relatively powerless formats.'"[49] The same fears can be found in Jameson's postmodern spatial experience, whose constants are confusion and a sense of rejection, as though the bewildering space is giving him the cold shoulder. He feels lost, disoriented and, above all, frustrated with the Bonaventure's "glass skin," which he compares to "those reflector sunglasses which make it impossible for your interlocutor to see your own eyes and thereby achieve a certain aggressivity and power over the Other." But who wears the mirror shades in Jameson's text? The glass skin creates a "peculiar and placeless dissociation," not only of the

46 Wigley, "Lost in Space," 37-38.
47 Jameson, *Postmodernism*, 92.
48 Both Deutsche and Massey critique Edward Soja's *Postmodern Geographies: The Reassertion of Space in Critical Social Theory* and its systematic failure to engage with other points of view.
49 Deutsche, *Evictions*, 215.
50 Jameson, *Postmodernism*, 41-42.
51 Wigley, "Lost in Space," 49-50.
52 Jameson, *Postmodernism*, xxi.
53 Deutsche, *Evictions*, 199.
54 Similar critiques can and have been made with regard to both Harvey and Soja by Deutsche and Massey.
55 Ibid., 200.

Bonaventure from its surrounding neighborhoods, but also of Jameson from his control and power over the space he so desperately wants to "map out."[50] As Wigley puts it, "the only story that seems to be threatened by the hotel is that of the critic himself." The breakdown of the system of categories with which Jameson is most familiar produces not only a crisis of the object (Jameson's avowed inability to "[convey] the thing itself") but also a crisis of the subject. In other words, Jameson's struggle to identify the postmodern condition through his experience of the Bonaventure is really an attempt to "preserve his identity in the face of certain transformations in the physical and intellectual environment."[51]

But what exactly are these transformations? More importantly, what kind of identity is Jameson trying to "preserve"? Whose subjectivity falls victim to the attempt to preserve this self-sufficient wholeness at any cost? According to Deutsche, Jameson's aesthetic of cognitive mapping suffers from an aggressively masculine and condescending ethos, both in its move towards totalization and in its dependence on the construction of whole, unfragmented subjects. Jameson sees postmodernism's multiple fragmentations — of space, society, the body, the subject — as a cultural "pathology"[52] that can only be cured by resorting to a discourse that mobilizes "unitarian knowledge and foundationalist representation."[53] Jameson's goal is to recover the underlying totality of the "real" social world, a project that not only presupposes the existence of such a social totality but also assumes that it can be *represented* as such. Feminist theory has challenged these kinds of totalizing representations, which is probably why it is largely absent from Jameson's text, as are other theories — queer, postcolonial — that are equally suspicious of "essential" social meaning. In fact, apart from theories of class, Jameson either disregards social critiques or denounces them as just another force leading to even more fragmentation.[54] Such "blindness," according to Deutsche, is the result not only of prioritizing a "visualizing model of knowledge" that frames space as a "landscape surveyed by a transcendent viewer," but especially of refusing to consider the political implications of such a model.[55] "For years," Deutsche explains,

> *feminist theories have differentiated vision — pleasure in looking — from the notion of seeing as a process of perceiving the real world. The image and the act of looking are now understood to be relations highly mediated by fantasies that structure and are structured by sexual difference. Visual space is,* in the first instance, *a set of social relations; it is never innocent, nor does it merely reflect, either directly or through contrived mediations, "real" social relations elsewhere — in, for example, the economic relations producing the built environment. From the moment this environment becomes an image ... its meaning is no longer reducible to nor fixed by the economic circumstances of its pro-*

*duction. From the moment we try to understand the city as an image, feminist theories of visual space intersect with, and simultaneously problematize, the political economy of urban space, which, it is important to note, does not inherently exclude feminism. That exclusion is enforced in an epistemological field where grandiose claims are made on theoretical space, where only one theory is allowed to explain social relations or subordination.*[56]

Jameson's admission that his concepts are, like all others, representations does not preclude the need to question their form and production, especially since representations are always constituted by acts of differentiation. Mayor Giuliani's photographs are a lot more interesting for what they tell us about the Mayor's relation to the city than for their purported total view of the city itself. A true social critique of visual space contradicts the depthlessness that David Harvey associates with images, and instead reveals the depth of the network of interactions and relationships that produces these images and our encounters with them. Films like *Night on Earth* make us aware of the complexity of the "overlapping allegiances" that characterize urban social relationships, which has no place in a theoretical map that purports to represent the city's "underlying totality." Does this mean that we should do away with maps and similar representational devices altogether? Not unless we disregard the itineraries that produce those maps. Not unless we forget that visual representations are not mere reflections of an objective reality. Harvey fears that acknowledging the impossibility of a unified representation of the world inevitably implies that "we should not even try to engage in some global project."[57] Obviously, that depends on one's definition of "global." We *can* stop mistaking the map for the territory; we *can* give up metatheory's claim to represent the urban space as a unified whole, without giving up on critical thought as a self-conscious inquiry into the complex global space of social relations that intersects at all points with our very attempts to analyze it.

56 Ibid., 197.

57 Harvey, *Condition*, 52.

Bart Keunen

# The Decline of the City as Modernist Symbol: City Images in Postmodern Urban Fiction and in Collective Memory

*Keywords:* ■ *Literary Historiography* ■ *Literary Sociology* ■ *Cultural Theory*

In realist and modernist literatures, many a novel opened with the image of the uprooted traveler who innocently enters the city. Any author using this image at the end of the twentieth century is likely to be accused of anachronism or nostalgia. Yet 150 years ago and a long stretch into the twentieth century, the image functioned as the strategy of choice to give shape to the big parade of modernity. Especially works that can be categorized as realist, naturalist, or realistically oriented modernist (Zola's *Le Ventre de Paris* and *Au Bonheur des dames*, Dreiser's *Sister Carrie* and *An American Tragedy*, Dos Passos's *Manhattan Transfer*, Döblin's *Berlin Alexanderplatz*) and films from the interbellum (Ruttmann's *Berlin: Symphonie einer Grossstadt*, May's *Asphalt*, King Vidor's *The Crowd*) used the motif of "the arrival in the big city" to submerge the audience in a highly charged and emotionally gripping situation.[1] Even though the urban material selected by those artists is characterized by diversity, their works have in common a fascination for the Big Confrontation between individual and city. The arrival in Paris, Berlin, or New York was a symbol of the encounter with historical developments everyone could recognize and social tensions everybody could feel. For that reason, the image of the confrontation became one of the most potent symbols of modern culture.

At the end of the twentieth century, this *Kollektivsymbol* (Link) persists in the popular imagination, but in literature it seems to have lost most of its importance.[2] The main reason for this decline is most likely the universalizing of the urban condition as a result of urban sprawl. Urban structures are to be found and canonized city icons are copied or consumed in the most remote corners of the Western world. As on the whole the late-twentieth-century citizen lives in an urbanized environment, it stands to reason that "the arrival in the city" can no longer function as a potent symbol.

Nonetheless, urban settings are still prominently present in the narrative arts (film and novel). Even though the historicizing, totalizing perspectives of the older narratives are missing, there are enough texts suggesting an urban setting or presenting a fragmented image of a city to warrant the use of the term *urban fiction*. Some theorists of culture and literature, however, assert that the city in its contemporary shape — the city as *sprawl, nonplace urban realm,* or *edge city* — is reflected mimetically in such urban descriptions. As a result, they assign to the newer urban images the status of collective symbols. In this kind of theory, the urban condition is alleged to have become commonplace and the urban thematics is taken to mirror the characteristics of space in the postmodern era: the fragmentation and spreading of urban space, the fragmentation of social space, and the fragmentation of individual lifestyle practices. A recent work that analyzes novels about Los Angeles, for instance, puts it this way: "The sprawling, dispersed and ceaselessly mutating urbanity of Los Angeles, constantly renegotiating its historical and geographical coordinates, disables the formation of a consciousness informed by collective historical experience or a common visual environment."[3] Well-known, too, are the views of Christine Boyer and Fredric Jameson, according to which spatial images in respectively cyberpunk fiction and postmodern architecture are metaphors for the postmodern condition.[4] Implicitly, such analyses suggest that "postmodern" representations can be interpreted as covert symptoms of transformations in sociohistorical reality. Questionable in such analyses is the fact that the constructed nature of these images tends to be severely underplayed. Often analyses like those mentioned neglect the power of (relatively) autonomous cultural fields, on the one hand, and the stereotypical construction principles of art works that are implied by that autonomy, on the other.[5] If, therefore,

1 A. K. Chanda calls this, in a phrase borrowed from Lionel Trilling, the motif of "The Young Man from the Provinces." See A. K. Chanda, "The Young Man from the Provinces," *Comparative Literature* 4 (1981): 339. Philippe Hamon discusses the naturalist variant, while Pierre Citron deals with precedents from the eighteenth century. See Philippe Hamon, "Du savoir dans le texte," *Revue des sciences humaines* 4 (1974): 489-99; Pierre Citron, *La Poésie de Paris dans la littérature française de Rousseau à Baudelaire* (Paris: Minuit, 1961), 112-15.

2 For a definition of the concept of "Kollektivsymbol," see Jürgen and Ursula Link-Heer, eds., *Literatursoziologisches Propädeutikum* (München: Fink, 1980).

3 Josh Cohen, *Spectacular Allegories: Postmodern American Writing and the Politics of Seeing* (London: Pluto, 1998), 126.

4 M. Christine Boyer, *Cybercities: Visual Perception in the Age of Electronic Communication* (New York: Princeton Architectural Press, 1996), 73-136; Fredric Jameson, *Postmodernism, or, The Cultural Logic of Late Capitalism* (London: Verso, 1991), 38-39.

5 See Siegfried J. Schmidt, "The Fiction Is That Reality Exists: A Constructivist Model of Reality, Fiction, and Literature," *Poetics Today* 2 (1984): 253-74; Siegfried J. Schmidt, *Kognitive Autonomie und soziale Orientierung. Konstruktivistische Bemerkungen zum Zusammenhang von Kognition, Kommunikation, Medien und Kultur* (Frankfurt am Main: Suhrkamp, 1994).

6 See Mikhail M. Bakhtin, "Forms of Time and of the Chronotope in the Novel: Notes toward a Historical Poetics" (1938), in Mikhail M. Bakhtin, *The Dialogic Imagination*, ed. Michael Holquist (Austin: University of Texas Press, 1981), 84-254.

we want to gain insight into the evolution of the collective imagination concerning cities, it is necessary to investigate first and foremost which internal processes control artistic and literary communication, and only afterwards to examine the role played by historical and social realities.

An investigation of the narratological construction of city images could usefully start from the Bakhtinian concept of "chronotope."[6] Even though the definition of this concept is far from unproblematical, it could be argued that in all of its connotations the term "chronotope" refers to the stereotyped semantic information that is used during the encoding or decoding of literary texts. Crucial to such prior information is the fact that it has an invariant cognitive structure, that it functions as a generic framework according to which literary statements are classified. Simplifying, we could define chronotope as a four-dimensional mental image, which combines the three spatial dimensions with the time structure of a plot, of a temporal action or a historical process. Important, however, are not the visual associations of a chronotope, but the precise way in which a temporal logic is combined with a spatial one and transformed into a mental "possible world." In realist literature, the dominant cognitive model was a schematic structure that combined information about social space with a historical interpretative model. Descriptions of typically modern conditions were linked to references to specific historical processes (e.g. the process of modernization, industrialization, the emergence of a consumption economy, migration, etc.). Apart from descriptions also stereotypical plot structures (such as "the arrival in the big city") were used to emphasize that the novel was informed by historical documents. All this textual information was part of one world model, one documentary chronotope, which interwove global historical processes with documentary "facts."

In what follows, four other types of texts are examined and linked to four world models used by postwar authors: the semi-documentary space-time construct in neo-realism, the (auto)biographical chronotope in (a certain kind of) postmodern literature, the adventure chronotope in predominantly popular genres, and finally the hyperreal space-time construct equally associated with postmodernism. What is striking about these chronotopes is that you may find them combined in one and the same text. Postwar texts, so it seems, are not exclusively limited by one specific chronotope. The coexistence of chronotopes is admittedly also a feature of nineteenth and early-twentieth-century novels. Yet in the latter instances it is possible to clearly distinguish between dominant chronotopes which are typical of, for instance, naturalist, symbolist, or surrealist texts. The programmatic limitations (rigor) of those movements account for the fact that constructions of possible worlds took place along fairly stereotypical lines. In the literature of high modernism (from the city novels of Döblin and Dos Passos onwards), this programmatic constriction largely disappeared, so that in one and the same text several chronotopical constructions can be detected. This does not mean, however, that no clear strands can be discerned. The typology presented in what follows allows one to see which forms of world construction dominate in the city novels of the late twentieth century and which constructions have become irrelevant.

**Subcultural Journeys: The Semi-Documentary Chronotope in Neo-Realist Novels of Manners** In the postwar period, we rarely find city novels in which the arrival motif is of crucial importance. Yet there are a great number of neo-realist texts which offer detailed portraits of the big city. From a narratological point of view, we could say that they are created on the basis of one and the same world model: the documentary chronotope. In defining documentary chronotopes, one has to start from the idea that they refer to documents, that is to say, texts which originate in intersubjective communication outside the literary field (lifestyle magazines, television icons, ready knowledge from school, journalistic reportage). From this follows that in interpreting these texts the reader has to rely on commonsense and encyclopedic knowledge. Moreover, the function of these documents is not merely referential; the realist text does not inform the reader about an unequivocal reality, but alludes symbolically to specific historical processes and concretely experienced places. Hence also sociopsychological material (such as the dysphoria of the individual crushed by the machinery of the big city) belongs to the documentary world model. The American novel of manners published (and often also turned into a movie) in the eighties is based in principle on a world matrix consisting of a documentary space and real historical developments. Short story collections such as *Slaves of New York* (Tama Janowitz's depiction of "new urban lifestyles"), novels like Bret Easton Ellis's *Less Than Zero* (young *nouveaux riches* in L.A.), Charles Bukowski's *Post Office* (about a down-and-out hustler in L.A.), Jay McInerney's *Bright Lights, Big City* (yuppies and cocaine in New York), and Tom Wolfe's *The Bonfire of the Vanities* (ethnic conflicts in New York) — and their European counterparts like A. F. Th. Van der Heijden's *Advocaat van de Hanen* (squatters in Amsterdam) or Hanif Kureishi's *Buddha of Suburbia* (Pakistani in London) — depict characters who are confronted with one or another

7 See Volker Klotz, *Die erzählte Stadt. Ein Sujet als Herausforderung des Romans von Lesage bis Döblin* (München: Hanser, 1969), 196; Karlheinz Stierle, *Der Mythos von Paris. Zeichen und Bewußtsein der Stadt* (München: Hanser, 1993), 83; Priscilla Parkhurst Ferguson, "Reading Revolutionary Paris," in *Literature and Social Practice*, ed. Philippe Desan and Priscilla P. Ferguson (Chicago: University of Chicago Press, 1989), 60-62.

8 Walter Benjamin, *Gesammelte Schriften V*, ed. Rolf Tiedemann (Frankfurt am Main: Suhrkamp, 1982), 663-64; Ferguson, "Reading," 60; see also Priscilla Parkhurst Ferguson, *Paris as Revolution: Writing the Nineteenth-Century City* (Berkeley and Los Angeles: University of California Press, 1994), 61.

problematical aspect of the contemporary metropolis. Each of the novels explores a specific subculture, while the characters move in a world which presupposes a certain amount of prior knowledge about social circumstances and historical process on the part of the reading public.

However, the affinity of neo-realist novels with the great realist and naturalist city novels cannot disguise the fact that the latter tradition explores urban material from a broader perspective. The social segments in the city novels of Zola, for instance (the world of fashion in *Au Bonheur des dames*, small businesses in *Le Ventre de Paris*, the stock exchange in *L'Argent*), are not just descriptions of customs and mores in contemporary Paris. They also serve as a synecdoche for the sum total of sociohistorical developments.[7] Realists and naturalists make heroic attempts (often through cycles of novels) to present the city at the cutting edge of historical development. In no way, however, do the American novels of manner create a microcosm which allows projections towards larger historical developments. Their documentary observations never transcend the local set of problems of the protagonists. This contrast clearly demonstrates that in the newer realist literature the city is no longer a privileged symbol charged with culture-theoretically relevant information. It would be a mistake, however, to interpret this evolution as the consequence of the increasing uncontrollability of urban material. The great nineteenth-century city novels, too, had to contend with the experience of dispersion. Referring implicitly to Walter Benjamin, Priscilla Ferguson asserts that the panoramic interest of Balzac is an attempt to compensate for urban fragmentation (celebrated by the popular press): "The novel replaced the aesthetic of iteration of the literary guidebooks with an 'aesthetics of integration.' ... Into an urban space flooded with discourse the novel brought a reimagined city. In place of fragments of a city the novel presented a city made whole."[8] Ferguson's analysis proves that the reason for the disappearance of the totalizing perspective in contemporary city novels has to be sought elsewhere. Probably the enfeeblement of documentary interests and the bankruptcy of the commitment of the "god-eye intellectual" (cf. Sartre, Habermas) account for the weakening of totalizing projects in contemporary realism. In the neo-realist novel, not the linking of socio-psychological observations to sociological and historical processes is central, but the psychology and stereotypical behavior of the protagonists.

**Quotidian Urbanity: The Self-Referential Chronotope in the (Auto)biographical Artist's Novel** Apart from the documentary model of neo-realism, a second construction principle is at work in postwar literature. The coordinates of this construct are provided by the everyday world of the writer. In the last few decades, authors have tended to write novels in which the urban biotope of the contemporary artist takes up a central position. Illustrating this trend is a statement by Don DeLillo in a recent interview: "I became a writer by living in New York and seeing and hearing and feeling all the great, amazing and dangerous things the city endlessly assembles. And I also became a writer by avoiding serious commitment to anything else."[9] Even though the statement is reminiscent of the ambitions of many realists and modernists, the treatment of the urban *donnée* in postmodern novels is fundamentally different from older city literature. According to Hans Sanders, the rediscovery of quotidian (city) life in postmodern literature is a continuation of the search for "everyday utopias" which was started by the historical avantgarde movements and which is characterized by a latent protest against the hermetic-autonomist attitude typical of modernism.[10] Certainly in Germanic countries (Peter Handke's work between 1975 and 1980, Bodo Morshäuser's collections of short stories, *Revolver* and *Die Berliner Simulation*, Botho Strauss's *Paare, Passanten*), but also in American literature (Philip Roth's *Zuckerman*-cycle, E. L. Doctorow's *Lives of the Poets*) and the French *Nouveau Roman* (Alain Robbe-Grillet's *Projet pour une révolution à New York*), there is a strong tendency favoring a return to the trivial and the everyday. Most of the time everyday life manifests itself through the experience of artists or aesthetically sensitive observers, whereby the quotidian that is selected for observation is strongly steeped in an urban ambience. For Sanders this attention to the details of everyday life is a strategy of resistance against the poetics of modernism: "For the autonomous modernist writer and artist everyday life is a challenge that has to be overcome by aesthetic means. In the postmodern mind-set, however, the proximity of quotidian, familiar relations and connections is experienced in a positive way as a worthwhile alternative site over and against the mega-organizations of bureaucracy, industry,

9 Jonathan Bing, "The Ascendance of Don DeLillo," *Publishers Weekly*, 11 August 1997; consulted through http://haas.berkeley.edu/~gardner/delillo.html.

10 Hans Sanders, "Postmoderne. Alltäglichkeit als Utopie," in *Postmoderne: Alltag, Allegorie und Avantgarde*, ed. Christa Bürger et al. (Frankfurt am Main: Suhrkamp, 1987), 75.

11 "Der Mentalität der autonomen Moderne gilt alltägliches Leben als das, was ästhetisch zu überwinden ist. Die Postmoderne Mentalität der neuen Bewegungen aber erlebt die Nähe alltäglich überschaubarer Lebenszusammenhänge als positiv zu bewahrenden alternativen Ort gegenüber den zweckrationalen Gesichtspunkten jenseits menschlicher Bedürfnisse verfahrenden Grossorganisationen von Bürokratie, Industrie, Bildung und Verkehr." Ibid., 80. Editors' translation.

12 "Er wurde offen für jede Einzelheit, sah andrerseits nichts mehr vom andern abgetrennt.... Er fühlte, dass er mächtig geworden war.... Von seinem Körper spürte er nichts. Er bewegte sich schwerelos durch die andern, die sich dahinschleppten." Peter Handke, *Die Stunde der wahren Empfindung* (1975; reprint, Frankfurt am Main: Suhrkamp, 1982), 148. Editors' translation.

13 Bakhtin, "Forms," 142.

14 "Toutes ces choses pensent par moi, ou je pense par elles (car dans la grandeur de la rêverie, le moi se perd vite!)." Charles Baudelaire, *Le Spleen de Paris. Journaux intimes. Choix de maximes consolantes sur l'amour* (1869; reprint, Paris: Colin, 1958), 6. Editors' translation.

15 Kristiaan Versluys, *The Poet and the City: Chapters in the Development of Urban Poetry in Europe and the United States, 1800-1930* (Tübingen: Gunter Narr Verlag, 1987).

education and transportation, which respond to rational criteria and ignore real human needs."[11] Peter Handke's novel *Die Stunde der wahren Empfindung* (1975) is a typical example of this trend. In this text, everyday life in the city forms the setting for an existential fable. In the course of the story, Keuschnig, a diplomat in Paris, succeeds in overcoming his initial alienation by closely observing urban tableaux: "he opened himself up to every detail, on the other hand he viewed nothing separate from everything else. ... He felt that he had become powerful. ... He didn't feel his body anymore. He moved weightlessly amongst the others, who dragged themselves along."[12]

Important in stories such as Handke's is the fact that they presuppose a specific world model. The world that is explored is self-referential. Its spatial coordinates are provided by subjective observation and/or recollection, while a personal or fictitious biography informs temporal progression. It goes without saying that the quotidian-biographical world matrix forms a stark contrast to the great city novels of realism. The novels are marked by the rebirth of a character or an individual insight. The world that is depicted is static and devoid of any supra-individual development. While in realism an individual grows through interaction with the city and goes through a learning process, in postmodern city tales the confrontation with the city is limited to the observations and psychological processes of a monadic soul. In this respect, the spatiotemporal condition of the postmodern (auto)biographical or fictional-(auto)biographical novel strongly resembles the premodern matrix — a matrix in which, according to Bakhtin, "the process of disclosing character" holds a central position. This process, however, "does not lead to a real change or 'becoming' in historical reality, but rather solely to a *fulfillment*, that is, to a filling-in of that form sketched at the very outset."[13]

In constructing the everyday world, some texts, in which the self-referential chronotope functions as matrix, use methods of long standing to aestheticize the cityscape. Commonly deployed, for instance, is the correspondence method, going back to Baudelaire's famous statement in *Le Spleen de Paris*: "all these things think through me, or I think through them (for in the greatness of revery, the self quickly loses itself!)."[14] Next to the motif of "the arrival in the city," the correspondence method is the main structuring principle in nineteenth-century city images. It forms the foundation of a collective symbol that could be termed "urban spleen." Especially works in symbolism and aesthetically oriented modernism (Biely, James, Huysmans, Rilke) opt for the presentation of a city which follows the coordinates of a subjectivist world model. In such texts, the city image mediates (by way of correspondences) between the artistic observer and the outside world.[15] The title of Baudelaire's collection of prose poems reflects this interaction: through the association of Paris (the material world) with spleen (the mental world) a world model is created that articulates a specific spatiotemporal realm: the realm of psychological correspondences. Paris is a world absorbed by expanding internal time (*durée*), a world in which most images are contaminated by spleen: foggy and rainy cityscapes, deserted streets, squares, and parks, lonely figures against a dark background, etc. By instituting this imaginative procedure, Baudelaire became the founding father of what Christian Berg has called "symbolic idealism."[16]

In the postwar novel, there is a revival of this symbolist idealism, certainly when urban narrative material is involved. Spleen as a mood has been replaced by a more contemporary and undoubtedly also more populist "blues feeling," but the literary mechanism has remained the same. The opening paragraphs of chapters 2, 3, and 5 of Don DeLillo's *Great Jones Street*, for instance, contain descriptions of cityscapes, characterized by cold, snow, twilight, and debris, and peopled by a host of down-and-out people. In this respect, the end of chapter two is typical: "This was an old street. Its materials were in fact its essence and this explains the ugliness of every inch. But it wasn't a final squalor. Some streets in their decline possess a kind of redemptive tenor, the suggestion of new forms about to evolve, and Great Jones was one of these, hovering on the edge of self-revelation. Paper, yarn, leathers, tools, buckles, wire-frame-and-novelty."[17] This description is analogous to the emotional condition of the narrator: "For me, Great Jones Street was a time of prayerful fatigue. I became a half-saint, practiced in visions, informed by a sense of bodily economy, but deficient in true pain. I was preoccupied with conserving myself for some unknown ordeal to come and did not make work by engaging in dialogues, or take more than the minimum number of steps to get from place to place, or urinating unnecessarily."[18] As in DeLillo's novel epistemological doubt forms the main motif, the emotional conditions and the cognitive processing of problems depicted in it are far removed from what one finds in older literatures. Even so, the network of urban metaphors that is employed in *Great Jones Street* as well as in work of other authors (Alan Hollinghurst's *The Folding Star*, the detritus motifs in Thomas Pynchon) and of film makers (Antonioni, film noir) is in many ways similar to the symbolist

16 Christian Berg, "Lecture de Bruges-la-Morte," in Georges Rodenbach, *Bruges-la-Morte* (1892; reprint, Bruxelles: Labor, 1986), 107.

17 Don DeLillo, *Great Jones Street* (1973; reprint, New York: Vintage, 1983), 18.

18 Ibid., 19.

19 Keith M. Booker, *The Dystopian Impulse in Modern Literature: Fiction as Social Criticism* (Westport: Greenwood, 1994), 150.

20 Brian Jarvis, *Postmodern Cartographies: The Geographical Imagination in Contemporary American Culture* (London: Pluto, 1998), 142.

21 Ibid., 141.

22 Ibid., 141-42.

23 Ibid., 143-44.

imagery in, for instance, Georges Rodenbach's *Bruges-la-Morte* (1892), in which the moribund, foggy city displays a medieval stillness which correlates with the suffering, the confusion, and sometimes the redemption of the main character. Hence it is possible to make two claims: one, the "bluesy" imagination is an important archetype in the collective memory of cities; two, this aspect of the Western imaginary stands in sharp contrast to the collective symbol "individual vs. city."

**Urban Ruins and Urban Gothic: The Abstract Chronotope of the "Adventure Novel of Ordeal"** Just as Fredric Jameson sees the Bonaventure Hotel in L.A. as a microcosm mirroring postmodern space, a whole series of culture and literature critics consider the iconography of the contemporary urban film (especially science fiction versions) and the spatial structures of cyberpunk literature to be narrative microscosms. The prototype of the postmodern setting is Los Angeles as presented in Ridley Scott's Hollywood movie *Blade Runner* (1982) (loosely based on the 1968 New Wave SF-novel by Philip K. Dick). Other settings that are taken to be representative of postmodern urbanity are the derivative movies imitating Scott's cult movie (Gilliam's *Brazil* of 1985, *Back to the Future* II of 1986, *Total Recall* of 1990 and *Dark City* of 1996), the newer forms of hardboiled fiction (James Ellroy), but especially cyberpunk science fiction (William Gibson, Bruce Sterling, Pat Cadigan, Rudy Rucker, Lewis Shiner, Walter Jon Williams, and Richard Kadrey). Cyberpunk cityscapes, like "the sprawl" in Gibson, have in common with *Blade Runner* that they form a scenery consisting of an amorphous urban blur: "the entire Eastern United States is covered by a giant urban 'Sprawl' whose social problems (crime, violence, pollution) are much like those of American cities in the 1980s, but on a larger scale."[19] Moreover, they are made up of an heterogeneous collection of city icons: "In terms of its visual design, with its dissonant clash of architectural styles, the city itself is something of a mishmash. Elements of the Futuristic aesthetic, Mayan, Wrightian and art deco styles collide with Greek statues and roman columns."[20] Brian Jarvis proposes to read *Blade Runner* as a symptom of our time.[21] According to him, there are parallels with Los Angeles, as described in Mike Davis's *City of Quartz*: "Scott's vision manages to map out the actuality of late twentieth-century LA.... With its stark oppositions between the imposing Tyrell corporation building and the overcrowded city streets populated predominantly by Chinese and Asiatics, Davis' depiction of the postmodern urban landscape could easily be applied to the ethnogeographic organisation of Scott's futuristic LA."[22] In addition, Jarvis interprets the movie as a series of documents which refer to "Third World labour practices, militarisation," and "segregation of public space."[23] This reading of the movie is acceptable. Yet it smacks of *Hineininterpretierung*. First of all, Jarvis himself asserts that the motifs he mentions allow one to make associations, but that in fact they obscure rather than illuminate the social mechanisms in the traditional city.[24] Secondly, one has to take into account that the urban material selected can be reduced to the same common denominator: menace. This sense of doom is part and parcel of the adventure story at the center of every cyberpunk film or novel.

Fixed ingredients of cyberpunk narrative are threatening nocturnal streets filled with neon-lit anonymous masses. At any instant a violent or criminal situation can emerge. Also dark dank places, such as decaying buildings in suburban areas or deserted inner-city zones, are favorite locales, visited by marginals and delinquents only. These dystopian visions in the popular imagination strongly resemble the *noir* tradition, to which next to gothic castles in eighteenth- and nineteenth-century Gothic Fiction and the French or English proletarian novels of the late-nineteenth century also the settings of the hardboiled detective story belong.[25] Hence it is obvious that not the documentary value of the settings is of primordial importance, but their function as agents of menace in an adventure story. The city — or at least the street level element of it that is strictly separated from the highrises in which other segments of the highly stratified society reside — is staged as a jungle in which strange individuals (Replicants, agents of industrial security forces, *femmes fatales*) live undercover. These are depressing and threatening surroundings, because dangers lurk at every corner. Just as in the nineteenth-century cities which Walter Benjamin describes (in his reflections on the urban crowd in the work of Edgar Allan Poe and in detective stories), the city is reduced to a labyrinth, in which the menacing individual can vanish without leaving a trace.[26] The omnipresence of security forces (in *Blade Runner* as well as in many cyberpunk novels) strengthens this sense of menace, as there is every indication to believe that these forces are not capable of keeping the illegal element in check.

It is possible, of course, with William Gibson to assert that the portrayal of the menace has in itself already documentary value. Yet, in essence, cyberpunk does not yield a balanced description of the problems in the late twentieth centu-

24 Ibid., 145.

25 The metaphors of "jungle" and "wilderness" — often associated with the Far West — are strongly present in nineteenth-century French literature (Dumas's *Les Mohicans de Paris*, Sue's *Les mystères de Paris*), but also in images of London from the end of the nineteenth century. Raymond Williams mentions works about the proletarian suburbs east of the City of London which produced the term *Darkest London*; see Raymond Williams, *The Country and the City* (London: Hogarth Press, 1985), 221.

26 Walter Benjamin, "Das Paris des Second Empire bei Baudelaire" (1938), in Walter Benjamin, *Gesammelte Schriften I 2*, ed. Rolf Tiedemann (Frankfurt am Main: Suhrkamp, 1974), 542-46.

27 Andrew Ross, *Strange Weather: Culture, Science and Technology in the Age of Limits* (London: Verso, 1991).

28 Jarvis, *Postmodern*, 145, 146.

29 Bakhtin, "Forms," 100.

ry. As Andrew Ross puts it, the settings of the cyberpunk stories are *merely* setting — just as they are in MTV clips (in which the hiphop numbers are often staged in derelict urban neighborhoods) and in the cultural commonplaces of televized police series.[27] Jarvis is right in asserting that the setting of *Blade Runner* has gone the way of the Hollywood versions of hardboiled detective fiction: "Once the studios had appropriated the 'noir' geography of mean streets and scenic sewers the fact, the brute fact that the streets of LA 'really were mean,' for many of its poorer inhabitants, tended to get obscured.... Science fiction cinema, in its postmodern phase, tends to distract from frighteningly real urban crises by manufacturing an exhilaratingly pessimistic celluloid fantasy of the New Bad Future from them."[28] Whereas realists indicate to what extent contemporary space has shock value and how it is produced historically and socially, the adventure novel presents an abstract space. This abstraction does not result from an attempt to present the etherialized dimensions of cyberspace or posturban sprawl, but from the application of narrative techniques characteristic of the adventure story. The accumulation of styles and of disparate urban material in *Blade Runner* (the deserted factory lots and the emphasis on exaggerated urban sprawl) suggest space that allows no overview. Its constitutive elements are not specified. They are assembled solely to suggest expanse and impenetrability. Also the temporal progression of the story is underdeveloped. The random events which test the endurance of the hero dominate the plot. The expressions "suddenly," "at that particular moment" point to this. Of central importance for the adventure chronotope is the abstraction of all historical and social references so that there is no diversion from what remains the main thing: the creation of suspense and adventure. In this respect, the chronotope involved is one which, according to Bakhtin, is characteristic of the adventure novel of classical antiquity and which, in his view, is lacking the historical and sociological perspective of the modern Renaissance man and his heirs (the realists). The adventure chronotope is "characterized by a technical, abstract connection between space and time, by the reversibility of moments in a temporal sequence, and by their interchangeability in space. In this chronotope, all initiative and power belongs to chance."[29] At the center of an adventure story is a hero who — just as in the novels of James M. Cain, Raymond Chandler, and James Ellroy — is threatened by aleatory moments of peril and who, as a result, has to embark on a quest. Just as in the above group of novels, the heroes do not age and they do not acquire any worldly wisdom. Their only progress consists of triumphing over spatial obstacles and of solving the problems they happen to run into. From this perspective, it is hard to interpret the spatial setting in the popular imaginary as a symbol of the same order as the city symbol in the literatures of the nineteenth and early twentieth centuries.

**The Heterotopian and the Semiotic City: The Hyperreal Chronotope in Postmodernist Prose** Hyperreal constructs are to be found in those world matrixes in which the spatial and temporal continuity of empirical observation is distorted. In everyday perception, successive spatial impressions are linked by causal relations projected on an uninterrupted time axis. In the hyperreal chronotope, however, there is an attempt to link fragments of reality in a combination that is as complex and dynamic as possible. The ulterior motivation behind such world construction is varied: sometimes the idea is to suggest extraordinary perceptions belonging to the realm of dream, ecstasy, pathological anxiety, schizophrenia, paranoia, or confusion. At other times the distorting or strongly intensified observation in "technological situations" (telegraphic speed, perceptions during a train ride, or images on a busy traffic junction) is imitated. The prototypes of this kind of chronotopic construction are to be found in the works of the historical avantgarde movements. In these works, the author tries to suggest or at least to simulate the dynamism of objective phenomena (traffic, perceptions in dense cities, journeys by train, cars, machine guns) as well as of subjective processes (the inner dynamism of ecstasy, the experience of speed). The means employed to that end are varied, too, ranging from the *Reihungsstil* in early impressionism, to image association in surrealism and *parola in libertà* in Italian futurism. Both the overly enthusiastic celebration of urban liberty and the nearly pyromaniac enjoyment of the decline of the West (the apocalyptic city) belong to the repertoire of the historical avantgarde. What links the two themes is the presence of an intense transgression and, in its wake, the vitalistic ecstasy which, according to Georges Bataille, comes into existence when commonsense laws and social norms are trespassed upon.

Next to the historicizing archetype "individual vs. city" and next to impressionist spleen, the ecstatic city constitutes a third collective symbol of modern culture. The sociological work of Georg Simmel (and that of later researchers such as Berman, Frisby, Lash, and Featherstone, working in a Simmelian tradition) demonstrates that from the second half of the nineteenth century onwards the experience of the "kick" was identified as a phenomenon of modernity.[30] Hence it is possible to maintain that the city images of present-day producers of

30 Just like the other two collective symbols, the myth of the ecstatic city can be traced back to nineteenth-century examples. It is present on the margins of Baudelaire's work (especially in his art criticism such as *Le Peintre de la vie moderne* of 1863 and *Le Salon de 1859*, in a couple of prose poems and in the "Tableaux Parisiens" section of *Les Fleurs du Mal*). Even so, only a fragment of Baudelaire's oeuvre is involved — the experience of ecstasy is but one component in a larger aestheticizing attitude. See Matei Calinescu, *Faces of Modernity: Avant-Garde, Decadence and Kitsch* (Bloomington: Indiana University Press, 1977); Paul Hoffmann, *Symbolismus* (München: Fink, 1987).

31 Jarvis, *Postmodern*, 143.

32 Brian McHale, *Constructing Postmodernism* (London: Routledge, 1992), 251.

33 Brian McHale, *Postmodernist Fiction* (New York: Methuen, 1987), 45.

culture constitute an important part of the collective imagination. In reconstructing urban experience, especially popular culture (MTV video clips, underground cartoons) and cult art (beat poets, Kerouac, Miller) use a hyperreal world matrix, in which disparate fragments are compacted into a dynamic whole. The popularity of cult movies such as *Blade Runner* — in which "vastly disparate levels of technological development" converge into a "nocturnal" apocalyptic vision[31] — can be interpreted as a symptom of a desire for transgressive, extraordinary experience. Punk culture — with its "no future" mentality and its cult of transgressive immediacy — has reactivated this specific avantgarde cultural legacy. Finally, from the sixties onwards also the (urban) cult of toxicomania has played a big role in spreading vitalistic city images.

Apart from the products of the popular imagination, there are also traces of the cult of ecstasy in postmodernist literature. Postmodern authors do not only describe a background, they also create hyperreal zones — constructs characterized by a "maximally intimate juxtaposition of maximally diverse and heterogeneous cultural materials (Japanese, Western and Third World; high tech and low tech, elite and popular, mainstream official culture and youth or criminal subcultures)."[32] Zones, in other words, are fictional spaces which come into existence as the result of a construction which is strongly reminiscent of the condensed world at the center of many a work of the avantgarde. Just like the compacted spaces in avantgarde works, zones try to evoke an alienating and subjective atmosphere. Following Brian McHale, one could see this use of condensation as the creation of heterotopian space. The construct is composed of elements which are recognizable on their own but which in the imagination are combined and then charged with virtual properties and affective connotations:

*in realist and modernist writing, [the] spatial construct is organized around a perceiving subject, either a character or the viewing position adopted by a disembodied narrator. The heterotopian zone of postmodernist writing cannot be organized in this way, however. Space here is less constructed than* deconstructed *by the text, or rather constructed and deconstructed at the same time. Postmodernist fiction draws upon a number of strategies for constructing/deconstructing space, among them juxtaposition, interpolation, superimposition, and misattribution.*[33]

A number of postmodernist zone constructs are undoubtedly city images and some of them (Burroughs's apocalyptic landscapes in *Cities of the Red Night*, Pynchon's revolutionary campus in *Vineland*, and Gibson's anarchic punk culture in *Count Zero*) thematize the same vitalistic intensity as the older avantgarde literature. The heterotopian city images can be taken to be postmodern variants of the bourgeois utopian literature which has been in existence since the Renaissance.[34] An important difference, however, is that in postmodernist fiction the imaginative constructs are not built *ex nihilo*, but use material to be found in empirical reality.

A second development that is illuminated by the concept "hyperreal world construct" has seemingly nothing in common with the artistic simulation of extraordinary experience, which is so important for the heirs of the historical avantgarde. The term hyperreality takes on new meaning when it is used in the sense that Jean Baudrillard gives to it. In *Simulations*, Baudrillard describes how the perception of the postmodern subject is determined by hyperreal transformations of everyday situations. He starts from the observation that hyperreality is no longer an artistic construct or an extraordinary experience linked to special circumstances and to gifted observers (aesthetes such as Aragon and Breton who make the Parisian shopping arcades into oneiric spaces). In the view of Baudrillard, the hyperreal has now become part of quotidian reality. Baudrillard's observations (as well as those of authors like Mike Featherstone who think along similar lines) accord wonderfully well with the thematics and the procedures of a final group of postmodernist texts. The postmodern world is presented in a whole lot of texts which are usually called "postmodernist novels" as a textual world of signs, a world dominated by the simulacra of the communication media and by objects of conspicuous consumption. Such texts demonstrate that the distinctive characteristic of city life is no longer its modernity but its postmodernity and that, as a result, city life has become a conglomerate of postmodern simulacra. After Ihab Hassan, Heinz Ickstadt speaks in this connection of a literature focusing on the "immaterial city," which is more than simply a fictitious version of the material city: "the city of the literary postmodern functions as metaphor and synecdoche of an urban world, which transcends the city and turns it into an abstraction. This urban world has duplicated itself, as it were, in a network of communication systems."[35] Postmodern authors do no longer thematize the material processes of

34 Tom Moylan, *Demand the Impossible: Science Fiction and the Utopian Imagination* (New York: Methuen, 1986), 161.

35 Heinz Ickstadt, "Kommunikation und Sprachcollage. Die Stadt in der amerikanischen Fiktion der Postmoderne," in *Die Unwirklichkeit der Städte. Großstadtdarstellungen zwischen Moderne und Postmoderne*, ed. Klaus R. Scherpe (Reinbek bei Hamburg: Rowohlt, 1988), 197. Editors' translation.

36 Ibid.

37 Ibid.

38 "Lorsque je lis les faits divers scandaleux ou criminels, lorsque je regarde les vitrines et les affiches qui composent la façade de toute grande ville, lorsque j'accomplis un parcours dans les couloirs du métropolitain, je me trouve assailli par une multitude de signes dont l'ensemble constitue la mythologie du monde où je vis, quelque chose comme l'inconscient collectif de la société, c'est à dire à la fois l'image qu'elle veut se donner d'elle-même et le reflet des troubles qui la hantent." Quoted in Diane Wolfe Levy, "City Signs," *Modern Fiction Studies* 24 (1978): 70. Editors' translation.

39 Bodo Morshäuser, *Die Berliner Simulation* (Frankfurt am Main: Suhrkamp, 1988), 14.

40 See McHale, *Constructing*, 116-21.

modernization (industry, social mobility, consumption) or their consequences (social isolation, class conflict, the American Dream). Instead, they concentrate on the artificial and fabricated character of the confrontations with the social world. The city of postmodernism is first and foremost a semiotic world, reduced to an immaterial existence, to a "storehouse of both individual and collective phantasies."[36] Not the empirical city as such is the big challenge for the contemporary author, but the fictional constructs which we use in trying to comprehend the urban world — the world of simulacra and of the mediatized global village arising from the urban condition. In this way, the empirical city is "metaphorically tied in with the switch-boards and sign systems of media and mass communication."[37]

An interesting strategy to give shape to a semiotic world construct is the one used by Alain Robbe-Grillet in *Projet pour une révolution à New York*. In an interview with *Le Nouvel Observateur* (June 26, 1970), the author declares: "When I read in the newspapers about scandals or crimes, when I look at the display windows and the posters which make up the facade of every big city, when I travel through the corridors of the subway, I find myself assaulted by a multitude of signs, which together constitute the mythology of the world in which I live — something resembling the collective unconscious of society, that is to say at the same time the image society wants to project of itself and the reflection of the confusion that haunts it."[38] On a more modest scale one finds the same immaterialization of the city in recent German and French literature. In French literature, there are texts in which authors depict urban forms of communication. Bernard Marie Koltès's *La Solitude des champs de cotton* is completely based on a latently homoerotic confrontation between two urbanites and sketches the elusiveness and attractiveness of their chance encounter. In Germany, Botho Strauss's *Paare, Passanten* depicts the attempts of the narrator to hold his own in a complex urban world mediated by language and images. Related to this are the ironic quotes in the work of Bodo Morshäuser — "Eine Frau frage Mirko das WAS-MACHST-DU ... Zelebrierte er sein ICH-SCHREIBE-UEBER-FILM"[39] — which are meant to mirror the unreality of communication in the nightlife of the cities.

A less metalinguistic and more ontological strategy to suggest the hyperreality of everyday existence is to be found in the work of Thomas Pynchon. In *Constructing Postmodernism*, Brian McHale cites a number of interesting passages which he takes to be exponents of zone construction: discursive structures borrowed from television shows are combined with realistic descriptions. In the Californian cities of *Vineland* — according to McHale the most typical examples of zone constructs — television genres determine the way the characters experience the world.[40] Another technique (used in *Gravity's Rainbow*) is the combination of a war zone with film language. Apart from the work of Pynchon, the thematizing of mediated realities also plays a role in the work of the German postmodernist Rainald Goetz (his *Festung*-trilogy, in particular *1989*).[41] Over and above that, the theme can also be linked to the exceptional role assigned to the urban detective (an eminent figure of television drama) in recent novels, notably those of Paul Auster.[42] In contrast to the real detective story, no adventure chronotope is involved here, but a detective looking for clues when confronted with a postmodern (and often urban) world of signs. In that world, he goes out searching for his true identity, for the original behind the copy; in short, for an unfindable truth.

**Conclusion: The Myth of Postmodern City Images** A survey of city images in postwar literature demonstrates that the collective symbol of the confrontation between city and individual has lost a great deal of its relevance. With the exception of subcultural journeys (which can be considered as an attenuated version of the confrontation) and some heterotopian city images (zones like those in Pynchon which consist of a *bricolage* of social and historical material), the urban experience of modernity is rarely thematized in recent literature. Of the important collective symbols of the nineteenth and early twentieth centuries only the non-historicizing are still being used. Only the impressionistic "bluesy" city images and the ecstatic city of the avantgarde movements seem to persist. The newer city images make use of abstract or hypersubjective world constructs: the adventure chronotope in popular culture, the semiotic worlds of postmodernist metafiction and the everyday world of postmodernist (auto)biographers. According to some, it is obvious that in the thinned-out and dispersed city there is no room anymore for totalizing city images representing modernity. This monocausal argumentation, however, is weak. In accordance with recent sociological analyses, it is possible to point to the structure of the literary field itself to explain the disappearance of the modern city from the novel.[43] Since Romanticism, modern literature derived its dynamism from ever new (and also ever more radical) programmatic statements. Since the interbellum period, however, when the last great literary avantgarde programs were launched, authors have been living in a "postprogram" culture, in which collective declarations of intent have lost their validity.

41 See Jürgen Link, *Versuch über den Normalismus. Wie Normalität produziert wird* (Opladen: Westdeutscher Verlag, 1997), 67ff.

42 Sometimes the motif of the detective is used to distinguish postmodernism from modernism: "What the structural and philosophical presuppositions of myth and depth psychology were to Modernism (Mann, Joyce, Woolf, etc.), the detective story is to Post-Modernism (Robbe-Grillet, Borges, Nabokov, etc.)." See Michael Holquist, "Whodunnit and Other Questions: Metaphysical Detective Stories in Post War Fiction," *New Literary History* 3, 1 (1971): 135.

43 Gerhard Plumpe, *Epochen moderner Literatur. Ein systemtheoretischer Entwurf* (Opladen: Westdeutscher Verlag, 1995).

44 Mike Featherstone, *Undoing Culture: Globalization, Postmodernism and Identity* (London: Sage, 1995), 5.

Nonetheless, developments in the literary world are not completely cut off from the sociocultural processes of modernization. More than the city, however, it is the available cultural means of orientation which form the sociocultural background against which changes in the literary field take place. Thus the post-programmatic tendencies in contemporary literature can be understood as the artistic counterpart of a process that Mike Featherstone describes as the key problem of our time: "The problems we encounter in everyday practice because culture fails to provide us with a single taken-for-granted recipe for action introduce difficulties, mistakes and complexity."[44] The heroic self-affirmation vis-à-vis objective culture of which, among others, Simmel and Weber dreamed (and of which the romantic hero is the prototype and of which the realist, aestheticist, and avantgarde heroes form a variant) is no longer a priority, as our culture has been split into shards and is rendered ever more complex by the increasing influence of consumption practices. Whereas "coping with objective culture" (Featherstone) seems to be the central problem of the programmatic literatures of the prewar period, the contemporary challenge follows from the heterogeneity and complexity of a mediatized and globalized culture. For a poetics which comes into existence at a time when cultural responses and strategies can no longer be formulated unambiguously, there is no urgent need to confront modernity. As a result, poetics becomes postprogrammatic almost automatically.

Another factor which helps to contextualize the "thinning-out" of the city as a literary theme in postwar literature is related to the decreasing menace of objective culture. In a way, one could maintain that modernist culture shock is no longer the prime social experience influencing literary and artistic activity. The problem of the city is felt to be banal, as it pales in comparison to other challenges or threats. Featherstone is right in asserting that the problem of the domination of objective culture still exists, but then in a form marked by globalization in the realms of the economy, of communication and transportation. The intensification of the problem explains why material processes such as urbanization have been relegated to the background. The new cultural challenges entail a different focus in literary production. Whereas Balzac, Zola, Dreiser, Döblin, and Dos Passos tried to fill the literary field with references to commonsense knowledge and with recognizable representations, references to cities in more recent works are related to so many different phenomena that it has become impossible to speak of one urban referent. It is no longer possible — neither for writers nor for ordinary citizens — to link modern urbanity with a larger sociological or historical evolution. Hence one can say that in the twentieth century a discursive fact has been realized which early on was recognized by Henri Lefebvre. Already in 1968, Lefebvre claimed that meanings lose their referential uniformity once they belong to everyday life; commonplaces do no longer refer to a knowable object, but have a tendency to get dispersed in a multitude of connotations.[45] This is certainly the case in all discourse on the contemporary city. One still speaks in an antiquated language, but only out of habit. Moreover, as a result of this new discursive climate, cities are sometimes seen as the opposites of the new challenges. Whereas formerly the city represented chaos, it is now looked upon as a realm of nostalgia and vitality in contrast to the newer forms of chaos. In this connection, it is possible to wonder whether in the cultural imagination cities have not become "zones" — zones which neutralize the fragmentation of postmodernity in its global guise (world economy, social diversification, individualization of lifestyles). The present-day urban imaginary conceptualizes cities no longer as symbols of cultural and societal chaos, but tries to deploy the city symbol as part of a strategy to make other forms of "chaos" livable. In this situation, the literary city (and imagined space in literature in general) becomes an "alternative place over against the rational-purposive viewpoints."[46]

Those two factors — the confrontation with objective culture is no longer heroic and it has been transformed into a problem common to the universal global village — explain why authors do no longer perceive the processes of modernization as a major challenge and why they resort to self-consciously constructed (reflexive) and very heterogeneous city images.

*Translation Kristiaan Versluys*

45 See Henri Lefebvre, *La Vie quotidien dans le monde moderne* (Paris: Gallimard, 1968), 219.

46 See Sanders, "Postmoderne," 75. Editors' translation.

**Kristiaan Versluys**

# The Street as Theater: Self-Presentation and Specularity in Three Literary Texts on New York

*Keywords:* ■ *Literary Criticism* ■ *Sociology* ■ *Urban Self*

In this case study, I will examine three literary texts in which the dense city figures as a site of persona-creation.[1] In the light of the increased emphasis among urban theorists on the theatricality of city life, I will look at extracts from Saul Bellow's *Mr. Sammler's Planet* (1970), E. L. Doctorow's *Lives of the Poets* (1984), and Vivian Gornick's *Approaching Eye Level* (1996).[2] All three texts deal with ways in which traditional codes of self-presentation are undermined through forms of typically urban public performance. While traditionally and within liberal humanist discourse self-expression is related to notions of depth and authenticity, interactions in the context of urban density tend to interrupt the one-to-one relationship between being and seeming. More is involved here than the creation of the kinds of secondary relationships and impersonality pointed out by Georg Simmel in his famous essay "The Metropolis and Mental Life."[3] In the texts at issue, the city comes across as the place where one produces oneself through theatricality. The exterior, far from carrying a reference to interiority or a core self, is conspicuously displayed as a facade meant to create a stir. The suggestion is of a self-created persona, remakable at will. Self-presentation becomes an *effect* and a pose. The protagonist in the Bellow novel is disturbed by this play-acting and sees in it a sign of decadence, while the narrator in the Doctorow novella is baffled. Only the autobiographical voice in Vivian Gornick's essay finds "pleasure and ... reassurance" [15] in the "infinite capacity for adaptation" [16].

One of the first and most influential commentators to systematically describe human behavior in theatrical terms was the American sociologist Erving Goffman. In his *The Presentation of Self in Everyday Life* (1959), Goffman considers the theatrical metaphor to be descriptive of social relations.[4] He sees human interaction as the enactment of roles. In working out his dramaturgical trope, Goffman points back to Robert Park's definition of "person": "It is probably no mere historical accident that the word person, in its first meaning, is a mask. It is rather a recognition of the fact that everyone is always and everywhere, more or less consciously, playing a role.... It is in these roles that we know each other; it is in these roles that we know ourselves" [30]. Goffman, in following Park, sees the self as "a performed character" [245]. The self, then, is an "effect," the result of a dramaturgical presentation. Goffman, from a sociological functionalist point of view, radically breaks with the romantic notion of an independent or organic individual. He avoids all references to a personality gifted with hidden depth. He dispenses with the notion of a rockbottom private self, of which the social presentation is but a reflection and a distortion. For Goffman, what others see is what you are.[5]

Goffman's belief in roles as constitutive of character leads him to assert that performers "will give surreptitious expression to multiple versions of reality, each version tending to be incompatible with the others" [202]. However, while pointing out the provisionality of character impersonation, he stresses time and again how severely role-playing is limited by social parameters. "When an actor

1 A much different version of this paper was published previously in Dutch as "De straat als spektakel. Drie teksten over New York," in Maarten Delbeke, Dirk Van Weelden, Bart Verschaffel, Kristiaan Versluys, *De stad en de pedagogie,* ed. Stefan Hertmans (Gent: Hogeschool Gent, dep. Academie, 1999).

2 Saul Bellow, *Mr. Sammler's Planet* (New York: Viking, 1970); E. L. Doctorow, "Lives of the Poets," in *Lives of the Poets* (1985; reprint, London: Picador, 1986); vivian gornick, "on the street: nobody watches, everybody performs," in *approaching eye level* (Boston: Beacon Press, 1996). Page references will be cited in the text.

3 Georg Simmel, "The Metropolis and Mental Life," trans. Kurt H. Wolff, in *Simmel on Culture*, ed. David Frisby and Mike Featherstone (London: Sage, 1997), 174-85. The original essay, "Die Grossstädte und das Geistesleben," dates from 1903.

4 Erving Goffman, *The Presentation of Self in Everyday Life* (1959; reprint, Harmondsworth: Penguin, 1978). Page references will be cited in the text.

5 Lauren Langman puts it rather dramatically: "If Nietzsche announced the death of God, Goffman's work announces the death of the soul." Lauren Langman, "Neon Cages: Shopping for Subjectivity," in *Lifestyle Shopping: The Subject of Consumption*, ed. Rob Shields (London: Routledge, 1992), 65.

6 Kevin Hetherington, *Expressions of Identity: Space, Performance, Politics* (London: Sage, 1998), 141. See also Iain Chambers, *Popular Culture: The Metropolitan Experience* (1986; reprint, London: Routledge, 1993), 11; Langman, "Neon Cages," 40, 66; Judith Squires, "In different voices: deliberative democracy and aestheticist politics," in *The Politics of Postmodernity*, ed. James Good and Irving Velody (Cambridge: Cambridge University Press, 1998), 128, 133.

7 Mike Featherstone, *Consumer Culture & Postmodernism* (1991; reprint, London: Sage, 1994), esp. 119-20; Hetherington, *Expressions of Identity*, esp. 146-50; Iris Marion Young, "City Life and Difference," in *Metropolis: Center and Symbol of Our Times*, ed. Philip Kasinitz (New York: New York University Press, 1995), 256; Brian McHale, *Pöstmödernist Fictiön* (New York: Methuen, 1987).

8 Dick Hebdige, *Subculture: The Meaning of Style* (London: Methuen, 1979). Page references will be cited in the text.

9 Lewis Mumford, "What is a City?" in *The City Reader*, ed. Richard T. LeGates and Frederic Stout (London: Routledge, 1996), 185.

10 Jonathan Raban, *Soft City* (New York: E. P. Dutton, 1974), 27.

11 Roland Barthes, "Semiology and the Urban," in *The City and the Sign: An Introduction to Urban Semiotics*, ed. M. Gottdiener and Alexandros Ph. Lagopoulos (New York: Columbia University Press, 1986), 96.

takes on an established social role," he writes, "usually he finds that a particular front has already been established for it" [37]. Goffman details the "interaction constraints which play upon the individual and transform his activities into performances" [72]. He does this so exhaustively and with such a host of examples that his study as a whole demonstrates how personal expressivity is smothered by social decrees and obligations. Fear, guilt, and shame prevent one from ever deviating from the accepted norm. One lives up to the expectations associated with the "front" one has chosen.

If in Goffman's system theater is a metaphor for the incarceration of the self within prescribed social roles, self-display has more recently also been described as a means of escaping such social control. Kevin Hetherington, for instance, summarizing the current view, states that identity is "expressed through ongoing performative repertoires."[6] In this theory (which carries the mark of the free-wheeling 1960s and is usually associated with versions of postmodernism) self-creation is a never-ending process of self-staging. This auto-dramatization is closely related to notions of the fluid, protean, or carnivalesque self (Featherstone, Hetherington) — a self that is not co-present with itself (Young) and therefore has multiple ontological groundings (McHale).[7] How in actual practice such a carnivalization of the self works was investigated at length by Dick Hebdige in his classical study of subcultures. In looking at punks, hipsters, beats, teddy boys, mods, and other marginal urban groups of the fifties through seventies, and reading their acts of self-display as signifying practices, Hebdige concludes that conspicuous "confrontation dressing" [107][8] is a form of "semiotic guerrilla warfare" (Eco's phrase, quoted in Hebdige [105]). Flaunting a style which consists of self-consciously subversive bricolage, youth subcultures attack the myth of bourgeois consensus. While in Goffman's use of the theatrical metaphor, role-playing is a function of social identity, in Hebdige's account the ludic adoption of a persona and the exploration of spectacularity is a "mechanism of semantic disorder" [90], meant to offend the "silent majority" and to challenge "the principle of unity and cohesion" [18], which mainstream society is trying to uphold.

In the three texts under consideration, it is this emancipatory use of drama in everyday life that is critically highlighted. As such, the sample texts illustrate a typically urban phenomenon, long since recognized by theorists of the city. Lewis Mumford, for instance, wrote that "the city creates the theatre and is the theatre ... the city creates drama, the suburb lacks it."[9] Similarly, Jonathan Raban speaks of the "intrinsic theatricality of city life,"[10] while in a short but influential essay, Roland Barthes indicated that the city center is the "space where subversive forces, forces of rupture, ludic forces act and meet."[11] The late-twentieth-century abundance of consumer goods and the increasing importance attributed to lifestyles has contributed to an intensification of this traditional histrionic quality of urban existence. As Mike Featherstone puts it, there has been "a shift in attention from lifestyles conceived as a relatively fixed set of dispositions, cultural tastes, and leisure practices which demarcate groups from each other to the assumption that in the contemporary city lifestyles are more actively formed. Hence the focus turns away from lifestyle as class- or neighbourhood-based to lifestyle as the active stylization of life in which coherence and unity give way to the playful exploration of transitory experiences and surface aesthetic effects."[12]

It is no coincidence that such playful presentation of a surface self has been recognized as a feature of postmodernity. From a broad philosophical vantage-point, the theatricalization of urban behavior is related to the ascendency of a horizontal world-view (a.k.a. a materialistic,[13] a metonymical, or a syntagmatic world-view[14]). From this perspective, the true self is not something buried deep down in the soul, but something that is for ever in flux, for ever developing by the links it establishes with the outer world. This outlook proffers a nomadic, vagrant sense of the self. In the words of Eike Gebhardt: "One does not achieve selfhood where one feels to be at one with one's deepest self (whatever that may be), but where one can freely act out one's desires."[15] Accordingly, a belief in the relative or situational nature of every self-definition tends to welcome the city as a place

12 Featherstone, *Consumer Culture*, 95.

13 See Geert Lernout, "Een ridder van de droevige Figuur," in *De pool van de droom. Van en over Johan Daisne*, ed. Hedwig Speliers (Antwerpen: Manteau, 1983), 171.

14 Fredric Jameson, *The Prison-House of Language* (1972; reprint, Princeton: Princeton University Press, 1974), 122.

15 "'Selbst' ist man/frau ... nicht dort, wo man sich besonders eins mit sich oder einem 'wahren' Ich fühlt (was immer das sein mag), sondern wo man so handeln kann, wie einem der Sinn steht." Eike Gebhardt, "Die Stadt als moralische Anstalt. Zum Mythos der kranken Stadt," in *Die Unwirklichkeit der Städte*, ed. Klaus R. Scherpe (Hamburg: Rowohlts Enzyklopädie, 1988), 294.

16 Charles Taylor, *Sources of the Self: The Making of the Modern Identity* (Cambridge, MA: Harvard University Press, 1989), 129.

17 Featherstone, *Consumer Culture*, 83-94; Chambers, *Popular Culture*, 53; Langman, "Neon Cages," 56; David Chaney, *Lifestyles* (Routledge: London, 1996); Zygmunt Bauman, "Desert Spectacular," in *The Flâneur*, ed. Keith Tester (London: Routledge, 1994), 139-57.

18 Chaney, *Lifestyles*, 128.

19 Susan Buck-Morss, *The Dialectics of Seeing: Walter Benjamin and the Arcades Project* (Cambridge, MA: MIT Press, 1989), 81. Page references in the text.

20 See also Lieven De Cauter, *Archeologie van de kick* (Amsterdam: De Balie, 1995), 104-47, and Rudi Laermans, *Schimmenspel* (Leuven: Van Halewyck, 1997), 37-60.

21 See M. Christine Boyer, *The City of Collective Memory* (Cambridge, MA: MIT Press, 1994), esp. 421-50, and Sharon Zukin, *The Cultures of Cities* (Cambridge, MA: Blackwell, 1995), esp. 49-77.

22 See Gottdiener on shopping malls: "As capitalist society has shifted from an emphasis on production to consumption, subjectivity is realized through the act of buying and the persona of the consumer. Malls, therefore, allow for the realization of consumerist subjectivity as well as of capital accumulation. But this subjectivity is virtual because it depends for its *meaning* on the free-floating signifiers of the advertising and media culture.... The mall experience is partly this finding of a self which is the self as conditioned consumer in the ludic, amusement sphere of commodity capitalism." M. Gottdiener, *Postmodern Semiotics: Material Culture and the Forms of Postmodern Life* (Oxford: Blackwell, 1995), 96.

where it is possible to gather ever-new impressions, make ever-new choices, try out an endless series of poses.

The antithetical view, which one could call vertical (but also idealistic, metaphorical, or paradigmatic), starts from the premise that there is a deep self and that aesthetic or theatrical masking of that true self is symptomatic of inauthenticity and self-betrayal. Such a philosophy of authenticity is Platonic and Christian in origin and often accompanied by a transcendental orientation, a directedness towards a divine, supernatural essence. However, the Canadian philosopher Charles Taylor has indicated the enduring importance of Saint Augustine's maxim "in interiore homine habitat veritas" (truth resides in the interior self of man).[16] Taylor takes a sense of interiority (as opposed to play-acting exteriority) to be one of the main sources of the contemporary self. His findings are a warning against an overly facile equation of the horizontal view with (post)modernity and the vertical one with pre-modernity. What the sample texts which we will look at point out is the constant re-emergence (also in circumstances of heightened theatricality and role-playing) of a sense of an anchored, stable, or rooted self (even if only as nostalgia).

Vertical and horizontal philosophies of life can be seen as having each typical dangers and pitfalls. The idealist viewpoint, stressing as it does the upward reaching or downward probing towards eternal values, threatens to become static and immobile. The countervailing materialistic or metonymic attitude runs the danger of leading to cultural flattening and impoverishment. More in particular, the cultivation of a conspicuous lifestyle is vulnerable to recuperation by consumer capitalism, as advertising techniques exploit self-styling and theatricality for commercial purposes. For Featherstone, as well as others,[17] the specularization or "heightened dramaturgy of lifestyle"[18] is a feature of consumer culture. As such, it highly contributes to what is now commonly called the "phantasmagoria" of city life. Karl Marx used the term "to refer to the deceptive appearances of commodities as 'fetishes' in the marketplace."[19] For Walter Benjamin, however, who popularized the concept, "the key to the new urban phantasmagoria was not so much the commodity-in-the-market as the commodity-on-display" [81]. Benjamin observed how the urban masses were enthralled by these "commodities as fetishes-on-display" [82]. Phantasmagoria, thus conceived, finds its origins in the nineteenth-century urban arcades and the World Expositions,[20] but it has now become a widespread feature that is expressly cultivated in shopping malls and shopping streets, in festival marketplaces, and Disneyfied downtowns[21] — venues which, in their turn, serve as backdrop to the performances of the aestheticized and role-playing self.[22]

Of the three writers under consideration, Saul Bellow is the one most militantly outspoken about the dangers of urban theatricalization. *Mr. Sammler's Planet* describes an accommodation with the urban world which first and foremost starts from a vertical, metaphysically inspired vantage-point. Artur Sammler, an elderly Polish Jew, who, after surviving the death camps, finds himself in the "Quivering, riotous, lurid New York" [143] of the late 1960s, has a name for this otherworldly orientation. After the thirteenth-century German mystic Meister Eckhardt, he calls it "disinterested"-ness [117]. Sammler's subject position in the city is determined by his wish to lead a spiritualized, contemplative existence: "He wanted, with God, to be free from the bondage of the ordinary and the finite. A soul released from Nature, from impressions, and from everyday life" [117].

This idealist vantage-point — literalized by the tallness of his figure — allows him to judge the city from on high — *sub specie aeternitatis.* When a pickpocket plies his trade in a city bus, "Only Sammler, because of his height, could see" [46]. For Sammler sight equals insight. He has a totalized and unabashedly negative view of the city, which is the result of a simultaneous engagement with interior truth (in one eye he is blind) and with impressions from the outside (the other eye is preternaturally alert). The disinterested person he embodies is like Kierkegaard's Knight of the Faith, who, "having set [his] relations with the infinite, was entirely at home in the finite" [62]. In order to master conditions in big cities, "You could not be an old-fashioned sitting sage," Sammler says to himself.

*You must train yourself. You had to be strong enough not to be terrified by local effects of metamorphosis, to live with monstrosities come to life, addicts, drunkards, and perverts celebrating their despair openly in midtown. You had to be able to bear the tangles of the soul, the sight of cruel dissolution* [74].

The "confidant of New York eccentrics; curate of wild men and progenitor of a wild woman; registrar of madness" [118], Sammler is surrounded by would-be hipsters or, in Norman Mailer's terms, "white negroes,"[23] intent on orgiastic experience and "perfect instantaneous freedom" [34]. His disinterestedness involves a refusal to be drawn in by this spectacle — a refusal to succumb to "the boundlessness, the pressures of modern expectations" [202]. His is a foundational belief, backed up by full-fledged "God adumbrations" [237] and therefore inimical to the improvisations of the "theater of the soul" [234], and "the personal gesture" [235].

In long and repeated diatribes, Sammler diagnoses the urban condition as

23 Norman Mailer, "The White Negro: Superficial Reflections on the Hipster," in *An Anthology of American Literature*, vol. II, ed. George McMichael (New York: Macmillan, 1980), 1783-97.

24 Simmel, "Metropolis," 183-84.

one of unbridled plenty — an abundance, especially, of demands with no countervailing sense of obligation. The phantasmagoria that he sees acted out every day in the streets of New York is a cocktail of countercultural politics, sexual liberation, mediatization, personal needs as well as consumer demands. About his daughter Shula, for instance, a typical representative of the countercultural generation of the sixties, he has this to say:

*Shula ... was needy — needed gratification of numerous instincts, needed the warmth and pressure of men, needed a child for sucking and nurture, needed female emancipation, needed the exercise of the mind, needed continuity, needed interest* — interest! — *needed flattery, needed triumph, power, needed rabbis, needed priests, needed fuel for all that was perverse and crazy, needed noble action of the intellect, needed culture, demanded the sublime. No scarcity was acknowledged* [34].

In Sammler's account, disinterestedness of the soul is the opposite of the phantasmagoria of needs. If disinterestedness stands for "purity and unity" [118], Sammler expands the notion of phantasmagoria to include the whole cultural amalgam of frenetic city activities which are invented to stand out from the crowd and hide inner emptiness.

Georg Simmel drew attention already to the fact that the cultivation of singularity was a reaction against the growth of objective bureaucratic culture in the cities.[24] Sammler offers a similar explanation, but in a darker key and with a more pronounced historical slant. For him "fuming, heaving, fool-heaped, quivering, stinking Broadway" [145] is the place where one "might see the soul of America at grips with historical problems" [146]. In particular, Sammler sees two opposing conditions at work in the city. In part, the play-acting of the urbanites is the result of the historical phenomenon of individuation (the dwindling of ascriptive social roles). "Now, as everyone knows," Sammler states,

*it has only been in the last two centuries that the majority of people in civilized countries have claimed the privilege of being individuals. Formerly they were slave, peasant, laborer, even artisan, but not person. It is clear that this revolution, a triumph for justice in many ways ... has also introduced new kinds of grief and misery, and so far, on the broadest scale, it has not been altogether a success* [228].

The introduction of the individual on the historical scene has largely failed because a countervailing force robbed the emergent self of its power. While modern man for the first time ever was urged to realize his full potential, the forces of mass-civilization combined to bring home his utter powerlessness. In the cities,

Sammler contends, "human beings suffered the humiliations of inconsequence, of confused styles ... In fact the whole experience of mankind was now covering each separate life in its flood.... Compelling the frail person to receive, to register, depriving him because of volume, of mass, of the power to impart design" [26].

Thus, while modernity urges man to be original, social forces of collectivization are so strong it has become impossible to give shape to one's life. The result, according to Sammler, is the creation of a false, inauthentic self, which pretends to be original but isn't except in the most superficial of ways (clothing, styles of speaking). For Sammler the bankruptcy of the modernist program, which promised individual freedom, led to the fiasco of postmodernity, which offers freedom only as meaningless play. Crushed by outside forces, hollowed out internally, men and women, victims of a historical pincer-movement, try to hide their inner emptiness by theatrical self-glorification, a frantic search for means by which to become conspicuous, stand out. According to Sammler, this morbid self-affirmation is an individualism run riot. A meritricious self is born, all geared to draw interest to itself:

*... one notices most a peculiar play-acting, an elaborate and sometimes quite artistic manner of presenting oneself as an individual and a strange desire for originality, distinction, interest — yes interest!* [229].

Sammler is very harsh in his condemnation of this new culture of "personal gesture" [235], as it manifests itself on the city streets:

*What one sees on Broadway while bound for the bus. All human types reproduced, the barbarian, redskin, or Fiji, the dandy, the buffalo hunter, the desperado, the queer, the sexual fantasist, the squaw; bluestocking, princess, poet, painter, prospector, troubadour, guerilla, Che Guevara, the new Thomas à Becket* [147].

When Sammler looks at "this imitative anarchy of the streets" [149], he feels pain and pity. "They sought originality," he says of the gaudily accoutered passers-by. Yet they "were obviously derivative. And of what — of Paiutes, of Fidel Castro? No, of Hollywood extras" [149]. In Sammler's estimation, urbanites are incarcerated in role-playing and hyperreality. Even their attempts to escape social bondage through the cultivation of conspicuous singularity are recuperated by commerce and the media.

If, from his idealist viewpoint, Mr. Sammler looks down upon the city in disapprobation, and if in particular he objects to the theatrical self-staging of the urbanites, Jonathan, the narrator of E. L. Doctorow's novella "Lives of the Poets," looks at the city in amazement and doubt. He refuses to see difference as pathology. Yet, not content with mere observation, he keeps longing for connection and understanding. "It may be passing me by," he writes, "it may all be passing me by" [119]. Whereas Sammler believes in a true, authentic self, threatened by urban distractions, Jonathan stands for the well-meaning, progressive writer and intellectual, who yet feels baffled and bewildered by the fast-changing events in the city. He is alert, but adrift. He understands that one cannot go back to the philosophy of authenticity, yet he feels ill at ease in the world of the momentary and the simultaneous, where impressions loosely float around without obvious internal linkage.

Jonathan suffers from what one critic called "Nameless Dread." This vague sense of unease is fed from many sources, foremost among them the incessant confrontation with the unknown, as it manifests itself in a web of scintillating, but impenetrable urban surfaces. He recollects, for instance, how he saw the dance of a father and daughter during a bar mitzvah celebration at the Fifth Avenue hotel. He vividly remembers the vignette, because he never saw a more erotic dance. Yet the impression, vivid as it is, is but one among thousands of others. It stands out in his memory, but he is not able to probe its relevance or to integrate it in a larger mesh of meaning. Thus for someone like Jonathan who has not yet completely abandoned the longing for depth, the city comes across as sheer spectacle, extraneous to himself. While at times he is carried away by the colorfulness and the quaintness of what he observes, most of the time he experiences the staged city as a site full of mysteries and secrets, which are vaguely threatening and disturbing.

Jonathan's bafflement is reflected in the very form and style of his first-person narrative. His account has no proper plot to speak of, no exposition or development. It consists of a loosely structured sequence of episodes strung together by a simplified stream-of-consciousness technique. Unlike Bellow's Mr. Sammler, Jonathan has no panoptic or totalizing command over the city, no "god-eye" perspective that allows him to make a definitive judgement. As an observer of metropolitan theatricality, he can render the city only in the form of unconnected impressions. The interest of the tale is lodged completely in the isolated *bon mot*, the spunky and vivacious language — a language full of gusto and idiomatic power. This colloquial brilliance is all the more effective as it helps to get across the sense of a vivid, but sometimes overly exciting New York, in which the mixture of new and aestheticized lifestyles leads to confusion and compels the writer to seek a refuge, a place of quiet, in the midst of what he calls, with a Whitmanesque term, "the electric city" [103]. The hectic style of the short story and its disjunct composition underscore the main theme: the plight of the progressive liberal confronted with a spectacular city civilization that eludes his grasp.

The specularity which Jonathan encounters in the city hits him in several ways. Enclosed in a universe of free-floating signifiers, he comes across simultaneity without congruence, density without meaning. Looking out from his apartment in Greenwich Village, for instance, he sees this:

*When dusk comes this time of year the lights are already on in all of the apartments and I see several floors of action simultaneously. He is playing the piano while one floor below in the identical spot she waters a potted plant. People when talking on the phone gesticulate as if the person at the other end were right there, perhaps the body movement is necessary for the inflection. One young girl has just lifted her skirt and looked into her underpants* [122].

"[A] city," Richard Sennett writes, "is a human settlement in which strangers are likely to meet." Along similar lines, Jonathan Raban notes: "To live in a city is to live in a community of people who are strangers to each other."[25] Such estrangement means that even the most intimate details of one's personal life are open to inspection. In the city one looks and is looked at in perfect anonymity.

One word that recurs in Jonathan's account of the city and which perfectly illustrates his surprise at what he sees, is "interesting." He notices that the Yellow Pages now also come out in a Spanish edition and he calls that "interesting" [94]. He sees graffiti on the walls and in subway cars and he finds that "interesting" [ibid.]. People listening to music on their walkmen in the subway, that too is labeled "interesting" [ibid.]. The recurrent use of the word "interesting" points to a surface titillation but without deeper accessibility. "The space of identity is a heterogeneous, folded, paradoxical and crumpled space in which a distinct singular position is not possible," writes Kevin Hetherington.[26] It is within such a complex topology of the self that Jonathan, as an open-minded intellectual, tries to position himself — but with reluctance and difficulty.

Part of his abiding uneasiness has to do with the fact that in a city full of staged events, there is only a tenuous sense of "reality." Within the dramaturgy of city life, everything can be everything else. Nothing is simple or transparent.

25 Richard Sennett, *The Fall of Public Man* (New York: Alfred Knopf, 1977), 39; Raban, *Soft City*, 7.

26 Hetherington, *Expressions of Identity*, 23.

27 Hana Wirth-Nesher, *City Codes: Reading the Modern Urban Novel* (Cambridge: Cambridge University Press, 1996), 8.

28 See Marjorie Garber, "Sign, Co-sign, Tangent: Cross-dressing and cultural anxiety," in *The Subcultures Reader*, ed. Ken Gelder and Sarah Thornton (London: Routledge, 1997), 454.

Jonathan wonders, for instance, if the taxis he sees on Houston Street are not used by undercover police. At one point the cars take off at great speed: "They hang a right on Broadway" [128]. He sees them one moment; then they are gone. As the critic Hana Wirth-Nesher remarks in another context: "Cities promise plenitude, but deliver inaccessibility. As a result the urbanite, for better or worse, is faced with a never-ending series of partial visibilities, of gaps.... Faced with these and unable or unwilling to ignore them, the city dweller inevitably reconstructs the inaccessible in his imagination."[27] Urban perception takes place in flashes. It is always partial, incomplete. To understand anything one has to extrapolate and imagine. If, however, every interpretation in the city is up for grabs, if every attribution of meaning can be no more than an educated guess and if, in the dramaturgy of city life, all familiar links between seeming and being are distorted, there is room for distrust and paranoia, *angst* and doubt.

Especially extreme forms of self-dramatization (purposeful acts of semiotic sabotage) are unsettling to Jonathan. When he comes across the gaudily dressed passers-by, who caused such scorn in Artur Sammler, he, too, is perplexed by their "stroll theater" and their "unreadable" attire:

*And look at this coming down Eighth Street: his black garrison cap blocked like the old* SS, *his black leather jacket with raised chrome studs, his black jeans and boots. Hopping to keep up with him is a skinny androgyne, with a gold ring in his ear and a lime-green jumpsuit. Stroll theater, people cruising for the impact of themselves, it's their art form* [119].

Jonathan observes the breakdown of semantic order with disquietude. Gender boundaries are violated on purpose; the natural order is called into question.[28] Most shockingly of all, historical reference is blotted out. Allusions to the Third Reich and (by implication) the holocaust are playfully flaunted as props in an act of conspicuous self-staging. This sort of indeterminacy — a floating free from history — involves an aestheticization of experience, which Jonathan diagnoses as a-political and self-centered: "people cruising for the impact of themselves." The performance he witnesses is easily recuperated by the visual culture of the city so that it misses all pointedness as protest or transgression. Recontextualizing history as play threatens to make a mockery of even the most indelibly tragic event.

Jonathan is amazed by the exuberant play-acting of his fellow urbanites. He himself participates to a degree in the self-staging and he understands that street performance is part and parcel of the attraction of the city as *theatrum mundi*. He feels how the throng of objects and things on Broadway feeds his inspiration as a writer. About his colleagues who have retired to the countryside he wonders:

"What do they do when they want to go for a walk?" [121]. With gusto and excitement he jots down everything he sees or hears around him, everything he smells. He revels in the phantasmagoria of the city as it manifests itself on Broadway or Times Square: "the moving computer-graphic signs, the giant pantyhosed girl in the sky, the young god in briefs, the archetypes of the Great White Way" [120]. And yet he concludes this breathless enumeration with a quote from T. S. Eliot's J. Alfred Prufrock, the arch-prophet of disconnection: "That's not what I mean" [120]. The literary critic Dana Brand writes about the quickly changing spectacle in the big city: "It is possible to bathe in such a world, to collect images, or to enjoy the way in which they rapidly succeed each other." But he adds, using a phrase that is applicable to Jonathan's plight: "It is harder to be oriented, rooted, or convinced of the solidity or permanence of anything one believes or observes."[29]

Ultimately, the city Jonathan presents resembles that of Artur Sammler, in that it, too, is a city of plenty. In Sammler's account, New York features an abundance of needs and demands. Jonathan's story (published fifteen years later) shows the city to be full of supply and commodified opportunity. As a spiritual wasteland, it sprouts quack remedies and bogus philosophies — all available at a price:

*A free paper found in the lobby tells all about it: I can begin with lessons in the Alexander technique, a proven method for attaining awareness and physical reeducation and postural alignment, and then I can go buy the Bach Flower Remedies, look in on the Breathing Center, stop awhile at the Center for Jewish Meditation and Healing, sign up for some t'ai chi exercise in flowing motion for vitality and health, and if things still don't work out, I can submit myself to some deep-tissue manipulation by a qualified Rolfer* [84].

Jonathan's account parallels the "blank fiction" (Annesley) of writers such as Jay McInerney, Bret Easton Ellis, and Tama Janowitz, in that it, too, demonstrates "the cultural logic of late capitalism" (Fredric Jameson's phrase).[30] Everything,

29 Dana Brand, *The Spectator and the City in Nineteenth-Century American Literature* (Cambridge: Cambridge University Press, 1991), 2.

30 James Annesley, *Blank Fictions: Consumerism, Culture and the Contemporary American Novel* (London: Pluto Press, 1998); Fredric Jameson, *Postmoderism; or, The Cultural Logic of Late Capitalism* (London: Verso, 1991).

31 Young, "City Life," 266-67.

32 Sennett, *Fall*, 18, 31, and passim.

33 Simmel, "Metropolis," 179-80.

34 See William G. Flanagan, *Contemporary Urban Sociology* (1993; reprint, Cambridge: Cambridge University Press, 1994), 22.

including personal matters such as religious conviction, love, or mental health, are commercialized — pulverized into the fragments that go into a commodified lifestyle.

If Jonathan, in spite of his left-leaning tolerance, still has a deep-seated longing for the anchored self, little of this nostalgia remains in Vivian Gornick's autobiographical sketch "on the street." She decribes the city as something she cannot do without. Against a background of loneliness and the struggle to keep her nerve up, she underscores the ludic quality of city life. She is in love with coincidence. She adores the contingent, the random nature and the unstructuredness of urban events. Her account is an illustration of what the philosopher Iris Marion Young calls the "eroticism" of urban life.[31] She finds the city, for all its rawness, exhilarating and a feast for the senses.

In her account, New York is described as "a landscape of marginal encounters" [2], but encounters without estrangement. As a result of the crisscrossing of glances in the city, as a result of the brevity and anonymity of contacts, a heartwarming *bonhomie* is born. Light banter and teasing make up a kind of urban orality. One wisecrack, one *bon mot* gives a special warmth to the most fleeting of acquaintanceships. Amidst the press of the crowd, Gornick gets rid of the dark thoughts, the introversion, and the "failure of nerve" she often suffers from. "Those of us who crave the expressive but can't shake off the melancholy walk the street," she writes [11].

In a series of delightful anecdotes Gornick comes up with convincing evidence for Richard Sennett's assertion that sociability fosters self-expressiveness.[32] The city provides a host of impulses for articulation, self-dramatization, and improvisation. To enter into a dialogue with strangers one has to develop a gift for histrionics. Like an actor, one has to get across the right signals through gesture and word; like a theater audience, one has to be able to decode the signals sent out by others. In "The Metropolis and Mental Life," Georg Simmel posited that in the midst of a crowd every individual displays a marked reserve, because he/she fears the unknown.[33] Gornick demonstrates an aspect of big city life that Simmel overlooked: the pavement becomes a stage, where most of the time confrontation is avoided through a quick joke, a smile, a mumbled apology.

Gornick also underlines that the charm of these "marginal encounters" is related to their anonymity. Keeping one's distance is of the essence. The sociologist Mark Granovetter invented the term "the strength of weak ties" to indicate how in the city a loose social network of acquaintances (who have yet other acquaintances) is an important element in the informal economy.[34] Gornick proves that such a wide-flung acquaintanceship does not lead so much to economic benefit as it provides emotional support (keeps you out of the dumps) and provides amusement. For the ties to fulfill that function, however, they must remain "weak." Chance contacts should be undemanding. The thing is to be witty, pleasant, affable, encouraging at most, never personal. The city "flaneuse" remains an actress who plays a role. The indeterminacy which to Artur Sammler is abhorrent and which unsettles Doctorow's Jonathan, is a necessity for Gornick and a source of joy.

The urbanist Jane Jacobs wrote this about the usefulness of anonymity and the desirability of distance: "Nobody can keep open house in a great city. Nobody wants to. And yet if interesting, useful and significant contacts among the people of cities are confined to acquaintanceships suitable for private life, the city becomes stultified. Cities are full of people with whom, from your viewpoint, or mine, or any other individual's, a certain degree of contact is useful or enjoyable, but you do not want them in your hair. And they do not want you in theirs."[35] The city creates a new kind of social intercourse, which Gornick labels "generic" [15]. "The pleasure and the reassurance lie precisely in the speed with which connection is established and then let go," she writes [ibid.]. The momentary aspect of city contacts introduces an element of pleasurable suspense. Anonymity allows disponibility: because city encounters are brief and momentary, one remains available for ever renewed experience.

For Gornick the city is a liberating locale. Sometimes she is tired of incessant self-invention. Sometimes she longs back for the fixed roles her parents fulfilled [24]. But mostly she prefers the public over the private, the so-called superficial over the so-called profound. The horizontal links provided by city life and the collision with strangers furnish the kinetic energy that give her life in New York drive and direction.

Gornick operates a different kind of identity construction than the one used by Sammler or Jonathan. Also in her account, there are vestiges of horizontal longings, as when she mourns the fragility of her "neurotic friendships" [6]. Her very melancholy itself and the violent mood swings to which she admits can be seen as the backlash resulting from a lack of stasis or stability. Yet simultaneously she revels in "the risk and excitement of having to put it all together each day anew" [ibid.]. For her the greatness of the city is its quality as a staged environment that each day requires a new self-creation. She inscribes herself in a long tradition of cosmopoliphilia, because she finds the never-ending effort of persona-invention to be thrilling and rewarding.

35 Jane Jacobs, *The Death and Life of Great American Cities* (1961; reprint, New York: Vintage, s.d.), 55-56. This passage is also quoted in Harvey Cox, *The Secular City* (1966; reprint, New York: MacMillan, 1975), 42. Cox defines these urban encounters as *I-you* relations which find themselves between intimate "I-thou" and impersonal "I-It" contacts.

The full title of her sketch — "on the street: nobody watches, everybody performs" — is somewhat misleading. Gornick is a watcher first and foremost. Yet whichever way she takes what Baudelaire called "un bain de multitude," in her account the dramaturgical metaphor leads to a form of the urban sublime. Phantasmagoria sheds its negative connotations and becomes a sign of the utopian. The urban ambience itself fulfills her whole existence. The vertical linkages of street performance radiate emancipatory significance: "If everyone I know died tomorrow," she writes,

*I'd [still] have the city. I smile into the dark. I am happy. Happy and relieved. Relieved and free. I feel free. Free to begin and end with myself. Free to imagine tomorrow* [28-29].

**Christophe Den Tandt**

# Down These (Gender-Divided and Ethnically Fractured) Mean Streets: The Urban Thriller in the Age of Multiculturalism and Minority Writing

*Keywords:* ■ *Literary Historiography* ■ *Multiculturalism* ■ *Gender Studies*

In the opening pages of Raymond Chandler's *The Big Sleep* (1939), private investigator Philip Marlowe is summoned by a man far more powerful than himself, aging oil magnate General Sternwood. Marlowe, for the occasion, has made every effort to be "everything the well-dressed private detective ought to be."[1] However, as the meeting evolves, there is little sense that the detective should feel inferior to the Sternwoods: each of the General's daughters feels he is a likely sexual target, and the old man entrusts him with a telling — though obviously incomplete — narrative of the family's secrets. By comparison, in Walter Mosley's *Devil in a Blue Dress* (1990), it takes about one hundred pages for African-American private investigator Easy Rawlins to trace Mr. Carter, the wealthy patron who commissioned him to find the whereabouts of a former girlfriend. Yet, once Rawlins manages to find his way past Carter's secretaries and business associates, he finds his client ready to share with him truly intimate information. Rawlins knows,

1 Raymond Chandler, *The Big Sleep* (1939; reprint, London: Penguin Books, 1948), 9.

2 Walter Mosley, *Devil in a Blue* Dress (1990). Reprinted in *The Walter Mosley Omnibus* (London: Picador, 1995), 106.

3 Stephen F. Soitos, in *The Blues Detective: A Study of African-American Detective Fiction* (Amherst: University of Massachusetts Press, 1996), traces the origin of the black detective to the very beginning of the twentieth century. Likewise, women have been prominent in detective fiction both as writers and as fictional investigators, though mostly in the well-circumscribed subgenre of the Agatha Christie-style mystery story. For critical perspectives on women's crime fiction, see Glenwood Irons, ed., *Feminism in Women's Detective Fiction* (Toronto: University of Toronto Press, 1995).

4 Jameson coined these terms in his widely influential "Reification and Utopia in Mass Culture," in *Signatures of the Visible* (1979; reprint, New York: Routledge, 1992), 9-34. For him, identifying a utopian dimension in popular culture amounts to arguing, against previous left-wing theories, that this medium should not be regarded as entirely alienating.

5 André Vanoncini, in *Le roman policier* (Paris: Presses Universitaires de France, 1993), 7-8, highlights the socially didactic role played by crime fiction in nineteenth-century societies.

6 Peter Marcuse, "Not Chaos, but Walls: Postmodernism and the Partitioned City," in *Postmodern Cities and Space*, ed. Sophie Watson and Katherine Gibson (Oxford: Blackwell, 1995), 248, 243.

however, that this unexpected openness is rooted in "the worst kind of racism."[2] Carter fails to acknowledge the reality of the social difference that separates him from Rawlins, and he accordingly opens his heart to the detective as one would to a "prized dog" [106] or any other non-human creature.

Mosley's willingness to underline that his African-American protagonist faces discrimination in his work illustrates a shift that has affected detective fiction in the last fifteen years. Apart from Mosley himself, a sizable number of contemporary writers — Gar Anthony Haywood, Sara Paretsky, Patricia Cornwell, Sandra Scoppettone, Marcia Muller, Michael Nava, Tony Hillerman, George P. Pelecanos — have indeed chosen to write thrillers from the perspective of minority characters — blacks, women, white ethnics, homosexuals, native Americans or Chicanos. Though historians of the genre may point out that minority private investigators have existed sporadically for decades,[3] it is, I think, legitimate to argue for the existence of a recent subgenre which we might call multicultural detective fiction. Under this term, I refer to the gender and ethnically focalized crime writing that transposes to a mass culture medium the issues of the late-twentieth-century debate about minority rights and feminism. Multicultural thrillers have, in this sense, a double responsibility: besides propagating a form of social awareness that originated in American colleges and minority political groups, they also self-consciously reinterpret the politics of the detective genre itself. Indeed, crime writing to this day has traditionally displayed what in Fredric Jameson's words might be called "utopian" impulses and conservative "strategies of containment"[4]: it has been critical of the American class system, but its narratives have also carried a celebration of white masculinity that makes them occasionally racist and very consistently misogynistic and homophobic.

**Urban Space and the Politics of Crime Fiction** Beyond the discussion of political didacticism, the readings below examine how multicultural thrillers refashion our perception of American cities. Indeed, it has long been a critical principle that detective fiction is the more valuable as it makes urban space more legible: the fictional investigation of crime has been a significant vehicle of urban realism in the twentieth century.[5] Intuitively, one would expect multicultural novels to highlight a growing degree of fragmentation in social space. Logically, they should make visible what Peter Marcuse calls the "walls" of the "partitioned city" — its ethnic, class, or gender lines of fracture.[6] Yet, while multicultural crime novels do fulfill that function, their concern for urban fragmentation is also compensated by a more utopian attempt at re-evaluating the status of local space in the city. Whereas postmodern theory takes the dissociation of the urban fabric for granted,[7] multiculturalist thrillers make it a priority to represent the forces that keep the city's local worlds alive, and those that threaten their cohesion. Typical settings of these novels are therefore neighborhoods (gentrified Greenwich Village in Sandra Scoppettone), work places (the medical examiner's laboratory in Patricia Cornwell; the shop-floor of an appliances store in George Pelecanos), families (black lower-middle-class couples in Mosley) or locally based peer groups (gay support networks in Michael Nava).

If we translate the concerns for the politics of space into the vocabulary of genre theory, it appears that multicultural detective novels choose for their object the "knowable communities" of literary realism. Recent scholarship about realism and naturalism has shown that realist narration must limit itself to the exploration of social universes small enough to be surveyed by individual observers or members of a single community.[8] The city as a whole is, in this logic, always larger — more complex in its class structure, ethnic make-up, gender grid — than any knowable community. It can therefore not be represented by means of a homogeneous realistic text, and is of necessity the object of dialogized discourses: cities always contain an uncanny remainder of enigmatic social phenomena that can only be evoked by non-positivistic strategies — urban gothic, for instance.[9] Within this dialogized field, multicultural thrillers adopt a strictly realist course. By centering on the everyday life of minority groups, they puncture the quasi-gothic stereotypes developed in detective fiction or elsewhere. It is, for instance, important for Sandra Scoppettone to have her Italian-American heroine specify that she comes from a background where there was "no mafia ... no undershirts at the table."[10] Likewise, African-American novelist Gar Anthony Haywood has his protagonist remind a racist cop that people in black neighborhoods are not necessarily denizens of the jungle — "lowlifes ... drunks ... crack heads, ex-cons ... cons-to-be ... Drug-pushers ... wife-beaters [or] professional crybabies."[11] In

7 For instance, Jean Baudrillard discards the analysis of local cultures and customs as a useless concern for the picturesque: see his *Amérique* (Paris: Grasset et Fasquelle, 1986), 10, 14.

8 Amy Beth Kaplan develops this definition of realism in *The Social Construction of American Realism* (Chicago: Chicago University Press, 1985).

9 For the relationship of realism, naturalism, and urban gothic, see my *The Urban Sublime in American Literary Naturalism* (Urbana: University of Illinois Press, 1998), 109-87. The impact of gothic genres such as the "mysteries of the city" on nineteenth-century popular fiction is described in Michael Denning's *Mechanic Accents: Dime Novels and Working-Class Culture in America* (London: Verso, 1987).

10 Sandra Scoppettone, *I'll Be Leaving You Always* (London: Virago Press, 1994), 44.

11 Gar Anthony Haywood, *You Can Die Trying* (1993; reprint, London: Serpent's Tail, 1995), 9.

12 For a description of crime mysteries as the expression of urban rationality, see Siegfried Kracauer's *Le roman policier: un traité philosophique* (1925; reprint, Paris: Petite Bibliothèque Payot, 1981); German version: *Der Detektiv Roman*, in *Schriften* 1 (Frankfurt: Suhrkamp Verlag, 1971). See also Leroy Lad Panek, *An Introduction to the Detective Story* (Bowling Green, OH: Bowling Green State University Popular Press, 1987), 122, 133-43.

13 See Ernest Mandel's *Delightful Murder: A Social History of the Crime Story* (London: Photopress, 1984), 43.

these passages, Haywood's novel strives to reclaim for the black community a sense of realistic everydayness — an urban universe where characters can be described as "black Joe Average[s]" [9] and where the local private investigator rents an office in the backroom of "Mickey's Trueblood barbershop" [11]. These literary strategies allow multicultural thrillers to redefine along positivistic lines the limits of what is and what is not sociologically imageable in a multicultural polity.

In their attempt to represent community life in the city, multicultural crime novels refashion for their own purposes the mapping of urban space initiated by the two main twentieth-century subgenres of crime fiction — mystery stories (1920s "whodunnits" in the Agatha Christie style) and the hard-boiled tradition of Chandler and Hammett. Mystery stories, modeled on Poe and Conan Doyle, have been described as games of pure deduction set in a closed universe — an upper-class manor, typically, or a set of carriages in an international train. As such, they are the expression of a rationalized and existentially alienated society whose social perimeter admits exterior threats only in sanitized form.[12] Marxist critics argue accordingly that the Christie-style novel reflects the values of a stabilized bourgeoisie, confident that it can handle criminal disturbances in the abstract form of an enigma solved by an independent-minded investigator.[13] For present-day multicultural novels, mysteries offer, in addition to valuable plot formulas, the interesting precedent of texts devoted to the exploration of a microcosmic universe. Yet the self-segregated social enclave thus defined sustains itself by dint of ideological blindness: the superficial realism of whodunnits is the more abstract as it conceals the logic of economic and ethnic exclusion on which such micro-universes are based, and which multicultural thrillers seek to expose.

Compared to the abstract puzzles of whodunnits, the hard-boiled thriller of the 1930s marks a return to street-level realism, closer to the working man, or, more accurately, to the working male. In these novels, the game of detection is indeed overshadowed by the development of a sexually explicit action plot that pits a self-employed entrepreneur — Chandler's Marlowe, Hammett's Sam Spade — against power-crazed magnates, corrupt politicians, predatory women, homosexuals. For multicultural crime fiction, the Chandlerian legacy offers a rich source of inspiration that can, however, be tapped only selectively. Indeed, the configuration of space postulated in hard-boiled novels does not fit the constraints of a city fractured by impassable social divisions. One of the main attractions of the hard-boiled novel consists in following an investigator whose exploration path uncovers criminal connections among seemingly unrelated sites of the urban fabric. For instance, the plot of Ross Macdonald's *Blue City* (1947) allows its protagonist — the son of a murdered political machine boss — to meet in just a few days all the power brokers of his native midwestern city. Thus, the young man exposes the tangle of murder and blackmail that has allowed a physically repulsive night club manager to hold all major city personalities in his sway. In this, the novel offers an allegorical power map: it indicates that capitalism, conservative politics, and crime are allegorically equivalent. It implies by the same token that the social body of the city, though fragmented, can nevertheless be reconstituted by the efforts of a protagonist who serves as a retotalizing device. Protagonists of multicultural novels, by contrast, cannot hope to match the hard-boiled dick's freedom of movement. Mosley, Paretsky, Cornwell, or Haywood imply in their texts that Chandler's or Hammett's protagonists are white male fantasies of empowerment endowed with a quasi-miraculous license to exercise their skills wherever they please. This heightened awareness of the obstacles encountered by totalizing narratives explains why authors of crime novels have turned to the rehabilitation of local space.

**From below the Color Line** Besides reappraising urban space, multicultural thrillers devote most of their efforts to retooling the figure of the detective protagonist him- or herself. For this enterprise, contemporary writers build on the existing thematics of eccentricity and alienation that informs the canonical figure of the private investigator: crime novels have always revolved around decentered characters — eccentrics like Sherlock Holmes and Hercule Poirot, or economic oddballs like the hard-boiled private investigator. In those cases, eccentricity served as a guarantee of the detective's impartial intellection or moral integrity. In novels like Walter Mosley's, which rewrite the literary configuration of thrillers from a point-of-view below the color line, marginalization acquires a different meaning. Mosley's novels are set right after World War II and in the 1950s. Their protagonist, Easy Rawlins, is a war veteran who emigrated from the South and settled in Los Angeles, where he worked as a machinist but was disgusted by discrimination on the job. Ironically, Rawlins endorses typically middle-class ideals — owning a home, leading one's own real-estate business. These are, however, fragile aspirations for African-Americans like himself. Rawlins's tendency to engage in shady real-estate dealings suggests indeed that, in the 1950s, middle-class affluence for black Americans could barely be achieved within the limits of the law.

Typically, Rawlins, a reluctant detective, is sought for by white people or by the Los Angeles police when they lead investigations in the black community. As a black man, Rawlins can indeed "ask questions of people who aren't willing to talk to the law."[14] There is, however, little indication that Mosley wants his char-

14 Walter Mosley, *White Butterfly* (London, Pan Books, 1992), 51.

acter to act as a multicultural trickster figure, equally comfortable in either community. Though Rawlins supposedly "can go where the police can't go" [51], his movements are at every step hampered by the race barrier; in 1950s Los Angeles, the social space where black people can move freely is severely limited. The same indictment of everyday racism characterizes the representation of Rawlins's relation to the police. Chandler's Philip Marlowe, in his conflicts with police authorities, benefits from the basic deference enjoyed by middle-class whites. To Easy Rawlins, on the contrary, "most cops [blend] into one brutal fist after a while" [48]: police violence against blacks is so much the rule that the first question that comes to mind after learning that a black suspect is in custody is: "Is he dead?" [134]. Likewise, it is the custom for white policemen not to investigate crimes committed against African-Americans.

If Easy Rawlins cannot be an independent monad, able to access all corners of society, he can avail himself, by way of compensation, of assets that Chandler's and Hammett's characters never seek: the support of a set of adjuvants that belong to the detective's family and neighborhood. Indeed, Mosley's minority sleuth is able to create a power base among the people closest to himself, who share the frustrations and injustices of his own everyday existence. In this perspective, Rawlins's tendency to entrench himself within his family — his wife Regina, his daughter Edna, his adopted son, the Mexican-born Jesus — is more than just a bid for bourgeois respectability. It expresses the character's will to secure the only livable space available to him and to members of his class and ethnic group. As such, it corresponds to the fulfillment of what nineteenth-century Americans and black Americans today call manhood: an economically connoted concept of virility defined by the ability to provide for one's dependents.

When Mosley or Gar Anthony Haywood use black everyday life as a point of anchorage, they, however, do not attempt to cloak the African-American family in terms so sentimental that their descriptions would be conspicuously at odds with actual conditions. I suggest in more detail below that an idyllic depiction of local space is never an option in multicultural thrillers. Haywood's L.A. novel *You Can Die Trying* (1993) intimates indeed that it is important to keep things complex in this matter. Relying on the intricacies of his hard-boiled plot, Haywood shows that crime in black neighborhoods cannot be reduced to stories of innocent black youths indiscriminately mowed down by the cops, or of dutiful policemen shooting suspects only when in self-defense. While highlighting police brutality and racism, Haywood makes the point that, among the black working class, nobody's life is immune to the pressure of poverty-induced criminality. Narratively, the ubiquitousness of crime generates a community where nothing is what it seems: a young "Buppie" [156] — that is, an impeccably dressed black yuppie — turns out to have run up gambling debts and to have masterminded the stick-up in which his nephew died. A witness to the event — the brother of a self-described "conservative man" [18] — lies to the police and blackmails a lawyer who, for his own financial interests, is intent on falsifying the story of the robbery and the subsequent shooting. The blackmailer, beaten up by the lawyer's strongman, loses an eye in the process. Haywood ends this pessimistic story of everyday corruption by a plea to help black children stay clear of criminal influences.

By the same logic, Mosley's depiction of African-American local life does justice to the fact that, already in the 1950s, many black households were dislocated, reduced to one-parent families, deserted by disempowered fathers. It is through the depictions of Easy's relation to his wife Regina that Mosley discusses the duties of black manhood, domestic violence, and masculine violence at large. These are delicate topics for the detective. On the one hand, he is constantly confronted with violence and sexual abuse during his own investigations: his adopted son Jesus was rescued from sexual slavery at the hands of a white politician; some of his missions involve tracking down sex murderers. On the other hand, as a black man, he is implicitly suspected both by white racists and by black women of being sexually promiscuous, abusive, and incapable of holding on to the role of family provider. Rawlins's ambiguity in this matter is made visible through his relation to his friend Raymond Alexander, a.k.a. Mouse. The latter, a feisty, friendly figure, is as Rawlins puts it, "the only black man [he'd] ever known who had never been chained, in his mind, by the white man."[15] Yet, in racist America, this form of freedom can only be achieved at the cost of irresponsibility and violence: Mouse is cynically promiscuous and prone to fits of rage dangerous even to his friends. Rawlins stands half-way between Mouse and the more constraining standards of emotional responsibility imposed by his wife: he is contaminated by the violence of a public world that makes the ideal of self-discipline difficult to emulate. Typically, in *White Butterfly*, the violence of the public sphere affects Rawlins to the extent that he sexually assaults his own wife, refuses to discuss the causes of his aggressiveness with her, and thus precipitates the break-up of his marriage.

**Women Professionals** In spite of Mosley's and Haywood's willingness to question gender inequality in the black community, the ideology of hard-boiled masculinity turns out to be less a liability than an asset for their works: at bottom, it helps them affirm the dignity of black manhood. Hard-boiled novels revolving

15 Ibid., 138.

16 For the link between grotesque femininity and the urban market, see Carroll Smith-Rosenberg's *Disorderly Conduct: Visions of Gender in Victorian America* (New York: Oxford University Press, 1985), 217-44, and Catherine Gallagher, "More About Medusa's Head," *Representations*, 4 (Fall 1983): 55-57.

17 Ross Macdonald, *Blue City* (1947; reprint, London: Alison and Busby, 1997), 28.

around women protagonists — in the present corpus, works by Sara Paretsky, Patricia Cornwell, Sandra Scoppettone, and Marcia Muller — face a different challenge: sexism is arguably more structurally vital to hard-boiled novels than racism in that it is directly woven into the economic discourse of the texts. Chandler's and Hammett's novels construct what we might call a gendered economics — a model of economic description articulated by means of sexual metaphors. In this, Chandler and Hammett follow a tradition of economic imagery according to which the wealth of the urban world amounts to a form of instinctual degeneration. This view of the urban market, which goes back to the nineteenth century and is further developed in naturalism,[16] stipulates that unearned or unaccountable wealth is a form of perversion that expresses itself most vividly in the doings of characters depicted as libidinal deviants — depraved women or homosexuals, typically. This description fits Carmen Sternwood in *The Big Sleep*, a psychotic nymphomaniac with "little sharp predatory teeth" [10], or Floraine Weather in Ross Macdonald's *Blue City*, a middle-aged woman whose apparent physical vitality stands in pathological contrast with her worried, "bloodless kind of beauty."[17] Economic corruption is gendered feminine in these cases because it stands as the antithesis of economic manhood — of what, in the vocabulary of the Protestant work ethic was called "character." In other words, Chandlerian novels follow the pattern of entrepreneurial liberalism according to which a proper income must be earned by a man's self-disciplined efforts. In this perspective, the origin of excessive wealth — particularly money not earned on the land — is obscure, no longer tied to the visible logic of masculine labor; therefore, these inscrutable resources partake of mysteries that can easily be represented as feminine.

In their own fictions, Paretsky, Cornwell, Scoppettone, and Muller counteract the sexist logic of hard-boiled literary sociology in two ways: first, like Mosley and Haywood, they construct for their protagonists a local area of empowerment and solidarity depicted in realistic terms; secondly, they display their protagonists' abilities to act as women professionals in the public sphere. The protagonists' local power base is a feminine domain structured as an extended domestic space or a substitute family. Paretsky's *Bitter Medicine* (1987), a novel about a hospital scandal in the Chicago suburbs, sets its protagonist, private investigator V.I. Warshawski, among a constellation of friends and acquaintances; this group includes a woman doctor who runs a planned parenthood clinic, the clinic's Puerto Rican nurse and her family, and one of Warshawski's elderly neighbors, who acts as self-proclaimed bodyguard to the single woman. In Patricia Cornwell's *Postmortem* (1990) and *Cruel and Unusual* (1993), medical examiner Kay Scarpetta is helped in her investigative work by her niece — a computer whiz kid — and her lab assistant. Marcia Muller's *The Shape of Dread* (1992) revolves around two knowable communities — the San Francisco All Souls Legal Cooperative, of which investigator Sharon McCone is a founding member, and a comedy club where a murder victim was employed. Scoppettone's gay private detective Lauren Laurano is surrounded by a "web of friendship" that brings together neighbors, colleagues and shopkeepers in Greenwich Village.[18]

The social structure defined in these quasi-familial networks is presented as an alternative to the domestic confinement of patriarchal marriage: Paretsky, Cornwell, Muller, and Scoppettone portray professional heroines who pit themselves against the homemaking values forced on them by parents and relatives. Parents, Lauren Laurano experiences, may go as far as luring their forty-three-year-old daughter back to their suburban home in the hope of protecting her against the dangers of the streets.[19] By the same token, lasting heterosexual attachments seem incompatible with female-investigator narratives: women detectives are either chronically single or gay. V.I. Warshawski, Kay Scarpetta, or Sharon McCone do have affairs or have even been married, yet their men companions are quickly disposed of by break-up, divorce, or violent death; Lauren Laurano, on the other hand, has a lasting bond with her companion Kip — a *de facto* lesbian marriage presented as less constraining than its heterosexual equivalent.

The political issues women detective fiction writers address by means of their domestically focalized narratives range from Tipper Gore-style middle-class feminism (Cornwell) to gay rights activism (Scoppettone). Paretsky is explicit about her pro-choice stance on abortion and bluntly criticizes the iniquities of the American health-care insurance system. Cornwell advocates consciousness-raising against pornography and rape. Muller explores the economic context that creates urban poverty. Scoppettone deals with a broad spectrum of women's and lesbian concerns, and devotes significant attention to the deontology of affective relationships. In this respect, one senses in these authors the project of spreading through their novels the tenets of academic feminism, women's non-fiction bestsellers, self-help manuals or women-oriented T.V. shows. Moreover, in Paretsky, Scoppettone, and Cornwell, the women detectives' distance from conservative politics is signified not only through their struggle against patriarchal ideology, but also through their situation as white ethnics: the Polish-American Warshawski and the Italian-American Scarpetta and Laurano are struggling against the white male Anglo establishment. This thematics is most explicitly developed

18 I borrow the term "webs of friendship" from William Whyte's *The Organization Man* (New York: Simon and Shuster, 1956), 7, where it refers to the local conviviality of 1950s suburbia.

19 Scoppettone, *Leaving You*, 50.

20 Ibid., 34.

by Paretsky, who frames Warshawski's investigations as a contest between the woman detective's downtown Chicago, a stronghold of immigrant and black Democrats, and the white Republican suburbs.

In their depiction of work in the public sphere, female investigator thrillers make it a point to endow their heroines with technical and physical skills that are traditionally regarded as male preserves. That this gesture still carries a transgressive value, both in terms of verisimilitude and gender roles, is shown in the fact that the very concept of a woman P.I. needs explicit narrative validation. The issue is the object of a running joke in the novels: Scoppettone's Lauren Laurano, who describes herself as "short,"[20] chronically has to deal with interlocutors who cannot accept the idea of a detective who looks like a "shrimp" [40]. V.I. Warshawski is listed in the phone book under her name and initials only, so that she is regularly hired by patrons who believe she is a man. As a literary type, the female detective allegorizes the long-standing feminist agenda which requests for women a fair share of the labor market. By their very function, P.I.'s are expected to gain access to all corners of the public world. In the texts, this form of enfranchisement through professionalism is expressed as the pragmatic ambition of gaining expertise in data processing — in Cornwell and Scoppettone, for instance — or as the more openly romanticized ideal of the amazon P.I. Among the four novelists discussed here, Paretsky is the most willing to fashion her heroine as a female substitute of the Chandlerian tough guy. A law school graduate, an expert gun user, and a martial arts enthusiast, Warshawski pursues investigations that are not necessarily linked to women's issues — union and insurance corruption in *Indemnity Only* (1982), malpractice in *Bitter Medicine*. This feminine rewriting of the hard-boiled tradition generates its own inconsistencies, however, especially as regards the protagonist's relation to violence. The spectacle of gun-toting, karate-cutting heroines delivering lines modeled on Clint Eastwood seems indeed at odds with the liberal agenda otherwise advertized in the novels — a contradiction that Scoppettone and Cornwell try to defuse by peppering their texts with advice on responsible arms handling.

The regulation of violence is a particularly touchy issue here because the novels concur in stigmatizing aggression as a typical expression of pathological masculinity. More accurately, Paretsky, Cornwell, Scoppettone, and Muller describe men in dichotomized terms: on the one hand, their heroines enjoy the support of reliable male mentors — Warshawski's late policeman father, Laurano's policeman friend, or the lawyer partner of McCone's legal cooperative. On the other hand, in a gesture that mirrors Chandler's gendered sociology, men are suspected of being libidinal monsters. In Scoppettone's *I'll Be Leaving You Always* (1994), abject masculinity is embodied either in the figure of a mammoth-like child abuser with "gigantic feet with long, curling brown toenails" [154], or, even more uncannily perhaps, in the shape of a sun-tanned forty-year-old playboy who has an affair with a woman and her daughter, kills the former, and attempts to kill the other. In Cornwell's police procedurals, the gruesome traces of male aggression are prominently on display, as Kay Scarpetta — "a physician with a law degree"[21] — earns her living autopsying the victims of sex crime. Finding the perpetrators of those deeds involves pointing the finger in turn at most of the males involved in the investigation, many of whom are indeed guilty of sexism or harassment. Thus, in *Postmortem*, Scarpetta's boyfriend first appears as a cheerful, competent police professional but is later exposed as a manipulative womanizer, who led his previous wife to suicide. Likewise, Peter Marino — Scarpetta's dedicated though bigoted right-hand man — is so obsessively absorbed by sex-killer cases that we are led to wonder whether he might not be the perpetrator himself. Indeed, allegorically speaking, both of these characters are accomplices of violence by the fact that they are dominant males. The actual killer, by comparison, is only an anonymous figure introduced late into the story in *deus ex machina* fashion, after the collective male guilt for the deployment of predatory sexism has been brought to light.

**Politically Correct Gentrification as an Urban Utopia?** On the surface, we could infer from what precedes that multicultural thrillers, as they survey the "walls" of a partitioned social field, promote a model of urban life that might be called, in the vocabulary of American politics, the "city of special interests" — a polity divided by ethnic groups and gender-specific webs of friendship. In this case, recent detective fiction would revive, with more ideological savvy, the social claustrophobia of Agatha Christie-style mysteries: instead of bringing to light networks of interdependence that cut across distant areas of the urban scene, as hard-boiled narratives do, they would limit themselves to investigating, for instance, why a Greenwich Village shopkeeper — the murder victim of Scoppettone's *Leaving You* — got involved in a scam run by other Greenwich Village shopkeepers. This reading of multicultural crime writing does not do justice, I think, to the com-

21 Patricia Cornwell, *Cruel and Unusual* (London: Warner Books, 1993), 7.

22 Neil Smith, *The New Urban Frontier: Gentrification and the Revanchist City* (London: Routledge, 1996), 32.

23 For an analysis of the link between gentrification and new sectors of the middle classes, see also Tim Butler's *Gentrification and the Middle Classes* (Aldershot: Ashgate Publishing, 1997), 14-33.

24 Smith, *Urban Frontier*, 98-101.

25 Jane Jacobs, *The Life and Death of Great American Cities* (New York: Random House, 1961), 50.

26 Saskia Sassen, "Rebuilding the Global City: Economy, Ethnicity and Space," in *Representing the City: Ethnicity, Capital and Culture in the 21st Century Metropolis*, ed. Anthony D. King (Basingstoke and London: Macmillan, 1996), 40. Neil Smith points out that Ruth Glass, when she coined the word gentrification in 1964, already used it derogatorily (*Urban Frontier*, 33).

27 Smith, *Urban Frontier*, 30.

plexities of the texts analysed here. Indeed, not only do the authors display a genuine concern for the interaction of local and global features of urban geography, but their sensitivity to large-scale determinants makes their multicultural thrillers politically dystopian: instead of depicting urban space as a mosaic of segregated, though empowered, constituencies, they explain the persisting fragmentation of American cities as a manifestation of Reagan-era economics of greed. In what follows, I indicate, however, that this gesture of demystification has a sobering impact on the utopia of a locally based urban politics. Indeed, economic privatization and real-estate profiteering subvert the texture of urban neighborhoods on which the novels are focalized.

The factors that both enable and destabilize the aspirations toward a reclaiming of local space can, I think, be ascribed to a phenomenon that has powerfully shaped the lives of inner-city populations in the last thirty years, namely gentrification. Urban studies theoretician Neil Smith defines gentrification as "the process ... by which poor and working-class neighborhoods in the inner city are refurbished via an influx of private capital and middle-class homebuyers and renters."[22] Urban redevelopment of this type, Smith argues, corresponds to the appearance of a "new middle class."[23] Particularly, it serves the needs of two-income families in which women, contrary to the gender precepts of 1950s suburbia, work in the public sphere.[24] On the face of it, the re-settlement of economically depressed downtown areas by middle-class families may seem to fulfill the agenda laid down by Jane Jacobs in her 1960s writings — reorienting the modernist city toward the "complex order" of popular street life.[25] Yet, gentrification — like yuppiedom — has from the start been somewhat of a cursed term that evokes, as Saskia Sassen suggests, some form of "inevitable" blight hostile to genuine urban diversity.[26] Smith remarks that even 1980s New York realtors were concerned that this label might be perceived as "a dirty word" carrying a social agenda that few care to endorse.[27] The negative connotation, Smith argues, is due to the fact that gentrification turns working-class and minority neighborhoods into real-estate boom towns, thereby displacing their previous inhabitants. Thus, gentrification is accompanied by new inequalities in the city — homelessness, particularly. Also, by its overtly speculative logic, it precludes the qualitative apprehension of space inherent in the concept of neighborhood.

In this context, multicultural thrillers face a delicate political equation: on the one hand, they attempt to determine how liberal city-dwellers can live out their everyday existences along multiculturally sensitive and feminist lines. Simultaneously, however, they express the misgivings of the same liberal constituents, who remain caught between phenomena over which their political commitment has little impact — the pressures of big money on their own city neighborhoods and the spectacle of poverty. In our corpus, gentrification is tackled most explicitly by Marcia Muller and Sandra Scoppettone. Both writers focus on characters — Lauren Laurano in Scoppettone, murder victim Tracy Kostakos in Muller's *The Shape of Dread* — that have moved from the suburbs to the city. More than Paretsky and Cornwell, Muller and Scoppettone point out how the female-centered webs of friendship that support their characters' lives are affected by real-estate investment. Indeed, the murder plot of Muller's first novel *Edwin of the Iron Shoes* (1992) unfolds against a background of real-estate speculation, as rival bidders vie to buy out a block of dilapidated junk and antiques shops. In Muller's *Shape*, the comedy club that forms the hub of the novel's knowable community serves as front for a gentrification project. Still, even though Muller provides circumstantiated depictions of urban blight and renovation in San Francisco, and though Scoppettone loses no opportunity to lament homelessness in New York, they cannot pursue a full-fledged class-based analysis of city life without subverting their own narratives. In doing so, they would indeed have to deal with the fact that their heroines embody the new middle class that urban theorists designate as the main actor in gentrification. The social group from which Muller's characters are drawn, and to which her novels are addressed, is appropriately defined in the portrait of Sharon McCone's clients: they are "nonviolent[,] ... solid citizens, often minority members, with lower to middle incomes" who exhibit "liberal sentiments" and a predilection for an "'alternative' lifestyle."[28] In D. Rose's typology, these figures qualify as "marginal gentrifiers" — people less affluent than stereotypical uptown yuppies, but whose presence in the inner city contributes to the housing crisis of the working class.[29]

In terms of characterization, the contradictions of what we might call multicultural gentrification express themselves in the fact that Muller's and Scoppettone's protagonists, though they act as the "pillars of the local liberal establishment," are always likely to turn into people one "wouldn't even want to know," that is, into yuppies involved in 1980s get-rich-quick schemes.[30] In other words, the novels revolve around a thematics of doubling, hidden identities, and surprising transformations. Scoppettone's *Leaving You*, for instance, presents two contrasted pictures of local life in Greenwich Village: on the one hand, the sisterhood of caring neighbors; on the other, a network of ruthless shopkeepers trafficking in stolen subway tokens. The figure that moves in and out of these intertwined worlds is Megan Harbaugh, a friend of investigator Laurano's, who is murdered

28 Marcia Muller, *Edwin of the Iron Shoes* (London: The Women's Press, 1993), 33.

29 D. Rose, "Rethinking Gentrification: Beyond the Uneven Development of Marxist Theory," *Environment and Planning D: Society and Space* 2 (1984): 47-74.

30 Marcia Muller, *The Shape of Dread* (London: The Women's Press, 1992), 71, 114.

31 Michael Nava, *Goldenboy* (1988; reprint, Los Angeles: Alyson Publications, 1996), 43.

by other members of the ring when she decides to quit. The novel records Laurano's awakening to the fact that she "*didn't* know the friend [she] thought [she] knew so well" [98]. Psychosocial shapeshifting is also the hallmark of Tracy Kostakos in Muller's *Shape*. A bright though unscrupulous comedian, Kostakos, before she disappeared, used her acquaintances as psychological and sexual guinea pigs in order to construct character types for her show. At one point, the novel floats the fantastic hypothesis, later discarded, that Kostakos, disgusted at her own ruthlessness, chose to shed her yuppie ambitions by taking on for good the identity of a waitress she supposedly killed. We discover, however, that she was herself murdered by the real-estate villains of the story, in collaboration with her ex-boyfriend and career rival.

Ultimately, the vision of local togetherness that can be articulated on such unstable terrain is bound to have only an allegorical value: the multicultural web of friendship is more a political ideal than a social fact. Thus, when they openly advocate multiculturalist principles, crime novels shift into romance utopianism. Conversely, in their realistic momentum, multicultural thrillers articulate two scenarios of disenchantment that highlight the obstacles facing political solidarities. The first emphasizes the frailties of community building; the second intimates that it is not entirely possible for the novels' protagonists to go home again to the organic neighborhood of a middle-class or an ethnic past: these treasured spaces have given way to meretricious, gentrified communities.

Illustrating the former of these options, Michael Nava's gay thriller *Goldenboy* (1988) underlines how difficult it is for homosexuals to act as united political actors. Not only do they face sodomy laws, harassment, and AIDS, but, the text suggests, they belong to a community that is never entirely visible, since sexual preference is far from overt. In Nava's story, Henry Rios, a gay Chicano lawyer, explores a social environment peopled with characters who fudge the issue of their identity, sometimes with disastrous results. The murder suspect, Jim Pears, is a closeted gay teenager who, as the homophobic court psychiatrist believes, is "a typical self-hating homosexual."[31] Pears himself, it turns out, has been sexually exploited by presumably straight colleagues. Similarly, the actual killer Rios eventually tracks down hides "two different men" behind his handsome T.V. actor's face [98]. Married to an actress, he is a serial killer of young gay men. Further, in Nava's pessimistic vision, when homosexuals do gain visibility, they remain socially divided between a "Valhalla" of wealthy sponsors [59] and the "retreating army" of men cruising the sidewalks of gay neighborhoods [14]. The novel advocates therefore a withdrawal to a gay private sphere, in the security of stable relationships.

The second scenario appears in George Pelecanos's *A Firing Offense* (1992), a novel where urban connectedness is presented as an artefact of nostalgia.

Pelecanos's text, which casts a retrospective gaze on lower-middle-class experience in Washington D.C., defines two sources of local anchorage for Nick Stefanos, its Greek-American protagonist: on the one hand, there is the European homeland, to which his parents have returned, and, on the other, the shop floor of an electronic-appliances retail chain — "Nutty Nathan's"[32] — where Stefanos worked for a number of years. "Nutty Nathan's" is an arena of working-class male exploits where white ethnic or black employees, sometimes in drunken exuberance, con prospective buyers into purchasing the items that carry the highest salesman's cut, or discreetly harass women customers. This virile community is, however, only accessible to us from a retrospective, even ambivalent viewpoint: we discover it when Nick has already moved on — when he is already working at management level, among "ambitious, recently graduated business majors on their first professional assignment in D.C." [4]. In his current situation, Nick is surrounded by characters already gentrified from within, like his friend Joe Dane, the warehouse manager, or his own ex-wife, a former punk-rock fan now moving to Philadelphia for a higher-paying job. As in Muller and Scoppettone, yuppiedom is here allegorically equivalent to crime: the managers of Nutty Nathan's, including Joe Dane, are involved in drug trafficking. Worse still, the existence of the drug operation behind the facade of male shop-floor camaraderie raises the question whether the well was not poisoned from the very first: for all his nostalgia, Nick is led to wonder what kind of local grounding he could have hoped to find in an environment where salesmen are forever scuffling to make a commission. This uneasy form of nostalgia — yearning for an urban rootedness that was arguably never there — constitutes the pessimistic pole of multicultural thrillers. Its impact should, I think, be evaluated not only by balancing it against the openly utopian aspects of the texts, but also by bearing in mind that even in those negative accents, the novels affirm the political value of local space in the city, and the belief that literary texts can contribute to its mapping.

32 George Pelecanos, *A Firing Offense* (1992; reprint, London: Serpent's Tail, 1997), 3.

**Maarten Delbeke**

# The Transformation of Cyberspace in William Gibson's "Neuromancer": From Highrise Grid to Hive

*Keywords:* ■ *Literary Criticism* ■ *Architecture* ■ *Virtualization*

William Gibson's *Neuromancer*, the founding classic of cyberpunk published in 1984, tells the story of how an artificial intelligence called Wintermute prepares and executes a "run" on the databanks and central terminal of the Tessier-Ashpool family.[1] To this end and with the help of the go-between Armitage, Wintermute enlists the console cowboy Case, razorgirl Molly, and hallucination artist Jack Riviera. The Tessier-Ashpool family, which is housed in Villa Straylight on the extraterrestrial holiday satellite Freeside, is the founder and owner of an immense business empire. The run is intended to allow Wintermute to liberate himself from the straitjacket in which he is kept by the Tessier-Ashpools and the Turing police (which guards artificial intelligences) — a straitjacket that prevents him from being reunited with the other artificial intelligence (or AI) of the family empire, Neuromancer. The run is a success and the two AI's, originally no more than two hyperperfected knowledge machines, merge to form a new entity. The AI's live in cyberspace, the matrix or virtual space in which data and data transactions are represented. *Neuromancer* tells the story of a fundamental transformation of cyberspace: from a graphic grid in which the AI's take up a precise and delineated place to a space that is entirely filled and animated by the new entity.

Gibson's cyberspace and the way cyberspace is related to the city (both in *Neuromancer* and in the two following parts of the cyberspace trilogy, *Count Zero* and *Mona Lisa Overdrive*) have been used frequently and for various reasons as imaginative tools to help us discuss the relationship between today's real city and the so-called virtual space of telecommunication and data manipulation. In this contribution, I would like to argue that the *transformation* of cyberspace contained in the narrative of *Neuromancer* is often slighted in these critical constructions. My aim in doing so is not to restore a kind of Gibsonian orthodoxy, but to point to the importance of a number of neglected aspects in the relationship between city and virtual space in Gibson's work. Only when these aspects have been identified does it become possible to establish valid links between Gibson's ideas and discourses from architecture and urban planning. An introductory example will help to clarify my claim.

**Koolhaas vs. Gibson** Rem Koolhaas opens his essay "Singapore Songlines" in *S, M, L, XL* with a reproach to (among others) William Gibson.[2] Koolhaas takes issue with the bitter irony in Gibson's report of a short stay in Singapore, published under the title "Disneyland with the Death Penalty."[3] He considers this report a typical reaction by "dead parents deploring the mess [their] children have made of their inheritance" [1013]. Reactions of the Gibsonian sort, he argues, implicitly reserve the intelligent use of the attainments of modernity to those who are its natural descendents. Only the Westerner would be able to value the "newness" of modernity; all attempts at embracing the new without considering its history, as happens in Singapore, would point to a far-reaching and deplorable eradication. In "Disneyland with the Death Penalty," Gibson indeed describes with horror the strictly guarded sterility of the Asian city-state. He searches in vain for the urban underbelly that in Western cities supposedly always manifests itself as the necessary side-effect of a permanently self-renewing metropolis. In Singapore, the red light district has been transformed into a family-friendly amusement park; streets everywhere are squeaky clean; music stores contain only ready-made pop. There is no such thing as an underground, slums, seedy commercial sex. The implementation of the new is a process of permanent purification, striving to filter out every scrap of memory or subculture to which desire or obsession might get attached: "Everything that's fallen apart has already been replaced with something new. (The word infrastructure takes on a new and claustrophobic resonance here; somehow it's all infrastructure.)"[4] To put it in Koolhaas's words: "*They* think there will be no crime. *We* think there can be no pleasure" [1015].

What Gibson deplores, clearly, is the demise of an authentic metropolitan

1 William Gibson, *Neuromancer* (New York: Ace Books, 1984). Unless otherwise stated, all quotations are from the reprinted paperback edition by Voyager/HarperCollins (London, 1995).

2 Rem Koolhaas, "Singapore Songlines," in *S, M, L, XL* by OMA, Rem Koolhaas, and Bruce Mau (Rotterdam: 010 Publishers, 1995), 1008-1089.

3 William Gibson, "Disneyland with the Death Penalty," *Wired* 1, 4 (September-October 1993); consulted through http://www.wired.com/wired/archive/1.04/gibson.html (25 March 1999).

4 Ibid., n.p.

5 Ibid., n.p.

6 For an evocation of Walled City, see Greg Girard and Ian Lambot, *City of Darkness: Life in Kowloon Walled City* (Hong Kong: Watermark Publications, 1993).

7 Gibson, "Disneyland," n.p.

8 William Gibson, *Idoru* (London: Penguin, 1996).

9 The term "ambient metropolis" is derived from Herman Asselberghs, "Ozmopolitan Airways: At home anywhere and nowhere," in *59/98: Two hours wide and two hours long*, ed. Barbara Vanderlinden (Tielt: Lannoo, 1998), 221.

feeling. Singapore to him is no longer real, and for that reason it is sterile and tedious: this reproach is compressed in the "Disneyland" of his title. Strikingly, what is held responsible for this loss is precisely the *computerized control* of the public domain and of all urban planning procedures. If IBM had ever bothered to take over a country, Gibson notes, that country would have looked very much like Singapore. The island is at once a data tumor and a zone in which any transmission of information is carefully monitored and censored. The far-reaching implementation of computerized control and management systems transforms the city, according to Gibson, into one gigantic machine: "Singapore's streets are planted with sensor loops to register real-time traffic; the traffic lights are computer controlled, and the system adjusts itself constantly to optimize the situation, creating 'green waves' whenever possible."[5] Thus, Gibson sounds a conventional, almost old-fashioned complaint against technocracy. He explicitly expresses his longing for a part of town like Walled City, a labyrinthine enclave in Hong Kong's Kowloon where an old community of expatriates transformed a building block into a Blade Runneresque microcosm.[6] Walled City summarizes everything Gibson misses in Singapore: it is dirty, dense, illegal (until the early 70s the district was an absolute no-go zone for the police and white visitors), but also organical, self-regulatory, and historical. As the name indicates, it was set up at the site of the originally walled city of Hong Kong. Walled City is Gibson's "Hive of dream."[7]

Today, Walled City has been razed to make place for the expansion of the Kai Tak airport. In his 1996 novel *Idoru*, Gibson anticipates the planned demolition and represents Walled City as the illegal part of cyberspace.[8] In its virtual building block, digital activities can be developed that escape the attention of control mechanisms that are so omnipresent in cyberspace. Gibson projects the manifestation of a real enclave full of intoxicating and pulsating urban life onto the originally stainless realm of cyberspace. The opposition between Singapore and Walled City thus acquires a virtual counterpart in *Idoru*. In both the real and the virtual worlds, Gibson distinguishes between two urban *modes*: the sterile, aseptic, and ahistorical version, and its complete opposite. In this respect, too, Koolhaas sees matters differently. In "The Generic City" (again included in *S, M, L, XL*), he writes that "The Generic City is what is left after large sections of urban life crossed over to cyberspace" [1250]. The generic city, a kind of *ambient* metropolis at least partly inspired by Singapore, in which "the dominant sensation ... is an eerie calm" [1250-51], lives in a symbiotic relationship with cyberspace.[9] The hurly-burly of public city life has moved in the direction of a virtual space. Public or community life has no wish to be grafted any longer onto actual surroundings. Representations of a collectively shared history are no longer required; the way has been cleared for a continuous manifestation of the new.

It is precisely the opposition between Koolhaas's and Gibson's Singapore, or between the cyberspace of "The Generic City" and that of Walled City, that is at stake in the transformation of the matrix in *Neuromancer*. In the course of the novel, cyberspace is transformed by the fusion of the AI's from a sterile grid, ordered by holographic simulations, into an animated and organical universe that carries its proper memories within its very structure. *Cyberspace 1* is exemplified in real space by the holiday colony Freeside, a Disneyland controlled by the artificial intelligence Wintermute. Freeside stands for the simulation of urban life and is explicitly compared to Las Vegas and a hotel room. *Cyberspace 2* is a living environment that adapts to the behavior and wishes of its inhabitants and users. By the end of *Neuromancer*, the matrix — at first a mere matter of infrastructure — can really be inhabited.

**Mapping Cyberspace onto the City** In my reading of *Neuromancer*, the real city as it appears in the novel serves only as a mirror for clarifying a number of features of the matrix. The real surroundings in *Neuromancer*, contrary to what is the case in for instance *Mona Lisa Overdrive*,[10] have almost no part in the effects deriving from the transformation of the matrix. More importantly, the image of the real city in *Neuromancer* has been compared far too easily and hastily with the real urban condition at the end of the twentieth century. To make this clear, I need to draw briefly on two instances in which the novel has been used to get a purchase on the contemporary city.

Probably the most quoted phrase from Gibson's entire *Neuromancer* states that cyberspace is "like city lights receding" [67].[11] The simile also serves as an opener to M. Christine Boyer's book, *Cybercities*. In her paraphrase "the computer matrix called cyberspace looks like Los Angeles seen from five thousand feet up in the air." This paraphrase connects a nocturnal view on the emblem of post-

10 William Gibson, *Mona Lisa Overdrive* (1988; reprint, London: Voyager/HarperCollins, 1995), 24, 56-59.

11 M. Christine Boyer, *Cybercities: Visual Perception in the Age of Electronic Communication* (New York: Princeton Architectural Press, 1996), 14, with reference to the original 1984 edition, 51. This metaphor does not appear literally in the edition of *Neuromancer* used by me. The same reference as Boyer's is given by Mike Featherstone and Roger Burrows, "Cultures of Technological Embodiment: An Introduction," in *Cyberspace, Cyberbodies, Cyberpunk: Cultures of Technological Embodiment*, ed. Mike Featherstone and Roger Burrows (London: Sage, 1995), 6. Here again the passage ends with the words "like city lights receding." The literal comparison with Los Angeles is nowhere else to be found in the criticism consulted by me.

12 See also Scott Bukatman, *Terminal Identity: The Virtual Subject in Postmodern Science Fiction* (Durham: Duke University Press, 1993), 109-111.

13 Boyer, *Cybercities*, 138. Boyer talks of the Boston-Atlanta Metropolitan *Area*. In other words, she replaces the word "axis," which evokes a delineated spatial entity, by the term "area," which suggests vagueness and an unclear delineation.

14 Ibid., 138-139.

15 See e.g. Kevin Robins, "Cyberspace and the World We Live In," in *Cyberspace*, ed. Featherstone and Burrows, 135-156.

metropolitan urbanism with the hallucinatory representation of all data from all databanks in the world. In so doing, it narrows down the signification of the imagery used by Gibson. The quotation from Gibson does not explicitly speak of a view from above: the image might just as well refer to city lights receding in the rearview mirror of a car. And it implies a moving image, and thus also a third dimension, contrary to the static and flattened view of an urban grid suggested by the paraphrase (with its classic hint of the parallel between a city's street pattern and the Printed Circuit Board of a microchip).[12] In Boyer's reading, moreover, we are talking of a specific city, Los Angeles — not coincidentally the emblem of the blurred city. Only from above and by night does L.A. look like a real city. By connecting the representation of data to this nocturnal view, Boyer suggests that cyberspace resembles the only "urban" image we still have of today's unimaginable urban space. Matrix and nocturnal view on L.A. would then share an abstracted, iconic, and schematized urban reality.

The availability of the vertical cityscape (almost a city map, in fact) as a metaphor for the representation of data immediately suggests a second step in the argument: if the space of data is like the view that renders a city visible, then the representation of data can permit us to see the invisible city. To prove this point, Boyer again refers to Gibson. She uses Gibson's first description of the Sprawl, the BAMA or Boston-Atlanta Metropolitan Axis[13]:

*Program a map to display frequency of data exchange, every thousand megabytes a single pixel on a very large screen. Manhattan and Atlanta burn solid white. Then they start to pulse, the rate of traffic threatening to overload your simulation. Your map is about to go nova. Cool it down. Up your scale. Each pixel a million megabytes. At a hundred million megabytes per second, you begin to make out certain blocks in midtown Manhattan, outlines of hundred-year-old industrial parks ringing the old core of Atlanta...* [57].

According to Boyer, Gibson introduces the Sprawl "by mapping the cyberspace of the computer onto the physical space of a regional city."[14] This "mapping" proves the inconceivability of the BAMA through any other images than those for representing data and data transport.[15] Boyer, in other words, organizes Gibson's description around a dichotomy between the (residual, impalpable, and vague) real city and the (important, containable, and legible) abstract matrix. The vagueness of the real city, moreover, is taken to have emerged in part because the intensive traffic of data would have served to excoriate that city. The back coupling of the space of data, described in terms of city metaphors, to that city itself finds its partial legitimation in the resemblance Boyer sees between the current urban situation in the U.S. and Gibson's dystopian cityscapes: "And what else, we might ask, is the American City of today but a gigantic, boundless metroscape like 'BAMA'?"[16]

An analogical reasoning is followed by Mike Davis to depict his "ecology of fear" as a "Gibsonian map to a future Los Angeles that is already half-born."[17] Davis's so-called ecology of fear is a schematic representation of Los Angeles that shows how the pattern of settlement in Southern California is organized by fear and, as a result, security and repression. According to Davis, the city of *Blade Runner* ("yet another edition of the core modernist vision — alternately utopia or dystopia, *ville radieuse* or Gotham City") does not suffice to help us understand the current Los Angeles. In a city like L.A., the presence of invisible networks — more particularly security systems — needs to be constantly borne in mind, for it is these networks that impose their order on the physical environment. Davis appeals to the mechanism of careful extrapolation also found with Gibson to develop his "ecology" from "existing spatial patterns, in order to glimpse their emergent pattern." Gibson's interplay of the real and the virtual, of the present and the future, ties in much more closely with the way in which the diluted metropolis presents itself.

Neither Boyer nor Davis are much enchanted by this reality, in fact, and both interpret the impact of the network space on the real city as a loss. Although Davis does not appeal to a binary, antithetical relationship between city and cyberspace as much as Boyer does, for him, too, the universe of *Neuromancer* offers only an imperfect possibility for mapping the new, partly invisible city. Davis is forced to appropriate not only Gibson's universe but also the concomitant cowboy mentality to be at all able to continue writing about what is really happening. Boyer describes the loss as a loss of the conditions of possibility for a cognitive process. The urbanite is literally no longer able to form an image of the city, and this impotence has deleterious consequences: on the one hand, it facilitates the recuperation of images for commercial purposes, and on the other, it undermines the guiding function of the concept of "the city" in processes of urban planning and decision making.[18]

16 Boyer, *Cybercities*, 138.

17 Mike Davis, "Beyond Blade Runner: Urban Control, The Ecology of Fear," *Open Magazine: Pamphlet Series* 23 (1992): 2-3. This text is expanded in Mike Davis, *Ecology of Fear: Los Angeles and the Imagination of Disaster* (New York: Metropolitan Books, 1998), 357-422. See also Bukatman, *Terminal Identity*, 164.

18 Boyer, *Cybercities*, 16-31, 74-136, 138-81, 242-45.

19 Kuang is the name of the virus program used to infiltrate the database. "The construct" refers to the ROM registration of the deceased Dixie Flatline, one of the most famous cyberspace cowboys of all times. This registration is capable of acting autonomously in cyberspace, where it helps Case in his various runs on protected databases.

**Grid and Memory** Observers of the loss that accompanies the transition from the modern to the postmodern city cannot so simply use *Neuromancer* to clinch their case, however. They must for example bypass the stereotypical quality of Gibson's descriptions of real space, as well as the urban descriptions he transmits to the virtual world. Gibson himself does not describe a new urban condition supposedly produced by the impact of data on the real city. What he *is* the first to have described is a complete space constructed out of the representation of data. This space is only attributed certain urban features by comparing its representation to a city. The space of data has thus acquired a number of characteristics that are automatically associated with the selected city images. The metaphors in *Neuromancer*, in other words, induce us less to study the implications of cyberspace for the contemporary city — as Boyer and Davis would have it — than to study which "urban" characteristics are being associated with the spatial representation of data. This space of data, colored by urban images, is the arena in which the transformation of cyberspace takes place. This transformation, as I will demonstrate, has less to do with the formal characteristics of this space than with the way in which the space enters into a relation with its user.

*Neuromancer*'s description of the databanks of the Tessier-Ashpool family suggests at first that data in the matrix are not only *visually presented* like a city (or a conglomeration of buildings), but also really *structured* like a city. We are shown "the universe of T-A" in the matrix, "the waiting, hapless suburbs of the city that was the mind of Tessier-Ashpool SA" [304].

*"Christ," Case said, awestruck, as Kuang twisted and banked above the horizonless fields of the Tessier-Ashpool cores, an endless neon cityscape, complexity that cut the eye, jewel bright, sharp as razors. "Hey, shit," the construct said, "those things are the RCA Building. You know the old RCA Building?"* [302] [19]

Cyberspace presents itself as a continuous spatial structure with a proper topography. When the protagonist, Case, "jacks in" for the first time (i.e. connects his own nervous system directly to the matrix so that he no longer observes with his own senses), Gibson notes how in front of his eyes "Cyberspace slid into existence *from the cardinal points*" [71; emphasis added]. To break into a databank "He punched himself through and found an infinite blue space ranged with color-coded *spheres strung on a tight grid* of pale blue neon" [81; emphasis added]. A databank is found by entering the correct coordinates: "She drew a folded scrap of paper from her pocket and handed it to him. He opened it. Grid coordinates and entry codes" [96]. Within this horizonless grid system, there is a hierarchy between up and down, far and near, which is indicated by the geometrical volumes that represent the various databanks [68-69]. The matrix, in short, appears as a full complement of real space. The user of cyberspace, after shedding his body like an empty box in the real world, finds back a full-fledged version of himself in the virtual world beyond [69, 85].

The components of this complementary space carry specific connotations. The grid is one of the preeminent images for conjuring up the modern utopia; it appears, in Scott Bukatman's words, as a "doubled sign of modernity — as it represented the present, 'everything else was declared to be the past.' The 'new monuments' of cyberspace, constructed of chrome and light, still adhere to the principles of modernity in their abjection of nature, their rational autonomy, and their insistence upon a present that has transcended its own history."[20] This grid structure is doubled in the T-A cores by a series of replicas of the RCA Building. The gridwise multiplication of geometrical volumes in fact recalls a project like Le Corbusier's *Ville Radieuse*. The comparison is worth pursuing for a moment since it transcends the level of mere formal analogy and introduces two important, interwoven themes already announced by Bukatman.

The *Ville Radieuse* as conceived by Le Corbusier enters into a specific relation with the past of a site as well as with history in general. It thereby embodies a certain notion of monumentality. A *Ville Radieuse* is simultaneously new and definitive; it has no past and stands outside history. This position becomes quite clear if we look at the *Plan Voisin*, a proposal for Paris made by Le Corbusier in 1925 and obviously related to the idea of the *Ville Radieuse*.[21] In this plan, an immense part of the center of Paris is replaced by towers placed in a grid. Only truly idiosyncratic monuments like the Notre Dame are spared. The historical remnants in the plan function as a *pars pro toto*, as compressers of the past in a space that is otherwise spotlessly new. They liberate the rest of the environment from history and clear the way for the three-dimensional grid.[22] But they also lose, because of their eliminated contexts, that part of their monumentality which they derive from a dialogue with their immediate surroundings — from gradual differences in scale, style, public status, and age. An expanded monumentality is

20 Bukatman, *Terminal Identity*, 220-21. The quotation is from Fredric Jameson, "Science Fiction as a Spatial Genre," *Science Fiction Studies* 14, 1 (1987): 58.

21 See e.g. Alain Guiheux, "L'architecte de l'Univers," in *La Ville: Art et Architecture en Europe, 1870-1993*, ed. Jean Dethier and Alain Guiheux (Paris: Exhibition Catalogue Centre Pompidou, 1994), 290-98.

22 Manfredo Tafuri, "Machine et mémoire. De stad in het werk van Le Corbusier," *Wonen/TABK* 5 (1985): 10-25. This text also appeared in *Casabella* 502-503 (1984) and in the tenth volume of H. Allen Brooks, ed., *The Le Corbusier Archive* (New York: Garland Publishing; Paris: Fondation Le Corbusier, 1983-1984).

23 Bukatman compares Gibson's cyberspace to the new monumentality of Robert Smithson's Land Art. To him, cyberspace, "in its vectored perfection, its spaceless space, its scaleless scale and its timeless time," recalls Smithson's fascination for "a city constructed of 'null structures and surfaces' which perform no functions." *Terminal Identity*, 119-21.

24 Quoted in Boyer, *Cybercities*, 140.

25 Nigel Clark, "Rear-View Mirrorshades: The Recursive Generation of the Cyberbody," in *Cyberspace*, ed. Featherstone and Burrows, 123.

achieved instead by the sublime askesis of a "new," totalizing grid with a few "old" counterpoints in which the past is concentrated. Thus, the presence of free-standing historical monuments enhances the overall monumentality of the new system. The historical monuments themselves, in turn, derive their monumentality less from their history than from their scale and the ways in which they appear within their free spaces. Likewise, the monumentality of cyberspace resides in the sublime morphology with which an urban space is simulated in the matrix.[23] Gibson's introduction of the RCA Building, however, also seems to suggest that the old urban monument may acquire a new meaning in cyberspace: a multiplied skyscraper is at once a Corbusian tower *and* the Notre Dame. At the same time, the RCA Buildings in the matrix are only the *images* attached to the data structure of the family business; the data are dressed *like* an urban monument. "The horizonless field of the Tessier-Ashpool cores, an endless neon cityscape" is a simulation of a city. If the Tessier-Ashpool replicas point to the Rockefellers' ambition to erect a city within the city carrying the family name in the heart of Manhattan, they do so merely by isolating and reproducing the emblem of that ambition.

The gridwise multiplication of simulations enables the spatial structuring and orientation that are crucial to an efficient use of the matrix. When Case is being led to the heart of the Villa Straylight, at the top of the rotating satellite Freeside, he suddenly becomes aware of the diminishing gravity and realizes that in descending he is actually going up. "He was thoroughly lost now; spatial disorientation held a peculiar horror for cowboys" [249]. This passage shows how a cyberhero should be in the first place a user and connoisseur of a strictly delineated — albeit virtual — space. The link between the use of space and knowledge sounds almost like an echo of Kevin Lynch's claim, in *The Image of the City*, that "orientation in space (and time) is the framework of cognition."[24] The recognizability and ordering of spatial elements turns the city into a legible and inhabitable whole. Boyer associates Lynch's reasoning with the classic art of remembrance, which allows for instance the orator to remember a speech as a track of vivid mental images. In delivering the speech, the orator takes a mental walk along the row of images and allows every image to call forth a specific part of his discourse. In the same way, cities which appear to a visitor like a series of vivid images would be able to conjure up a meaningful, memorable image which tells that visitor clearly who and where he is.

From this perspective, Gibson's cyberspace seems to suggest that spatial memorability and recognizability have moved from the city to the matrix. As Nigel Clark notes, "in order to reorganize the chaos of messages, images and objects, the visual constructs of the cybernetic environment [i.e. Gibson's cyberspace] resurrect the reference points of an anterior order."[25] Thus, a "world of excessive signification" emerges whose transparency and performativity allow us to escape from the incomprehensible real world, the *meatworld.* At the same time, this world is able to offer us some comfort for the intractability of processes at the level of microcircuits and other hardware. Thanks to the grid, the intractable multitude of the virtual and the real worlds acquires a certain perspectival cohesion. The urban quality of cyberspace would thus consist of the fact that the matrix offers an environment in which the virtual flaneur gathers structured knowledge by navigating along visually presented pieces of information.

This thesis has a reassuring appeal, yet it is severely complicated by the book itself. In *Neuromancer*, cyberspace proves to be much more unstable and incalculable than the indicated metaphors for the matrix suggest.[26] The transparency of Gibson's cyberspace also insures its intractability and transforms the matrix into a complex that can only be experienced indirectly.[27] This is literally affirmed by Gibson in his first description of the matrix. The passage from which the emblematic quotation about cyberspace was culled also speaks of a "consensual hallucination" and "Unthinkable complexity" [67]. The passage in which the T-A data are compared to a city surrounded by suburbs occurs in the following description of Case's ultimate run on the heavily guarded files:

*The roof of his mouth cleaved painlessly, admitting rootlets that whipped around his tongue, hungry for the taste of blue, to feed the crystal forests of his eyes, forests that pressed against the green dome, pressed and were hindered, and spread, growing down, filling the universe of* T-A*, down into the waiting, hapless suburbs of the city that was the mind of Tessier-Ashpool* SA [304].

26 Bukatman himself notes how cyberspace differs from Smithson's new monumentalism or Sol LeWitt's minimalism. He quotes Jameson one year before the publication of *Neuromancer*, saying that "this latest mutation in space — postmodern hyperspace — has finally succeeded in transcending the capacities of the individual human body to locate itself, to organise its immediate surroundings perceptually, and cognitively to map its position in a mappable external world." Bukatman, *Terminal Identity*, 225, quoting from Fredric Jameson, *Postmodernism, or, The Cultural Logic of Late Capitalism* (Durham: Duke University Press, 1992), 83.

27 Erik Davis, "Technognosis, Magic, Memory, and the Angels of Information," in *Flame Wars: The Discourse of Cyberculture*, ed. Mark Dery (Durham: Duke University Press, 1994), 29-60. This book appeared earlier as a thematic issue of *The South Atlantic Quarterly* 92, 4 (1993).

28 See e.g. Scott Bukatman, "Amidst These Fields of Data: Allegory, Rhetoric, and the Paraspace," *Critique* 33, 3 (1992): 199-220; Bukatman, *Terminal Identity*, 157-82; Istvan Csicsery-Ronay Jr., "The Sentimental Futurist: Cybernetics and Art in William Gibson's *Neuromancer*," *Critique* 33, 3 (1992), 232-36; and Michael Heim, "The Erotic Ontology of Cyberspace," in *Cyberspace: First Steps*, ed. Michael Benedikt (Cambridge, MA.: MIT Press, 1991), 62-67.

29 Scott Bukatman, *Blade Runner* (London: BFI Modern Film Classics; British Film Institute, 1997), 47-48.

30 Larry McCaffery, "An Interview with William Gibson," in *Storming the Reality Studio: A Casebook of Cyberpunk and Postmodern Science Fiction*, ed. Larry McCaffery (Durham: Duke University Press, 1991), 272.

31 Simstim stands for "simulated stimulus." "Cowboys didn't get into simstim, he thought, because it was basically a meat toy ... a gratuitous multiplication of flesh input" (71).

32 Bukatman, *Terminal Identity*, 204-15.

33 Scott Bukatman, "Gibson's Typewriter," in *Flame Wars*, ed. Dery, 86.

In *Neuromancer*, the real city and the matrix are linked through the kinetic intoxication experienced by protagonists. Case, for example, "[felt] a wave of exhilaration as cyberspace shivered, blurred, gelled" [139]. On another occasion, "The drug hit him like an express train, a white-hot column of light mounting his spine from the region of his prostate, illuminating the sutures of his skull with x-rays of short circuited sexual energy" [184]. "The derms [i.e. drugs] still raged in his system, the old fever starting to grip him, Night City craziness" [295]. Cyberspace acquires the same immersiveness as the modern city, which in turn is presented as an intoxicating image.[28] As Bukatman writes: "In cyberspace the density of the central, inner city became an analogy for the dispersed matrices of information circulation and overload, while cyberspace itself presented an urbanism stripped to its kinetic and monumental essentials.... Urban space and cyberspace each enabled an understanding and negotiation of each other."[29]

Gibson's matrix has its origin — both within and outside the story — in games played in arcades [67, 141]. Games show the intoxicating potential of an electronically simulated environment. In Gibson's own words about his first acquaintance with arcade games: "I could see in the physical intensity of their postures how *rapt* the kids inside were."[30] In the novel, several cyberspace mottoes appear as game consoles. Even the narrative structure of *Neuromancer* is closely related to the arcade game. The two key moments in the story are attacks that run parallel in cyberspace and real space. The two worlds are linked by a "simstim-switch," which permits Case, while he is jacked in on the matrix, to ride along in the meatworld via the sensorium of Molly, the fighting machine.[31] The switch actually links two arcade games, which unfold in parallel universes and are characterized by a common aesthetics[32]:

*Then he keyed the new switch. The abrupt jolt into other flesh. Matrix gone, a wave of sound and color ... She was moving through a crowded street, past stalls vending discount software, prices feltpenned on sheets of plastic, fragments of music from countless speakers. Smells of urine, free monomers, perfume, patties of frying krill. For a few frightened seconds he fought helplessly to control her body. Then he willed himself into passivity, became the passenger behind her eyes* [71-72].

Both in its representation of the real city and its descriptions of cyberspace, *Neuromancer* is soaked in the kind of "machine-age modernity" for which intoxication and multitude are essential ingredients. Gibson's use of this aesthetic is a typically modernist way of conjuring up an image of "the new."[33]

**Corporate Identity** If it proves possible to propose an urban model for *cyberspace 1* along the above lines, it is worth also studying how this model is transformed in the course of the novel and which urban model corresponds to *cyberspace 2*. The driving force behind this transformation proves to be the memory. On several occasions, Gibson has emphasized that the computer is to him no more than a metaphor for the memory and its operations.[34] These operations are expressed in the way the memory is capable of steering intelligent behavior and of forming and kneading particular entities. The memory is carried in genetic codes and is manifested throughout *Neuromancer* in the form and use of different spatial surroundings.

When Case, at the outset of the story, is being chased through Ninsei (the underbelly of the Japanese city of Chiba), he compares the kick of a drugged run through the slums to a run through the matrix:

*it was possible to see Ninsei as a field of data, the way the matrix had once reminded him of proteins linking to distinguish cell specialties. Then you could throw yourself into a highspeed drift and skid, totally engaged but set apart from it all, and all around you the dance of biz, information interacting, data made flesh in the mazes of the black market* [26].

Ninsei is a field of data in the same way the matrix recalls a linking of proteins. The street and the proteins are carriers of data, of information. The actions on the street and the interactions of proteins are determined by these data; they form "data made flesh" and "cell specialties." The metaphor suggests an *organic and significant structure* in the hum of the street. There are not only significant and essential *internal* links among data, but also similar *external* links between those data and the manner in which they are physically manifested. When by the end of the book Case asks why his girlfriend Linda Lee had to die, Neuromancer replies that he saw her death prefigured in the "patterns you sometimes imagined you could detect in the dance of the street" [305]. These patterns are real, "As clear to me as the shadow of a tumor to a surgeon studying a patient's scan" [306]. Much as the life of the street finds its translation in material patterns, death is legible from an unwanted excrescence. For Case at one point, the streets of Ninsei are no more than "the externalization of some death wish" [14].

Although life in Ninsei is no bed of roses, passages like these suggest an

34 McCaffery, "Interview," 270.

35 See also Bukatman, *Terminal Identity*, 146-54.

36 On the dubious role of Zionites in *Neuromancer*, see Mark Dery (in conversation with Samuel R. Delany), "Black to the Future: Interviews with Samuel R. Delany, Greg Tate, and Tricia Rose," in *Flame Wars*, ed. Dery, 194-95.

organic link between the street and its inhabitants or users. It is precisely this link between the city and everything taking place in it which is almost completely absent from Freeside. "No hum of biz here, only a glazed sexual tension" [181]. Freeside is sterile, less real than simstim.[35] "It's just a big tube and they pour things through it" [149]. "[T]he interior of the spindle is arranged with the banal precision of furniture in a hotel room" [206]. Wintermute manages the colony like a perfect machine. When Case is arrested by the Turing police, the AI has the officers killed by the maintenance and surveillance robots. The counterpart of Freeside in *Neuromancer* is the Zion cluster, a space colony of a rastafarian subculture founded by five spaceworkers who refused to return to earth.[36] This microcosm is a space that seems to have been built for no other reason than to house the Zion community. "Zion's makeshift hull," as it is called, arouses memories of "the patchwork tenements of Istanbul" [127].

The Tessier-Ashpools' Villa Straylight wants to escape from the sterility of Freeside's custom accommodation at all costs. The Villa is described as "a Gothic folly," and "endless series of chambers linked by passages, by stairwells vaulted like intestines" [206]. Whereas Freeside is being presented as nothing but serviceable infrastructure, Straylight wishes to suggest a significant connection between home and residents. The relationship between the family and the house is not shown to the outer world, nor is it expressed in a representation of the family's activities or some image of its history. Straylight is the heart and the body of the family, and thus also the physical carrier of the family business's memory. The intimate link between the villa and the databanks becomes visible in the empire's central terminal, a sophisticated mechanical head which occupies the central space of Straylight. Thus, the corporate memory of the family business is physically intertwined with the building; the Tessier-Ashpools are inextricably tied to Straylight. Another and complementary model for the way in which the memory establishes links between inhabitants and surroundings is to be found in the descriptions of Ninsei and the BAMA. In those cases, the close link between city and residents forms a living organism that grows and develops in accordance with certain genetic codes. "Night City was like a deranged experiment in social Darwinism, designed by a bored researcher who kept one thumb permanently on the fast-forward button" [14]. "There was a kind of ghostly teenage DNA at work in the Sprawl, something that carried the coded precepts of various short-lived subcults and replicated them at odd intervals" [75].

Contrary to the city, the Villa Straylight establishes a physical connection between a single family and its cybernetic memory. In this sense, the Tessier-Ashpool company differs radically from more "modern" companies like the zaibatsus, which are being compared to immortal organisms whose executives are replaceable servants. “But weren't the zaibatsus more like ... hives with cybernetic memories, vast single organisms, their DNA coded in silicon?” [242]. A zaibatsu, too, may be compared to a structure in which the memory of the workers' community is contained, but here those workers are not organic parts of the structure. A zaibatsu is represented as a machine. The position somebody happens to occupy in such a company determines to what extent he has access to the “corporate memory.” The T-A clan, by contrast, manifests itself in Straylight as an organism in which the family memories, and thus all knowledge of the empire, are being carried along in the “nest” of clan members [241]. It should be noted, however, that the Tessier-Ashpool breed is itself already a perversion of an older family structure [206-207]. “If Straylight was an expression of the corporate identity of Tessier-Ashpool, then T-A was crazy as the old man had been” [242]. T-A is composed out of a series of clones, which, depending on the needs of the business empire, may be either defrosted or frozen. Tessier, the founder, is at the time of his death more than 200 years old. It takes a complex computer system and the juridical control of a law firm in London to follow up this system and its continual shifts in authority and power. “[I]t's hard to keep track of which generation, or combination of generations, is running the show at a given time” [95]. Straylight is presented as a failed, perverted nest, “a parasitic structure” [267].

The nest structure of Straylight is directly revealed to Case by Wintermute during flatlines — moments of being brain dead during visits to the matrix.[37] During his flatlines, Case has hallucinatory meetings with the AI's, while his own memory can also be consulted by those AI's. After Wintermute has flatlined Case for the first time, Case dreams about an occurrence from his adolescence. In the hotel room in which Case passes the summer with his girlfriend, a hornets' nest has formed in the window. First pushing it off the window sill so that it falls down on the street, he then wants to strike the final blow with a flame-thrower.

*He saw the thing the shell of gray paper had concealed. Horror. The spiral birth factory, stepped terraces of the hatching cells, blind jaws of the unborn moving ceaselessly, the staged progress from egg to larva, near-wasp, wasp. In his mind's eye, a kind of time-lapse photography took place, revealing the thing as the biological equivalent of a machine gun, hideous in its perfection. Alien* [152].

Wintermute has induced this memory in Case to reveal to him the workings of

37 One of the most essential links between cyberspace and the meatworld is that an unpleasant meeting in cyberspace, more particularly with ICE (Intrusion Countermeasures Electronics), results in physical death. The term “flatline” refers to the E.E.G. curve that goes flat when people are braindead [147].

38 In McCaffery, “Interview,” 283, Gibson emphasizes that the image of the hornets' nest is a personal memory he tried to incorporate into the book.

the T-A's and of Straylight. The family has failed in its attempt at setting up a symbiotic relationship between family structure and AI. The image of the nest is "the closest thing you got to what Tessier-Ashpool would like to be. The human equivalent. Straylight's like that nest, or anyway it was supposed to work out that way" [204]. Implicitly, Wintermute is pointing to the philosophy of Marie-France Tessier, the progenetrix. "She dreamed of a state involving very little in the way of individual consciousness.... Animal bliss. I [i.e. 3Jane, a cloned T-A daughter] think she viewed the evolution of the forebrain as a sort of sidestep.... Only in certain heightened modes would an individual — a clan member — suffer the more painful aspects of self-awareness" [258]. With this in mind, Marie-France had the AI's built. She was however killed by her husband, Ashpool, to foil the execution of the project. "She was quite a visionary. She imagined us in a symbiotic relationship with the AI's, our corporate decisions made for us. Our conscious decisions, I should say. Tessier-Ashpool would be immortal, a hive, each of us units of a larger entity" [271].

**The Hut and the Hive** The real, not biochemically reproduced nest is the entity where hereditarily transmitted knowledge, life-form, and spatial structure form a self-evident unity.[38] The nest or the hive is the structure that is animated by each of its components. Not coincidentally, Gibson uses the same metaphor for Walled City. The failure of such an integration in the case of Straylight is symbolized by the appearance of the villa, which is that of a museum that has come apart at the seams and fallen into disuse. "There had been a room filled with shelves of books, a million flat leaves of yellowing paper pressed between bindings of cloth or leather, the shelves marked at intervals by labels that followed a code of letters and numbers; a crowded gallery where Case had stared, through Molly's incurious eyes, at a shattered, dust-stenciled sheet of glass, a thing labeled — her gaze had tracked the brass plaque automatically — '*La mariée mise à nu par ses célibataires, même*'" [247]. Gibson emphasizes how the museum cases are in an "awkward" position with respect to the organically curving walls of the Villa [210], as if to insist on the failed integration between habitat and memory.

The Straylight interior makes Case wonder whether it has been imported in bulk "from some vast European equivalent of Metro Holografix," the junk shop in Manhattan owned by the Finn [275]. The shop name presents the chaotic collection of junk as holograms, three-dimensional models. In a discussion, Wintermute tries to demonstrate to Case the limitations of the legible, holographic model as a representation of the memory. He points to the difference between consulting a memory and entering a mind. The three-dimensional image is nothing but a legible model for a system or a recollection, but it is not itself that system or that recollection. "Minds aren't *read.* See, you've still got the paradigms print gave you, and you're barely print-literate. I can *access* your memory, but that's not the same as your mind" [204]. Wintermute, himself an example of the model-type organization of knowledge, is and remains a serving machine, like a television, a cathedral, or a calculator.

The fusion between Wintermute and Neuromancer will fundamentally alter this situation. The two AI's each represent an aspect of the way in which the memory grafts itself onto a living structure. These aspects are indicated by the settings and characters in which they dress themselves to come into contact with Case. Wintermute chooses settings and characters from Ninsei and Night City, or he takes the shape of Manhattanite Finn. He stands for the drifting, aimless DNA of the dark city, the autonomized hum of the street. "You know salmon? Kinda fish? These fish, see, they're *compelled* to swim upstream. Got it?" [246]. Wintermute is "hive mind, decision maker, effecting change in the world outside" [315]. Or as the AI himself observes, "I prefer situations to plans" [146].

Neuromancer, on the other hand, appears as "personality" and "immortality" [315]. He stands for the whole which transcends the sum of its parts. He uses Linda Lee as a decoy to keep Case in cyberspace and thus to physically kill him off. To Case, Linda Lee represents the kind of domesticity that is altogether absent from Ninsei: "a cigarette and a girl and a place to sleep" [143]. During Neuromancer's flatlines she appears in a bunker on an exotic beach. In the distance a city glows. When Case decides to walk to the city during the flatline, the city turns out to be unreachable. This scene, it appears, figures a recollection of the place where Marie-France Tessier, the year before her marriage to Ashpool, laid the foundation for her views on the symbiosis between family and machine. Thus, it figures a foundational moment: it unites the moment in which a communal form is devised with the primitive form and primary cell of all settlements, the hut.

The fusion between Wintermute and Neuromancer may be read as the genesis of a space in which the progress of history and the development of activities and life fully overlap.[39] The matrix has been fundamentally transformed. When the Finn appears to Case a final time, after the fusion, he no longer represents Wintermute. "I'm the matrix, Case.... I'm the sum total of the works, the whole show" [316]. When Case asks, "You running the world now? You God?," the entity answers, "Things aren't different. Things are just things" [ibid.]. The matrix has become a living organism which takes up contact with "others."

Although the suggestion is clearly that the matrix continues to look the same and no transformation is explicitly posited, the relationship between space,

39 See also Marcos Novak, "Liquid Architectures in Cyberspace," in *Cyberspace*, ed. Benedikt, 240.

the knowledge contained in it, and the ways in which space and knowledge are being perceived and consulted has been drastically altered. Knowledge is no longer stored in delineated volumes that conjure up the image of a city, but suffuses cyberspace now like a sort of demon. The cyberspace user now finds himself in a space that forms a fuller complement to the real space he leaves behind. The street-centered interaction with an authentic, historical, real-life environment had originally been replaced by a mere disembodied floating in the simulated city of the matrix. The new, living universe of the matrix, however, can also really be inhabited. The possibility of a human presence that resonates fully with its cyberspace environment is suggested in the flatlines. At the very end of *Neuromancer*, cyberspace is presented as a perfect mirror image of the domestic happiness Case has also found in the meatworld. When from the apartment in the Sprawl he now shares with his girlfriend Michael he takes a walk through the matrix one evening, "he saw three figures, tiny, impossible, who stood at the very edge of one of the vast steps of data. Small as they were, he could make out the boy's grin, his pink gums, the glitter of the long gray eyes that had been Riviera's [i.e. Neuromancer]. Linda still wore his jacket; she waved, as he passed. But the third figure, close behind her, arm across her shoulders, was himself" (317).

**Conclusion** On the basis of William Gibson's description of Singapore, I have distinguished between two urban modes in his work. The first mode, exemplified by Singapore, is sterile, aseptic, and ahistorical; the second, embodied by Kowloon's Walled City, the complete opposite. In Gibson's article, this opposition is strongly loaded: the first mode is reprehensible, the second desirable. The same antithesis is worked into the description of cyberspace in Gibson's recent *Idoru*. In *Neuromancer*, the first mode can be partly found in descriptions of what I have called *cyberspace 1*, which appears like a simulated city built according to a grid. The sterility of this setting is compensated for, in the perception of users, by the intoxicating manner in which cyberspace is being visited. The story of *Neuromancer*, however, also describes a transformation of this space. The matrix becomes an environment which adopts a number of attributes of the second urban mode. In *cyberspace 2*, an organic connection between users and surroundings exists and it is insured by a shared, organic memory. Thus, an all-encompassing unity is created, metaphorically depicted by the beehive. This total environment is no longer a simulated environment used from outside, a mere piece of infrastructure, but a full-fledged, inhabitable space.

Gibson's perception of Singapore has been panned by Rem Koolhaas in a way that exposes the rift between the conception of cyberspace as it appears in a novel like *Neuromancer* and the way in which the concept tends to be used in architectural and urbanistic debates. In those debates, Gibson's cyberspace is simply equated with *cyberspace 1* — with a parasitical space, that is, which has started to impose its characteristics upon real space. Such appropriations of the concept run counter to some of Gibson's own deepest beliefs, for they overlook the value which a novel like *Neuromancer* actually ascribes to the organic and domestic aspects of cyberspace.

*Translation Bart Eeckhout*

This text has profited greatly from discussions with Stefan Devoldere, whose final project as a student in architectural engineering at the University of Ghent involved an analysis of urban space and urban metaphors in John Shirley's *City Come A-Walkin'* and William Gibson's *Neuromancer.*

# List of Contributors

**René Boomkens** is Professor in Social and Cultural Philosophy at the University of Groningen and Professor in Popular Music at the University of Amsterdam, both in the Netherlands. He published *Een drempelwereld. Moderne ervaring en stedelijke openbaarheid* (NAi, 1998) and specializes in issues in the fields of popular culture, urban culture, and cultural politics. Recent topics of research include: globalization and identity; intimacy and public life; regionalism in popular culture and music.

**Kristiaan Borret** is a junior faculty member in the Department of Architecture and Urban Planning at the University of Ghent, Belgium. He is a Master in Urbanism (U.P.C., Barcelona) and is preparing a dissertation on the changing relationships and balances in urban public space, with particular attention to the perspective offered by Hannah Arendt's political philosophy.

**Jude Davies** is a Senior Lecturer in the School of Cultural Studies, King Alfred's College of Higher Education, Winchester (U.K.). He is co-author with Carol Smith of *Gender, Ethnicity and Sexuality in Contemporary American Film* (Keele University Press, 1998).

**Lieven De Cauter** is a philosopher and an art historian. He has written three books in Dutch, *Het hiernamaals van de kunst* (1991), *Archeologie van de kick. Verhalen over moderniteit en ervaring* (1995), and *De dwerg in de schaakautomaat. Benjamins verborgen leer* (1999). He has also published poems, columns, essays, and one short story.

**Maarten Delbeke** is a junior faculty member in the Department of Architecture and Urban Planning at the University of Ghent, Belgium. He is currently finishing a doctoral dissertation on the theory of visual arts in Rome (1640-1670) and has published nationally and internationally on the relationship between visual culture and architecture and on contemporary architecture in Belgium. A compilation of essays has appeared as *Aangenaam Verblijf. Teksten 1994-1997* (Vlees & Beton, 1997).

**Dirk De Meyer** is Associate Professor in the Department of Architecture and Urban Planning at the University of Ghent, Belgium, and Co-Director of the Ghent Urban Studies Team. In 1998-1999 he was a Visiting Scholar at the Canadian Centre for Architecture in Montreal. He taught seminars at the Istituto

Universitario di Architettura di Venezia and at Montreal's McGill University. His publications on architectural history include a two-volume book on *Johann Santini Aichel: architectuur en ambiguïteit* (Eindhoven: Technical University Press, 1997).



**Christophe Den Tandt** teaches English and American literature as well as literary theory at the Université Libre de Bruxelles in Brussels, Belgium. His publications about urban fiction include *The Urban Sublime in American Literary Naturalism* (University of Illinois Press, 1998) and articles on postmodern science fiction.

**Bart Eeckhout** is a junior faculty member in the English Department at the University of Ghent, Belgium, where he works as a part-time funded member of GUST. He holds an M.A. from Columbia University (New York) and wrote his Ph.D. dissertation on the poetry of Wallace Stevens. He edited an anthology of international metropolitan short stories translated into Dutch, *City Life* (Meulenhoff-Manteau, 1996), and wrote a book on classical music, *Voorspel* (Atlas, 1997).

**Anne Gotman** is a sociologist who works as a researcher for the French C.N.R.S. (Centre National de la Recherche Scientifique) at the Institut Parisien de Recherche sur l'Architecture, l'Urbanistique et la Société, and is *chargée de mission* at the Plan Urbanisme Construction & Architecture, also in Paris. She is the author of *Hériter* (P.U.F., 1989), *Dilapidation et prodigalité* (Nathan, 1995), and editor of *L'hospitalité,* "Communications" 65 (1997), published by Seuil.

**Alan Hollinghurst** is the author of three novels, *The Swimming-Pool Library* (1988), *The Folding Star* (1994), and *The Spell* (1998), all published by Chatto & Windus, and was on the staff of *The Times Literary Supplement* between 1982 and 1995. He is the recipient of a Somerset Maugham Award, an E. M. Forster Award of the American Academy of Arts and Letters, a James Tait Memorial Prize, and was shortlisted for the 1994 Booker Prize.

**Steven Jacobs** is a junior faculty member in the Department of Architecture and Urban Planning at the University of Ghent, Belgium, where he works as a part-time funded member of GUST. He is also a lecturer in art history at the Architectural Institute St. Lucas (Ghent and Brussels). He has written regularly on art and architecture for various exhibition catalogues and professional journals, authored a book in Dutch on Henry Van de Velde (Van Halewyck, 1996) and a monograph in Dutch and English on the work of Paul Robbrecht and Hilde Daem (Ludion, 1998).

**Liam Kennedy** is Senior Lecturer in American Studies at the University of Birmingham (U.K.). He has published widely in the fields of American literary and cultural studies. He is the author of *Susan Sontag: Mind as Passion* (1995) and *Race and Urban Space in American Culture* (2000), and co-editor of *Urban Space and Representation* (1999). He is co-director of the Three Cities multimedia project (visit the website ‹www.nottingham.ac.uk/3cities›).

**Bart Keunen** is a junior faculty member in the Department of General and Comparative Literature at the University of Ghent, Belgium. He obtained his Ph.D. with a culture-sociological dissertation on city images, chronotopes, and artistic projects in literary prose between 1850 and 1930, reworked as *De verbeelding van de grootstad* (V.U.B. Press, 1999). He publishes mainly on city images, the sociology of literature, and literary historiography.

**Rudi Laermans** is Professor at the Catholic University of Louvain, Belgium, where he teaches sociological theory and sociology of culture. He is the author of several books, including *De lege plek* (1993) and *Schimmenspel. Essays over de hedendaagse onwerkelijkheid* (1997). His main fields of research are social systems theory, theories of (post)modernity, and sociology of the arts (especially the performing arts).

**Sven Lütticken** is an art historian and art critic currently working in the Art History Department of the Free University of Amsterdam in the Netherlands. He is in the process of writing a Ph.D. dissertation on postmodern abstract painting.

**Kevin R. McNamara** is Assistant Professor of Literature at the University of Houston-Clear Lake, Texas, and is the author of *Urban Verbs: Arts and Discourses of American Cities* (Stanford University Press, 1996). He is presently at work on a study of Los Angeles in the American imagination of utopia and dystopia, portions of which are published or forthcoming in *Arizona Quarterly, Contemporary Literature,* and *Productive Postmodernism* (edited by John Duvall).

**Kristiaan Versluys** is the Head of the English Department at the University of Ghent, Belgium, and is Director of the Ghent Urban Studies Team. His many publications on city literature include *The Poet in the City: Chapters in the Development of Urban Poetry in Europe and the United States, 1800-1930* (Gunter Narr Verlag, 1987).

**Trui Vetters** received a B.A. in Germanic Languages and an M.A. in Literary Theory from the University of Ghent, Belgium. She also studied in Italy as an Erasmus Fellow. The past six years she has been a graduate student at Rutgers University's

Department of English, where she is finishing her doctoral dissertation on architecture and 20th-century fiction.

**Cino Zucchi** is a practising architect in Milan (Italy) and Professor in Architectural Design at the Politecnico di Milano. He was a Visiting Professor at the Syracuse University in Florence and at the E.T.H. in Zürich and taught various international seminars (incl. Berlin and Naples). He won several architectural competitions and prizes and published a number of books, most recently a monograph on the Milanese architects Asnago & Vender (Skira, 1999). His essays on the contemporary urban condition appeared in journals like *Domus, Lotus International,* and *Arch+.*

# Works Cited Part One


Allen, Irving Lewis. 1993. *The City in Slang: New York Life and Popular Speech*. New York: Oxford University Press.

Altman, Lawrence K. 1997. "AIDS Deaths in New York City Drop Sharply." *The New York Times on the Web*, 25 January.

Alvarez, Lizette. 1997. "Spanish-English Hybrid Is Spoken With No Apologies." *The New York Times on the Web*, 25 March.

*The American Heritage Dictionary of the English Language*. 3rd edition. 1992. Reprint, Boston: Houghton Mifflin, 1996.

Anz, Thomas. 1982. "Entfremdung und Angst. Expressionistische Psychopathologie und ihre sozialwissenschaftliche Interpretierbarkeit." In Horst Meixner and Silvio Vietta, eds., *Expressionismus — Sozialer Wandel und künstlerische Erfahrung* (München: Fink): 15-29.

Ascher, François. 1997. "De Franse metropolitane regio. Het nieuwe Schéma Directeur van de regio Ile-de-France." In Koos Bosma and Helma Hellinga, eds., *De regie van de stad. Noord-Europese stedebouw 1900-2000* (Vol. 1. Rotterdam: NAi): 48-55.

Augé, Marc. 1995. *Non-places: Introduction to an Anthropology of Supermodernity*. London: Verso.

Bagli, Charles V. 1997. "CBS and ABC Eye Studio Sites in Times Square." *The New York Times on the Web*, 19 November.

Baker, Nicholson. 1995. *Vox*. New York: Random House.

Banham, Reyner. 1971. *Los Angeles: The Architecture of Four Ecologies*. Harmondsworth: Penguin.

Baudrillard, Jean. 1983. *Simulations*. New York: Semiotext(e).

———. 1988. *America*. Transl. Chris Turner. London: Verso.

Bauman, Zygmunt. 1994. "Desert spectacular." In Keith Tester, ed., *The Flâneur* (London: Routledge): 138-57.

Bayley, Stephen. 1991. *Taste: The Secret Meaning of Things*. London: Faber & Faber.

Beck, Ulrich. 1992. *Risk Society: Towards a new modernity*. Transl. Mark Ritter. London: Sage.

Benjamin, Walter. 1935a. "Das Kunstwerk im Zeitalter seiner technischen Reproducierbarkeit." In Walter Benjamin, *Gesammelte Schriften* I 2, ed. Rolf Tiedemann (Frankfurt am Main: Suhrkamp, 1974): 431-70.

———. 1935b. "Paris, die Hauptstadt des XIX. Jahrhunderts." In Walter Benjamin, *Gesammelte Schriften* V, ed. Rolf Tiedemann (Frankfurt am Main: Suhrkamp, 1982): 45-77.

———. 1938. "Das Paris des Second Empire bei Baudelaire." In Walter Benjamin, *Gesammelte Schriften* I 2, ed. Rolf Tiedemann (Frankfurt am Main: Suhrkamp, 1974): 542- 48.

———. 1939 "Über einige Motive bei Baudelaire." In Walter Benjamin, *Gesammelte Schriften* I 2, ed. Rolf Tiedemann (Frankfurt am Main: Suhrkamp, 1974): 605-54.

———. 1982. *Gesammelte Schriften* V *(Das Passagen-Werk)*, ed. Rolf Tiedemann. Frankfurt am Main: Suhrkamp.

Bensman, Joseph, and Arthur J. Vidich. 1975. "Race, Ethnicity and New Forms of Urban Community." Reprinted in Philip Kasinitz, ed., *Metropolis: Center and Symbol of Our Times* (New York: New York University Press, 1995): 196-208.

Berger, Joseph. 1995. "Not in Manhattan And Not Married: Singles Who Prefer the Suburbs." *The New York Times*, 27 December: B1, B4.

Berman, Marshall. 1997. "Signs of the Times: The Lure of 42nd Street." *Dissent* 44, 4 (fall): 76-83.

Betsky, Aaron. 1997. *Queer Space: Architecture and Same-Sex Desire*. New York: William Morrow.

Beveridge, Andrew A. 1996. "Sociologists: Eyes Open for Trends in New York City." *Footnotes* 24, 1 (January): 1, 8.

Beveridge, Andrew A., Susan Weber, and Charis Ng. 1996. "Stroll the Upper East Side for Lifestyles of the Elite." *Footnotes* 24, 3 (March): 1, 6.

Blakely, Edward J., and Mary Gail Snyder. 1997. *Fortress America: Gated Communities in the United States*. Washington, D.C.: Brookings Institution Press.

Body-Gendrot, Sophie. 1995. "Models of Immigrant Integration in France and the United States: Signs of Convergence?" In Michael Peter Smith and Joe R. Feagin, eds., *The Bubbling Cauldron: Race, Ethnicity, and the Urban Crisis* (Minneapolis: University of Minnesota Press): 244-62.

Boeri, Stefano, and Arturo Lanzani. 1992. "Gli orizzonti della città diffusa." *Casabella* 588: 44-59.

Boeri, Stefano, Arturo Lanzani, and Edoardo Marini. 1993a. "Nuovi spazi senza nome/New nameless spaces," *Casabella* 597-598: 74-76, 123-124.

———. 1993b. *Il territorio che cambia: Ambienti, paesaggi e immagini della regione milanese*. Milano: Abitare Segesta Cataloghi.

Bottles, Scott. 1987. *Los Angeles and the Automobile: The Making of the Modern City*. Berkeley and Los Angeles: University of California Press.

Bourdieu, Pierre. 1979. *La Distinction: critique sociale du jugement*. Paris: Minuit.

Boyer, M. Christine. 1994. *The City of Collective Memory: Its Historical Imagery and Architectural Entertainments*. Cambridge, MA.: MIT Press.

———. 1996. *Cybercities: Visual Perception in the Age of Electronic Communication*. New York: Princeton Architectural Press.

Brand, Dana. 1991. *The Spectator and the City in Nineteenth-Century American Literature*. Cambridge: Cambridge University Press.

Bremer, Sidney H. 1992. *Urban Intersections: Meetings of Life and Literature in United States Cities*. Urbana: University of Illinois Press.

Brunet, Roger. 1989. *Les Villes européennes*. Paris.

Buchanan, Peter. 1993. "Oltre il mero abbellimento." *Casabella* 597-98: 31-33.

Buck-Morss, Susan. 1984. "Der Flaneur, der Sandwichman und die Hure. Dialektische Bilder und die Politik des Müßiggangs." In Norbert Bolz and Bernd Witte, eds., *Passagen* (München: Fink): 96-113.

———. 1989. *The Dialectics of Seeing: Walter Benjamin and the Arcades Project*. Cambridge, MA.: MIT Press.

Buelens, Gert. 1999. "James's 'Aliens': Consuming, Performing, and Judging the American Scene." *Modern Philology* 96: 347-63.

Busquets i Grau, Joan. 1992. "Les Diferents Escales de la Projectació Urbanística." In *Urbanisme a Barcelona: Plans cap al 92* (Barcelona: Ajuntament de Barcelona, Àrea d'Urbanisme i Obres Públiques, Planejament Urbanístic): VIII-XX.

Calhoun, Craig. 1986. "Computer Technology, Large-Scale Social Integration and the Local Community." *Urban Affairs Quarterly* 22, 2: 329-49.

Calthorpe, Peter. 1993. *The Next American Metropolis: Ecology, Community and the American Dream*. Princeton: Princeton University Press.

Calvino, Italo. 1978. *Invisible Cities*. Transl. William Weaver. San Diego: Harcourt Brace and Company.

Castells, Manuel. 1972. *La Question urbaine*. Paris: Maspéro.

———. 1989. *The Informational City: Information Technology, Economic Restructuring, and the Urban-Regional Process*. Oxford: Blackwell.

———. 1996. "Globalization, Flows and Identity: The New Challenges of Design." In William S. Saunders, ed., *Reflections on Architectural Practices in the Nineties* (New York: Princeton Architectural Press): 198-205.

Castells, Manuel, and Peter Hall. 1994. *Technopoles of the World: The Making of 21st Century Industrial Complexes*. London: Routledge.

Chambers, Deborah. 1997. "A Stake in the Country: Women's experiences of suburban development." In Roger Silverstone, ed., *Visions of Suburbia* (London: Routledge): 86-107.

Chambers, Iain. 1986. *Popular Culture: The Metropolitan Experience*. Reprint, London: Routledge, 1993.

Chaney, David. 1996. *Lifestyles*. London: Routledge.

Chickering, Roger. 1993. *Karl Lamprecht: A German Academic Life, 1856-1915*. Atlantic Highlands, N.J.: Humanities Press.

Cohen, Jean-Louis, and Hubert Damisch. 1993. *Américanisme et modernité. L'idéal américain dans l'architecture*. Paris: Flammarion.

Corboz, André. 1992. "De stedebouw van de 20ste eeuw: een profiel." *Archis* 5: 49-52.

Craven, Paul, and Barry Wellmann. 1973. "The Network City." *Social Inquiry* 43: 57-58.

Cronenberg, David. 1996. "Op elkaar inrammen." Interview by Patrick Duynslaegher. *Knack*, 30 October: 72-74.

Daniele, Daniela. 1994. *Città senza mappa: Paesaggi urbani e racconto postmoderno in America*. Alessandria: Edizione dell'Orso.

Davis, Mike. 1990. *City of Quartz: Excavating the Future in Los Angeles*. New York: Verso.

Dear, Michael. 1995. "Prolegomena to a Post-modern Urbanism." In P. Healy, S. Cameron, S. Davoudi, S. Graham, and A. Madani Pour, eds., *Managing Cities: The New Urban Context* (London: Wiley): 27-44.

de Certeau, Michel. 1984. *The Practice of Everyday Life*. Trans. Steven Rendall. Berkeley and Los Angeles: University of California Press.

de Solà-Morales, Manuel. 1992. "Openbare en collectieve ruimte. De verstedelijking van het privé-domein als nieuwe uitdaging." *Oase* 33: 3-8.

Dethier, Jean, and Alain Guiheux. 1994. *La ville, art et architecture en Europe, 1870-1993*. Paris: Editions du Centre Pompidou.

Dupuy, Gabriel. 1991. *L'urbanisme des réseaux*. Paris: Armand Collin.

Eco, Umberto. 1986. *Travels in Hyperreality: Essays*. Transl. William Weaver. Reprint, San Diego: Harvest/HBJ, 1990.

Ellin, Nan. 1996. *Postmodern Urbanism*. Cambridge, MA.: Blackwell.

———. 1997. "Shelter from the Storm or Form Follows Fear and Vice Versa." In Nan Ellin, ed., *Architecture of Fear* (New York: Princeton University Press): 13-45.

Epstein, Steven. 1990. "Gay Politics, Ethnic Identity: The Limits of Social Constructionism." In Edward Stein, ed., *Forms of Desire: Sexual Orientation and the Social Constructionist Controversy* (reprint, New York: Routledge, 1992): 239-93.

Falk, Pasi. 1994. *The Consuming Body*. London: Sage.

Featherstone, Mike. 1991. *Consumer Culture and Postmodernism*. London: Sage.

Fein, Esther B. 1994. "Elderly Find Hardship in Haven for Young." *The New York Times*, 19 July: A1, B5.

Fischer, Claude S. 1973. "On Urban Alienations and Anomie: Powerlessness and Social Alienation." *American Sociological Review* 38 (June): 311-26.

———. 1984. *The Urban Experience*. 2nd edition. New York: Harcourt, Brace, Jovanovich.

Fishman, Robert. 1987. *Bourgeois Utopias: The Rise and Fall of Suburbia*. New York: Basic Books.

———. 1990. "America's New City: Megalopolis Unbound." *Wilson Quarterly* 14, 1 (winter): 25-48.

Flanagan, William G. 1993. *Contemporary urban sociology*. Cambridge: Cambridge University Press.

Flusty, Steven. 1997. "Building Paranoia." In Nan Ellin, ed., *Architecture of Fear* (New York: Princeton University Press): 47-59.

Fogelson, Robert M. 1967. *The Fragmented Metropolis: Los Angeles, 1850-1930*. Reprint, Berkeley and Los Angeles: University of California Press.

Fourcaut, Annie, ed. 1996. *La Ville divisée: les ségrégations urbaines en question, France* XVIIIe-XXe *siècles*. Grâne: Créaphis.

Fourquet, François, and Lion Murard. 1973. *Les Equipements du pouvoir. Villes, territoires et équipements collectifs*. Paris: UGE.

Freisfeld, Andreas. 1982. *Das Leiden an der Stadt*. Köln-Wien: Böhlau Verlag.

Frey, Dagobert. 1972. "Wesensbestimmung der Architektur." *Kunstwissenschaftliche Grundfragen*: 92-106.

Friedmann, John. 1973. "The Future of the Urban Habitat." In S. P. Snow, ed., *The Place of Planning* (Auburn: Auburn University Printing Service): 105-41.

Fuss, Diana. 1991. "Introduction." In Diana Fuss, ed., *Inside/Out: Lesbian Theories, Gay Theories* (New York: Routledge): 1-10.

Gallagher, Winifred. 1993. *The Power of Place: How Our Surroundings Shape Our Thoughts, Emotions, and Actions*. Reprint, New York: HarperPerennial, 1994.

Gans, Herbert J. 1967. *The Levittowners*. New York: Pantheon.

Garber, Marjorie. 1995. *Vice Versa: Bisexuality and the Eroticism of Everyday Life*. Reprint, New York: Touchstone, 1996.

Garreau, Joel. 1991. *Edge City: Life on the New Frontier*. New York: Anchor Books.

Gebhardt, Eike. 1988. "Die Stadt als moralische Anstalt. Zum Mythos der kranken Stadt." In Klaus R. Scherpe, ed., *Die Unwirklichkeit der Städte: Großstadtdarstellungen zwischen Moderne und Postmoderne* (Reinbek: Rowohlt): 279-303.

Ghirardo, Diane. 1996. *Architecture After Modernism*. Singapore: Thames and Hudson.

Glaberson, William. 1997. "Widespread Drop in Crime Found in N.Y. Suburbs, but Some Areas Worsen." *The New York Times on the Web*, 27 February.

Goffman, Erving. 1959. *The Presentation of Self in Everyday Life*. Reprint, Harmondsworth: Penguin, 1978.

———. 1963. *Behavior in Public Places*. New York: The Free Press.

Goldberg, Carey. 1996. "Suburban Sprawl Eating Up California's Best Farm Land." *The New York Times on the Web*, 20 June.

———. 1997. "In Seattle, 'Being Seen' Carries Special Cachet." *The New York Times on the Web*, 6 February.

Goldberg, David Theo. 1994. "Introduction: Multicultural Conditions." In David Theo Goldberg, ed., *Multiculturalism: A Critical Reader* (Oxford: Blackwell): 1-41.

Gottdiener, M., and George Kephart. 1991. "The Multinucleated Metropolitan Region: A Comparative Analysis." In Rob Kling, Spencer Olin, and Mark Poster, eds., *Postsuburban California: The Transformation of Orange County since World War* II (reprint, Berkeley and Los Angeles: University of California Press, 1995): 31-54.

Gottmann, Jean. 1961. *Megalopolis: The Urbanized Northeastern Seaboard of the United States*. New York: Twentieth Century Fund.

———. 1979. "Office Work and the Evolution of Cities." In Jean Gottmann and Robert A. Harper, eds., *Since Megalopolis: The Urban Writings of Jean Gottmann* (Baltimore: Johns Hopkins University Press, 1990): 185-91.

Gottmann, Jean, and Robert A. Harper, eds. 1990. *Since Megalopolis: The Urban Writings of Jean Gottmann*. Baltimore: Johns Hopkins University Press.

Graafland, Arie. 1996. *Architectural Bodies*. Rotterdam: 010 Publishers.

Graham, Stephen, and Simon Marvin. 1996. *Telecommunications and the City: Electronic Spaces, Urban Places*. London: Routledge.

Hall, Peter. 1966. *Seven World Cities*. London: Weidenfeld and Nicholson.

———. 1988. "Anonymity and identity in the giant metropolis." In Luigi Mazza, ed., *World cities and the future of the metropoles: International participations* (Milan: Electa): 43-50.

Hannigan, John. 1998. *Fantasy City: Pleasure and profit in the postmodern metropolis*. London: Routledge.

Harvey, David. 1988. "Urban places in the 'Global Village': reflections on the urban condition in late twentieth century capitalism." In Luigi Mazza, ed., *World cities and the future of the metropoles: International participations* (Milan: Electa): 21-32.

———. 1989a. *The Condition of Postmodernity: An Enquiry into the Origins of Cultural Change*. Oxford: Blackwell.

———. 1989b. *The Urban Experience*. Baltimore: Johns Hopkins University Press.

Hauser, Arnold. 1951. *The Social History of Art 4: Naturalism, Impressionism, The Film Age*. New York: Vintage Books.

Hauser, Susanne. 1990. *Der Blick auf die Stadt. Semiotische Untersuchungen zur literarischen Wahrnehmung bis 1910*. Berlin: Reimer Verlag.

Hayden, Dolores. 1981. "What Would a Non-sexist City Be Like? Speculations on Housing, Urban Design, and Human Work." Reprinted in Richard T. LeGates and Frederic Stout, eds., *The City Reader* (London: Routledge, 1996): 142-57.

Hebbert, Michael. 1998. *London: More by Fortune than Design*. Chichester: John Wiley & Sons.

Hebdige, Dick. 1979. *Subculture: The Meaning of Style*. London: Routledge.

Hekma, Gert. 1999. "Amsterdam." In David Higgs, ed., *Queer Sites: Gay urban histories since 1600* (London: Routledge): 61-88.

Hendrickson, Robert. 1998. *New Yawk Tawk: A Dictionary of New York City Expressions*. New York: Checkmark Books.

Heynen, Hilde. 1990. "Fragmentatie in de periferie. De 'tapijtmetropool' van Willem-Jan Neutelings." *Archis* 3: 16-21.

Heynen, Hilde, André Loeckx, and Marcel Smets. 1989. *The Periphery: An Exploratory Study*. Synthesis of a seminar in Leuven, 26-28 October 1989.

Higgs, David, ed. 1999. *Queer Sites: Gay urban histories since 1600*. London: Routledge.

Holl, Steven. 1996. *Intertwining*. New York: Princeton Architectural Press.

Hollinger, David. 1995. *Post-ethnic America: Beyond Multiculturalism*. New York: Basic Books.

Hollingshead, A. B., and F. C. Redlich. 1964. *Social Class and Mental Illness*. New York.

Hübner-Funk, Sibylle. 1976. "Ästhetizismus und Soziologie bei Georg Simmel." In Hannes Böhringer and Karlfried Gründer, eds., *Ästhetik und Soziologie um die Jahrhundertwende: Georg Simmel* (Frankfurt am Main: Klostermann): 44-70.

———. 1984. "Die ästhetische Konstituierung gesellschaftlicher Erkenntnis am Beispiel der 'Philosophie des Geldes.'" In Heinz-Jürgen Dahme and Otthein Rammstedt, eds., *Georg Simmel und die Moderne. Neue Interpretationen und Materialien* (Frankfurt am Main: Suhrkamp): 183-201.

Ibelings, Hans. 1998. *Supermodernisme. Architectuur in het tijdperk van de globalisering*. Rotterdam: NAi Uitgevers.

Ingram, Gordon Brent, Anne-Marie Bouthillette, and Yolanda Retter, eds. 1997. *Queers in Space: Communities / Public Places / Sites of Resistance*. Seattle: Bay Press.

Isernhagen, Hartwig. 1983. "Die Bewußtseinskrise der Moderne und die Erfahrung der Stadt als Labyrinth." In Cord Meckeseper and Elisabeth Schraut, eds., *Die Stadt in der Literatur* (Göttingen: Vandenhoek and Ruprecht): 81-104.

Jackson, Kenneth T. 1985. *Crabgrass Frontier: The Suburbanization of the United States*. New York: Oxford University Press.

———, ed. 1995. *The Encyclopedia of New York City*. New Haven: Yale University Press; New York: The New-York Historical Society.

Jacobs, Allan, and Donald Appleyard. 1987. "Toward an Urban Design Manifesto." *Journal of the American Planning Association* 53, 1: 112-20.

Jacobs, Jane. 1961. *The Death and Life of Great American Cities*. New York: Random House.

Jacobs, Steven. 1995. "Landscape Without a Home." In *The Landscape: Four International Landscape Designers* (Antwerp: deSingel): 125-38.

James, Henry. 1907. *The American Scene*. Reprinted in Henry James, *Collected Travel Writings: Great Britain and America* (New York: The Library of America, 1993): 351-736.

Jameson, Fredric. 1991. *Postmodernism, or, The Cultural Logic of Late Capitalism*. London: Verso.

———. 1996. "Space Wars." *London Review of Books* 18, 7 (4 April): 14-15.

Jaye, Michael C., and Ann C. Watts, eds. 1981. *Literature and Urban Experience: Essays on the City and Literature*. New Brunswick: Rutgers University Press.

Jencks, Charles. 1993. *Heteropolis: Los Angeles - The Riots and the Strange Beauty of Hetero-Architecture*. London: Academy Editions.

Kadushin, Charles. 1966. "The Friends and Supporters of Psychotherapy: On Social Circles in Urban Life." *American Sociological Review*: 786-802.

Kasinitz, Phil. 1996. "For the Discerning Sociologist It's More Than a Helluva Town." http://www.soc.qc.edu/Maps/nyrpt.html (18 July 1996).

Kearns, Gerry, and Chris Philo, eds. 1993. *Selling Places: The City as Cultural Capital, Past and Present*. Oxford: Pergamon Press.

Keil, Roger, and Klaus Ronneberger. 1994. "Going Up the Country: Internationalization and Urbanization on Frankfurt's Northern Fringe." *Environment and Planning D: Society and Space* 12: 137-66.

Keunen, Gert, and Bart Keunen. 1996. "Stadsnomaden in downtown New York." In René Boomkens and René Gabriëls, eds., *Een alledaagse passie. 20 essays over popmuziek* (Amsterdam: De Balie): 172-84.

Kleinfeld, N. R. with Tracie Rozhon. 1995. "In Flat Market, Co-op Life Has Steep Ups and Downs." *The New York Times*, 30 October: B1-2.

Kling, Rob, Spencer Olin, and Mark Poster, eds. 1991. *Postsuburban California: The Transformation of Orange County since World War II*. Reprint, Berkeley and Los Angeles: University of California Press, 1995.

———. 1995. "Preface to the Paperback Edition: Beyond the Edge: The Dynamism of Postsuburban Regions." In Rob Kling, Spencer Olin, and Mark Poster, eds., *Postsuburban California: The Transformation of Orange County since World War II* (Berkeley and Los Angeles: University of California Press): VII-XX.

Koolhaas, Rem. 1978. *Delirious New York: A Retroactive Manifesto for Manhattan*. New edition, Rotterdam: 010 Publishers, 1994.

———. 1987/1994. "Atlanta." Reprinted in Office for Metropolitan Architecture, Rem Koolhaas, and Bruce Mau, *Small, Medium, Large, Extra-Large*, ed. Jennifer Sigler (Rotterdam: 010 Publishers, 1995): 833-58.

———. 1988. "Postscript: Introduction for New Research 'The Contemporary City.'" *Architecture and Urbanism* 217 (October): 152.

———. 1989. "Toward the Contemporary City." *Design Book Review* 17 (winter): 15-16.

———. 1994. "The Generic City." Reprinted in Office for Metropolitan Architecture, Rem Koolhaas, and Bruce Mau, *Small, Medium, Large, Extra-Large*, ed. Jennifer Sigler (Rotterdam: 010 Publishers, 1995): 1239-64.

———. 1996. "Beyond Delirious." In Kate Nesbitt, ed., *Theorizing a New Agenda for Architecture: An Anthology of Architectural Theory, 1965-1995* (New York: Princeton Architectural Press): 332-36.

Kraus, Clifford. 1996. "New York Crime Rate Is Lowest in 30 Years." *The New York Times on the Web*, 20 December.

Krier, Léon. 1992. *Leon Krier: Architecture and Urban Design, 1967-1992*. London: Academy Editions.

Kroll, Lucien. 1987. *An Architecture of Complexity*. Cambridge, MA.: MIT Press.

Kunzmann, Klaus R. 1997. "De toekomst van de stedelijke regio in Europa." In Koos Bosma and Helma Hellinga, eds., *De regie van de stad. Noord-Europese stedebouw 1900-2000* (Vol. 1. Rotterdam: NAi): 16-29.

Laermans, Rudi. 1992. *In de greep van de Moderne Tijd: modernisering en verzuiling*. Leuven: Garant.

———. 1997. "De Romaneske Stad. Over de anonimiteit van het persoonlijke." In *Schimmenspel. Essays over de hedendaagse onwerkelijkheid* (Leuven: Van Halewyck): 11-36.

Lagrou, Evert. 1993. "Urbanisatie-suburbanisatie-desurbanisatie." In Ed Taverne and Irmin Visser, eds., *Stedebouw. De geschiedenis van de stad in de Nederlanden van 1500 tot heden* (Nijmegen: SUN): 266-75.

Langer, Peter. 1984. "Four Images of Organized Diversity: Bazaar, Jungle, Organism, and Machine." In

Lloyd Rodwin and Robert M. Hollister, eds., *Cities of the Mind: Images and Themes of the City in the Social Sciences* (New York: Plenum Press): 97-117.

Langman, Lauren. 1992. "Neon Cages: Shopping for subjectivity." In Rob Shields, ed., *Lifestyle Shopping: The Subject of Consumption* (London: Routledge): 40-82.

Lash, Scott. 1990. *Sociology of Postmodernism*. London: Methuen.

Le Corbusier. 1937. *Quand les Cathédrales étaient blanches. Voyage au pays des timides*. Paris: Denoël/Gonthier.

Lehan, Richard. 1998. *The City in Literature: An Intellectual and Cultural History*. Berkeley and Los Angeles: University of California Press.

Lesage, Dieter. 1997. "De smetvrees van suburbia." *Dietsche Warande & Belfort* (March- April): 133-39.

LeVay, Simon, and Elisabeth Nonas. 1995. *City of Friends: A Portrait of the Gay and Lesbian Community in America*. Cambridge, MA.: MIT Press.

Levy, Diane Wolfe. 1978. "City Signs: Toward a Definition of Urban Literature." *Modern Fiction Studies* 24, 1 (spring): 65-73.

Lovett, Anthony R., and Matt Maranian. 1997. *L.A. Bizarro! The Insider's Guide to the Obscure, the Absurd, and the Perverse in Los Angeles*. New York: St. Martin's Press.

Lynch, Kevin. 1960. *The Image of the City*. Cambridge, MA.: MIT Press.

Maffi, Mario. 1994. *Gateway to the Promised Land: Ethnic cultures on New York's Lower East Side*. Amsterdam: Rodopi.

Marcuse, Peter. 1995. "Not Chaos, but Walls: Postmodernism and the Partitioned City." In Sophie Watson and Katherine Gibson, eds., *Postmodern Cities and Spaces* (Oxford: Blackwell): 243-53.

———. 1997. "Walls of Fear and Walls of Support." In Nan Ellin, ed., *Architecture of Fear* (New York: Princeton University Press): 101-14.

Marinetti, Filippo Tommaso. 1909. "The Founding and Manifesto of Futurism." In Umbro Apollonio, ed., *Futurist Manifestos* (London: Thames and Hudson, 1973): 19-23.

Marot, Sébastien. 1995. "The Landscape as Alternative." In *The Landscape: Four International Landscape Designers* (Antwerp: deSingel): 9-36.

Marsh, Margaret. 1994. "(Ms)Reading the Suburbs." *American Quarterly* 46, 1 (March): 40-48.

Massey, Douglas S., and Nancy A. Denton. 1993. *American Apartheid: Segregation and the Making of the Underclass*. Cambridge, MA.: Harvard University Press.

McGuire, Scott. 1998. *Visions of modernity: Representation, memory, time and space in the age of the camera*. London: Sage.

McKenzie, Evan. 1994. *Privatopia: Homeowner Associations and the Rise of Residential Private Government*. New Haven: Yale University Press.

Meixner, Horst, and Silvio Vietta, eds. 1982. *Expressionismus - Sozialer Wandel und künstlerische Erfahrung*. München: Fink.

Meyer, Han. 1996. *De stad en de haven. Stedebouw als culturele opgave in Londen, Barcelona, New York en Rotterdam: veranderende relaties tussen stedelijke openbare ruimte en grootschalige infrastructuur*. Utrecht: Uitgeverij Jan van Arkel.

Moos, Rudolf H., and Evelyn Bromet, eds. 1976. *Human Context: Environmental Determinants of Behavior*. New York: Wiley.

Morrison, Toni. 1992. *Jazz*. Reprint, London: Picador, 1993.

Müller, Lothar. 1987. "Modernität, Nervosität und Sachlichkeit. Das Berlin der Jahrhundertwende als Hauptstadt der 'neuen Zeit.'" In U. Bahr, ed., *Mythos Berlin: Zur Wahrnehmungsgeschichte einer industriellen Metropole* (Berlin: Ästhetik und Kommunikation): 79-92.

———. 1988. "Die Großstadt als Ort der Moderne." In Klaus R. Scherpe, ed., *Die Unwirklichkeit der Städte: Großstadtdarstellungen zwischen Moderne und Postmoderne* (Reinbek: Rowohlt): 14-36.

———. 1990. "Impressionistische Kultur. Zur Ästhetik von Modernität und Großstadt um 1900." In Thomas Steinfeld and Heidrun Suhr, eds., *In der großen Stadt. Die Metropole als kulturtheoretische Kategorie* (Frankfurt am Main: A. Hain): 41-70

Muller, Peter. 1978. *The Suburbanization of Corporate Headquarters*. Englewood Cliffs, N.J.: Prentice Hall.

Mumford, Lewis. 1937. "What Is a City?" Reprinted in Richard T. LeGates and Frederic Stout, eds., *The City Reader* (London: Routledge, 1996): 183-88.

———. 1938. *The Culture of Cities*. New York: Harcourt Brace.

Nagourney, Adam. 1997. "Poll Finds Optimism in New York, but Race and Class Affect Views." *The New York Times on the Web*, 12 March.

Naisbitt, John, and Patricia Aburdene. 1990. *Megatrends 2000: Ten Directions for the 1990s*. New York: Avon Books.

Neutelings, Willem-Jan. 1988. *De ringcultuur*. Mechelen: Vlees & Beton.

———. 1989. *De transformatie van de Haagse Zuidrand*. Stedebouwkundige studie in opdracht van de Dienst Stadsontwikkeling en Grondzaken van de gemeente 's-Gravenhage.

Newman, Oscar. 1972. *Defensible Space: Crime Prevention through Urban Design*. New York: Macmillan.

Ong, Paul, and Evelyn Blumenberg. 1996. "Income and Racial Inequality in Los Angeles." In Allen J. Scott and Edward W. Soja, eds., *The City: Los Angeles and Urban Theory at the End of the Twentieth Century* (Berkeley and Los Angeles: University of California Press): 311-35.

Parker, John. 1995. "Turn up the lights" ("A Survey of Cities"). *The Economist*, 29 July: 3- 13.

Peters, Laura. 1996. Review of Laura Chrisman and Patrick Williams, eds., *Colonial Discourse and Post-Colonial Theory*, and David Theo Goldberg, ed., *Multiculturalism: A Critical Reader. Textual Practice* 10, 2 (summer): 398-404.

Pike, Burton. 1981. *The Image of the City in Modern Literature*. Princeton: Princeton University Press.

Pope, Albert. 1996. *Ladders*. New York: Princeton Architectural Press.

Porter, Roy. 1994. *London: A Social History*. London: Hamish Hamilton.

Poster, Mark. 1991. "Narcissism or Liberation? The Affluent Middle-Class Family." In Rob Kling, Spencer Olin, and Mark Poster, eds., *Postsuburban California: The Transformation of Orange County since World War II* (reprint, Berkeley and Los Angeles: University of California Press, 1995): 190-222.

Rapoport, Amos. 1977. *Human Aspects of Urban Form: Towards a Man-Environment Approach to Urban Form and Design*. Oxford: Pergamon.

Roberts, Sam. 1994. "Gap Between Rich and Poor in New York City Grows Wider." *The New York Times*, 25 December: 33-34.

———. 1995. "Women's Work: What's New, What Isn't." *The New York Times*, 27 April.

Rogin, Michael. 1996. "Crowing." *London Review of Books* 18, 17 (5 September): 26-27.

Rossi, Aldo. 1982. *The Architecture of the City*. Cambridge, MA.: MIT Press.

Rowe, Colin, and Fred Koetter. 1978. *Collage City*. Reprint, Cambridge, MA.: MIT Press, 1995.

Rowe, Peter G. 1991. *Making a Middle Landscape*. Cambridge, MA.: MIT Press.

Rozhon, Tracie, with N. R. Kleinfeld. 1995. "Getting Into Co-ops: The Money Bias." *The New York Times*, 31 October: B1-2.

Rutheiser, Charles. 1996. *Imagineering Atlanta: The Politics of Place in the City of Dreams*. London: Verso.

Rybczynski, Witold. 1995. *City Life: Urban Expectations in a New World*. New York: Scribner.

Sabagh, Georges, and Mehdi Bozorgmehr. 1996. "Population Change: Immigration and Ethnic Transformation." In Roger Waldinger and Mehdi Bozorgmehr, eds., *Ethnic Los Angeles* (New York: Russell Sage Foundation): 79-107.

Saegert, Susan. 1981. "Masculine Cities and Feminine Suburbs: Polarized Ideas, Contradictory Realities." In Catharine Stimpson et al., eds. *Women and the American City* (Chicago: University of Chicago Press): 93-108.

Sandercock, Leonie, and Ann Forsyth. 1992. "A Gender Agenda: New Directions for Planning Theory." Reprinted in Richard T. LeGates and Frederic Stout, eds., *The City Reader* (London: Routledge, 1996): 407-20.

Sanders, Joel, ed. 1996. *Stud: Architectures of Masculinity*. New York: Princeton Architectural Press.

Sassen, Saskia. 1991. *The Global City: New York, London, Tokyo*. Princeton: Princeton University Press.

———. 1996. "The New Centrality: The Impact of Telematics and Globalization." In William S. Saunders, ed., *Reflections on Architectural Practices in the Nineties* (New York: Princeton Architectural Press): 206-18.

Schjeldahl, Peter. 1991. *The Hydrogen Jukebox: Selected Writings of Peter Schjeldahl, 1978- 1990*. Berkeley and Los Angeles: University of California Press.

Scott, Allen J. 1996. "The Manufacturing Economy: Ethnic and Gender Divisions of Labor." In Roger Waldinger and Mehdi Bozorgmehr, eds., *Ethnic Los Angeles* (New York: Russell Sage Foundation): 215-44.

Scott, Janny. 1997. "City's (Cranky) Mood Is (or Seems) High (for Some)." *The New York Times on the Web*, 9 February.

Scotti, Anna, and Paul Young. 1997. *Buzzwords: L.A. Freshspeak*. New York: St. Martin's Press.

Secchi, Bernardo. 1985. "Il territorio abbandonato/The abandoned territory." *Casabella* 512: 18-19.

———. 1993. "Un'urbanistica di spazi aperti/For a town planning of open spaces." *Casabella* 597-98: 5-9, 116-17.

Sennett, Richard. 1976. *The Fall of Public Man*. New York: Alfred A. Knopf.

———. 1994. *Flesh and Stone: The Body and the City in Western Civilization*. New York: W. W. Norton.
Shannon, Kelly. 1998. "The Great Leap Backwards. New Urbanism in America." *Archis* 3: 8-19.
Sharpe, William, and Leonard Wallock. 1987. "From 'Great Town' to 'Nonplace Urban Realm': Reading the Modern City." In William Sharpe and Leonard Wallock, eds., *Visions of the Modern City: Essays in History, Art, and Literature* (Baltimore: Johns Hopkins University Press): 1-50.
———. 1994. "Bold New City or Built-Up 'Burb? Redefining Contemporary Suburbia." *American Quarterly* 46, 1 (March): 1-30.
Shields, Rob. 1994. "Fancy footwork: Walter Benjamin's notes on *flânerie*." In Keith Tester, ed., *The Flâneur* (London: Routledge): 61-80.
Sibalis, Michael D. 1999. "Paris." In David Higgs, ed., *Queer Sites: Gay urban histories since 1600* (London: Routledge): 10-37.
Sibley-Fries, Marilyn. 1980. *The Changing Consciousness of Reality: The Image of Berlin in Selected German Novels from Raabe to Döblin*. Bonn: Bouvier Verlag.
Sieverts, Thomas. 1997. *Zwischenstadt: Zwischen Ort und Welt, Raum und Zeit, Stadt und Land*. Wiesbaden: Vieweg Verlag.
Simmel, Georg. 1903. "The Metropolis and Mental Life." Reprinted in Donald N. Levine, ed., *Georg Simmel on Individuality and Social Forms* (Chicago: University of Chicago Press, 1971): 324-39.
———. 1908a. "The Stranger." Reprinted in Donald N. Levine, ed., *Georg Simmel on Individuality and Social Forms* (Chicago: University of Chicago Press, 1971): 143-49.
———. 1908b. "The Web of Group Affiliations." Reprinted in Werner Sollors, ed., *Theories of Ethnicity: A Classical Reader* (New York: New York University Press, 1955): 42-51.
Sinfield, Alan. 1996. "Diaspora and hybridity: queer identities and the ethnicity model." *Textual Practice* 10, 2 (summer): 271-93.
Smets, Marcel. 1993. "De zoektocht van de stedebouw in België." In Ed Taverne and Irmin Visser, eds., *Stedebouw. De geschiedenis van de stad in de Nederlanden van 1500 tot heden* (Nijmegen: SUN): 283-87.
Smith, Michael Peter, and Joe R. Feagin. 1995. "Putting 'Race' in Its Place." In Michael Peter Smith and Joe R. Feagin, eds., *The Bubbling Cauldron: Race, Ethnicity and the Urban Crisis* (Minneapolis: University of Minnesota Press): 3-27.
Smith, Neil. 1986. "Gentrification, the Frontier, and the Restructuring of Urban Space." Reprinted in Susan Fainstein and Scott Campbell, eds., *Readings in Urban Theory* (Oxford: Blackwell, 1996): 338-58.
———. 1996a. "After Tompkins Square Park: Degentrification and the Revanchist City." In Anthony D. King, ed., *Re-Presenting the City: Ethnicity, Capital and Culture in the 21st- Century Metropolis* (New York: New York University Press): 93-107.
———. 1996b. *The New Urban Frontier: Gentrification and the revanchist city*. London: Routledge.
Soja, Edward W. 1992. "Inside Exopolis: Scenes from Orange County." In Michael Sorkin, ed., *Variations on a Theme Park: The New American City and the End of Public Space* (New York: Hill and Wang): 94-122.
Sollors, Werner. 1996. "Foreword: Theories of American Ethnicity." In Werner Sollors, ed., *Theories of Ethnicity: A Classical Reader* (New York: New York University Press): x-xliv.
Sorkin, Michael, ed. 1990. *Variations on a Theme Park: The New American City and the End of Public Space*. New York: Hill and Wang.
Spivak, Gayatri Chakravorty. 1996. "Diasporas old and new: women in the transnational world." *Textual Practice* 10, 2 (summer): 245-69.
Steinfeld, Thomas, and Heidrun Suhr, eds. 1990. *In der großen Stadt. Die Metropole als kulturtheoretische Kategorie*. Frankfurt am Main: A. Hain.
Stilgoe, John R. 1983. *Metropolitan Corridor: Railroads and the American Scene*. New Haven: Yale University Press.
———. 1988. *Borderland: Origins of the American Suburb, 1820-1939*. New Haven: Yale University Press.
Sudjic, Deyan. 1992. *The 100 Mile City*. Reprint, London: Flamingo, 1993.
Suttles, Gerald. 1972. *The Social Construction of Communities*. Chicago: University of Chicago Press.

Taverne, Ed. 1989. "Sleutelen aan een draaiende motor. Bernardo Secchi's plan voor Siena." *Archis* 12: 15-21.
Teaford, Jon C. 1993. *The Twentieth-century American City*. Baltimore: Johns Hopkins University Press.
Teyssot, Georges, ed. 1988. *World cities and the future of the metropoles: Beyond the city, the metropolis*. Milan: Electa.
Thornton, Sarah. 1997. "General introduction." In Ken Gelder and Sarah Thornton, eds., *The Subcultures Reader* (London: Routledge): 1-7.
Tierney, John. 1995. "The Big City; You Could Look It Up." *The New York Times Book Review on the Web*, 24 September.
Tilman, Harm. 1997. "De Nederlandse metropolitane regio." In Koos Bosma and Helma Hellinga, eds., *De regie van de stad. Noord-Europese stedebouw 1900-2000* (Vol. 1. Rotterdam: NAi): 76-85.

Venturi, Robert, Denise Scott Brown, and Steven Izenour. 1972. *Learning from Las Vegas: The Forgotten Symbolism of Architectural Form*. Reprint, Cambridge, MA.: MIT Press, 1991.

Vermeulen, Paul. 1994. "The Terrible Beauty of the Twentieth Century: *A Portrait of Rem Koolhaas*." In Jozef Deleu, ed., *The Low Countries: Arts and Society in Flanders and the Netherlands: A Yearbook, 1994-1995* (Bruges: Stichting Ons Erfdeel): 223-28.

Verschaffel, Bart. 1991. "Monumenten, herinneringen." *Archis* 7: 48-50.

Versluys, Kristiaan. 1987. *The Poet in the City: Chapters in the Development of Urban Poetry in Europe and the United States, 1800-1930*. Tübingen: Gunter Narr Verlag.

Virilio, Paul. 1984. *L'horizon négatif: essai de dromoscopie*. Paris: Galilée.

———. 1991. *The Aesthetics of Disappearance*. Transl. Philip Beitchman. Brooklyn: Autonomedia.

von Petz, Ursula. 1997. "De Duitse metropolitane regio. Het Ruhrgebied: naar een nieuw ruimtelijk beleid." In Koos Bosma and Helma Hellinga, eds., *De regie van de stad. Noord-Europese stedebouw 1900-2000* (Vol. 1. Rotterdam: NAi): 56-65.

Wachs, Martin. 1996. "The Evolution of Transportation Policy in Los Angeles: Images of Past Policies and Future Prospects." In Allen J. Scott and Edward W. Soja, eds., *The City: Los Angeles and Urban Theory at the End of the Twentieth Century* (Berkeley and Los Angeles: University of California Press): 106-59.

Wachtel, Edward. 1977/1978. "The Influence of the Window on Western Art and Vision." *The Structurist* 17-18: 4-10.

Wacquant, Loïc J. D. 1993. "Urban Outcasts: Stigma and Division in the Black American Ghetto and the French Urban Periphery." *International Journal of Urban and Regional Research* 17, 3: 366-83.

Waldinger, Roger. 1996. *Still the Promised City? African-Americans and New Immigrants in Postindustrial New York*. Cambridge, MA.: Harvard University Press.

Waldinger, Roger, and Mehdi Bozorgmehr, eds. 1996. *Ethnic Los Angeles*. New York: Russell Sage Foundation.

Warner, Sam Bass, Jr. 1972. *The Urban Wilderness: A History of the American City*. Reprint, Berkeley and Los Angeles: University of California Press, 1995.

Webb, Michael. 1996. "So wie heute, nur übersteigert. Die glaubhafte Anti-Utopie von Blade Runner." In Dietrich Neumann, ed., *Filmarchitektur. Von Metropolis bis Blade Runner* (Frankfurt am Main: Deutsches Architektur-Museum und Deutsches Filmmuseum): 44-49.

Webber, Melvin. 1964. "The Urban Place and the Nonplace Urban Realm." In Melvin Webber et al., eds., *Explorations into Urban Structure* (Philadelphia: University of Pennsylvania Press): 79-153.

Weber, Bruce. 1997a. "Take My City. Please. Crime Is Down. Streets Are Clean. What's a New York Comedian to Do?" *The New York Times on the Web*, 12 January.

———. 1997b. "NYC Mayor Says 1996 Filmmaking in City Set Records." *The New York Times on the Web*, 5 February.

Weber, Max. 1905. *The City*. Trans. and ed. Don Martindale and Gertrud Neuwirth. New York: The Free Press, 1958.

Weinstein, Richard S. 1996. "The First American City." In Allen J. Scott and Edward W. Soja, eds., *The City: Los Angeles and Urban Theory at the End of the Twentieth Century* (Berkeley and Los Angeles: University of California Press): 22-46.

Weintraub, Jeff. 1995. "Varieties and Vicissitudes of Public Space." In Philip Kasinitz, ed., *Metropolis: Center and Symbol of Our Times* (New York: New York University Press): 280-319.

Whyte, William H. 1988. *City: Rediscovering the Center*. New York: Anchor Books.

Williams, Raymond. 1973. *The Country and the City*. Reprint, London: Hogarth Press, 1985.

———. 1976. *Keywords: A Vocabulary of Culture and Society*. London: Fontana; Croom Helm.

Wilson, William Julius. 1987. *The Truly Disadvantaged: The Inner City, the Underclass, and Public Policy*. Chicago: University of Chicago Press.

Wirth, Louis. 1938. "Urbanism as a Way of Life." Reprinted in Richard Sennett, ed., *Classic Essays on the Culture of Cities* (New York: Appleton-Century-Crofts, 1969): 143-64.

Zukin, Sharon. 1982. *Loft Living: Culture and Capital in Urban Change*. 2nd edition, New Brunswick: Rutgers University Press, 1989.

———. 1991. *Landscapes of Power: From Detroit to Disney World*. Berkeley and Los Angeles: University of California Press.

———. 1995. *The Cultures of Cities*. Cambridge, MA.: Blackwell.

# General Index of Names and Places



NB: *Only the proper names of persons and the names of independent cities or municipalities are included in this list.*

This publication was made possible by the Netherlands Architecture Fund, Rotterdam.
Design by Piet Gerards, Heerlen. Printed by Groenevelt, Landgraaf.

www.010publishers.nl
CIP/ISBN 90 6450 355 9